A Year in a Cottage Kitchen

A Year in a Cottage Kitchen

Madeleine Olivia

Plant-based Recipes from the Heart of Cornwall

Contents

My Life in Cornwall 06
About the Book 09
Kitchen Essentials 10
Seasonal Eating 14

— *one* Spring 16

— *two* Summer 70

— *three* Autumn 122

— *four* Winter 172

About the Author 218
Index 220

My Life in Cornwall

Looking out the window, I saw hedgerow after hedgerow pass as the roads got narrower and the sun began to set. After a long journey from Surrey, we crossed a small bridge over a river and climbed a winding hill that reached an old farmhouse on the edge of Bodmin Moor. I was just three years old when my parents decided to move to Cornwall, and it has been my home ever since. I've lived in Scotland and Brighton, travelled the world, and yet there is nowhere else that I love more than this county. As I've gotten older I've moved further into the depths of Cornwall, where the two coastlines narrow closer to one another. Where farmland, moorland, woodland and white sandy beaches are abundant. In spring the granite hedgerows explode into multicoloured displays of wildflowers, while the sun of high summer reflects on the aqua blue waters of small coastal villages. Wild mushrooms pop up their heads in ancient woodlands in autumn as the leaves fall to create carpets of red and orange. The rugged coastlines are beaten by crashing waves in winter, as the crowds disperse and the locals cosy up next to a fire in an old pub.

As I write this, I look out of the window to rainy late spring showers, the wisteria hanging down and the green bushy trees swaying in the wind. Just 15 minutes away is the north and south coasts, home to the most beautiful beaches I've ever seen in my life. Crystal clear shorelines, long stretches of beautiful white sand and dramatic rock formations that never fail to take my breath away. This is my home.

We moved to our 200-year-old Georgian farmhouse a few years ago, after deciding West Cornwall was where we wanted to settle. This home was something I had always dreamed of: a huge wisteria growing up the back of the cottage, an old-world kitchen complete with exposed beams, granite surround fireplace and Aga range, and cosy rooms that we could make our own. We have renovated and redecorated throughout to bring life and colour into the cottage, starting with my sanctuary: the kitchen. This is where I created all the recipes in this book, filmed every one of my videos, shared meals with my nearest and dearest, and spent countless mornings enjoying my coffee. A forever home that feels like an extension of our family.

We felt the pull to return to Cornwall after a trip to the other side of the world and a short stint in Brighton, to slow down our pace of life. The feeling of being cut off from the world is one I quite like; where the distractions and conveniences of modern life don't quite reach the depths of this part of the country. While I live a lot of my life

online, trying to keep up with the fast-paced nature of social media and algorithms, I can switch off at weekends to potter around the garden and buy secondhand trinkets from the local car boot sales (swap meets). I wouldn't change a thing and I invite you in to share a slice of Cornwall in my cottage kitchen for a moment of quiet among the chaos.

About the Book

Where I live weaves into everything I create. Throughout the book you'll find my favourite dishes growing up in Cornwall, the comfort foods that I crave, and plant-based alternatives to cosy cooking. Each chapter of this book follows the rhythm of the seasons, using the vegetables that are abundant and small rituals that make each time of year feel distinct, such as it's a slow soup for a stormy evening in winter, or something light and refreshing for a sun-dappled afternoon in spring.

I've invited people (maybe you reading!) into my world through my vlogs, and shared plant-based recipes that feed my soul since 2016. Cooking for me is about love for you, your body and those around you. I love foods that recall a memory from childhood, nourish my body or bring me comfort when I need it most.

All the recipes in this book are totally plant-based because my food philosophy is one that celebrates vegetables and plants, therefore avoiding animal products due to their current impact on the Earth, and exploitative nature of farming animals for fast consumption. We are farming and consuming animal products at a rate that is totally unsustainable, fuelling my passion to share how easy and delicious it is to cook with plants.

However, this book is for everyone, whether you are vegan or a meat-lover. Everyone can benefit from eating more plant-based meals and understanding how to widen their appreciation for new and different ways of cooking. I want to open your eyes to how many different ways we can all enjoy the abundance of vegetables we have available to us. Meals, desserts and snacks made entirely from plants are not only good for you but are totally and utterly delicious. Eating seasonally, knowing where your food comes from and making it comforting is at the heart of these recipes.

Join me for a year in Cornwall of cosy dishes, easy staples and sweet treats made from the heart.

Kitchen Essentials

EQUIPMENT

Cake and loaf tins
Have a few varying sizes of tins (pans), including springform ones, so you can whip up delicious sweet treats whenever you fancy.

Cast-iron pans with lids
One of the first things I bought for our new kitchen when moving into the cottage was a new set of cast-iron pans. They will last a lifetime and have so many uses, plus I find they stop things from sticking!

High-speed blender
I swear by my Vitamix blender, and probably use it every other day if not every day. Smoothies, dips, sauces, soups, you name it, it will blend it to the smoothest consistency. Any high-speed blender in your budget is worth it for the assistance these give in the kitchen.

Citrus juicer
Make your life easier and buy a hand-held citrus juicer, which catches all of the seeds. Lemons feature in so many of my recipes this is an absolute must for me.

Wire rack
For bread, cakes and bakes to cool after baking.

Stand-up colander
Make sure to opt for one that can sit in the sink for hands-free pouring and rinsing.

Dough scraper
If you enjoy making your own bread (try my recipes on page 202 and page 53), a dough scraper is so useful to scrape the dough out of the mixing bowl, and even to knead on a work surface. I prefer a plastic one.

Food processor
Many of the recipes in this book call for a food processor because they are essential for making your own sauces, pestos, toppings or bases from scratch. I have a large food processor and also a smaller one for different uses, and any extra cost buying one is worth it for the money you save making more things at home.

Garlic press
Of course you can chop your garlic, but I only ever use a garlic press. You can buy a million different kinds, but I have a plastic one that doesn't have any removable parts and is easy to clean.

Glass storage containers
I recently switched to mainly glass storage containers so that I can use them as packed lunchboxes, to heat things up in the microwave or store in the refrigerator. Plastic is fine for cold foods, so don't throw these out, but I prefer to use glass jars for anything hot to avoid microplastics leaching into the food. Save any large glass jars or containers from things like passata (sieved tomatoes) or beans to use.

Gratin and casserole dishes
Traybakes, casseroles, gratins and roasts are all made in these types of dishes and I personally love a ceramic or cast-iron one.

SMEG
HERBS & SPICES
autumn and winter veg

Hand and mini whisk
Instead of using my large mixer, sometimes I prefer to simply use my hand whisk because the attachments can be washed in the dishwasher. A mini whisk is underrated but super useful for removing any lumps in small amounts of sauces or mixes.

Immersion blender
If room in the kitchen or the wallet doesn't allow for a large high-speed blender, an immersion blender can work amazingly well for blending soups and sauces in a bowl or pan. I've had mine since university, when it was a hand-me-down from my mum!

Indian spice tin
I got this as a gift from my sister over 10 years ago and I will never look back. It means I can buy my spices in bulk and store in the cupboard, and have all my essential spices in one tin ready to use. I have one for main spices such as cumin, turmeric, cayenne, paprika, garam masala, and one for herbs and seasonings such as oregano, thyme, basil, garlic granules, chilli (hot pepper) flakes and onion powder.

Large mixing bowls
You can never have too many of these because I always seem to run out. I have glass, ceramic and stainless steel in different sizes in my kitchen for easy food preparation.

Measuring cups and jugs
Though I prefer to measure in grams, I still use my measuring cups and jugs all the time for ease, including teaspoon and tablespoon measures. For all my recipes I also share cup measurements to make things simpler. I've dropped and broken my fair share of pretty ceramic ones to know that metal is best!

Microplane
Purchase a microplane and freeze your garlic and chilli! It means you will always have these staples available, and you can Microplane them straight into your dish without having to chop them up.

Non-stick pans
This can be a stainless-steel pan, cast-iron or your classic non-stick. I opt for ones that are without the harmful chemicals that can come with non-stick, and make sure to replace them when they chip.

Proving basket
Not necessarily an essential for everyone, but definitely for the bread baker. It helps to shape the bread before baking in the oven, creating a beautiful round shape and helping it to rise to achieve a delicious soft and fluffy inside.

Sharp knives
You don't have to spend loads of money on knives. Mine are mostly pretty basic! But I make sure to sharpen them on a regular basis and look after them.

Stand mixer
If you are really into cooking and baking then a stand mixer is an essential for baking bread and vegan desserts. It just makes life so much easier.

Silicone utensils
Spatulas, mats, spoons, tongs, whisks, reusable bags, etc. I have them all to save scratching my beloved pans and to reduce waste with silicone mats or storage bags as they are reusable.

Stainless-steel pans
A great alternative to non-stick pans, as when used correctly, they are amazing for non-stick and crisping your food!

Tofu press
I've had my tofu press for over 10 years. It was probably one of the first things I bought when I went vegan. It saves the faff of piling things up on top of the tofu to press all the liquid out, and makes tofu so much more delicious as it can soak up all the delicious flavours you are marinating it in or cooking with.

Wood chopping boards
I only use wooden chopping boards for the best hygiene and longevity for my knives! Plus they look great when used for serving.

Seasonal Eating

Over the following pages, you will find a list of when different fruits and vegetables are in season and therefore at their best.

SPRING

Asparagus
Broad (fava) beans
Carrots
Chard
Elderflower
Kohlrabi
Lettuce
New potatoes
Pak choi
Peas
Peppers
Radishes
Rhubarb
Salad leaves
Salad potatoes
Spinach
Spring onions (scallions)
Spring greens
Strawberries
Watercress
Wild garlic (Ramps)

SUMMER

Aubergine (eggplant)
Broccoli
Beetroot (beets)
Blackberries
Blackcurrants
Blueberries
Broad (fava) beans
Cauliflower
Celery
Chard
Cherries
Chillies
Courgette (zucchini)
Cucumber
Elderflower
Fennel
French/green and runner beans
Gooseberries
Hispi cabbage
Lettuce
New potatoes
Mangetout
Radishes
Raspberries
Pak choi
Peas
Peppers
Potatoes
Rhubarb
Rocket (arugula)
Salad leaves
Samphire
Spinach
Sugar snap peas
Strawberries
Swiss chard
Sweetcorn
Tomatoes
Watercress

AUTUMN

Apples
Beetroot (beets)
Broccoli
Blackberries
Brussels sprouts
Carrots
Cauliflower
Cavolo nero/kale
Celery
Chard
Chestnuts
Cranberries
Fennel
French/green and runner beans
Leeks
Onions
Pears
Peas
Parsnips
Potatoes
Pumpkins
Plums
Kohlrabi
Mangetout
Onions
Savoy cabbage
Spinach
Squash
Sweetcorn
Swede (rutabaga)
Swiss chard
Turnips
Watercress
White cabbage

WINTER

Apples
Beetroot (beets)
Broccoli
Brussels sprouts
Carrots
Cauliflower
Celeriac (celery root)
Celery
Cranberries
Jerusalem artichokes
Kale
Leeks
Onions
Parsnips
Pears
Potatoes
Purple sprouting broccoli
Red cabbage
Savoy cabbage
Spring greens
Spring onions (scallions)
Squash
Swede (rutabaga)
Turnips
Watercress
White cabbage

— one

Spring

My Favourite Breakfast

SERVES 1

40 g (1½ oz/ ⅓ cup) chickpea flour (gram or *besan*)
2 tablespoons nutritional yeast
pinch of bicarbonate of soda
1 teaspoon black pepper
2 tablespoons non-dairy yoghurt
100 ml (3½ fl oz/ scant ½ cup) water
1–2 chestnut mushrooms, finely chopped
½ shallot, finely chopped
1 tablespoon olive oil
grated vegan cheese
pinch of black salt (kala namak)
chopped herbs, for sprinkling
splash of hot sauce (my favourite is Tabasco)

I've been eating a version of this vegan omelette using chickpea flour for the past few years, and it remains my favourite breakfast. It's known as a *besan chilla*, which is a traditional Indian recipe. Recently I learnt a tip from one of my followers to add non-dairy yoghurt and bicarbonate of soda to make it extra fluffy, and it works a treat!

---

1. Mix the chickpea (gram) flour, nutritional yeast and bicarbonate of soda together in a small jug, then season with the black pepper. Add the yoghurt and water and whisk vigorously until smooth. Add the mushrooms and shallot and stir to combine.
2. Heat the olive oil in a medium frying pan over a medium heat. Pour in the omelette mixture and tip the pan to evenly spread it across the pan. Cook for 5–8 minutes. You can check it is cooked and ready to fold when the sides come up easily with a spatula.
3. When ready, grate over a little vegan cheese, then fold in half with a spatula and cook for another 1–2 minutes on each side on a slightly higher heat to crisp up and turn golden.
4. Serve hot with black salt, fresh herbs and some hot sauce.

Notes

— Black salt adds an eggy taste to the omelette. It is optional but really adds an extra element to the dish! It's available to buy online.

— Feel free to swap the vegetables out for your favourites. I often use tomatoes, peppers or spinach, but mushrooms are definitely a winner!

Homemade Crumpets

MAKES 6 CRUMPETS

½ teaspoon granulated sugar
1 teaspoon (4 g) dried active yeast
300 ml (10 fl oz/1 ¼ cups) lukewarm water
200 g (7 oz/1⅔ cups) plain (all-purpose) flour
1 teaspoon salt
1 teaspoon baking powder
neutral oil, such as vegetable oil, for greasing

Crumpets are an English classic, which are perfect for breakfast or an afternoon snack, with a steaming cup of tea. Enjoyed with homemade blackberry jam (page 156), this is my husband's ultimate favourite brekkie!

---

1. Start by adding the sugar and yeast to the lukewarm water in a medium bowl, then whisk together and leave to stand for 5 minutes until frothy.
2. Next, add the flour and salt to a large mixing bowl, then pour in the yeast liquid and whisk together to create a smooth batter (this will take a few minutes). Stir through the baking powder. Cover the bowl with a damp tea (dish) towel and leave to rise in a warm spot for 15 minutes.
3. Grease biscuit cutters or crumpet rings with a little oil. I used four 8 cm (3¼ in) ones, but you can use any cutters you have, and place them in a large frying pan. Place the pan over a high heat. Stir through the batter to remove air bubbles, then using a ladle, add around 60 ml (2 fl oz/¼ cup) of batter to the cutter. Cook for 10 minutes, or until the crumpet has risen and small holes form in the top.
4. Quickly toast the other side of the crumpet by flipping over. Carefully lift off the ring, and remove the crumpet from the pan. Repeat for the remaining batter. You can do this for multiple crumpets at a time.

   Top with butter and jam, or my favourite, Marmite!

Notes

— You can weigh the batter on kitchen scales, and measure out how much you are using if you want crumpets that are all the same size.

First Harvest Soup

SERVES 4

2 tablespoons sunflower oil
2 medium leeks, chopped
2 garlic cloves, grated or chopped
pinch of cayenne pepper
1 medium carrot, diced
1 large potato, peeled and cut into 2–3 cm (¾–1¼ in) cubes
900 ml (30½ fl oz/3⅔ cups) vegetable stock
300 g (10½ oz/2⅓ cups) fresh or frozen peas
450 g (1 lb) young spinach (can substitute for kale)
3 tablespoons chopped herbs (I used a mix of mint and parsley leaves)
sea salt and freshly ground black pepper
crusty bread, to serve

This soup is perfect for the days of spring when the weather is still brisk, and the first vegetables are ready for harvesting from the kitchen garden.

---

1. Heat the oil in a large saucepan and fry the leeks for about 10 minutes, stirring occasionally until softened. Add the garlic and cayenne pepper and cook for a further 2 minutes.
2. Add the carrot, potato and stock, then season and bring to the boil. Reduce to a simmer and cook, stir occasionally for about 20 minutes, or until the potatoes are soft.
3. Finally, add the peas and spinach, heat through, then add the herbs, and blitz in a blender (or using an immersion blender) until smooth. Check the seasoning and serve with crusty bread.

Notes

— This is an easy vegetable soup recipe that can be made at any time of the year with the harvests from your garden or seasonal vegetables from your local market or farm shop. Try swapping the peas and spinach for vegetables abundant at a different time of year – you could go for green beans in summer or broccoli in autumn, for example.

Tofu, Leek and Herb Tart

SERVES 4

320 g (11¼ oz) sheet of ready-rolled shortcrust pastry
2 tablespoons olive oil
3 large leeks, washed and sliced
300 g (10½ oz) silken tofu
zest of 1 lemon, juice of ½
½ teaspoon caraway seeds
½ teaspoon coriander seeds
pinch of ground turmeric
15 g (½ oz) nutritional yeast
2 tablespoons finely chopped parsley
2 tablespoons finely chopped coriander (cilantro)
pinch of black salt (kala namak, optional)
sea salt and freshly ground black pepper

A celebration of early spring when the leeks are sweet and fresh herbs are peeking through the soil. Silken tofu works perfectly to create a creamy and dairy-free tart that is delicately spiced. This dish is perfect for a slow weekend lunch or a weekday light supper.

---

1. Preheat the oven to 190°C fan (400°F).
2. Press the ready-rolled pastry into a 20–25 cm (8–10 in) round flan dish, leaving any excess pastry that goes over the sides. Line the pastry with baking parchment and cover with baking beans (pie weights), then blind bake for 10 minutes before removing from the oven.
3. Meanwhile, add the olive oil to a frying pan and gently fry the leeks over a medium heat for 7–8 minutes until softened. Remove from the heat and leave to cool for a few minutes.
4. Blend the silken tofu and the lemon juice together in a food processor until smooth, then add to the pan with the remaining ingredients and stir to combine. Gently heat for a few minutes, stirring constantly.
5. Pour the mixture into the flan dish and bake for 35–40 minutes until golden and set. Remove from the oven and leave to cool for 10–15 minutes, then trim around the pastry to neaten and serve.

Roasted Asparagus Salad

SERVES 4

2 bunches asparagus, trimmed and sliced into 5 cm (2 in) pieces
1 tablespoon vegetable oil
mixed salad leaves (I used red little gem and rocket/arugula)
50 g (1¾ oz/⅓ cup) cashews or peanuts, roughly chopped
½ red chilli, finely chopped
2 tablespoons finely chopped coriander (cilantro)
sea salt and freshly ground black pepper
sesame seeds, for sprinkling

FOR THE DRESSING

2 teaspoons toasted sesame oil
1 tablespoon rapeseed oil, or similar
1 teaspoon miso
1 teaspoon brown sugar
1 teaspoon grated ginger
1 garlic clove, grated
zest and juice of 1 lime

Although asparagus is in season for a short period, I look forward to cooking and eating it every year. One of my favourite ways is to simply roast the aspargus, which allows it to shine, then pair it with a zingy Asian-inspired dressing with nutty sesame and a gentle kick of chilli. It's perfect as a light lunch or a vibrant side dish.

1. Preheat the oven to 200°C fan (425°F).
2. Arrange the asparagus on a baking tray (pan), add a little oil and lightly season. Toss to coat, then roast in the oven for 10 minutes, or until softened.
3. Meanwhile, whisk all the dressing ingredients together in a small bowl. Season with black pepper.
4. Once the asparagus is ready, remove from the oven and place in a serving dish on top of the salad leaves. Add the nuts, chilli and coriander, then pour over the dressing and toss to combine.
5. Serve with a sprinkle of sesame seeds.

Pizza Rolls

MAKES 12 ROLLS

FOR THE BASIC DOUGH

25 g (scant 1 oz) granulated or caster (superfine) sugar
21 g (¾ oz) fast-action dried yeast or 3 sachets (7 g/¼ oz each)
450 ml (16 fl oz/generous 1¾ cups) lukewarm water
500 g (1 lb 2 oz/4 cups) plain (all-purpose) flour, plus extra for dusting
500 g (1 lb 2 oz/4 cups) strong white bread flour, plus extra for dusting
25 g (scant 1 oz) salt

FOR THE PIZZA TOPPINGS

3 tablespoons tomato purée (paste)
50 g (1¾ oz) vegan cheddar cheese, grated
4–5 olives, halved
6 cherry tomatoes, halved
½ red onion
small handful of rocket (arugula)
small handful of basil leaves
olive oil, for brushing

These rolls are ideal to make ahead for spring picnics, lunchboxes or to accompany a family spread. With familiar flavours of tomato, herbs and melty vegan cheese rolled up in pillowy dough, they are mouth-wateringly delicious warm or cold.

---

1. Add the sugar and yeast to the lukewarm water in a bowl, stir and leave for 5 minutes.
2. Meanwhile, mix the flours and salt together in a large mixing bowl, then add the yeast mixture. If using a stand mixer, attach the dough hook and mix on medium-fast speed for 3 minutes. Alternatively, knead by hand for 10 minutes until a smooth dough forms.
3. Cover the bowl with a damp tea (dish) towel and leave to rise in a warm place for 1 hour, or until doubled in size. Meanwhile, lightly flour a 12-hole muffin tray.
4. Once risen, knock the dough back (30 seconds in a mixer or 1–2 minutes by hand) to get rid of any large air bubbles, then roll the dough out flat on a lightly floured work surface. As a guide, 46 x 23 cm (18 x 9 in) will make 12 rolls.
5. Spread the tomato purée two-thirds of the way over the dough, then add half of your toppings on top of the tomato. Fold the dough in half lengthways, rotate 90 degrees and roll out flat again. Repeat this topping, folding and rolling process again, then cut 6 strips down the rolled-out dough lengthways and one across to make 12 equal strips. Roll each piece up and place vertically in the prepared muffin tray. Lightly brush the tops with olive oil and leave to prove for 20 minutes at room temperature.
6. Preheat the oven to 200°C fan (425°F).
7. Bake for 15 minutes, or until golden brown. Enjoy warm out of the oven.

Notes

— Play around with your favourite toppings, making sure not to overfill.

Spring Frittata

SERVES 6–8

150 g (5½ oz) potatoes (new or waxy both work here), peeled and diced into 2–3 cm (¾–1¼ in) cubes
100 g (3½ oz) purple sprouting broccoli, trimmed and cut into 10 cm (4 in) pieces
1 tablespoon olive oil
1 medium leek, sliced
1 medium courgette (zucchini), chopped
2 garlic cloves, grated
10 cherry tomatoes, halved
sea salt and freshly ground black pepper
chopped herbs (such as dill, chives, parsley, basil), to serve

FOR THE 'EGG' MIX
360 g (12¾ oz) block firm tofu
100 ml (3½ fl oz/scant ½ cup) non-dairy milk
1 tablespoon chickpea (gram or *besan*) flour
2 tablespoons nutritional yeast
1 tablespoon cornflour (cornstarch)
¼ teaspoon ground turmeric
¼ teaspoon black salt (kala namak, optional)
good pinch of red chilli (hot pepper) flakes
50 g (1¾ oz) vegan cheese, grated

This is a colourful and fresh vegetable frittata to welcome the warmer longer days. With a hint of kala namak for an eggy flavour, and tofu and chickpea flour to mimic an eggy texture, this is delicious served warm for brunch, or cold with a crisp salad on a sunny afternoon.

---

1. Preheat the oven to 180°C fan (400°F).
2. Boil the potatoes in a medium saucepan of lightly salted water for 10 minutes, or until just tender. Halfway through cooking, add the broccoli to the pan. Drain and set aside to steam.
3. Meanwhile, blitz all the 'egg' ingredients, except the vegan cheese, in a blender until smooth. Stir through the vegan cheese.
4. Heat the oil in a medium ovenproof frying pan or sauté pan, add the leek, courgette and garlic and fry for 10 minutes over a medium heat, or until softened. Add the boiled potatoes, broccoli and tomatoes to the pan and cook for a few more minutes. Then pour over the 'egg' mixture and gently combine. Season with salt and pepper.
5. Transfer the pan to the oven and bake for 30–35 minutes until the frittata is firm to touch. Remove from the oven and leave to cool for 5 minutes before slicing into triangles and serving with chopped herbs.

Notes

— This is a very flexible recipe that can be made throughout the year, so change up the vegetables for each season, or opt for those you enjoy the most!

Stuffed Chard Rainbow Rolls with Peanut Dip

MAKES 8–10 ROLLS

8–10 rice paper wrappers
1 bunch of rainbow chard, ends of stalks chopped
1 medium beetroot (beet), peeled and finely grated
1 carrot, thinly sliced
4 spring onions (scallions), halved and cut into strips
large bunch of mint leaves
large bunch of coriander (cilantro) leaves, stems removed

FOR THE PEANUT AND COCONUT DIPPING SAUCE

100 g (3½ oz) vegan coconut yoghurt
1 tablespoon peanut butter
1 tablespoon soy sauce
juice of ½ lime
3–6 tablespoons warm water
splash of chilli oil
sea salt and freshly ground black pepper

I brought these back into my kitchen after eating vegetarian summer rolls when I visited Southeast Asia. They are packed with crisp spring vegetables, wrapped in delicate rice paper and dipped in a creamy tangy peanut sauce.

---

1. Whisk all the dipping sauce ingredients together in a bowl, adding more or less warm water depending on how thick the sauce is. Set aside.
2. Heat a large saucepan of water until warm. The pan needs to be big enough to submerge the rice paper wrappers. Submerge a rice paper wrapper into the warm water for 10–20 seconds to soften, making note of the smooth side (this is the outside of the roll). Don't allow it to become too soft as they will be too fragile to roll.
3. Place the rice paper wrapper on a slightly damp wooden chopping board and in the centre add your fillings: chard, beetroot, carrot, spring onions, mint and coriander. Fold the bottom over the fillings, gently roll over once, then fold over the sides and finish by rolling over to seal. Set aside and repeat with the remaining rice paper wrappers to make 8–10 rolls.
4. Serve straight away with the dipping sauce.

Notes

— The first time you do this, it may take a couple of rolls to get the hang of it! If you have rolled a burrito before it is similar. To make them easier to roll and seal, make sure not to under- or overfill.

Roasted Garlicky Radishes and New Potatoes

SERVES 4

2 tablespoons olive oil
2 garlic cloves, grated
1 teaspoon Dijon mustard
zest of 1 lemon, wedged to serve
bunch of radishes, about 250 g (9 oz), trimmed
500 g (1 lb 2 oz) new potatoes, any larger ones halved
small handful of parsley, chopped (you can substitute rocket/arugula or watercress instead)
sea salt and freshly ground black pepper

Buttery new potatoes and red radishes are roasted until golden and crisp and then tossed with garlic, lemon zest and a hint of mustard for a simple side dish – perfect for a garden supper.

---

1. Preheat the oven to 220°C fan (4725°F).
2. Line a large baking sheet with baking parchment.
3. In a large bowl, mix the olive oil with the grated garlic, mustard, lemon zest, salt and pepper.
4. Then add the radishes and potatoes to the bowl, and toss together to combine.
5. Tumble the potatoes and radishes onto the baking sheet and roast for about 25–30 minutes, tossing halfway through, until golden, then remove from the oven.
6. Transfer the potatoes and radishes to a serving dish and sprinkle over the fresh parsley and lemon wedges before serving.

Wild Garlic and White Bean Bake

SERVES 4

2 leeks, trimmed and sliced
1 celeriac (celery root), peeled and cubed
small handful of wild garlic (ramps), roughly chopped
1 tablespoon olive oil
250–300 ml (8–10 fl oz/ 1–1 ¼ cups) vegan cream or coconut cream
2 x 400 g (14 oz) tins cannellini beans
juice of 1 lemon
1 tablespoon wholegrain mustard
sea salt and freshly ground black pepper

FOR THE BREADCRUMB TOPPING

50 g (1¾ oz/⅓ cup) whole almonds
4 tablespoons nutritional yeast
150 g (5½ oz/1¾ cups) fresh breadcrumbs
zest of 1 lemon
100 g (3½ oz) wild garlic (ramps), roughly chopped
1 tablespoon olive oil
sea salt and freshly ground black pepper

Every year I wait eagerly for the first signs of wild garlic popping up, tucked along the woodland paths and shaded lanes around my home. I see it as the first real sign of spring on its way after a long, cold winter. While I make a hundred batches of wild garlic pesto, I also love adding it to dishes for a garlicky kick. Creamy cannellini beans, tender leeks and earthy celeriac (celery root) make this comforting traybake ideal for the chilly early spring days that cling to winter.

---

1. Preheat the oven to 180°C fan (400°F).
2. Add the leeks, celeriac and a small handful of chopped wild garlic to a deep baking tray (pan). Drizzle over the olive oil and season with salt and pepper. Roast in the oven for 20 minutes.
3. Meanwhile, blitz the almonds in a food processor or high-speed blender until they are fine and dusty. Add the remaining topping ingredients and pulse to combine. Set aside.
4. After 20 minutes, remove the tray from the oven and give the leeks and celeriac a stir. Pour over the cream, then add the beans, lemon juice and mustard. Stir to mix, then sprinkle over the breadcrumb topping.
5. Return the tray to the oven and roast for a further 30 minutes, or until golden brown and crispy. Cover the top with foil for the last 10 minutes if it starts to look a little too golden on top.

Notes

— When foraging for wild garlic, stick to paths that are less busy with dog walkers, and not on the side of the road. Make sure to be familiar first with the shape and smell of wild garlic so as not to confuse it with Lily of the Valley, which is poisonous. The best way to be safe is by rubbing the leaves between your fingers as wild garlic has a very distinctive garlic smell. Wild garlic is usually one leaf per stem growing from the base, while Lily of the Valley usually has two leaves further up the stem.

— If making this out of season, you can substitute the wild garlic for garlic and/or basil.

Tofu, Coconut and Purple Sprouting Broccoli Curry

SERVES 4

1 onion, finely chopped
400 ml (14 fl oz) tin coconut milk
400 g (14 oz) tin chopped tomatoes
1 teaspoon brown sugar
2 tablespoons tomato purée (paste)
300 g (10 ½ oz) block extra firm tofu, pressed (see page 74), drained and cubed
250 g (9 oz) purple sprouting broccoli
sea salt and freshly ground black pepper
rice and/or naan, to serve
chopped coriander (cilantro), for sprinkling

FOR THE CURRY PASTE

1 teaspoon coriander seeds
2 teaspoons cumin seeds
thumb-sized piece of ginger, peeled and finely chopped
1 red chilli, finely chopped
1 lemongrass stalk, outer skin and tough ends removed, roughly chopped
2 garlic cloves, grated
1 shallot, roughly chopped
½ teaspoon ground turmeric
zest and juice of 1 lime
3 tablespoons vegetable oil, plus extra for frying
bunch of coriander (cilantro), including the stalks
sea salt and freshly ground black pepper

Gently spiced and fragrant, this curry is rich, creamy and refreshingly light. In-season purple sprouting broccoli is the perfect addition for the cusp of spring. I enjoy a tofu curry most weeks, and, for this one, the homemade curry paste can easily be made in batches, stored and used again for another quick and easy dinner.

---

1. Start by making the curry paste. Lightly toast the coriander and cumin seeds in a dry frying pan for 2 minutes over a low heat. Add them to a food processor with the remaining paste ingredients and blend until smooth. Set aside.
2. Fry the onion in a little oil in a large pan for 10 minutes over a medium heat, or until softened. Add the curry paste and fry for 2 minutes, or until fragrant. You can add all the paste for a spicier curry, or reduce the amount to half depending on your spice preference.
3. Pour in the coconut milk, chopped tomatoes, sugar and tomato purée and bring to the boil. Add the tofu and stir everything through. Reduce to a simmer and cook for 5–10 minutes until the sauce has thickened a little. Season with salt and pepper.
4. Meanwhile, add the purple sprouting broccoli to a separate pan and cover with boiling water. Simmer for 2 minutes, or until softened, then drain. Sprinkle with a little salt and set aside.
5. Serve the curry with steamed rice, topped with the broccoli and a sprinkling of coriander. Enjoy with a side of naan, if you like.

Notes

— Store any extra curry paste in an airtight container in the fridge for up to a week. If you want to make extra for another curry, simply double up the ingredients and freeze the paste.
— For crispy tofu, you can fry this separately in oil and season, then stir through once the sauce has thickened.

Spring Greens Filo Pie

SERVES 3–4

spray oil, for greasing
1 tablespoon olive oil
1 onion, chopped
1 garlic clove, grated
200 g (7 oz) young spinach
250 g (9 oz) asparagus, trimmed and cut into 3–4 cm (1¼–1½ in) pieces
100 g (3½ oz/¾ cup) frozen peas, defrosted
2 tablespoons finely chopped parsley
1 tablespoon finely chopped mint
zest of 1 lemon
250 g (9 oz) vegan cream cheese
270 g (9½ oz) packet of filo pastry
50 g (1¾ oz) vegan butter, melted
1 tablespoon sesame seeds, for sprinkling
sea salt and freshly ground black pepper

I just love the look and taste of crispy filo pastry. Filled with vibrant green asparagus, peas and spinach, and bound together with lemon zest, fresh herbs and vegan cream cheese, this is a light yet satisfying meal, and one made to be shared.

1. Preheat the oven to 180°C fan (400°F). Lightly spray a 20 cm (8 in) pie dish with oil.
2. Heat the olive oil in a frying pan over a medium heat, add the onion and cook for 10 minutes until softened. Add the garlic and cook for another minute, then transfer to a large bowl.
3. Add the spinach to a colander and wilt by pouring a kettle of boiling water over. Rinse with cold water and leave to drain. Squeeze as much of the water out of the spinach and dry in a tea (dish) towel. Roughly chop and add to the bowl with the onions and garlic.
4. Add the asparagus and peas to the bowl with the parsley, mint, lemon zest and cream cheese. Season with salt and pepper and stir to thoroughly combine.
5. Brush each of the filo sheets (do this one by one as you use each sheet) with the melted vegan butter and layer into the prepared dish. Do this by moving around the bowl, overhanging the edges by about 12 cm (4½ in).
6. Spoon in the filling and fold the filo over the top, scrunching to seal it. Brush all over with more of the melted butter and add a sprinkling of sesame seeds on top. Bake in the oven for 25–30 minutes until golden, making sure to keep an eye on it at the end so it does not burn. Remove from the oven and leave to cool for 5–10 minutes before serving.

Watercress and Pea Pesto Hasselback Potatoes

SERVES 2–3

500 g (1 lb 2 oz) new potatoes (waxy potatoes can also be used)
2 tablespoons vegetable oil
1 garlic clove, grated
sea salt and freshly ground black pepper

FOR THE WATERCRESS AND PEA PESTO
50 g (1¾ oz) watercress
200 g (7 oz/1¼ cups) frozen peas, defrosted by running under the hot tap and draining
2 tablespoons pine nuts or sunflower seeds
2 garlic cloves
juice of 1 lemon
2 tablespoons vegan Parmesan-style cheese or nutritional yeast
4 tablespoons olive oil, or more if needed

Growing up, my favourite potato was a hasselback. I adore how they soak up all the flavour and are both crispy and fluffy at the same time. These are dressed with a punchy green pesto made from peppery watercress and sweet springtime peas. The leftover pesto will be perfect to spoon over your meals for the rest of the week.

---

1. Preheat the oven to 200°C fan (425°F).
2. Place each potato into the hollow of a wooden spoon, and using a sharp knife, cut vertical slices across the potato. The spoon will stop you cutting all the way through to create the hasselback cuts.
3. Add the potatoes to a roasting tin (pan), turning the potatoes so the slices are facing up.
4. Mix the oil, garlic, salt and pepper together in a small bowl, then brush the potatoes with the mixture, taking care to get between the slices. Roast in the oven for 45 minutes, basting halfway through with the remaining garlic oil mixture.
5. Meanwhile, blitz all the ingredients for the pesto in a food processor until smooth. Add a little extra olive oil if it needs it.
6. When the potatoes are golden, remove them from the oven and sprinkle with a little extra sea salt. Drizzle with the pesto and toss to coat.

Notes

— There will be some pesto leftover, which you could use with pasta. The pesto can be stored in an airtight container in the refrigerator for 3–5 days.

— This dish would work well with some extra vegetables thrown into the tin alongside the potatoes towards the end of their cooking. For example, some broccoli or green beans could be added for the last 15 minutes of roasting.

Potato and Broccoli Gratin

SERVES 4–6

600 g (1 lb 5 oz) potatoes, peeled and finely sliced
1 head of broccoli, cut into small florets
1 medium onion, sliced
10–15 cherry tomatoes, halved
olive oil, for drizzling
sea salt and freshly ground black pepper

FOR THE TOPPING
50 g (1¾ oz) vegan Cheddar-style cheese
50 g (1¾ oz/generous ¾ cup) panko breadcrumbs
1 tablespoon finely chopped parsley
1 teaspoon paprika

FOR THE WHITE SAUCE
500 ml (17 fl oz/generous 2 cups) non-dairy milk
3 heaped tablespoons cornflour (cornstarch)
25 g (scant 1 oz) vegan butter, plus extra for greasing
1 teaspoon dried oregano
2 teaspoons garlic granules
3 tablespoons nutritional yeast

Gratins are the definition of comfort food. This one is creamy, topped with crispy breadcrumbs and layered with potatoes and broccoli for a simple and nourishing dish. I love this with some vegan sausages on the side!

---

1. Preheat the oven to 190°C fan (400°F). Grease a large gratin dish with a little vegan butter.
2. Mix all the ingredients for the topping in a small bowl. Set aside.
3. Next, make the white sauce. Add about 2 tablespoons of non-dairy milk to a bowl with the cornflour and mix to a runny paste. Set aside.
4. Pour the remaining milk into a saucepan over a low–medium heat. Add the butter and salt and pepper to taste and stir with a hand-held whisk to melt the butter. As it starts to boil, add the cornflour and milk paste and whisk to form a smooth sauce, taking care to make sure it isn't sticking to the bottom of the pan.
5. Once boiling, reduce the heat and cook for a further 1–2 minutes, stirring to thicken into a smooth sauce. Stir in the dried oregano, garlic granules and nutritional yeast, then remove from the heat and set aside.
6. Arrange a layer of potatoes in the prepared gratin dish, then add layers of the broccoli, onions and tomatoes, lightly seasoning each layer with salt and pepper. Repeat a couple more times, finishing the gratin with a layer of potatoes. Pour over the sauce to coat all the ingredients.
7. Sprinkle the breadcrumb topping over and finish with a light drizzle of oil. Bake in the oven for 40–45 minutes until golden brown.

Wild Garlic and Pine Nut Focaccia

SERVES 8

500 g (1 lb 2 oz/4 cups) strong white bread flour
10 g (½ oz) sea salt
7 g (¼ oz) sachet fast-action dried yeast or 15 g (½ oz) fresh yeast
about 50 ml (1¾ fl oz/3½ tablespoons) olive oil, plus extra for oiling and drizzling
370 ml (12½ fl oz/1½ cups) warm water

FOR THE WILD GARLIC AND PINE NUT TOPPING
50 g (1¾ oz) wild garlic (ramps), roughly chopped (saving a small handful of whole leaves for topping the focaccia)
25 g (1 oz/2 tablespoons) pine nuts
2 tablespoons olive oil
sea salt and freshly ground black pepper

The process of making focaccia from scratch is very satisfying, with dimpling the dough with your fingers being the particular highlight. I learnt this focaccia method (in particular the kneading technique) from a bread course with Rupert Cooper at Philleigh Way Cookery School in Cornwall and have been making it this way ever since. What makes this even better is the addition of wild garlic (ramps), plucked straight from a nearby path.

1. Add the flour, salt, yeast, olive oil and warm water to a large bowl, making sure that the yeast and salt are separate from each other so the salt doesn't kill the yeast. Stir with a wooden spoon or your hands to form a dough, then scrape out onto a lightly oiled work surface.
2. You can knead the dough in a mixer, or try the technique we learnt at Philleigh Way Cookery School: 'walk' your dough with a dough blade by scooping the blade under the dough, moving it around and forwards, then scraping, spinning and tucking. Keep the bottom of the dough ball at the bottom, rather than rolling it around over itself.
3. Lift the dough up into the air with your fingertips on either side of the dough, slap the bottom back down onto the surface and fold it over itself away from you. Do this five times to knead and then walk your dough again. The dough should start to come together and feel more elastic. It's ready when it appears smooth and comes easily away from the surface.
4. Place the dough back into the bowl, drizzle with olive oil, cover with a damp tea (dish) towel and leave in a warm spot to rise for 45–60 minutes until doubled in size.
5. Meanwhile, make the wild garlic topping. Add the chopped wild garlic and pine nuts to a pestle and mortar with the olive oil and bash together until a paste is created. Season with salt and pepper. The paste can also be made in a bowl with a rolling pin, or in a food processor.

6. Line a large baking tray (pan) with baking parchment and drizzle with more olive oil. Tip the dough onto the baking tray. Press the dough into the corners and create dimples with wet fingers. Cover and allow to prove in a warm spot until doubled in size again (another 45–60 minutes).
7. Preheat the oven to 200°C fan (425°F).
8. When the dough has risen, spread the top evenly with the wild garlic paste, then roll the few saved wild garlic leaves and push these into the dough. Agitate and dimple the focaccia again with wet fingers, then bake for 20–25 minutes until golden brown. Remove from the oven and allow to cool slightly before serving.

Notes

— When foraging for wild garlic, stick to paths that are less busy with dog walkers, and not on the side of the road. Make sure to be familiar first with the shape and smell of wild garlic so as not to confuse it with Lily of the Valley, which is poisonous. The best way to be safe is by rubbing the leaves between your fingers as wild garlic has a very distinctive garlic smell. Wild garlic is usually one leaf per stem growing from the base, while Lily of the Valley usually has two leaves further up the stem.

— With this focaccia recipe you can use whatever toppings you like throughout the seasons. Some other favourites could be rosemary, oregano, tomatoes, garlic, fried courgette (zucchini) or aubergine (eggplant), caramelized onions, olives, thinly sliced potatoes or some vegan cheese.

— You can use different methods for kneading the dough, or use an electric mixer to knead.

Hot Cross Buns

MAKES 12 BUNS

50 g (1¾ oz) vegan butter, plus extra to serve
300 ml (10 fl oz/1¼ cups) unsweetened non-dairy milk, at room temperature
75 g (2½ oz/⅓ cup) caster (superfine) sugar
7 g (¼ oz) sachet of fast-action dried yeast
500 g (1 lb 2 oz/4 cups) strong white bread flour, plus extra for dusting
1 teaspoon salt
2 teaspoons mixed spice
1 teaspoon ground cinnamon
100 g (3½ oz/generous ¾ cup) sultanas (golden raisins)
50 g (1¾ oz/¼ cup) mixed peel
zest of 1 orange
oil, for greasing
maple syrup, for drizzling

FOR THE CROSS

50 g (1¾ oz/scant ½ cup) plain (all-purpose) flour
3 tablespoons water

A true marker of spring with their roots in Easter tradition, hot cross buns are one of my favourite things to eat at this time of year with their soft pillowy texture and spiced fragrant flavour. These are best enjoyed toasted with vegan butter and a cup of tea.

---

1. Start by melting the vegan butter in a pan over a medium heat. Once melted, remove from the heat and add the room temperature milk*, sugar and yeast and stir together to mix. Leave to stand for 10 minutes, or until bubbles start to form.
2. In a separate large bowl, mix the flour, salt, mixed spice and cinnamon together.
3. If using a stand mixer, add the milk mixture to the bowl with 125 g (4½ oz/1 cup) of the flour mixture at a time, mixing on high speed for 4 minutes, or until the dough is beaten and no longer sticky but elastic and smooth.
4. If not using a mixer, then add the flour to a large mixing bowl. Make a well in the middle of the flour, then pour in the milk mix. Using a wooden spoon, stir together, then using your hands, bring it all together to form a sticky dough. Tip the dough out on a lightly floured work surface and knead for 5 minutes by stretching the dough with one hand and kneading with the heel of the other, folding back on itself. Repeat until you have a smooth and elastic dough ball.
5. Transfer the dough back to the bowl and cover with a damp tea (dish) towel, then leave to rise in a warm spot for 1½ hours, or until doubled in size.
6. Line a large baking tray (pan) with baking parchment and set aside. When the dough has risen, roll the dough out again and knock back by flattening it with your hands. Scatter over the sultanas, mixed peel and orange zest and knead again for 5 minutes to distribute them. Place the dough back in the bowl and leave to rise again in a warm spot for a further 1½ hours, or until doubled in size.
7. Knock the dough back again, then divide it into 12 and roll into buns. Do this by gathering the edges of each ball in the middle and rotating around until you have a tight ball. Flip the ball over so the seal is on the base.

8. Arrange the buns on the lined baking tray, about 2.5 cm (1 in) apart. Cover with lightly oiled cling film (plastic wrap) and leave to prove for 45 minutes–1 hour until doubled in size.
9. Preheat the oven to 200°C fan (425°F).
10. For the cross, mix the flour with and water together in a small bowl to form a paste. Fill a piping bag fitted with a small nozzle with the paste and decorate each bun with a cross.
11. Bake the buns in the oven for 15–20 minutes until golden brown. You may need to turn them halfway to make sure they are evenly baked. Remove from the oven and brush with maple syrup for a glossy shine. Leave to cool on a wire rack to cool and serve toasted with vegan butter and a cup of tea!

Notes

— *If the milk isn't at room temperature yet, just heat it with the butter to get it to the right temperature. It needs to be this temperature so that the yeast can activate.

— If you don't have a piping bag, you can make your own from a triangular piece of baking parchment with a cut at the point.

Easter Biscuits

MAKES 18–20 BISCUITS

200 g (7 oz) vegan butter
1 teaspoon vanilla extract
100 g (3½ oz/scant ½ cup) caster sugar (superfine), plus extra for sprinkling
zest of 1 orange
300 g (10½ oz/scant 2½ cups) plain (all-purpose) flour, plus extra for dusting
½ teaspoon mixed spice
½ teaspoon ground cinnamon
70 g (2½ oz/½ cup) currants

FOR THE GLAZE

2 teaspoons maple syrup
3 teaspoons vegan milk

These delicate biscuits (cookies) are a nod to the traditions of Easter Sunday. The dough is crumbly and short, dotted with curtants, and has a sugar-glazed top.

---

1. Start by whisking the butter, vanilla, sugar and orange zest together in a large bowl until pale and creamy. This can be done by hand, or with a stand mixer fitted with a whisk attachment to make things easier.
2. Sift in the flour and stir through, then add the spices and currants and mix into a ball of dough. Make sure not to overwork the dough as it should be crumbly.
3. Wrap the dough in cling film (plastic wrap) and leave to chill in the refrigerator for 30 minutes.
4. Meanwhile, preheat the oven to 160°C fan (350°F) and line a baking sheet with baking parchment or a silicone sheet.
5. Roll out the chilled dough onto a floured work surface, to about 5 mm (¼ in) thick. Using a small biscuit (cookie) cutter, cut out individual biscuits. Once you've cut shapes out of the first roll of dough, bring it together, roll out again and cut the remaining, so nothing goes to waste. This should make around 18–20 biscuits.
6. Place the biscuits spaced apart onto the lined baking sheet and bake for 10 minutes.
7. Meanwhile, for the glaze, mix the maple syrup and milk together in a small bowl.
8. Remove the biscuits from the oven, gently brush with the glaze and sprinkle with caster sugar. Return to the oven for 2–5 minutes until golden brown at the edges. (You can turn the biscuits the opposite way for a perfectly even bake.)
9. Remove from the oven and leave to cool on a wire rack for 10–15 minutes to set before serving. These can be stored in an airtight container for up to a week (if they last that long!).

Rhubarb Eton Mess

SERVES 4–6

aquafaba (liquid) from 400 g (14 oz) tin chickpeas (garbanzos)
½ teaspoon lemon juice, white wine or apple cider vinegar, plus a squeeze of lemon juice
125 g (4½ oz/½ cup) caster (superfine) sugar
400 g (14 oz) rhubarb stalks, cut into 3 cm (1¼ in) pieces
1 recipe quantity Vegan Coconut Cream (page 110) or vegan coconut yoghurt

A fun way to use up the water from a tin of chickpeas (garbanzos), known as aquafaba, is to make meringue! Eton Mess was a pudding my mum would always do for after a barbecue on those first sunny days of the year. Making the most of the first harvests of rhubarb is my favourite way to enjoy this British classic.

---

1. Preheat the oven to 100°C fan (250°F) and line a baking tray (pan) with baking parchment.
2. Whisk the aquafaba in a stand mixer fitted with a whisk attachment, or in a large bowl with an electric whisk. Keep mixing, adding the ½ teaspoon of lemon juice or vinegar, until the water becomes fluffy, white and has stiff peaks.
3. Add 100 g (3½ oz/scant ½ cup) of the caster sugar, a little at a time, whisking as you go. The mixture will become glossy and thick.
4. Arrange the meringue in little dollops onto the lined baking tray and bake for 90 minutes. Switch the oven off and leave the meringues in the oven for a further 90 minutes to fully dry out before removing from the oven and setting aside.
5. Preheat the oven to 200°C fan (425°F). Place the rhubarb on a large baking tray, sprinkle over 25 g (1 oz/scant 2 tablespoons) of the sugar and pour over the squeeze of lemon juice. Roast for 15 minutes, or until the rhubarb is softened. Leave to cool.
6. Make the Vegan Coconut Cream, if using, following the instructions on page 110.
7. To assemble the Eton Mess, add a layer of broken-up bits of the meringue in individual glasses or bowls, then a layer of Vegan Coconut Cream or coconut yoghurt, then another layer of the stewed rhubarb. Enjoy!

Saffron Buns

MAKES 8–10 ROLLS

very good pinch of saffron threads (about 5 g/¼ oz)
300 ml (10 fl oz/1¼ cups) oat milk
140 g (5 oz) vegan butter
500 g (1 lb 2 oz/4 cups) strong white bread flour, plus extra for dusting
1 teaspoon ground cinnamon
7g (¼ oz) sachet of fast-action dried yeast
1 teaspoon salt
50 g (1¾ oz/¼ cup) caster (superfine) sugar
100 g (3½ oz/generous ¾ cup) sultanas (golden raisins) or raisins

FOR THE GLAZE

50 g (1¾ oz/¼ cup) caster (superfine) sugar
3 tablespoons water

Saffron buns are a cherished Cornish classic. Delicate, buttery and sweet, infused with aromatic saffron, I remember loving these when I was growing up. There is also a cake version.

1. Heat the milk in a saucepan to almost boiling point. Remove from teh heat. Crumble the saffron threads between your fingers over the pan and stir through. Add the butter and stir until melted, then leave to infuse for 15–20 minutes.
2. If using a stand mixer, add the flour, cinnamon, yeast, salt (keeping the salt separate from the yeast) and sugar to the mixer fitted with a dough hook and pour in the saffron-infused milk. Mix slowly and knead for about 5 minutes.
3. If kneading by hand, in a large bowl, add the flour, cinnamon, yeast, salt (keeping it separate from the yeast) and sugar. Make a well in the centre and pour in the saffron-infused milk. Stir to combine, then turn out onto a lightly floured work surface and knead for 5–7 minutes until the dough is soft and elastic.
4. Add the sultanas and knead for a few more minutes until the dough is springy (it should bounce back when pressed).
5. Cover the bowl with a damp tea (dish) towel and leave the dough to rise in a warm spot for 45–60 minutes until doubled in size. Line a large baking sheet with baking parchment.
6. Turn the risen dough out onto a lightly floured work surface, then knock back (taking the air out of the dough) and knead for 1 minute. Cut the dough into 8–12 pieces. Using your hands, roll each piece into a ball: fold the outside of the dough into the middle, rotate and repeat until you have formed a tight ball. Arrange the dough balls on the lined baking sheet, leaving enough space between each bun, then cover and leave in a warm spot to prove for a further 30 minutes, or until risen.
7. Meanwhile, preheat the oven to 200°C fan (425°F).
8. Bake the risen buns for 18–20 minutes until beautifully golden.
9. Meanwhile, make the glaze. Bring the sugar and water to the boil in a pan for about 1 minute to dissolve the sugar. When the buns are ready, remove them from the oven and place on a wire rack to cool. Brush the glaze over the top of each bun straight away.

Ginger, Turmeric and Lemon Tonic

MAKES 2–3 LITRES (68–102 FL OZ/8½–12¾ CUPS)

juice of 4 lemons
2–3 tablespoons maple syrup
1 tablespoon apple cider vinegar
2.5 cm (1 in) piece of fresh ginger, peeled and sliced
2.5 cm (1 in) piece fresh turmeric, peeled and sliced
¼ teaspoon freshly ground black pepper
¼ teaspoon sea salt
still or sparkling water, for topping up

This soothing tonic is to be enjoyed first thing in the morning as it contains nourishing lemon, ginger, turmeric and apple cider vinegar. Simply top up with ice and enjoy diluted with sparkling or still water.

1. Add all the ingredients, except the still or sparkling water, to a large jug and stir to combine. Leave to chill in the refrigerator for at least 1 hour, or overnight to infuse.
2. Pour the tonic through a sieve (strainer) into a large, clean bottle to filter out any bits.
3. Top up with sparkling or still water to your desired dilution. You can do this with individual servings in the glass, using the tonic like a cordial, or top up in 1–2 large bottles ready for use.
4. I like mine with 2 litres of water for this mixture, making approximately 2 large jugs of tonic.

Notes

— Store in an airtight bottle in the refrigerator. You can recycle a glass or plastic bottle with a tight-fitting lid for this.
— If diluting in the bottle, I would dilute with 2 litres (68 fl oz/ 8½ cups) water.

— *two*

Summer

Tofu Sarnie

SERVES 4

300 g (10½ oz) block firm tofu
2 tablespoons neutral-tasting oil, such as vegetable oil
2 tablespoons soy sauce
1 teaspoon smoked paprika
1 tablespoon maple syrup
1 teaspoon garlic granules

TO SERVE

4 slices of bread of choice
vegan butter, for spreading
lettuce leaves
1 large tomato, sliced
vegan mayonnaise, ketchup, mustard or hot sauce (whatever you like)
sea salt and freshly ground black pepper

There are plenty of plant-based alternatives to bacon available in the shops these days, but my absolute favourite is made with tofu: it crisps beautifully in the oven, and when layered in between toasted bread, with juicy tomato, fresh lettuce and vegan mayo, it really hits the spot.

1. Start by draining and pressing the tofu to make sure all the liquid has been removed. I like to use a tofu press, but this can also be done by slicing the tofu, wrapping in a paper towel and placing something heavy on top then leaving it for up to 30 minutes to squeeze out any excess liquid.
2. Meanwhile, preheat the oven to 200°C fan (425°F) and line a large baking sheet with baking parchment.
3. Mix the oil, soy sauce, paprika, maple syrup and garlic granules together in a small bowl. Using a sharp knife or a mandoline, slice the tofu as thinly as possible, then carefully dip each slice into the soy sauce mixture, allowing the excess to drip off and place on the lined baking sheet. Take care not to overlap each strip.
4. Bake the tofu for 20 minutes, then turn the slices over and bake for a further 15–20 minutes, checking every 10 minutes to make sure the edges do not blacken. If you do see that happening, remove the tofu slices from the oven and leave to cool. The tofu will crisp up even more as it cools.
5. Enjoy in a sandwich loaded up with butter, lettuce, sliced tomato and your favourite sauce!

Notes

— Tofu is perfect for a whole host of recipes and can be enjoyed in sandwiches, wraps, rice bowls, on pasta, etc.
— If you have made more tofu than you need, store it in an airtight container in the refrigerator to enjoy the next day!

Summer Smoothie

SERVES 1

1 banana
150 g (5½ oz/approx scant ½–1 cup)) fresh or frozen summer berries (strawberries, raspberries, blackberries, blueberries)
1 heaped tablespoon of vegan coconut yoghurt
1 tablespoon pumpkin seeds
juice and zest of 1 orange
1 tablespoon maple syrup
150 ml (approx ½–¾5 fl oz/ scant ⅔ cup) non-dairy milk
large handful of ice, if using fresh berries

When the weather gets warmer, all I crave is a refreshing morning smoothie to get the day started. The best thing about smoothies is how many nutrients and vitamins you can pack into one glass. Use either fresh or frozen berries to start the summer.

---

1. Add all of the ingredients to a high-speed blender and blend.

Notes
— Swap the berries for any fruit you like!

Mediterranean Grilled Summer Vegetables

SERVES 2–4

1 aubergine (eggplant), sliced lengthways
1 red (bell) pepper, cored and sliced into quarters
1 fennel bulb, sliced lengthways into 1 cm (½ in) pieces, fronds saved for garnish
2 tablespoons olive oil
vegan feta-style cheese, crumbled, for topping
sea salt and freshly ground black pepper

FOR THE DRESSING
1 tablespoon olive oil
1 teaspoon agave syrup
1 garlic clove, minced
juice of 1 orange
1 tablespoon finely chopped dill

Charred vegetables from under the grill (broiler) is sometimes the simplest and most delicious way to enjoy summer vegetables. The combination of earthy aubergine (eggplant), aniseed fennel and sweet (bell) pepper blends perfectly when enjoyed with a bright lemon and herb dressing atop peppery rocket (arugula).

---

1. Preheat the grill (broiler).
2. Arrange the aubergine, pepper and fennel out on a large baking tray (pan), then brush or drizzle with the olive oil and season with salt and pepper on both sides. Grill (broil) for 5 minutes on each side until charred and browned.
3. Meanwhile, whisk all the dressing ingredients together in a bowl.
4. Add the grilled vegetables to a platter or in individual bowls, then pour over the dressing. Sprinkle with crumbled vegan feta and the saved fennel fronds and enjoy warm or cold!

Coronation Chickpeas

SERVES 4

2 tablespoons olive oil
1 red onion, finely sliced into half-moons
2 tablespoons flaked (slivered) almonds
400 g (14 oz) tin chickpeas (garbanzos), rinsed and drained
2 teaspoons medium curry powder
pinch of dried chilli (hot pepper) flakes (optional)
1 teaspoon tomato purée (paste)
1 tablespoon mango chutney
zest of 1 lemon
2 teaspoons lemon juice
50 g (1¾ oz/¼ cup) dried apricots or use raisins, sultanas (golden raisins) or dried mango
2 tablespoons vegan mayonnaise
pinch of caster (superfine) sugar
1 tablespoon vegan yoghurt
2 tablespoons finely chopped coriander (cilantro)
sea salt and freshly ground black pepper

A playful take on a very British classic, this plant-based version swaps chicken for chickpeas (garbanzos), keeping all the sweet, spiced richness of the original. It's the kind of recipe that feels just right for a summer picnic or a lazy lunch in the garden.

---

1. Heat the oil in a large saucepan over a low-medium heat, add the onion and cook for 10 minutes, or until softened.
2. Meanwhile, toast the flaked almonds in a dry frying pan over a low to medium heat, stirring frequently until lightly browned. Set aside.
3. Add the chickpeas to the onion, mash just a little, so there's a mixture of textures, then add the curry powder and chilli flakes. Season and stir to combine. Reduce the heat to low and cook for another minute, then remove from the heat and add to a large bowl. Leave to cool for 2 minutes, then add all the remaining ingredients, holding back a little of the coriander to sprinkle over later, and stir to combine.
4. Check the seasoning, sprinkle over the toasted flaked almonds and the remaining coriander and serve in a sandwich or with a fresh green salad.

BBQ Shredded Tofu Taco

<u>*SERVES 4 (MAKES 8 TACOS)*</u>

300 g (10½ oz) block extra firm smoked tofu, drained and pressed as per the instructions on page 74 (you can use unsmoked tofu)
1 teaspoon smoked paprika
1 teaspoon ground coriander
1 teaspoon ground cumin
½ teaspoon ground cinnamon
pinch of chilli (hot pepper) flakes
2 tablespoons olive oil
1 onion, finely chopped
3 garlic cloves, very finely chopped
2 tablespoons barbecue sauce
2 tablespoons tomato purée (paste)
sea salt and freshly ground black pepper

<u>*TO SERVE*</u>
avocado, sliced or mashed
salsa of choice
finely chopped coriander (cilantro)
lime wedges
shredded lettuce (optional)
vegan cheese, grated (optional)
8 tortillas

Grating tofu makes for the ideal texture for a shredded barbecue taco. It's fast to whip together in under 30 minutes, made with warming spices and assembled with creamy avocado, zesty lime, spicy salsa and crunchy lettuce.

---

1. Start by grating the tofu coarsely using a box grater.
2. Mix all the spices together in a large bowl, add the grated tofu and toss to combine until evenly coated.
3. Heat the oil in a large frying pan over a medium heat, add the onion and fry for 5–10 minutes until softened. Stir in the garlic and fry for a minute or two.
4. Next, add the spiced tofu and the remaining ingredients. Stir to combine, then cook for 5 minutes, or until crisp on one side. Once starting to brown, use a spatula to flip the shredded tofu and crisp up on the other side for a further 5 minutes. Continue to flip a few more times to reach the desired crispiness.
5. Meanwhile, prepare your toppings of choice. I love some mashed avocado, salsa and coriander finished with a squeeze of lime.
6. Warm the tortillas up either in the microwave or by quickly heating each side of the tortilla in a hot pan for 5–10 seconds. Keep them warm inside a tea (dish) towel as you go.
7. Load up your taco with the crispy shredded tofu and your favourite toppings, and enjoy!

Notes
— This recipe would work well with mushrooms or beans instead of the tofu (minus the grating)!

Multigrain Bean Salad with Mint and Pomegranate Dressing

SERVES 6–8

150 g (5½ oz/¾ cup) brown, black or wild rice
150 g (5½ oz/generous ¾ cup) whole grains (such as buckwheat, quinoa, barley, amaranth, farro, burghul)
400 g (14 oz) tin beans (such as kidney beans, black beans, chickpeas (garbanzos), black-eyed beans butter (lima) beans, pinto beans), drained and rinsed
10 cherry tomatoes, quartered
6 radishes, very thinly sliced (I used a mandoline)
1 small red onion, thinly sliced into half-moons
1 tablespoon pumpkin seeds
handful of lamb's lettuce or use rocket (arugula) or young spinach
pomegranate seeds, for topping (optional)
lemon wedges, to serve

FOR THE DRESSING

1 tablespoon finely chopped mint
2 teaspoons Dijon mustard
1 teaspoon pomegranate molasses
zest and juice of 1 lemon
2 tablespoons olive oil
sea salt and freshly ground black pepper

A fresh and vibrant multigrain salad that is full of goodness. It's delicious warm or cold as a nutritious lunch or shared at a gathering. The final touch of pomegranate molasses in the dressing and pomegranate seeds for topping takes the flavour to another level.

---

1. Cook the rice and whole grains according to the packet instructions. Set aside to cool.
2. Meanwhile, whisk all the dressing ingredients together in a small bowl. Taste and adjust the seasoning.
3. When the rice and whole grains are cool, add to a large bowl with the remaining salad ingredients, adding the lamb's lettuce last and tossing everything together.
4. Pour over the dressing, sprinkle over the pomegranate seeds, if using, and serve with lemon wedges.

Notes

— This salad works as a great base depending on what grains or beans you want to add, or have in your store cupboard.
— Double up the dressing ingredients and store the extra in an airtight container or jar in the refrigerator to use at a later date. Simply give it a shake before using.

Our BBQ Potato Salad

SERVES 6

750 g (1 lb 10 oz) new potatoes, large ones cut in half
30 ml (1 fl oz/2 tablespoons) olive oil
zest and juice of 1 lemon
1 red onion, finely chopped
2 tablespoons finely chopped parsley
3 tablespoons finely chopped mint
2 tablespoons finely chopped dill
1 pomegranate, deseeded
1 teaspoon sumac
sea salt and freshly ground black pepper

I prefer a lighter and fresher version of the classic potato salad, something with lemony olive oil, aromatic herbs and juicy pomegranate to accompany a barbecue. This is super easy to make ahead and serve cold for hosting in the summer.

1. Cook the potatoes in large saucepan of boiling salted water until tender, then drain and leave to steam.
2. Mix the olive oil, lemon juice and zest and salt and pepper to taste in a small bowl with a hand whisk.
3. Add the remaining ingredients to a large bowl, then add the potatoes and dressing, and mix to combine. Leave to chill in the refrigerator until ready to serve.

Harissa Roasted Tomatoes and Mushrooms

<u>*SERVES 3–4*</u>

500 g (1 lb 2 oz) cherry tomatoes
500 g (1 lb 2 oz) chestnut mushrooms, cleaned and stalks trimmed
2 tablespoons harissa paste
2 tablespoons olive oil
2 garlic cloves, minced
squeeze of lemon juice

<u>*TO SERVE*</u>
drizzle of balsamic glaze
1 tablespoon chopped coriander (cilantro)

Coating tomatoes and mushrooms with a harissa-based spicy marinade and roasting until caramelized makes my mouth water just thinking about it. They are delicious with flatbreads or spooned over whole grains for an effortless lunch or light dinner.

---

1. Preheat the oven to 180°C fan (400°F).
2. Pierce each cherry tomato with the tip of a sharp knife to allow the flavours to be absorbed, and tumble into a large baking tray (pan) with the mushrooms.
3. Mix the harissa paste, olive oil, garlic and lemon together in a small bowl, then add to the baking dish and toss through so everything is covered. Bake for 25–30 minutes until the tomatoes have softened.
4. Serve with a drizzle of balsamic glaze and a sprinkle of coriander. Add some warmed flatbreads for an ideal lunch.

Notes

— Replace the mushrooms with courgette (zucchini), aubergine (eggplant) or (bell) pepper for something different next time.

Baked Green Falafel with Courgette and Tahini Dip

SERVES 2–3

400 g (14 oz) tin chickpeas (garbanzos), drained and rinsed
1 small onion, roughly chopped
large handful (25–30 g/1 oz) of parsley, roughly chopped
large handful (25–30 g/1 oz) of coriander (cilantro), roughly chopped
large handful (25–30 g/1 oz) of mint, roughly chopped
½ teaspoon chilli (hot pepper) flakes, to taste
2 garlic cloves, grated
1 teaspoon ground cumin
squeeze of lemon juice
2 tablespoons chickpea (gram or *besan*) flour
½ teaspoon bicarbonate of soda (baking soda)
sea salt and freshly ground black pepper

FOR THE COURGETTE AND TAHINI DIP

2 tablespoons olive oil, plus extra for frying
1 courgette (zucchini), roughly chopped
zest and juice of 1 lemon
1 garlic clove, grated
2 tablespoons tahini
150 g (5½ oz) vegan coconut yoghurt
small handful of mint, roughly chopped
small dash of maple syrup, to taste

These herby falafels are packed with vibrant green goodness in the parsley, coriander (cilantro) and mint, and served with a fresh and creamy courgette (zucchini) tahini yoghurt. Baking them in the oven instead of deep-frying makes them easy and lighter to eat.

---

1. To make the falafels, add the chickpeas to a food processor with the onion, parsley, coriander, mint, chilli flakes, garlic, cumin, lemon juice, 1 teaspoon of salt and plenty of black pepper and pulse until mixed, making sure not to overblend.
2. Next, add the mixture to a large bowl and add the flour and bicarbonate of soda and mix thoroughly. Cover and chill in the refrigerator for 30 minutes.
3. Preheat the oven to 200°C fan (425°F). Line a baking sheet with baking parchment or a silicone mat.
4. Wet your hands and divide the falafel mixture into 10 portions, then roll them into balls, about 4 cm (1½ in) diameter and 25 g (scant 1 oz) each. Place each ball onto the prepared baking tray and bake for 25 minutes, turning halfway.
5. Meanwhile, make the dip. Heat a little olive oil in a large frying pan over a medium heat and fry the courgettes until softened.
6. Add the courgettes to a food processor together with the remaining dip ingredients and blitz to combine, adding a dash of warm water to loosen if needed.
7. Serve the falafels with the courgette and tahini dip, warmed flatbread or pitta bread.

Notes

— For a crispier coating, you can deep-fry the falafels. Heat enough oil in a large saucepan (don't fill it more than two-thirds full) and fry the falafels for a few minutes until golden, taking care not to overcrowd the pan.

Mushroom Satay Kebab

MAKES 6–8 KEBABS

400 g (14 oz) oyster mushrooms (if you can't find oyster mushrooms, this can be subbed for shiitake)
50 g (1¾ oz) vegan coconut yoghurt
2 garlic cloves, very finely chopped
½ tsp ground coriander
½ teaspoon ground cumin
½ teaspoon ground turmeric
½ teaspoon curry powder
1 tablespoon dark soy sauce
2 tablespoons vegetable oil
sea salt and freshly ground black pepper

FOR THE PEANUT SAUCE

3 tablespoons smooth peanut butter
1 tablespoon light soy sauce
juice of 1 lime
1 tablespoon maple syrup
thumb-sized piece of ginger, peeled and grated
small handful of coriander (cilantro), chopped
1–2 teaspoons chilli sauce

Mushrooms might be my favourite food on the planet, and one of the best mushrooms out there is the oyster mushroom. They are meaty, tender and soak up flavours so beautifully, making them ideal for a chargrilled kebab dipped in a spicy peanut sauce.

---

1. Depending on how they come, tear the oyster mushrooms into bite-sized strips using your hands if needed (this is best rather than using a knife to get the right texture).
2. Mix the yoghurt, garlic, spices and soy sauce together in a large bowl and season with salt and pepper.
3. Add the torn mushrooms to the yoghurt mixture and toss to coat evenly. Cover with cling film (plastic wrap) and leave to chill in the refrigerator for at least 2 hours or overnight.
4. Before you start cooking, soak 6–8 wooden skewers in a large bowl of warm water for about 30 minutes. This prevents the skewers from burning while cooking.
5. Preheat the grill (broiler) or light a barbecue.
6. Meanwhile, prepare the peanut sauce for dipping by whisking all the ingredients together in a bowl. You could also use a food processor. Taste and adjust the seasoning, adding the hot sauce to your spice preference.
7. Load the marinated mushrooms onto the skewers and brush with oil.
8. Grill (broil) or barbecue on both sides for 8–10 minutes, rotating as you go until golden brown and crispy.
9. Enjoy dipped in or drizzled with the peanut sauce straight away!

Notes

— You could try this recipe with a 300 g (10½ oz) block of cubed tofu instead of mushrooms for some loaded tofu satay.

Black Bean Burgers with Summer Hot Sauce

MAKES 6 BURGERS

400 g (14 oz) tin black beans, drained, and carefully dried in a tea (dish) towel
1 garlic clove, grated
½ red onion, chopped
1 tablespoon milled (ground) flaxseed
3 tablespoons water
125 g (4½ oz/1½ cups) breadcrumbs
200 g (7 oz/1 cup) cooked long-grain brown rice
1 red chilli, chopped
1 teaspoon Cajun seasoning
2 tablespoons cornflour (cornstarch)
1 tablespoon chopped coriander (cilantro)
1 tablespoon barbecue sauce
vegetable oil, for frying
sea salt and freshly ground black pepper

FOR THE SUMMER HOT SAUCE

100 g (3½ oz) red chillies, chopped
1 medium onion, chopped
2 garlic cloves, chopped
200 g (7 oz) tomatoes, chopped
2 teaspoons tomato purée (paste)
150 ml (5 fl oz/scant ⅔ cup) apple cider vinegar
2 tablespoons lime juice (about ½ lime)
1 tablespoon maple syrup
1 tablespoon vegetable oil

Black beans make the absolute best burgers. They have the right texture to hold their shape in a patty and have a delicious depth of flavour when combined with all the seasonings. Pair with a homemade summer hot sauce that is as vibrant as it is punchy.

---

1. Add all the burger ingredients, except the vegetable oil, to a food processor and pulse to mix, making sure not to blend to a paste, but simply to combine. Alternatively, using your hands, combine the mixture so it clumps together (if using your hands, you may want to chop the ingredients more finely).
2. Shape the mixture into 6 burger patties, then place on a plate, cover with cling film (plastic wrap) and leave to chill in the refrigerator while you make your hot sauce.
3. For the hot sauce, add all the ingredients to a food processor and blitz, then taste and adjust the seasoning.
4. To cook the burgers, heat a dash of oil in a large frying pan, and once hot, add half of the patties and cook for a few minutes over a medium heat until browned. Turn over and repeat on the other side. Reduce the heat to low and continue to cook for a few more minutes until they have cooked through into the middle. Keep an eye to make sure they don't burn on the base. You can keep them warm in the oven while you finish the second batch.
5. Serve in a burger bun or flatbreads with salad and accompanying hot sauce.

Notes

— The hot sauce recipe makes more than you need for this dish, so store the sauce in a sealed sterilized jar in the refrigerator for about 2 weeks to enjoy with other meals.

Lemony Green Bean Linguine

SERVES 4

25 g (scant 1 oz/2 tablespoons) pine nuts
75 g (2¾ oz/scant 1 cup) fresh breadcrumbs, toasted
olive oil, for toasting the breadcrumbs
1 teaspoon garlic granules
handful of basil, chopped
handful of parsley, chopped
zest and juice of 1 lemon
400 g (14 oz) dried linguine
500 g (1 lb 2 oz) green beans, cut into 3–4 cm (1 ¼–1½ in) lengths
sea salt and freshly ground black pepper
1 teaspoon chilli (hot pepper) flakes (optional), to serve
vegan Parmesan- or Cheddar-style cheese, grated, to serve

This is a light and zesty simple pasta dish that celebrates the season's green beans. Plus it can be ready in just 15–20 minutes, making it ideal for a simple midweek summer dinner.

---

1. Toast the pine nuts in a dry frying pan over a medium heat until golden brown, then transfer to a bowl and set aside. In the same pan, toast the breadcrumbs in a little oil until crisp and golden.
2. Add the breadcrumbs to the bowl with the pine nuts, then add the garlic granules, herbs, lemon zest, salt and pepper and mix to combine.
3. Bring a large saucepan of salted water to the boil and add the linguine. Return to the boil, then reduce to a simmer and cook for 8–10 minutes until al dente. Add the green beans 2 minutes before the end of cooking. Drain, reserving 50 ml (1¾ fl oz/3½ tablespoons) of the pasta cooking water. Return the pasta and beans to the pan, along with the pasta water and lemon juice and stir through.
4. Mix in the herby breadcrumbs, saving a handful for the topping. Serve in bowls topped with the reserved breadcrumbs, a sprinkle of chilli flakes (if using) and a little vegan cheese.

Notes

— You could add a tub, about 250 ml (8 fl oz/1 cup) of vegan cream to the pasta for a creamy sauce!

Veg Sausage and Courgette Pilaf

SERVES 4

250 g (9 oz/1¼ cups) basmati rice
500 ml (17 fl oz/generous 2 cups) vegetable stock
handful of flaked (slivered) almonds
2 tablespoons olive oil
8 vegan sausages, each cut into 4 pieces
2 medium courgettes (zucchini), sliced into half-moons
1 red onion, chopped
1 medium white onion, finely chopped
2 garlic cloves, grated
1 teaspoon nigella seeds
10 cherry tomatoes, halved
200 g (7 oz/1¼ cups) frozen peas
1 tablespoon pomegranate molasses or balsamic vinegar
2 tablespoons chopped mint
3 tablespoons chopped parsley
sea salt and freshly ground black pepper

TO SERVE

vegan coconut yoghurt
balsamic glaze, for drizzling

This is my idea of comfort food for the summer with juicy, seasonal garden courgettes (zucchini), herby veggie sausages and bursts of peas mingled in fluffy rice. It's a brilliant way to use up a glut of summer veg, and comes together with little fuss.

---

1. Cook the rice in the vegetable stock in a large saucepan according to the packet instructions.
2. Meanwhile, toast the flaked almonds in a dry frying pan over a medium heat for a few minutes. Set aside.
3. Next, heat 1 tablespoon of oil in a large frying pan over a medium heat, add the sausages and cook until they have lightly browned. Remove from the pan and set aside.
4. Add the remaining oil to the frying pan over a medium heat, then add the courgettes and black pepper and fry until the courgettes have browned and the water from them has evaporated.
5. Add the onions, garlic and nigella seeds to the pan and cook for a couple of minutes until they have just started to soften. Add the tomatoes and peas and fry for a further few minutes until the onions and tomatoes are softened.
6. Add the cooked sausages, cooked rice, pomegranate molasses and herbs to the pan and stir through to combine all the ingredients. Taste to check the seasoning.
7. Transfer to a serving dish and serve with a dollop of vegan yoghurt, a drizzle of balsamic glaze and the toasted almonds.

Notes

— Try swapping the vegan sausages for a 400 g (14 oz) tin of your favourite beans.

Five Green Pasta

SERVES 4

1 tablespoon olive oil
1 leek, roughly chopped
1 courgette (zucchini), roughly chopped
3 garlic cloves, grated
100 g (3½ oz/scant ⅔ cup) frozen peas
100 g (3½ oz) spinach
400 g (14 oz) pasta of choice
handful of basil leaves
75 g (2¾ oz/½ cup) cashews
75 ml (2½ fl oz/5 tablespoons) extra virgin olive oil
zest and juice of ½ lemon
sea salt and freshly ground black pepper

TO SERVE
lemon juice, for drizzling
handful of basil leaves
pistachios, roughly chopped, for sprinkling

The easiest way to eat enough greens is by blending them into a delicious sauce to be enjoyed with pasta. This pasta packs in five different greens blitzed into a velvety creamy cashew sauce. Plus it's ready in under 30 minutes.

1. Heat the olive oil in a large frying pan over a medium heat, add the leek and fry for 5 minutes, or until softened.
2. Add the courgette and cook for a further 5 minutes until the leek and courgettes start to brown and caramelize. Stir through the garlic, then add the peas and spinach and cook for 1–2 minutes until fragrant and wilted.
3. Bring a large saucepan of salted water to the boil, add the pasta and cook according to the packet instructions until al dente.
4. Meanwhile, transfer the leek, courgette, spinach and garlic mix to a food processor or blender, along with the remaining ingredients and a ladleful of the pasta cooking water and blend until smooth, adding more water if it needs it. Taste, then season with salt and pepper if needed.
5. Once the pasta is ready, drain and stir through the sauce straight away. Serve in bowls with a drizzle of lemon juice, basil leaves and a sprinkling of pistachios.

Notes
— If you have any sauce left over, store in an airtight container in the refrigerator for up to 3 days.

Warm Butter Bean, New Potato and Tomato Salad

SERVES 2–4

400 g (14 oz) new potatoes, any large ones halved
400 g (14 oz) tin butter (lima) beans, drained and rinsed
300 g (10½ oz) mixed tomatoes, halved
1 red onion, finely sliced into half-moons
small bunch of basil, torn
1 tablespoon finely chopped mint
sea salt

FOR THE DRESSING
4 tablespoons olive oil
1 garlic clove, finely chopped
zest of ½ lemon
1 teaspoon za'atar
1 teaspoon maple syrup
1 tablespoon balsamic vinegar or red wine vinegar
sea salt and freshly ground black pepper

This comforting warm salad combines potatoes, butter (lima) beans and summery fresh tomatoes with a herby, zesty dressing. This is the sort of salad to be enjoyed after a long day in the sun.

---

1. Bring a large saucepan of salted water to the boil, add the potatoes and cook for 15 minutes, or until softened. Drain and add to a large bowl with the beans. Toss to combine and warm the beans.
2. Meanwhile, whisk all the dressing ingredients together in a small bowl and season with salt and pepper. Set aside.
3. Add all the remaining salad ingredients to the potatoes and gently mix. Just before serving, add the dressing and toss through.

Tear and Share Cheesy Bread

MAKES 24 BALLS

500 g (1lb 2 oz/4 cups) strong white bread flour, plus extra for dusting
7g (¼ oz) sachet fast-action dried yeast
1 teaspoon granulated sugar
1 teaspoon salt
1 tablespoon olive oil, plus extra for greasing
150 ml (5 fl oz/scant ⅔ cup) unsweetened non-dairy milk, at room temperature
175 ml (6 fl oz/¾ cup) lukewarm water
1 garlic clove, very finely chopped
3 thyme sprigs, finely chopped
150 g (5½ oz) vegan cheese, grated
100 g (3½ oz/¾ cup) pitted black olives, halved
sea salt and freshly ground black pepper

These soft, golden dough balls are filled with melty vegan cheese, thyme and black olives and baked together in a round that's made for pulling apart at the table. This bread is best enjoyed warm and shared with friends and family.

---

1. Add the flour, yeast and sugar to a large mixing bowl (or the bowl of a stand mixer). Add the salt to the other side of the bowl (the salt and yeast cannot mix yet as the salt may deactivate the yeast).
2. Next, add the olive oil, milk and water and knead with the dough hook on medium speed for 5 minutes, or by hand on a lightly floured work surface for 10 minutes, until soft and elastic.
3. Place the dough in a bowl, cover with a damp tea (dish) towel and leave in a warm spot to rise for 1 hour, or until doubled in size.
4. Meanwhile, mix the garlic, thyme, vegan cheese and olives together in a bowl and season with salt and pepper. Set aside.
5. Grease a 22–25 cm (9–10 in) round springform cake tin (pan) with a little olive oil and set aside.
6. Remove the dough from the bowl and place on a lightly floured work surface. Using your fingertips, press all over the dough to knock back.
7. Cut the dough in half, then roll each piece into a ball. Cover with a damp tea (dish) towel and leave to rise on the work surface for 10 minutes.
8. After 10 minutes, cut the two dough balls in half, then in half again. Keep going until you have 24 even-sized pieces.
9. Flatten each piece into a small ball, and add 1 tablespoon of the cheese mixture to the centre. Gather the edges by bringing them into the middle over the filling. Move around in a circle until you form a tight ball. Flip the dough ball over so the seal is on the base. Repeat for all 24 pieces.
10. Arrange the balls in the prepared cake tin in a circle, starting from the middle. Cover and leave to prove for 1 hour, or until doubled in size.
11. Preheat the oven to 200°C fan (425°F). Bake in the oven for 25–30 minutes until golden brown. Enjoy warm torn apart with friends and family.

Fruit Scones with Coconut Cream

MAKES 8–10 SCONES

350 g (12 oz/generous 2¾ cups) self-raising flour, plus extra for dusting
40 g (1½oz/scant ¼ cup) granulated sugar
good pinch of salt
1 teaspoon baking powder
90 g (3¼ oz) vegan butter
1 teaspoon vanilla extract
150 ml (5 fl oz/scant ⅔ cup) non-dairy milk, plus extra for brushing
50 g (1¾ oz/¼ cup) mixed dried fruit
homemade Blackberry Jam (page 156), to serve

FOR THE VEGAN COCONUT CREAM

75 ml (2½ fl oz/5 tablespoons) coconut cream
3 tablespoons vegan butter
2 tablespoons icing (powdered) sugar

Warm scones straight out of the oven, loaded up with homemade jam and coconut cream (jam first of course – the only and Cornish way) is one of the best sweet treats there is!

---

1. Line a large baking tray (pan) with baking parchment and set aside. In a stand mixer bowl fitted with a paddle attachment, or mixing bowl if not using a mixer, measure out the flour, sugar, salt and baking powder and stir together. Then add the vegan butter and mix until you have fine breadcrumbs (if you don't have a stand mixer, you can also pulse it in a food processor or rub it with your fingers).
2. Next, in a jug, add the vanilla extract to the milk and stir together. Slowly pour the milk into the flour mixture, combining (either with the mixer on low or by hand) until you have a smooth dough. Add the dried fruit and give it a final mix to combine.
3. Gently roll out the dough on a lightly floured work surface until it is about 2 cm (¾ in) thick. Don't play with the dough too much, just a quick roll to flatten. Transfer the dough to the lined baking tray and chill in the refrigerator for about 25–30 minutes.
4. Using 8 cm (3 in) biscuit (cookie) cutters, cut out 8–10 scones from the chilled dough, making sure not to twist the cutter as this will stop the scones from rising properly. Simply place the cutter on the dough, bash down and remove. Gently roll out any dough trimmings and cut out more scones.
5. Place each scone on the baking sheet, leaving a 2 cm (¾ in) gap between each. Brush the tops gently with a little milk, making sure it doesn't drip down the sides (they may rise unevenly if it does), then freeze for 15 minutes.
6. Preheat the oven to 200°C fan (425°F). Bake the chilled scones for 15 minutes, or until they are golden brown.
7. Meanwhile, make the coconut cream. Using a stand mixer fitted with a whisk attachment, or an electric whisk on high speed, whisk all the ingredients together for 5 minutes, until light and fluffy.
8. Serve the scones warm, cut in half, spread with jam first (the Cornish way) and topped with a dollop of coconut cream.

Lemon and Elderflower Cake

SERVES 8–10

150 ml (5 fl oz/scant ⅔ cup) vegetable oil, plus extra for oiling
400 g (14 oz/scant 3¼ cups) self-raising flour
300 g (10½ oz/1⅓ cups) golden caster (superfine) sugar
1½ teaspoon baking powder
zest of 2 lemons, half for inside, half to decorate
250 ml (8 fl oz/1 cup) water
wild elderflowers (just the flowers, not the leaves), to decorate

FOR THE DRIZZLE
3 tablespoons elderflower cordial (see page 120 for homemade)
juice of 1 lemon

FOR THE ICING
500 g (1 lb 2 oz/4 cups) icing (powdered) sugar, sifted
250 g (9 oz) vegan butter or margarine, softened
zest of 1 lemon
2 tablespoons elderflower cordial (see page 120)
1 tablespoon non-dairy milk

Elderflower starts to come into bloom in late May to June, filling up the hedgerows and attracting the bees. This sponge cake is delicately infused with lemon and Elderflower Cordial (see page 120) and is beautifully fluffy and deliciously moist.

---

1. Preheat the oven to 180°C fan (400°F). Oil two 20 cm (8 in) cake tins (pans) and line the base and sides with baking parchment.
2. For the cake, add all the dry ingredients to a large bowl and mix together. Add the lemon zest, then pour in the oil and water and stir everything together until completely combined. Divide the batter equally between both cake tins and bake for 30 minutes, or until golden brown and a skewer inserted into the centre of the cake comes out clean.
3. Mix all the drizzle ingredients together in a small bowl.
4. When the cakes are baked, remove from the oven and leave to cool in the tins for about 10 minutes, then turn out onto a wire rack. Pierce small holes all over the cakes with a skewer or cocktail stick (toothpick) and brush or pour the drizzle over. Leave to cool.
5. For the icing, add half of the icing sugar to a large bowl, together with the butter and beat with an electric whisk until light and fluffy. Whisk in the remaining icing sugar, the lemon zest, cordial and milk until light and fluffy again.
6. Pour about half of the icing over the top of one of the cakes and spread out evenly with a spatula. Add the second cake on top, then add the rest of the icing to the top with a spatula. Smooth out, but don't worry about it looking perfect.
7. Decorate with some extra grated lemon zest and some wild foraged elderflowers, if you like. Alternatively, add the flowers around the edge of the plate for decoration.*

Notes

— The foraged elderflowers in this recipe are for decoration. While the flowers are edible in small amounts, the elderflower plant does contain toxins, so I would advise picking the flowers off when enjoying a slice.

Blackcurrant Ice Cream

SERVES 8

400 g (14 oz) fresh blackcurrants
1 tablespoon water
2 x 400 ml (14 fl oz) tins coconut milk (with the cream)
120 g (4 oz/½ cup) caster (superfine) sugar
pinch of sea salt
1 teaspoon cornflour (cornstarch)
splash of cold non-dairy milk
1 teaspoon vanilla extract

It's surprisingly easy to whip up ice cream at home. Using coconut cream makes it rich and complements the sharpness of blackcurrants. You can also try this recipe with other fresh berries throughout the summer months, if you like.

---

1. Soften the blackcurrants with the water in a small saucepan over a medium heat. Pour into a sieve (strainer) and push through into a bowl to make a purée. Set aside.
2. Add the coconut milk, sugar and salt to a large pan and heat over a medium heat until the sugar has dissolved.
3. In a small bowl, mix the cornflour with a little cold non-dairy milk, then add to the pan and cook for a few minutes whisking constantly until slightly thickened.
4. Remove from the heat and stir in the vanilla extract and blackcurrant purée, then leave to cool. Once cooled, transfer to a freezer-proof container with a lid and set in the freezer for at least 3–4 hours.
5. After 3–4 hours, when the ice cream looks set, stir it through and return to the freezer. Leave overnight to be enjoyed the next day.

Notes

— If you have an ice-cream machine, pour it into the machine and let it do its work according to the instructions, then store in the freezer.
— Add a tiny amount (25 ml/scant 2 tablespoons) of alcohol (crème de cassis is ideal) to the ice cream to keep it softer in the freezer.
— This recipe will work well with any berries. You can also use frozen berries.

Elderflower Cordial

MAKES 2 LITRES (68 FL OZ/8½ CUPS)

25 elderflower heads, stalks trimmed
1.5 litres (50 fl oz/ 6 ¼ cups) water
1.5 kg (3 lb 5 oz/6½ cups) granulated sugar
zest and juice of 3 lemons
50 g (1¾ oz) citric acid

I tried this recipe a few years ago when I wanted to get more into foraging, and realized I could make my favourite drink from scratch! I've referenced both the Good Food and the River Cottage recipe with a few extra tips I've learnt along the way!

---

1. Forage the elderflower heads in the morning on a sunny dry day when they are the most fragrant and the pollen is fresh. The best time of year to do this is late May to mid-June when the flowers are in bloom. Remove the stalks and check for any small insects. Wash very gently in cold water by swirling them around (don't rinse them under the tap or mess around with them too much as this will take away lots of flavour), then lift them out carefully and set aside.
2. Bring the water to the boil in a large saucepan, add the sugar and heat gently, but don't boil, until the sugar is completely dissolved. Once it has dissolved, bring to the boil and simmer for a minute or two, then turn off the heat.
3. Add the elderflowers, lemon zest (you can zest the lemons quite coarsely with a vegetable peeler or coarse grater), juice and citric acid to the pan. I also throw the lemons in there too to infuse. Cover the pan with a lid and leave to stand overnight.
4. The next day, strain the liquid through a muslin (cheesecloth) or tea (dish) towel. I find this easiest to do over a sieve (strainer) or colander over a jug (pitcher) with a spout, gently with a ladle.
5. Pour the cordial through a funnel into sterilized bottles with lids (screw top or swing-top, for example) and store in the refrigerator. It lasts for about 6 weeks.

Notes

— To sterilize the bottles, either run them through the dishwasher, or wash with hot soapy water, then place in the oven at 160°C fan (350°F) for 15 minutes.

— three

Autumn

Leftover Squash Pancakes

<u>*MAKES 6 PANCAKES*</u>

100 g (3½ oz) leftover squash or pumpkin, puréed (or use shop-bought pumpkin purée)
125 g (4½ oz/1 cup) plain (all-purpose) flour (or use gluten-free flour)
2 tablespoons caster (superfine) sugar
1 teaspoon ground cinnamon
½ teaspoon mixed spice
1 tablespoon baking powder
pinch of sea salt
240 ml (just over 8 fl oz/scant 1 cup) non-dairy milk
1 tablespoon apple cider vinegar
1 teaspoon vanilla extract
vegetable oil, for cooking

<u>*TO SERVE*</u>
maple syrup
fresh fruit, such as blueberries or apples

These cosy pancakes are a great way to use any lingering pumpkins or squash from festive decorations or autumn (fall) meals. I often also make a batch of my own pumpkin purée at this time of year, which makes these pancakes super easy to whip up. You can also easily find pumpkin purée in the supermarket.

---

1. Prepare your leftover squash by roasting in the oven and puréeing ahead of time. You can do this with any squash or pumpkins you've used for decoration, or leftovers from meals you have made. Alternatively, this can be substituted with shop-bought pumpkin purée.
2. Sift the flour into a large bowl, add the sugar, spices, baking powder and salt and stir together with a wooden spoon.
3. Pour the milk, vinegar and vanilla into a measuring jug and stir together. Leave to stand for 10 minutes, then add the squash or pumpkin purée and stir. Pour the wet mixture into the dry mixture bowl and whisk until combined, making sure not to over mix (it's fine if there are a few lumps). Leave the pancake batter to rest for a further 10 minutes.
4. Heat a non-stick frying pan over a medium heat with a small drizzle of vegetable oil. Using a ladle or a measuring jug, add the batter to the pan, about 120 ml (4 fl oz/½ cup) per pancake. When you can see bubbles forming on the top of the pancake, it's ready to flip. So, have a little peek underneath to see if it's golden, and flip! Cook until brown on both sides, then remove to a plate. Repeat the process until all batter is used up. It should yeild about 6 pancakes.
5. Serve with a drizzle of maple syrup and some fresh blueberries or apples.

Cornish Potato Cakes

SERVES 8

600 g (1 lb 5 oz) potatoes, peeled and roughly chopped
200 g (7 oz/1⅔ cups) plain (all-purpose) flour, plus extra for dusting
75 g (2½ oz) non-dairy butter or vegetable oil
small handful of herbs (parsley, chives, dill, basil for example), finely chopped, plus extra for sprinkling
oil cooking spray or vegetable oil, for cooking
sea salt and freshly ground black pepper

Simple, humble and rustic, these potato cakes are made with fluffy boiled potatoes, thickened with flour and seasoned with fresh herbs. They go perfectly with a hearty cooked breakfast, or as a side to a soup crisped up in a pan with a dollop of butter on top. They can be baked or fried, and are irresistibly comforting Cornish fare.

---

1. Bring a large saucepan of salted water to the boil, add the potatoes and cook for 20 minutes. Drain and allow to steam in the colander for 5 minutes until completely cold.
2. Preheat the oven to 200°C fan (425°F). Line a large baking tray (pan) with baking parchment.
3. Add the cold potatoes to a large bowl with the flour and butter or oil and mash until smooth. Season with salt and pepper, then add the chopped herbs and stir to combine.
4. On a lightly floured work surface, roll the dough out into a circle or rectangle, 2.5–3 cm (1–1¼ in) thick, then cut into triangles (like pizza slices) or divide into rectangles. You can also shape them into patties, if you prefer.
5. Arrange on the lined baking tray and spray or drizzle with oil, then bake for 30–35 minutes until golden brown, turning them halfway through cooking. Alternatively, fry in a pan with oil for 5–7 minutes on each side until golden brown. Serve hot with some extra herbs sprinkled on top. These go perfectly with a full English breakfast!

Cider and Onion Soup with Croutons

SERVES 4

60 ml (¼ cup) sunflower oil
5 large onions, sliced
2 bay leaves
1 teaspoon white miso paste
1 tablespoon apple cider vinegar
1 teaspoon garlic granules
500 ml (17 fl oz/generous 2 cups) scrumpy cider
700 ml (24 fl oz/scant 3 cups) vegetable stock
1 large floury potato, peeled and diced into 2 cm (¾ in) pieces
2 slices of rustic bread, cubed or torn into 2 cm (¾ in) cubes
sea salt and freshly ground black pepper

Sweet, slow-cooked onions simmered with proper Cornish scrumpy cider, it's everything I crave when the season starts to switch to grey, blustery days. This soup is best served cosied up indoors with woolly socks and a dog snoozing at your feet.

---

1. Heat 2 tablespoons of the oil in a large saucepan over a low–medium heat, add the onions and bay leaves and fry for 20 minutes, or until the onions are soft and golden.
2. Next, add the miso paste, vinegar and garlic granules and stir through. Pour in the cider, vegetable stock and potato and bring to the boil. Reduce the heat slightly, partially cover the pan with a lid and simmer for 20 minutes, or until the potato is soft. Press some of the potato against the side of the saucepan to mash, to help thicken the soup. Season with salt and pepper.
3. Meanwhile, add the remaining oil to a separate frying pan and add the cubed bread. Lightly season and fry over a medium heat for 5–10 minutes until crispy, take the pan off the heat and set aside until ready to serve.
4. Ladle the soup into individual bowls and top with the croutons.

Potato and Spinach Stuffed Flatbreads

SERVES 4

FOR THE FLATBREADS

200 g (7 oz) vegan plain yoghurt
200 g (7 oz/1⅔ cups) plain (all-purpose) flour, plus extra for dusting
½ teaspoon paprika
1 teaspoon instant dried yeast
olive oil, for frying
sea salt and freshly ground black pepper

FOR THE FILLING

2 medium potatoes, peeled and quartered
100 g (3½ oz) spinach
1 teaspoon ras el hanout
½ onion, finely chopped
1 garlic clove, grated
20 g (¾ oz) dried apricots, finely chopped
a pinch of chilli (hot pepper) flakes
zest of ½ lemon
1 tablespoon nutritional yeast
50 g (1¾ oz) vegan Cheddar-style cheese, grated
sea salt

TO SERVE

coriander (cilantro), roughly chopped
squeeze of lemon juice

Homemade flatbreads are super easy to make, and these ones are stuffed with a comforting mix of mashed potato, earthy spinach, sweet apricot and warming ras el hanout. Finish them off with a generous squeeze of lemon and a sprinkling of coriander (cilantro).

---

1. For the filling, bring a large saucepan of salted water to the boil, add the potatoes and cook for 15–20 minutes until softened. Drain, return the potatoes to the pan and mash.
2. Meanwhile, pour a kettle full of boiling water over the spinach in a colander or sieve (strainer) and stir until wilted. Quickly run under the cold tap and leave to drain. Squeeze in a dry tea (dish) towel to get rid of all the water, then roughly chop and set aside.
3. For the flatbreads, combine the yoghurt, flour, paprika, yeast, salt and pepper in a large mixing bowl, then using your hands, knead the ingredients into a soft dough. Cover with a damp tea (dish) towel and set aside for a few minutes.
4. For the filling, mix the mashed potatoes, spinach, ras el hanout, onion, garlic, apricots, chilli flakes, lemon zest, nutritional yeast and vegan cheese together in another large bowl.
5. Divide the dough into 4 even portions, then roll out each portion on a generously floured work surface into a flat round. Be generous with extra flour for dusting, as the dough can be sticky.
6. Place a quarter of the filling onto the middle of each flatbread and shape into a round.
7. Using wet fingers, lift the edges of the flatbread up over the filling into the centre, working your way around the circle, overlapping each piece of dough as you go and sealing with your fingers.
8. Heat a little olive oil in a large frying pan over a medium heat, add 1–2 stuffed flatbreads and cook for about 5 minutes on each side until golden brown. Repeat with all the flatbreads, then serve with a sprinkling of coriander and a squeeze of lemon juice.

Roasted Tomato and Sweet Potato Soup

SERVES 4

1 kg (2 lb 4 oz) cherry tomatoes, halved
2 medium sweet potatoes, chopped
3 garlic cloves, kept whole and slightly crushed
1 carrot, roughly chopped
2 celery stalks, chopped
2 red onions, roughly chopped
3–4 thyme sprigs
olive oil, for drizzling
½ teaspoon dried oregano
1 teaspoon paprika
½ teaspoon cayenne pepper
500 ml (17 fl oz/generous 2 cups) vegetable stock
200 ml (7 fl oz/scant 1 cup) coconut milk
splash of balsamic vinegar
handful of parsley
sea salt and freshly ground black pepper

TO SERVE

crusty bread
1 tablespoon chopped parsley
toasted pumpkin or sunflower seeds

This soup toes the line between late summer and early autumn (fall), when tomatoes are still sweet but you are craving something warm. Roasting the tomatoes, sweet potatoes and garlic takes the soup to another level.

1. Preheat the oven to 200°C fan (425°F).
2. Add the tomatoes, cut-sides up, the sweet potatoes and garlic to 2 large roasting tins (pans). Add the carrot, celery, onions and thyme and drizzle all over with olive oil. Sprinkle with the dried oregano, paprika and cayenne pepper, then season with salt and pepper and toss to coat.
3. Roast in the oven for 45–50 minutes until everything is softened and starting to brown. Remove from the oven and leave to cool for 10 minutes.
4. Add all the vegetables to a food processor with the stock, coconut milk, balsamic vinegar and parsley and blend until smooth. Alternatively, add everything to a large saucepan and use an immersion blender. Taste and adjust the seasoning, if necessary.
5. Serve the soup warm with crusty bread, a grind of black pepper, the chopped parsley and a sprinkling of toasted pumpkin or sunflower seeds.

Sunflower Super Seed Butter

MAKES 1 X 500 ML (17 FL OZ) JAR

500 g (1 lb 2 oz/4 cups) sunflower seeds
2 tablespoons chia seeds
2 tablespoons flaxseeds
2 teaspoons sea salt
1 teaspoon ground cinnamon
2–4 teaspoons granulated brown sugar

I love making homemade seed butter because you can add so much extra goodness to it! This one has a delicious depth of flavour because the sunflower seeds are roasted and the chia and flax add extra fibre and nutrients. You can sweeten to taste, depending on how you like it, or even leave the sugar out altogether. It's perfect on toast or dolloped on top of porridge.

1. Preheat the oven to 180°C fan (400°F). Line a baking tray (pan) with baking parchment.
2. Spread the sunflower seeds out on the lined baking tray and roast in the oven for 10 minutes, or until golden.
3. Transfer the roasted sunflower seeds to a high-speed blender or food processor and blend until completely smooth. This may take a bit of time, but can be helped along by scraping down the sides as you go until the seeds are a butter consistency. First the seeds will turn sandy, then they will come together into a paste and finally become buttery and creamy.
4. When the sunflower seeds have turned to butter, add the remaining ingredients and blend again until smooth. Taste and adjust the seasoning, if necessary. You may prefer a little more salt or sugar.

Notes

— Store in an airtight jar or container in the cupboard for a couple of weeks, or a month in the refrigerator.
— Why not try adding 1 tablespoon of cocoa (unsweetened chocolate) powder along with the extra seeds for a delicious chocolate seed butter?

Mini Cornish Pasties

MAKES 12 MINI PASTIES

500 g (1 lb 2 oz/4 cups) strong bread flour, plus extra for dusting
1 teaspoon salt
250 g (9 oz) vegan butter, cubed
175 ml (6 fl oz/¾ cup) cold water

FOR THE FILLING

2 tablespoons olive oil
300 g (10½ oz) potatoes, peeled and diced into 1 cm (½ in) pieces
150 g (5½ oz) swede (rutabaga), peeled and diced into 1 cm (½ in) pieces
1 carrot, peeled and diced
1 parsnip, peeled and diced
1 onion, finely chopped
sea salt and freshly ground black pepper

TO GLAZE

1–2 tablespoons non-dairy milk
1 tablespoon olive oil

I couldn't write this book without including a traditional Cornish pasty. All my favourite Cornish bakeries have incredible plant-based versions, and my favourite flavour is always a classic peppery filling of root vegetables inside a flaky pastry. Making these into mini versions is perfect for grabbing on the go.

1. Add the flour and salt to a stand mixer fitted with the paddle attachment. Add the cubed butter and mix until it looks like fine breadcrumbs. Add the cold water and mix until it becomes a pliable dough. This may take a few minutes. (Alternatively, make the dough by hand by rubbing the flour and butter together in a large mixing bowl with your fingertips to create breadcrumbs, then adding the water and mixing until combined.)
2. Transfer the dough to the work surface and roll into a ball, then cover with a tea (dish) towel and leave to rest in the refrigerator for about 3 hours. This can also be done the night before.
3. Preheat the oven to 180°C fan (400°F) and line a large baking sheet with baking parchment.
4. For the filling, combine the olive oil, potatoes, swede, carrot, parsnip and onion together in a large bowl. Season with salt and a generous amount of black pepper. Set aside.
5. Remove the dough from the refrigerator and roll out on a lightly floured work surface. Cut the dough into twelve 20 cm (8 in) rounds.
6. Spoon the filling evenly on half of each of the pastry rounds, piling it up as it will reduce with cooking. Use a little water to dampen around the edges of the round, then fold over and crimp to seal. Glaze the tops of each pasty with a little non-dairy milk mixed with oil and arrange on the lined baking sheet. Bake for 45 minutes, or until golden. Leave to cool a little before serving.

Notes

— You can look up traditional Cornish pasty crimping methods and styles online, or just roll with it!
— Why not add some vegan or vegetarian meat alternatives such as soy mince or sausage if you fancy a few meaty chunks in there too?

Bonfire Not Dogs

SERVES 12–16

300 g (10½ oz) block extra firm tofu, drain and pressed to remove extra moisture (see page 74)
90 ml (3 fl oz/⅓ cup) water
2 tablespoons olive oil
2 tablespoons maple syrup
3 tablespoons barbecue sauce, plus extra for frying
1 tablespoon Dijon mustard
1 tablespoon dark soy sauce
1 teaspoon smoked paprika
1 teaspoon ground cumin
½ teaspoon ground cinnamon
1 teaspoon onion powder
½ teaspoon garlic granules
2 tablespoons tomato purée (paste)
300 g (10½ oz) vital wheat gluten
vegetable oil, for cooking
sea salt and freshly ground black pepper
plain (all-purpose) flour, for dusting

TO SERVE
hot dog buns
piccalilli or ketchup
crispy onions

At this time of year there is nothing better than evenings by the fire – whether inside or outside – with BBQ-style food. Plant-based sausages are surprisingly simple to make from scratch and are ideal served in a bun with ketchup, mustard and crispy onions.

---

1. Break the tofu into pieces and add to a food processor with all the other ingredients, except the flour, vital wheat gluten and oil. Blitz for a few seconds until smooth. Add the gluten and blend until it comes together to form a dough.
2. Turn the dough out onto a lightly floured work surface and knead for 20–25 minutes, rotating as you go.
3. Divide the dough into 4 portions, then divide each piece into 3–4 portions to make 12–16 sausages (either large or regular-sized dogs). You can weigh the dough out if you want all the sausages to be the same size, but I usually eye-ball it!
4. Shape each hot dog with your hands by creating a log shape, then rolling them on the work surface. Place a sausage on a sheet of foil, about 13–15 cm (5–6 inch) wide, and roll up inside the foil. Twist the ends to seal and repeat this for all the sausages.
5. Place the foil-wrapped sausages in a steamer (stack them up if necessary) and steam for 30 minutes. When ready, carefully remove the foil.
6. Heat a little oil in a large frying pan over a medium-high heat, add the sausgaes with a squeeze of barbecue sauce for some extra flavour and moisture and fry until golden on all sides. Alternatively, you can toss them in a bowl with some barbecue sauce and grill (broil) them.
7. Enjoy served in a hot dog bun, topped with a helping of piccalilli or ketchup and crispy fried onions for bonfire night!

Notes

— These not dogs are perfect for making in advance. You can freeze them after steaming in their foil for up to 3 months to be fried and enjoyed later.

AGA

Chana (Chickpea) Squash Curry

SERVES 4

1 small squash, around 1 kg/ 2 lbs (I used butternut, but you can use any), peeled, deseeded and cut into 2 cm (¾ in) chunks
1 teaspoon black mustard seeds
1 teaspoon cumin seeds
60 ml (¼ cup/4 tablespoons) sunflower oil
1 onion, chopped
2 garlic cloves, finely chopped or grated
1 tablespoon grated ginger
1 teaspoon turmeric
1 teaspoon ground coriander
1 teaspoon ground cumin
2 teaspoons chilli powder (can add more for extra spice, less for not so spicy)
2 tablespoons tomato purée (paste)
200 ml (7 fl oz/scant 1 cup) vegetable stock
1 tablespoon brown sugar
4 tomatoes, chopped
small handful of chopped nuts
small handful of pumpkin seeds
400 g (14 oz) tin chickpeas (garbanzos), drained and rinsed
small bunch of coriander (cilantro), chopped
sea salt
naan or rice, to serve

Sweet roasted squash is paired with soft chickpeas (garbanzos), rich tomatoes and warming spices. This curry can easily be thrown together with just storecupboard (pantry) staples and a seasonal squash.

---

1. Preheat the oven to 200°C fan (425°F).
2. Arrange the squash chunks in a large roasting tin (pan) with the mustard and cumin seeds, sea salt to taste and 2 tablespoons of the oil. Roast for 30–35 minutes until the squash has softened. Remove from the oven.
3. Meanwhile, heat the remaining oil in a large saucepan over a medium heat, add the onion and cook for 10 minutes until softened. Add the garlic and ginger and cook for another minute. Stir in the spices and cook for 1 minute, then season with salt and add the tomato purée, vegetable stock, sugar and tomatoes. Give everything a good mix and cook for a further 10 minutes, stirring frequently, until the curry has thickened slightly.
4. Meanwhile, lightly toast the chopped nuts and pumpkin seeds in a dry frying pan. Set aside.
5. Add the chickpeas and roasted squash to the large saucepan mixture with half of the coriander, then cover with a lid and cook for 5 minutes.
6. Serve with the remaining coriander sprinkled over the top, with a side of naan or rice, and the toasted chopped nuts and pumpkin seeds sprinkled over.

Notes

— You can swap the squash for 2 sweet potatoes, and the chickpeas for kidney or butter (lima) beans, or even tofu.

Mushroom Meatballs

SERVES 4

2 tablespoons flaxseeds
6 tablespoons water
1 onion, chopped
2 garlic cloves, chopped
2 tablespoons olive oil
500 g (1 lb 2 oz) chestnut or wild mushrooms, roughly chopped
100 g (3½ oz/1⅔ cups) panko breadcrumbs
50 g (1¾ oz/scant ½ cup) walnuts
75 g (2½ oz/¾ cup) rolled oats
1 tablespoon miso paste
2 tablespoons nutritional yeast
½ teaspoon chilli (hot pepper) flakes
sea salt and freshly ground black pepper

FOR THE SIMPLE TOMATO SAUCE
1 onion, chopped
3 tablespoons olive oil
2 garlic cloves, very finely chopped
2 x 400 g (14 oz) tins chopped tomatoes
1 tablespoon dark brown sugar
1 teaspoon dried oregano
splash of Tabasco sauce or pinch of chilli (hot pepper) flakes

TO SERVE
300 g (10½ oz) dried spaghetti or pasta of choice
handful of herbs (basil, thyme, oregano), roughly chopped
vegan Parmesan-style cheese, finely grated

I just adore mushrooms, and using them for meatballs creates a comforting and crowd-pleasing dish that's ideal served atop a swirl of tomato spaghetti or tucked into a crusty sub roll.

1. Whisk the flaxseeds and water together in a small bowl. Set aside to thicken into a gel consistency.
2. In a large frying pan over a medium heat, cook the onion and garlic in olive oil for around 10 minutes until softened. Add the mushrooms and cook for a further 10–15 minutes until the liquid has evaporated and the mushrooms are starting to brown.
3. Preheat the oven to 220°C fan (475°F) and line a baking tray (pan) with baking parchment.
4. Blend the breadcrumbs, walnuts and oats in a food processor until they form a fine meal.
5. Transfer the onion, garlic and mushrooms to the food processor with the remaining ingredients and pulse until everything starts coming together. Make sure not to overblend. Transfer to a bowl and stir through the flax mixture until combined.
6. Roll and shape the mixture into 16–20 meatballs and arrange on the lined baking tray (pan). Bake for 20–25 minutes until browned, turning halfway through.
7. Meanwhile, prepare the simple tomato sauce. In a large saucepan over a medium heat, fry the onion in oil for 5–10 minutes until softened. Add the garlic and fry for few minutes more. Add the tomatoes, then the brown sugar and dried oregano. Season with a little Tabasco or chilli flakes, and salt and pepper to taste. Bring to the boil, then simmer for 5–10 minutes until the sauce is thickened.
8. When the meatballs are ready, add them to the sauce, cover with a lid and cook for 10 minutes. Don't move them about so they hold their shape.
9. Meanwhile, cook your pasta in a large pan of boiling water for 8–10 minutes until al dente. Drain and return to the pan.
10. Spoon a little of the tomato sauce into the spaghetti and stir to combine. Serve the spaghetti in bowls topped with a large helping of the tomato sauce and meatballs. Finish with a sprinkle of extra herbs and some vegan Parmesan.

Stuffed Cauliflower

SERVES 2–4

1 whole cauliflower, trimmed and leaves removed
bunch of spring onions (scallions), chopped
1 garlic clove, chopped
1 teaspoon paprika
3 tablespoons vegan pesto (or see page 150)
4–6 sundried tomatoes, chopped
zest of 1 lemon
100 g (3½ oz) vegan Cheddar-style cheese, grated
2 tablespoons vegan butter
2 tablespoons apple sauce
sea salt and freshly ground black pepper

FOR THE TOPPING

3 tablespoons fresh breadcrumbs
1 teaspoon paprika
2 tablespoons nutritional yeast
2 tablespoons olive oil

The humble cauliflower can get a bad rep, but stuffed with a mix of pesto, sundried tomatoes, and melty vegan Cheddar, then finished with a crunchy breadcrumb topping, you will have a centrepiece-worthy dish.

---

1. Carefully cut out as much of the stalk and core from the cauliflower as possible, leaving the florets still intact.
2. Bring a large saucepan of salted water to the boil, add the cauliflower and cook for 6–8 minutes until tender (taking care not to overcook to avoid it falling apart when you stuff it). Remove and set aside to steam.
3. Preheat the oven to 200°C fan (425°F).
4. Meanwhile, add the remaining ingredients to a food processor and pulse until finely chopped.
5. For the topping, mix the breadcrumbs with the paprika, nutritional yeast and oil together in a medium bowl. Set aside.
6. Fill a large piping bag with the processed ingredients and cut a small hole in the corner of the bag. Gently turn the cauliflower stem-side up and pipe the filling into the cauliflower, poking it in as you go. Place the cauliflower head upside down in a roasting tin (pan) and cover with a square of baking parchment. Roast upside down for 15 minutes – this allows the stuffing to sink down further into the cauliflower.
7. Remove the cauliflower from the oven, turn it right-side up, keeping the baking parchment in place to help keep the stuffing in and sprinkle the top and sides with the breadcrumb mix. Bake for a further 45 minutes, or until knife tender. Leave to cool for about 10 minutes before slicing into wedges to serve.

Roasted Butternut Squash and Sausage Gnocchi

SERVES 3–4

500 g (1 lb 2 oz) small butternut squash, peeled, deseeded and diced
1 packet (about 280–300 g/ 10–10½ oz) vegan sausages, sliced into 1–2 cm (½–¾ in) pieces
4 garlic cloves
1 large onion, quartered
2 tablespoons olive oil
chilli (hot pepper) flakes, for sprinkling (optional)
500 g (1 lb 2 oz) packet gnocchi
150 ml (5 fl oz/scant ⅔ cup) non-dairy milk
15 g (½ oz/ ¼ cup) nutritional yeast
1 tablespoon finely chopped sage, plus extra to serve
4 thyme sprigs, stalks removed and finely chopped, plus extra to serve
sea salt and freshly ground black pepper
handful of pecans, optionally toasted and roughly chopped, to serve

Roasted squash and garlic are blended into a creamy sauce, tossed with gnocchi, herby, vegan sausages and a scattering of toasted pecans. This cosy one-pan supper is for when the kitchen feels like the warmest place to be on a drizzly day.

---

1. Preheat the oven to 200°C fan (425°F).
2. Tumble the butternut squash, sausages, garlic cloves and onion into a large baking tray (pan) with 1 tablespoon of the olive oil. Sprinkle with the chilli flakes, if using, and season with salt and pepper. Bake for 30 minutes, or until softened and slightly caramelized, turning halfway through.
3. When the squash is a couple of minutes from ready, bring a large saucepan of water to the boil. Add the gnocchi and cook for 2 minutes, or according to the packet instructions. Drain, reserving some of the pasta water, and return to the pan.
4. Remove the baking tray from the oven, take out the sausages and add them to the pan with the gnocchi.
5. Add the rest of the tray veg to a food processor, along with the milk and nutritional yeast and blend until creamy and smooth, adding a little extra milk or gnocchi cooking water, if needed. Taste and adjust the seasoning, if necessary.
6. Pour the squash sauce into the pan with the sausages and gnocchi, then sprinkle over the herbs and stir through over a medium heat.
7. Serve topped with the pecans and an extra sprinkling of herbs

Notes

— Try adding some vegan cream at the end for an even creamier taste!

Kale Pesto and Sundried Tomato Babka Knots

MAKES 8 ROLLS

175 ml (6 fl oz/¾ cup) non-dairy milk, at room temperature, plus extra for brushing
2 teaspoons caster (superfine) sugar
7 g (¼ oz) sachet of fast-action dried yeast
300 g (10½ oz/scant 2½ cups) strong white bread flour, plus extra for dusting
1 teaspoon salt
1 tablespoon olive oil, plus extra for greasing

FOR THE PESTO
50 g (1¾ oz/½ cup) walnuts
2 garlic cloves
30 g (1 oz/½ cup) nutritional yeast
zest of 1 lemon, juice of ½
75 g (2½ oz) kale, tough stalks removed and leaves chopped
100 ml (3½ fl oz/scant ½ cup) olive oil
sea salt and freshly ground black pepper

Green kale and zesty lemon fill these soft, pillowy savoury babkas – a twisted bread shaped into yummy knots. Any leftover kale pesto with walnuts can be saved and stored in a container in the refrigerator to stir through pasta, or spread onto a toasted sandwich.

---

1. Add the milk, sugar and yeast to a stand mixer or large mixing bowl and leave to stand for about 5 minutes to froth.
2. Add the flour and salt to a separate mixer bowl (or combine with a spoon or your hands in a large mixing bowl if you are kneading by hand). Then pour the milk mix into the same bowl with the olive oil.
3. Fix the dough hook to the stand mixer, turn on and knead for about 3–4 minutes. If you don't have a stand mixer, add the dough to a floured work surface and knead by hand for 10 minutes until soft and springy.
4. Place the dough in a large lightly oiled bowl, cover with a damp tea (dish) towel and leave in a warm spot for 1 hour, or until roughly doubled in size.
5. Meanwhile, make the pesto. In a food processor, pulse the walnuts and garlic until finely chopped. Then add the nutritional yeast and lemon zest, season with salt and black pepper and pulse again. Add the kale and lemon juice, and while the processor is running, drizzle in the olive oil, until everything is combined.
6. Line a large baking tray (pan) with baking parchment or lightly grease with oil.
7. Remove the dough from the bowl and knock back on a lightly floured work surface. Divide the dough into 8 balls, then roll each ball into a long rectangle shape, about 20 cm (8 in) long. Spread about 1 tablespoon of the pesto on top of each rectangle and roll up from one side until it's a long log. Pinch the ends together and turn over so that the fold is underneath.

8. Using a sharp knife, cut each roll in almost half to just reveal the filling, leaving about 2 cm (¾ in) uncut at the bottom. Gently tie into a knot, twisting at the same time. I twisted the rolls around two of my fingers to make a hole in the middle for the end to go through.
9. Arrange the knots on the prepared baking tray, cover again with a tea (dish) towel and leave to prove for 45 minutes, or until doubled in size.
10. Preheat the oven to 180°C fan (400°F).
11. Brush the babkas with milk and bake for 15 minutes, or until lightly golden. Leave to cool for 5–10 minutes before serving.

Notes

— Store any extra pesto in an airtight container in the refrigerator for up to a week.

Tofu Goujons with Coconut Chilli Mayo

SERVES 4

300 g (10½ oz) block extra firm tofu
125 g (4½ oz/1 cup) plain (all-purpose) flour, plus 5 tablespoons
1 teaspoon paprika
1 teaspoon garlic granules
120 ml (4 fl oz/½ cup) non-dairy milk
125 g (4½ oz/1½–2 cups) breadcrumbs (either use homemade or panko)
1 tablespoon nutritional yeast
vegetable oil, for cooking
sea salt and freshly ground black pepper
lime juice, to serve

FOR THE COCONUT CHILLI MAYO

75 ml (2½ fl oz/5 tablespoons) vegan coconut yoghurt
zest and juice of ½ lime
2 teaspoons your favourite hot sauce

These crispy tofu goujons are coated in a spicy crumb and dipped into a creamy coconut chilli mayo. They can be fried, oven-baked or air fried for a deliciously crispy coating.

1. Drain and press the tofu to make sure all the liquid has been removed (see page 74), then slice it into chunky slices.
2. Meanwhile, make your coconut mayo (this can also be done while your tofu is in the oven or air-fryer if baking) by mixing all the ingredients together in a medium bowl. Set aside.
3. Prepare your coating station by whisking the 5 tablespoons of flour, paprika, garlic and salt and pepper with the milk in one bowl. In another bowl, add the breadcrumbs, nutritional yeast and a little more salt and pepper. Finally, in a third bowl, add the remaining flour. You can optionally add a fourth bowl with some water to keep your hands clean as you go, making sure to use one hand for wet ingredients, and one for dry.
4. First, dip the sliced tofu into the flour, making sure to coat all sides, then into the milk and flour mix and finally, in the breadcrumbs, making sure the sides are coated evenly.
5. The goujons can be fried, air-fried or oven-baked. For frying, add a generous amount of neutral oil, about 2 cm (¾ in) deep to a large frying pan over a medium heat and fry the tofu in batches until golden brown and crispy.
6. To bake, preheat the oven to 200°C fan (425°F) and line a baking tray (pan) with baking parchment. Arrange the tofu on the lined baking tray, spray or drizzle with a little oil and bake for 30–35 minutes, flipping halfway, until golden brown. For the air-fryer, set it to the same temperature as the oven and place the goujons in for 20 minutes.
7. Serve hot with a squeeze of lime juice and dipped into your delicious coconut chilli mayo.

Notes

— You can season the goujons in different ways, such as switching the paprika for chilli powder, dried herbs or a spice mix.

Blackberry Jam

MAKES 4–5 X 300–500 ML (10–17 FL OZ) JARS

1 kg (2 lb 4 oz) blackberries
1 kg (4⅓ cups) jam sugar
juice of 1 lemon

Nothing beats homemade jam. It's one of life's simple pleasures. This jam goes beautifully on top of my scones (page 110) or crumpets (page 24).

---

1. Add the blackberries and sugar to a large bowl. Cover with a tea (dish) towel and leaving to stand overnight.
2. The next day, add the berries and sugar to a large wide-based saucepan and squeeze over the lemon juice (to help the jam gel together you can also add the lemon pips – which contain pectin – in a small muslin or cheesecloth tied with some kitchen string as you cook the jam). Cook over a low heat until the sugar has completely dissolved. Bring to the boil, stirring so it doesn't stick to the base and cook on a rolling boil for a couple of minutes. Reduce the heat to a simmer for 5 minutes, stirring again to avoid any sticking on the base of the pan.
3. Test if your jam is set: either use a spoon to scoop out some of the jam and hold it horizontally over the pan, allowing it to drip off the spoon. It is set if the jam forms a long drip and hangs without dropping from the spoon. Alternatively, before starting your jam, place a saucer in the freezer. Remove from the freezer once cold and your jam is cooked, and add a spoonful of the jam to the saucer. Push the jam with your finger and if it wrinkles, it is set.
4. Once your jam is set, turn off the heat, spoon any scum off the top and leave to stand for 10–15 minutes.
5. Ladle the jam into warm, sterilized jam jars, removing the lemon pip bag if used, and seal immediately with an airtight lid. Store the jam for up to a year in a dark cupboard, and, once opened, store in the refrigerator and consume within a month.

Notes

— Lemon pips contain pectin, which acts as a gelling agent for the jam. For this recipe I have used jam sugar, which also contains pectin, so adding the lemon pips is entirely optional here.

— Use jars with lids and sterilize by washing in hot, soapy water and then drying in a fan oven at 150°C (300°F) for 10 minutes. Make sure to label your jars with the date. Jam will keep for 6 months, and should be stored in the fridge once opened.

Apple Crumble Loaf

SERVES 8

FOR THE LOAF

250 ml (8 fl oz/1 cup) non-dairy milk
1 tablespoon apple cider vinegar
2 tablespoons apple sauce
1 teaspoon vanilla extract
60 ml (¼ cup/4 tablespoons) sunflower oil, plus extra for greasing
350 g (12 oz/generous 2¾ cups) plain (all-purpose) flour
150 g (5½ oz/generous ¾ cup) light brown sugar
1 teaspoon ground cinnamon
1 teaspoon baking powder
1 teaspoon mixed spice
pinch of sea salt
1 crisp eating (dessert) apple, peeled and diced

FOR THE CRUNCH TOPPING

50 g (1¾ oz/¼ cup) soft brown sugar
50 g (1¾ oz/scant ¼ cup) granulated sugar
60 g (2 oz/½ cup) plain (all-purpose) flour
50 g (1¾ oz/generous ⅓ cup) mixed nuts of your choice, chopped
1 teaspoon ground cinnamon
60 g (2 oz) vegan butter, melted

This apple crumble loaf is a family favourite from this book, and a standout that everybody loved through the testing phase. It brings together everything I love about autumn (fall) bakes – soft spiced sponge, chunks of sweet apple and a golden, nutty crumble top. Your kitchen will smell incredible.

1. Preheat the oven to 200°C fan (425°F), and grease and line a 15 x 23 cm (6 x 9 in) loaf tin (pan) with lightly greased baking parchment.
2. Make your batter by adding the milk and vinegar together in a bowl and leaving to stand for 5–10 minutes to activate and thicken.
3. Next, prepare your crunch topping by mixing the sugars, flour, nuts and cinnamon together in a large bowl. Add the melted butter and, using a spatula, mix until well combined and crumble-like.
4. Once thickened, pour into a large mixing bowl along with the apple sauce, vanilla extract and oil. Add the remaining ingredients, exluding the apple pieces, and mix together. Take good care not to overmix the batter.
5. Tumble in the apple pieces and fold through, then pour the batter into the prepared loaf tin.
6. Sprinkle the crumble topping over the batter and bake for 45 minutes, or until golden brown and a skewer inserted comes out clean (allowing for the apple pieces).
7. Remove from the oven and place the tin on a wire rack. Leave to cool for about 30 minutes before removing the loaf from the tin to slice and enjoy.

Chocolicious Muffins

MAKES 6–8 MUFFINS

220 ml (7½ fl oz/generous ¾ cup) non-dairy milk
1 tablespoon apple cider vinegar
1 teaspoon vanilla extract
2 tablespoons non-dairy plain yoghurt
½ teaspoon sea salt
1 teaspoon instant coffee
95 ml (3 ¼ fl oz/generous ⅓ cup) vegetable oil
200 g (7 oz/1⅔ cups) plain (all-purpose) flour
75 g (2½ oz/⅔ cup) cocoa (unsweetened chocolate) powder
2 teaspoons baking powder
½ teaspoon bicarbonate of soda (baking soda)
200 g (7 oz/generous 1 cup) vegan chocolate chips
150 g (5½ oz/generous ¾ cup) light brown sugar

These rich and flufy muffins loaded with chocolate chips are melt-in-the-mouth delicious!

1. Preheat the oven to 220°C fan (475°F) and line 12 muffin cases in a 12-hole muffin tin (pan).
2. Combine the milk, vinegar, vanilla, yoghurt, salt and coffee together in a large bowl. Leave to stand for 5–10 minutes, then add the oil.
3. In a separate bowl, sift the flour, cocoa powder, baking powder and bicarbonate of soda together. Add the chocolate chips and sugar and stir through. Fold the dry ingredients into the wet ingredients. Don't worry if there are a few lumps.
4. Fill the muffin cases up to top with the batter. This mix should make about 6–8 muffins. Transfer to the oven and bake for 5 minutes. Reduce the oven temperature to 180°C fan (400°F) and continue baking for a further 20 minutes. Check to see if the muffins are ready by inserting a skewer into the middle of one and if it comes out clean they are done.
5. Remove from the oven, leave to cool for a few minutes, then remove the muffins from the tray and place on a wire rack to cool completely.

Notes

— Take care not to open the oven too much during the cooking time to avoid the muffins collapsing.

Spiced Toffee Apples

MAKES 4 APPLES

200 g (7 oz/generous ¾ cup) caster (superfine) sugar
60 ml (¼ cup) water
2 tablespoons golden syrup
1 teaspoon ground cinnamon
1 teaspoon apple cider vinegar
4 crisp medium apples

FOR THE TOPPINGS
100 g (3½ oz) vegan chocolate, melted
50 g (1¾ oz/½ cup) chopped hazelnuts

Growing up, a toffee apple on a cold bonfire night was one of my favourite treats that I looked forward to every year. Dipping them in melted chocolate and coating them in chopped nuts takes them to another level, which is the perfect treat for a fireside night at home.

---

1. Line a baking sheet with baking parchment.
2. Add the sugar and water to a medium saucepan and set over a medium–high heat. Stir together and bring to the boil. Once the mixture begins boiling, stop stirring and pour in the golden syrup, cinnamon and vinegar. Use a thermometer to keep an eye on the mixture until it reaches 150°C (302°F). This is known as the hard crack stage and will likely take between 10–15 minutes.
3. Meanwhile, skewer each apple with a lolly stick or skewer, then prepare your toppings in two separate bowls.
4. Once the syrup reaches temperature, remove the pan from the heat.
5. Working quickly so the syrup doesn't set, dip the apples into the sugar syrup, then into the melted chocolate, and finally the hazelnuts. Arrange on the lined baking sheet and leave to set. Enjoy!

Notes

— Make sure the toffee is not too runny so it doesn't run off the apples, or too thick, so it's easy to fully and evenly coat the apples.

— Don't store the toffee apples in the refrigerator as sugar can attract water and make the coating soft. Instead, I would advise you eat these immediately.

Pear Upside Down Cake

SERVES 8–10

FOR THE POACHED PEARS

125 ml (4 fl oz/½ cup) water
125 g (4½ oz/½ cup) caster (superfine) sugar
2 large ripe (but firm) pears, peeled (or 3 medium) and cut into quarters or eighths
juice of ½ lemon

FOR THE PEAR SAUCE

60 g (2 oz) vegan butter
60 g (2 oz/⅓ cup) light brown sugar
2 tablespoons maple syrup
½ teaspoon ground cinnamon
½ teaspoon ground ginger

FOR THE CAKE

100 g (3½ oz) vegan butter, melted, plus extra for greasing
160 g (5¾ oz) unsweetened apple sauce (if using sweetened apple sauce reduce amount of sugar by 50 g/1¾ oz)
60 ml (¼ cup/4 tablespoons) non-dairy milk
1 teaspoon vanilla extract
1 teaspoon very finely chopped ginger or 1 teaspoon dried ground ginger
125 g (4½ oz/1 cup) self-raising flour
100 g (3½ oz/scant ½ cup) caster (superfine) sugar
½ teaspoon baking powder
pinch of salt

Caramelized pears tucked beneath a soft, gently spiced sponge, this cake turns out beautifully every time, as it's made extra moist by the poached pears.

---

1. Preheat the oven to 180°C fan (400°F). Grease a 22 cm (8½ in) cake tin (pan) with butter and line the base and sides with baking parchment.
2. Start by poaching the pears. Heat the water and caster sugar in a large saucepan over a medium heat, stirring until the sugar is dissolved. Add the pears and lemon juice and cook for 5–10 minutes until the pears are just soft. Remove the pears from the pan and leave to cool, then slice. If the pears are very ripe you can omit this stage.
3. To make the pear sauce, add the butter and sugar to a small saucepan and cook over a medium heat, stirring until dissolved. Stir constantly for a few minutes until nicely thickened, then add the maple syrup, cinnamon and ginger.
4. Pour the sauce over the base of the prepared cake tin to cover (save any extra to drizzle over the top once served). Arrange the pear slices evenly overlapping each other on the base in a pretty pattern.
5. For the cake, add the melted butter, apple sauce, milk, vanilla and ginger to a large bowl and stir until just combined.
6. Sift the flour into a separate bowl, then add the sugar, baking powder and salt and mix to combine. Pour the wet mixture into the dry ingredients and stir until just combined. Pour the batter over the pears in the tin and bake for 35–40 minutes until a skewer inserted into the centre comes out clean.
7. Remove from the oven and leave to cool in the tin for 10 minutes. Place a plate over the cake and turn upside down onto the plate. The pears should now be on top, if any are stuck in the tin, gently remove and put back in place. Enjoy warm straight away, with a side of vegan vanilla ice cream, if you like.

Orange, Pistachio and Cranberry Cookies

<u>*MAKES 24 COOKIES*</u>

150 g (5½ oz/1½ cups) rolled oats
100 g (3½ oz/generous ¾ cup) plain (all-purpose) flour
½ teaspoon baking powder
½ teaspoon bicarbonate of soda (baking soda)
75 g (2½ oz/⅓ cup) caster (superfine) sugar
75 g (2½ oz/scant ½ cup) light brown sugar
½ teaspoon salt
50 g (1¾ oz/⅓ cup) pistachios, roughly chopped
50 g (1¾ oz/scant ½ cup) dried cranberries
75 ml (2½ fl oz/5 tablespoons) unsweetened non-dairy milk
100 ml (3½ fl oz/scant ½ cup) coconut oil, melted
1 teaspoon vanilla extract
zest of 1 orange

Chewy, zesty and just the right amount of sweet, I love using the flavours of orange, pistachio and cranberry to make these cookies. They are best enjoyed straight out of the oven when they are still a little gooey and warm!

---

1. Preheat the oven to 190°C fan (400°F) and line two baking sheets with baking parchment.
2. In a large bowl, mix together the oats, flour, baking powder, bicarbonate of soda, sugars and salt. Stir through the nuts and cranberries to combine.
3. In a separate bowl, mix the milk, coconut oil and vanilla together. Add the wet ingredients to the dry ingredients, along with the orange zest and mix through.
4. Using your hands, shape the dough into about 24 small balls and arrange on the lined baking sheets, spaced out. Gently flatten each cookie a little with your hand and bake for 10–15 minutes until golden.
5. Remove from the oven, leave to cool on the baking sheet for 10–15 minutes to harden, then move to a wire rack to cool. Enjoy!

Notes

— If you bake closer to 10 minutes, the cookies will be gooey; if closer to 15 minutes then you will have a crispier cookie, so go with what you like best.

Apple Tree Mulled Cider

MAKES 2 LITRES (68 FL OZ/8½ CUPS)

- 2 litre (68 fl oz) bottle of Cornish cider
- 2 apples, sliced
- 1 orange, sliced with the peel still on (gently squeeze a little of the juice into the pan)
- 2 teaspoons allspice
- 2 cinnamon sticks
- 6 cloves
- 2 star anise
- 1 tablespoon caster (superfine) sugar (optional)
- good glug of brandy or Calvados (optional)

In winter we all love mulled wine, but in autumn (fall) why not give mulled cider a go? Serving it warm and spiced is my favourite way to drink this Cornish cultural staple.

1. Pour the cider into a large saucepan and add the apples. Then add the orange, allspice, cinnamon, cloves, star anise and sugar, and stir to mix. Heat until almost boiling (be careful not to boil), stirring a few times. Gently simmer for 30 minutes.
2. For an extra kick, before removing from the heat, add the brandy and serve warm!

— four

Winter

Smoky Beans

SERVES 6

1 large onion, finely chopped
2 tablespoons oil
2 garlic cloves, grated or crushed
2x 400g tin of beans (I used haricot/navy), drained and rinsed
400 g (14 oz) tin of chopped tomatoes
200 g (7 oz) vegetable stock
2 tablespoons apple cider vinegar
1 tablespoon smoked paprika
1 teaspoon chilli powder (can adjust for less or extra heat)
1 teaspoon ground cumin
2 tablespoons pomegranate molasses (can substitute with maple or agave syrup)
dash of vegan Worcestershire sauce (or soy sauce)
sea salt and freshly ground black pepper

While baked beans from the tin is a staple, making them from scratch elevates them to another level that's totally worth the effort. These smoky beans are hearty, wholesome and just a little bit fiery.

---

1. Start by adding the onions to a large pan, and fry for around 5 minutes in the oil until softened, add the garlic and cook for a further minute.
2. Add the beans, tinned tomatoes, vegetable stock, apple cider vinegar, spices and pomegranate molasses. Splash a little Worcestershire sauce in and season to taste.
3. Cook for around 20 minutes, to reduce the sauce and enhance the flavour. Once cooked, adjust the seasoning and add any extra sweetness or chilli to taste.
4. Serve on toast topped with vegan cheese, or alongside a vegan full English!

Notes

— You can have this as hot as you like, just add any extra chill, chilli flakes or cayenne pepper to taste.
— For extra goodness, add a couple of handfuls of young spinach at the end, and stir through until wilted.

Winter Porridge with Stewed Pears

SERVES 2

FOR THE PEARS
1 tablespoon brown sugar
50 ml (1¾ fl oz/ 3½ tablespoons) water
squeeze of lemon juice
1 cinnamon stick or ½ teaspoon ground cinnamon
4 ripe pears, peeled, cored and quartered

FOR THE PORRIDGE
100 g (3½ oz/1 cup) rolled oats
500 ml (17 fl oz/generous 2 cups) boiling water
250 ml (8 fl oz/1 cup) non-dairy milk
¼ teaspoon ground cinnamon

Nothing beats porridge in the winter. I pretty much eat it every single day. I absolutely love stewing pears to accompany my morning porridge for the kind of sweet and warming breakfast you dream about as you fall asleep the night before.

1. Bring the sugar, water, lemon and cinnamon to a low simmer in a large saucepan over a medium heat until the sugar dissolves. Add the pears (making sure they are covered), then bring to the boil. Reduce to simmer for 10–15 minutes until the pears have softened. If your pears are less ripe, cook for longer, if overripe, cook for less time. Remove from the heat and set aside to soak up the liquid.
2. Meanwhile, add the rolled oats, boiling water and non-dairy milk to a large saucepan over a medium heat and bring to an almost boil, then reduce to a simmer for 10 minutes, stirring frequently until perfectly creamy.
3. Stir in the cinnamon and remove from the heat. Pour into bowls, top with the stewed pears and a drizzle of their sweet syrup.

Notes

— The stewed pears are also delicious with yoghurt, ice cream, pancakes or granola.
— You could also swap out the pears with crisp eating (dessert) apples.

Broccoli Chowder with Roasted Seeds

SERVES 4

2 tablespoons olive oil
1 onion, finely chopped
1 carrot, finely chopped
2 garlic cloves, grated
1 teaspoon paprika
¼ teaspoon celery salt
900 ml (30 fl oz/3¾ cups) vegetable stock
1 large potato or 2 medium potatoes, cut into 2–3 cm (¾–1¼ in) cubes
1 large head of broccoli, chopped into florets (I chop the stalk into small pieces and add it with the potatoes)
150 g (5½ oz) frozed or tinned sweetcorn
75 g (2½ oz) vegan cheese, grated
250 g (9 oz/1 cup) vegan crème fraîche (can substitute for coconut cream)
1 tablespoon cornflour (cornstarch) mixed in a little non-dairy milk (optional)
sea salt and freshly ground black pepper

TO SERVE

mixed seeds (I used sunflower, pumpkin and sesame), lightly toasted
crusty bread

This broccoli chowder is comfort in a bowl, with chunks of potato, bursts of sweetcorn and a creamy base. I love finishing it off with a handful of toasted seeds for a crunch, and of course some fresh bread out of the oven (page 202).

---

1. Heat the olive oil in a large saucepan over a medium heat, add the onion and carrot, then season and fry for 5–10 minutes until softened. Add the garlic, paprika and celery salt and fry for a further minute.
2. Pour in the vegetable stock, then add the potato, with any broccoli stalk pieces. Bring to the boil, then reduce the heat and simmer gently for about 10 minutes. Add the broccoli florets and simmer for a couple more minutes, making sure that the potato is cooked through.
3. Remove half of the vegetables with a sieve (strainer), and roughly blitz the remaining chowder with either a hand-held or immersion blender. Return the saved vegetables to the saucepan with the blended soup. Alternately, gently mash most of the potatoes against the side of the pan to easily thicken the chowder.
4. Finally, add the sweetcorn, cheese and crème fraîche and simmer for a couple of minutes while stirring. If the chowder is not as thick as you would like, add the cornflour mixture and stir constantly over a gentle heat until it reaches the desired thickness.
5. Check the seasoning and serve with a sprinkling of toasted mixed seeds and crusty bread.

Roasted Parsnip, Rosemary and White Bean Soup

SERVES 4

3 large parsnips, peeled and roughly chopped
1 onion, cut into wedges
400 g (14 oz) tin white beans (such as cannellini, butter/lima or haricot/navy beans), drained and rinsed
3 rosemary sprigs, 1 with the leaves chopped and reserved for serving
3 garlic cloves, unpeeled
3 tablespoons olive oil, plus 1 tablespoon to serve
750 ml–1 litre (25–34 fl oz/3–4¼ cups) vegetable stock
sea salt and freshly ground black pepper

Soups are a must throughout winter, and parsnip soup is one of my all-time favourites. This one is earthy, mellow and fragrant, and blended with creamy white beans for extra depth. Roasting the parsnips makes it even more delicious.

---

1. Preheat the oven to 180°C fan (400°F).
2. Arrange the parsnips, onion, beans, rosemary and garlic cloves on a baking tray (pan). Toss with the olive oil and season with salt and pepper. Bake for 25–30 minutes, then remove from the oven.
3. Remove and discard the rosemary and reserve some of the beans for the topping, then add the remaining roasted ingredients (making sure to squeeze out the roasted garlic from their skins) into a food processor. Pour in the vegetable stock and blend until smooth. Reheat in a saucepan, if necessary.
4. Adjust the seasoning and serve topped with the reserved beans, a drizzle of olive oil and a little fresh rosemary and black pepper.

Notes

— Store in the refrigerator in an airtight container for up to four days, or freeze for another day.

— You can also use an immersion blender instead of the food processor, by adding the roasted ingredients to a saucepan along with the vegetable stock and blending.

Caramelized Cabbage Steaks

SERVES 4

90 ml (3 fl oz/6 tablespoons) olive oil
1 medium Savoy or hispi cabbage, cut into wedges
2 tablespoons tomato purée (paste)
2 garlic cloves, finely chopped
1 teaspoon caster (superfine) sugar
1 teaspoon cayenne pepper
1 teaspoon smoked paprika
1 medium onion, chopped
400 g (14 oz) tin chopped tomatoes
2 tablespoons finely chopped coriander (cilantro)
sea salt

FOR THE DIP

200 g (7 oz) vegan crème fraîche (or substitute with vegan coconut yoghurt)
1 tablespoon za'atar
pinch of chilli (hot pepper) flakes (optional)
zest of 1 lemon
1 tablespoon coriander (cilantro), finely chopped
pinch of sea salt

Savoy cabbage turns into something truly special when roasted until golden and tender with deliciously caramelized edges, infused with warming spices and a spicy zingy dip.

---

1. Preheat the oven to 180°C fan (400°F).
2. Heat 60 ml (2 fl oz/4 tablespoons) of the oil in a large ovenproof frying or sauté pan over a medium heat. Add half the cabbage wedges, cut-side down, to the pan and season with salt. Fry until the sides are charred, then remove and repeat with the remaining wedges. Set aside.
3. Mix the tomato purée, garlic, sugar, spices and 1 tablespoon of oil together in a small bowl.
4. Heat the remaining tablespoon of oil in a large saucepan, add the onion and cook for 5 minutes, or until softened. Add the spicy tomato paste along with the tinned tomatoes and stir through. Simmer for 5 minutes.
5. Meanwhile, combine all the ingredients for the dip in a bowl.
6. Add the wedges to the pan with the sauce, cover with a lid and cook over a medium heat for 5–8 minutes until the cabbage has softened. Uncover and cook for another few minutes to thicken the sauce. Check the seasoning, sprinkle over the coriander and serve with the dip on the side.

Caramelized Onion and Lentil Sausage Rolls

MAKES 24 SAUSAGE ROLLS

1 tablespoon olive oil
4 red onions, finely chopped
1 teaspoon light brown sugar
2 garlic cloves, chopped
400 g (14 oz) chestnut mushrooms, finely chopped or minced (ground) in a food processor
handful of thyme leaves, roughly chopped or 1 tablespoon dried thyme
1 tablespoon miso paste
400 g (14 oz) tin green lentils, drained and rinsed
2 tablespoons caramelized onion chutney, plus extra to serve
50 g (1¾ oz) vegan cheese, grated
25 g (scant 1 oz/¼ cup) nutritional yeast
60 g (2 oz/¾ cup) fresh breadcrumbs
sea salt and freshly ground black pepper

FOR THE ROLLS
2 x 320 g (11 oz) sheets of ready-rolled vegan puff pastry, cold
2 tablespoons non-dairy milk, plus extra for brushing
1 tablespoon maple syrup
2 tablespoons sesame seeds, for sprinkling

Sausage rolls are such a comfort food, perfect for making in big batches to freeze for later, or to share with the family as the Christmas season nears. These are filled with sweet caramelized onions, savoury protein-rich lentils and earthy mushrooms for a moreish filling. You really don't miss the meat!

---

1. Preheat the oven to 180ºC fan (400ºF) and line two baking trays (pans) with baking parchment.
2. Heat the olive oil in a large saucepan, add the onions and fry over a medium heat for 10 minutes, or until softened. Add the sugar, garlic and seasoning and cook for a further 1–2 minutes.
3. Next, add the mushrooms and cook over a medium-high heat for 10–15 minutes until reduced.
4. Transfer the mushroom mixture to a large bowl and add the remaining filling ingredients. Combine everything together using your hands or a spoon.
5. Lay out the puff pastry sheets on a work surface and cut across lengthways to make 4 rectangles. Divide the filling into 4 portions and add to the centre of each rectangle. Using your hands, mould into a sausage shape lengthways, leaving a gap around the edge. Brush the edges with a little milk, then fold and join the pastry into the middle lengthways, gently pressing each side together. Flip the roll over so the seal is on the bottom.
6. For a vegan egg wash, mix the milk and maple syrup together in a bowl, then use to brush along the top of the rolls lightly. Sprinkle with sesame seeds, then using a sharp knife, cut each roll into 6 pieces. Arrange on the prepared baking trays and bake for 25–30 minutes until golden and flaky. Leave to cool for 5–10 minutes, then enjoy warm dipped in some extra caramelised onion chutney.

Notes

— Store in the refrigerator for 3 days, or freeze for up to three months before baking for another day.

Mushroom, Chestnut and Apricot Hand Pies

SERVES 12

10 g (¼ oz) dried porcini mushrooms
2 tablespoons olive oil
1 small onion, finely chopped
1 small-medium carrot, finely chopped
2 garlic cloves, grated
300 g (10½ oz) chestnut mushrooms, sliced
3 teaspoons finely chopped thyme leaves
50 ml (1¾ fl oz/3½ tablespoons) vegetable stock
1 tablespoon Marmite
2 teaspoons balsamic vinegar
2 teaspoons tomato ketchup
50 g (1¾ oz/generous ¼ cup) cup) dried apricots, roughly chopped
50 g (1¾ oz) vacuum-packed chestnuts, roughly chopped
50 g (1¾ oz/⅓ cup) frozen peas
1 teaspoon cornflour (cornstarch)
1 teaspoon maple syrup
2 tablespoons finely chopped parsley
2 x 320 g (13 oz) sheets of ready-rolled vegan shortcrust pastry
non-dairy milk and oil, for glazing
sea salt and freshly ground black pepper

These hand pies are gently flavoured with thyme and balanced with a touch of balsamic and maple syrup, making them a comforting treat for wintry days. Using pre-rolled supermarket pastry makes it really easy to whip these up – an ideal snack or warming lunch on the go.

---

1. Preheat the oven to 180°C fan (400°F). Soak the porcini mushrooms in boiling water for 20–30 minutes.
2. Meanwhile, heat the olive oil in a large saucepan, add the onion and carrot and cook over a medium heat for 5 minutes, or until softened. Add the garlic and cook for another minute. Season with salt and pepper.
3. Add the chestnut mushrooms to the pan and cook over a medium heat until all the water has evaporated and the mushrooms have reduced. Sprinkle in the thyme and pour in the porcini mushrooms along with their soaking water.
4. Next, add the vegetable stock to the pan, together with the Marmite, balsamic vinegar, ketchup, apricots, chestnuts, peas, cornflour and maple syrup, stirring through. Bring to the boil, then reduce to a simmer for a few minutes to thicken the sauce. Once reduced, stir through the parsley, adjust the seasoning and set aside to cool.
5. Roll out the pastry on a work surface and cut into 2 halves vertically. Once the mushroom filling has cooled, add the filling to one-half of each pastry.
6. Dampen the edges of the pastry, then fold one-half over the mushroom filling, sealing by crimping or using a fork. Glaze the top of the pies with a little non-dairy milk mixed in with a little oil. Bake for 25 minutes, or until golden. Remove from the oven and leave for 5 minutes to cool, then serve.

Garlic and Herb Cashew Cheese

SERVES 6–8

200 g (7 oz/generous 1 ¼ cups) cashews, soaked overnight in cold water or 1 hour in boiling water, and drained
3–5 tablespoons non-dairy plain yoghurt
1 garlic clove, very finely chopped
½ teaspoon garlic granules
juice of ½ lemon
1 tablespoon apple cider vinegar
2 tablespoons nutritional yeast
pinch of black salt (kala namak)
bunch of chives, finely chopped
bunch of dill or parsley, finely chopped
sea salt and freshly ground black pepper
crispy toast or crackers, to serve

My favourite vegan cheese is always a cream cheese. Cashews work so well for this as they are super creamy and, when soaked overnight, blend beautifully for a delicious texture that commands space on any cheese board. Flavoured with garlic, chives and dill or parsley, it's reminiscent of a classic Boursin.

---

1. Add all the ingredients, except the herbs, to a food processor or high-speed blender and blend on low speed until smooth. As you blend you will need to scrape the sides and continue blending until it comes together (this will take a bit of time).
2. Scoop into a bowl, and stir through the herbs. Leave to set in the refrigerator for an hour, then serve with crispy toast or crackers.

Notes

— Store in an airtight container in the refrigerator for up to a week.

Every Mushroom Bourguignon

SERVES 4–6

2 tablespoons olive oil
8–10 shallots, peeled and cut any larger ones in half
750 g (1 lb 10 oz) mixed mushrooms (I used button, chestnut shiitake and oyster mushrooms), cleaned, stems removed and cut or torn into bite-sized pieces
2 garlic cloves, finely sliced
2 bay leaves
2 tablespoons cornflour (cornstarch)
500 ml (17 fl oz/generous 2 cups) vegan red wine
2 tablespoons tomato purée (paste)
1 teaspoon Marmite
500 ml (17 fl oz/generous 2 cups) vegetable stock
10 baby carrots, peeled and trimmed
small bunch of parsley, finely chopped
sea salt and freshly ground black pepper
mashed or boiled potatoes or pasta, to serve

I wonder if you can tell my obsession with mushrooms. They're one of my favourite foods, and I try to sneak them in everywhere I can. I knew I had to make a recipe for the book that featured all of the best: chestnut, oyster, shiitake or whatever else you can get your hands on. Here, they are simmered with red wine, shallots, carrots and a touch of Marmite for that umami depth to create the ultimate rich, veggie bourguignon.

---

1. Gently heat the olive oil over a low heat in a large saucepan, add the shallots and cook for a few minutes until softened. Add the mushrooms with a pinch of salt and cook for around 15–20 minutes until reduced and the mushrooms have a good colour.
2. Add the garlic and bay leaves and cook for 1 minute, then sprinkle over the cornflour and stir through for 1 minute. Pour in the wine, stirring constantly to deglaze the pan. Simmer for a couple of minutes, stirring constantly, then add the tomato purée, Marmite, stock and carrots, then season.
3. Reduce to a gentle simmer, cover with a lid and cook for 35 minutes. Keep an eye on the pan, stirring and adding a splash of water if necessary. Stir through most of the parsley, leaving a little for serving.
4. Remove from the heat and serve with your choice of mashed, boiled potatoes or pasta, and an extra sprinkle of parsley.

Pantry Cupboard Stew

SERVES 4

1 small sweet potato, peeled and chopped
2 carrots, cut into 3 cm (1¼ in) chunks
2 tablespoons sunflower oil
1 teaspoon ground cumin
1 teaspoon ground cinnamon
1 teaspoon smoked paprika
1 large onion, chopped
1 green (bell) pepper, chunkily chopped
1 red (bell) pepper, chunkily chopped
1 teaspoon garlic purée (or 2 garlic cloves, grated)
400 g (14 oz) tin chopped tomatoes
2 x 400 g (14 oz) tins beans (whatever you have), drained and rinsed
200 ml (7 fl oz/scant 1 cup) vegetable stock
1 teaspoon granulated sugar
2 tablespoons tomato purée (paste)
10 olives of choice, pitted and halved
4 preserved lemons, roughly chopped
handful of coriander (cilantro), chopped
sea salt and freshly ground black pepper

TO SERVE

handful of flaked (slivered) almonds, toasted
handful of dried apricots, roughly chopped
couscous or crusty bread

Designed for the days where you have no clue what to make, and want to just reach into the storecupboard (pantry) and refrigerator to throw something together with the random ingredients available. I always have tinned beans, chopped tomatoes, spices and a few spare vegetables like sweet potatoes, carrots and (bell) peppers knocking around. Use this recipe as a base to make your own pantry cupboard stew with what you have!

---

1. Preheat the oven to 200°C fan (425°F).
2. Add the sweet potato and carrots to a roasting tin (pan), drizzle with 1 tablespoon of oil and a pinch of the cumin, cinnamon and paprika, then lightly season and toss. Roast in the oven for 25 minutes, or until softened.
3. When the vegetables are nearly finished roasting, heat the remaining tablespoon of oil in a large saucepan, add the onion and peppers and cook over a medium heat until softened. Add the garlic and remaining spices and cook for another minute.
4. Remove the vegetables from the oven and add to the pan with the chopped tomatoes, beans, vegetable stock, sugar, tomato purée, olives and preserved lemons, then season to taste. Bring to the boil, then reduce the heat to a simmer and cook for 10 minutes. Add most of the coriander.
5. Serve with the remaining coriander, flaked almonds and chopped apricots with a side of couscous or crusty bread.

Notes

— The benefit of this recipe is that you can use what you have in your pantry and refrigerator, so feel free to substitute the ingredients. For example, if you have potatoes instead of sweet potatoes, or other vegetables that need using up.

BREAD

Mushroom and Lentil Pie

SERVES 6

1 tablespoon olive oil
1 tablespoon vegan butter
1 large onion, finely sliced
400 g (14 oz) mixed mushrooms, such as oyster, shiitake, chestnut, etc.
20 g (¾ oz) dried porcini mushrooms, soaked in boiling water for 20–30 minutes)
3 garlic cloves, finely chopped
2 rosemary sprigs, finely chopped or 1 teaspoon dried
1 tablespoon finely chopped oregano
pinch of cayenne pepper (optional)
50 ml (1¾ fl oz/3½ tablespoons) red wine (or 1 tablespoon red wine vinegar)
400 g (14 oz) tin lentils (brown, green or beluga), drained and rinsed
1 teaspoon brown sugar
2 tablespoons tomato purée (paste)
1 tablespoon dark soy sauce
1 tablespoon light soy sauce
2 tablespoons plain (all-purpose) flour
125 ml (4 fl oz/½ cup) non-dairy milk, plus extra for brushing
100 g (3½ oz) vegan cheese, grated (optional)
2 sheets of vegan ready-rolled puff pastry
1 tablespoon vegetable oil, for brushing
sea salt and freshly ground black pepper

It's pie season, and there is nothing more hearty than mushrooms and lentils. This combination simmers in a glossy, thickened sauce, tucked into a flaky puff pastry. Drool-worthy.

---

1. Preheat the oven to 200°C fan (425°F).
2. Heat the olive oil and butter in a large frying pan over a medium heat, add the onion and fry for 5–10 minutes until softened.
3. Add the mushrooms, along with the liquid from the porcini mushrooms and cook for 15 minutes, or until reduced and browned. Season with salt and pepper, then add the garlic, rosemary, oregano and cayenne pepper and fry until fragrant.
4. Pour in the wine and stir through until evaporated. Add the lentils, sugar, tomato purée and soy sauces and stir through to combine. Sprinkle in the flour and stir to combine, cooking for a few minutes. Add the milk and cook for a couple of minutes until glossy and thick like gravy. Add a splash more of the milk if it is a little too thick. Add the vegan cheese, if using, and stir through to mix.
5. Line a 25–28 cm (10–11 in) pie tin (pan) with one of the sheets of pastry and trim the edges. Pour in the pie filling, then dampen the edges of the pastry base. Layer the second sheet of pastry on top and cut to size. Crimp the edges with a fork and pierce a small hole in the middle to let steam escape.
6. Brush the top with a mix of non-dairy milk and vegetable oil and bake in the oven for 20–25 minutes until golden brown.

Notes

— Depending on the size of the tin you are using, you can layer up multiple rolls of ready-rolled pastry to fill the space if needed.

Christmas Day Nut Roast

SERVES 6

vegetable oil, for greasing
1 tablespoon vegan butter
125 g (4½ oz) chestnut mushrooms, roughly chopped
1 medium red onion, chopped
300 g (10½ oz) carrots, finely chopped
1 celery stalk, finely chopped
2 garlic cloves, chopped
200 g (7 oz/2 cups) ground almonds
125 g (4½ oz/1 cup) dried cranberries, chopped
125 g (4½ oz/generous ⅔ cup) dried apricots, roughly chopped
200 g (7 oz/1½ cups) nuts, chopped (I used pecans and walnuts)
125 g (4½oz/1½ cups) fresh breadcrumbs
1 tablespoon water
1 teaspoon mixed spice
zest and juice of ½ orange
2 tablespoons tahini
1 teaspoon Marmite
handful of herbs (rosemary, thyme and parsley work well)
sea salt and freshly ground black pepper

Every year I make a nut roast for Christmas day, and the whole family loves it. I have tested many different versions over the years, and this recent iteration is my absolute favourite. It is packed with sweet dried fruit, crunchy toasted nuts, zesty orange, mixed spices and a medley of herbs for a vibrant vegan centrepiece for Christmas!

1. Preheat the oven to 180°C fan (400°F). Grease a large 900 g (2 lb) loaf tin (pan) with vegetable oil and line with baking parchment.
2. Melt the butter in a large frying pan over a low heat, add the mushrooms and cook for 5–10 minutes until reduced. Add the onion, carrots, celery and garlic and soften for 5 minutes.
3. In a large bowl, combine all the remaining ingredients, then stir through the onion mixture. Spoon into the prepared tin, pressing everything down and flattening the top. Cover with foil and roast in the oven for 40 minutes. Uncover after 30 minutes and roast for the final 10 minutes.
4. Remove from the oven and leave to cool in the tin for 10 minutes before carefully turning out to serve sliced.

Notes

— For serving on Christmas day, I prepare this the day before, leaving the final 10 minutes of roasting for the actual day.

Farmhouse Loaf

<u>*MAKES 1 LARGE LOAF*</u>

375 g (13 oz/3 cups) strong bread flour, plus extra for dusting
125 g (4½ oz/1 ¼ cups) rye flour
7 g (¼ oz) sachet fast-action dried yeast
10 g (½ oz) salt
330 ml (11 fl oz/1⅓ cups) lukewarm water
50 g (1¾ oz/scant ½ cup) mixed seeds

We don't buy bread in our house because my husband makes a loaf or two every week. Over time he has adapted the recipe slightly, and this is the most up-to-date version of his perfectly fluffy and crusty farmhouse loaf. It is far tastier and cheaper than anything you can buy in the shops!

---

1. Either in a stand mixer or a large bowl, combine the flours, yeast and salt, making sure the yeast and salt don't touch. Pour in the lukewarm water and either mix on medium speed with a dough hook for 5 minutes until it forms a smooth dough, or mix with a spoon until combined and then knead by hand on a work surface for around 10 minutes until smooth and elastic. Add the seeds gradually as the dough comes together.
2. Cover the dough with a damp tea (dish) towel (or lightly oiled cling film/plastic wrap) and leave in a warm spot to rise for 1–1½ hours until doubled in size.
3. Once risen, turn out onto a lightly floured work surface, and knock back with your hands. Create a ball by pinching the edge furthest away from you and folding over three-quarters of the way. Rotate and repeat to create a ball and tuck the bottom under. Cover with a damp tea (dish) towel. Leave in a warm spot to prove for 30 minutes, then repeat this step. If you have a proving basket, do this second proof in the basket. Sprinkle the basket with flour and tip the dough into it with the top facing downwards into the basket.
4. Preheat the oven to 230°C fan (475°F) and line the base of a Dutch oven or cast-iron casserole pot with baking parchment. Place the pot in the oven to heat up. You don't need to use one, but it helps with the rise. Alternatively, line a large baking tray (pan) with baking parchment.
5. Remove the hot pan from the oven. Tip the basket upside down so that the bread falls into your hand, then tip into the pot, seam-side down. If you aren't using a pan, simply place the dough onto the lined baking tray instead. Lightly score the top with a sharp knife or bread knife.

6. Bake in the oven for 30 minutes with the lid on, then uncover and bake for a final 5 minutes.
7. Transfer the bread to a wire rack to cool for 20–30 minutes before serving.

Notes

— The bread will last 3–4 days (though you'll likely eat it before then!).

— You can do the first proof of the dough overnight in the refrigerator for convenience.

Cottage Kitchen Dauphinoise Pie

SERVES 4

2 tablespoons olive oil
1 large onion, chopped
2 carrots, finely chopped
1 celery stalk, finely chopped
1 teaspoon paprika
250 g (9 oz) vegetarian mince
400 g (14 oz) tin green lentils (or use any colour), drained
400 g (14 oz) tin chopped tomatoes
2 tablespoons tomato purée (paste)
2 teaspoons Marmite
500 ml (17 fl oz/generous 2 cups) vegetable or mushroom stock
good splash of vegan Worcestershire sauce (or use soy sauce)
2–3 thyme sprigs, leaves picked and chopped (or use dried mixed herbs)
200 g (7 oz/1¼ cups) frozen peas
500 g (1 lb 2 oz) white potatoes, peeled and very finely sliced
25 g (scant 1 oz) vegan butter, melted
50 g (1¾ oz) vegan cheese, finely grated (optional)
sea salt and freshly ground black pepper

I loved when my mum announced that cottage pie or potato dauphinoise was on the menu for the evening. So I've combined my childhood favourites and made them totally plant-based for a blend of comfort foods that is deeply satisfying. It's a proper cottage kitchen dish – rustic, warming and cosy.

---

1. Preheat the oven to 200°C fan (425°F).
2. Heat a large frying pan over a medium heat, add the oil, onion, carrots and celery and fry gently for about 10 minutes. Sprinkle in the paprika and cook for a couple of minutes, stirring constantly.
3. Add the mince, lentils, chopped tomatoes, tomato purée, Marmite, stock, Worcestershire sauce and thyme, then season to taste. Bring to the boil, then reduce the heat and simmer for 5 minutes, or until the sauce has reduced. Finally, add the peas and stir through.
4. Spoon the lentil mixture into a large gratin dish.
5. Add the sliced potatoes to a large bowl and pour over the melted butter. Season with salt and black pepper and gently toss the potatoes until they are all coated with the butter.
6. Arrange the sliced potatoes overlapping on top of the lentil mixture, then top with the grated cheese, if using. Place the dish onto a baking tray (pan) and bake for 30–40 minutes until the potato is cooked through and golden brown.

Chocolate Torte

SERVES 8

250 g (9 oz) digestive biscuits (graham crackers)
100 g (3½ oz) vegan butter, melted
350 g (12 oz) dark vegan chocolate (at least 70% cocoa solids)
300 ml (10 fl oz/1¼ cups) coconut milk from a 400 ml (14 oz) tin (if the coconut milk has separated, strain off the excess water and use the creamy part for this recipe)
1 teaspoon vanilla bean paste
pinch of sea salt

TO SERVE
fresh raspberries
vegan ice cream

A chocolate torte was the start of every Christmas dessert table growing up. I am a chocolate fiend, and the likes of a pavlova or trifle were of no interest to me! After I went vegan, my mum made sure to create a plant-based version that tastes just as indulgent as the original. A no-bake dessert with a crisp biscuit (cookie) base and glossy chocolate filling is the best finish to a festive feast.

1. Blitz the biscuits in a food processor until they are fine crumbs, then add the melted butter and blitz again. Pour into a 20–22 cm (8–8½ in) loose-bottom cake tin (pan) and press down firmly over the base. Leave to chill in the refrigerator while you prepare your torte filling.
2. Break the chocolate into a heatproof bowl, set over a saucepan of simmering water and stir until completely melted, making sure the base of the bowl doesn't touch the water. Alternately, you can melt the chocolate in the microwave in 10–15 second bursts, stirring between each blast.
3. Gently warm the coconut milk in a medium pan, then add to the chocolate with the vanilla paste and salt and whisk together until thoroughly combined.
4. Pour the mixture onto the biscuit base and tap the tin gently on the work surface. This helps remove all the air bubbles. Leave to set in the refrigertaor for at least 2 hours, or overnight.
5. Serve with some fresh raspberries and vegan ice cream.

Notes

— You will have around 100 ml/3½ fl oz/scant ½ cup) of leftover coconut milk, which you can save to add to your morning coffee or smoothie.

Apple Sticky Toffee Pudding

SERVES 4

90 g (3 ¼ oz) vegan butter, softened, plus extra for greasing
125 g (4½ oz) Medjool dates, pitted and roughly chopped
75 ml (2½ fl oz/ 5 tablespoons) water
180 ml (6 fl oz/¾ cup) non-dairy milk
2 teaspoons bicarbonate of soda (baking soda)
pinch of salt
90 g (3 ¼ oz/½ cup) light brown soft sugar
150 g (5½ oz/1 ¼ cups) self-raising flour
3 red apples, peeled, cored and sliced

FOR THE TOFFEE SAUCE

120 g (4 oz) vegan butter
150 g (5½ oz/generous ¾ cup) light brown sugar
75 g (2½ oz) maple syrup
120 ml (4 fl oz/½ cup) vegan cream
pinch of sea salt

This is a twist on the classic sticky toffee pudding by simply adding apples. The golden toffee sauce soaks right through for the most melt-in-the-mouth delectable dessert.

---

1. Preheat the oven to 180°C fan (400°F). Grease the sides and base of a 22–23 cm (8½–9 in) square cake tin (pan) with vegan butter and line with baking parchment.
2. Add the dates, water and milk to a large saucepan and cook over a very low heat until the dates have softened. Remove from the heat, add the bicarbonate and salt and stir to combine.
3. In a separate bowl, cream the light brown sugar and butter together with a wooden spoon until light and fluffy, then stir into the dates. Gently fold in the flour.
4. Pour the batter into the prepared tin, place the apples neatly on top of the batter and bake for 15–20 minutes (30 minutes for a larger tin) until a skewer inserted into the centre comes out clean. Leave to cool in the tin while making the sauce.
5. For the sauce, add the butter, sugar and maple syrup to a pan and simmer over a medium heat until smooth. Add the cream and continue to simmer for a couple of minutes. Remove from the heat and add the sea salt.
6. Using a skewer, make holes all over the top of the cake and pour over the toffee sauce. Cut into portions and serve warm with extra sauce to drizzle on top!

Chocolate, Ginger and Pecan Tiffin

MAKES 16 TIFFINS

150 g (5½ oz) coconut oil or vegan butter, plus extra for greasing
300 g (10½ oz) ginger biscuits (cookies) (these are usually accidentally vegan)
3 tablespoons maple syrup
3 tablespoons light soft brown sugar
3 tablespoons cocoa (unsweetened chocolate) powder
300 g (10½ oz) non-dairy milk chocolate (or use dark)
1 teaspoon vanilla extract
100 g (3½ oz/generous ¾ cup) pecans, roughly chopped
1 teaspoon ground cinnamon
½ teaspoon ground ginger

This no-bake treat is ideal to give to friends and family for something thoughtful and special. Warming with ginger biscuits (cookies) and cinnamon, crunchy pecans and a thick layer of chocolate on top, I promise it won't last long in the refrigerator!

---

1. Grease a 20 cm (8 in) square tin (pan) with coconut oil or vegan butter and line the base and sides with baking parchment.
2. Crush the ginger biscuits into small pieces in a bowl with a rolling pin, leaving some chunks. Set aside.
3. Melt the coconut oil or vegan butter, maple syrup, brown sugar and cocoa powder together in a large saucepan over a medium heat. Break in 100 g (3½ oz) of the chocolate and stir through to melt until glossy.
4. Pour the melted chocolate mix into a large bowl with the ginger biscuits, together with vanilla extract, pecans, cinnamon and ginger and mix everything together. Spoon the mixture into the prepared tin. Pack in and press down firmly with a spoon, smoothing the top.
5. Melt the remaining chocolate either in the microwave or in a heatproof bowl set over a pan of simmering water, then pour over the tiffin mixture. Smooth the melted chocolate evenly with a spoon and leave to set in the refrigerator for 2–3 hours. Once set, dip a knife into boiling hot water and slice into 16 squares.

Notes

— You can substitute the pecans for any of your favourite nuts, or leave out for a nut-free alternative.

Spiced Cranberry Mocktail

MAKES 2–4 (DEPENDING ON GLASS SIZE) MOCKTAILS

200 ml (7 fl oz/scant 1 cup) cranberry juice
¼ teaspoon ground cinnamon
¼ teaspoon ground nutmeg
1 tablespoon maple syrup
juice of 1 lime
500 ml (17 fl oz/generous 2 cups) tonic water

TO GARNISH

3–5 fresh cranberries
cinnamon sticks

Being pregnant this past Christmas made me crave a festive mocktail that would get me in the spirit without any of the alcohol. The mix of cranberry, cinnamon, nutmeg and lime blend brings a little sparkle to a festive evening.

1. Fill a cocktail shaker with ice cubes, then pour in the cranberry juice. Add the cinnamon, nutmeg, maple syrup and lime juice. Shake to combine the ingredients until the outside of the shaker is cold.
2. Pour into individual glasses, top up with tonic water and garnish with fresh cranberries and a cinnamon stick.

Ultimate Hot Chocolate

SERVES 2

400 ml (14 fl oz) tin coconut milk, refrigerated overnight
30 g (1 oz/⅓ cup) icing (powdered) sugar, sifted
500 ml (17 fl oz/generous 2 cups) non-dairy milk
50 g (1¾ oz) vegan dark chocolate, plus extra grated, to finish
1 teaspoon ground cinnamon
1 heaped teaspoon cocoa (unsweetened chocolate) powder
vegan marshmallows, to serve (optional)

You cannot beat homemade hot chocolate. It is realms above any powdered version and doesn't require much more effort. Simply melt dark chocolate and milk and top with a sweet coconut cream for the most delicious warming cup to be sipped by the fire.

---

1. Spoon out the hard cream from the top of the chilled tin of coconut milk and leave behind the water. Add the cream to a large bowl and whisk with an electric whisk until creamy, about 30 seconds. Add the icing sugar and whisk until fluffy.
2. Pour the leftover coconut water and milk into a large saucepan over a low–medium heat. Break in the chocolate, then add the cinnamon and cocoa and simmer, stirring constantly, making sure not to boil.
3. When the chocolate has melted, pour into two mugs to serve. Spoon over the coconut cream and top with a few vegan marshmallows if using. Grate over some extra chocolate to finish and enjoy.

Notes

— I would recommend looking at the ingredients on the label of the coconut milk you are using. Go for one with a higher amount of coconut to get a creamier texture.

About the Author

Madeleine Olivia is a full-time content creator whose aim is to make a plant-based lifestyle easy and attainable. She provides her 550,000 YouTube subscribers with delicious, simple and affordable vegan recipes and is the author of *Minimal*, *Versatile Vegan*, *Plant Kitchen Comforts* and *Make it Vegan*.

Index

A

apples: apple crumble loaf 160
  apple sticky toffee pudding 211
  apple tree mulled cider 170
  spiced toffee apples 164
apricots: mushroom, chestnut and apricot hand pies 189
asparagus: roasted asparagus salad 30
  spring greens filo pie 47

B

babka knots, kale pesto and sundried tomato 150–3
bake, wild garlic and white bean 43
BBQ potato salad 86
BBQ shredded tofu taco 82
beans: multigrain bean salad 85
  pantry cupboard stew 194
  roasted parsnip, rosemary and white bean soup 182
  smoky beans 177
  wild garlic and white bean bake 43
  see also individual types of beans
berries: summer smoothie 76
biscuits, Easter 60
black bean burgers 96
blackberry jam 156
blackcurrant ice cream 118
Bonfire Night dogs 140
bourguignon, every mushroom 193
bread: farmhouse loaf 202–3
  kale pesto and sundried tomato babka knots 150–3
  potato and spinach stuffed flatbreads 132
  tear and share cheesy bread 108
  tofu sarnie 74
  wild garlic and pine nut focaccia 53–4
breakfast, my favourite 20
broccoli: broccoli chowder 181
  potato and broccoli gratin 50
buns: hot cross buns 56–8
  saffron buns 67
burgers, black bean 96
butter (lima) beans: warm butter bean, new potato and tomato salad 107

C

cabbage: caramelized cabbage steaks 184
cakes: apple crumble loaf 160
  chocolicious muffins 163
  lemon and elderflower cake 115
  pear upside down cake 167
cashews: garlic and herb cashew cheese 190
cauliflower, stuffed 147
chana (chickpea) squash curry 143
cheese, vegan: tear and share cheesy bread 108
chestnuts: mushroom, chestnut and apricot hand pies 189
chickpeas (garbanzos): baked green falafel 91
  chana (chickpea) squash curry 143
  Coronation chickpeas 80
chilli sauce: coconut chilli mayo 154
chillies: summer hot sauce 96
chocolate: chocolate, ginger and pecan tiffin 212
  chocolate torte 208
  chocolicious muffins 163
  ultimate hot chocolate 216
chowder, broccoli 181
Christmas Day nut roast 200
cider: apple tree mulled cider 170
  cider and onion soup 130
coconut cream, vegan 110
  rhubarb Eton mess 62
coconut milk: blackcurrant ice cream 118
  chocolate torte 208
  tofu, coconut and purple sprouting broccoli curry 44
  ultimate hot chocolate 216
coconut yoghurt: coconut chilli mayo 154
  peanut and coconut dipping sauce 38
cookies, orange, pistachio and cranberry 168
Cornish pasties, mini 138
Cornish potato cakes 129
Coronation chickpeas 80
cottage kitchen dauphinoise pie 206
courgettes (zucchini): courgette and tahini dip 91
  five green pasta 102
  veg sausage and courgette pilaf 100
cranberries: orange, pistachio and cranberry cookies 168
cranberry juice: spiced cranberry mocktail 214
crumpets, homemade 24
curry: chana (chickpea) squash curry 143
  Coronation chickpeas 80
  tofu, coconut and purple sprouting broccoli curry 44

D

dauphinoise pie, cottage kitchen 206
digestive biscuits (graham crackers): chocolate torte 208
dips and dipping sauces: coconut chilli mayo 154
  courgette and tahini dip 91
  peanut and coconut dipping sauce 38
dried fruit: Christmas Day nut roast 200
  fruit scones 110
  see also individual types of dried fruit
drinks: apple tree mulled cider 170

elderflower cordial 120
ginger, turmeric and lemon tonic 68
spiced cranberry mocktail 214
summer smoothie 76
ultimate hot chocolate 216

E

Easter biscuits 60
elderflower cordial 120
lemon and elderflower cake 115
equipment 10–13
Eton mess, rhubarb 62

F

falafels, baked green 91
farmhouse loaf 202–3
filo pastry: spring greens filo pie 47
first harvest soup 26
five green pasta 102
flatbreads, potato and spinach stuffed 132
focaccia, wild garlic and pine nut 53–4
frittata, spring 34
fruit scones with coconut cream 110

G

garlic: garlic and herb cashew cheese 190
roasted garlicky radishes and new potatoes 41
ginger, turmeric and lemon tonic 68
ginger biscuits: chocolate, ginger and pecan tiffin 212
gnocchi, roasted butternut squash and sausage 148
goujons, tofu 154
grains: multigrain bean salad 85
gratin, potato and broccoli 50
green beans: lemony green bean linguine 99

H

hand pies, mushroom, chestnut and apricot 189
harissa roasted tomatoes and mushrooms 88
herbs: baked green falafel 91
garlic and herb cashew cheese 190
tofu, leek and herb tart 29
hot chocolate, ultimate 216
hot cross buns 56–8

I

ice cream, blackcurrant 118

J

jam, blackberry 156

K

kale pesto 150–3
kebabs, mushroom satay 92

L

leeks: tofu, leek and herb tart 29
leftover squash pancakes 126
lemons: ginger, turmeric and lemon tonic 68
lemon and elderflower cake 115
lemony green bean linguine 99
lentils: caramelized onion and lentil sausage rolls 186
cottage kitchen dauphinoise pie 206
mushroom and lentil pie 196

M

meatballs, mushroom 144
Mediterranean grilled summer vegetables 79
meringues: rhubarb Eton mess 62
mince, vegetarian: cottage kitchen dauphinoise pie 206
mocktail, spiced cranberry 214
muffins, chocolicious 163
mushrooms: caramelized onion and lentil sausage rolls 186
every mushroom bourguignon 193
harissa roasted tomatoes and mushrooms 88
mushroom and lentil pie 196
mushroom, chestnut and apricot hand pies 189
mushroom meatballs 144
mushroom satay kebab 92

N

nut roast, Christmas Day 200

O

oats: winter porridge with stewed pears 178
omelettes: my favourite breakfast 20
onions: caramelized onion and lentil sausage rolls 186
cider and onion soup 130
orange, pistachio and cranberry cookies 168

P

pancakes, leftover squash 126
pantry cupboard stew 194
parsnips: roasted parsnip, rosemary and white bean soup 182
pasta: five green pasta 102
lemony green bean linguine 99
peanut butter: mushroom satay kebab 92
peanut and coconut dipping sauce 38
pears: pear upside down cake 167
winter porridge with stewed pears 178
peas: first harvest soup 26
watercress and pea pesto 48
pecans: chocolate, ginger and pecan tiffin 212
pesto: kale pesto 150–3
watercress and pea pesto 48
pies: cottage kitchen dauphinoise pie 206
mushroom and lentil pie 196
mushroom, chestnut and apricot hand pies 189
spring greens filo pie 47
pilaf, veg sausage and courgette 100
pine nuts: wild garlic and pine nut focaccia 53–4
pistachios: orange, pistachio and cranberry cookies 168
pizza rolls 32
porridge: winter porridge with stewed pears 178

potatoes: Cornish potato cakes 129
cottage kitchen dauphinoise pie 206
mini Cornish pasties 138
our BBQ potato salad 86
potato and broccoli gratin 50
potato and spinach stuffed flatbreads 132
roasted garlicky radishes and new potatoes 41
spring frittata 34
warm butter bean, new potato and tomato salad 107
watercress and pea pesto hasselback potatoes 48
puff pastry, vegan: caramelized onion and lentil sausage rolls 186
mushroom and lentil pie 196
purple sprouting broccoli: spring frittata 34
tofu, coconut and purple sprouting broccoli curry 44

R

radishes: roasted garlicky radishes and new potatoes 41
rainbow chard: stuffed chard rainbow rolls 38
rhubarb Eton mess 62
rice: multigrain bean salad 85
veg sausage and courgette pilaf 100

S

saffron buns 67
salads: multigrain bean salad 85
our BBQ potato salad 86
roasted asparagus salad 30
warm butter bean, new potato and tomato salad 107
sarnies, tofu 74
satay kebabs, mushroom 92
sauces: simple tomato sauce 144
summer hot sauce 96
toffee sauce 211
sausage rolls, caramelized onion and lentil 186
sausages: Bonfire Night dogs 140
roasted butternut squash and sausage gnocchi 148
veg sausage and courgette pilaf 100
scones, fruit 110
seasonal eating 14–15
seed butter, sunflower super 137
smoky beans 177
smoothie, summer 76
soup: broccoli chowder 181
cider and onion soup 130
first harvest soup 26
roasted parsnip, rosemary and white bean soup 182
roasted tomato and sweet potato soup 134
spiced cranberry mocktail 214
spiced toffee apples 164
spinach: first harvest soup 26
five green pasta 102
potato and spinach stuffed flatbreads 132
spring greens filo pie 47
spring frittata 34
spring greens filo pie 47
spring rolls: stuffed chard rainbow rolls 38
squash: chana (chickpea) squash curry 143
leftover squash pancakes 126
roasted butternut squash and sausage gnocchi 148
stew, pantry cupboard 194
sticky toffee pudding, apple 211
sultanas (golden raisins): hot cross buns 56–8
saffron buns 67
summer hot sauce 96
summer smoothie 76
sunflower super seed butter 137
swede (rutabaga): mini Cornish pasties 138
sweet potatoes: roasted tomato and sweet potato soup 134

T

tacos, BBQ shredded tofu 82
tahini: courgette and tahini dip 91
tart, tofu, leek and herb 29
tear and share cheesy bread 108
tiffin, chocolate, ginger and pecan 212
toffee: spiced toffee apples 164
toffee sauce 211
tofu: BBQ shredded tofu taco 82
Bonfire Night dogs 140
spring frittata 34
tofu, coconut and purple sprouting broccoli curry 44
tofu goujons 154
tofu, leek and herb tart 29
tofu sarnie 74
tomatoes: harissa roasted tomatoes and mushrooms 88
kale pesto and sundried tomato babka knots 150–3
pizza rolls 32
roasted tomato and sweet potato soup 134
simple tomato sauce 144
smoky beans 177
warm butter bean, new potato and tomato salad 107
tonic, ginger, turmeric and lemon 68
torte, chocolate 208
tortillas: BBQ shredded tofu taco 82
turmeric: ginger, turmeric and lemon tonic 68

V

vegetables, Mediterranean grilled summer 79

W

watercress and pea pesto 48
wild garlic: wild garlic and pine nut focaccia 53–4
wild garlic and white bean bake 43
winter porridge with stewed pears 173

Y

yoghurt, coconut: coconut chilli mayo 154
peanut and coconut dipping sauce 38

Quadrille, Penguin Random House UK, One Embassy Gardens, 8 Viaduct Gardens, London SW11 78W

Quadrille Publishing Limited is part of the Penguin Random House group of companies whose addresses can be found at globalpenguinrandomhouse.com

Penguin Random House UK

Published by Quadrille in 2026

www.penguin.co.uk

A CIP catalogue record for this book is available from the British Library

ISBN 9781837833788

10 9 8 7 6 5 4 3 2 1

Managing Director, Publishing: Sarah Lavelle
Publishing Director: Kajal Mistry
Senior Commissioning Editor: Kate Burkett
Copy Editor: Kathy Steer
Proofreader: Laura Rowe
Indexer: Vanessa Bird
Designer: Studio Polka
Photographer: Ali Green
Food Stylist: Polly Webb-Wilson
Food Stylist Assistant: Georgia Rudd
Head of Production: Stephen Lang
Production Manager: Sabeena Atchia

Colour reproduction by F1 Colour Ltd.

Printed in China by C&C Offset Printing Co., Ltd.

The authorised representative in the EEA is Penguin Random House Ireland, Morrison Chambers, 32 Nassau Street, Dublin 002 YH68.

FSC www.fsc.org MIX Paper | Supporting responsible forestry FSC® C018179

Penguin Random House is committed to a sustainable future for our business, our readers and our planet. This book is made from Forest Stewardship Council® certified paper.

Unity in Diversity: Perspectives on the Law of International Organizations

Unity in Diversity: Perspectives on the Law of International Organizations

Liber Amicorum for Niels M. Blokker

Edited by

Rick Lawson
Ramses A. Wessel

BRILL | NIJHOFF

LEIDEN | BOSTON

The Library of Congress Cataloging-in-Publication Data is available online at https://catalog.loc.gov

Typeface for the Latin, Greek, and Cyrillic scripts: "Brill". See and download: brill.com/brill-typeface.

ISBN 978-90-04-69992-2 (hardback)
ISBN 978-90-04-69993-9 (e-book)
DOI 10.1163/9789004699939

This book is printed on acid-free paper and produced in a sustainable manner.

Contents

Introduction: Niels Blokker's Contribution to International Institutional Law 1
Rick Lawson and Ramses A. Wessel

PART 1
Preserving the Peace

1 Restoring Justice Step 1: The Register of Damage for Ukraine 11
Roeland Böcker

2 The UN Liability Rules and General International Law: *Lex Specialis?* 23
Thomas Henquet

3 Security Council Oversight of Non-UN Operations
Law, Policy and Practice 41
Ian Johnstone

4 Operational Lawmaking within the UN: The Origins of the Legal Framework for Peacekeeping 57
Giserd Marqeshi and Nigel D. White

5 'Uniting against Impunity' in the New Cold War: Will the UN General Assembly Come of Age? 74
Michael Ramsden

6 The Amazing Resurrection of NATO: Problems and Prospects 88
Alfred van Staden

PART 2
Preserving the Planet

7 Regime Complexity in Global Health: The Search for Multilateral Pandemic Governance 103
Gian Luca Burci

8 The UN Security Council and a Warming World: Coming to Terms with the Security Implications of Climate Change 119
Daniëlla Dam-de Jong

9 Inter-organizational Collaboration: The World Organization for Animal Health and the One Health Initiative 132
Jan Klabbers

10 Weathering a Perfect Storm: Fundamental Questions of Institutional Law in Ocean Governance 144
Brian McGarry

11 The Quadripartite: Building Alliances between the WHO, the FAO, WOAH and UNEP 157
André Nollkaemper

12 The International Tribunal for the Law of the Sea and the Meeting of States Parties to the 1982 UN Convention on the Law of the Sea
Mare Ignotum *for the Law of International Organizations?* 176
Meagan S. Wong

PART 3
Preserving Justice

13 The Contribution of International Organizations to the Settlement of International Disputes 193
Eric De Brabandere and Jason Rudall

14 The EU's Foreign and Security Policy and Legal Remedies
Three Remarkable Cases before the EU Courts 207
Mielle Bulterman and Larissa van den Herik

15 Statement Decisions as Institutional Authority 222
Jacob Katz Cogan

16 The International Court of Justice in Conflict
Reflections on the Role and Impact of the Palestine Litigation 232
Helen Duffy and Giulia Pinzauti

17 The United Nations Criminal Tribunals: Terminable Yet Independent? 249
Huw Llewellyn

18 When the Whole Becomes More than the Sum of Its Parts
How the ICC Re-Invented Itself through Complementarity 265
Carsten Stahn

19 Governing International Justice: Whence the Unified Principles? 281
Sergey Vasiliev

PART 4
Preserving International Cooperation

20 Relations between 'European Courts'
Towards Civilized Dialogue? 297
Laurence Boisson de Chazournes and Pieter Jan Kuijper

21 The World Intellectual Property Organization's New Strategic Direction
Serving Underserved Communities and Helping Transform IP into a Tool That Works for Building a More Sustainable Future 310
Edward Kwakwa and Irina Chicu

22 The New Roles of the WTO 324
Gabrielle Marceau and Maria George

23 Between Restraint and Enthusiasm
International Organizations' Participation in Advisory Proceedings before the ICJ and ITLOS 339
Pierre Klein

24 Anticipation, or the People That Make the Law of the Sea Convention Work 353
Liesbeth Lijnzaad

25 Falling through the Cracks
Exploring the Role of Law in the Interaction between International Organizations 366
René Urueña

PART 5
Preserving International Organizations

26 The European Union as a Democratic International Organization 379
Laurens-Jan Brinkhorst and Jaap Hoeksma

27 Unity within Diversity: The Continuing Rise of Consensus 390
Helena Loutas-Paraskeva and Anmol Gulecha

28 Attaching Member State's Financial Contribution to the Organization to Circumvent the Organization's Immunity from Execution
Let the State Pay? 402
Paolo Palchetti

29 The Privileges and Immunities of International Organizations and Equality
Some Reflections on Their Justifications from an Egalitarian Perspective 412
August Reinisch

30 The Personality and Responsibility of International Organizations 423
Dan Sarooshi

31 The Great Unknown
General Principles Governing the Law of International Organizations 438
Kirsten Schmalenbach

32 *We the Peoples* in International Organizations: An Unfinished Agenda 451
Nico Schrijver

PART 6
Some Concluding Reflections on the Discipline of International Institutional Law

33 International Institutional Lawyers as Masters of Modern Philosophy 465
Jean d'Aspremont

34 Reading International Organizations
Between Legal Construction and Social Existence 476
Catherine Brölmann

35 Law and Lawyering in International Organizations 487
Edward Chukwuemeke Okeke

Index 499

Introduction: Niels Blokker's Contribution to International Institutional Law

Rick Lawson and Ramses A. Wessel

The retirement of our friend and colleague Professor Niels Blokker implies nothing less than the end of an era. Over the years, his work – and in particular his handbook on international institutional law[1] – has influenced students, scholars and practitioners alike. The handbook was first published by Niels' mentor, Hein (or Henry, as he was known abroad) Schermers, in 1972. The book served to support the course on international institutional law that had already started in 1963 at the University of Amsterdam and that was taught from 1978 onwards at the University of Leiden. Also for the editors of the present volume, *International Institutional Law* was the book they read during their own university studies in Leiden and Groningen respectively in the 1980s (albeit at the time half the size of the current version). Despite the somewhat encyclopaedic approach of the book (sometimes referred to as a 'telephone directory'), the topic appealed to ideas we both had in the field of international law: the (only) way forward is through international cooperation; and how to do that in a world of sovereign states remains a fascinating topic until this very day. The 'love for international organizations' – to quote a recent special issue of the *International Organizations Law Review*[2] – is difficult to explain but has something to do with a genuine interest in institutional solutions for global problems.

In 1984, at the age of 26, Niels was appointed as an assistant at the *Europa Instituut* in Leiden. He worked on his PhD and meanwhile assisted Schermers in teaching the course on the law of international organizations. It was perhaps only logical, but still an immense honour, that Schermers asked him in 1995 to join him as co-author of the handbook. Who could have predicted at the time that Niels was to continue the project after Schermers' retirement – and indeed after the latter passed in 2006 – until 2025? It is telling for Niels'

1 The most recent, sixth, edition is Henry G. Schermers and Niels M. Blokker, *International Institutional Law* (Brill Nijhoff, 2018). A new edition, again meticulously revised, is due to appear in 2025.

2 Niels M. Blokker and Ramses A. Wessel (eds.), "The Love for International Organizations", Special Issue, *International Organizations Law Review* (IOLR) vol. 21 (2024), p. 3.

 | DOI:10.1163/9789004699939_002

modesty as well for his devotion to Schermers that he kept the name of the original author on later editions.

In a way, links between the two have always been clear. Just like Schermers, who started his career at the Ministry for Foreign Affairs, Niels was appointed legal counsel at the same Ministry in the year 2000. In this capacity he represented the Netherlands, together with Hans Lammers, before the International Court of Justice in the *Legality of Use of Force* case.[3] Niels would continue in his position at the Ministry for more than a decade, being involved, *inter alia*, in the negotiations that led to the Kampala amendments to the ICC Statute. Yet, he never lost his interest in academia. He returned to Leiden in 2003 on a part-time basis. In doing so he was the first to be appointed on the *Schermers Chair*, which had been made possible due to an exceptionally generous donation by Hein Schermers. In 2013 Niels returned to academia full-time. In a few years' time, a new edition of *International Institutional Law* would see the light of day.

But it is not just the *Schermers and Blokker* book that makes people mention Niels' name first when the topic of the law of international organizations comes up. In 2003 Niels Blokker and Ramses Wessel met to discuss the possibility of establishing a journal on the law of international organizations, the *International Organizations Law Review* (*IOLR*, also published by Brill).[4] In a way, the foundations for this cooperation had been laid in the so-called 'LURIO' meetings that we had organised between the two research groups in Leiden and Utrecht on what in Dutch is called *recht der internationale organisaties* (*RIO*). Celebrating the 20th birthday of the journal in Vienna in 2023, it became clear that we could not have foreseen its impact when it was created. *IOLR* functions not only as a forum to exchange ideas, but also strengthened the formation of a community of scholars and practitioners working on the legal aspects of international organizations. In addition, it offered an opportunity to explore more theoretical dimensions of the law of international organizations – to which Niels contributed both as an editor and as an author.[5] This was a welcome and very much needed exercise, also

3 ICJ, *Legality of Use of Force (Serbia and Montenegro v. Netherlands)*, [2004] ICJ Reports, p. 1011. See N.M. Blokker, "From a Dispute About the Use of Force to a Non-Dispute About Jurisdiction: The Case Concerning Legality of Use of Force (Yugoslavia *v.* Netherlands) before the International Court of Justice", in N.M. Blokker a.o. (eds.), *The Netherlands in Court: Essays in Honour of Johan G. Lammers* (Brill, 2007), pp. 19–50.

4 First talks were with Jan Klabbers, who immediately accepted to be on the Board and offered to become the first book review editor (and has wonderfully performed that role for almost 20 years).

5 See for instance Niels Blokker, "International Organizations and their Members", in *IOLR* vol. 1 (2004), pp. 139–161, or his "Comparing Apples and Oranges? Reinventing the Wheel?

to enrich a discipline that arguably had a rather 'factual' or 'encyclopaedic' image, based on the various handbooks. Even a fundamental notion as the definition of an international organization had not been developed thoroughly.[6] When, in 2020, Jan Klabbers and Guy Fiti Sinclair introduced a symposium on Theorizing International Organizations Law in the *European Journal of International Law*, their starting point was the observation by Schermers and Blokker that "there is no strongly established tradition of developing theories on international organizations in the land of legal science".[7]

Yet, despite complaints of a lack of theory in the field, most studies dealing with the question of whether something can be seen as an 'international organization' quote the book by Schermers and Blokker. The three elements the book mentions have become somewhat of a standard: "international organizations are defined as forms of cooperation (1) founded on an international agreement; (2) having at least one organ with a will of its own; and (3) established under international law".[8] The second element indeed seems crucial and differentiates international organizations from, for instance, international conferences. While the handbook's theoretical notion is largely based on the ideas of Viraly (whom Niels greatly admires) and his concept of 'function' – essentially boiling down to the idea that "the existence of international organizations is entirely instrumental, directly related to the performance of certain functions"[9] – the idea of an entity with separate international legal personality can of course be traced back to the famous *Reparation for Injuries* case of the International Court of Justice.[10] The notion of international institutions not being merely centres "for harmonizing the actions of nations" (in the words of the Court) still seems to be at the root of most current debates on post-national rule-making, global administrative law, the exercise of public authority, informal international lawmaking and global constitutionalism.

Schermers' Book and Challenges for the Future of International Institutional Law", in *IOLR* vol. 5 (2008), pp. 197–213, or again "International Organizations and Customary International Law – Is the International Law Commission Taking International Organizations Seriously?", in *IOLR* vol. 14 (2017), p. 1.

6 See also Lorenzo Gasbarri, *The Concept of an International Organization in International Law* (Oxford UP, 2021).

7 Jan Klabbers and Guy Fiti Sinclair, "On Theorizing International Organizations Law: Editors' Introduction", in *European Journal of International Law* (*EJIL*) vol. 31 (2020), pp. 489–496.

8 Schermers and Blokker (*supra* note 1), p. 41 (or to use the book's characteristic referencing style: §33).

9 *Ibidem*, at p. 20.

10 ICJ, *Reparation for Injuries Suffered in the Service of the United Nations* (Advisory Opinion), [1949] ICJ Reports p. 174.

The (in)famous *volonté distincte* of international organizations (as the basis for the idea by Schermers and Blokker that international organizations have "a will of their own"), triggered debates on how to control these creations.[11] This reveals that legal personality is not just about the capacity to bring claims or to engage in other legal actions; it is part of the defining nature of international organizations, despite the fact for some organizations it is not yet clear that being an international organization and having legal personality (existing as an entity in a certain legal system) indeed coincide.[12]

Apart from his contribution to these more theoretical notions, Niels always had a keen eye for the realities that international organizations have to cope with. This combination of theoretical groundings and a practical approach was already present at the very beginning of his academic career: his PhD thesis *International Regulation of World Trade in Textiles* had as a subtitle "Lessons for practice – a contribution to theory".[13] The same combination was reflected, exactly 35 years later, in Niels' monumental summer course for the Hague Academy of International Law.[14]

It comes as no surprise that the fine combination of a solid theoretical basis, extensive practical experience and a healthy dose of common sense made Niels a popular *ad hoc* advisor for international organizations, as well as for a wide range of entities that were aspiring for that status. This broad international exposure, combined with intellectual curiosity, enabled him to collect – and use – examples of international organizations and situations that no one had ever heard of, but that gradually fuelled the discipline's coming of age. Rumour has it that Niels has a special drawer[15] in which he collects examples of obscure international organizations to be later used in a new edition of the handbook. And in class, because Niels is a great teacher who has the gift of triggering his students' interest and bringing even the most technical subjects to life. With

11 Cf. the Frankenstein reference in Klabbers' *An Introduction to International Institutional Law* (Cambridge UP, 2009).

12 Niels M. Blokker and Ramses A. Wessel, "Revisiting Questions of Organizationhood, Legal Personality and Membership in the OSCE: The Interplay Between Law, Politics and Practice", in Mateja Platise Steinbrück, Carolyn Moser, Anne Peters (eds.), *The Legal Status of the OSCE* (Cambridge UP, 2019), pp. 135–164.

13 Niels Blokker, *International Regulation of World Trade in Textiles: Lessons for practice – a contribution to theory* (Martinus Nijhoff Publ., 1989). The *promotores* were professors Hein Schermers (Leiden) and Kamiel Mortelmans (Utrecht).

14 Niels M. Blokker, "Legal Facets of the Practice of International Organizations", in *Collected Courses of The Hague Academy of International Law – Recueil des cours*, vol. 435 (Brill, 2024), pp. 73–324.

15 That this is not a folder on a computer testifies to his character.

his human interest and warm personality he was always popular amongst his students – and warmly respected by his colleagues.

So, theory *and* practice, institutions *and* human beings. Indeed, rather than a narrow focus on theoretical approaches to international organizations, which are sometimes vulnerable to the risk of becoming detached from reality, Niels Blokker's extensive contribution to the field can be found in a critical analysis of the various functions of international organizations and, perhaps above all, how these functions differ between organizations. What his work shows is that when we talk about an international organization, we may mean different things and use different starting points as no organization can be compared to another. It is in the comparison of different roles of organs, different decision-making rules, different (numbers of) members, and different accountability rules that we understand how international organizations work. Yet, despite the fact that the European University Institute, the World Meteorological Organization, or the Asian Infrastructure Investment Bank are all international organizations,[16] there is not so much they have in common. And this variation is only likely to grow in an era of proliferation of international organizations.[17] Niels Blokker's life's work, however, is to find 'unity in diversity' – which therefore rightfully inspired the subtitle of his main book. Paraphrasing his own words, there *is* something like international institutional law as there *is* some unity within diversity. After all, we also have international law, despite the many variations between states. Thus, while each international organization is unique, they have sufficient characteristics in common to justify a comparison and to consider international institutional law to be a sub-discipline within the larger field of public international law.[18]

We would not do justice to Niels, however, if we were taken to suggest that his academic interests were limited to international institutional law in a narrow sense. Quite to the contrary, he has published extensively on a wide range of subjects. We already mentioned his PhD thesis about the international regulation of world trade in textiles. His experience at the Dutch Ministry of Foreign Affairs allowed him to explore other areas. Based on his involvement in the negotiations towards the Kampala amendments to the ICC Statute, Niels was able to publish extensively, and authoritatively, on the crime of

16 Again borrowing examples from Klabbers and Sinclair (*supra* note 7).

17 Niels M. Blokker and H.G. Schermers, *Proliferation of International Organizations: Legal Issues* (Kluwer Law International, 2000).

18 See Blokker's arguments on pages 24–31 of his handbook.

aggression.[19] Several publications address issues of international peace and security.[20] In recent years Niels turned to the governance of international courts and tribunals.[21]

This broad range of interest, centred around international organizations but with an open eye to the global problems that we face today, is clearly reflected by the current edited volume, which is a true *liber amicorum* – a worthy successor, we would hope, to the *liber amicorum* that Niels himself edited three decades ago for his mentor, Hein Schermers.[22] The contributors to the present volume come from all corners of the globe. They have closely worked with Niels in different settings or have had the pleasure of having him as a supervisor. The list of authors also reveals the width of Niels' national and international network, and the high esteem that he commands. The various chapters address some of the core issues of international institutional law, combining classic themes and contemporary issues. The contributions have been organised around five of the most pressing themes of our times: *preserving the peace* (covering both classic issues such as peacekeeping and new challenges such as the war in Ukraine), *preserving the planet* (addressing climate change, animal welfare and the law of the sea), *preserving justice* (focussing on the settlement of international disputes, for instance by the International Court of Justice or the International Criminal Court), *preserving international cooperation* (both

19 See, e.g., Niels Blokker, "The Crime of Aggression and the United Nations Security Council", in *Leiden Journal of International Law* vol. 20 (2007), pp. 867–894; Niels Blokker, "Prosecuting the crime of aggression: the role of the UN Security Council", in Stephanie Bock and Eckart Conze (eds.), *Rethinking the Crime of Aggression: international and interdisciplinary perspectives* (T.M.C. Asser Press, 2022), pp. 255–267; Niels Blokker and Stefan Barriga, chapters 17–19 in Claus Kreß and Stefan Barriga (eds.), *The Crime of Aggression: A Commentary*, Vol. 1 (Cambridge UP, 2016), pp. 621–674.

20 See, e.g., N.M. Blokker "Is the authorization authorized? Powers and practice of the UN Security Council to authorize the use of force by 'coalitions of the able and willing'", in *EJIL* vol. 11 (2000), pp. 541–568; Niels M. Blokker and Nico J. Schrijver (eds.), *The Security Council and the Use of Force: Theory and Reality – A Need for Change?* (Martinus Nijhoff Publ., 2005), Niels M. Blokker, *Saving Succeeding Generations from the Scourge of War: The United Nations Security Council at 75* (Brill Nijhoff, 2020); Nico J. Schrijver and Niels M. Blokker (eds.) *Elected members of the Security Council: Lame Ducks or Key Players?* (Brill Nijhoff, 2020).

21 See, e.g., Niels M. Blokker, "The Governance of International Courts and Tribunals: Organizing and Guaranteeing Independence and Accountability", in Andreas Føllesdal and Geir Ulfstein (eds.), *The Judicialization of International Law: A Mixed Blessing?* (Oxford UP, 2018).

22 Niels Blokker and Sam Muller (eds.), *Towards More Effective Supervision by International Organizations – Essays in Honour of Henry G. Schermers* vol. I (Martinus Nijhoff Publ., 1994).

between States and among international organizations), as well as *preserving international organizations* (with recurring topics such as privileges and immunities, legal personality and responsibility of international organizations, as well as general principles governing the law of international organizations). The volume ends with some concluding reflections on the discipline of international institutional law.

Together, the contributions make abundantly clear that the discipline of international institutional law is alive and kicking. Indeed, as one of the contributors in this volume asserts: "The modern history of international law comprises the history of States. The future history of international law will likely be written to a greater extent by international organizations". This is perhaps not obvious in an era where support for a 'rule-based international order' is eroding. As the pendulum swings away from international cooperation, and nationalist forces focus on self-interest, one might expect to see international organizations dwindle. But the global problems remain and do not stop at national borders. The need for international cooperation remains. As the contributions to this volume illustrate, the work of Niels has inspired, and continues to inspire, many across the globe to find institutional solutions for global problems.

Based on all this, only one statement seems appropriate to conclude this short introduction: Niels Blokker has become an institution.

PART 1

Preserving the Peace

CHAPTER 1

Restoring Justice Step 1: The Register of Damage for Ukraine

*Roeland Böcker**

1 *"Buurman"* Blokker

Somewhere in the middle of our respective professional lives – Niels Blokker and the author were born in the same year – I had the tremendous pleasure of working with Niels for some eight years in the International Law Division of the Dutch Ministry of Foreign Affairs, where Niels was the deputy legal adviser. What's more, we were ministerial neighbours in an era when government employees of a certain seniority were entitled to an office of their own. This provided me with an excellent opportunity to observe Niels' unbeatable good humour, even on dreary Monday mornings in mid-winter. His cheerful "*Goedemorgen buurman!*" (Good morning neighbour!) resonated in my head long after his departure from the Ministry. A departure, by the way, which amply demonstrated Niels' passion for academia, overshadowing even his crucial role for eight years in the cradle of Dutch international law policy. It is therefore with the greatest pleasure that I contribute to this *liber amicorum* for Niels on the occasion of a new step in life.

2 War in Europe, the World's Response

On 24 February 2022, Russia brutally invaded Ukraine and took control over large parts of the East and South of the country. In addition to the annexation of the Ukrainian Crimea, eight years before, this amounted to the largest incident of aggression by one European state against another since the Second World War. The international mechanism designed specifically to act as required to maintain international peace and security, the United Nations

* The author has worked for the Dutch Ministry of Foreign Affairs since 1987, *inter alia* as Government Agent to the European Court of Human Rights and as Permanent Representative to the Council of Europe. He is currently adviser to the Ukraine accountability team in the Human Rights and Multilateral Affairs Directorate (DMM) of the Ministry.

 | DOI:10.1163/9789004699939_003

Security Council, was unable to do so, due to the right to veto of the aggressor, the Russian Federation, being a permanent member of the Council. The Security Council did, however, adopt a procedural resolution[1] calling for an emergency special session of the General Assembly on the matter, as a corollary of the Assembly's "Uniting for peace" resolution.[2] On 28 February 2022, the General Assembly opened its eleventh emergency special session, on the Russian invasion of Ukraine. On 2 March 2022, the Assembly by a large majority adopted Resolution ES-11/1, in which it deplored in the strongest terms the Russian aggression against Ukraine in violation of Article 2(4) of the United Nations Charter, and demanded that the Russian Federation immediately cease its use of force against Ukraine and refrain from any further unlawful threat or use of force against any Member State.[3] Five further resolutions were adopted in the course of the emergency special session.[4]

A large number of initiatives in support of Ukraine, including in the legal field, were taken in the meantime, both bilaterally and multilaterally. In order not to exceed the scope of this article, reference is limited to the Order of 16 March 2022 of the International Court of Justice on provisional measures in the case of *Allegations of Genocide under the Convention on the Prevention and Punishment of the Crime of Genocide* (*Ukraine v. Russian Federation*), the referral of 2 March 2022 by forty-three states of the situation in Ukraine to the prosecutor of the International Criminal Court (ICC) and the ensuing arrest warrants of 17 March 2023[5] and 5 March 2024[6] by the ICC's pre-trial chamber against the president of the Russian Federation and other Russian high

1 UN Security Council Resolution 2623 of 27 February 2022.

2 UN General Assembly (UNGA) Resolution 377 of 3 November 1950, "Uniting for peace".

3 UNGA Resolution ES-11/1 of 2 March 2022 on Aggression against Ukraine.

4 UNGA Resolution ES-11/2 of 24 March 2022 on Humanitarian consequences of the aggression against Ukraine; UNGA Resolution ES-11/3 of 7 April 2022 on Suspension of the rights of membership of the Russian Federation in the Human Rights Council; UNGA Resolution ES-11/4 of 12 October 2022 on Territorial integrity of Ukraine: defending the principles of the Charter of the United Nations; UNGA Resolution ES-11/5 of 14 November 2022 on Furtherance of remedy and reparation for aggression against Ukraine; UNGA Resolution ES-11/6 of 23 February 2023 on Principles of the Charter of the United Nations underlying a comprehensive, just and lasting peace in Ukraine.

5 Arrest warrants for Vladimir Putin, the president of Russia, and Maria Lvova-Belova, Russian commissioner for children's rights, alleging responsibility for the war crime of unlawful deportation and transfer of children from the occupied areas of Ukraine to the Russian Federation.

6 Arrest warrants for Sergei Ivanovich Kobylash, lieutenant general in the Russian armed forces, and Viktor Nikolayevich Sokolov, admiral in the Russian navy, for the war crimes of directing attacks at civilian objects and causing excessive incidental harm to civilians or damage to civilian objects, and the crime against humanity of inhumane acts.

authorities, as well as two initiatives which aimed at investigating and prosecuting the crime of aggression, in the absence of the ICC's jurisdiction to do so,[7] notably, the establishment of an International Centre for the Prosecution of the Crime of Aggression (ICPA), and ongoing talks about the creation of a special tribunal for the crime of aggression.

3 Dutch Policy on Accountability for Ukraine

On 14 July 2022, the Dutch minister of Foreign Affairs hosted the ministerial Ukraine Accountability Conference in The Hague, marking the commitment of forty-five countries to upholding international law. The participants agreed on a political declaration, pledging further support for efforts to ensure accountability for international crimes and committing to establish a Dialogue Group on Accountability for Ukraine. This Dialogue Group, a coordinating mechanism for all national and international efforts aimed at the investigation and prosecution of international crimes committed in the context of the war against Ukraine, has become fully operational in the meantime. Since the Accountability Conference, the Dutch government has expressed its availability to host a number of new international organizations. The ICPA, referred to above, was launched on 3 July 2023 at the Eurojust offices in The Hague. In the same month, a host state agreement between the Kingdom of the Netherlands and the Council of Europe was concluded on the establishment in The Hague of the Register of Damage for Ukraine, followed by the actual opening of the Register in The Hague. Also, the government expressed its willingness to host a future special tribunal for the crime of aggression, provided such an initiative will receive sufficient international political and financial support, will not interfere with the work of the ICC and will be manageable in terms of security and related capacity. Finally, under similar conditions, the government expressed its availability to host a future compensation mechanism, which is the logical follow-up to the Register of Damage. The Register and the compensation mechanism will be further discussed below.

On 4 May 2023, Ukrainian president Volodymyr Zelenskyy visited The Hague and met with then Prime-Minister Mark Rutte and a number of other domestic and international authorities. The visit was concluded by a bilateral Declaration on Accountability for Ukraine, which, *inter alia*, confirmed the leading role of the Netherlands in implementing item 7 of president Zelenskyy's

7 See Article 15bis, paragraph 5, Rome Statute of the International Criminal Court.

Peace Formula of 11 October 2022, "Restoring justice". This role inspires Dutch policy on accountability for Ukraine and led to a further ministerial conference on 2 April 2024 on Restoring Justice for Ukraine. That conference was concluded by a political declaration, supported by forty-four states, which committed themselves to the investigation and prosecution of international crimes, including the crime of aggression, to the compensation of damage at the expense of the Russian Federation, and to the promotion of international dialogue on accountability for Ukraine.

4 General Assembly Resolution ES-11/5

One of the resolutions adopted by the United Nations General Assembly in the course of its emergency special session on Ukraine was Resolution ES-11/5 of 14 November 2022, entitled *"Furtherance of remedy and reparation for aggression against Ukraine"*.[8] This resolution serves as the legal starting point for the ensuing activities of the international community, aimed at reaching compensation for war victims. Resolution ES-11/5 recognised that the Russian Federation must bear the legal consequences of all of its internationally wrongful acts in or against Ukraine, including making reparation for the injury, and for any damage, caused by such acts. The resolution also recognised the need for the establishment of an international mechanism for reparation, and recommended the creation of an international register of damage in co-operation with Ukraine.[9] For a proper assessment of what followed, it is important to note that – unlike most of the other emergency special session resolutions concerning the war in Ukraine, which generated majorities of over 140 votes – Resolution ES-11/5 was supported by ninety-four member states. This is still a substantial number, but less than half of the membership of the United Nations. The supporting group included virtually all European and western states. Though the number of votes against was reassuringly low, only fourteen, the large number of abstentions and absentees, almost exclusively made up of states from the global south, gave more reason for concern. Given the primordial interest by European and western states, it is perhaps not

8 See *supra* note 4.

9 A similar initiative was taken by the General Assembly in its Resolution A/RES/ES-10/17 of 15 December 2006, which established, as a subsidiary organ of the Assembly, the United Nations Register of Damage Caused by the Construction of the Wall in the Occupied Palestinian Territory (UNRoD), following the issuance on 9 July 2004 by the International Court of Justice of its advisory opinion on *the Legal Consequences of the Construction of a Wall in the Occupied Palestinian Territory*.

surprising that the Council of Europe appeared on the scene soon after the adoption of Resolution ES-11/5.

5 The Council of Europe and the Russian Federation

In the course of a radical expansion of the Council of Europe – until the fall of the Berlin wall a mostly West-European organization – the Russian Federation joined the Council in 1996. Those within the political organs of the organization who considered that, due to its lack of any democratic tradition, Russia could by no standards be considered a democracy worthy of joining the Council of Europe, were eventually outnumbered by those who were primarily driven by the Council of Europe's pan-European mission and by the hope and expectation that Russian democracy and rule of law, albeit unsatisfactory at the time, would benefit from Russia's membership of the family of European democracies. Despite undeniable benefits emanating from this membership – for instance the moratorium on executions of the death penalty and payment of just satisfaction to successful applicants before the European Court of Human Rights – Russia never failed to severely challenge the Council of Europe and its values. Shortly after its accession it waged an internal war in Chechnya. In 2008 it attacked fellow member state Georgia and upheld puppet governments in the Georgian breakaway regions of Abkhazia and South-Ossetia. And during the quarter of a century of its membership, Russia made clear that human rights were, at best, a marginal issue within its domestic and foreign policies.

It was not, however, before the annexation of the Crimea and the interference in the Donbass in 2014 – the latter leading, *inter alia*, to the tragic downing of Flight MH17 – that the Council of Europe showed Russia its teeth. Russia's hostile and unlawful behaviour in fellow member state Ukraine led the Parliamentary Assembly, one of the two statutory bodies of the Council of Europe, to deprive its Russian members of their right to vote, first in 2014 and again in 2015. This in turn led the Russian Duma to terminate participation of its delegation in the Assembly altogether. The Council of Europe, however, did not bite. The Committee of Ministers, the other statutory body and highest decision-making organ of the organization, remained passive, to the extent that it left Russia's membership untouched. Thus, *de facto*, the situation after 2015 came down to a kind of half membership, where Russia participated in one statutory body, but not in the other. This situation became more and more untenable as time passed. While it deprived Russia of the opportunity to participate in some of the important decision-making in the Parliamentary Assembly – notably the election of the Secretary-General and deputy Secretary-General of the Council of Europe, the Commissioner for Human Rights and the judges of the European Court of Human Rights – it provided Russia at the same time with an excellent pretext to criticize and neglect any decisions taken, or views expressed, by those authorities. Since in the interval between the Russian interference in Ukraine in 2014 and its full-scale war against Ukraine in 2022 the prevailing view in both statutory organs of the Council of Europe was still in favour of Russia's membership, the return of the Russian delegation to the Parliamentary Assembly in 2019 was, *de facto* at least, facilitated by the creation of the so-called "complementary joint procedure". In short, this procedure aimed at ensuring that no decision affecting membership of the Council of Europe (including suspension and the deprivation of the right to vote for political reasons) could be taken without prior consultation between the statutory bodies.[10]

Five years on, one can only conclude that these and other efforts to "domesticate" the Russian Federation within the family of European democracies have failed completely. The full-scale aggression of Russia against a fellow member state as of 24 February 2022 led the Council of Europe to act with unprecedented speed in suspending, and subsequently terminating, Russia's membership. By 16 March 2022, Russia was no longer a member of the organization and six months later it stopped being a party to the European Convention on Human Rights. The latter is particularly relevant to the issue of compensation for human rights violations, since the Russian Federation may be held accountable under the Convention for any such violations committed before 16 September 2022, thus including the first semester of the war.[11] One day before the expiration of that period, the Committee of Ministers called for efforts, in co-operation with Ukraine, to secure full reparation for the damage, loss or injury caused by violations by the Russian Federation of international law in Ukraine. The Committee repeated this call on 24 February 2023,

10 Remarkably, apart from the Russia context, the complementary joint procedure would appear not to have passed a first test: on 24 January 2024, the Parliamentary Assembly unilaterally resolved not to pass the credentials of the delegation of Azerbaijan for political reasons and suspended the Azerbaijani delegation from participating in the Assembly until further notice.

11 Mindful of the challenge of the execution of judgments of the European Court of Human Rights against a non-member state of the Council of Europe, the Committee of Ministers, on 7–8 February 2024, invited the Committee of Legal Advisers on Public International Law (CAHDI) to explore all possible avenues consistent with international law aimed at securing the payment by the Russian Federation of just satisfaction awarded by the European Court of Human Rights, while respecting the immunities of States and their property (CM/Del/Dec(2024)1488/10.5). At the time of writing, the CAHDI report is expected.

one year after the start of the aggression, and bearing in mind United Nations General Assembly Resolution ES-11/5 that had been adopted in the meantime. Similarly, the Parliamentary Assembly, on 26 January 2023, called on member states to set up an international compensation mechanism and, as a first step, an international register of damage.[12]

6 The (Enlarged) Partial Agreement

In response to these calls by the Council of Europe's statutory organs, the Council's secretariat proposed setting up a register of damage for Ukraine by way of a so-called Enlarged Partial Agreement. The concept of Partial Agreements dates from an early Committee of Ministers resolution.[13] It is designed to avoid deadlock in situations where unanimity is required but out of reach, while the non-supporting member states do not object to other states taking a decision, on the understanding that such decision binds only the latter, but not the former. Thus, the Partial Agreement is a fairly light and flexible form of international cooperation, allowing progress even where unanimity is absent. In order to avoid situations where a mere handful of states initiate all manner of activities under the flag of the Council of Europe, a certain minimum of supporting member states is required, presently one-third of the total membership, or sixteen member states.

The *Enlarged* Partial Agreement (EPA) further develops the concept of the Partial Agreement in that it recognises that in some cases the problems dealt with in the Council of Europe exceed the geographical framework of the territory of the member states, and that the organization must be ready to allow non-member states to participate in relevant intergovernmental activities..[14] Examples of EPA's are the Council of Europe Development Bank and the Pompidou Group.[15] Should an EPA be acceded to by all member states, its name will change to Enlarged Agreement proper. Examples of Enlarged Agreements are the Venice Commission[16] and GRECO.[17]

12 PACE Resolution 2482 (2023) of 26 January 2023.

13 Resolution adopted by the Committee of Ministers at its 9th Session, August 1951.

14 Statutory Resolution (93)28, adopted by the Committee of Ministers on 14 May 1993, builds on the early CM resolution of August 1951.

15 International Cooperation Group on Drugs and Addiction.

16 European Commission for Democracy through Law.

17 Group of States against Corruption.

7 The EPA Register of Damage for Ukraine

In the present case, it was recognised from the outset that unanimity within the Council of Europe on setting up a register of damage was unlikely, since not all member states were equally convinced of the responsibility of the Russian Federation for compensating damage emanating from its aggression, or had abstained from UNGA Resolution ES-11/5 or been absent during the vote.[18] On the other hand, it was considered important to broaden support for this initiative well beyond Europe, given the global impact of the Russian aggression. This led the Committee of Ministers, on 12 May 2023, to establish the EPA Register of Damage Caused by the Aggression of the Russian Federation Against Ukraine.[19] A few days later, on 17 May 2023, the heads of state and government of the Council of Europe, meeting in Reykjavik for the fourth time in nearly seventy-five years, confirmed the establishment of the Register of Damage for Ukraine.[20] Following the expression by the government of the Netherlands of its availability to host the Register, it was decided that the Register would have its seat in The Hague.

The Register of Damage serves as a record of evidence and claims information on damage, loss or injury caused, on or after 24 February 2022, by Russia's internationally wrongful acts in the territory of Ukraine within its internationally recognised borders, extending to its territorial waters.[21] Claims may be submitted to the Register by all natural and legal persons having suffered such damage, loss or injury, as well as by the State of Ukraine, including its regional and local authorities.

With regard to membership of the Register, two distinctions may be made. Firstly, a distinction between, on the one hand, the group of ninety-four United Nations member states that supported Resolution ES-11/5 of 14 November 2022 and, on the other hand, other states or international organizations. The first group may join the Register by a simple notification to the Secretary General of

18 Armenia and Serbia abstained on UNGA Resolution ES-11/5. Azerbaijan was absent during the vote.

19 Resolution CM/Res(2023)3 of 12 May 2023 establishing the Enlarged Partial Agreement on the Register of Damage Caused by the Aggression of the Russian Federation Against Ukraine.

20 The Conference of Participants allowed the use of the abbreviation "RD4U" for official purposes.

21 Article 1.1 of the Statute of the Register of Damage Caused by the Aggression of the Russian Federation Against Ukraine. The Statute appears as an appendix to Resolution CM/Res(2023)3.

the Council of Europe.[22] The second group may, upon request, be authorised by the Conference of Participants to join the Register, taking into particular account the position of the government of Ukraine.[23] This provision is clearly intended to avoid the Russian Federation and its allies joining the Register and interfering with its work, or at least, in case of a future peace agreement, to control such an accession.

The second distinction to be made is the distinction between Participants and Associate Members. The first group shall pay a fixed annual contribution and have the right to vote in the Conference of Participants.[24] The second group shall pay a voluntary contribution and shall not have the right to vote.[25] This distinction is inspired in particular by the expectation that non-member states of the Council of Europe sympathizing with the aim of the Register, might shy away from becoming too involved in Council of Europe administrative affairs and carrying the ensuing burden of responsibilities. The distinction, however, is somewhat blurred by the provision that those Associate Members having voluntarily contributed at the level of the annual contribution of the Participants, shall have the full range of rights of Participants during the financial year for which they made such a contribution.[26]

Participation in the Register stands at forty-four at the time of writing. This concerns a large majority of member states of the Council of Europe,[27] three observer states to the Council of Europe[28] and the European Union. The observer states joined the Register as Associate Members.

The Register is composed of several organs. The highest authority is the Conference of Participants, to which Associate Members may participate, but without the right to vote.[29] The Conference meets as often as is necessary, but at least once a year.[30] At its first meeting on 27 June 2023, the Conference, upon a proposal by the government of Ukraine, designated the Executive Director of the Register as the head of the Register's secretariat.[31] Since the duration

22 Articles 4.1 and 4.2 of the Statute.

23 Article 4.3 of the Statute.

24 Articles 4.1 and 10.2 of the Statute.

25 Articles 5.6 and 10.2 of the Statute.

26 Article 5.7 of the Statute.

27 Forty out of forty-six member states, the exceptions being Armenia, Azerbaijan, Bosnia-Herzegovina, Hungary, Serbia and Türkiye.

28 Canada, Japan and the United States.

29 Subject to Article 5.7 of the Statute.

30 Article 5.4 of the Statute. The Conference has met three times in 2023 and, so far, once in 2024.

31 Markiyan Kliuchkovskyi, who had so far been the chief negotiator on the Register on behalf of Ukraine.

and intensity of the ongoing war justifies the expectation that the number of claims submitted will run into the millions, it is self-evident that exclusively digital working methods and, hence, an adequate knowledge of information technology within the Register's secretariat are absolutely required.

At its third meeting on 16 November 2023, the Conference, furthermore, appointed the seven members of the Board of the Register, a group of independent experts having the ultimate authority in determining the eligibility of claims to be recorded in the Register, based on the recommendation of the Executive Director.[32] At its first meeting in The Hague from 11 to 15 December 2023, the Board started its work on the required rules and regulations for the determination of the categories of claims, the procedures for receiving, processing and recording of claims, the format of the claim forms and the requirements for evidence with respect to each category of claims.

The Register of Damage for Ukraine was opened for the submission of claims at the ministerial conference Restoring Justice for Ukraine in The Hague on 2 April 2024. This launch concerned, at first instance, only one category of claims, notably damage to housing. The launch of twelve further categories of claims took place in August 2024, while 18 to 20 further categories are expected to be operational before the end of 2024. The launch is expected to be completed by April 2025. Meanwhile, the influx of claims in the first months after the launch in April 2024 stands at a few thousands of claims. This modest number may be explained by several reasons: first, the limited scope of the launch at first instance: one claims category only; second, the deliberate absence of a wide-scale publicity campaign, in order to give the Register the opportunity to test its technology and procedures and, third and more importantly, a widespread belief among potential claimants that the international community will not be able to ensure real compensation of damage. It is the latter argument which particularly highlights the international community's responsibility for pursing its efforts on the path to a fully-fledged compensation mechanism for Ukraine. The next chapter is devoted to this issue.

8 Next Steps

United Nations General Assembly Resolution ES-11/5 not only recommended the creation of an international register of damage for Ukraine, but also

32 Robert Spano (Iceland, chair), Chiara Giorgetti (Italy, Vice-Chair), Veijo Heiskanen (Finland), Yulia Kyrpa (Ukraine), Aleksandra Mężykowska (Poland), Lucy Reed (United States) and Norbert Wühler (Germany).

recognised the need for the establishment of an international mechanism for reparation for the injury, and for any damage, caused by the internationally wrongful acts of the Russian Federation. It goes without saying that merely registering claims of damage, essential as this activity may be for preserving the necessary information and evidence, cannot by itself qualify as such a mechanism. It can only be the first limb of a mechanism, that should have the capacity to assess the validity of claims registered and enable payment of compensation for valid claims, lest reparation will remain an idle promise. In the same vein, in Resolution CM/Res(2023)3, referred to above, the member states of the Council of Europe agreed to continue working towards the establishment, by a separate international instrument, of a future international compensation mechanism, which may include a claims commission and a compensation fund, of which the work of the Register, including its digital platform, with all data about claims and evidence recorded, is intended to constitute an integral part.

It goes without saying that the nature of a compensation mechanism – although useful for setting up a database of claims – makes the light structure of the EPA unfit for a much more far-reaching mechanism that must be able to impose binding decisions upon claimants, but also on a non-member state, even more so in the absence of that state's cooperation and with the war that gave rise to the damage claimed still ongoing at high intensity. Hence the reference in Resolution CM/Res(2023)3 to a separate international instrument. Though there may be a scarce precedent for a compensation mechanism,[33] it does not apply to such a situation, as a result of which there is a high level of pioneering involved and creativity required.

With that in mind, the Netherlands, in cooperation with Ukraine and the Register of Damage, hosted and chaired a first preparatory meeting in The Hague on 9 and 10 July 2024, on an international instrument to establish a claims commission for Ukraine. At the meeting, fifty-three participating states and the European Union agreed to focus on such a claims commission as the second step towards a fully-fledged compensation mechanism, inspired by the success of the first step, the Register of Damage. It was also agreed to set 2025 as the foreseen year of establishment of the claims commission.

33 The United Nations Compensation Commission (UNCC) was created to process claims and pay compensation for losses and damage suffered as a direct result of Iraq's unlawful invasion and occupation of Kuwait in 1990–1991. It was, however, set up as a subsidiary organ of the United Nations Security Council under Security Council resolution 687 (1991), which fundamentally distinguishes this precedent from the present situation.

In parallel, particularly within the EU and the G7, the feasibility is being examined for not only freezing Russian assets present within the relevant states, which has already been achieved under EU sanctions against the Russian Federation, but also for seizing such assets or, alternatively, seizing proceeds stemming from such assets, for the benefit of Ukraine. Obviously, these endeavours extend far beyond the goal of compensation of damage, since any assets seized could in principle be used for a variety of goals, such as procurement of weapons or reconstruction. Nevertheless, they will be highly relevant once the time is ripe for taking the third and last step to a fully-fledged compensation mechanism: setting up a compensation fund.

9 Conclusion

This article is not about warfare. It has left the military dimension of the war in Ukraine untouched. It goes without saying that military support by the international community to Ukraine is and should remain the first priority as long as the Russian aggression continues. Only if Ukraine emerges from this horrific situation as a free and independent state, accountability stands a chance of becoming more than an idle promise. That said, it is never too early to start work on institutions and processes that are capable – if only in a distant future – of restoring justice where justice has been denied. Not only can there be no safe havens for those responsible for the appalling violations of international law committed in Ukraine, as long as they live, also some form of compensation for all victims of the war must be secured. In this respect, despite the tragedy still unfolding today in Ukraine, the energetic establishment of the Register of Damage for Ukraine and the first endeavours towards a claims commission give a glimmer of hope.

CHAPTER 2

The UN Liability Rules and General International Law: *Lex Specialis*?

*Thomas Henquet**

1 Introduction

This contribution concerns the rules promulgated by the United Nations General Assembly (UNGA) in resolution 52/247 (1998), regarding the liability of the UN towards third parties for claims arising in connection with peacekeeping operations ('UN Liability Rules').[1] These rules entail financial and temporal liability limitations, and an exemption from liability in the case of 'operational necessity'.

By way of background, the UN Liability Rules form part of the UN's implementation of Section 29(a) of the General Convention ('Section 29(a)'), which requires the UN – like other international organizations subject to similar provisions – to "make provisions for appropriate modes of settlement of … disputes of a private law character" to which the organization is a party. Elsewhere,[2] originally in his doctoral dissertation, written under supervision of Niels Blokker, the present author has interpreted Section 29(a), and proposed a structural revision of its implementation. This entails the development of adequate alternative remedies to counterbalance, and thereby bolster, the jurisdictional immunity of international organizations, and increase these organisations' legitimacy. To this end, the author has proposed the establishment of a comprehensive mechanism: the 'Mechanism for the Settlement of Disputes of a Private Law Character' (hereinafter referred to as the Mechanism). The Mechanism would be established by the UNGA and operated under the auspices of the Permanent Court of Arbitration (PCA).

---

* The author is Chief of the Legal Office and Senior Legal Adviser at the Registry of the International Criminal Court. The views expressed herein are those of the author alone and do not reflect the views of the International Criminal Court.

1 Third parties, or private parties, are defined for present purposes as persons or legal entities outside the international organization, thus excluding its staff and officials.

2 T.S.M. Henquet, *The Third-Party Liability of International Organisations: Towards a 'Complete Remedy System' Counterbalancing Jurisdictional Immunity* (Brill Nijhoff, 2023).

 | DOI:10.1163/9789004699939_004

The proposal builds on the scholarship of Niels Blokker who, in underscoring the significance not only of the jurisdictional immunity of international organizations but also of closing the 'accountability gap' by way of procedural remedies,[3] recognised a potential role for the PCA.[4] This illustrates how Niels Blokker's scholarship, notwithstanding its theoretical rigour, is coupled with pragmatism, drawing on his broad experience in practice. This is but one way in which Niels has inspired students and colleagues alike, not least the present author, who had the privilege of being both.

Returning to the Mechanism proposed by the author, it would consolidate and enhance the procedural remedies for the implementation of Section 29(a). This would include standing claims commissions, which are envisaged in status of forces agreements (SOFAs) for the settlement of third-party disputes arising in the context of peacekeeping operations. However, in reality, such commissions have never been established, while their legal frameworks give rise to several problems.[5] In addressing such problems, the Mechanism would provide for the adequate settlement of third-party disputes in connection with peacekeeping operations, while facilitating the development of the UN Liability Rules governing such disputes.

As part of that development, several outstanding questions regarding those rules remain to be resolved.[6] One question of particular significance concerns their relationship to general international law. This has come to the fore in the context of the Articles on the Responsibility of International Organizations (ARIO) of the International Law Commission (ILC).[7] In commenting on a draft version of the ARIO, the UN Secretariat stated:

> The most notable examples of *lex specialis* in the practice of the United Nations include the principle of "operational necessity", which precludes responsibility for property loss or damage caused in the course of United Nations peacekeeping operations under the conditions set out by the Secretary-General and endorsed by the General Assembly ... and the temporal and financial limitations adopted in the same resolution for injury or damage caused in the course of the same operations.

---

3 N.M. Blokker and N.J. Schrijver, "Afterwords", in N.M. Blokker and N.J. Schrijver (eds.), *Immunity of International Organizations* (Brill Nijhoff, 2015), p. 342 at p. 357.

4 N.M. Blokker, "Member State Responsibility for Wrongdoings of International Organizations: Beacon of Hope or Delusion?", in *International Organizations Law Review* (IOLR) vol. 12 (2015), p. 319, at p. 331.

5 Henquet (*supra* note 2), at pp. 244–256.

6 *Ibidem*, at 261–290.

7 UN Doc. A/66/10 (2011), Ch. V.E.1.

> Resolution 52/247 on third-party liability: temporal and financial limitations, adopted on 26 June 1998, sets temporal and financial limitations on the liability of the United Nations in respect of third-party claims arising out of United Nations peacekeeping operations, and *as such* prevails over the duty to provide full reparation under draft article 33.[8]

The UN Secretariat made this comment in connection with, what would become, Article 64 of the ARIO (*lex specialis*):

> These articles do not apply where and to the extent that the conditions for the existence of an internationally wrongful act or the content or implementation of the international responsibility of an international organization, or a State in connection with the conduct of an international organization, are governed by special rules of international law. Such special rules of international law may be contained in the rules of the organization applicable to the relations between an international organization and its members.

Doubts have been expressed in the literature as to the *lex specialis* status of the UN Liability Rules,[9] and the present author has concluded that that purported status "remains to be tested".[10] The purpose of the present contribution is to explore the matter further.

This contribution is structured as follows. Chapter 2, by way of background, provides a brief introduction to the UN Liability Rules. In discussing *lex specialis*, Chapter 3 begins by questioning the existence of *lex generalis* on point (Section 3.1), and then discusses *lex specialis* and its conceptual attractiveness in the context of international organizations (Section 3.2). Thereafter, the analysis turns to consider Article 64 of the ARIO and the requirements for *lex specialis*, which the UN Liability Rules may seem to meet on their face (Section 3.3). However, as discussed next (Section 3.4), the crux of the matter is the creation of a binding legal regime *vis-à-vis* third parties. To this end, the UN Secretary

8 UN Doc. A/CN.4/637/Add.1 (2011), at p. 35, para. 2 (fn. omitted; emphasis added).

9 P. Klein, "Responsibility", in J. Katz Cogan, I. Hurd and I. Johnstone (eds.), *The Oxford Handbook of International Organizations* (Oxford UP, 2016), p. 1026 at p. 1028, referring to P. Bodeau-Livinec, "Les Faux semblants de la *lex specialis* – l'exemple de la résolution 52/247 de l'Assemblée générale des Nations Unies sur les limitations temporelles et financierès de la responsabilité de l'ONU", *Revue Belge de Droit International* vol. 46 (2013), p. 117; C. Ferstman, "Reparations for Mass Torts Involving the United Nations: Misguided Exceptionalism in Peacekeeping Operations", in *IOLR* vol. 16 (2019), p. 42.

10 Henquet (*supra* note 2), at p. 273.

General (UNSG) and the UNGA, at the time, adopted a pragmatic approach to operationalise the UN Liability Rules. While this approach offers arguments in favour of the *lex specialis* nature of the UN Liability rules, there are counterarguments as well. These various arguments remain to be explored more fully, potentially in litigation before the proposed Mechanism.

2 The UN Liability Rules

By way of background, the issue of the third-party liability of the UN has come to the fore notably in the context of peacekeeping operations. That is no surprise as such operations entail a significant risk of personal injury, illness and death, and property loss or damage. Against the backdrop of a report by the UNSG in 1995 on the implementation of Section 29 of the General Convention,[11] the UNSG produced two reports, in 1996 and 1997, respectively,[12] specifically concerning third-party claims in connection with UN peacekeeping operations. The latter two reports set forth the UN Liability Rules, which were subsequently promulgated by the UNGA in resolution 52/247 of 17 July 1998. Like the 1996 Report and the 1997 Report, UNGA resolution 52/247 was channelled through the Fifth (Administrative and Budgetary) Committee, apparently without involvement of the Sixth (Legal) Committee. There UNGA did not debate the resolution and adopted it without a vote.[13]

To provide context, the policy rationale underlying the UN Liability Rules is to preserve the public funds contributed by UN member states. That is, according to the 1997 Report: "To the extent that funds are used to pay third-party claims, lesser amounts may be available to finance additional peacekeeping or other United Nations operations".[14] At the same time, according to the 1997 Report: "In limiting the liability of the Organization with regard to third-party claims arising from peacekeeping operations it is expected that the host Government will assume responsibility for providing any additional compensation that may appear warranted under the circumstances".[15] However, this

11 UN Doc. A/C.5/49/65 (1995) ('1995 Report').

12 UN Doc. A/51/389 (1996) ('1996 Report'); UN Doc. A/51/903 (1997) ('1997 Report').

13 UN Doc. A/52/PV.88 (1998), at p. 16.

14 1997 Report, para. 12.

15 *Ibidem*, stating also: "The limitation on the liability of the Organization as a means of allocating the risks of peacekeeping operations between the United Nations and host States is premised on the assumption that consensual peacekeeping operations are conducted for the benefit of the country in whose territory they are deployed, and that having expressly or implicitly agreed to the deployment of a peacekeeping operation in its territory, the

premise of 'shared liability', which does not seem to have been operationalised, is arguably flawed.[16]

As regards the substance of the UN Liability Rules,[17] in resolution 52/247 of 17 July 1998, the UNGA, among others:

> Decided that the financial and temporal limitations set out in the 1997 Report shall apply (para. 5). Thus, among others, as to the former limitations, compensable types of injury or loss shall be limited to economic loss, thus excluding non-economic loss (para. 9(a) and (b)). And, as a rule, the amount of compensation payable for injury, illness or death of any individual shall not exceed a maximum of 50,000 USD (para. 9(d)). As to the latter limitations, as a rule, claims must be submitted within six months of sustaining the damage, loss or injury, or six months after the claimant discovered it, and in any event within a year of the termination of the mandate of the operation (para. 8);
>
> Endorsed the view of the UNSG in the 1997 Report that no limitations on liability apply in the case of gross negligence or wilful misconduct (para. 7); and
>
> Endorsed the view of the UNSG in the 1996 Report that the liability of the UN is not engaged in the case of operational necessity (para. 6). According to the 1996 Report, 'within the discretionary power of the force commander':[18]

> In deciding upon the operational necessity of any given measure the following must be taken into account: (a) There must be a good-faith conviction on the part of the force commander that an 'operational necessity' exists; (b) The operational need that prompted the action must be strictly necessary and not a matter of mere convenience or expediency. It must also leave little or no time for the commander to pursue another, less destructive option; (c) The act must be executed in pursuance of an operational plan and not the result of a rash individual action; (d) The damage caused should be proportional to what is strictly necessary in order to achieve the operational goal.[19]

---

host country must be deemed to bear the risk of the operation and assume, in part at least, liability for damage arising from such an operation".

16 See Henquet (*supra* note 2), at pp. 276–277.

17 *Ibidem*, at pp. 115–116 and 133–140.

18 1996 Report, para. 14.

19 *Ibidem*.

3 *Lex specialis*

For the UN Liability Rules to have *lex specialis* status under Article 64 of the ARIO, they would need to qualify as "special rules of international law",[20] and they would need to govern the conditions for the existence of an internationally wrongful act or the content or implementation of the international responsibility of an international organization. However, above all, for these rules to have the status of *lex specialis*, there must necessarily exist *lex generalis*. Thus, the question arises as to the existence of 'more general rules',[21] regarding the international responsibility of the UN *in its relationship with private parties*.

3.1 *Lex generalis?*

Under the ARIO, considering the scope of Part Two ("The internationally wrongful act of an international organization"), it is conceivable for an international organization to incur international responsibility towards *private parties*.[22] However, the scope of the ARIO is otherwise limited when it comes to such parties.[23] Specifically, Article 33(1) of the ARIO provides that Part Three of the ARIO ("Content of the international responsibility of an international organization") is limited to obligations owed to "one or more States, to one or more other organizations, or to the international community as a whole".[24] Notwithstanding, Article 33(2) adds that this is "without prejudice to any right, arising from the international responsibility of an international organization, which may accrue directly to any person or entity other than a State or an international organization".[25] In this connection, with reference to UNGA resolution 52/247 (1998), the ARIO Commentaries point to "breaches committed by peacekeeping forces and affecting individuals" as a "significant area in which rights accrue to persons other than States or organizations".[26]

These saving clauses leave unresolved as to what are the 'more general rules' on point. There is debate in scholarship about the state of general international

20 See Henquet (*supra* note 2), at p. 271.

21 Draft Articles on the Responsibility of International Organizations, with Commentaries, UN Doc. A/66/10 (2011), Ch. V.E.2, ('ARIO Commentaries'), Art. 64, at p. 100, para. 1.

22 Henquet (*supra* note 2), at pp. 34–35.

23 *Ibidem*, at pp. 35–45.

24 Part Three includes, for example, Article 31, which provides for the obligation to make 'full reparation' for injury.

25 Article 50 of the ARIO, contained in Part Four ('The implementation of the international responsibility of an international organization'), provides likewise as regards the 'invocation of the responsibility of an international organization'.

26 ARIO Commentaries, Art. 33, at p. 59, para. 5.

law as regards the responsibility of international organizations towards private parties, and this largely turns on the purported 'right to a remedy'.[27] This author has concluded that while general international law arguably entitles private parties to an effective procedural remedy, a substantive right to a remedy arguably has yet to crystallise.[28]

Returning to the ARIO, as seen, Part Two thereof *does* apply in the relationship between international organizations and private parties. Its Chapter V concerns "circumstances precluding wrongfulness", one such circumstance being "necessity" pursuant to Article 25 of the ARIO, paragraph 1 of which provides:

> Necessity may not be invoked by an international organization as a ground for precluding the wrongfulness of an act not in conformity with an international obligation of that organization unless the act:
>
> (a) is the only means for the organization to safeguard against a grave and imminent peril an essential interest of its member States or of the international community as a whole when the organization has, in accordance with international law, the function to protect that interest; and
>
> (b) does not seriously impair an essential interest of the State or States towards which the international obligation exists, or of the international community as a whole.

That arguably is a higher threshold than the one for "operational necessity" under the UN Liability Rules, such that the UN might be exempt from liability under its own rules, but not under the ARIO. The issue is inconsequential so long as general international law does not recognise a substantive right to a remedy. However, to the extent that right develops from *lex ferenda* to *lex lata* (potentially including a right to full reparation, as per Article 31 of the ARIO), the corresponding obligations for international organizations would reflect the relevant 'more general rules' for present purposes. The question then arises: are those rules (including "necessity" as a circumstance precluding wrongfulness), being *lex generalis*, set aside by the UN Liability Rules (including "operational necessity" as a liability exemption), as *lex specialis*?

---

27 Henquet (*supra* note 2), at pp. 70–96.

28 *Ibidem*, pp. 96–97. But see, e.g., K. Wellens, *Remedies against International Organisations* (Cambridge UP, 2002), at p. 17; D. Shelton, *Remedies in International Human Rights Law* (Oxford UP, 2015), at p. 432; and Ferstman (*supra* note 9), at p. 67 ("the purpose of the general law ... is to ensure that victims of violations receive adequate and effective reparation. ... The general law on reparations should continue to apply to the extent that the goals of reparations are not fulfilled by the 'special' rules").

3.2 *International Organizations and lex specialis*

An appropriate starting point for this purpose in the context of international organizations is the Advisory Opinion of the International Court of Justice (ICJ) in the *Legality of the Use by a State of Nuclear Weapons in Armed Conflict* case:

> International organizations are governed by the 'principle of speciality', that is to say, they are invested by the States which create them with powers, the limits of which are a function of the common interests whose promotion those States entrust to them.[29]

In this light, it is perhaps no surprise that it emerged from the comments submitted by international organizations to the ILC on the topic of the responsibility of international organizations that, as Boon recalled,

> there is very little consensus on the genus of international organizations, and consequently on the application of general rules to these increasingly important and pervasive bodies. Indeed, most organizations took the position that the founding premise of the international legal framework applicable to them should be speciality not generality.[30]

Specifically, the UN Secretariat commented that the ILC "should be guided by the specificities of the various international organizations: their organizational structure, the nature and composition of their governing organs, and their regulations, rules and special procedures – in brief, their special character".[31]

This, then, brings the principle of *lex specialis* into sharp focus.[32] According to the ILC Study Group on Fragmentation of International Law: Difficulties Arising from the Diversification and Expansion of International Law (the ILC Study Group):

29 ICJ, *Legality of the Use by a State of Nuclear Weapons in Armed Conflict*, Advisory Opinion of 8 July 1996, [1996] ICJ Reports, p. 66, para. 25.

30 K. Boon, "The Role of *Lex Specialis* in the Articles on the Responsibility of International Organizations", in M. Ragazzi (ed.), *Responsibility of International Organizations: Essays in Memory of Sir Ian Brownlie*, (Martinus Nijhoff, 2013), p. 135.

31 UN Doc. A/CN.4/637/Add.1, 4, para. 1.

32 The principle of *lex specialis*, which is not codified in the VCLT, is not uncontroversial. See, e.g., T. Irmscher, "Immunities and the Right of Access to Court: Conflict and Convergence", in D. Sarooshi (ed.), *Mesures de Réparation et Responsabilité à Raison des Actes des Organisations Internationales: Remedies and Responsibility for the Actions of International Organizations* (Brill Nijhof, 2014), p. 443 at p. 466.

> The maxim *lex specialis derogat legi generali* is a generally accepted technique of interpretation and conflict resolution in international law. It suggests that whenever two or more norms deal with the same subject matter, priority should be given to the norm that is more specific.[33]

In terms of the principle's rationale, the ILC Study Group explained:

> That special law has priority over general law is justified by the fact that such special law, being more concrete, often takes better account of the particular features of the context in which it is to be applied than any applicable general law. Its application may also often create a more equitable result and it may often better reflect the intent of the legal subjects.[34]

Notwithstanding, as Boon commented in the context of the ARIO,

> there remains substantial murkiness with regards to the *lex specialis* mechanism under the articles. Important work remains to be done in clarifying the concept of *lex specialis* which the International Law Commission in another context has acknowledged is vague, heavily context-dependent, and impossible to codify.[35]

3.3 *Lex specialis under Article 64 of the ARIO*

The ILC Commentaries to Article 64 of the ARIO are rather brief. They focus particularly on the existence of special rules in the relationship between an international organization, notably the then European Community, and its member states. Of note, the ILC Commentaries do not refer to the UN Liability Rules in this context.

Boon set forth four cumulative requirements for the application of *lex specialis* in the context of Article 64 of the ARIO:

33 UN Doc. A/CN.4/l.702 (2006), para. 14(5). Relatedly, the ILC Study Group' also referred to 'special (self-contained) regimes', that is: "a group of rules and principles concerned with a particular subject matter may form a special regime ('Self-contained regime') and be applicable as *lex specialis*". *Ibidem*, para. 14(11).

34 *Ibidem*, para. 14(7). Cf. S.C. Neff (ed.), *Hugo Grotius on the Law of War and Peace: Student Edition*, (Cambridge UP, 2012), Book II, pp. 28–9, at p. 250 ("Among agreements, ... that should be given preference which is most specific and approaches most nearly to the subject in hand; for special provisions are ordinarily more effective than those that are general").

35 Boon (*supra* note 30), at p. 138 (fn. omitted).

> (i) the actual inconsistency between the rules; (ii) one body of law is more specific than the other; (iii) the sources of law leading to the conflict support the application of *lex specialis*; and (iv) the application of *lex specialis* does not alter the rights or obligations of the beneficiaries of the agreement.[36]

The first requirement entails that "there is actual inconsistency between the rules, or there is a discernable intention that one provision is to exclude the other".[37] As regards the second requirement, "the party would need to prove that one instrument or body of law is more specific, and that there was a deliberate attempt by the parties to derogate from general rules".[38] As to the third requirement, "*lex specialis* invites an analysis of hierarchy of sources".[39] According to the fourth requirement, "derogation will be limited in situations where it might affect the balance between the rights and obligations of the parties under a treaty".[40]

Notwithstanding Klein's observation as regards Article 64 of the ARIO that "[t]he adoption of such special rules does not … seem to constitute a very common phenomenon for the time being",[41] on their face, the UN Liability Rules may be deemed largely to meet the foregoing requirements, to the extent relevant.[42] As to the first requirement, as seen, there arguably is an inconsistency between 'operational necessity' under the UN Liability Rules, and 'necessity' as a circumstance precluding wrongfulness under Article 25 of the ARIO.

Regarding the second requirement, the UN Liability rules arguably meet the specificity requirement insofar as these rules apply to the UN in the specific context of peacekeeping operations and they are detailed in several respects. There is no evidence that the UNGA considered the UN's third-party liability under general international law, but the UNSG touched on the issue in general terms.[43] And there arguably is a discernable determination on the UNGA's part for the UN's third-party liability in this context to be governed exclusively by

36 *Ibidem*, at p. 141.

37 *Ibidem*.

38 *Ibidem*.

39 *Ibidem*, at p. 142.

40 *Ibidem*, at p. 144.

41 Klein (*supra* note 9), at p. 1028.

42 The fourth requirement would not be relevant in the case in point insofar as the inconsistency arises under two non-treaty standards.

43 See 1997 Report, para. 37 ("Financial limitations on the liability of the Organization … constitute an exception to the general principle that when tortious liability is engaged compensation should be paid with a view to redressing the situation and restoring it to what it had been prior to the occurrence of the damage").

the UN Liability Rules. This is suggested by the wording of resolution 52/247 (1998); for example, pursuant to paragraph 6 of the resolution, the UNGA: "Endorses the view of the Secretary-General that *liability is not engaged* in relation to third-party claims resulting from or attributable to the activities of members of peacekeeping operations arising from 'operational necessity'" (emphasis added).

As to the third requirement, in terms of hierarchy of sources, the normative value of the UN Liability Rules, as 'internal rules',[44] arguably is considerable in light of the 'principle of speciality' articulated by the ICJ in its aforementioned *Advisory Opinion in the Legality of the Use by a State of Nuclear Weapons in Armed Conflict* case.[45]

It may, therefore, be tempting to conclude that the UN liability Rules have *lex specialis* status. In this respect, according to Bodeau-Livinec:

> La résolution 52/247 semble donc organiser un véritable régime juridique spécifique, presque auto-suffisant (*self-contained*), puisqu'il a vocation à couvrir l'ensemble du champ de la responsabilité des Nations Unies à raison des activités des [opérations de maintien de la paix], sans s'appuyer, au moins explicitement, sur les principes de droit commun.[46]

However, there is more than meets the eye when considering the UN Liability Rules in terms of *lex specialis*. According to Bodeau-Livinec, "la proclamation d'une *lex specialis* ne suffit pas à établir un régime juridique spécifique en droit".[47] Bodeau-Livinec casts doubt as to the qualification of the UN Liability Rules as *lex* and as *specialis*. The former aspect, which is the primary focus of the remainder of this contribution, turns on the creation of a binding legal regime *vis-à-vis* third parties.

3.4 *A Binding Legal Regime vis-à-vis Third Parties*

The issue here is whether the legal regime governing the UN Liability Rules, as Bodeau-Livinec put it, "peut faire droit dans les rapports entre l'Organisation et les tiers".[48] Indeed, according to the 1997 Report:

---

44 Boon (*supra* note 30), at p. 142.

45 In this connection, Boon recalled that in their comments to the ILC in the context of the ARIO, NATO and the World Bank emphasised the significance of internal rules. Boon (*supra* note 30), at p. 143.

46 Bodeau-Livinec (*supra* note 9), at p. 128.

47 *Ibidem.*

48 *Ibidem*, at. p. 130. Otherwise put, according to Bodeau-Livinec, the issue is whether "le régime de responsabilité invoqué soit, notamment, opposable à ceux qu'il vise". *Ibidem*, at p. 117.

> The need to establish these limitations in a legally binding manner is ... imperative. The United Nations must ensure that potential claimants, whether the host State or the individual, consent to the limitations or are otherwise bound by them regardless of their consent.[49]

Bodeau-Livinec considered the matter, amongst others, from the perspective of Article 17 of the UN Charter. That provision concerns the budgetary powers of the UNGA, which according to the 1997 Report, entail the power to limit financial liability.[50] Bodeau-Livinec suggested that as Article 17 of the UN Charter is limited to the internal management of the Organization, a resolution based on that provision cannot create legally binding obligations for third parties. However, the adoption of such a resolution was but one of three modalities proposed by the UNSG in the 1997 Report,[51] as endorsed by the UNGA in resolution 52/247 (1998).[52] According to the UNSG, these modalities were "both necessary and sufficient" to establish limitations on the UN's liability "in a legally binding manner".[53]

In addition to a resolution adopted by the UNGA – which would become resolution 52/247 (1998) – the second modality is the inclusion of a liability clause in SOFAS, to which end the UNGA explicitly requested the UNSG to "take the necessary measures".[54] The third modality is the inclusion of a liability clause in the terms of reference of claims review boards, which the UNGA requested the UNSG to ensure.[55]

At the time, therefore, the UN's position was that the promulgation of the UN Liability Rules in resolution 52/247 (1998) *as such* would not suffice to create a legally binding liability regime *vis-à-vis* third parties or that these rules would *as such* qualify as *lex specialis*.[56] This may indeed be taken to contrast with the aforementioned suggestion by the UN Secretariat in the context of Article 64 of the ARIO.[57]

---

49 1997 Report, para. 37.

50 *Ibidem*, para. 39. Cf. Henquet (*supra* note 2), at p. 262, submitting that, arguably, the UNGA was empowered under Article 17 of the UN Charter to limit liability and that, alternatively, the power to do so might exist under the doctrine of 'implied powers'.

51 See Section IV of the 1997 Report.

52 UN Doc. A/RES/52/247 (1998), para. 3, referring specifically to Section IV of the 1997 Report.

53 1997 Report, para. 38.

54 UN Doc. A/RES/52/247 (1998), para. 12.

55 *Ibidem*, para. 13.

56 Cf. Bodeau-Livinec (*supra* note 9), at p. 131 ("Partant, l'Organisation reconnaît que la résolution 52/247 ne crée pas *per se* une *lex specialis* mais a besoin de relais conventionnels").

57 In fact, however, the UN Secretariat went on to comment that "pursuant to paragraph 12 of General Assembly resolution 52/247, the Secretary-General consistently includes

The 'layered' approach, involving the modalities proposed in the 1997 Report, as adopted by the UNGA, was foreshadowed by the technique used to limit the UN's liability within UN Headquarters District. Article III, Section 8, of the Headquarters Agreement between the UN and the US empowered the former to adopt regulations operative within UN headquarters district.[58] The UNGA, having requested the UNSG to present any such draft regulation for approval to the UNGA,[59] adopted Headquarters Regulation No. 4, limiting the UN's third-party liability within UN headquarters.[60]

The three modalities combined create a legally binding system pursuant to which the UN Liability Rules apply *vis-à-vis* third parties. The workings of this system are illustrated by the United Nations Stabilisation Mission in Haiti (MINUSTAH) SOFA, Paragraph 54 of which provides as follows:

> Third-party claims for property loss or damage and for personal injury, illness or death arising from or directly attributed to MINUSTAH, except for those arising from operational necessity, which cannot be settled through the *internal procedures* of the United Nations, shall be settled by the United Nations in the *manner provided for in paragraph 55* of the present Agreement, provided that the claim is submitted within six months following the occurrence of the loss, damage or injury, or, if the claimant did not know or could not have reasonably known of such loss or injury, within six months from the time he or she had discovered the loss or injury, but in any event not later than one year after the termination of the mandate of MINUSTAH. Upon determination of liability as provided for in the present Agreement, the United Nations shall pay compensation within such financial limitations as are approved by the General Assembly in its resolution 52/247 of 26 June 1998.[61]

The "internal procedures" mentioned are understood to refer to the mission's claims review board, whose terms of reference include the UN Liability Rules,

the limitations on liability in the status-of-force agreements concluded between the United Nations and the States where peacekeeping operations are deployed". UN Doc. A/CN.4/637/Add.1 (2011), at p. 35, para. 2.

58 Agreement between the United Nations and the United States of America regarding the headquarters of the United Nations, 26 June 1947, approved by the General Assembly of the United Nations, on 31 October 1947, with an exchange of Notes, dated 21 November 1947, 11 UNTS 11.

59 UN Doc. A/RES/481(V) (1950).

60 UN Doc. A/RES/41/210 (1986). Of note, these limitations are in part reflected in the UN Liability Rules. Henquet (*supra* note 2), at p. 281.

61 2271 UNTS 235; *United Nations Juridical Yearbook* 2004, at pp. 28 ff. (emphasis added).

as per resolution 52/247 (1998). The "manner provided for in paragraph 55" of the SOFA entails the settlement of third-party claims by a standing claims commission, with the UN Liability Rules being the applicable law.[62]

The dispute settlement clause in the SOFA may be understood as a standing offer of arbitration, with an arbitration agreement coming into existence upon a third-party claimant commencing dispute settlement proceedings. The same technique is used in bilateral investment treaties (BITs), pursuant to which each state party consents to investor-state dispute settlement with nationals of the other state party. Like SOFAs, BITs typically set forth the law governing investment relations, which is the applicable law in investor-state dispute settlement proceedings.[63]

The peculiarity of third-party dispute settlement with the UN under a SOFA is that it cannot be seen in isolation from the jurisdictional immunity of the UN. Indeed, Paragraph 55 of the MINUSTAH SOFA provides that

> any dispute or claim of a private-law character, not resulting from the operational necessity of MINUSTAH, to which MINUSTAH or any member thereof is a party *and over which the courts of Haiti do not have jurisdiction because of any provision of the present Agreement* shall be settled by a standing claims commission to be established for that purpose. (Emphasis added.)

62 Paragraph 54 does not actually determine that the UN Liability Rules are the applicable law in dispute settlement proceedings – it merely envisages the 'determination of liability' by the standing claims commission, followed by the payment of compensation by the UN in accordance with the UN Liability Rules. However, insofar as liability can only be determined with reference to substantive standards, the claims commission would presumably resort to the UN Liability Rules. Cf. K. Schmalenbach, "Dispute Settlement (Article VIII Sections 29–30 General Convention)", in A. Reinisch (ed.), *The Conventions on the Privileges and Immunities of the United Nations and its Specialized Agencies: A Commentary* (Oxford University Press, 2016), p. 529 at p. 570, para. 83 ("the standing claims commission will apply the resolution as it is integrated into the sofa/soma dispute settlement clauses").

63 S. Riegler *et al.*, *Applicable Law in Investment Treaty Arbitration*, available at <https://globalarbitrationreview.com/guide/the-guide-investment-treaty-protection-and-enforcement/first-edition/article/applicable-law-in-investment-treaty-arbitration#footnote-086>, accessed 18 March 2024 ("Many, although not all, investment protection treaties lay down an explicit choice of law. Those treaties that do stipulate the laws that apply often set out that the dispute is to be resolved in accordance with the provisions of the treaty itself. However, due to the specific role that the underlying treaty usually has in investment arbitration, the treaty is considered to be the main source of law, even if it does not contain such a self-reference". [fn. omitted]).

Article III of the MINUSTAH SOFA, in conjunction with Article II of the General Convention, confers upon the UN "immunity from every form of legal process". As a result of this 'absolute' immunity, the courts of the host state are barred from adjudicating third-party claims against the UN. The only available option for claimants, therefore, is to avail themselves of the dispute settlement mechanisms under the SOFA. Indeed, the "claimant is faced with a *fait accompli*".[64]

Thus, it is the combination of the modalities proposed in the 1997 Report, as endorsed and decided on by the UNGA in resolution 52/247 (1998), together with the UN's jurisdictional immunity as counterbalanced by alternative recourse under the SOFA, that operationalises the UN Liability Rules *vis-à-vis* third parties. It is perhaps in this sense that the following statement by Bodeau-Livinec is to be understood:

> Quant aux personnes privées, qui peuvent être directement lésées par les activités des [opérations de maintien de la paix], leur sort sera largement tributaire de la juridiction dont elles dépendent. Si elles relèvent de celle de l'État hôte, les dispositions de l'accord de statut des forces devraient pouvoir être appliquées à leur situation sans difficulté particulière.[65]

However, the next part of the statement is more difficult to follow:

> Dans le cas contraire (celui d'investisseurs étrangers par exemple, qui ne sont pas nécessairement soumis par l'effet des contrats ou traités bilatéraux d'investissement au droit de l'État d'accueil), l'opposabilité des limites prévues par la Resolution 52/247 apparaît fort aléatoire.[66]

As per Paragraph 55 of the MINUSTAH SOFA, the alternative remedies under the SOFA would be available in case of "*any* dispute or claim of a private-law character ... over which the courts of Haiti do not have jurisdiction" (emphasis added). This is irrespective of the nationality of the third-party claimant, or the provisions of host state law.

In dispute settlement proceedings under the SOFA, a private party could seek to challenge the lawfulness of the UN Liability Rules on the basis that the limitation of the UN's liability contravenes general international law. It would be for the claims commission to determine whether it is competent to rule on that challenge. In the event that it does, the UN could argue that general

64 Henquet (*supra* note 2), at p. 278.
65 Bodeau-Livinec (*supra* note 9), at p. 133.
66 Ibidem.

international law (to the extent it is *lex lata* – see above) was derogated from by operation of the SOFA, that is, an agreement under international law between the UN and the host state.

In this respect, it is widely accepted that parties may in principle 'contract out' of general international law.[67] As the ICJ ruled in *North Sea Continental Shelf Cases*: "it is well understood that, in practice, rules of [general] international law can, by agreement, be derogated from in particular cases or as between particular parties".[68] According to Lindroos, this is an expression of the "idea of *lex specialis*".[69] Specifically with respect to the ARIO, according to Boon: "In a situation where there is a conflict between the articles and a treaty, the treaty prevails".[70]

Yet, the freedom to derogate from general international law by agreement is not without limitation, as the ILC Study Group explained:

> Whether derogation by way of *lex specialis* is permitted will remain a matter of interpreting the general law. Concerns that may seem pertinent include at least the following: the normative status of the general law (is it *jus cogens*?), *who the beneficiaries of the obligations are (prohibition to deviate from law benefiting third parties, including individuals or non-State entities)*; whether non-derogation may be otherwise inferred from the terms of the general rule (for instance its "integral" or "interdependent" nature, its *erga omnes* character, or subsequent practice creating an expectation of non-derogation).[71]

The reference to "law benefiting third parties", in particular, invites further debate on whether it is permissible for any rules of general international law on the responsibility of international organizations towards third-parties to be derogated from by the UN Liability Rules.[72] In this respect, due regard is

67 A. Lindroos, "Addressing Norm Conflicts in a Fragmented Legal System: The Doctrine of *Lex Specialis*", in *Nordic Journal of International Law* vol. 74 (2005), p. 27, at p. 37.

68 ICJ, *North Sea Continental Shelf cases* (*Federal Republic of Germany v. Denmark and Federal Republic of Germany v. Netherlands*), Judgment of 20 February 1969, [1969] ICJ Reports, p. 3, para. 72.

69 Lindroos (*supra* note 67), at p. 37.

70 Boon (*supra* note 30), at p. 142.

71 UN Doc. A/CN.4/L.682, para. 109 (emphasis added).

72 Cf. Ferstman (*supra* note 9), at p. 63 ("is the international organization capable of agreeing with its Member States on rules modifying its obligations on reparation, when injured individuals (as opposed to Member States) are the ultimate beneficiaries?"). See also *ibidem*, at pp. 66–67 ("It is questionable whether UN practice has crystallised sufficiently to ground a *lex specialis* rule. While it might be possible for the organization and its members to agree rules to govern specific scenarios, and they have done so regularly, is

moreover to be paid to the following observation of the ILC Study Group as regards the *lex specialis* technique of legal reasoning:

> Its power is entirely dependent on the normative considerations for which it provides articulation: sensitivity to context, capacity to reflect State will, concreteness, clarity, definiteness. Its functioning cannot be assessed independently of the role of considerations of the latter type in specific context of legal reasoning. How does a particular agreement relate to the general law around it? Does it implement or support the latter, or does it perhaps deviate from it? Is the deviation tolerable or not? *No general, context-independent answers can be given to such questions.*[73]

The foregoing may provide arguments *pro* and *contra* the *lex specialis* nature of the UN liability Rules. Insofar as the nature of those rules may be clarified in litigation, this further underscores the significance of the implementation of the dispute settlement procedures under SOFA's,[74] as well as the improvement of such procedures by way of the proposed Mechanism.

The establishment of the Mechanism would moreover address Bodeau-Livinec's distinct criticism that, while a welcome policy statement,[75] the UN Liability Rules fall short of establishing "un cadre juridique suffisamment précis et spécifique pour correspondre pleinement aux exigences de la *lex specialis*'.[76] This lack of precision and specificity as regards the legal framework, according to Bodeau-Livinex, is specifically the case where the UN Liability Rules defer to the discretionary powers of the UNSG.[77]

The present author has submitted that the UN Liability Rules are indeed "succinct and rudimentary",[78] and "give rise to several legal questions".[79] Apart

it less legitimate and arguably *ultra vires* for it to develop abridged frameworks when the responsible organization owes reparation not to its members, but to injured individuals. The injured individuals have not voluntarily agreed to the special regime, even though their States of nationality may have done so" [fn. omitted]).

73 UN Doc. A/CN.4/L.682, para. 119 (emphasis in original).

74 Cf. Ferstman (*supra* note 9), at p. 45 ("where there is no independent court with the mandate to adjudicate claims, the UN's (mis)framings of the law are incapable of challenge. The more these (mis)framings are asserted without challenge, the more credence they receive – in this sense the 'fake' law progressively becomes 'real'. But this does not make those framings legally correct, just or appropriate").

75 Bodeau-Livinec (*supra* note 9), at p. 136.

76 *Ibidem*, at p. 135.

77 *Ibidem*, referring, for example, to the discretionary power of the UNSG to accept claims filed out of time under UN Doc. A/RES/52/247 (1998), para. 8.

78 Henquet (*supra* note 2), at p. 279.

79 *Ibidem*, at p. 293.

from issues like "the legal basis for the adoption of these rules, their legal nature and their scope of application",[80] questions that arise as regards the contents of these rules include the definition of 'personal property', and the causality requirements for damage to be compensable.[81] This has led the present author to submit:

> If the UN Liability Rules are to mature into a fully fledged liability regime, they are in need of clarification and development through consistent interpretation and application, just as domestic tort law regimes develop through regulation, jurisprudence and scholarship. From the perspective of the rule of law, as understood by the UN, that development is required to foster legal certainty.[82]

The proposed Mechanism would cater for the consistent interpretation and application of the UN Liability Rules,[83] thereby contributing to their increased precision and specificity.

4 Conclusion

The UN Secretariat's suggestion, in the context of the ARIO, that the UN Liability Rules would, as such, constitute *lex specialis* does not correspond to the position of either the UNSG or the UNGA when these rules were promulgated. The promulgation of the UN Liability Rules at the time evidenced a clear determination that these rules would govern the UN's third-party liability in the context of peacekeeping operations. The approach taken to operationalise the rules was pragmatic, involving the interplay between an UNGA resolution, amended terms of reference of claims review boards and, importantly, amended SOFAS in conjunction with the UN's jurisdictional immunity before host state courts. In keeping with Niels Blokker's scholarship, this pragmatism ought to be coupled with fuller legal scrutiny of the legal nature of the UN Liability Rules, with due regard for context. Contentious proceedings before the proposed Mechanism may serve that purpose.

80 *Ibidem*, at p. 426.
81 *Ibidem*, at pp. 279–280.
82 *Ibidem*, at p. 280.
83 Namely by way of the extended jurisdiction of its Appellate Tribunal, see *ibidem*, at p. 455.

CHAPTER 3

Security Council Oversight of Non-UN Operations

Law, Policy and Practice

*Ian Johnstone**

1 Introduction

In 1990, the United Nations (UN) Security Council authorized a coalition led by the United States (US) to take military action in response to Iraq's invasion of Kuwait. That triggered lively debate in the policy and scholarly communities about whether such "authorized" operations were lawful and, if so, whether the Council was legally required to retain some control over delegated enforcement action. Niels Blokker joined that debate in an article published in the year 2000, surveying the practice of the Security Council in the 1990s.[1] He concurred with the weight of legal opinion on the first point, namely that authorizing member states to use force was an implied power of the Council and therefore within its competence. On the second question, he argued "the Charter system and principles of delegation reject *carte blanche* delegations and favour authorizations which respect the authority and responsibility of the Security Council in the UN collective security system".[2] In that article and a later book chapter he laid out a set of principles that ought to guide the Council in exercising this implied power and reviewed the practice up to 2011. In both contributions, he identified a trend towards increasing oversight of such operations in the years since 1990 but argued that more could be done.[3]

In his characteristically thoughtful analysis, Blokker balances the legal requirement for control against the broad discretion granted to the Council. Three recent developments add a new sense of urgency to the questions he addressed. First, the line between "enforcement action" and so-called "robust

* The author is Professor of International Law, Fletcher School of Law and Diplomacy, Tufts University.

1 Niels Blokker, "Is the Authorization Authorized?", in *European Journal of International Law* vol. 11 (2000), p. 541.

2 *Ibidem.*

3 *Ibidem*, pp. 565–566, and Niels Blokker, "Outsourcing the Use of Force: Towards More Security Council Control of Authorized Operations", in Marc Weller (ed.), *The Oxford Handbook on the Use of Force in International Law* (Oxford UP, 2015), p. 224.

 | DOI:10.1163/9789004699939_005

peacekeeping" or "peace enforcement" has become blurred, generating uncertainty about when Security Council authorization is required. Second, the decline of enthusiasm for large-scale UN peacekeeping means we may see more operations undertaken by regional organizations and coalitions. Third, geopolitical tensions in the Council will likely make it harder for the Security Council to control (or even authorize) such operations. Together these developments raise two questions: what types of operations require Security Council authorization? What level of UN oversight over these operations is needed and appropriate?

The answer to the first question would seem to be clear: Article 53 of the UN Charter stipulates that "enforcement action" must be authorized by the Security Council whereas consent-based peacekeeping need not be. However, because the line between enforcement and peacekeeping has become blurred, it is not so straightforward. Nor is the answer to the second question. Practice since 1990 has been inconsistent and neither the scope nor form of Security Council oversight has been specified with any precision. Moreover, even for some operations that the Security Council *does not* authorize, a case can be made that *some* UN oversight is nevertheless required.

This article builds on Blokker's insights to provide tentative answers to those questions. It does so, first, by considering why Security Council oversight is important and why contemporary practice has made the legal issues more complex than in the past. It then addresses when Security Council authorization is required for an operation that uses force, focusing on two categories: 'grey area' peace operations and 'intervention by invitation'. The final section considers the practice of the Security Council in providing oversight, highlighting various mechanisms that have been employed. In these turbulent times, this variegation is important. For the Council to fulfil its primary responsibility for the maintenance of international peace and security, member states will have to be especially adept at improvisation – drawing on and moving beyond the body of practice that exists.

2 Why Security Council Oversight Is Important

The UN Charter envisions a more structured collective security system than what exists in practice. Military action undertaken pursuant to Article 42 was meant to employ forces provided to the organization on the basis of Article 43 agreements. The superpower rivalry made it impossible to negotiate those agreements and attempts to revive the idea in the immediate post-Cold War era gained little traction.[4] Instead, the Council has 'delegated' enforcement action to coalitions of the willing, as it did with respect to North Korea in 1950 and Iraq in 1990–91, or to regional organizations, as it did by authorizing NATO to use force to protect civilians against the Libyan army in 2011. Yet full-blown enforcement action against government forces has been rare. More common is when the Security Council authorizes a peace operation conducted by a regional organization or *ad hoc* coalition to use of force for limited purposes.

As Christine Gray points out, the constitutional propriety of these authorizations is no longer debated.[5] Yet UN member states have from the start expressed discomfort with the Security Council divesting itself of all responsibility when it delegates. In the 1991 Gulf War, states were concerned about the lack of UN control over the timing of the start to the operation, the scope of the mandate, and when it would end. Scholars worried that, if enforcement action was going to be delegated to powerful states or regional organizations with robust military capacity, what would prevent them from using Security Council authorization as a cover to pursue their own agendas.[6]

This discomfort has roots in the UN Charter. Article 24 stipulates that the Council must act on behalf of the membership as a whole, in accordance with the purposes and principles of the UN. Article 53(1) requires not only that the Security Council must authorize enforcement action by a regional organization, but also that the action occurs "under [it's] authority". As Blokker points out, this does not significantly restrict the Security Council's discretion,[7] but it does generate an expectation that the Security Council will not wash its hands of missions it authorizes. At a minimum, the Council should be well enough informed about the progress of the operation to know whether the mandate is being adhered to, and whether it should be renewed, revised, or terminated.

The UN Charter suggests the Security Council has a role even with respect to operations it does not authorize. Article 54 requires that the Council be kept informed of actions by regional organizations, including "activities" regional operations undertake without Security Council authorization. Article 51

4 UN Secretary-General Boutros Boutros-Ghali proposed this: Report of the Secretary-General, *An agenda for peace: preventive diplomacy, peacemaking and peace-keeping* (1992) UN Doc [ST/]DPI/1247, para. 43.

5 Christine Gray, *International Law and the Use of Force* (4th ed., Oxford UP, 2018), p. 342.

6 Karine Bannelier and Theodore Christakis, "Between Flexibility and Accountability: How Can the Security Council Strengthen Oversight of Use of Force Measures?", in Jeremy Farrall and Hilary Charlesworth (eds.), *Strengthening the Rule of Law through the UN Security Council* (Routledge, 2016).

7 Blokker (*supra* note 1), p. 552.

requires states to report on action they take in self-defence, which does not require Security Council authorization. There is a rationale for these reporting requirements. Suppose, for example, a firmly consent-based regional peace operation deployed without Security Council authorization loses the consent of the host government and begins to use offensive force. The Security Council should know this so it can decide whether, pursuant to Article 53(1), the operation now requires Security Council authorization. With respect to Article 51 self-defence, the Council should be informed of the progress of the military action to know whether it should step in. These provisions do not impose rigid legal requirements but suggest the Security Council has some responsibility to remain attentive even to operations that do not initially require its authorization.

Blokker, Dan Sarooshi, and others claim that general legal principles as well as the UN Charter constrain the ability to the Council to delegate *carte blanche*. These are among the general principles they identify:

- An organization cannot delegate more powers than it possesses.[8] The Council can delegate powers expressly granted in the Charter as well as those that "are conferred upon it by necessary implication as being essential to the performance of its duties", such as peacekeeping.[9] But it cannot delegate powers that are beyond its competence, for example, military action that would blatantly violate fundamental Charter principles (Article 24(2)).
- In delegating power, an international organization must not change the distribution of functions within the organization, nor can it nullify an existing explicit power in so doing, unless exercising that existing power is impossible.[10]
- The Council cannot transfer or "delegate away" overall responsibility for an operation.[11] According to Sarooshi, the Security Council can delegate Chapter VII discretionary power only if it "retains such a degree of control and authority (…) that it can change the decision of its delegate at any time".[12]

8 *Ibidem*, p. 552. See also Daniel Sarooshi, "The United Nations System for the Maintenance of International Peace: What Role for Regional Organizations Such as NATO?", in *Current Legal Problems* (1999), pp. 473, 480, and Daniel Sarooshi, *The United Nations and the Development of Collective Security* (Oxford UP, 1999), pp. 22–44.

9 ICJ, *Reparations for injuries suffered in the service of the United Nations*, Advisory Opinion [1949] ICJ Reports, p. 174.

10 Blokker (*supra* note 1), p. 549.

11 Henry Schermers and Niels Blokker, *International Institutional Law* (6th ed., Brill, 2018), p. 185, para. 227C.

12 Sarooshi, "The UN System" (*supra* note 8), p. 480.

The notion of international organization "responsibility" has two connotations in the context of military operations. On one level, it is a factual matter about who oversees the operation. On another level, it is about legal liability for wrongs an operation may commit. It is beyond the scope of this article to address the many complexities and controversies that surround the responsibility of international organizations for internationally wrongful acts.[13] It is important to observe, however, that the more control the Security Council seeks to exercise over regional or coalition operations, the more likely it is that it will be held responsible for wrongs. In principle, that is as it should be: with power comes responsibility. In practice, it could be a problem if Security Council "control" absolves the regional organizations or member states that conduct the operation from liability.[14]

What about the regional organizations themselves? Presumably, they provide political oversight of operations conducted under their banners. Does that mitigate the need for Security Council oversight? Not entirely. The constitutional authority of regional organizations to engage in peace operations or enforcement action is a hodgepodge of implied and express powers.[15] The African Union (AU), Collective Security Treaty Organization (CSTO), Economic Community of West African States (ECOWAS), European Union (EU), and Organization for Security and Cooperation in Europe (OSCE) all have language in their constitutive instruments that contemplates peace operations. For the North Atlantic Treaty Organization (NATO), the Organization of American States (OAS), and League of Arab States, it is an implied power. Most of those organizations have institutional structures to provide political oversight, but they do not do so consistently. Thus, in the 1990s, ECOWAS engaged in several operations without going through the normal decision-making processes.[16] The Commonwealth of Independent States sent peacekeeping operations to Tajikistan and Georgia in 1993 and 1994 respectively, without a formal decision to do so and with little or no oversight. In the case of Georgia, that lack of oversight was apparent during the 2008 war when Russian 'peacekeepers' in South Ossetia and Abkhazia were joined by thousands more Russian

13 Draft Articles on the Responsibility of States for Internationally Wrongful Acts, adopted by the International Law Commission at its fifty-third session (2001).

14 Moritz Moelle reviews the debate over "overall control" versus "effective control" in the context of peace operations that potentially engage the responsibility of multiple organizations and proposes an alternative standard of "normative control". Moritz Moelle, *The International Responsibility of International Organizations: Cooperation in Peacekeeping Operations* (Reprint ed., Cambridge UP, 2018), Chapters 3 and 4.

15 Gray (*supra* note 5), pp. 416–424.

16 *Ibidem*, pp. 423–444.

troops, 6000–8000 of which stayed behind without Georgia's consent after the war ended.

In any case, regional organization oversight of an operation does not absolve the Security Council from exercising its Charter-based responsibilities. This is especially true if the UN is providing operational, political, or financial support. Consider ATMIS (formerly AMISOM) in Somalia. This AU operation authorized by the Security Council is, in some ways, a peace operation with a mandate to provide security and stability. In other ways, it is a counter-terrorism operation with a mandate to defeat Al-Shabab. The UN has supported it, logistically and financially. When ATMIS engages in combat operations, it is subject to humanitarian law, and in all its activities it is bound by human rights law. The UN – because it is supporting the mission – has responsibility to prevent or at least not be complicit in violations of humanitarian and human rights law, given effect through the application of its Human Rights Due Diligence Policy.[17]

Even when the UN supports a mission not authorized by the Security Council, these considerations would kick in. As discussed below, the Security Council did not authorize the G5 Sahel counter-terrorism operation, but the UN peacekeeping mission in Mali (MINUSMA) provided it with some support.

3 What Types of Operations Require Security Council Authorization?

There is no law requiring the UN Security Council to authorize the entire spectrum of peace operations conducted by regional organizations and coalitions of the willing. At one end of the spectrum, civilian or firmly consent-based observer missions do not require such authorization. Examples include the political missions and training/advisory missions by the EU in Armenia, Central African Republic, Libya and Mali; by the OSCE in Albania, Moldova and Serbia; by NATO in Iraq; and by the OAS in Colombia. Even large monitoring missions, such as the EU Monitoring Mission in Georgia (over 200 personnel) and the OSCE Special Monitoring Mission in Ukraine from 2014 to 2022 (800 personnel) do not require Security Council authorization. Nor does the Multinational Force and Observers (over 1000 uniformed personnel) on the Sinai Peninsula.

At the other end of the spectrum, Article 53 stipulates that full-scale enforcement action does require Security Council authorization. Operation Desert

17 United Nations, *Human rights due diligence policy on United Nations support to non-UN security forces*, A/67/775, S/2013/110 (5 March 2013).

Storm in 1991 (a US-led coalition) was based on a Security Council mandate, as was the NATO-led operation in Libya in 2011.

Between those extremes is a spectrum of operations, two types of which merit special attention.

3.1 *Grey Area Peace Operations*

First are operations that blur the line between peacekeeping and enforcement. Militarily 'robust' peace operations by regional organizations or coalitions are often authorized by the Security Council under Chapter VII of the UN Charter, even when they have the consent of the host government. Examples include: UNITAF in Somalia in 1992; Multinational Forces in Haiti in 1994 and 2004; IFOR/SFOR in Bosnia in the late 1990s; INTERFET in East Timor in 1999; KFOR in Kosovo from 1999 to the present; the IEMF in the DRC in 2003; ECOMOG in Sierra Leone (after 1999); ISAF in Afghanistan from 2001 to 2014; AMISOM and now ATMIS in Somalia since 2005; AFISMA in Mali in 2012; MISCA in the CAR in 2013; and the Multinational Security Support mission in Haiti in 2024. Because these operations had or have both the consent of the host government and authorization by the Security Council, questions about their legality have not arisen.

However, there are a handful of cases where neither host government consent nor Security Council authorization was clear. In Liberia from 1990–97, ECOWAS intervened at the request of former President Samuel Doe, but not with the consent of Charles Taylor and the NPLF, which controlled 90% of the country. While deployed, ECOMOG drove the NPLF out of Monrovia twice, and occupied parts of the territory the group had controlled. The Security Council never authorized the operation but did "commend" it after the fact.[18] In Sierra Leone, ECOMOG was deployed with the consent of President Tejah Kabbah and, after he was thrown out of office in a coup in 1997, used force to remove the junta from power and restore the democratically elected President. It did not have Security Council authorization to use force until October 1997, and even then only to enforce an arms embargo. As with the Liberia operation, the Security Council "commended" it after the fact.

Some scholars have argued that the Liberia and Sierra Leone cases suggest that after-the-fact approval by the Security Council satisfies the requirements of Article 53. Yet Christine Gray and others argue persuasively there is insufficient practice to support that.[19] To eliminate any uncertainty the 2004 High

18 UNSC Res. 788 (19 November 1992), UN Doc S/RES/788.

19 Gray (*supra* note 5), pp. 425–445; Christian Henderson, *The Use of Force in International Law* (2nd ed., Cambridge UP, 2023), pp. 202–207.

Level Panel on Threats Challenges and Change proposed that Security Council authorization should be required for *all* such peace operations.[20] But the Secretary-General did not endorse that in his report to the World Summit, nor was it endorsed by member states at the World Summit itself.[21] In any case, the question remains: what sort of oversight can be envisioned when the Security Council is unable or unwilling for political reasons to authorize these "grey area" operations? While Liberia and Sierra Leone are anomalous cases, we may see more in the future. As UN operations withdraw from Mali, Sudan and the DRC, will a regional organization or coalition deploy a mission to replace them? If so, it is not clear the Security Council would authorize that given the prospect of a veto.

3.2 *Intervention by Invitation*

A related phenomenon is so-called 'intervention by invitation'. As a general proposition, a government that invites another government to send forces to deal with an internal security threat does not violate Article 2(4) of the UN Charter. On the other hand, if an insurgent group invites that intervention, it is illegal. The law becomes more complicated when the 'government' is not in full control of the entire territory or lacks legitimacy. According to the traditional rule, the government that can do the inviting is the entity that has 'effective control' of a country, regardless of how it came to power.[22] Yet standards of legitimacy are creeping into this area of the law.[23] In The Gambia in 2016, former President Jammeh refused to step down after losing elections. At the invitation of President-elect Barrow, who was in exile in Senegal at the time, ECOWAS sent forces to install him. The Security Council did not explicitly approve the intervention but expressed "full support to the ECOWAS in its commitment to ensure, *by political means first*, the respect of the will of the people of The Gambia as expressed in the results of 1st December elections".[24]

20 United Nations High Level Panel on Threats Challenges and Change, *A more secure world: our shared responsibility*, A/59/565 (2 December 2004), para. 213. Rosemary Durward, "Security Council Authorization for Regional Peace Operations: A Critical Analysis", in *International Peacekeeping* vol. 13 (2006), p. 350.

21 Dace Winther, *Regional Maintenance of Peace and Security under International Law* (Routledge, 2014), p. 231.

22 Gregory Fox, "Intervention by Invitation", in Weller (*supra* note 3), p. 817.

23 Mohamed Helal, "The ECOWAS Intervention in the Gambia – 2016", in Tom Ruys, Oliver Cortens and Alexandra Hofer (eds.) *International Law on the Use of Force: A Case Based Approach* (Oxford UP, 2018), pp. 922–932.

24 UNSC Res. 2337 (9 January 2017), UN Doc S/RES/2337, para. 6, emphasis added.

In that resolution, as well as those adopted by ECOWAS and the AU, Barrow was deemed to be the legitimate president.

Moreover, even applying the 'effective control' test, the law on who gets to invite an intervention is not straightforward. If the insurgency rises to the level of a civil war and the insurgents control substantial territory, one school of legal thought holds that no state can intervene on either side.[25] The logic is that, when a government loses effective control of the entire territory, the people should be allowed to determine their future free from outside interference.[26] But what if state X continues to arm the government forces? Can state Y arm the rebels? There is considerable scholarly and some state support for a so-called "right of counter-intervention", but it does lend itself to the possibility of abuse.[27] Moreover, it is hard to make the case that such a right exists as a matter of customary law because states that arm rebel groups in other states often do so covertly. The covert nature of the practice makes it hard to identify the requisite *opinio juris* for the customary rule to have developed.

Thus, we have two categories of cases where the need for Security Council authorization is legally uncertain: robust peace operations in which the quality of host government consent to the operation is questionable; and third-party interventions in internal conflicts when the authority of the entity inviting the intervention is questioned. Those two situations suggest that Security Council oversight is an issue not only for SC-authorized operations by a regional organization or a coalition, but also for operations that were not authorized but perhaps should have been.

4 Oversight Mechanisms in Theory and Practice

In his two reviews of Security Council practice on authorized uses of force, Blokker identifies three elements of control: the breadth of the mandate, whether there is a time limit on the authorization, and reporting requirements. In his 2000 article, he lists sixteen cases (the Korea war, the Iraq war and 14 after that). In his 2015 chapter he lists 13 more cases between 2000–2011. In both publications, he detected a tend towards increasing control: mandates were more precisely defined, the authorizations would typically require periodic renewal, and the obligation to report was usually written into the resolution. Writers since then have confirmed the trend, with some notable

25 Fox (*supra* note 22), pp. 827–29.
26 Henderson (*supra* note 19), p. 462.
27 *Ibidem*, pp. 469–72.

exceptions.[28] Regional and coalition operations have not been consistent in keeping the Security Council informed, either because they do not report or do so only in a perfunctory manner.[29] The resolution authorization military action in Libya in 2011 set no time limit and the scope of the authorization became the subject of great debate, specifically, whether the authorization to protect civilians encompassed the military action that led to the removal of Gaddafi from power.[30] The most controversial cases have involved implied and so-called 'revived' authorizations: Kosovo in 1999, Iraq in 2003, Côte d'Ivoire in 2011, and Mali in 2012.[31] It is not necessary here to revisit the legal debates those cases provoked, but simply to observe that the issue of Security Council 'control' is at the heart of them all. A key element of the Iraq case, for example, is whether, having determined in Security Council resolution 1441 that Iraq was in "material breach" of its disarmament obligations and been given one more chance to come into compliance, it was up the Council as a whole or individual member states to decide whether there was a further material breach justifying the use of force.[32]

While there is clearly room for strengthening the language in Security Council resolutions to reinforce these three elements of control, there are also other means of doing so. One approach is through institutional cooperation; another is mission-by-mission support.

4.1 *Inter-institutional Cooperation*

The New Agenda for Peace affirms a widely held view that for "peace enforcement" and "enforcement action", the Security Council should look to regional and sub-regional organizations or multinational coalitions, not UN operations. It goes on to state "peace enforcement action authorized by the Security Council must be fully in line with the Charter of the United Nations and international humanitarian and human rights law, and involve effective and transparent accountability measures, including to the Security Council".[33] Appeals for closer cooperation between the UN and regional organizations go back to Secretary-General Boutros-Ghali's *Agenda for Peace*, reiterated in multiple

28 Gray (*supra* note 5), p. 350; Henderson (*supra* note 19), pp. 176–179.

29 Charlotte Ku, "Transparency, Accountability and Responsibility for Internationally-Mandated Operations", in Weller (*supra* note 3), p. 420.

30 Gray (*supra* note 5), pp. 377–380.

31 Ian Johnstone, "When the Security Council is Divided: Imprecise Authorizations, Implied Mandates and the 'Unreasonable' Veto", in Weller (*supra* note 3), pp. 234–244.

32 Gray (*supra* note 5), pp. 367–377.

33 United Nations, *A New Agenda for Peace*, Our Common Agenda Policy Brief No. 9 (July 2023), p. 25.

Secretariat reports since then, including the SG's report to the World Summit of 2005.[34] The World Summit itself expressed support for a stronger relationship between the UN and regional and sub-regional organizations and called for "formalized agreements" between the respective secretariats "and, as appropriate, the involvement of regional organizations in the work of the Security Council".[35] The Security Council began adopting resolutions on cooperation in 2005, starting with resolution 1631, which expressed an intention to hold regular meetings with heads of regional and sub-regional organizations, as well as high level inter-governmental meetings. That resolution pointedly reiterated the obligation in Article 54 for regional organizations to keep the Security Council informed of their activities.[36] In resolution 2167 of 2014, the Security Council reiterated the obligation to keep the Security Council informed not only of activities undertaken but also those contemplated.[37]

Since then, the UN has signed cooperation agreements with the AU and EU.[38] In 2010, the UN General Assembly established an Office to the AU (UNOAU) to "further a more systematic, streamlined and structured partnership between the AU and the UN, through implementation of the Joint UN-AU Framework for Enhanced Partnership in Peace and Security".[39] Every year since then the SG has issued a report on strengthening the UN and AU relationship.

The 2023 report, which focuses on UN financing of AU peace support operations, has interesting things to say about accountability mechanisms.[40] Discussion of such mechanisms can be traced to Security Council resolutions in 2016 and 2017, which called for "effective accountability and compliance frameworks" in AU operations.[41] The UN and AU have been working for several years on developing a "reporting framework that would establish clear,

34 *Agenda for Peace* (*supra* note 4), paras. 60–65; United Nations Report of the Secretary-General, *In Larger Freedom: towards development, security and human rights for all*, A/59/2005 (21 March 2005), paras. 213–215.

35 UN General Assembly, *World Summit Outcome*, A/Res/60/1 (24 October 2005), para. 17c.

36 UNSC Res. 1631 (17 October 2005), UN Doc S/RES/1631, paras. 7 and 9.

37 UNSC Res. 2167 (28 July 2014), UN Doc S/RES/2167, para. 1.

38 See for example the *Framework Agreement Between the United Nations and the European Union for the Provision of Mutual Support in the context of their respective missions and operations in the field* (2020) and the *Joint UN-AU Framework for Enhanced Partnership* (2017).

39 See UNOAU website <https://unoau.unmissions.org/>.

40 United Nations Report of the Secretary-General, *Implementation of Security Council resolutions 2320 (2016) and 2378 (2017) and considerations related to the financing of African Union peace support operations mandated by the Security Council*, S/2023/303 (1 May 2023).

41 UNSC Res. 2320 (18 Nov. 2016), UN Doc S/RES/2320, para. 6; UNSC Res. 2378 (20 Sept. 2017), UN Doc S/RES/2378, preambular para. 17.

consistent and predictable reporting channels between the [UN] Secretariat, the [AU] Commission and the [Security Council and the AU Peace and Security Council]". By May 2023, the AU Commission had made substantial progress in developing accountability, transparency and compliance frameworks that address not only financial accountability but also compliance with human rights and humanitarian law (para. 15). Oversight mechanisms for the AU Peace Fund have been put in place (para. 20). And a consultative planning and mandating process has been developed both to reflect the prerogatives of the AU Peace and Security Council and "to ensure sufficient oversight by the Security Council over any potential AU peace support operation for which UN assessed funding was being sought" (para. 23). Two financing models were highlighted – joint UN-AU missions and UN support packages to AU missions – both of which would facilitate the application of UN standards for "financial oversight, accountability mechanisms, and requirements for human rights due diligence" (para. 31).

Tellingly, the cooperation agreements with the EU do not include similar language about accountability, perhaps because the UN does not finance or support these missions in the same way. Nevertheless, the possibility of EU operations violating human rights and/or humanitarian law is real. As is the possibility of such violations by NATO, the CSTO, ECOWAS, SADC, and other regional or sub-regional organizations, with whom the UN has a less institutionalized relationship than with the EU and AU.[42]

4.2 *UN Support to Particular Missions*

As the UN engages in more "partnership peacekeeping", it exercises oversight in various ways. The most direct is deployment of a parallel observer mission. For example, in July 1994 the Security Council mandated the United Nations Observer Mission in Georgia to, among other things, "observe the operation of the CIS peacekeeping force within the framework of the agreement".[43] Having (reluctantly) welcomed the operation, some members of the Council wanted to ensure it behaved as a *peacekeeping* force. That is the only case where the Council used such explicit language, but the UN Observer Mission in Liberia was deployed alongside ECOMOG to verify "impartial application" of the peace agreement and to report on any major violations of international humanitarian law.[44]

42 Moelle (*supra* note 14), p. 154.

43 UNSC Res. 937 (21 July 1994), UN Doc S/RES/937.

44 UNSC Res. 866 (22 September 1993), UN Doc S/RES/866. UNOMSIL had a similar mandate in Sierra Leone.

Co-deployed UN peacekeeping missions can also play an oversight role. Thus, while UNMIK was not tasked directly with monitoring KFOR in Kosovo, the Secretary-General was requested to instruct his Special Representative "to coordinate closely with the international security presence to ensure that both presences operate towards the same goals and in a mutually supportive manner" and to "report to the Council at regular intervals on the implementation of this resolution, including reports from the leaderships of the international civil and security presences".[45] The resolution authorizing INTERFET in East Timor requested the leadership of that mission to report to the Security Council through the Secretary-General, pending his recommendations on establishing a UN peacekeeping mission to take over INTERFET's functions.[46]

Co-deployed missions in Mali are another example. There, MINUSMA was deployed alongside French-led Operation Barkhane and the G5 Sahel Joint Force – two counter-terrorism operations. Resolution 2391 requests UN support to the G5 Sahel and calls upon the latter "to establish a robust compliance framework to prevent, investigate, address and publicly report violations and abuses of human rights law and violations of international humanitarian law".[47] It calls on regional and international partners (including the UN) to support the establishment and implementation of the compliance framework (para. 22). The SG was tasked with ensuring strict compliance with the Human Rights Due Diligence Policy and the G5 Sahel was urged to ensure "the relevant monitoring and reporting mechanisms are in place and functional" (para. 23). On paper, these arrangements were designed to ensure greater levels of transparency and compliance by G5 Sahel with international humanitarian and human rights law.[48] MINUSMA did not support Barkhane but did cooperate with it, and the Security Council authorized the French forces to use "all necessary means" to intervene in support of elements of the UN operation when facing imminent threats. It also requested France "to report to the Council on the implementation of this mandate in Mali and to coordinate its reporting with the reporting by the Secretary-General (…)".[49]

---

45 UNSC Res. 1244 (10 June 1999), UN Doc S/RES/1244.

46 UNSC Res. 1264 (15 September 1999), UN Doc S/RES/1264.

47 UN Security Council resolution 2391 (8 December 2017) UN Doc S/RES/2391, paras. 12–17.

48 Haidi Willmot and Scott Sheeran (eds.), *United Nations Security Council Conflict Management Handbook* (Anwar Gargash Diplomatic Academy, 2023), p. 410. However, in his 2023 report on financing AU operations, the SG pointed out a "lack of clarity on reporting and accountability [by the G5 Sahel] to either the UN Security Council or the Peace and Security Council of the AU". Secretary-General, *Implementation of Res. 2320* (*supra* note 40), para. 37.

49 UNSC Res. 2295 (29 June 2016), UN Doc S/RES/2295, para. 45.

In other situations, UN political missions have been deployed alongside large multinational peace operations. In the resolution establishing the UN Assistance Mission in Afghanistan (UNAMA), the Security Council requested the International Security Assistance Force (ISAF) "to work in close consultation with the Secretary-General and his Special Representative" and requested the latter to report to the Council every four months on the implementation of this resolution.[50] In 2023, the Security Council authorized deployment of a Multinational Security Support Mission (MSS) to Haiti, which Kenya volunteered to lead. The authorizing resolution includes this paragraph:

> 18. Requests the leadership of the Multinational Security Support mission to ensure the highest standards of transparency and conduct, and to report every three months once the MSS is operational on the ground, as a part of regular reporting to the Security Council, through the Secretary-General, on the implementation of the resolution, including but not limited to composition of the mission, measures to ensure appropriate conduct and discipline, and to prevent sexual exploitation and abuse; and on investigations of allegations of misconduct and excessive use of force.[51]

The MSS operates alongside the UN Integrated Office in Haiti (BINUH), which could have an indirect role in ensuring respect for paragraph 18.[52]

Finally, the UN has on two occasions provided "support packages" to operations by regional organizations. In Darfur, from 2007, the UN provided "light" and "heavy" support packages to assist the AU mission (AMIS).[53] These packages involved a mix of personnel and equipment funded out of the UN peacekeeping budget, developed mainly as a stopgap pending the transition of AMIS into a hybrid UN-AU operation called UNAMID.[54] In Somalia in 2009 the Security Council established the UN Support Office for AMISOM (UNSOA, later called UNSOS) to provide logistical and other forms of operational support to AMISOM.[55] In resolution 2628, the Security Council called on the AU to monitor and investigate allegations of human rights violations by ATMIS forces, and to

50 UNSC Res. 1401 (28 March 2002), UN Doc S/RES/1401.

51 UN Security Council Res. 2669 (2 October 2023), UN Doc S/RES/2669.

52 See generally Eugene Chen, *How Can the UN Best Support Kenya's Mission to Haiti* (IPI Global Observatory, 31 January 2024).

53 UNSC Res. 1769 (31 July 2007), UN Doc S/RES/1769.

54 Willmot and Sheeran (*supra* note 48), p. 400.

55 Paul D. Williams, *UN Support to Regional Peace Operations: Lessons from UNSOA* (International Peace Institute, 2017), p. 2.

ensure "the highest standards of transparency, and conduct and discipline".[56] It also requested the AU to keep the Security Council informed, through the SG, on the implementation of ATMIS' mandate, including "accountability measures taken to address previously identified underperformance, including command and control, and conduct and discipline".[57] The UN's support (and oversight) was formalized in memorandums of understanding and letters of assist between the UN and AU, enabling the AU to perform its "oversight, accountability and compliance responsibilities" and the UN to implement its Human Rights Due Diligence Policy.[58]

Even when there is no UN presence in the mission area, it sometimes provides support to regional and coalition operations. For example, the UN Office in Central Africa (UNOCA) provided support to the AU Regional Task Force on the Lord's Resistance Army (as did a UN peacekeeping missions in the region). The UN Office in West Africa (UNOWA) provided support to the G5 Sahel from 2017–2023 and may play a more significant role in support of ECOWAS and AU efforts in Mali in the future.

5 Conclusion

As Blokker observed, since 1990 Security Council oversight of authorized operations has grown, although there is room for improvement. The challenge is likely to become greater in the years ahead, as the result of convergence of three factors: geopolitical tensions in the Security Council; declining enthusiasm for robust UN peacekeeping missions; and continuing demand for peace enforcement, counterterrorism, and counter-insurgency operations. If regional organizations or coalitions fill the gap, the Security Council has a responsibility to do what it can to exercise some oversight over operations it authorizes and those it does not.

Past practice suggests multiple mechanisms for supplying that oversight. Clear, time-bound mandates on the purpose for which force can be used is one. Systematic reporting to the Security Council is a another. Institutional cooperation agreements with *all* regional and sub-regional organizations are a third. Agreed compliance and accountability frameworks for particular missions is a fourth. Structures for implementing the UN's HRDDP is a fifth. These ideas are not new. Nor, in this political climate, is it possible to construct an

56 UNSC Res. 2628 (31 March 2022), UN Doc S/RES/2628, para. 32.

57 *Ibidem*, para. 53.

58 S/2023/303 (*supra* note 40), para. 14.

oversight template that can be pulled off the shelf whenever force is used. Yet some comfort can be derived from the fact that, from the earliest days of the UN, the Security Council managed to improvise in how it went about fulfilling its primary responsibility for the maintenance of international peace and security: from the invention of peacekeeping, to delegated enforcement action, to "partnership" peace operations. The ability to continue improvising will be put to the test in the years ahead, as Security Council members struggle to find common ground on future peace operations and enforcement actions. If they fail to do so, accountability for these valuable conflict management tools will suffer, and the Security Council risks fading into irrelevance.

CHAPTER 4

Operational Lawmaking within the UN: The Origins of the Legal Framework for Peacekeeping

Giserd Marqeshi and Nigel D. White***

1 Introduction

In 1962 the International Court of Justice (ICJ) delivered possibly its most expansive interpretation of the United Nations (UN) Charter. In the context of serious disputes over whether the UN General Assembly could mandate armed peacekeeping operations in the Middle East (United Nations Emergency Force (UNEF) I) and the Congo (*Opération des Nations Unies au Congo* (ONUC)), the Court concluded that the UN General Assembly could so act in the exercise of its subsidiary responsibility for international peace and security.[1] Reflecting on the Court's acceptance of the Assembly's competence, Schermers and Blokker expressed the view that "the advisory opinion of the International Court of Justice may encourage the acceptance of the principle that operational activities are permitted, but it does not solve the problem of limiting such activities".[2] It must be remembered that the ICJ was concerned with whether the UN General Assembly had the competence to mandate a peacekeeping operation. From that there is a tendency, fuelled by the predominance of a functionalist approach to the developments of the powers of UN organs,[3] to assume that the ICJ approved of the legality of peacekeeping operations per se. However, as Schermers and Blokker indicate, there must be limits on that power. In particular, it is reasonable to state that if the UN General Assembly has the power to mandate consensual peacekeeping operations, then so should the UN Security Council, which after all has the primary competence in matters of peace and security.[4] However, while the Assembly's competence is

* Giserd Marqeshi is a Ph.D. candidate, School of Law, University of Nottingham, UK.
** Nigel D. White is Professor of Public International Law, University of Nottingham, UK.

1 ICJ, *Certain Expenses of the United Nations*, [1962] ICJ Reports, p. 151.

2 Henry Schermers and Niels M. Blokker, *International Institutional Law* (6th ed., Brill Nijhoff, 2018), para. 1215.

3 Jan Klabbers, "The Transformation of International Organizations Law", in *European Journal of International Law* (EJIL) vol. 26 (2015) pp. 9, 15–19.

4 UN Charter, Article 24(1).

 | DOI:10.1163/9789004699939_006

arguably confined to quite a narrow conception of peacekeeping (consensual and non-coercive),[5] can the same limitations apply to the Security Council when it mandates a peacekeeping operation? After all, the Security Council not only has the power to work with the parties to a conflict to seek a solution based on consent utilising a range of powers attributed to it under Chapter VI (which would accommodate consensual peacekeeping), it also has powers to make binding decisions and impose measures upon states under Chapter VII including a range of non-forcible and forcible measures.[6]

This contribution will explore how peacekeeping, which has been developed operationally without a clear constitutional basis in the UN Charter, nevertheless operates within a legal framework, albeit an evolving, contested and functionally driven one. In particular, an emphasis on the latter category might suggest that the legal theory and practice of peacekeeping is indicative of the "enduring theory of functionalism" which has "shaped" the "body of international organizational law".[7] After all, as Niels Blokker has written, international organizations have to "deal with real problems that have to be solved".[8] However, as this chapter will suggest, the 'legal' power to create and to regulate peacekeeping has also been quite contingent on the historical context. On the one hand, the material manifestation of UN peacekeeping hinged quite conspicuously on its Cold War historical genesis. Peacekeeping was conditioned by fractious Cold War international relations, which when contextualised against its indeterminate Charter location, produced fierce contestation on the precise contours of its legality. As a result, the legal basis for peacekeeping was thus also simultaneously predicated, to an arguably significant extent, on the arguments put forth by specific individuals within the UN involved in its institutionalisation: namely the then UN Secretary General Dag Hammarskjöld and the Director of the UN Secretariat's General Legal Division – Oscar Schachter – both of whom not only had to articulate, and indeed justify, a Charter basis for UN peacekeeping powers, but also suggest normative legal restraints on this power in line with the rules and principles of international law. This chapter will thus revisit the seminal article written by Oscar Schachter in 1964 which articulated a legal framework for UN peacekeeping in the midst of these circumstances, after the first two peacekeeping operations showed both the

5 *Certain Expenses* (*supra* note 1), pp. 163–4.

6 UN Charter, Articles 41 and 42.

7 Laurence Boisson de Chazournes, "Functionalism! Functionalism! Do I Look Like Functionalism?", in *EJIL* vol. 26 (2016), p. 951.

8 Niels Blokker, "Comparing Apples and Oranges? Reinventing the Wheel? Schermers' Book and Challenges for the Future of International Institutional Law", in *International Organizations Law Review*, vol. 5 (2008) pp. 197, 209.

benign and coercive potential of peacekeeping, and it asks whether Schachter and Hammarskjöld's conception of peacekeeping law continues to have relevance today.

2 Historical Context

The broader historical context is vital in conceptualizing the legal debate. Doctrinal debates on the competencies of the Council *vis-à-vis* the Assembly aside,[9] as Branca writes, peacekeeping has fundamentally "evolved around certain landmark events" in the divided world of the Cold War.[10] Yet as aptly put by Blokker, this might be a mere truism given the inevitability that the world's premier international organizations would have to solve "real problems".[11] Having said that, the significance of these broader contextual factors is amplified in the context of peacekeeping because of the nature in which they engage with, and indeed arguably significantly condition, peacekeeping's legal basis *and limitations*. Indeed, even in the aforementioned ICJ jurisprudence, it is worth recalling that the reason the first two peacekeeping missions were mandated by the Assembly was because the UN became "entangled in the global Cold War".[12] With the Council gridlocked because of superpower induced antinomies,[13] "the plans for UNEF reflected a desire to accommodate small states' concerns about the direct involvement of European great powers in the crisis … the gathering of UN-led forces in the Sinai was powerfully symbolic of the organization's commitment to protect its smaller and more vulnerable members against domination by would-be imperialist powers".[14] Perhaps as

9 Dan Ciobanu, "The Power of the Security Council to organize Peace-Keeping Operations", in Antonio Cassese (ed.), *United Nations Peace-Keeping: Legal Essays* (Sijthoff and Noordhoff, 1978), pp. 15–17.

10 Eleonara Branca, *Responsibility Regimes for International Peace Operations* (Scientific Editorial, 2023), p. 11.

11 Blokker (*supra* note 8), p. 209.

12 Guy Fiti Sinclair, *To Reform the World: International Organizations and the Making of Modern States* (Oxford UP, 2017), p. 142.

13 The Soviet Union submitted that the power to establish peacekeeping force lay in the exclusive competence of the Council. See *Memorandum of the USSR Government* delivered by Grigory Tunkin. The memorandum stated that "Chapter VII of the Charter envisaged that it was the Security Council alone and not the General Assembly that may set up international armed forces and take such action as might be necessary to maintain or restore international peace and security, including the use of such armed forces" – see *Certain Expenses: Memoranda, Pleadings and Documents* (1962), p. 271.

14 Sinclair (*supra* note 12), p. 146.

significantly, the temporal significance of Cold War relations extended beyond the mere prefiguration of the particular peacekeeping operation, for it was also reflected in the actors who were emboldened as a result.[15] Of note in particular, was the increasingly animated role of the then UN Secretary General Dag Hammarskjöld.[16] As Sinclair writes:

> In a summary study of the operation that he submitted to the General Assembly on October 9, 1958, Hammarskjöld acknowledged that UNEF represented "a new and in many ways unique experiment," and had been undertaken in conditions that demanded "a new approach and a new type of operation". The study distilled several "basic principles and rules" that "would provide an adaptable framework for later operations that might be found necessary". These principles – often summarised as consent, minimum use of force in self-defence, and neutrality – comprised a "kind of blueprint, master texts of the kind needed for this kind of operation," and remain central to how peacekeeping operations are conceived and conducted today.[17]

Indeed, Branca concludes that "the first theorisation" of the now habitually invoked triad of norms or principles that legally structures peacekeeping to this day "dates back to the 1958 Hammarskjöld Report of the UNEF mission".[18] Each of these norms distinguished UNEF from mandatory action under Chapter VII of the UN Charter. Nevertheless, in providing for armed forces, UNEF had moved beyond the four corners of Chapter VI, which concerned peaceful and non-operational methods of dispute settlement. Although the first of its kind, the UNEF experience had proven valuable, and Hammarskjöld suggested the possibility of "an agreed standby plan for a [UN] peace force that could be activated on short notice in future emergencies to serve in similar ways". In fact, Hammarskjöld had previously envisioned more opportunities for enhancing the role of the UN in this area. He expressed the hope that "this evolution of emphasis and practice will be pursued and broadened in the

15 Rosalyn Higgins, "A General Assessment of United Nations Peace-keeping", in Cassese (*supra* note 9), pp. 7–12.

16 Douglas Hurd writes: "Article 99 of the Charter, by his own liberal interpretation, gave him a right to intervene where he thought it necessary" – see Douglas Hurd, *Memoirs* (Little, Brown, 2003), p. 142.

17 Sinclair (*supra* note 12), p. 146, citing Dag Hammarskjöld, "Summary study of the experience derived from the establishment and the operation of the force: report of the Secretary-General" (October 9, 1958) UN Doc A/3943.

18 Branca (*supra* note 10), p. 25.

future", rather than what seemed to be the less urgent task of attempting "formal constitutional changes".[19] However, his efforts to apply the same principles in the Congo only three years later would prove considerably more challenging. ONUC is commonly conceptualized as a sort of precarious extension of peacekeeping powers and practice,[20] often justified on the basis of the lessons the UN purportedly drew from their first peacekeeping experiment in UNEF.[21] A notion thus seemingly in line with the "enduring theory of functionalism" which has "shaped" the "body of international organizational law".[22] However, it is worth recalling that the legality of the UN's peacekeeping endeavours, as well as the emboldened role of the Secretary General, was not only fiercely challenged at the time,[23] but also exacerbated in the context of ONUC.[24] In particular, peacekeeping's legal grounds were consistently opposed by the Soviet Union as an illegal, distinctly 'western' co-option of the Charter.[25] And Hammarskjöld himself often drew the visceral ire of the Soviets in polemical debates premised not just on the supposed political proclivities which the Secretary General apparently harboured through his leadership of the UN Secretariat,[26] but the manner in which these proclivities in fact prefigured the merely ostensibly benign, neutral nature of UN peacekeeping which Hammarskjöld introduced.[27]

---

19 Dag Hammarskjöld, "Introduction to the Annual Report of the Secretary-General on the Work of the Organization" (UNGA Twelfth Session, 1957) UN Doc A/3594/Add.1, p. 3.

20 Nigel D. White, "Peacekeeping Doctrine: An Autonomous Legal Order?", in *Nordic Journal of International Law* (2019), pp. 1, 18–23.

21 Oscar Schachter, *The Relation of Law, Politics and Action in the United Nations* (Hague Collected Courses, 1963), p. 62.

22 De Chazournes (*supra* note 7), p. 951.

23 See Tunkin (*supra* note 13).

24 On the 'UN operations in Korea and Congo,' the Soviet jurist Morozov wrote: "It was thus a question of justifying the use of the Organisation [the UN] as a weapon of the colonialists and the imperialists who could railroad through the decisions they wanted with the aid of parliamentary methods … to help the reactionary imperialists quarters make use of the U.N. to suppress the national liberations movements in the colonies … such are the far reaching practical conclusions drawn from the distorted interpretation of the legal nature of the Charter". See G.I. Morozov, "International law and the UN", in Grigory Tunkin (ed., translated by G. Ivanov-Mumjiev), *Contemporary international law: collection of articles* (Progress Publishers, 1969), p. 140.

25 *Ibidem.*

26 In particular, see Khruschev's scathing attack on Hammarskjöld at the General Assembly, an account of which may be found at Harlan Cleveland, "The Man Who Wasn't There", *American Society for International Law Proceedings* vol. 55 (1961), p. 206.

27 Frielingsdorf writes: "Regardless of how Hammarskjöld's actions in the Congo are viewed, Khrushchev was right on this – the UN was no longer an organization where the Soviets were treated as equal members. The Secretary-General was actively pursuing an

All this notwithstanding, it might be argued that in spite of Soviet antinomies, peacekeeping had functionally passed a sort of 'formal' legal test in the context of the *Certain Expenses* opinion. However, that opinion was predicated on the determination that peacekeeping did not constitute enforcement action.[28] Yet owing to the considerably different nature between UNEF and ONUC, the latter in fact pointing in the direction of further exponential growth of peacekeeping powers beyond the criteria of consensual and non-coercive operations, the case left an "ambiguous legacy".[29] For instance, while it might be possible to identify some of the limitations upon Chapter VI-type peacekeeping (paradoxically derived from the framework placed around UNEF I by the UN General Assembly and Secretary General), it is more difficult to identify those applying to Chapter VII-type peacekeeping deployed following a Security Council resolution. The ICJ's opinion, therefore, whilst legally legitimating the practice of peacekeeping simultaneously left open significant questions on the precise contours of its supposed limitations. Questions which, importantly, even its chief architect Hammarskjöld was reticent to engage with given the precarious situation UNEF and ONUC were operating within both practically, and legally. Interestingly, however, this lacuna was to be addressed outside the formal channels of international law by the main protagonist of the then emerging 'invisible college' of international lawyers, and personal friend and legal advisor to Hammarskjöld, Oscar Schachter.[30]

3 Operational Lawmaking within the UN

It might seem odd that an analysis of peacekeeping should seek answers in part in an academic article, albeit one written by one of the most recognisable international lawyers.[31] However, it is a lesser-known fact that Oscar Schachter was at the heart of the development of UN peacekeeping, working closely with the UN Secretary General Dag Hammarskjöld. The obituary for Oscar Schachter published in the *New York Times* in 2003 contained the following endorsement

anti-Soviet goal as the very basis of his Congo policy". Per-Axel Frielingsdorf, *"Machiavelli of Peace" – Dag Hammarskjöld and the Political Role of the Secretary-General of the United Nations* (PhD Thesis, London School of Economics 2016, unpublished), p. 186.

28 *Certain Expenses* (*supra*, note 1), pp. 163, 177.

29 Sinclair (*supra*, note 12), 158.

30 See Oscar Schachter, "Invisible College of International Lawyers", in *Northwestern University School of Law Review* vol. 72 (1977–1978), p. 217.

31 Oscar Schachter, "The Uses of Law in International Peace-Keeping", in *Virginia Law Review* vol. 50 (1964), p. 1096.

by the UN Secretary General Kofi Annan: "Professor Schachter did more than any other official of the United Nations to help shape the rule of law", noting in particular that he was the "architect of the legal framework which has guided United Nations peacekeeping for more than 50 years".[32] Therefore, it is appropriate to explore that legal framework through the work of Schachter, alongside that of the Secretary General and, moreover, evaluate the continued relevance of that framework given the evolution of peacekeeping.

In his seminal article Schachter provided one of the few in-depth and holistic accounts of the legal framework governing peacekeeping, going far beyond the usual concern of international lawyers as to the precise Charter basis for such operations. Peacekeeping is characterized by Schachter as "measures taken by the United Nations to preserve the peace in its most immediate sense, that is to extinguish the local fires that threaten to ignite the rest of the globe". His purpose "is to show that these emergency 'fire-brigade' activities are more complicated and subtle than may seem to be the case".[33] To this end he expounds a legal framework derived from the Charter both expressly and impliedly, but also from the purposes of the UN, the wider context of Cold War international relations, and the idea of law as found in liberal democracies. It is in this latter sense that the dynamic, binary interplay between Schachter *and* Hammarskjöld is perhaps most conspicuous, with important connotations in conceptualizing peacekeeping's legal limitations. Of particular note was the combination of Schachter's role in the legal institutionalisation of peacekeeping alongside the philosophical convictions of Hammarskjöld. As Giblin writes, "peacekeeping doctrine also fundamentally epitomised" the "personal philosophical beliefs" of its chief architect Hammarskjöld.[34] A notion which might initially seem as a considerably large *proviso* given the *prima facie* constant appeal to fundamental international legal concepts such as consent, impartiality and the non-use of force implicit in Hammarskjöld's explanatory framework for UN peacekeeping. Add to this the fact that these doctrines were then further elaborated in a similarly neutral and benign way reflective of international law and interpretations of the Charter by one of the exemplary scholars of the time – Schachter.

On the one hand, there is perhaps a simple explanation here in the relatively straightforward notion that a concept such as peacekeeping, in this consensual, impartial and non-coercive form at least, is indeed merely uncontroversially

32 *New York Times*, 17 December 2003.

33 Schachter (*supra* note 31), p. 1098.

34 Jennifer Giblin, *United Nations Peacekeeping and the Principle of Non-Intervention: A TWAIL Perspective* (Routledge Press, 2024).

compatible with the terms of the Charter, as well as broader international law.[35] After all, Hammarskjöld, according to Schachter no less, was a man "… imbued with the spirit of law".[36] Seen in a different light, it could be suggested that this conventional account perhaps somewhat overlooks the critique that between UNEF and ONUC, UN peacekeeping was "neither neutral nor impartial [but] based mainly on clearly defined Cold War objectives shared by the General Secretary and Western permanent members of the Security Council … many of the principles that have guided the UN were created to serve certain Cold War objectives rather than being based on neutrality and impartiality".[37] As outlined in the previous section, from the very beginning, peacekeeping was intensely criticized as being practically constructed and legally buttressed by a particular form of western *liberalism* implicit in its Cold War custodians, which in turned conditioned the practical application of the 'holy trinity' of consent, neutrality/impartiality and the non-use of force, which defined its legitimacy and limitations.

Indeed, it was often quite conspicuous that the Soviets were not entirely wrong in arguing much of Hammarskjöld's 'vision' for the UN happened to fundamentally align with powerful liberal proclivities and Western state agendas.[38] This ideological convergence might even have been precisely the reason Hammarskjöld got the job.[39] This is why it is worth exploring the argument that Hammarskjöld's theoretical vision of international law and the UN in turn prefigured peacekeeping doctrine. Ove Bring writes:

> Dag Hammarskjöld was appointed Secretary-General five years after Hans Morgenthau had published his influential realist opus *Politics*

35 See Oscar Schachter, *International Law in Theory and Practice* (Martinus Nijhoff Publishers, 1991), p. 406.

36 Oscar Schachter, "Dag Hammarskjöld and the Relation of Law to Politics", in *AJIL* vol. 56 (1962), pp. 1–2.

37 Frielingsdorf (*supra* note 27), pp. 11–12.

38 One only has to look at Hammarskjöld's previous occupation in the Swedish ministry to observe a conspicuously 'liberal economic orientation'. See Anne Orford, "Hammarskjöld, economic thinking and the United Nations", in Carsten Stahn and Henning Melber (eds.), *Peace Diplomacy, Global Justice and International Agency: Rethinking Human Security and Ethics in the Spirit of Dag Hammarskjöld* (Cambridge UP, 2014), p. 160. In a similar vein, it could be said that the influence on international institutional law of liberal lawyer/academics such as Schachter has been significant. In a different and uncontroversial sense, this can also be said of Niels Blokker whose work at the Dutch Foreign Ministry is reflected in the practical, analytical and comprehensive approach taken in seminal works such as Schermers and Blokker (*supra* note 2).

39 Hurd (*supra* note 16), p. 142.

> *among Nations*. In a speech in 1956 Hammarskjöld had reason to comment on the divide between idealism and realism. Assertions that the UN had failed were often misleading, he said: "Do we refer to the purposes of the Charter? They are expressions of universally shared ideals which cannot fail us, though we, alas, often fail them. Or do we think of the institutions of the United Nations? *They are our tools. We fashioned them. We use them.* It is our responsibility to remedy any flaws there may be in them." And he continued: "This is a difficult lesson for both idealists and realists, though for different reasons. I suppose that, just as the first temptation of the realist is the illusion of cynicism, so the first temptation of the idealist is the illusion of Utopia." Hammarskjöld was an idealist in the sense that he believed in the purposes and principles of the UN Charter and in the possibilities of the UN Organization. At the same time, he was a realist the sense that he did not want to stretch the potential capacities of the Organization too much if member states were not ready for it.[40]

Interestingly, this notion of a sort of mediation between a polarity of international legal idealism and legal realism is also fundamental to the writings of Schachter.[41] Whilst similarly critiquing realist schools of international law sceptical of any invocation of 'autonomous' international law,[42] Schachter simultaneously maintained "all law involves the pursuit of social ends through the exercise of legitimated power and that in this sense it is reasonable to consider it as an aspect of the broader political process influenced by the factors that operate in politics generally".[43] On interpretation of the Charter, Schachter writes:

> to emphasize that law in the United Nations (or elsewhere, for that matter) is not to be approached as a set of autonomous norms which dictate decisions but as a process through which States and peoples pursue

40 Ove Bring, "Hammarskjöld's dynamic approach to the UN Charter and international law", in Stahn and Melber (*supra* note 38), p. 149.

41 For a fascinating insight into the manner Schachter perhaps prefigured the later seminal work of Martii Koskenniemi on dualism and polarity, see José E. Alvarez, "Commemorating Oscar Schachter, The Teacher", in *Colombia Law Review* vol. 104 (2004), pp. 556, 558.

42 Although Schachter was concerned with Myres McDougal rather than Hans Morgenthau. For an overview of the shift between the two in international legal realist approaches, see Gregory Shaffer, "Legal Realism and International Law", in Jeffrey L Dunoff and Mark A Pollack (eds.), *International Legal Theory: Foundations and Frontiers* (Cambridge UP, 2021).

43 Schachter (*supra* note 35), p. 3.

> their interests and undertake joint action in accordance with felt necessities and values … of what use are legal principles in the conditions of crisis, deep-seated mistrust, the bipolar concentration of power and the demands for radical change that characterize the intensely political atmosphere of the United Nations?[44]

To a significant extent therefore both Hammarskjöld and Schachter exhibited powerful convictions, perhaps inherent in the pathology of a sort of distinctly 'Cold War' liberalism, quite the orthodoxy at the time,[45] that the inherent indeterminacy of the Charter[46] ought to be interpreted and indeed constitutionally animated to achieve the considerably important organizational aims of peace and security.[47] The organization's development of peacekeeping powers was necessary but the role of international law was also vital. The abstract to Schachter's 1964 article in the *Virginia Law Review* entitled: "The Uses of Law in International Peace-Keeping", states:

> Mr. Schachter points out that legal precepts and precedents are essential to effective on-the-spot peacekeeping action by the United Nations. For they, on the one hand, provide a framework within which the peace-keeping agency and its members may operate and, on the other hand, make possible confidence in the legality and impartiality of the agency. He proceeds to examine United Nations peace-keeping operations as occasioned both by frontier conflicts and internal turmoil, tracing the role of legal principles in the evolution of an effective peace-keeping apparatus and drawing to light the importance, over and above the principles themselves, of their impartial, consistent, and reasoned application in a manner characteristic of 'law'.[48]

Peacekeeping is thus to retain a "characteristic of law" in a manner which seems to imply a desire for legal normativity rather than anything necessarily

---

44 Schachter (*supra* note 21), p. 169.

45 For a recent inquiry into the distinctiveness of 'Cold War' liberalism, see Samuel Moyn, *Liberalism Against Itself: Cold War Intellectuals and the Making of Our Times* (Yale UP, 2023).

46 Schachter (*supra* note 21), pp. 193–196.

47 Indeed, Schachter writes "… no account of the role of law can be adequate without considering the impact of ideals of peace and security" – Schachter (*supra* note 35), pp. 2–3.

48 Schachter (*supra* note 31), p. 1096.

concrete.[49] However, the fundamental question remains as to what each factor of the trinity determinatively means and thus, how they would apply in concrete situations. As Jennifer Giblin duly articulates in a TWAIL inspired critique of ONUC, the mere idea that consent, impartiality and the non-use of force were textually transposed into peacekeeping's structuring doctrines from broader international law might have done much towards bolstering the modalities' formal legal legitimacy, but the evidence is quite damning in suggesting it does very little as to providing a determinative framework for their actual application in practice.[50] This is clearly problematic in the context of attempting to define peacekeeping's purported legal limitations. Particularly given that, despite Schachter's delicate balance between international law and the need for innovative UN organizational powers for ensuring peace and collective security, Hammarskjöld might have been only invoking the triad as part of a broader game of "reigning by ambiguity", which allowed him "to control the UN" and introduce peacekeeping in the midst of a Cold War hegemonic lacuna.[51]

4 Legal Framework, Legitimation and Limits

In much of the preceding discussion, the legal justification, and legitimization of UN peacekeeping practice have emphasised the tripartite criteria of consent, impartiality and the non-use of force as foundational doctrines. Their significance to peacekeeping can hardly be overstated, given the paramountcy they are afforded not only in the scholarly reflections on peacekeeping's legal basis,[52] but also the UN itself.[53] The UN seldom engages with questions of peacekeeping theory, but seems to be conspicuous about the holy trinity

49 Branca (*supra* note 10), p. 25, makes the argument that the Holy Trinity is a "normative model".

50 Giblin (*supra* note 34).

51 Frielingsdorf (*supra* note 27), p. 168.

52 Alejandro Posada Téllez, "Explaining the Endurance of the 'Holy Trinity' in United Nations Peacekeeping", in *Oxford Political Review* (June 9 2022), available at <https://oxfordpoliticalreview.com/2022/06/29/explaining-the-endurance-of-the-holy-trinity-in-united-nations-peacekeeping/>, last accessed 18th February 2024.

53 Special Committee on Peacekeeping Operations, *Comprehensive Review of the Whole Question of Peacekeeping Operations in all their Aspects*, UN Doc A/57/767 (2003), para. 46; United Nations Peacekeeping Operations: Principles and Guidelines (UNDPKO, 2008), pp. 31–33.

whenever it does so.[54] As the last section concluded however, given the development and expansion of peacekeeping powers, there is an emerging orthodoxy from across the international legal spectrum which scrutinizes the UN's fidelity to this doctrine. With the implication that from the very beginning, the holy trinity presented indeterminate, normative criteria prone to co-option by hegemonic actors and political manipulation, rather than a set of necessarily 'legal' limitations.[55]

Equally, however, there is also a comparably permissible, perhaps more functionalist, argument that the model of peacekeeping which characterized the UN's early practices in UNEF and ONUC is simply not as relevant in explaining modern mandates. These, by the UN's own admission,[56] have been forced to evolve into more expansive, robust and militarized operations in response to the practical issues created by the increasingly complicated contemporary conflicts in which they are deployed.[57] Furthermore, it is important to note that the creation and oversight of peacekeeping mandates has institutionally migrated from their original loci in the Assembly to now being under the almost exclusive purview of the Council (and indeed is very predominant in its agenda). It is thus not merely a case of practical functionality which has expanded the nature of contemporary peacekeeping missions, but also, as this chapter previously queried, the powers derived from the relevant Charter basis at the heart of the mandate's constitution. This in turn, brings us full circle back into Niels Blokker's guiding prognosis, what are the precise legal limits on peacekeeping powers created by the Council? Is the holy trinity still relevant here?

Quite often, there is a temptation, principally amongst scholars, to resolve this distinctly binary impasse between Council and Assembly mandated peacekeeping powers by delineating, and thus compartmentalizing, them into

54 This point is made by Branca: "While an intense scholarly debate on the matter has attempted to identify the legal basis of peace operations, the UN and other organizations have not shown any interest in the inquiry. For many years, all the relevant UN documents on peace operations have completely omitted the discourse on their legal basis" – Branca (*supra* note 10), p. 38.

55 Giblin (*supra* note 34).

56 "Success of United Nations Peacekeeping Depends on Adapting to Changing Nature of Conflict, Assistant Secretary-General Tells Fourth Committee" <https://press.un.org/en/2017/gaspd646.doc.htm> last accessed 16 September 2024>.

57 James Sloan, *Militarisation of Peacekeeping in the Twenty-First Century* (Hart Publishing, 2011), p. 295.

a complex schemata of broader 'peace operations'.[58] In this manner, the holy trinity is retained for 'traditional' peacekeeping mandates, whilst mandates with greater enforcement powers are legally distinguished under different terminologies. The problem, of course, is that because peacekeeping is not in the Charter, it is often unclear which chapter is underpinning the mandate in question. Yet, the holy trinity is still habitually invoked in an almost vernacular way, despite being attached to the sort of mandates which stretch the lexical confines of consent, impartiality, and non-use of force to such an extent that it can conceivably argued they lose any meaningful explanatory value,[59] assuming, of course, they ever had any to begin with.

The question thus develops, given that there is no formal legal requirement which innately restricts Security Council mandated peacekeeping to the trinity, and the theoretical and operational applicability of consent, impartiality and non-use of force to modern peacekeeping is becoming increasingly strenuous, why are they still invoked in a manner which suggests the relationship is innate, or indeed, inherently necessary? Particularly given, as this chapter has discussed, there is a powerful argument to suggest that the holy trinity of peacekeeping was a historical contingency, as much as anything necessarily organic to international law, the UN and the collective security system. Recall, for instance, that the UN's predecessor, the League of Nations, did also produce something akin to 'peacekeeping', and it ought to be considered that it did so with a legal basis quite different to the holy trinity.[60] Can the uses of international law in peacekeeping thus extend beyond invocations of the holy trinity? Arguably, a kernel of this is already implicit in the work of Hammarskjöld and Schachter. In the aforementioned 1958 summary study which Hammarskjöld submitted to the Assembly, it might be relevant to note that only consent is explicitly mentioned.[61] Now the remaining criteria of impartiality and the non-use of force are certainly implied, but they are not directly expressed. And more importantly, they are implied in the context of other factors. Similarly, in his seminal 1964 article, Schachter begins with the *proviso* of

58 See for example Patryk Labuda, "UN Peacekeeping as Intervention by Invitation. Host State Consent and the Use of Force in Security Council-Mandated Stabilization Operations", in *Journal on the Use of Force and International Law* vol. 7 (2020), p. 317.

59 *Ibidem*, p. 317.

60 Alan James, "The peacekeeping role of the League of Nations", in *International Peacekeeping Journal* vol. 6 (1999), pp. 154, 160.

61 Dag Hammarskjöld, *Summary study of the experience derived from the establishment and the operation of the force: report of the Secretary-General* (October 9, 1958) UN Doc A/3943.

"general observations about the role that law can perform in the processes of peacekeeping",[62] in which, analogous to the framework discussed by Hammarskjöld, the holy trinity is conspicuous by its explicit, textual absence.

An illustrative point is the manner in which 'impartiality' is interpreted in Schachter's article.[63] According to Nicholas Tsagourias, impartiality in the peacekeeping context is now construed as "an operational term and refers to the *conduct* of the operation".[64] The legal principle thus has a distinct operational value in this context, requiring peacekeeping missions to structure their mandate in a manner which ensures the "equal treatment of the parties in material terms".[65] Yet Schachter's conceptualisation is much more holistic, which is perhaps quite emblematic of his distinctly liberal conception of law.[66] In the 1964 article, Schachter observes that "in certain situations, the required guidance for international officials has to be sought in the recognized precepts of international law and in the general principles of law accepted by states".[67] Impartiality, in the context of Schachter's article, seems to be situated more closely to operating as a general precept of *international law*, rather than a definitive criteria for guiding the practice of the mission.[68] Put more simply, although Schachter mentions impartiality, it is seen as an attribute of the legal approach rather than a separate legal principle derivative of peacekeeping. When framed in this manner, it evidently alters the contours of impartiality. Since law, by its very nature, is supposed to be impartial, and much of the legal rhetoric deployed by Schachter privileged the idea that compliance with international law and principles derived from the Charter prevented UN peacekeeping from being a form of arbitrary, discretionary or political action, the criterion of impartiality might be construed as an empty vessel of legitimation rather than a principle requiring operative application. This is why in the

62 Schachter (*supra* note 31), p. 1098.

63 Which is perhaps notable from a lexical standpoint in itself given the formal and academic literature on peacekeeping privileging the term 'neutrality' early on. See for example Marianne von Grünigen, "Neutrality and Peacekeeping", in Cassese (*supra* note 9).

64 Nicholas Tsagourias, "Consent, Neutrality/Impartiality and the Use of Force in Peacekeeping: Their Constitutional Dimension", in *JCSL* vol. 1 (2007), pp. 465, 478.

65 *Ibidem*.

66 See, for instance, his invocations of Kant in balancing between the "nature and reality of international law" – Schachter (*supra* note 35), pp. 2–6.

67 Schachter (*supra* note 31), p. 1100.

68 Schachter emphasises an application of the Kantian notion of precepts and concepts informing peacekeeping practice. He clarifies, more broadly, that the "nature and reality" of international law requires relating "concepts to practice" to give them content, but also relating "practice to concepts" in order to give "practices meaning and direction" – Schachter (*supra* note 35), pp. 2–6.

context of ONUC, for instance, lip service to 'impartiality' was indeed fundamental, even as UN action was anything but.[69] Frielingsdorf writes:

> The argument is circular. The definition becomes subjective in the extreme: impartial is whatever Hammarskjöld decides is impartial. Ergo, Hammarskjöld's actions are per definition impartial ... the principles followed the actions; not the other way around. Rather than adopting a policy that was derived from principles of impartiality and non-intervention in an internal conflict, Hammarskjöld's policy was to intervene in the internal conflict. The principles of impartiality were created afterwards to defend actions that were motivated by partiality.[70]

5 Conclusion – The Relevance of Schachter and Hammarskjöld Today?

Overall, Schachter's theoretical synthesis of law and peacekeeping maintained that the law "provided the common frame of reference and the standards of mutual interest that are necessary for collective effort in today's divided world".[71] And as a result, law contributed in a positive manner to the development of international authority and responsibility for the UN and its relevant actors, all in the midst of a tense and critical political context.[72] Whether, however, the law also prescribed limitations in a sense which would satisfy the fundamental question posed by Blokker, as to the legal limits of the power to mandate peacekeeping forces, is slightly more precarious. Particularly given, as we have seen, the way in which this "common frame of reference and the standards of mutual interest"[73] in the peacekeeping context coincided with, or perhaps were co-opted by, the Secretary General Dag Hammarskjöld. Having said that, it is worth referring back to the question as to whether the vision of peacekeeping and international law articulated by Schachter and Hammarskjöld is even still relevant at largely capturing the legal and practical dynamics of contemporary peacekeeping. After all, the point was made previously that the legal principles which characterized early missions such as UNEF and ONUC, "often

69 Von Grünigen (*supra* note 63), pp. 138–140.

70 Frielingsdorf (*supra* note 27).

71 Schachter (*supra* note 31), pp. 1098, 1114.

72 On this, see Antonio Cassese, "Recent Trends in the Attitude of the Superpowers towards Peace-Keeping", in Cassese (*supra* note 9), pp. 224–228.

73 Schachter (*supra* note 31), p. 1114.

summarized as consent, minimum use of force in self-defence, and neutrality/impartiality, remain central to how peacekeeping operations are conceived and conducted today".[74] Yet, at the same time, the precise extent of these principles, in the words of both Schachter and Hammarskjöld themselves no less, had to remain adaptable to the "critical political context" in which UN peacekeeping was to be situated.[75] This left open the possibility of consequential changes to peacekeeping doctrine if missions developed within, and had to respond to, situations vastly different to the sort of circumstances in which early mandates were crafted.[76] Indeed, perhaps no better account of this is offered by the UN Department of Peacekeeping itself:

> With the end of the Cold War, the strategic context for UN Peacekeeping changed dramatically. The UN shifted and expanded its field operations from "traditional" missions involving generally observational tasks performed by military personnel to complex "multidimensional" enterprises ... UN Peacekeepers were now increasingly asked to undertake a wide variety of complex tasks, from helping to build sustainable institutions of governance, to human rights monitoring, to security sector reform, to the disarmament, demobilization and reintegration of former combatants.[77]

Clearly, the sort of measures discussed above extend well beyond the analogy of Schachter which likened peacekeeping to "measures taken by the United Nations to preserve the peace in its most immediate sense, that is to extinguish the local fires that threaten to ignite the rest of the globe".[78] Yet even in the face of these exponential changes to the function and telos of peacekeeping since

74 Sinclair (*supra* note 14), p. 146, citing Dag Hammarskjöld, *Summary study of the experience derived from the establishment and the operation of the force: report of the Secretary-General* (October 9, 1958) UN Doc A/3943.

75 Cassese (*supra* note 72).

76 In fact, there is argument to suggest this change occurred immediately upon Hammarskjöld's untimely death. Sloan writes that "following Secretary-General Hammarskjöld's death in September 1961, the ground shifted somewhat (...) the new Secretary-General, U Thant, was less averse to the use of force and more willing to take sides in internal questions", thus departing from the legal tripartite in a significant way. Regarding ONUC, Sloan continues that "as circumstances on the ground changed, the operation moved away from all three of these [peacekeeping] principles, arguably abandoning them altogether". See Sloan (*supra* note 57), pp. 129–130.

77 See "United Nations Peacekeeping: Our History", available at <https://peacekeeping.un.org/en/our-history>, last accessed 21 September.

78 Schachter (*supra* note 31), p. 1098.

the Cold War, the legal tripartite of consent, impartiality and the non-use of force are often said to have ostensibly remained,[79] but have also "broadened and reinterpreted over time", in order to provide "an adaptable framework".[80] Modern 'stabilization' mandates given to peacekeeping operations in Africa are characterized by "robust force, counter-terrorism, and increased cooperation with host state forces", as well as including "returning basic services, building the capacity of the host state to enforce the rule of law, and an inclusive peace process".[81] In a number of ways, it seems as though peacekeeping's fidelity to the legal tripartite has become stretched beyond the point of reconciliation with early mandates.

79 Commentators often make the point that the traditional principles of peacekeeping are constantly accentuated by official UN doctrine, despite the seemingly incontestable reality of practice suggesting otherwise. See Sloan (*supra* note 57), pp. 62–63.

80 Kseniya Oksamytna and John Karlsrud, "Introduction", in Kseniya Oksamytna and John Karlsrud (eds.) *United Nations Peace Operations and International Relations Theory* (Manchester UP, 2023), p. 4.

81 Alexander Gilder, "The Effect of 'Stabilization' in the Mandates and Practice of UN Peace Operations", in *Netherlands International Law Review* vol. 66 (2019), p. 48.

CHAPTER 5

'Uniting against Impunity' in the New Cold War: Will the UN General Assembly Come of Age?

*Michael Ramsden**

1 Introduction

The political and armed conflicts over the past 10 years have, to numerous commentators, produced a 'new Cold War'.[1] Robert Levgold's prediction in 2014 that this new Cold War "will affect nearly every important dimension of the international system" has played out within the United Nations (UN) system, with the Security Council being deadlocked in responding to some of the gravest humanitarian crises in recent history, including in Syria, Ukraine and Gaza.[2] Within the UN itself much expectation is placed upon the Security Council given the wide scope of its powers under Chapter VII of the UN Charter to authorise states to take coercive measures against other states.[3] Yet, the failure of the Security Council to exercise these powers in situations which called for action has led to renewed attention on the extent to which the General Assembly is able to fill the void.[4] The famous 1950 *Uniting for Peace* resolution has classically occupied the scholarship on the scope of Assembly powers, especially in the context of authorising the use of force.[5] But the rise of international criminal law and a growing impetus in ensuring accountability

* The author is a Professor of Law, The Chinese University of Hong Kong.

1 See Michael Scharf, "Power Shift: The Return of the Uniting for Peace Resolution", in *Case Western Reserve Journal of International Law* vol. 55 (2023), pp. 1, 3 (and citations there).

2 Robert Legvold, "Managing the New Cold War", in *Foreign Affairs* (2014), p. 74.

3 As to these powers, see e.g. Erika de Wet, *The Chapter VII Powers of the United Nations Security Council* (Hart, 2004).

4 See e.g. Carsten Stahn, "From 'United for Peace' to 'United for Justice'? Reflections on the Power of the United Nations General Assembly to Create Criminal Tribunals or Make Referrals to the ICC", in *Case W. Res. J. Int'l L.* vol. 55 (2023), p. 251; Michael Ramsden and Tomas Hamilton, "Uniting against Impunity: The UN General Assembly as a Catalyst for Action at the ICC", in *International and Comparative Law Quarterly* vol. 66 (2017), p. 893.

5 See e.g. Michael Ramsden, "Uniting for Peace and Humanitarian Intervention: The Authorising Function of the UN General Assembly", *Wash. International Law Journal* vol. 25 (2016), p. 267.

 | DOI:10.1163/9789004699939_007

for atrocity situations now justifies a renewed focus on the potential role of the Assembly in not only uniting for peace but also against impunity.

With a focus on General Assembly practice over the past decade the following chapter – which builds upon the PhD dissertation I had the great fortune of completing under the exceptional guidance and mentorship of Professor Blokker – considers the potential roles that the plenary is capable of playing in uniting against impunity. It first considers the scope of the Assembly's legal powers and then proceeds to broadly evaluate its anti-impunity practice in the context of challenging Security Council inaction, pronouncing upon the occurrence of atrocities in resolutions on country situations, and its involvement in empowering investigative mechanisms. It considers that while the Assembly has taken strides forward in uniting against impunity, there remains potential for it to go even further in fashioning creative solutions to coordinate state responses as well as to overcome Security Council deadlock.

2 The Legal and Factual Significance of General Assembly Resolutions

The nature and extent of the General Assembly's powers turns upon interpretation of the UN Charter. A narrow construction has been to place an emphasis on the Charter text as a means to challenge perceived expansionist tendencies of the Assembly as *ultra vires*.[6] However, identifying *vires* purely by reference to the Charter text does not reflect UN practice, with different organs, including the International Court of Justice (ICJ), recognising the scope for institutional powers to evolve.[7] Indeed, this is reflected in the drafting history itself, where delegates resolved that it was "inevitable" that each UN organ would define its own powers, a process that was "inherent in the functioning" of an international organization.[8]

The power of the General Assembly to furnish recommendations to states or to the Security Council has perhaps most faithfully adhered to the language in the Charter, in the sense that a 'recommendation' is generally interpreted

6 UNGA, Seventy-first session, 66th plenary meeting UN Doc A/71/PV.66 (21 December 2016), p. 33 (Russia).

7 ICJ, *Legal Consequences of the Construction of a Wall* (Advisory Opinion), [2004] ICJ Reports, pp. 136, 149.

8 *UNCIO* XIII 633–634, 668–669 (1945).

as non-binding.[9] Being 'non-binding' denotes the freedom of the recipient to refuse to observe them without legal consequence.[10] Blaine Sloan did famously argue in 1948 that states in the Assembly may through practice instill in its recommendation a mandatory requirement to comply, particularly in areas where an international regulatory vacuum existed, such as the protection of human rights.[11] However, it is clear that Assembly recommendations practice has not developed as Sloan argued (perhaps with the exception of colonial matters).[12] While there are numerous occasions where the Assembly has used obligatory-type language in its resolutions ("demanding" that its recommendations are followed and condemning states when they have failed to do so), there is a distinct lack of uniformity of approach, nor underlying debate amongst members evincing an intention to develop recommendations into mandatory instruments.[13]

However, this lack of development should not be overstated, nor should the absence of a mandatory binding power undermine the legal significance of General Assembly resolutions in certain instances. As the International Law Commission (ILC) noted in identifying international obligations, "special attention should be placed" on resolutions of the Assembly, being "a plenary organ of the [UN] with virtually universal participation, that may offer important evidence of the collective opinion of its Members".[14] A distinction can be drawn in this respect between the legal status of a resolution and the primary obligations external to the resolution that it interprets in such instruments. For example, numerous resolutions have "demanded" that Israel cooperate with the Assembly's Special Committee as required "in accordance with its obligations as a State Member of the United Nations".[15] The value of resolutions of this nature is its interpretation of these underlying Charter obligations and the scope of the Assembly's powers: as the then UN Secretary-General noted

9 Michael Ramsden, *International Justice in the United Nations General Assembly* (Edward Elgar, 2021), pp. 152–180 (albeit that there is still a duty of good faith within the UN Charter on the part of states to consider it).

10 *Ibidem*, 154.

11 Blaine Sloan, "The Binding Force of a Recommendation of the General Assembly of the United Nations", in *British Yearbook of International Law* vol. 25 (1948), pp. 1, 24.

12 Ramsden (*supra* note 9), at p. 180.

13 *Ibidem*.

14 ILC, *Draft Conclusions on Identification of Customary International Law, with Commentaries*, UN Doc A/73/10 (2018).

15 See e.g. UNGA Res 72/84 (2017), at [2]; Michael Ramsden, "Cooperation with United Nations Atrocity Inquiries", *Fordham International Law Journal* vol. 45 (2022), pp. 473, 491 (and citations there).

in 1957, a recommendation that seeks to implement the Charter would itself "have behind it the force of the Charter".[16]

The specific legal principles at play here are those specified in the Vienna Convention on the Law of Treaties, as a "supplementary" means of interpretation though "subsequent agreement" and "subsequent practice".[17] As the ILC has surmised, both interpretive approaches "may arise from or be expressed in, the practice of an international organization in the application of its constituent instrument".[18] Furthermore, it is clear that these evolutive approaches to interpretation need not be limited to clarifying ambiguous or general terms in a treaty, but also applies to constructions that have the effect of reading down or even establishing a new institutional power.[19] The ICJ has at least implied that the Friendly Relations Declaration (Resolution 2625) was a subsequent agreement; the ILC and other commentators have also identified other resolutions in these terms.[20] Similarly, there are various General Assembly practices that have been recognized to be "subsequent practice", including the "increasing tendency over time" for the Assembly and Security Council to deal "in parallel with the same matter" (despite this being apparently inconsistent with Article 12(1) of the UN Charter).[21]

The legal significance of General Assembly resolutions can also be appreciated outside of the UN system. Thus, Assembly 'declarations' and other resolutions that articulate abstract legal principles constitute evidence in the identification of customary international law.[22] Furthermore, where a multilateral treaty is interpreted in a resolution, such interpretation might constitute a subsequent agreement or practice in the application of the treaty (given

16 UN Secretary-General, *Question Concerned by the First Emergency Special Session of the General Assembly from 1 to 10 November 1956*, UN Doc A/3527 (1957), at [20].

17 Vienna Convention on the Law of Treaties (entered into force 27 January 1980), 1155 UNTS 331, Art. 31.

18 ILC, *Draft Conclusions on Subsequent Agreements and Subsequent Practice in Relation to the Interpretation of Treaties, with Commentaries*, UN Doc A/73/10 (2018), conclusion 12(2).

19 *Ibidem*, conclusion 7; ILC, *First report on subsequent agreements and subsequent practice in relation to treaty interpretation* (2013), UN Doc A/CN.4/660, at [49]–[50].

20 ICJ, *Military and Paramilitary Activities in and Against Nicaragua (Nicaragua v US)* (Merits), [1986] ICJ Reports, pp. 14, 100; ILC (*supra* note 18), p. 99, fn. 545; Henry Schermers and Niels Blokker, *International Institutional Law: Unity Within Diversity* (Brill, 2018), p. 891.

21 ICJ (*supra* note 7), p. 149. See also ICJ, *Legal Consequences for States of the Continued Presence of South Africa in Namibia* (Advisory Opinion), [1971] ICJ Reports, pp. 16, 22; ILC (*supra* note 18), p. 100.

22 Ramsden (*supra* note 9), at pp. 86–98.

that Assembly members are also parties to such multilateral treaties).[23] In this regard, there is a large body of practice from international and *ad hoc* tribunals in relying upon Assembly resolutions in support of a particular interpretation of international criminal law.[24] On some occasions, an Assembly resolution itself was taken as an authoritative exposition of custom, including in providing the legal foundation for certain crimes prosecuted in the post-World War II trials.[25]

Finally, a brief word is also due for the significance of General Assembly resolutions in another way, in carrying factual value within international affairs, as 'quasi-judicial' instruments. Being quasi-judicial denotes the Assembly's practice in making factual determinations in the application of legal norms.[26] These vary considerably but have included findings over the occurrence of human rights violations within the territory of a member state; the responsibility of a member state for violations of international law; and the recognition of states of affairs, particularly in relation to statehood and territorial disputes.[27] The extent to which the Assembly has effectively asserted quasi-judicial authority will turn upon how such resolutions have influenced the decisions of actors on the same subject matter, as the following section covers.

3 Uniting against Impunity in the New Cold War

Having outlined the legal foundation for General Assembly powers, demonstrating a broad latitude to develop its powers to address changing exigencies, the question is how the events of the past decade have led to the UN's plenary organ to assert itself in a manner that advanced accountability for international crimes.

3.1 *Challenges to Security Council Inaction and Permanent Member Veto*

Over the past decade, it is apparent that the General Assembly has become more pointed in its criticism of Security Council deadlock on accountability for atrocity crimes as well as to explore creative solutions to overcome such deadlock.

23 *Ibidem*, p. 84.
24 *Ibidem*, pp. 22–65.
25 *Ibidem*, p. 26.
26 *Ibidem*, p. 100.
27 *Ibidem*, pp. 145–149.

The *Uniting for Peace* resolution, first adopted in 1950, is the most famous example of General Assembly challenge to the Security Council, providing scope for the plenary body to take measures in circumstances of Council failure.[28] Precisely what these measures entail has been the subject of much debate. A stronger reading of *Uniting for Peace* permits the Assembly to step into the shoes of the Council and exercise powers analogous to those found in Chapter VII, including to provide legal justification for members to take coercive measures, up to and including the use of force.[29] This reading finds most support in the first such situation in which it applied, Korea (1950), where the continued UN military operations there appeared to be under the legal authority of Assembly resolutions.[30] A weaker reading, on the other hand, treats *Uniting for Peace* as a procedure to allow the Assembly to convene an emergency special session on a matter that the Council was also acting; but with the plenary body still being confined to its non-binding discursive powers.[31] This weaker version seems to be prevalent in Assembly resolutions under this mechanism, including over recent years.[32] Thus, while Assembly resolutions in the 2022 Ukraine crisis have condemned Russian aggression and demanded Russia's unconditional withdrawal, the plenary organ has not purported to provide legal justification for states to take coercive measures, including sanctions or the use of force.[33]

That *Uniting for Peace* has been largely confined to the 'weaker' approach above itself has prompted recent debate on whether it still serves a useful purpose. On the one hand, *Uniting for Peace* is said to be redundant given that the General Assembly now routinely acts on a situation alongside the Security Council, a practice confirmed by the ICJ in *Wall*.[34] Furthermore, the Assembly has on many occasions condemned Council inaction and made recommendations to members to address security threats without invoking *Uniting for Peace*.[35] On the other hand, the value of *Uniting for Peace* is in the optics it produces when an emergency special session is convened; the 2022 Ukraine session and the resolution it produced was headline news around the world. There is also another potential value, in supplying the solemnity of occasion

28 UNGA Res 377 A (1950).

29 Ramsden (*supra* note 5), p. 279.

30 *Ibidem*, at pp. 282–285.

31 *Ibidem*, at pp. 279–282.

32 *Ibidem*.

33 UNGA Res. ES-11/1 (2022), [2]–[3]; Michael Ramsden, "Uniting for Peace: The Emergency Special Session on Ukraine", in *Harvard International Law Journal* (online, 2022), p. 1.

34 *Wall* (*supra note* 7), p. 149.

35 See e.g. UNGA Res 66/253 B (2012), preamble; UNGA Res 31/6 D (1976), at [10].

for members to make stronger legal interpretive claims in the adoption of resolutions to maintain international peace and security in the face of an absent Security Council. In recent years, the possibility for the Assembly to authorise states to impose sanctions (that might otherwise be unlawful); to establish an *ad hoc* tribunal vested with the same powers as one created by the Security Council; and the fashioning of a referral power to the International Criminal Court ('ICC'), have all been put forward as potentially creative developments of the plenary organ's power under the auspices of *Uniting for Peace*.[36] Practice under this mechanism (particularly the Korea (1950) situation) together with the legal framework of the Assembly's ability to interpret the scope of its own powers (see section 2 above) both provide avenues for the plenary organ to advance a stronger interpretation of *Uniting for Peace*. However, this potential has yet to be realised so far in this new Cold War.

Instead, the General Assembly has pivoted towards a new initiative to pressure the Security Council into discharging its functions via the creation, in April 2022, of a standing mandate to convene a debate whenever a veto was cast by a Council permanent member.[37] This standing mandate, adopted in Resolution 76/262, appeared to have been prompted by two objectives: first, to enhance Council accountability to the Assembly; second, to prompt the Assembly to engage more robustly in matters of international peace and security in circumstances of Council failure.[38] Unlike *Uniting for Peace*, considered as an exceptional measure premised first upon a finding of Council failure, Resolution 76/262 envisages a debate whenever the veto is cast.[39] The standing mandate initiative thus has the potential for a more systematic scrutiny of veto power than that provided under *Uniting for Peace* and, with this, greater attention being place on issues around the veto including its possible legal limits. In turn, although still early days, members have engaged with the implications of veto misuse, albeit in political rather than legal terms.[40] Some members have also underlined the Assembly's "duty to react to violations of

36 See Scharf (*supra note* 1); Stahn (*supra note* 4); Tom Hamilton and Michael Ramsden, "The Politicisation of Hybrid Courts: Observations from the Extraordinary Chambers in the Courts of Cambodia", in *International Criminal Law Review* vol. 14 (2014).

37 UNGA Res. 76/262 (2022).

38 See Rebecca Barber, "The U.N. General Assembly's Veto Initiative Turns One: Is it Working?", in *Just Security*, 26 April 2023 (and citations there), available at <https://www.justsecurity.org/86140/the-u-n-general-assemblys-veto-initiative-turns-one-is-it-working/>.

39 See e.g. UNGA, Seventy-sixth session, 68th plenary meeting, UN Doc. A/76/PV.69 (26 April 2022), 7 (Brazil) (noting that Resolution 76/262 goes too far and *Uniting for Peace* better reflects the need for balance between the Council and the Assembly).

40 Barber (*supra* note 38) (and citations there).

international law" and "responsibility to uphold the principles of the United Nations Charter".[41]

These broad assertions have yet, however, to manifest themselves into an General Assembly asserting itself as an alternative to the Security Council in providing legal justification for states to take measures (that might otherwise be unlawful) in seeking to maintain international peace and security, including in the specific context of securing accountability for atrocity crimes.[42] In recent years there are areas where the Assembly could have bolstered the legal case for certain measures taken by states against other states, including to support the legality of sanctions imposed on Russia and North Korea.[43] There are, in short, areas where the Assembly could do more to act, using its unique position as being comprised a near universal membership of states, to advance interpretive claims that support the legality of state action to advance accountability for atrocity crimes outside of Council authorisations.

3.2 *Rise in General Assembly Quasi-Adjudication of International Situations*

A significant development in the new Cold War has been the readiness of the General Assembly to make legal determinations in its resolutions dealing with country situations.[44] In the space of accountability for atrocity crimes these have arisen in two main ways. First, the Assembly has incorporated the established crimes making up international criminal law – war crimes, crimes against humanity, genocide and aggression – in their country consideration of situations.[45] The Assembly has been inconsistent in its use of these criminal norms, with some criticising the narrow focus on particular situations in history (such as Israel and South Africa).[46] But there has been a trend towards the greater engagement over the past decade in using these crimes to describe events in particular country situations.[47] This has included the legal characterisation of some conduct in terms that the Assembly has previously tended to avoid: genocide and aggression, which found a return in resolutions on the

41 *Ibidem.*

42 *Ibidem.*

43 *Ibidem* (similarly, the Assembly could have also supported the legal basis for cross-border humanitarian aid from Turkey and Syria as justified by necessity, including also to declare that humanitarian assistance does not constitute unlawful intervention in a state's internal affairs).

44 Ramsden (*supra note* 9), pp. 100–151.

45 *Ibidem.*

46 *Ibidem.*

47 *Ibidem*, p. 151.

Myanmar and Ukraine situation respectively.[48] Second, the Assembly has also formed a view on certain international affairs that, although not perhaps directly intending to secure accountability, inadvertently assist in doing so. In this regard, the Assembly has a long history of declaring certain entities to be states (e.g. the right of Palestine to statehood), to recognise territory as belonging to particular states (e.g. South Ossetia as part of Georgia), and to deny the validity of referenda that have been used by aggressor states to claim territory (e.g. the Crimea).[49]

Both types of resolution have had an appreciable impact both on the atrocity crime characterisation of situations as well as the wider context in which conflicts have taken place. A primary place in which these quasi-judicial resolutions have produced impact is in the judicial sphere, where courts have relied upon them to support certain conclusions aimed at addressing the consequences of atrocity crimes.[50] Recently, the ICJ's provisional measures jurisdiction in particular has become a fertile terrain for strategic litigations to wage 'lawfare', whereby often the weaker adversary turns to the Court in order to obtain a remedy with the goal to support their wider narrative on a situation and to exert pressure on its stronger adversary to alter its preferences.[51] In this regard, General Assembly resolutions noting the possible occurrence of genocide in Myanmar, and the occurrence of Russian aggression against Ukraine, have been used to support the plausibility of claims for provisional measures in these situations.[52] In a similar manner, the Assembly's determination that Palestine met the definition of statehood was integral to the ICC being able to act on crimes alleged to have occurred within this territory; Resolution 67/19 (2012) (recognising the right to Palestinian statehood) was thus treated as "… *determinative* of Palestine's ability to accede to the [ICC] Statute", thereby supporting the opening of an investigation.[53]

48 UNGA Res. ES-11/1 (2022), [2]; UNGA Res. 73/264 (2018), [1]. As to the avoidance of the genocide label in Assembly resolutions: Michael Ramsden, "The Crime of Genocide in General Assembly Resolutions: Legal Foundations and Effects", in *Human Rights Law Review* vol. 21 (2021), p. 671.

49 Ramsden (*supra note* 9), pp. 145–149.

50 *Ibidem*, p. 151.

51 See further Michael Ramsden, "Strategic Litigation Before the International Court of Justice: Evaluating 'Impact' in the Campaign for Rohingya Rights", in *European Journal of International Law* vol. 33 (2022), p. 441; Michael Ramsden, "Strategic Litigation in Wartime: Judging the Russian Invasion of Ukraine through the Genocide Convention", in *Vanderbilt Journal of Transnational Law* vol. 56 (2023), p. 181.

52 *Ibidem*.

53 ICC, *The Prosecutor of the International Criminal Court, Fatou Bensouda, opens a preliminary examination of the situation in Palestine* (Press Release, 16 January 2015), available at <https://www.icc-cpi.int/Pages/item.aspx?name=pr1083>, emphasis added.

To be sure, the General Assembly has a long history of what is described here as 'quasi-judicial' practice, involving a political body in forming a view on legal issues and situations; but recent practice does show the plenary's evolution into a body that seeks to advance accountability for atrocity crimes to a much greater extent than before.[54] In this regard, the rise in the use of international criminal law norms in Assembly resolutions has tracked the growth of this area of law in itself, including the creation of commissions of inquiry, *ad hoc* tribunals and the ICC.[55] In turn, the clearer definition given to international crimes and their applicability in certain situations has allowed the Assembly to incorporate these norms into its country resolutions accordingly. But the Assembly has also created institutions (i.e. commissions of inquiry) that have facilitated this quasi-judicial practice (as addressed in the next section in more detail). The number of such commissions has grown considerably over the past two decades, with their findings often being referred to in Assembly resolutions.[56]

In this regard, it can be said that the General Assembly has made strides forward in support of its mandate to advance atrocity crimes accountability, although the full potential of this quasi-judicial role remains unrealised. In particular, there still remains a disconnect between the Assembly's characterisation of a state being responsible for mass atrocities and the action that the plenary takes within its institutional competence. At a minimum, it is open to the Assembly to not recognise the credentials of a state that it has previously adjudged to have seriously violated international law.[57] Credentials challenges usually only arise where there are competing governmental claims to represent a state; but there is also practice where the Assembly has factored in a regime's adherence to the UN Charter in deciding whether to accept or reject credentials (i.e. South Africa).[58] While some challenge the Assembly's legality in doing so, the fact remains that the plenary has broad latitude to interpret its own powers, including who it allows to participate in the Assembly (see section 2 above).

3.3 *Empowering*

Another area which has seen development in the past decade has been the creation of commissions of inquiry with powers that seemingly go beyond those typically found in such bodies. The General Assembly has a practice of establishing commissions in response to a wide variety of situations throughout

54 Ramsden (*supra note* 9), p. 151.
55 *Ibidem*, p. 149.
56 *Ibidem*, pp. 100–151.
57 *Ibidem*, pp. 141–145.
58 *Ibidem*, pp. 143–145.

its history.[59] In this regard, the International, Impartial and Independent Mechanism for Syria (IIIM-Syria), established by the Assembly in 2016, was particularly innovative in being vested with a power to collect and analyse evidence to identify specific perpetrators to facilitate criminal prosecutions.[60] This went beyond the typical commission which was confined to collecting evidence of human rights violations generally rather than preparing case files against individual suspects.[61] This shows a readiness on the part of the Assembly to develop its powers in a manner that addresses gaps that arise in securing accountability for international crimes, particularly in relation to events of the gravest international concern. The context here was the failure of the Security Council to refer the Syria situation to the ICC.[62] The IIIM-Syria was thus created as a means to both support and stimulate creative solutions outside of the ICC, such as prosecutions in national courts under the doctrine of universal jurisdiction.[63]

The analysis in section 2 above shows a legal foundation for the creation of the IIIM-Syria, and further iterations of this model, either as being justified within the text of the UN Charter, as grounded in subsequent practice, or as a subsequent agreement. The last option here is, admittedly, on weak ground: the resolution that underpinned the IIIM-Syria was supported by 105 Member States, with 15 voting against, 52 abstentions and 21 not voting.[64] The difficulty here is whether the resolution commanded the 'general acceptance' of the membership to constitute a subsequent agreement, in contrast to the much larger numbers in support of resolutions that have been said to command general acceptance.[65] A clearer basis can be reasonably implied in the text of the Charter. Despite being engaged in a quasi-prosecutorial function, the fact still remains that the IIIM-Syria facilitates the General Assembly's powers under the UN Charter in informing their discussion and content of

59 *Ibidem*, pp. 182–183 (and citations there).

60 UN Secretary General, *Report of the Secretary General on the Implementation of the resolution establishing the International, Impartial and Independent Mechanism to Assist in the Investigation and Prosecution of Persons Responsible for the Most Serious Crimes under International Law Committed in the Syrian Arab Republic since March 2011*, UN Doc. A/71/755 (2017), at [30]–[31].

61 Ramsden (*supra* note 9), p. 184.

62 *Ibidem*.

63 *Ibidem*.

64 UNGA Res. 71/248 (2016).

65 See *supra* note 20.

recommendations.[66] This remains the case even though specific individuals are identified for prosecution; in fact, doing so allows for finer texture to be given to Assembly recommendations.[67] But even if a grounding in prior practice is considered necessary then it is also clear that this is not the first occasion in which the Assembly has identified individual perpetrators and sought their prosecution, having done so in relation to the South Africa situation.[68] Similarly, the Assembly has also assisted national prosecutions of individuals in the situation of Cambodia and Guatemala, further adding to the weight of practice concerning the facilitation of prosecutions.[69]

While there is some practice in the General Assembly performing or delegating a quasi-prosecution function, the IIIM-Syria was an important milestone in the plenary body's attempt to assert itself in securing accountability for atrocity crimes in the new Cold War. While the degree to which the IIIM-Syria will produce impact will ultimately be measured by the prosecutions that it yields within international or domestic courts (a process which is ongoing), it is also apparent that this mechanism has set new standards for the next generation of investigative mechanisms within the UN system, integrating new approaches to evidence collection, incorporating victims' perspectives, and in facilitating justice within the accountability ecosystem generally.[70] In this respect, the Human Rights Council has been guided by the IIIM-Syria precedent and established similar mechanisms, vested with powers to prepare case files on individual suspects, in the Myanmar and Ukraine situations.[71] The Security Council also followed in these footsteps by establishing a comparable mechanism to prosecute crimes committed by Da'esh/ISIL, showing the scope for Assembly innovations to influence Council solutions.[72]

At the same time, it is apparent that the General Assembly has not fully come of age in empowering subsidiary organs, especially in going that next

66 Ramsden (*supra* note 5), p. 185.

67 *Ibidem.*

68 UNGA Res 41/103 (1986), at [6], [7].

69 UNGA Res 57/228 B (2003); UNGA Res 63/19 (2008); UNGA Res 64/293 (2010), at[4].

70 Anni Pues, "The UN General Assembly as a Security Actor: Appraising the Investigative Mechanism for Syria", in *Max Planck Yearbook of United Nations Law* vol. 26 (2022), pp. 553, 571; UN Secretary-General, *International, Impartial and Independent Mechanism to Assist in the Investigation and Prosecution of Persons Responsible for the Most Serious Crimes under International Law Committed in the Syrian Arab Republic since March 2011*, UN Doc. A/77/751 (16 February 2023).

71 UNHRC Res. 39/2 (2018), at [22]; UNHRC Res. 49/1 (2022), ay [11] (albeit that the Ukraine commission mandates it to endeavour to "identify, where possible" those responsible).

72 UNSC Res. 2379 (2017), at [2].

step to establish *ad hoc* tribunals (without the consent of the host state) with the power to prosecute and convict suspects for international crimes.[73] The Security Council has traditionally performed this role. Yet, Council deadlock over accountability for the MH17 airline disaster, Syrian crimes and Russian aggression all provided opportunities to explore the possibility for the Assembly to step into the breach and create *ad hoc* tribunals in these situations.[74] Certainly, there would be no legal impediment for the Assembly to establish such an organ following the approach to legal powers set out in section 2 above. The complicated aspect would be in legally obliging states to cooperate and to impose binding judgments on individual suspects; yet, both of these impediments can be overcome through a members' delegation of their universal jurisdiction to the tribunal and an application of the customary international obligation upon states to cooperate with international criminal tribunals.[75] However, the Assembly has so far failed to take the opportunity to go that next step in its evolution as a justice actor within the international system.

4 Conclusion

The General Assembly's role in advancing accountability for atrocity crimes has undergone evolution over time. From its early practice in challenging Security Council inaction, the Assembly has increasingly played a role in providing an alternative forum in which to pronounce upon its members' priorities in relation to ongoing atrocity situations. The creative use of Assembly powers to establish the IIIM-Syria was a significant moment in supporting the view that the plenary could advance other creative solutions to address impunity gaps, including in establishing *ad hoc* tribunals and making referrals to the ICC. This Chapter argued, in this respect, that the Assembly has a broad discretion in defining the scope of its own powers, including, by virtue of its near universality of membership, a unique position in being able to advance legal interpretive claims and to certify the existence of particular states of affairs that support atrocity crime accountability efforts.

73 The Assembly has facilitated tribunal creation, but premised upon state consent (Cambodia): Hamilton and Ramsden (*supra* note 36), p. 115.

74 Stahn (*supra note* 4), pp. 259–261; Michael Ramsden, "Uniting for MH17", in *Asian Journal of International Law* vol. 7 (2017), p. 337.

75 Stahn (*supra note* 4), pp. 270–271.

Rather, as Carsten Stahn has noted, a limitation on General Assembly power (in the context of *ad hoc* tribunal creation) lies in the political arena rather than UN institutional law.[76] This might be due to a mixture of reasons, including the preference some states have to strengthen ICC capacity or regional initiatives instead.[77] Some states will also share a concern that such initiative becomes a double edged sword with the possibility that creative expansions of Assembly power is used against them in the future. Still, this Chapter has outlined the rise of an anti-impunity focus within the Assembly and growing frustration over the failure of the Security Council to fulfil its functions where it matters most. Within this growing sentiment, and as states continue to negotiate the so-called new Cold War in the years ahead, there is a legal basis for the Assembly to fill the void created by Security Council deadlock to unite against impunity.

76 *Ibidem*, p. 276.
77 *Ibidem*, p. 285.

CHAPTER 6

The Amazing Resurrection of NATO: Problems and Prospects

*Alfred van Staden**

1 Introduction

It is Niels Blokker's lasting achievement to have analysed the legal structure of international organizations in a lucid and cogent way. Among those organizations, the North Atlantic Treaty Organization (NATO) occupies a special place. To be sure, the Atlantic Alliance, too, is grounded on the principle of legal equality, but its practical functioning is largely contingent on American leadership as well as the acceptance thereof by the lesser member states. Ever since NATO's foundation, the United States (US) has taken a disproportionate share of the common defence burden.[1] The willingness of the US administration to make vast American resources available to the protection of member states was highly instrumental in solving the collective action problem. This problem is paralysing many international organizations. At the root of it is that those organizations are producing 'goods' (in the case of NATO security or stability) that all member states have access to. In principle, none of its members can be excluded from the benefits of their mutual cooperation.

Thus, if an external party is deterred from aggression to member state X, then it is likewise deterred vis-à-vis member state Y and Z. The metaphor of the nuclear umbrella aptly captures the reality of states sharing their fate in an age of weapons of mass destruction. The characteristic of jointness of supply, which is essential to public goods, implies that participating states may be tempted not to pay their fair share in the sacrifices required for achieving common goals. Whether or not individual members deliver their full contribution

* Professor Alfred (Fred) van Staden is emeritus professor of international relations at Leiden University, and a former director of the Netherlands Institute of International Relations Clingendael (The Hague).

1 During most of the Cold War years the US accounted for 50 percent of total NATO military spending. In the post-Cold War period the American share grew to as much as 75 percent.

 | DOI:10.1163/9789004699939_008

is not relevant to the opportunity of consuming the public good. This gives rise to the well-known free-rider problem emanating from collective action.[2]

The role of the United States has been indispensable for successfully organising collective action in NATO for two reasons at least. First, NATO's overall military strength depends to a great extent on American forces being assigned to allied tasks. Without US military assistance Europe had been defenceless during the Cold War. Second, the US administration is able to exert pressures on the free riders in the Alliance. Those pressures may take different forms, from cajoling to the threat of withdrawal or disengagement.

As widely recognised, at the heart of the basic treaty of NATO, the North Atlantic Treaty, is the much-cited Article 5. This Article considers an armed attack on one member state to be an attack on all members. The wording of the Article is a masterpiece of calculated ambiguity. On the one hand It unconditionally obliges member states to assist the Party or Parties subject to attack, but on the other it leaves to them to determine what action is deemed necessary.[3] This ambiguity is a clear illustration of what has been called the security dilemma in alliance politics.[4] Weaker allies fear to be abandoned by the strongest ally when the chips come down, i.e. when war breaks out and the protection of the strongest is needed. Therefore, it is in the weaker allies' interest to formulate the assistance clause as strictly as possible. By contrast, the strongest ally fears to be entrapped by the weaker ones into quarrels where its vital interests are not at stake. That is why the strongest seek some leeway in the clause concerned. The formulation of Article 5 is a compromise between the opposing interests of stronger and weaker allies, or – putting it differently – of the protector and protected states.

Furthermore, the linkage with the Charter of the United Nations deserves attention. One should recall that the drafters of the North Atlantic Treaty

---

2 The classical study of the collective action problem is Mancur Olson, *The Logic of Collective Action: Public Goods and the Theory of Groups* (1965). See also Todd Sandler, *Collective Action: Theory and Applications* (1992).

3 The full text of the first paragraph of Art. 5 reads as follows: "The Parties agree that an armed attack against one or more of them in Europe or North America shall be considered an attack against them all and consequently they agree that, if such an armed attack occurs, each of them, in exercise of the right of individual or collective self-defence recognized by Article 51 of the Charter of the United Nations, will assist the Party or Parties so attacked by taking forthwith, individually and in concert with the other Parties, such action as *it deems necessary* (*italics* added), including the use of armed force, to restore and maintain the security of the North Atlantic area".

4 Glenn H. Snyder, "The Security Dilemma in Alliance Politics", in *World Politics* vol. 36 (1984), at pp. 461–496.

deliberately decided to refer to Article 51 concerning individual or collective self-defence under Chapter VII[5] and not to Chapter VIII regarding Regional Arrangements. The judgement was made that by defining the newly established Alliance as an UN Regional Arrangement the requirement of prior authorization by the UN Security Council had to be met should any enforcement action be contemplated.[6] With the Cold War already broken out and the looming threat of Soviet vetoes in the Council, the risk of paralysis in decision-making was deemed too big.[7]

NATO has been hailed, at least by its supporters, as the most successful military alliance in history. Still, in the previous decade several western leaders had called the future of the organization into doubt. Thus, just after his election in 2016 as president of the United States, Donald Trump qualified the Alliance as "obsolete"[8] and, in November 2019, president Macron of France diagnosed it with "brain death".[9] Several years earlier retiring US defence secretary Robert Gates had warned that NATO faced "a dim if not dismal future" and even "irrelevance".[10] The decision by the Russian president Putin to launch a military attack on Ukraine on 24 February 2022 had led in western capitals to an agonising reappraisal of the security situation in Europe. The attack revitalised the belief in the indispensability of the Alliance while restoring the commitment to its original core task, i.e. collective defence towards external aggression. After a long period of engaging in crisis management and stabilisation operations outside its treaty area, NATO had come to full circle.

In this chapter, the evolution of the Alliance since the end of the Cold War will be described and analysed. In addition, current problems and future prospects are discussed.

5 See the text quoted *supra* note 3.

6 Art. 53, para. 1, of Chapter VIII stipulates that "no enforcement action shall be taken under regional arrangements or by regional agencies without the authorization of the Security Council (…)".

7 See on the foundation of NATO, Lawrence S. Kaplan, *NATO 1948: The Birth of the Transatlantic Alliance* (2007).

8 In an interview with the London *Times* and the German newspaper *Bild* three days before his inauguration as president on 20 January 2017.

9 In an interview with *The Economist*, 7 November 2019.

10 Robert Gates, "Has the Atlantic alliance outlived its usefulness?", in *The New York Times*, 10 June 2011.

2 Evolution Since the End of the Cold War

2.1 *The Russia Factor*

It is platitudinous to state that common perceptions of threat are the midwife of the formation of military alliances. It is equally commonplace to assert that once those perceptions are beginning to fade or disappear, alliances tend to disintegrate. The second proposition is the logical corollary of the first. So, on the face of it, NATO had lost its rationale with the collapse of the Soviet Union in 1991 and the following dismantlement of the Warsaw Pact. The survival of the Alliance to date is closely intertwined with the assessment by western countries of the aspirations of post-Soviet Russia. Did the end of Soviet communism offer the historic opportunity to integrate the Russian Federation into an all-European security system? Building a Common European Home? Or, rather, was post-Soviet Russia to be considered heir to traditional Russian imperialism, waiting for opportunities to restore the former Soviet empire?

Clearly, western governments were faced with a dilemma. On the one hand, they could not put the existence of NATO in jeopardy for the sake of an untested new security system with Russia as a close partner. Apart from the shadow of Russia's imperial past, it was felt that the domestic situation of the country was too precarious. The polarisation between the nationalist right and the leftovers of the old communist party made Russia less and less stable. The country proved to be increasingly resentful to the outside world. Moreover, Boris Yeltsin, the first president of the Russian Federation, did not instil much confidence because of his capricious behaviour. On the other hand, western governments had to take account of the emergence of feelings of marginalisation in Russia. Those feelings had taken root under the influence of the loss of large chunks of territory of the former Soviet Union as well as of the declining influence over Central and Eastern Europe. Russian foreign policy was pervaded by a sense of humiliation and, as a consequence, drive to revenge.[11] Western countries tried to solve this dilemma by establishing a number of institutional forms of cooperation with Russia. In spite of the prevalence of mutual suspicion, they recognised that no stable security order in Europe could be built without some form of Russian participation.

First of all, western governments actively supported the proposal to beef up the Conference on Security and Cooperation in Europe (CSCE), the pre-eminent platform for cooperation of the West with Russia. At the Budapest

11 On the background of the fall of the Soviet Union, see Vladislav M. Zubak, *Collapse: The Fall of the Soviet Union* (2021).

Summit of December 1994, the CSCE was transformed into the Organization for Security and Cooperation in Europe. This implied the upgrading from a permanent conference to a full-fledged international organization under the aforementioned Chapter VIII of the United Nations (UN) Charter. As early as November 1990, the participating countries (among which all NATO members) had agreed in the French capital to the so-called 'Charter of Paris for a New Europe'. Following on the principles of the Helsinki Final Act (1975) this Charter provided a framework for cooperation between the western states and the former communist countries, first and foremost Russia.

Secondly, Russia was invited to take part in NATO's 'Partnership for Peace' (PfP) programme. This was aimed at creating trust and developing practical cooperation between the member states of NATO and other states mostly in Europe, particularly post-Soviet states. The programme, formally launched early 1994, was focused on military-to-military cooperation on training, exercises, disaster planning and response. In June 1994, Russia joined PfP.

Thirdly, three years later, the NATO-Russia Founding Act was concluded. This Act further institutionalised collaboration of the Alliance with Russia. Thus, a permanent NATO-Russia Council (NRC) was established to provide the forum, as was stated, for consultation, transparency and consensus-building. However, the NRC had little practical effect. Significantly, it was not used to prevent the 2008 Russo-Georgian War broken out after Russia had actively supported militarily two self-proclaimed Georgian republics.[12] This could be seen as a bad omen of the later deterioration of NATO-Russian relations.

In public and scholarly debate on relations between Russia and the West the issue of NATO expansion towards Central and Eastern Europe played a prominent part. Had the Russian leadership reason to feel betrayed given promises made by some western leaders? The most important one was the suggestion made that after German reunification NATO would not move "one inch Eastward" (dixit US secretary of state James Baker[13]). Or should it be emphasised that western governments never gave written assurances to that effect? Likewise, was enlargement not to be regarded as the natural response of an Alliance that had embraced an open-door policy vis-à-vis any European state in a position to further the principles of the North Atlantic Treaty and 'to contribute to the security of the North Atlantic area'?[14] In the considerations of

12 South Ossetia and Abkhazia.

13 On this subject, see Mary E. Sarrote, *Not one inch. America, Russia, and the Making of post-Cold War Stalemate* (Yale UP, 2021).

14 Art. 10 of the North Atlantic Treaty. This article pertaining the accession of new members is the only place in the Treaty prescribing the rule of unanimity in decision-making among member states.

western leaders the latter argument clearly outweighed the counter-argument of antagonising Russia. For the sake of credibility, it was argued, NATO could not be but remain faithful to the legitimate right of the peoples in the region to determine their own fate. Additionally, NATO membership of unified Germany was believed to be in the interest of stability of Europe as a whole.

However justified concerns about the possibility of Russia moving in an adversarial direction, the country did not pose a clear and present danger in the short term. After all, in the 1990s, Russia was badly weakened economically while its military forces had become in poor shape. Therefore, western governments had trouble in convincing the public at large of the cause of NATO's continued existence. They were forced to search for new missions in order to show NATO's *raison d'être* and, in doing so, retain popular support.

2.2 *NATO's New Missions*

In the Summer of 1993, the Democratic senator Richard Lugar threw a stone in the Atlantic pond by launching the phrase "Out of Area or Out of Business", meaning that if NATO was not able to find meaningful tasks outside its treaty area it was bound to outlive its usefulness.[15] The influential senator echoed a sentiment widely shared in NATO circles. A first step to widening NATO's mission was the involvement of the Alliance with the Balkan wars (1992–95) on Europe's periphery. Although the initial American response to the wars was one of reticence – secretary of state Baker declared: 'We don't have a dog in that fight'[16] – winds were changing when the Democratic Clinton administration entered the political scene. With the blessing of the US, NATO was going to support the world organization by monitoring and enforcing a UN no-fly zone over Bosnia and Herzegovina. In 1994, the Alliance launched its first-ever combat operation. The military actions against Serbia turned out to be decisive in ending the Bosnian war. The US also took an active part in the making of the so-called Dayton peace agreement of 1995. Similarly, four years later, NATO's air campaign stopped large-scale Serbian ethnic cleansing against Albanians in Kosovo, the province that had seceded from Serbia.[17] The campaign was contested in the legal community, since it was carried out without an explicit mandate of the UN Security Council.[18]

---

15 Richard Lugar, *Remarks delivered to the Open Forum of the U.S. State Department* (2 August 1993).

16 Elizabeth Drew, *On the Edge: The Clinton Presidency* (Simon & Schuster, 1994), at p. 139.

17 On the conflict, see Tim Judah, *Kosovo: War and Revenge* (Yale UP, 2002).

18 Governments in NATO countries nevertheless held that the campaign was legitimate.

NATO's Strategic Concept of 1999[19] had identified new security risks such as terrorism, ethnic conflict and political instability. Three different tasks for the Alliance were designated: 1. collective defence, 2. crisis management and peace support, and 3. cooperative security. The latter task was briefly defined as engaging security partnerships with non-members and international organizations. Though the three tasks were put on an equal footing of importance, crisis management and peace support operations clearly were going to dominate NATO's overall performance at the early stage of the 21st century. Indeed, the Alliance had evolved in an organization whose main function was the conduct of out-of-area stabilisation missions. Wars of necessity were replaced by wars of choice. This was exemplified by NATO's efforts to stabilise Afghanistan through the International Security Assistance Force (ISAF), which lasted from 2001 to 2014.[20] To a lesser extent, it also became visible in allied assistance to Iraq in the field of military and police training. Besides, it is interesting to note that just after the terrorist attacks on targets in New York and Washington on 11 September 2001, NATO members invoked Article 5 of the Treaty for the first time in the history of the Alliance.

The Russian annexation of the Crimean peninsula in 2014 and the war in the Donbas prompted NATO to reconsider the emphasis previously laid on expeditionary operations out-of-area. The Wales summit of that year was marked by a strategic reorientation. It was decided to terminate the ISAF operation and refocus on contingencies in Europe. To this end proposals were adopted for large-scale reinforcement and reorganisation of defence capabilities. With his decision to invade Ukraine Vladimir Putin, in spite of himself, pushed NATO to go back to its original primary mission: countering the Russian threat. The Alliance regained popular support to such a degree that most allied governments were able to honour the promise made on the aforementioned Wales summit to spend at least two percent of their gross domestic product (GDP) on defence within a decade. In addition, Finland's and Sweden's application for membership in the aftermath of the Russian invasion underscored NATO's renewed force of attraction.

2.3 *NATO's Enlargement Process*

As stated above, in conformity with the founding treaty, NATO has pursued an open-door policy on the admittance of new member states. Unlike what

19 NATO's Strategic Concepts are intended to equip the Alliance to respond to current security threats and challenges and guide its political and military development so that it is equally prepared to face future threats and challenges.

20 NATO formally assumed command of ISAF mission in August 2003.

is sometimes asserted the US, under the Clinton administration, initially took a cautious approach on this matter. Obviously, Washington wanted to spare Russian sensitivities shortly after the absorption of the former German Democratic Republic into the Alliance.[21] In an attempt to forge consensus NATO published a study on enlargement in 1995. The study set standards (such as democratic reforms and the rule of law) to be met by candidate members. A so-called Membership Action Plan (MAP) was created for helping prepare non-members for eventual membership. Candidate countries were also urged to closely cooperate with NATO members participating in international peace missions. Most importantly, they had to show the capacity of being producers of security rather than mere consumers.

As it happened, Poland, Hungary and the Czech Republic were the first former Warsaw Pact countries to join NATO in 1999. Five years later, they were followed by the so-called Vilnius Group, composed of Estonia, Latvia, Lithuania, Romania, Bulgaria, Slovakia and Slovenia.[22] On the Bucharest summit of 2008, the application for membership by Ukraine and Georgia provoked divisions among NATO members. Whereas the US administration of George W. Bush was strongly in favour of admitting the two countries, particularly France and Germany were adamantly opposed. The fear of adversely impacting the relationship with Russia motivated the opponents' position. Ultimately, it was agreed that Ukraine and Georgia 'will become members of NATO',[23] without specifying concrete steps to make that happen. The decision drew sharp criticism from some commentators. Thus, for example, the British historian Timothy Garton Ash argued that the compromise represented the worst of both worlds: 'It increased Putin's sense of a U.S.-led threat to the remains of the Russian empire without guaranteeing the security of Ukraine or Georgia.'[24] Nevertheless, the same wording was used at the 2023 Vilnius summit when NATO reaffirmed the commitment to admit Ukraine, meanwhile at war with Russia, in the future.[25]

No doubt, NATO's enlargement process fundamentally changed Europe's security landscape. All but a handful of European states had become members of the Atlantic Alliance. NATO considered the process an historic success, as

---

21 See *supra* note 13.

22 Croatia and Albania formally acceded to NATO in 2009, Montenegro in 2017, North Macedonia in 2020, Finland in 2023 and Sweden in 2024. The total membership of NATO amounted to 32.

23 *Declaration of the Bucharest Summit*, 3 April 2008, para. 23.

24 Timothy Garton Ash, "Postimperial Empire. How the War in Ukraine is Transforming Europe", in *Foreign Affairs* (May–June 2023), at p. 68.

25 *Vilnius Summit Communiqué*, 11 July 2023, para. 11.

it had contributed, allegedly, to the advancement of stability and cooperation on the continent. By contrast, enlargement was very much resented by Russia. Moscow proclaimed to be encircled by a ring of hostile states that were said to pose a danger to its interests. The striking contradiction signified the widened cleavage between NATO and Russia.

3 Current Problems

Despite NATO's new lease of life, a number of serious problems affecting its performance and cohesion cannot be ignored. The focus will be on three topics: (1) the implementation of NATO's strategy under changed circumstances; (2) the involvement of NATO with China; and (3) Europe's quest for strategic autonomy.

3.1 *Implementation of Military Strategy*

The basic tenet of NATO's strategy is to deter an outside attack. To this end a mixture of military capabilities have been developed and sustained. One leg is made up of classical defence forces in order to deny the opponent the option of seizing any piece of NATO territory. The other are retaliatory capabilities to punish acts of aggression with strikes on the opponent's heartland. The hard core of the latter are the nuclear forces of the US. However, too much reliance on retaliation is raising the question of credibility. How credible is it to respond to even a minor infringement of the treaty area with the use of nuclear weapons? This question is highly relevant in the context of the security of the Baltic states, which are very much exposed to Russian military power.

Initially, the Alliance sufficed to deploy small battalion-sized tripwire forces in the new member states bordering Russia. With the growing military threat by that country it was realised that such a small military presence was inadequate to prevent war in Europe. The reliance on mere retaliation by nuclear strikes had become too big. As said before, Russia's annexation of Crimea prompted a transformation of NATO's force structure, which was further boosted by the war in Ukraine. Important decisions in this regard were made at the NATO summits of Madrid (2022) and Vilnius (2023). Thus, the so-called military enhanced Forward Presence was reinforced. Concretely, the number of multinational battlegroups on the Alliance's Eastern flank were doubled, from four to eight. At the same time, it was also decided to strengthen those units up to brigade level. What's more, a new multinational Allied Reaction Force was established to replace the 40,000-military strong NATO Response Force. The new force was to provide a high readiness pool of over 100,000 troops with a notice of up to 10 days. The force could be expanded to a strength of around 200,000 within a time frame of 10–30 days and to as many as 500,000 in 30–180 days. On top of that, the commitment was made to invest in more heavy pre-positioned equipment and forward-deployed capabilities.

The New Force Model, as outlined above, represented the most radical restructuring of NATO's armed forces since the end of the Cold War. Its main feature was the shift from highly mobile and lightly armed units geared for expeditionary operations to robust and heavily armed forces prepared for possible military confrontation with Russia.[26]

3.2 *Involvement with China*

The rise of China had become a matter of concern to all NATO members. However, most of them were not following the US position to describe the Asian mastodon as a direct threat to national security. It was the Democratic president Barack Obama who had ordered a major strategic review of US security policy, paving the way to the so-called pivot to Asia. The greater part of American military forces was earmarked for deployment in the Indo-Asian military theatre. China was prioritised America's main strategic opponent in the global arena.[27] Obama's successors Donald Trump and Joe Biden stepped up efforts to contain China's drive to expand its influence outside its borders, first of all in the Indo-Pacific.

Although the challenge of China had also become part of European strategic thinking,[28] European governments were wary to be drawn into any escalatory policies of the US vis-à-vis its rival superpower. Whereas the US tended to favour a globalisation of NATO to ensure that resources of its allies (like naval forces) could be used to discourage Chinese aggression, its Atlantic partners were inclined to stick to geographical limits on NATO's reach. With the revival of the Russian threat they were concerned to see NATO's strategic focus on Europe diffused.

In the economic domain, too, transatlantic differences came to the surface. Instead of *de-coupling* economic links with China, the European Union proposed a strategy of *de-risking*, meaning that only economic transactions with explicit security implications should be reduced.[29] The European view of China was more nuanced than the American one. Indeed, the EU had defined

26 On this topic, see Dick Zandee, "NATO's Vilnius summit: the consequences for the Allies", *Atlantisch perspectief* vol. 47 (2023), at pp. 23–24.

27 See on this subject William T. Tow and Douglas Stuart (eds.), *The New US Strategy towards Asia. Adopting to the American Pivot* (Routledge, 2015).

28 See Ian Bond a.o., *Rebooting Europe's China Strategy* (Centre for European Reform, 2022).

29 See, for instance, speech by the president of the European Commission, Ursula von der Leyen, on EU-China relations to the Mercator Institute and the European Policy Centre, 30 March 2023.

the country simultaneously as 'a partner', 'a competitor' and 'a systemic rival'.[30] In order to deal with their differences, American and European allies had agreed to turn NATO into the primary forum for a closer trans-Atlantic dialogue on China. It is not a foregone conclusion that this dialogue will yield a common China strategy.

3.3 *Europe's Quest for Strategic Autonomy*

The concept of strategic autonomy was articulated by president Macron in particular during and after the years of the Trump presidency (2017–2021). It refers to Europe's ambition to lessen its dependence on the US while enhancing its ability to defend Europe and carrying out operations in its neighbourhood.[31] The idea of Europe acting as an autonomous international actor was widened to non-security and defence fields such as energy supply and economic value chains in general.[32] Though various motives were at the basis of the concept, it has been fuelled of late by wide-spread fear that the US might be losing its long-term interest in guaranteeing Europe's security. That fear has been reinforced once again by Donald Trump who as a presidential contender in the election campaign of 2024 caused outrage in NATO-minded circles by stating that, if re-elected, he would encourage Russia "to do whatever the hell they want to any member state that doesn't pay enough".[33] Indeed, those inflammatory words could not but undermine the credibility of Article 5. In this respect, the European autonomy goal may be seen as a strategic hedge should any future American president put all his eggs in the basket of Asian security or retreat to a course of neo-isolationism.

It should be stressed, however, that European allies by no means were equally enthusiastic to loosen the bonds with the US. Especially Central and Eastern states were afraid of negative repercussions on cooperation within NATO. They (and for that matter the United Kingdom and some other NATO members) seriously doubted both Europe's will and ability to conduct major military operations absent American leadership. To be sure, as early as 1994 NATO had adopted the so-called European Security and Defence Identity (ESDI) allowing for the possibility of developing a European pillar within the Alliance.[34] But it remains an open question of whether European strategic

30 *Fact Sheet on EU-China Relations*, European External Action Service (December 7, 2023).

31 For an overview of this subject, see Dick Zandee a.o., *European Strategic Autonomy in Security and Defence* (Clingendael Report, 2020).

32 See European Council, *Versailles Declaration*, 11 March 2022.

33 Mr. Trump made his remarks at a political rally in South Carolina on February 10, 2024. See further *The Guardian*, February 11, 2024.

34 Decisions made at the NATO summit in Brussels.

autonomy can be reconciled with the political unity and strategic integrity of NATO. Its advocates believed in the complementarity of Atlantic and European military cooperation, its opponents were convinced that the two are antithetical. Sceptics may argue that the very concept is a pipe dream, since the gap in military capabilities between the two sides of the Atlantic is unbridgeable for many years to come.

4 The Future

Will NATO still be a cornerstone of the future security order? Probably it will. But in light of the problems sketched above the Alliance is not likely to preserve its present shape. Different paths to NATO's future are imaginable. A valuable contribution to the debate about this subject was made by the Norwegian defence analyst Jo Inge Bekkevold. He distinguishes three scenarios.[35] The first one is what he calls *a Europe-only NATO*. The main characteristic of this scenario is the American withdrawal from the Alliance, either because – as the author puts it – the US shifts all of its resources to the Indo-Pacific in order to take on China or due to domestic change in the country. This scenario may be criticised on the ground that its denotation represents a contradiction in terms. Indeed, the Alliance embodies the transatlantic link. Without American participation NATO actually ceases to exist.

The name of the second scenario is *a global NATO*. As the name would suggest, in this image of NATO's future both the US and its European allies shift their energies and resources from Europe to Asia. The weakness of this scenario is twofold. First, the optimistic assumption that the Russian Federation would not pose a security threat to European nations any longer. Second, the thought that those nations would overcome their reluctance to be part of a classical great-power struggle between the US and China. Neither assumption is plausible.

The third scenario is labelled *a fragmented NATO*. Though the US remains committed to the defence of Europe, European allies are no longer pursuing a single coherent strategy. The reasons for the latter are supposed to be the following: different threat perceptions, the singular interests of new members, or domestic pressures. As to the latter, a big unknown would be the impact in various European countries of the rise of political parties of the far right. The

35 Jo Inge Bekkevold, "NATO's Remarkable Revival", in *Foreign Policy* (Fall 2023), available at <https://foreignpolicy.com/2023/09/11/nato-alliance>.

loyalty to NATO of some of those parties should be questioned, particularly given hidden sympathies for Putin's Russia.

Clearly, none of the scenarios under discussion promises a bright and carefree future for the Alliance. But, in this context, optimists may point out that the history of NATO is littered with many crises that eventually could be overcome. Common bonds of solidarity and a deep sense of mutual interest proved to be strong.

5 Conclusion

During its existence NATO has demonstrated much resilience. Its ability of adaptation to a radically changing security environment is remarkable. After a relatively long period of lingering doubts about its rationale, it resurrected as a military alliance directed at collective defence when relations with the Russian Federation deteriorated. This resurrection is amazing since the Alliance was repeatedly declared moribund by western leaders in the 2010s. Its underlying cause should be clear: the emergence of revanchist impulses in Putin's foreign policy. The Russian leader, quite paradoxically, may be called NATO's life saviour. Clearly, the Alliance has regained widespread popularity amongst the large majority of voters in its member states. Not surprisingly, despite deep concerns over the ongoing war in Ukraine, NATO could celebrate rather jubilantly its 75th anniversary on the Washington summit of July 2024. Nevertheless, the Atlantic Alliance is by no means an unsinkable Titanic, mainly because enduring US support cannot be taken for granted. Indeed, Donald Trump's resounding victory in the Presidential elections of November 2024 ushered in a new era of uncertainty for NATO. It is an uncomfortable thought that the future of NATO is held hostage by the whims of domestic politics on the other side of the Atlantic.

PART 2

Preserving the Planet

CHAPTER 7

Regime Complexity in Global Health: The Search for Multilateral Pandemic Governance

*Gian Luca Burci**

1 Introduction

Global health is a field of international governance that has been studied by international law and international relations scholars only recently. The increasing politicization of global health has become particularly visible since the 1990s, in good part because of its overlaps and tensions with questions of human rights, economy and security. Precisely those tensions have contributed to the formation of regime complexes among international instruments and institutions that have become systemic characteristics of global health governance. The need to navigate across different regimes and institutions has created areas of tension and uncertainty that have inter alia been delaying the adoption of a new pandemic agreement. This contribution aims at framing in general terms regime complexity in global health and providing some examples that are at the centre of the discussions on a pandemic agreement as of late 2024. As will be discussed below, regime complexity implies the existence of multiple institutional regimes and requires a thorough study of their building blocks as well as of the political considerations underpinning them. Niels Blokker's monumental reconstruction of the field of international organizations has been and will remain an indispensable tool in this endeavour.[1]

2 Global Health and Regime Complexity

2.1 *International Regime Complexity in a Few Words*

My working assumption is that international regime complex and complexity theories provide an insightful analytical tool to understand the normative and

* The author is Senior Visiting Professor of International Law and Academic Adviser of the Global Health Centre, Geneva Graduate Institute.

1 Henry G. Schermers and Niels M. Blokker, *International Institutional Law* (6th rev. ed., Brill, 2018).

 | DOI:10.1163/9789004699939_009

political framework of global health. Unlike other international legal regimes,[2] however, global health is surprisingly understudied from this perspective.[3] The present contribution aims at hopefully drawing the attention of international law and international relations scholars to the use of regime complexity as an analytical tool to open up original perspectives in global health law and governance.

It is not possible here to provide a detailed overview of regime complex and complexity, theories that are in fact well-known and have been developed and popularized by scholars such as Karen Alter, Kal Raustiala and David Victor.[4] Alter and Raustiala famously defined regime complex as "an array of partially overlapping and non-hierarchical institutions that includes more than one international agreement or authority" and regime complexity as "the international political systems of global governance that emerge because of the coexistence of rule density and regime complexes".[5] The rise of regime complexity is attributed to the increasing density of partially overlapping and non-hierarchical international 'elemental regimes', making it impossible to deal with a particular issue in a single institutional venue and equally impossible to rely on a 'clean slate' to design normative solutions to the problems at hand. Rules and institutional density, and consequently the proliferation of regime complexes and situations of regime complexity, can be explained *inter alia* by shifts in power and preferences among states and the search for representation and agency that may lead to the creation of new institutions and instruments coexisting alongside previous ones. Global health offers a good example in this connection: the existence of the World Health Organization (WHO) as the sole global health agency has not prevented states and other stakeholders from establishing partially overlapping and often competing institutions dealing with specific aspects of global health such as the Joint United Nations Programme on HIV/AIDS (UNAIDS), the Global Fund to Fight AIDS, Tuberculosis and Malaria, and multiple public-private partnerships.[6]

2 Kal Raustiala and David G. Victor, "The Regime Complex for Plant Genetic Resources", in *International Organization* vol. 54 (2004), p. 277.

3 The main contribution I am aware of is Thurid Bahr, Anna Holzscheiter and Laura Pantzerhielm, "Understanding Regime Complexes through a Practice Lens – Repertoires of Interorganizational Practices in Global Health", in *Global Governance* vol. 27 (2021), p. 71.

4 Classical references are Karen J. Alter and Kal Raustiala, "The Rise of International Regime Complexity", in *Annual Review of Law and Social Sciences* vol. 14 (2018), p. 329; Karen J. Alter and Sophie Meunier, "The Politics of International Regime Complexity", in *Perspectives on Politics* vol. 7 (2009), p. 13.

5 Alter and Raustiala (*supra* note 4), p. 333.

6 Gian Luca Burci, "Public Private Partnerships in the Public Health Sector", in *International Organization Law Review* (IOLR) vol. 6 (2009), p. 359.

The effects of regime complexity are equally not linear and often contested. Negotiating on particular issues across institutions and regimes is a challenging task that intuitively benefits more powerful states with the resources to navigate different institutions, rules and policy objectives. At the same time, it may empower groupings of weaker states that use their strength in numbers and the strategic value of the resources they can offer to direct negotiations towards friendlier institutional and normative settings. Forum shopping and regime shifting are frequent manifestations of such power dynamics. The outcomes are not always positive and may result in stalemate, legal indeterminacy or "strategic inconsistencies".[7] It has also been argued that regime complexity may enhance the influence and role of other actors such as experts, secretariats of international organizations, civil society organizations and corporations that can become skilled navigators of regime complexes, advocates of particular perspectives or orchestrators of political compromises.[8] For these reasons, regime complexity analysis has to move beyond 'classic' international law and institutions and use a transnational law approach that factors in the normative role of non-state actors and networks.

It is not a foregone conclusion who are the 'winners and losers' of regime complexity. It is also empirically evident that international regime complexity is usually not an expression of rational design in addressing collective action problems. It is rather the pragmatic result of progressive legalization and institutionalisation of international governance, of the coexistence of numerous overlapping and non-hierarchical regimes and how it becomes inevitable to address new or emerging problems by negotiating across those regimes, in particular when there are different and competing interests. Global health by its nature offers many examples and the current negotiations towards a new pandemic agreement and amending the International Health Regulations (IHR) represent a convergence and layering of various regime complexes.

2.2 *Global Health as Multiple Regime Complexes*

It is fair to say, even with some unavoidable oversimplification, that the political and legal complexification of global health begins in earnest in the 1990s. Global health has always been political, and its history shows how much geopolitical and ideological dynamics and tensions have influenced its development.[9] However, from the vantage point of WHO as the central organization in global health governance, the main normative and policy functions used to focus on protection from the international spread of disease – including through the

7 Alter and Raustiala (*supra* note 4), p. 341.

8 *Ibidem*.

9 Randall M. Packard, *A History of Global Health* (Johns Hopkins UP, 2016).

legally binding IHR – as well as the harmonisation of public health practices and pharmaceutical markets through soft law instruments.

The global spread of HIV/AIDS starting in the mid-1980s changed this paradigm, abruptly increased the politicization of global health and the formation of regime complexes across which states and other actors operate. Reactions by civil society and an increasing number of states to criminalizing and discriminatory measures against HIV/AIDS victims that did not solve the public health problem used human rights as a normative weapon. The progressive involvement of global and regional human rights institutions as well as the role played by the United Nations (UN) General Assembly confirm this observation.[10] The cross-cutting nature of the HIV-AIDS problem, that fundamentally transcended a pure public health dimension, also led in the early 1990s to an uncoordinated involvement of many UN system organizations that resulted in contradictory messages and competition for limited resources. Such unproductive situation and the weakness of WHO led to the establishment of UNAIDS as an advocacy and coordinating mechanism, and in 2002 to the creation of the Global Fund dedicated in large part to funding HIV-AIDS interventions. As an example of resulting regime complexity in the HIV-AIDS space, a number of states have been using WHO and other 'traditional' international organizations to dilute or oppose culturally unacceptable references (e.g. to LGBTQ+ communities) that would otherwise be more uncontroversially used in UNAIDS.

One of the most overt and analyzed situations of regime complexity in global health is the highly controversial and unresolved tension between the protection of pharmaceutical innovation through intellectual property rights (IPR) on the one hand, and the availability and affordability of essential medicines on the other hand, both in terms of their prices as well as of the lack of investment in research for medicines addressing 'neglected' and unprofitable diseases.[11] This imbalance, which is not a new problem in public health, acquired a global political dimension in the 1990s because of the development of life-saving but unaffordable antiretrovirals (ARV) at around the same time as the creation of the World Trade Organization (WTO) in 1995 with its single undertaking of trade obligations as well as the proliferation of free trade and investment agreements. The WTO Agreement on Trade-Related Aspects of

10 Daniel Tarantola and Sofia Gruskin, "The recognition and evolution of the HIV and human rights interface: 1981–2017", in Gian Luca Burci and Brigit Toebes (eds.), *Research Handbook on Global Health Law* (Elgar, 2018), p. 303.

11 Frederick M. Abbott, "Health and intellectual property rights", in Burci and Toebes (*supra* note 10), p. 135.

Intellectual Property Rights (TRIPS), in particular, with its first-ever comprehensive regulation of IPR represented a victory for the research-based pharmaceutical industry and the states upholding their interests. The pushback against the industry's overreach in its pricing of ARV and the human misery it contributed to create in the developing world did not only materialize through bottom-up contestation of WTO and neoliberal ideology, but also through the antagonistic use of other international organizations with an appropriate mandate and friendlier decision-making processes. Developing countries, in particular middle-income countries with a strong generic medicines industry such as Brazil and India, successfully framed the problem as a question of equity, human rights and public health and raised it in WHO, the Human Rights Council and the UN General Assembly. Soft instruments such as strategies, plans of action, resolutions establishing reporting and accountability arrangements and the constant use of agreed language promoting the use of TRIPS 'flexibilities' were mobilized to attack the legitimacy of the hard law of TRIPS, its implementation and its aggressive use to chill regulatory measures in developing countries.[12] This has led to a rebalancing of private entitlements and public objectives but also to 'strategic inconsistencies', uncertainties in the boundaries of IPR law and a 'hardening of soft law' for its political implications, thus rendering the negotiation of new policy instruments as difficult and long as negotiating a new treaty.[13]

The peculiarity of the formation of regime complexes in global health is that, unlike other international law fields such as environment and human rights, there are relatively few binding international instruments having the protection and promotion of human health as their primary object and purpose.[14] Consequently, rule and institutional density is mostly built around other international regimes and the role that health plays in them or across them as a normative value. The position of WHO in these regime complexes relies only in part on the few binding instruments it has adopted so far – the Framework Convention on Tobacco Control and the IHR – and for the most part on soft normative instruments such as frameworks and codes, policy documents such as strategies and plans of action,[15] and even on the epistemic

12 Sharifah Sekalala, *Soft Law and Global Health Problems* (Cambridge UP, 2017), p. 29.

13 Lawrence R. Helfer, "Regime Shifting: The TRIPS Agreement and New Dynamics of Intellectual Property Lawmaking", in *Yale Journal of International Law* vol. 29 (2004), pp. 1, 42.

14 Gian Luca Burci, "Global health law: present and future", in Burci and Toebes (*supra* note 10), p. 486.

15 Gian Luca Burci and Claude-Henri Vignes, *World Health Organization* (Kluwer, 2004), p. 141.

authority exercised by the organization in defining parameters and boundaries for other organizations and national actions.[16] This systemic characteristic of global health makes it essential to factor the influence of soft normative instruments, non-state actors and international secretariats in the unfolding of regime complexity. It also points to the fact that global health is characterized by multiple regime complexes that partly overlap and compete and see the involvement of several international organizations and instruments, with WHO roughly at the centre of such firmament. Regime complexity is the inevitable consequence of this situation.

3 The Normative Response to the COVID-19 Pandemic and Regime Complexity

The COVID-19 pandemic, like some previous health emergencies but at a much higher order of magnitude, shows the inherent complexity of international outbreaks of infectious diseases. The numerous international review and inquiries that have been published since 2021 have emphasized this point and called for holistic policy interventions to address such complexity and avoid an ineffective silos approach.[17] Regime complexity characterizes both the causes of the pandemic as well as its short- and long-term effects.

The proposal for a new treaty to prevent pandemics initially came from the European Union, but its initiative garnered the support of a growing number of "friends of the treaty" and was immediately raised in the 2020 World Health Assembly (WHA).[18] After protracted discussions and hesitations about the need for a new instrument rather than the revision of the IHR, the Assembly launched negotiations in December 2021 and established an Intergovernmental Negotiating Body (INB) for that purpose.[19] Even though negotiations are still

16 A recent example is the role played by WHO's Director-General through his frequent and regular press briefings and other statements during the COVID-19 pandemic: see Jan Klabbers, "The Normative Gap in International Organization Law – The Case of the World Health Organization", in *IOLR* vol. 16 (2019), p. 272.

17 The Independent Panel for Pandemic Preparedness and Response, *COVID-19: Make it the Last Pandemic* (2021), available at <https://theindependentpanel.org/wp-content/uploads/2021/05/COVID-19-Make-it-the-Last-Pandemic_final.pdf> (accessed 27 February 2024).

18 WHO, *COVID-19 response* (19 May 2020), doc. WHA73.1.

19 WHO, *The World Together: Establishment of an intergovernmental negotiating body to strengthen pandemic prevention, preparedness and response* (1 December 2021), doc. SSA2(5).

underway as of the time of writing (and are tentatively expected to conclude by May 2025), the directions taken on the issues reviewed below confirm the insights from the regime complexity scholarship mentioned above about the need for states to navigate within and across different institutional and legal regimes to pursue their political goals on issues that cannot be reduced to a single instrument and organization.

A final but important introductory point is the framing of COVID-19 and the normative response to it as a question of human health to be dealt with through WHO as the default international organization. Even though an international agreement on such a cross-cutting issue could have been plausibly negotiated for example in the context of the UN General Assembly, the political consensus immediately pointed to WHO as the appropriate institutional and conceptual frame. That choice creates path dependency and has evident consequences for a regime complexity analysis, as it requires states to position themselves in other institutions that can promote their political interests while remaining within a human health frame.

Among the causes of the pandemic, the likely animal origin of the SARS-COV-2 virus has again confronted humanity in stark terms with its vulnerability to the spread of animal pathogens (zoonoses) in a globalized and environmentally compromised world where animals and humans are often in close and unregulated proximity and pathogens and their vectors spread northwards due to global warming. The frequency and dramatic implications of zoonotic spillovers, including most dramatically HIV/AIDS, pandemic influenza, coronaviruses infections including COVID-19 and haemorrhagic fevers (e.g. Ebola and Marburg viruses) has confirmed the importance of addressing normative gaps, lack of capacities at national level and a fragmented institutional landscape at international level. The need to prevent or quickly control zoonotic spillovers requires looking beyond human health and factor in animal health, food production (especially intensive farming) and environmental factors in a holistic approach referred to a "One Health".[20] This concept and approach are intrinsically complex substantively and linked *inter alia* to questions such as food safety and the prevention of antimicrobial resistance. They are also intrinsically complex institutionally, operating at the interface of the mandates of WHO, the Food and Agriculture Organization (FAO), the World Organization on Animal Health (WOAH), the UN Environment Programme

20 WHO, *One Health*, at <https://www.who.int/health-topics/one-health#tab=tab_1> (accessed on 19 February 2024).

(UNEP) and various environmental conventions.[21] Joint cooperation among WHO, FAO and WOAH was formalized in a number of agreements at the secretariat level but remained uncoordinated and at times competitive. Political pressure increased substantially as a result of COVID-19 and led to the inclusion of UNEP and the formation of the so-called "Quadripartite" as well as a more productive cooperation that culminated in the joint establishment of a One Health High-Level Expert Panel,[22] and the adoption in 2022 of the One Health Joint Plan of Action to set out future shared activities.[23] It is interesting that most activities have been conducted among secretariats without their governing bodies asserting the organizations' positions, even though each of the Quadripartite organizations has maybe complementary but certainly different perspectives in the light of their respective mandates and the interests of the communities they represent.[24] The draft forming the basis for negotiating the pandemic agreement as of September 2024[25] approaches the problem from a human health protection perspective but reflects the difficulty of regulating an issue at the interface of multiple international organizations. While previous drafts required parties to take into account recommendations and policies developed by Quadripartite organizations, they did not purport to establish an institutional mechanism for the development of joint recommendations and even those references have been watered down to simply refer to support for Parties "from WHO and other relevant intergovernmental organizations".[26]

21 Stefania Negri & Mark Eccleston-Turner, "One Health and Pathogen Sharing: Filling the Gap in the International Health Regulations to Strengthen Global Pandemic Preparedness and Response", in *IOLR* vol. 19 (2022), p. 188; Ginevra Le Moli, "One Health and the Prevention of Pathogens' Spillover", in *Yearbook of International Disaster Law* vol. 4 (2023), p. 334. See also Hélène de Pooter, Gian Luca Burci, Pedro A. Villarreal, "*One Health*" ILA White Paper 22 (2022), available at <https://www.ilaparis2023.org/wp-content/uploads/2022/12/SANTE-EN.pdf>.

22 WHO Press Release of 20 May 2021, available at <www.who.int/news/item/20-05-2021-new-international-expert-panel-to-address-the-emergence-and-spread-of-zoonotic-diseases> and <https://www.who.int/groups/one-health-high-level-expert-panel> (accessed 19 February 2024).

23 FAO-UNEP-WHO-WOAH, *One Health Joint Plan of Action* (2022–2026). *Working together for the health of humans, animals, plants and the environment* (2022), available at <https://www.who.int/publications/i/item/9789240059139>.

24 As an example, FAO has included One Health in its programmatic documents as one of many aspects of its activities or the challenges for agriculture and food production. FAO, 'Strategic Framework 2022–2031', pp. 25, 36, available at <https://www.fao.org/3/cb7099en/cb7099en.pdf> (accessed 22 February 2024).

25 WHO, *Intergovernmental Negotiating Body to draft and negotiate a WHO convention, agreement or other international instrument on pandemic prevention, preparedness and response*, doc. A/77/10 (27 May 2024).

26 *Ibidem*, Article 5.3.

Among the effects of the pandemics largely responsible for the unacceptable level of morbidity and mortality reported between 2020 and 2023 in developing countries, probably the most controversial has been the inequitable global allocation of initially scarce medical countermeasures, in particular vaccines but also masks and other protective equipment. The events in question are too well-known to require an overview or summary here, but it is undeniable that the cause of the unequal and inequitable availability of vaccines (as the most urgent medical countermeasure) lies firstly with the limited global manufacturing capacity concentrated in few companies and countries, and secondly with the behaviour of developed countries that used their financial and political resources to purchase most of the available vaccines. The ambitious public-private platform set up in April 2020 by WHO and other actors to pool the procurement of medical countermeasures – in particular its vaccine pillar COVAX – represented an interesting experiment in institutional complexity in its own right but managed to improve the situation only partially and was later subject to much criticism.[27] The equity and solidarity failure in full display during the pandemic have sharpened the controversies around the effects of pharmaceutical patents and other proprietary rights on the availability of affordable life-saving medicines, as well as the clash between regimes, mentioned above. The best-know example has been the initiative taken in October 2020 by India and South Africa, supported by over 60 countries, for a WTO waiver of IPR over COVID-19 medical countermeasures under the TRIPS Agreement.[28] The highly polarized discussion generated by that request led to a disappointingly watered down decision by the WTO General Council in May 2022,[29] which confirms the inertial effects of decision-making practices in WTO and the difficulty for developing countries to catalyse substantive changes. At the same time, however, the same groups have been using the WHO negotiations on a pandemic agreement to push aggressively for a commitment by parties towards time-bound waivers of IPR as well as encouraging companies to grant free licences of their IPR. Developing countries have relied on the heavy public funding by developed countries of research and development of COVID-19 vaccines and therapeutics as the legal and political basis to justify waiving otherwise private rights. Developed countries, heavily lobbied by their respective pharmaceutical companies, have articulated their so far

27 WHO, *COVAX*, at <https://www.who.int/initiatives/act-accelerator/covax#cms> (accessed 22 February 2024). Ann Danaiya Usher, "A beautiful idea: how COVAX has fallen short", in *The Lancet* (2021), p. 2322.

28 WTO, *Waiver from certain provisions of the TRIPS Agreement for the prevention, containment and treatment of COVID-19 – Communication from India and South Africa* (2 October 2020), doc. IP/C/W/669.

29 WTO, *Ministerial decision on the TRIPS Agreement* (17 June 2022), doc. WT/MIN(22)/30.

hostile reaction in part on challenging the mandate of WHO to regulate issues falling squarely under the jurisdiction of WTO and that should be discussed in that context. This argument implies a form of hierarchy between regimes, with developing countries opposing the same hierarchical claim on a *lex specialis* basis because of the exceptional and specific health needs during a pandemic, and by using equity, solidarity and right to life and health arguments for political and normative support. Positions are far apart on this issue, and it would not be surprising if any outcome would strengthen the 'strategic inconsistencies' that try to weaken the hold of developed countries over patents and other rights but at the cost of an unclear and uncertain overall normative landscape.

The third highly controversial issue from a regime complexity perspective concerns the sharing of pathogens samples and their genetic sequences to jumpstart research into diagnostics, therapeutics, vaccines and protective equipment, as well as the sharing of the benefits deriving from their utilization. This has become one of the major stumbling blocks for the pandemic agreement negotiations, and the regime complexes weighing on its regulation from a WHO perspective form part of the problem. Once again, there is a risk in analysing regime complexity at a time when rules are changing rather than describing a more settled normative situation, but the main purpose here is to show a sense of direction in the building of regime complexes regardless of specific possible outcomes.

The sharing of human pathogens for public health purposes has been reportedly a common practice among laboratories, research institutions and public health agencies in different countries for a long time, guided by uncodified professional norms of scientific collaboration and ethics, with biosafety and biosecurity considerations as the main legal limit. There is little scholarly literature on sharing practices besides influenza, where the existence of a network of laboratories loosely coordinated by WHO on a voluntary basis enabled the selection of strains for influenza vaccines. Anecdotal evidence points to the development of informal norms generated within groups of scientists and institutions specialized in sharing specific pathogens such as HIV/AIDS, poliomyelitis and tropical diseases.[30] There is no evidence of an interest in states claiming proprietary or sovereignty rights on pathogens, and the fact that the

30 Anthony Rizk *et al.*, "'Everybody knows this needs to be done, but nobody really wants to do it' – governing pathogens- and benefit-sharing (PBS)", in *Global Health Centre Working Paper* No. 23 (2021), p. 397, available at <https://www.graduateinstitute.ch/library/publications-institute/everybody-knows-needs-be-done-nobody-really-wants-do-it-governing> (accessed 25 February 2024).

movement of pathogens was largely from developing to developed countries did not seem to raise issues of biopiracy or inequity.[31]

The regime complex for pathogens emerges as an unintended consequence of the progressive shift in the consideration of genetic resources in general, from common heritage to the object of sovereign and private rights. This process culminated in the adoption in 1992 of the UN Convention on Biological Diversity (CBD)[32] and the later adoption in 2010 of its "Nagoya Protocol".[33] Pathogens and public health were totally absent from the politics behind the CBD, whose main purposes were encouraging the conservation of threatened ecosystems and biological resources, fighting biopiracy and securing sovereignty and wealth for developing countries rich in the resources needed by many industries in the developed world. For that reason, the CBD regime places access on an equal footing with "the fair and equitable sharing of the benefits arising out of the utilization of genetic resources";[34] its default structure is bilateral and transactional, with access conditioned on the prior informed consent of the contributing state and on mutually agreed terms with the entity providing access.[35] The Nagoya Protocol regulated in some detail the modalities for benefit sharing, including a non-exhaustive list of monetary and non-monetary benefits.[36] The governance of the CBD and the Nagoya Protocol became the institutional focus not only for the further development of global biodiversity conservation policies but also for addressing incomplete or unpredictable aspects of their legal regimes as explained below.

The increasingly legalized biodiversity regime abruptly intruded in the voluntary and informal pathogen sharing regime in 2007, when Indonesia notified WHO that it would no longer share human samples of H5N1 avian pandemic influenza because of the intrinsic inequity of providing free samples that would enable pharmaceutical companies to manufacture very expensive vaccines without compensation, including for the providing country. The declared legal basis for this move was precisely the CBD's assertion of sovereignty over

31 Similar considerations are attributed to other genetic organisms, e.g. in the case of plant genetic resources that were reportedly considered "a resource that was shared in common and accessible to all". See Raustiala and Victor (*supra* note 2), p. 281.

32 Convention on Biological Diversity (adopted 5 June 1992, entered into force 29 December 1993), 1760 *UNTS* 79.

33 Nagoya Protocol on Access to Genetic Resources and the Fair and Equitable Sharing of Benefits Arising from their Utilization to the Convention on Biological Diversity (adopted 29 October 2010, entered into force 12 October 2014), 3008 *UNTS* 3.

34 Convention on Biological Diversity (*supra* note 32), Article 1.

35 *Ibidem*, Article 15.

36 Nagoya Protocol (*supra* note 33), Articles 1, 5 and Annex.

genetic resources, which was applied by Indonesia for the first time to pathogens.[37] Even though that claim was initially rejected by a number of developed countries as a perversion of the object and purpose of the CBD, it gathered increasing consensus among developing countries as a way to strengthen the leverage enabled by the CBD in a politically crucial area. This successful assertion resulted in an indirect expansion of the scope of the CBD into an area fundamentally different from those originally intended for regulation.

The fear of a devastating avian influenza pandemic precipitated a difficult negotiation in WHO that culminated with the adoption in 2011 of the non-binding Pandemic Influenza Preparedness Framework (PIP Framework).[38] The PIP framework is an innovative instrument regulating the entire cycle of pandemic influenza surveillance and response through the tracking and sharing of viruses as well as of benefits deriving from the production of diagnostics, antiviral medicines, and vaccines. It purports to create a closed multilateral system whereby companies obtaining virus strains or otherwise benefiting from it have to conclude a binding agreement with WHO and agree to share certain benefits with it for distribution according to needs and public health principles.

The negotiation of the PIP Framework coincidentally unfolded in parallel with that of the Nagoya Protocol that was adopted in 2010 and entered into force in 2014. While the Protocol elaborates the essentially bilateral structure of the CBD, it provides flexibilities that have influenced the parallel development of the WHO regime. In particular, Article 4(4) provides that the Protocol shall not apply to an "access and benefit-sharing instrument" consistent with the objectives of the Protocol with regard to the parties and the genetic resources covered by it. While this provision was probably intended to safeguard the FAO International Treaty on Plant Genetic Resources for Food and Agriculture,[39] it

37 Michelle E. Rourke, "Restricting Access to Pathogen Samples and Epidemiological Data: A Not-So-Brief History of 'Viral Sovereignty' and the Mark It Left on the World", in Mark Eccleston Turner and Ian Brassington (eds.), *Infectious Diseases in the New Millennium* (Springer, 2020) p. 167; Gian Luca Burci, "Health and Infectious Diseases", in Thomas G. Weiss and Sam Daws (eds.), *The Oxford Handbook on the United Nations* (2nd ed., Oxford UP, 2018) pp. 679, 689. According to Rourke, Indonesia's claim was preceded by a number of more veiled and indirect statements by some states and WHO that hint at a recognition of the sovereignty or at least the control over pathogens by the countries that held physical control over them.

38 WHO, *Pandemic influenza preparedness Framework for the sharing of influenza viruses and access to vaccines and other benefits* (2011), at <http://apps.who.int/gb/pip/> (accessed 26 February 2024).

39 International Treaty on Plant Genetic Resources for Food and Agriculture (adopted 3 November 2001, entered into force 29 June 2004), 2400 *UNTS* 303.

has been at the centre of WHO's normative discourse as a reaction to the perceived inadequacy of the bilateral and transactional model embodied by the CBD for public health, in particular for responding to disease outbreaks that require prompt and unconditional multilateral sharing rather than bilateral case-by-case negotiations. The priority of many developing countries has been instead seeking guarantees of benefits as a precondition for sharing pathogens under their control, hence the appeal of the Nagoya Protocol as the default legal reference and as an instrument that can provide necessary clarity and predictability to the international sharing of pathogens.

The normative developments of the last few years in WHO and within the CBD governance confirm the findings of the scholarship on regime complexity about the potentially chilling effect of increasing legalization and institutional density and the consequent uncertainty. Fragmentation in national representation in different institutions and at times divergent priorities between national agencies add to the complexity. It can be added that WHO has proved reluctant to move ahead of the protracted and cumbersome discussions in the CBD and Nagoya Protocol governance, thus creating a sense of dependency and hierarchy between regimes based on functional specialization.

Developments on this issue, that converge in the current negotiations of the pandemic agreement,[40] have moved in a number of directions:

1) Whether the PIP Framework constitutes a specialized international instrument (SII) under Article 4(4) of the Nagoya Protocol, an important step affected by the disagreement under the latter on the criteria, process and authority for designation of SIIs.[41] Still, it seems that that Parties to the Nagoya Protocol implicitly consider the PIP Framework as an SII as

---

40 WHO, "Article 12: Vice Chair and Co-Facilitators' proposed PABS design elements". The text has not been posted on WHO's website but has been released by an online media outlet: Health Policy Watch, *EXCLUSIVE: Read Latest Pandemic Agreement Draft Ahead of Monday's Negotiations* (15 February 2024), available at <https://healthpolicy-watch.news/exclusive-read-latest-pandemic-agreement-draft-ahead-of-mondays-negotiations/> (accessed 23 February 2024). As of the time of writing, negotiators have only been able to discuss a number of building blocks of the article rather than actual text.

41 CBD, "Specialized international access and benefit-sharing instruments in the context of Article 4, paragraph 4, of the Nagoya Protocol" (19 December 2022), doc. NP-4/11. The text on Article 12 of the pandemic agreement (*supra* note 38) provides that "The PABS System is intended as a specialized international access and benefit-sharing instrument within the meaning of Article 4.4 of the Nagoya Protocol, and the Parties will implement it as such at the domestic level through the necessary legislative, administrative or policy measures". It seems therefore to leave the qualification of the system to each party, which is clearly unsatisfactory and can increase uncertainties in case of divergent decisions.

there have not been claims that its functioning breaches the CBD, thus creating another layer of uncertainty;

2) The search within WHO for a multilateral approach to share pathogens beyond pandemic influenza. The PIP Framework has been used as a default blueprint because of its multilateral and non-transactional nature and of its presumed consistency with Article 4 (4) of the Nagoya Protocol. However, the absence of an established international network of laboratories besides influenza and uncertainties about the criteria and process for identifying dangerous pathogens cast doubts about how a multilateral framework open to unspecified pathogens can qualify as an SII that is limited under the Nagoya Protocol to "specific genetic resources". Also the pharmaceutical industry, prime addressee of any pathogen sharing framework, repeatedly expressed its reluctance to commit to an ambiguous legal arrangement that could result in onerous obligations and expose it to charges of breaching the Nagoya Protocol.
3) A particularly complex aspect of the search for a multilateral pathogen and benefit-sharing regime is overcoming the transactional and bilateral nature of the CBD and designing a multilateral regime where both access to pathogens and the sharing of benefits run in parallel and are both supported by clear and enforceable obligations. Not only states but also most importantly the pharmaceutical industry should contribute to a measure of equity in allocating equitably vaccines and other medical countermeasures to developing countries. The bitter lessons of COVID-19 explain the absolute priority given by developing countries on this aspect of the negotiations of the pandemic agreement. The draft pandemic agreement addresses this and the previous question by institutionalizing a new Pandemic Access and Benefit Sharing (PABS) system, with most details to be negotiated in a later protocol.[42] This approach, if eventually agreed, may lead to increased regime complexity and be used by developed countries to weaken the impact of the CBD for example by insisting on the status of the PABS as an SII that can be carved out of the transactional approach of the Nagoya Protocol;
4) A final and further complicating factor is the spread of affordable biotechnology that makes it increasingly possible to sequence the genomes of pathogens and turn them into digital files. Genetic sequence data (GSD according to WHO's terminology, or digital sequence information – DSI – in CBD parlance) are progressively replacing physical samples for

42 WHO doc. A/77/10 (*supra* note 25), Article 12.

a variety of public health functions and are therefore acquiring a similar value for the purpose of sharing and generating benefits. Genetic sequencing technology was in its infancy when the CBD was adopted and is not explicitly mentioned either there or, for that matter, in the Nagoya Protocol and the PIP Framework. This omission has created a yawning normative vacuum about the international legal status of GSD and the conditions for its use, which has been partly filled by a growing number of public or private databases where sequences are loaded and accessed by users under different conditions.[43] This situation has injected a transnational and contractual law aspect in the regime complex of pathogen, situating database operators as international institutional actors rather than just corporate entities to be regulated in accordance with the international obligations of their host states.[44] The WHO secretariat has tried to discourage an excessive privatization of GSD by adopting a set of non-binding guiding principles on genomic data sharing.[45] Most importantly, the Conference of the Parties to the CBD has stepped in to fill the void by setting a general normative and policy framework that takes into account the special characteristics of GSD but conditions their sharing to the general principle of fair and equitable sharing of benefits. The decision established a multilateral mechanism for benefit sharing including a global fund, as well as a working group to address a large number of governance and operational issues.[46] Through this decision, the CBD has asserted the inclusion of GSD within its scope and planted the seeds for further layers of regime complexity. The draft elements of the pandemic agreement under discussion include the sharing of GSD within the PABS also as a trigger of benefit sharing obligations, but its design and implementation will very probably depend on the content of the forthcoming CBD multilateral mechanism with the concrete possibility of

43 Examples include GISAID, a private database which became the main platform for uploading sequences of the COVID-19 virus (<www.gisaid.org>, accessed 26 February 2024), and the International Nucleotide Sequence Database Collaboration (INSDC), a consortium of public databases located in the United Kingdom, Japan and the United States (<https://www.insdc.org>, accessed 26 February 2024).

44 Anthony Rizk, Adam Strobejko, Gian Luca Burci and Suerie Moon, "What are the options? Pathogen-, GSD- and benefit-sharing in an international instrument", Geneva Graduate Institute Global Health Centre discussion paper (2022), at <https://repository.graduateinstitute.ch/record/301010> (accessed 26 February 2024).

45 WHO, 'Guiding principles for pathogen genome data sharing' (2022), available at <https://www.who.int/publications/i/item/9789240061743> (accessed 26 February 2024).

46 Conference of the Parties to the Convention on Biological Diversity, *Digital sequence information on genetic resources* (15th session, 19 December 2022), doc. CBD/COP/DEC/15/9.

different groups of states navigating either or both regimes for their own political ends.[47]

4 Conclusions

The normative and policy responses to COVID-19, in particular the ongoing negotiations in WHO since 2022 on a 'pandemic agreement', unsurprisingly build on the multiple legal regimes that address the issues raised by the pandemic and point to regime complexity 'in the making'. While the outcome of the negotiations is still uncertain, they undeniably point to a situation of regime complexity cutting across several elemental regimes and institutions and raising a concrete risk of failure to adopt practical operational measures to prevent and respond to future health emergencies. It is hoped that this short overview will stimulate the attention of scholars in analyzing more in depth the many facets of regime complexity in global health, some of which are still developing as in the case of the pandemic agreement.

---

47 The latest CBD input as of the time of writing is *Further development of the multilateral mechanism for benefit-sharing from the use of digital sequence information on genetic resources, including a global fund*, CBD doc. CBD/WGDSI/2/L.2 (16 August 2024).

CHAPTER 8

The UN Security Council and a Warming World: Coming to Terms with the Security Implications of Climate Change

*Daniëlla Dam-de Jong**

1 Introduction

When I received an invitation to contribute to this *Liber Amicorum* for Niels Blokker, I immediately knew that I wanted to write about the United Nations (UN) Security Council, as this is a theme in which we share a mutual interest. I have fond memories of the many conversations we have had on topics relating to the functioning of the Security Council, whether this concerned the delimitation between Chapters VI and VII of the UN Charter, the Council's role in formulating subsequent practice relevant for the interpretation of the Charter or questions of procedure. In addition, it was a true pleasure to co-author a chapter with Niels Blokker on the use of force for an undergraduate textbook that we wrote together with several other colleagues working at the Grotius Centre for International Legal Studies.[1] Throughout all these exchanges, I have benefitted immensely from Niels' thorough knowledge of and passion for the law and practice of the UN and other international organizations. Having decided on the theme, the next question concerned the angle for this chapter. For this, I decided to challenge Niels Blokker by choosing a topic he is slightly less familiar with, namely climate security. I hope this topic will inspire future discussions.

Climate change – and environmental degradation more generally – are increasingly posing challenges to societies' adaptive capacities. Global temperatures and sea levels are on the rise, the availability of natural resources

---

* The author is Professor of International Sustainable Development Law, Grotius Centre for International Legal Studies, Leiden University. This chapter is partly based on research undertaken for a presentation at a pre-event of the Stockholm+50 conference on the Integration of Environmental Security Risks in Peace Operations, as well as on a chapter on the Security Council and Environmental Peacebuilding, published in D.A. Dam-de Jong and B. Sjöstedt (eds.), *Research Handbook on International Law and Environmental Peacebuilding* (Edward Elgar, 2023).

1 C. Rose *et al.*, *An Introduction to Public International Law* (Cambridge UP, 2022).

 | DOI:10.1163/9789004699939_010

is rapidly declining and extreme weather events have become more frequent and intense. The effects of these environmental changes also pose threats to international peace and security: environmental stress exacerbates competition over access to scarce natural resources and catalyse conflicts between communities (e.g., between nomadic herders and pastoralist groups competing for land and water); it leads to mass population movements (e.g., caused by drought or sea level rise); and it provides fertile breeding grounds for terrorist groups to recruit youth due to a loss of alternative livelihoods.[2] According to the 2023 *Ecological Threat Report*, "[f]or an average increase of one degree in temperature there is a 13 per cent associated increase in intergroup conflict."[3]

The interconnections between environmental stress and peace and security have long been recognized at the strategic level. Already in his 1992 *Agenda for Peace*, former UN Secretary-General Boutros Boutros-Ghali signalled a need to synthesise information from early warning systems developed by the UN with "political indicators to assess whether a threat to peace exists and to analyse what action might be taken by the United Nations to alleviate it".[4] He further stated his intention to make available to the Security Council and other UN organs "analyses and recommendations for preventive action" emerging from these systems.[5]

Three decades after this pioneering report, current UN Secretary-General Antonio Guterres released his *New Agenda for Peace* in July 2023. The new agenda again emphasises the connections between environmental stress and peace and security, focusing on climate change.[6] Among the recommendations for action "to achieve more effective multilateral action for peace",[7] the report contains five recommendations for institutional responses to addressing the interlinkages between climate, peace and security. Only one of these specifically addresses the Security Council as the body with primary responsibility for the maintenance of international peace and security. More specifically,

2 See, e.g., the climate-related security risk assessments conducted by SIPRI on Iraq, Somalia, Lake Chad and Central Asia, available at <https://www.sipri.org/research/peace-and-development/climate-change-and-risk/expert-working-group-climate-related-security-risks>. See also International Crisis Group, *Stopping Nigeria's Spiraling Farmer-Herder Violence*, Africa Report No. 262 (2018).

3 Institute for Economics & Peace, *Ecological Threat Report 2023: Analysing Ecological Threats, Resilience & Peace* (2023), p. 41.

4 *An agenda for peace: Preventive Diplomacy, Peacemaking and Peace-keeping*, Report of the Secretary-General pursuant to the statement adopted by the Summit Meeting of the Security Council on 31 January 1992, para. 26.

5 *Ibidem*.

6 United Nations, *Our Common Agenda*, Policy Brief 9: *A New Agenda for Peace* (2023).

7 *Ibidem*, p. 15.

the report recommends the Council to "systematically address the peace and security implications of climate change in the mandates of peace operations and other country and regional situations on its agenda".[8] The other four recommendations highlight the role of other actors – within and outside of the UN system – in addressing the interlinkages between climate, peace and security, implying that addressing these interlinkages is considered a shared responsibility.

Guterres' recommendations raise a critical question: given the multidimensional nature of climate change and the need for an integrated approach across UN organs and other multilateral bodies in addressing the impacts of climate change and other ecological changes on security, which aspects – if any – should be addressed by the UN Security Council as the primary organ responsible for the maintenance of international peace and security? This question has surfaced in many Security Council debates over the past decades, with some members advocating an enhanced role for the Security Council in addressing climate change and others taking a more conservative approach, arguing that climate change is primarily a sustainable development issue that is best addressed through the UN climate change regime.[9] The objective of this chapter is to provide a snapshot of the institutional questions that dominate these debates and to propose ways forward, based on a division of responsibilities between various UN organs. As such, it aims to build on existing scholarship that focuses on the mandate and powers of the UN Security Council in relation to climate change, while shifting the focus to a broader organizational perspective.[10] For this purpose, section 2 will first discuss the practice of the UN Security Council in relation to climate change. Section 3 will critically assess this practice in light of the *New Agenda for Peace* and other strategic UN approaches, most notably the sustaining peace approach. Section 4 will offer

8 *Ibidem*, p. 21.

9 For an analysis of the positions of the permanent members of the Security Council with respect to a climate role for the Council, see Shirley Scott, "The Attitude of the P5 Towards a Climate Change Role for the Council", in Shirley Scott and Charlotte Ku (eds.), *Climate Change and the UN Security Council* (Edward Elgar, 2018), p. 209.

10 See, e.g., Shirley Scott and Charlotte Ku (eds.), *Climate Change and the UN Security Council* (Edward Elgar, 2018); Anne Dienelt, "The Climatization of International Peace and Security – A Missed Opportunity?", in Sandrine Maljean-Dubois and Jacqueline Peel (eds.), *Climate Change and the Testing of International Law*, Centre for Studies and Research in International Law and International Relations Series, vol. 26, (Brill 2023); Lucile Maertens, "Climatizing the UN Security Council", in *International Politics* vol. 58 (2021), p. 640; Eliana Cusato, "Of violence and (in)visibility: the securitisation of climate change in international law", in *London Review of International Law* vol. 10 (2022), pp. 2, 203.

final reflections on the interconnections between climate change and other environmental factors on the one hand and international peace and security on the other.

2 UN Security Council Practice in Relation to the Security Implications of Climate Change

The question of whether and to what extent the UN Security Council should address the security implications of climate change is a hotly debated issue. A key controversy relates to the question of whether such implications fall within the mandate of the Security Council, given that climate change is a problem of a multidimensional nature and the connections between climate change and conflict are often indirect. In other words, it is not climate change itself that causes or triggers conflicts, but rather its effects on, for instance, precipitation patterns and the implications thereof for livelihood opportunities, sparking violence between communities. Likewise, the effects of climate change can have an impact on the resilience of communities in conflict situations, for instance when a government is not able to provide support to communities affected by climate-induced drought because its capacities are reduced due to an (ongoing) armed conflict. Climate change is therefore connected with both root causes and drivers of conflict, but it is never a direct cause of conflict. It is precisely for this reason that its consideration by the Security Council has proved controversial, prompting accusations that the Council oversteps its mandate in addressing climate change and encroaches on the mandates of other UN organs.[11]

This controversy also explains why the topic has been addressed notably through open (thematic) debates and so-called informal Arria Formula meetings with civil society at the initiative of individual members of the Security Council.[12] The very first thematic debate on the security implications of

11 See Loraine Sievers and Sam Daws, *The Procedure of the UN Security Council* (2014), pp. 582–584.

12 See *ibidem*, at pp. 19–97 on the Council's working methods. For an overview of meetings on climate change, see Security Council Report, *The UN Security Council and Climate Change*, Research Report No. 2, 21 June 2021, Annexes I–III; and Security Council Report, *The UN Security Council and Climate Change: Tracking the Agenda after the 2021 Veto*, Research Report No. 4, 30 December 2022, Annexes I and II. For an overview of climate language in Security Council resolutions and presidential statements between 2009 and 2023, see <https://www.securitycouncilreport.org/atf/cf/%7B65BFCF9B-6D27-4E9C-8CD3-CF6E4FF96FF9%7D/climate_change_language.pdf>.

climate change within the Security Council dates to 2007 and was initiated by the UK.[13] The debate did not produce any results and mostly demonstrated the controversy surrounding the topic.[14] A second thematic debate organized by Germany in 2011 was more constructive: it marked the Security Council's first actual engagement with the climate security nexus. This debate introduced the important notion of "threat multiplier" to designate the impact of climate change on international peace and security.[15] By the end of the debate, the Council adopted a Presidential Statement in which it set out its position towards the security implications of climate change and to which it has since referred in several country-specific resolutions.[16] In this statement, the Council underlined the role of the United Nations Framework Convention on Climate Change and of other UN organs, notably the General Assembly and the Economic and Social Council (ECOSOC), in addressing climate change, "including its possible security implications".[17] The Council further indirectly embraced the notion of "threat multiplier" by expressing its concern "that possible adverse effects of climate change may, in the long run, aggravate certain existing threats to international peace and security".[18] Finally, the Council defined its own role, by clarifying the circumstances in which it intended to consider the security implications of climate change in its practice, namely "when such issues are drivers of conflict", when they "represent a challenge to the implementation of Council mandates" or when they "endanger the process of consolidation of peace".[19] For these purposes, it requested the Secretary-General to include contextual information on the possible security implications of climate change in its reports to the Council.[20]

---

13 Annex to the letter dated 5 April 2007 from the Permanent Representative of the United Kingdom of Great Britain and Northern Ireland to the United Nations, addressed to the President of the Security Council, UN Doc. S/2007/186, paras. 3 and 7.

14 Meeting record debate on energy, security and climate, UN Doc. S/PV.5663, 17 April 2007.

15 Meeting record debate on impact of climate change, UN Doc. S/PV.6587, 20 July 2011, at 4.

16 Statement by the President of the Security Council, UN Doc. S/PRST/2011/15, 20 July 2011.

17 *Ibidem* para. 3. The Council hereby also responded to a resolution adopted by the General Assembly on Climate change and its possible security implications in 2009, which invited "the relevant organs of the United Nations, as appropriate and within their respective mandates, to intensify their efforts in considering and addressing climate change, including its possible security implications". This resolution enhanced the legitimacy of the Council to consider climate security matters. See General Assembly Resolution 63/281 (2009). See also Shirley Scott and Charlotte Ku, "The UN Security Council and global action on climate change", in Scott and Ku (*supra* note 9), p. 13.

18 Statement by the President of the Security Council, UN Doc. S/PRST/2011/15, 20 July 2011.

19 *Ibidem*, para. 8.

20 *Ibidem*.

The Security Council's country-specific practice has in fact increasingly engaged with the security implications of climate change, albeit cautiously. First, presidential statements and resolutions often refer to climate change or its effects in general terms. For instance, several presidential statements in relation to the Sahel refer to the adverse effects of climate and ecological changes as being interrelated with security challenges in the region.[21]

Second, the Council often calls on the UN more broadly and individual states to conduct risk assessments. Resolution 2349 (2017) on Lake Chad, adopted following a visiting mission by Security Council members to the Lake Chad Basin Region in March 2017, is a key resolution in this respect. Under the heading 'root causes and development', the Security Council:

> *Recognises* the adverse effects of climate change and ecological changes among other factors on the stability of the Region, including through water scarcity, drought, desertification, land degradation, and food insecurity, and emphasises the need for adequate risk assessments and risk management strategies by governments and the United Nations relating to these factors.[22]

Similar references to the effects of climate change and other ecological changes on stability were included in subsequent resolutions relating to Somalia, Mali, the Central African Republic, the Democratic Republic of the Congo, South Sudan and Iraq,[23] including calls on governments and the UN to conduct risk assessments and to develop risk management strategies.

---

21 See several of the Council's Presidential Statements on Peace and Security in Africa, including UN Doc. S/PRST/2012/26 of 10 December 2012, UN Doc. S/PRST/2013/10 of 16 July 2013, UN Doc. S/PRST/2013/20 of 12 December 2013 and UN Doc. S/PRST/2015/24 of 8 December 2015; its Presidential Statement on Threats to International Peace and Security Caused by Terrorist Acts of 27 August 2014, UN Doc. S/PRST//2014/17; and its Presidential Statement on Peace Consolidation in West Africa of 28 July 2016, UN Doc. S/PRST/2016/11.

22 Resolution 2349 (2017), 31 March 2017, para. 26. It should be noted that references to risk assessments and risk management strategies also appear in a Presidential Statement on Peace Consolidation in West Africa adopted on 20 January 2017 (UN Doc. S/PRST/2017/2).

23 See, e.g., Resolutions 2408 (2018), 2431 (2018), 2461 (2019), 2472 (2019), 2520 (2020), 2540 (2020), 2568 (2021) and 2592 (2021) on Somalia; Resolutions 2423 (2018), 2480 (2019), 2531 (2020) and 2584 (2021) on Mali; Resolution 2429 (2018) on Darfur; Resolutions 2448 (2018), 2552 (2020) and 2605 (2021) on the Central African Republic; Resolution 2499 (2019) on the Central African Region; Resolutions 2524 (2020), 2579 (2021) on Sudan; Resolution 2556 (2020) on the DR Congo; Resolution 2567 (2021) on South Sudan; and Resolution 2576 (2021) on Iraq.

Third, peace operations and political missions are increasingly mandated with climate-related tasks. The UN Assistance Mission in Somalia (UNSOM) was the first to receive an express mandate to provide strategic advice in relation to climate change, including in relation to mitigation and adaptation measures.[24] Since then, responsibilities in relation to climate change have also been included in the mandates of other peace operations, such as the UN Assistance Mission in Iraq (UNAMI) and the UN Mission in South Sudan (UNMISS). For instance, UNMISS is requested to provide "gender-sensitive risk assessments on the adverse effects of climate change" as part of its responsibilities for creating the conditions conducive to the delivery of humanitarian assistance,[25] while UNAMI is requested to "advise, support, and assist […] the Government of Iraq on facilitating regional dialogue and cooperation, including on […] adverse impacts of climate change in particular those contributing to desertification and drought, resilience building, infrastructure, public health, and refugees".[26] Interestingly, these newer resolutions consistently refer to the UN climate change regime in the preamble, most likely to appease the members opposing climate language in Security Council resolutions.[27]

Where cautious progress can therefore be observed in the country-specific practice of the UN Security Council, controversy over the Council's role has

24 Resolution 2540 (2020), paras. 5(l) and 13. The primary focus of UNSOM has been on mainstreaming environment and security approaches across the UN and its partners; to form partnerships with local and international organizations to deliver interventions on the ground around mitigation and adaptation approaches; and to gather data and evidence and to conduct research on the climate security nexus. These tasks are expressly connected to supporting Somalia's efforts to advance the 2030 Sustainable Development Agenda and its peacebuilding programmes. See also <https://unsom.unmissions.org/environment-and-climate-security>.

25 Resolution 2625 (2022), 15 March 2022, para. 3(b)(i). Resolution 2677 (2023) of 15 March 2023 added a request to the UN Secretary-General to report on "risks associated with climate change that may adversely impact peace and security in South Sudan, and implementation of the UNMISS mandate".

26 Resolution 2632 (2022), 26 May 2022, para. 2(b)(iv).

27 See for instance Resolution 2631 (2022), which contains the following preambular paragraph: "Recognizing that the adverse effects of climate change, ecological changes, and natural disasters, among other factors, can contribute to desertification and drought, adversely impact the humanitarian situation, and aggravate any existing instability, emphasizing the need for comprehensive risk assessments by the Government of Iraq with the support of the United Nations, upon the request of the Government of Iraq, to take meaningful actions to adapt to or mitigate challenges posed by climate change and ecological change, and acknowledging the United Nations Framework Convention on Climate Change and the Paris Agreement". See also Security Council Report, *The UN Security Council and Climate Change: Tracking the Agenda after the 2021 Veto*, Research Report No. 4 (30 December 2022), p. 5.

remained, both at the country-specific and the thematic level. For instance, both India and China expressed serious concerns over the inclusion of climate language in resolution 2625 (2022) on UNMISS mandate renewal, with China accusing the US as penholder for "fail[ing] to heed and take on board [...] reasonable suggestions" by other members.[28] Attempts by both permanent and elected members to drive the agenda forward at the thematic level have also met with fierce resistance by other permanent and elected members. A 2021 draft resolution proposed by Ireland and Niger, which had the support of twelve Council members and was co-sponsored by 113 member states, was vetoed by Russia, with India voting against and China abstaining. Russia's opposition related to four issues, including the Western approach to tackling the climate crisis. More specifically, Russia reproached the West of using the security framing as a diversion to mask a lack of political will to make available funds for climate adaptation projects and loss and damage in the context of the UN climate change regime.[29] It emphasised this point again in a ministerial high level debate organised by the United Arab Emirates in June 2023, with China and Brazil expressing similar concerns.[30] While these concerns are valid to the extent that they point to the need to step up efforts under the UN climate change regime, I would argue that the Security Council still has an important role to play in addressing the security implications of climate change. The following section will assess the Security Council's practice in light of the *New Agenda for Peace* and the sustaining peace approach developed by the UN with the aim of providing suggestions for system-wide institutional responses to the climate crisis, including its security implications.

3 A New Agenda for Peace

As emphasised throughout this chapter, climate change is a multidimensional problem that affects the whole of society. Although it does have security

28 Meeting record debate on the Reports of the Secretary-General on the Sudan and South Sudan, UN Doc. S/PV.8994, 15 March 2022, p. 4.

29 Meeting record debate on Maintenance of international peace and security, UN Doc. S/PV.8926, 13 December 2021. Russia's other concerns related to a perceived one-sided focus on climate change and disregard of other conflict-related environmental issues, the (in)suitability of peace operations in conducting analyses on the complex interactions between climate change and security and the potential broad implications of strengthening the climate-security connections with respect to the types of situations that come within the Security Council's purview.

30 See the Meeting record of the high-level ministerial meeting on Climate change, peace and security of 13 June 2023, UN Doc. S/PV.9345.

implications, the problem can only be effectively tackled through mitigation of greenhouse gas emissions, as covered by the UN climate change regime. This regime also plays a key role in promoting adaptation projects to help affected communities cope with the effects of climate change on their livelihoods. As such, the UN climate change regime, more specifically the UN Framework Convention on Climate Change (UNFCC) and the Paris Agreement, is indeed the primary framework for addressing climate change and its effects on society, including in relation to conflict prevention. Significantly, this regime is founded on notions of equity, which determine the respective (differentiated) obligations of States parties to the conventions.[31] These include obligations for 'developed' states to provide financial and technical assistance to 'developing' states and to compensate these states for damage that has already occurred (loss and damage).

Yet, while the UN climate change regime is a key framework for devising and implementing systemic responses to addressing the causes and effects of climate change, the Security Council arguably has a separate responsibility to address the effects of climate change on security alongside other UN organs. In my view, the *New Agenda for Peace* provides a good basis for a viable approach to climate security, as it embeds this theme in a broader strategy aimed at preventing conflict and sustaining peace. As such, it is based on the sustaining peace approach that was introduced almost a decade ago by the Advisory Group of Experts for the 2015 Review of the United Nations Peacebuilding Architecture and which was subsequently endorsed by both the UN General Assembly and the UN Security Council.[32] In their respective resolutions, they defined sustaining peace as "a goal and a process to build a common vision of a society, ensuring that the needs of all segments of the population are taken into account, which encompasses activities aimed at preventing the outbreak, escalation, continuation and recurrence of conflict, addressing root causes, assisting parties to conflict to end hostilities, ensuring national reconciliation, and moving towards recovery, reconstruction and development".[33] The twin resolutions further explicitly referred to the 2030 *Agenda for sustainable*

31 See Lavanya Rajamani, *Innovation and Experimentation in the International Climate Change Regime* (Brill Nijhoff, 2020), at p. 175.

32 The Challenge of Sustaining Peace: Report of the Advisory Group of Experts for the 2015 Review of the United Nations Peacebuilding Architecture, UN Doc. A/69/968 – S/2015/490, 29 June 2015. For endorsement by the Security Council and the General Assembly, see UNSC Resolution 2282 (2016) on 'sustaining peace', 27 April 2016; UNGA Resolution 70/262 on 'Review of the United Nations peacebuilding architecture', 27 April 2016.

33 *Ibidem*, 8th preambular paragraph.

development and to the concept of sustainable development more broadly as being relevant to a comprehensive approach to sustaining peace.[34]

The significance of the sustaining peace approach is twofold. First, it proposes a strategy characterized by flexibility across the full conflict spectrum, emphasising that "[m]any of the priorities and the tools for preventing lapse or relapse into conflict are similar and it makes little sense to divide limited energies and resources artificially".[35] Second, it proposes further integration of the UN's three foundational pillars: peace and security, human rights and development. Although the mutual dependence of these pillars has long been recognized,[36] the sustaining peace approach effectively brings them together in a single overarching framework.

The flexibility and integration that characterize the sustaining peace approach has implications for the UN as an organization. While the sustaining peace approach does not affect the respective mandates of the UN's principal organs as such, its fluidity does require them to cooperate more closely. This, as the Advisory Group of Experts for the 2015 Review of the United Nations Peacebuilding Architecture noted, is a major challenge, given "the fragmentation of the United Nations, born of the distribution of responsibilities contemplated in the Charter between the Security Council and the General Assembly, with the Economic and Social Council occupying an intermediate and somewhat ambiguous space in-between".[37] This challenge is acutely felt in the context of climate security, as effectively addressing the security implications of climate change does indeed require a multifaceted and coordinated approach across UN organs.

The *New Agenda for Peace* provides the tools to do this. Its recommendations on addressing the interlinkages between climate, peace and security appeal to a broad range of actors. In addition to its call on the Security Council to "systematically address the peace and security implications of climate change in the mandates of peace operations and other country or regional situations on its agenda",[38] the Agenda calls for the strengthening of "connections between multilateral bodies to ensure that climate action and peacebuilding reinforce each other", the establishment of a "dedicated expert group on climate action, resilience and peacebuilding to develop recommendations

34 *Ibidem*, 11th and 12th preambular paragraphs.

35 *The Challenge of Sustaining Peace*, Report of the Advisory Group of Experts for the 2015 Review of the United Nations Peacebuilding Architecture, UN Doc. A/69/968 – S/2015/490, 29 June 2015, para. 26.

36 *An agenda for peace* (*supra* note 4).

37 *Ibidem*, para. 40.

38 United Nations (2023) *Our Common Agenda*, Policy Brief 9: *A New Agenda for Peace*, p. 21.

on integrated approaches to climate, peace and security" under the aegis of the Intergovernmental Panel on Climate Change; the establishment of a "new funding window within the Peacebuilding Fund for more risk-tolerant climate finance investments" and finally the establishment of "joint regional hubs on climate, peace and security to connect national and regional experiences, provide technical advice to Member States and help accelerate progress" on the climate, peace and security agenda.[39] Furthermore, related action points in the New Agenda for Peace address the prioritization of prevention strategies at the national level and the contribution of the 2030 Agenda for Sustainable Development to addressing the underlying drivers of violence and insecurity.[40] It is noteworthy that only part of these issues is reflected in the proposal for a Pact for the Future,[41] which will be submitted to the UN member states when they convene at the Summit of the Future in September 2024. Notably, where the zero draft urged the Security Council "to address the peace and security implications of climate change in the mandates of peace operations and during discussions on other country or regional situations on its agenda, where relevant,"[42] the third revision only contains a general call on the Security Council to "ensure that peace operations [...] [are] part of a comprehensive approach to sustaining peace".[43] These revisions demonstrate a continuing commitment to remove the silos to make the UN more effective in addressing today's challenges, yet they also underscore the controversies regarding the Security Council's role in addressing the nexus between climate change and international peace and security.

4 Concluding Remarks

There is no doubt that climate change poses an existential threat to humanity and other life on this planet. It is also clear that climate change (indirectly) poses a threat to international peace and security through its effects on livelihoods and territory. It is for these reasons that this chapter argues that climate security does fall within the purview of the Security Council's mandate, while recognizing that the Council can only effectively address the security

39 *Ibidem.*

40 *Ibidem*, pp. 19 and 20.

41 Pact for the Future: Rev.3 (27 August 2024), paras. 39, 42 and 43, available at <https://www.un.org/sites/un2.un.org/files/sotf-pact-for-the-future-rev.3.pdf>.

42 Zero Draft of the Pact for the Future (26 January 2024), para. 69.

43 Pact for the Future: Rev.3 (27 August 2024), para. 43(a).

implications of climate change if it cooperates with other UN organs and multilateral bodies, including the UN climate change regime.

The Security Council can make an important contribution to preventing further conflict escalation in countries on its agenda if it systematically considers the risks that the effects of climate change may have on conflict dynamics. For this purpose, the Security Council needs reliable data. The Climate Security Mechanism, an interdepartmental agency established by the UN Department of Political and Peacebuilding Affairs, the UN Development Programme and the UN Environment Programme in 2018, to assist the UN system in addressing climate-related security risks,[44] can (and already does) play a key role in providing the Security Council with the necessary data.

Furthermore, the UN Secretary General's suggestion of equipping the UN climate change regime with a dedicated expert group on climate action, resilience and peacebuilding under the aegis of the Intergovernmental Panel on Climate Change is valuable, as it would enhance the UN system's capability to effectively tackle the security implications of climate change. This expert group may be in a good position to advise the various UN organs on their respective responsibilities. Hopefully, its embedding in the UN climate change regime may also help alleviating tensions within the Security Council over its role in relation to climate security.

While a stronger embedding of climate security in the UN system is crucial, it does raise questions regarding the UN's approach to addressing the connections between environmental factors and peace and security more broadly. For instance, we are currently witnessing enormous losses in biological diversity, to the extent that some authors predict a sixth mass extinction.[45] Climate change certainly plays a role in driving and accelerating these processes, but their causes are more diverse. Significantly, biodiversity loss is largely caused by land conversion and other destructive practices driven by (mostly Western) consumption patterns. Yet, unlike climate change, biodiversity loss has never been placed on the Security Council's agenda, even though it is an existential threat to humanity's survival in much the same way as climate change. Interestingly, the third revision of the Pact for the Future recognizes these broader connections, where it seeks to

> [e]nsure that relevant United Nations' intergovernmental organs consider and address within their respective mandates, the implications for

44 See <https://www.unep.org/topics/fresh-water/disasters-and-climate-change/climate-security-mechanism-csm>.

45 See Elizabeth Kolbert, *The Sixth Extinction: An Unnatural History* (Bloomsbury, 2015).

> international peace and security of the adverse effects of climate change, loss of biodiversity, desertification, water scarcity and water risks and other environmental challenges where relevant.[46]

This is a hopeful development, signalling that the time has come for a UN system-wide reappraisal of the interconnections between security and the environment. It only seems natural that the Security Council will play its part in this effort.

46 Pact for the Future: Rev.3 (27 August 2024), para. 42(a).

CHAPTER 9

Inter-organizational Collaboration: The World Organization for Animal Health and the One Health Initiative

*Jan Klabbers**

1 Introduction

Like all other political communities, international organizations both collaborate and compete with one another. The international legal literature has only recently come to grapple with this, having traditionally directed much of its energy to relations between states and studying such relations from the perspective of states – though there are exceptions.[1] Incomplete though as such a state-centric perspective is, it is even more popular among International Relations scholars, though here too exceptions can be found.[2]

* The author is Professor of International Law, University of Helsinki.

1 Evelyne Lagrange, "Les relations entre les organisations internationals", in Michele Vellano (ed.), *Il Futuro delle Organizzazioni Internazionali: Prospettive Giuridiche* (Editoriale Scientifica, 2015); Jan Klabbers, "Transforming Institutions: Autonomous International Organisations in Institutional Theory", in *Cambridge International Law Journal* vol. 6 (2017), p. 105; René Uruena, "Interaction between International Organizations", in Jan Klabbers (ed.), *The Cambridge Companion to International Organizations Law* (Cambridge UP, 2022). A study of one particular joint venture (the progeny of FAO and WHO) is Mariëlle Masson-Matthee, *The Codex Alimentarius Commission and Its Standards* (TMC Asser Press, 2007); and some work has been done on the position of the EU towards other international organizations: see Rachel Frid, *The Relations between the EC and International Organizations: Legal Theory and Practice* (Martinus Nijhoff, 1995). In turn, the fragmentation debate devoted relatively little attention to international organizations and their relations, more or less assuming that the sources of fragmented rules were less worthy of attention than those rules and their interactions themselves. The debate culminated in the publication of Martti Koskenniemi, *Fragmentation of International Law: Difficulties Arising from the Diversification and Expansion of International Law* (Erik Castrén Institute, 2007).

2 Very useful is Benjamin Faude, *Von Konkurrenz zu Arbeitsteilung: Komplexität und Dynamik im Zusammenspiel internationaler Institutionen* (Campus, 2015); there are some studies on collaboration in the global health domain where also the private sector plays an important role; see, e.g., Chelsea Clinton and Devi Sridhar, *Governing Global Health* (Oxford UP, 2017); Liliana Andonova, *Governance Entrepreneurs* (Cambridge UP, 2017). Some relevant work is done under the heading regime complexity; a fine overview is Karen Alter and Kal Raustiala, "The Rise of International Regime Complexity", in *Annual Review of Law and Social Science*

 | DOI:10.1163/9789004699939_011

The focus on states leaves a gaping research hole: how is it that international organizations collaborate and compete? This brief contribution in honour of Niels Blokker, one of the world's leading (and nicest!) international organization lawyers, zooms in on collaboration involving an international organization that, while a century old, has remained largely unknown: the World Organization for Animal Health (WOAH). For much of its existence it lived in a twilight zone, far removed from the public view and known, at best, to professionals in the field of animal health: veterinarians, farmers, and likewise. This now seems to have changed, perhaps in part due to a growing interest in animal welfare and animal rights, including in the legal profession.[3]

This contribution will provide a brief introduction to the WOAH and will use this organization as a platform for looking at a particular form of collaboration involving several international organizations: the One Health project, emanating from WOAH, the World Health Organization (WHO), the Food and Agriculture Organization (FAO) and the United Nations Environment Program (UNEP). Despite having been launched in 2008 by a (slightly different[4]) group of international organizations and having been widely embraced in circles of health policy makers, One Health has not yet been the subject of much academic analysis beyond the fields of medicine and veterinary medicine,[5] never mind legal analysis.

2 The World Organization for Animal Health

In 1924, representatives of a number of states met in Paris in order to establish an international organization that few have ever heard of: the *Office International des Epizooties* (OIE), since 2003 re-branded as the World Organization for Animal Health (WOAH) and currently comprising 183 member states.[6] Studying

---

vol. 14 (2018), p. 329, while some other work views some organizations as leading others: Kenneth Abbott *et al.* (eds.), *International Organizations as Orchestrators* (Cambridge UP, 2015).

3 By way of example, my own employer, the University of Helsinki, houses an Animal Law Centre: <https://www.helsinki.fi/en/researchgroups/animal-law-centre/about> (visited 6 August 2024).

4 Earlier partners included UNICEF and the World Bank.

5 It is not at all discussed, e.g., in a recent book-length study of the WHO. See Marcos Cueto, Theodore Browne and Elizabeth Fee, *The World Health Organization: A History* (Cambridge UP, 2019).

6 A very useful historical discussion of the emergence of the 'international veterinary order' is Cornelia Knab, *Pathogens Crossing Borders: Global Animal Diseases and International Responses, 1860–1947* (Routledge, 2022). The OIE is hardly present in studies of international

this organization can be interesting for a variety of reasons. Dealing, as it does, with animal diseases, it seems to be a textbook example of the functionalist approach to international organizations: addressing a single topic, exercising a single function, seemingly hugely technical in nature, and without any highly obvious political undertones or overtones – after all, who would be opposed to studies on *Rinderpest*? Who could possibly object to warnings concerning hoof and mouth disease? This alone makes a closer acquaintance worthwhile. The OIE also sparks interest because of the policy domain in which it operates. Initially, its job was mostly to protect humans against diseases spread by animals; and thus it operates somewhere in the interstices between the domains of the World Health Organization, the Food and Agriculture Organization, the World Trade Organization, and a handful of others.[7] And it does so by concluding all sorts of agreements, a practice which may or may not rest on firm legal foundations. Third, it underwent a makeover a number of years ago, complete with a new name and, it seems, a remodeled mission: since 2003 it is referred to as the World Organization for Animal Health. And then there is the prosaic circumstance that in January 2024, it celebrated its centenary. It is not the first international organization to do so, but still, such longevity is relatively rare.

Hence, the OIE (WOAH; I will mostly use the latter abbreviation) may offer a useful prism through which to study international organizations, and yet, this has rarely been done, it seems. There appears to be no monograph in English available, neither from the discipline of international law nor that of international relations, and academic articles or book chapters on the OIE are likewise hard to find. This is hardly a unique situation: much the same applied to a hugely policy-relevant organization such as the International Organization for Migration;[8] in recent years this lacuna has been filled to some extent.[9] But at least as surprising is that the recent popularity of animal rights as a topic for academic reflection has not simultaneously seen an increase of work

organizations. It is not mentioned, for instance, in the monumental and otherwise comprehensive reference work by Bob Reinalda, *Routledge History of International Organizations: From 1815 to the Present Day* (Routledge, 2009).

7 Note, e.g., that there several references to OIE in the WTO's Agreement on the Application of Sanitary and Phytosanitary Measures.

8 Jan Klabbers, "Notes on the Ideology of International Organizations Law: The International Organization for Migration, State-Making, and the Market for Migration", in *Leiden Journal of International Law* vol. 32 (2019), p. 382.

9 Megan Bradley, *The International Organization for Migration: Challenges, Commitments, Complexities* (Routledge, 2020); Megan Bradley, Cathryn Costello and Angela Sherwood (eds.), *IOM Unbound? Obligations and Accountability of the International Organization for Migration in an Era of Expansion* (Cambridge UP, 2023).

on OIE – even Anne Peters' *tour d'horizon* (and *tour de force*) on animals in international law devotes no more than a dozen pages to the organization.[10] Likewise, Alejandro Lorite offers but a few sparing glimpses into the OIE, and then mostly into its output rather than its structure or role.[11]

The creation of the OIE owes, as so often, much to considerations of time and place. Throughout history, mankind had been plagued by infectious diseases, and in response regional health offices had been set up at the edges of Europe: in Tangier, Tehran, Constantinople, Alexandria – so as to protect Europe and the Europeans. And once the US had gained global prominence, a pan-American sanitary bureau was likewise established – this time to protect Americans against infectious diseases. Still, this could not prevent the 'Spanish flu' (so-called because it had seemed to originate in Spain) from wreaking havoc right after World War I, between 1918 and 1920. The flu effectively outdid the war in terms of numbers of casualties, and was thought to have originated in animals. A subsequent outbreak of *Rinderpest*, in 1920 in Belgium, provided France with the incentive to convene an international conference on veterinary medicine, in Paris in 1921. Surprisingly, at least to the French, it turned out that a year earlier in Buenos Aires an International Institute of Foot-and-Mouth Disease (*Instituto Internacional de la Fiebra Aftosa*) had already been set up between a number of Latin American and European states. While this had a more limited mandate (only foot-and-mouth disease), it was nonetheless deemed a competitor, so much so that the French eventually declined to participate.[12]

While the early 1920s saw the Spanish flu and *Rinderpest* result in many deaths, this was nonetheless a period of modernist optimism.[13] The period inaugured a 'move to institutions', signaling a different style of politics and testifying to a belief that the world could be managed and perhaps re-made.[14] After the devastations of World War I, the League of Nations and the International Labour Organization had just been established, as well as the world's first standing and quasi-universal court, the Permanent Court of

10 Anne Peters, *Animals in International Law* (Hague Academy of International Law, 2021), pp. 85–96.

11 Alejandro Lorite Escorihuela, "Global Animal Law, Pain, and Death: An International Law for the Dominion", in Vincent Chapaux, Frédéric Mégrét and Usha Natarajan (eds.), *The Routledge Handbook of International Law and Anthropocentrism* (Routledge, 2023).

12 Knab (*supra* note 6), p. 101.

13 Berman refers to it as a time of international legal modernism: Nathaniel Berman, "Modernism, Nationalism, and the Rhetoric of Reconstruction", in *Yale Journal of Law and the Humanities* vol. 4 (1992), p. 351.

14 David Kennedy, "The Move to Institutions", in *Cardozo Law Review* vol. 8 (1987), p. 841.

International Justice. The *Office Internationale d'Hygiene Publique* (OIHP) had just seen the day, and its benefactor John D. Rockefeller likewise sponsored the establishment of an International Health Office within the League of Nations. And in medicine broadly the future also seemed to smile, given that something as vital as insulin had just been discovered.[15] The Wall Street crash was still a few years away; these were the roaring twenties of champagne and the Charleston. Against this background, setting up an organization for animal protection could potentially kill two birds with a single stone. The 1918 Spanish flu was still fresh in the collective memory, and had avian origins: it was transmitted from birds to humans. The immediate reason, the outbreak of *Rinderpest* (also known as cattle plague), had not been uncommon in Europe, and had also spread to Europe's colonial possessions, leading to a response of sorts in colonies with relatively large groups of white settlers – and less so elsewhere.[16] In other words: doing something against *Rinderpest* might come to protect human life and would make economic sense to boot. Based on objectives formulated in Paris in 1921, states met again three years later to set up the OIE, which became fully operational another three years later, in 1927.

While WOAH's standards are eventually decided upon by member states representatives, they tend to be prepared by experts; WOAH grew out of more or less regular veterinarian expert meetings, and exercises considerable epistemic authority. Those 28 states meeting in 1924 concluded the International Agreement for the Creation of an *Office International des Epizooties*, an instrument which nowadays likely would be labeled 'Final Act' or perhaps 'Framework Agreement'. Quite a few of these states hailed from Europe (and included Monaco), but the meeting also welcomed delegations from Argentina, Brazil, Guatemala, Mexico, and Peru, and even Siam. Morocco and Tunisia also took part, despite not being fully independent states.[17] While the International Agreement announces the establishment of the organization and places it under command of a committee of delegates of the member states, most of the constitutional provisions are found in the simultaneously adopted Organic Statutes, considered an integral part of the International Agreement. The brief International Agreement (eight articles) mainly sees to funding and

---

15 Nick Rennison, *1922: Scenes from a Turbulent Year* (Oldcastle, 2021), pp. 25–26.

16 As suggested by Thaddeus Sunseri, "The Entangled History of *Sadoka* (Rinderpest) and Veterinary Science in Tanzania and the Wider World, 1891–1901", in *Bulletin of the History of Medicine* vol. 89 (2015), p. 92.

17 This was not an uncommon practice: the League of Nations, e.g., counted India as a member state prior to independence.

amendment and its own entry into force, and was initially concluded for a period of seven years, to be tacitly renewed.

The Organic Statutes, rather brief too (16 articles), actually set up the Office and provided a little more detail, e.g. with regard to the composition of the International Committee (its plenary, composed of national delegates with a certain expertise) and the composition of the Office itself, complete with a Director, technical staff, and 'employees' (the latter presumably referring to clerical staff). Most importantly, the Organic Statutes in Article 4 listed the main powers of the new OIE (the text itself spoke of 'objects'): promoting and coordinating relevant research work; collecting information on the spread of zoonotic diseases and the ways to control them; and examining draft agreements. Article 10 further instructed the Office to produce a bulletin, at least once a month, providing information on domestic laws and regulations, information concerning the spread of animal diseases, and statistics as well as bibliographical references. Equally important, under Article 5 member states were required ("by telegram") to alert the Office of any outbreak of *Rinderpest* and foot and mouth diseases, and to provide regular reports on the local situation with respect to nine selected diseases. The main idea was clear: the OIE was to function as a clearing house for information, an administrative agency shared between a number of states with a view to regulating and managing animal health.

Nothing in either document suggests that the OIE can make law. Quite the opposite: Article 2 of the Organic Statutes provides that the organization "may not intervene in any way in the administration of the various States". Accordingly, the Terrestrial Animal Health Code, a thick document in two volumes, refers in its Foreword to the Code as a set of recommendations. The Code is accompanied by a Manual of Diagnostic Tests and Vaccines aimed more specifically at laboratories, comprising itself close to 2000 pages. The same structure is followed with respect to aquatic animals: a detailed Code with provisions on risk, disease prevention and control, and trade-related measures followed by provisions for specific categories (fish, crustaceans and mollusks), accompanied by a Manual of Diagnostic Tests for Aquatic Animals.[18]

The initial focus on farm animals suggests that, as with so many other multilateral activities in the nineteenth and first decades of the twentieth century, the main priority was to protect people (and especially European people)

18 The standard-setting process is explained in Sarah Kahn, "The Role of the World Organisation for Animal Health in the Development of International Standards for Laboratory Animal Welfare", in *Proceedings of the 6th World Congress on Alternatives and Animal Use in the Life Sciences* (2007), p. 727.

against all sorts of mishaps – Knab recalls that this was even the main motive behind the establishment of the first schools for veterinary medicine, in the 1760s.[19] Therewith, the early WOAH fits neatly in a whole string of initiatives, including the establishment of mid-nineteenth century sanitary bureaus at the edges of Europe. The year 1902 saw the conclusion of a Convention for the Protection of Birds that are Useful to Agriculture, concluded in Paris and seemingly still in force in the 2020s. Modernity was all about protecting the human against her environment: taming nature was part of the rationale for establishing river commissions in nineteenth century Europe, complemented by commercial motives in the colonies.[20]

Having been highjacked by German veterinary medicine during the 1930s, the OIE had a hard time finding its feet again after the war. Dissatisfaction with the focus on Europe slowly culminated in a move towards the name change: the French name was replaced by an Anglophone name, already in itself marking a break with Europe's imperial past, with more attention for animal health rather than the much narrower concept of epizooties, and adding the geographical denominator 'world', so as to underline that this was not just about Europe.

3 Collaboration: One Health

Ironically perhaps, one of the big items for discussion during the creation of the WOAH, in the early 1920s, was its relationship to other international organizations. One option was to attach it to the League of Nations and have it become something of a specialized agency in accordance with Article 24 of the League Covenant, but this would exclude (or so it seemed) states that were non-members of the League from participating – and major among these was the USA. Another option had been to attach it to the OIHP, and though the French had floated a proposal to this effect, it quickly transpired that other prospective members were less than interested.[21] At the end of the day then, the OIE, as it then was, became an independent international organization: independent from its host state, as provided for in the Organic Statutes, but also independent from any existing organization. Not surprisingly perhaps, neither the International Agreement nor the Organic Statutes contains any

19 Knab (*supra* note 6), p. 3.

20 Joanne Yao, *The Ideal River: How Control of Nature Shaped the International Order* (Manchester UP, 2022).

21 Knab (*supra* note 6), p. 102.

provision acknowledging the existence of an outside world, not in the form of a competence to engage with other organizations, and not in the form of a treaty-making competence or grant of international legal personality either.[22]

And yet, the WOAH does engage in collaboration with others. One example is the adoption of guidelines concerning meat safety together with the Paris-based International Institute of Refrigeration (established in 1920) during the late 1920s; another is that inter-agency attempts to eradicate rabies date back to the 1920s. Still, it had already earlier become clear that there was a functional need to collaborate. Among the first things the International Labour Organization (ILO) paid attention to, immediately after it had been set up in 1919, was the regulation of the occupational disease of anthrax. Anthrax is a bacterial infection originating in animals but transmittable to humans, through animal products, and turned out to be prevalent in such industries as the wool industry or the leather industry. Hence, the ILO took steps to combat anthrax, as did, at the time, the International Institute of Agriculture (IIA; forerunner of today's FAO) with respect to the protection of agricultural workers, even before the OIE was established.[23]

Most prominently perhaps in the early twenty-first century, the WOAH works together with the World Health Organization (WHO), the Food and Agriculture Organization (FAO) and the United National Environmental Program (UNEP) on an initiative referred to as One Health.[24] The underlying idea is quite straightforward: health has various dimensions, and should thus be approached holistically, or at least from various angles: it relates both to humans and to animals (and reflexively so), and it relates to food and the environment. Hence, health cannot be addressed in self-contained bureaucratic silos, but needs to be subject to inter-agency cooperation.

This creates a legal difficulty, at least from certain theoretical vantage points. Few international organizations are specifically empowered to engage in inter-institutional collaboration, and even less so when it comes to establishing legally binding relations. The WOAH itself lacks such powers. UNEP's powers, as provided in its constituent resolution, facilitate some kind of cooperation, but are not very specific: other international organizations, as well as

22 On this, see Jan Klabbers, "The Vacuum Assumption in International Organizations Law", in Jan Klabbers (ed.), *International Organizations Engaging the World* (Cambridge UP, forthcoming).

23 Knab (*supra* note 6), pp. 113–119. Other organizations involved in the war on anthrax were the League of Nations Health Office and the *Office International d'Hygiène Publique*.

24 On its intellectual antecedents, see Angela Cassidy, "Humans, Other Animals and 'One Health' in the Early Twenty-First Century", in Abigail Woods *et al.* (eds.), *Animals and the Shaping of Modern Medicine: One Health and Its Histories* (Palgrave MacMillan, 2018).

non-governmental organizations, are invited to "lend their full support and collaboration" to the UN, while organizations within the UN system (this covers the FAO and WHO, but not WOAH) are invited to adopt measures that "may be required to undertake concerted and co-ordinated programmes" – this sees to parallel action rather than collaboration per se.[25] The 1997 Nairobi Declaration on the Role and Mandate of UNEP did little to change this, merely adding that its coordinating role within the UN system should be strengthened and that it should "facilitate effective cooperation among all sectors of society".[26]

Far more specific are the external mandates of both WHO and FAO. The constitution of the WHO provides, in Article 70, that the Organization "shall establish effective relations and co-operate closely with such other international organizations as may be desirable." What is more, the same article even contains a partial procedural provision. While it does not specify who shall negotiate agreements on behalf of WHO, it does specify that any "formal agreement" shall be subject to approval by the plenary World Health Assembly, by a two-thirds majority. The FAO Conference (its plenary) is competent to make recommendations to other international organizations on matters pertaining to the FAO's purpose (Article 4 § 5 FAO), and under Article 12 § 1, it may enter into agreements with international organizations "with related responsibilities".[27] In other words, while the WHO has a proper competence to enter into formal agreements, and arguably the FAO as well, things are considerably less clear with respect to UNEP and WOAH.

In this light, it is not surprising that the collaboration is based not on a treaty (an instrument usually considered formal, giving rise to legally binding rights and obligations and thus, ideally, subject to some kind of scrutiny prior to conclusion), but rather on a Memorandum of Understanding (MoU). These are sometimes said to be not so much legally binding, but rather politically binding (which may well be a vacuous category).[28] The most recent version of the

---

25 UNEP, it should be noted, is not an independent international organization, but a program of the UN. It was established by General Assembly Resolution 2997 (1972); the provisions referred to can be found in Art. 4, §§ 5 and 3, respectively.

26 The Nairobi Declaration was adopted at the Nineteenth session of UNEP's Governing Council and can be found in UN Document A/52/25, p. 29.

27 Paragraph 2 of the same article sees to cooperation in matters of procurement, staff exchange, and the like.

28 See generally the conflicting views of Anthony Aust, *Modern Treaty Law and Practice* (Cambridge UP, 2000), embracing the non-legal yet binding MoU, and Jan Klabbers, *The Concept of Treaty in International Law* (Martinus Nijhoff, 1996), arguing that the idea of a non-binding purposive agreement is philosophically highly implausible and lacks judicial support.

MoU was concluded on 17 March 2022, initially for a period ending in May 2023 but subject to renewal – and such renewal seems to have taken place.[29]

Substantively, the text of the MoU is not particularly spectacular. It provides for cooperation and coordination mechanisms and, just in case, provides in Article 11 that each of the four parties can only be held responsible for their own work. It further contains some provisions on intellectual property and the use of names and logos. More interesting though, for current purposes, is that the point of the MoU is "to provide a formal and legal framework for the longstanding collaboration between the Parties".[30] In other words, despite the use of the term MoU, this is clearly meant to be legally binding – it would be nonsensical to create a "formal and legal framework" that would be merely politically binding. This impression is strengthened by Article 1, where under the heading "Interpretation" the MoU is given the status of something akin to secondary law, itself very interesting:[31] "This MoU does not supersede, replace or amend any prior agreements or arrangements between the Parties …". It defers to earlier agreements, which in itself suggests that the drafters recognized the possibility of conflicting rights and obligations.

One Health may well be a brilliant idea, whose establishment was long overdue. Yet, it raises a few questions. First, while two of its parties (WHO and FAO) can plausibly claim a competence to enter into such a venture, this is considerably less clear with respect to UNEP and WOAH. If these are thought to exercise delegated powers, it would seem that the power delegation to participate in One Health is missing or, alternatively, needs to be pieced together by linking various other powers together and constructing an implied powers argument. The one problem with this, however, is that it stands on shaky foundations with respect to delegation theory (or principal/agent theory): where a power needs to be implied, it is by definition not clearly delegated. And the widespread use of implied powers, especially in the broad conceptualization

29 I have not been able to find formal confirmation, but as there have been no reports of the termination of One Health, it may well be presumed that the MoU has been renewed. It would be nice though (and possibly not bad for the legitimacy of global governance) if such things would be reported in accessible form.

30 MoU, Art. 2, § 1. The MoU can be found at <https://www.fao.org/3/cb9403en/cb9403en.pdf> (visited 8 January 2024).

31 International organizations law, such as it is, lacks a proper doctrine of secondary law, relating to the adoption, effects, validity, and termination of the normative acts of international organizations.

of *Reparation for Injuries*,[32] cannot but undermine the idea that international organizations exercise delegated powers.

Second, even where a substantive competence can be found, few international organizations have something like a regular treaty-making procedure. The WHO does have one, to some extent (with the plenary having to approve), but even here one has to guess who decides on the mandate; how a mandate to negotiate comes about; who negotiates on behalf of the organization; and who gets to sign or express consent to be bound. These are regular staples of treaty-making but, with the exception of the EU, conspicuously absent from nigh-on all international organizations, including the UN.

And third, while it is useful to attribute responsibility in advance, the MoU's specification that each organization remains responsible for its own action suggests that there will be very little that can truly be deemed common or joint action. One Health, if Article 11 is to be taken seriously, puts an automatic brake on any far-reaching ambitions; and this, in turn, may well signify that One Health is not so much an attempt to overcome the fragmentation of social life into various regimes or policy domains, but is better seen as a public relations exercise, with each of the parties jealously guarding its autonomy and its own position and prerogatives. The irony then is that when they act autonomously, international organizations start to act like states – so much for the blessings of international cooperation.

4 To Conclude

The WOAH and its ecology provide a nice example of what may perhaps be referred to as functionalism's Achilles heel. Many international organizations are set up to perform a particular, specific function, but most are incapable of doing this properly on their own. The world, after all, is a holistic place, where everything is related, directly or indirectly, actually or potentially, to everything else. As a result, those specialized entities have no choice but to collaborate with each other if they want to do some justice to their mandates, and yet the legal structures for doing so (express powers, prescribed procedures) tend to be extremely limited.

32 Under the *Reparation* doctrine, a power can be deemed implied if it can be seen to be necessary to make the organization function effectively, and that is an argument that can very quickly be made. See *Reparation for Injuries Suffered in the Service of the United Nations* (advisory opinion), [1949] ICJ Reports, p. 174. For further discussion, see Jan Klabbers, *An Introduction to International Organizations Law* (4th ed., Cambridge UP, 2022).

This is highly visible with respect to the WOAH. Already at the time of its creation, a century ago, it was working together with other organizations to come to terms with anthrax and *Rinderpest*, and has done so quite successfully. But from a public law perspective, doing so has come at a price, as it lacks the formal powers to do so. Its member states, to put it plainly, never considered to delegate collaboration with other international organizations to WOAH; and yet it does so left, right and center. What is more: it would be unable properly to perform its main task if it were to refrain from collaboration.

The theoretical problem then is that such an organization cannot meaningfully be seen as exercising delegated powers. The political problem is that such an organization will be beyond any form of control. As long as it stays out of public view, this may not be considered too much of a problem, but the increasing social attention for animal welfare will inevitably also mean that WOAH will be touched by the spotlights. At a time when in western Europe the role of farming has come under scrutiny, one can just imagine what the populist narratives will be.

CHAPTER 10

Weathering a Perfect Storm: Fundamental Questions of Institutional Law in Ocean Governance

*Brian McGarry**

1 Introduction

As Niels Blokker often imparted to his countless students, international institutional law is "a field of study full of themes with variations".[1] This is an ideal context in which to consider the unique rhythms and inherent flexibility of the modern law of the sea: a dynamic interpretation of the classical composition of international law. But is today's institutional framework of ocean governance – which States have pursued so doggedly since the mid-20th century – a harmonious symphony, or a siren song luring us to the depths in a perfect storm?

The present contribution considers the law of the sea in the light of the broader historical trend toward the proliferation of international institutions.[2] One of the key reasons why robust law-making in this field has resisted the periods of stagnation found in other areas of multilateral cooperation is that the United Nations Convention on the Law of the Sea (UNCLOS) and related conventions establish a multiplicity of institutions to address complex and sensitive questions not fully resolved in the treaties themselves. While the landmark achievements of codifying the law of the sea have been lauded by key figures in

* The author is Assistant Professor of Public International Law, Grotius Centre for International Legal Studies, Leiden University. The author wishes to thank Eliza Shyhapova, LL.M., for her dedication and excellent research support during the preparation of this chapter. The usual disclaimer applies.

1 See Niels Blokker, "International Organizations and Their Members: 'International Organizations Belong to All Members and to None' – Variations on a Theme", in *International Organizations Law Review*, vol. 1 (2004), pp. 139–161.

2 See Niels Blokker, "Proliferation of International Organizations: An Exploratory Introduction", in Niels Blokker and Henry Schermers (eds.), *Proliferation of International Organizations: Legal Issues* (Brill Nijhoff, 2001), pp. 1–49.

 | DOI:10.1163/9789004699939_012

the negotiation of the Convention[3] and more recent commentators,[4] a closer look reveals a somewhat more troubling phenomenon: the prevalence of fundamental questions of institutional law emerging across the range of treaty bodies in this field.

This chapter briefly illustrates some of these questions in turn, regarding (2) the competence of treaty bodies, (3) the sources of their applicable law, (4) the exercise of their powers, (5) their independence and neutrality, and (6) their legal status and personality, in addition to (7) as-yet untested questions. The author (8) concludes that this phenomenon arises because of the challenges endemic to treatymaking in the law of the sea and, indeed, the manner in which institution-building has been used to overcome – without fully resolving – protracted negotiations in this field.

2 Competence of Treaty Bodies

A fundamental aspect of international organizations and their organs is the circumscribed nature of their respective mandates and functions. This principle of limited competence or 'speciality' provides that such bodies are entrusted to act only as far as the powers attributed to them allow, and that these powers must be used for defined purposes.[5] In the multifaceted institutional landscape of the law of the sea, questions concerning the limits of these treaty bodies' competence emerge in two respects: firstly, division of jurisdiction between a treaty body and the individual States Parties; and secondly, division of jurisdiction between treaty bodies.

The first phenomenon has recently arisen in the relationship between the International Seabed Authority (ISA) and the flag States of vessels engaged in the exploration of the International Seabed Area. In 2023, activists with Greenpeace International engaged in the "disruption of permitted exploration activities" being conducted in the Pacific Ocean by Nauru Ocean Resources Inc. (NORI), which had applied to the ISA for mining contracts in the deep seabed. This incident has given rise to conflicting views on the scope of the

3 See Tommy T.B. Koh, *A Constitution for the Oceans* (United Nations, 1982), available at <https://www.un.org/depts/los/convention_agreements/texts/koh_english.pdf>.

4 See, e.g., Tim Stephens, "Law of the Sea: UNCLOS as a Living Treaty", in *British Yearbook of International Law* vol. 86 (2016), pp. 225–231; Andreas Motzfeldt Kravik, "An analysis of stagnation in multilateral law-making – and why the law of the sea has transcended the stagnation trend", in *Leiden Journal of International Law* vol. 34 (2021), pp. 935–956.

5 Henry Schermers and Niels Blokker, *International Institutional Law* (6th ed., Brill Nijhoff, 2018), p. 168.

ISA's jurisdiction to take measures to deal with interference in deep seabed operations (including ordering the States and organizations concerned to take actions),[6] and has been the subject of proceedings before the courts of the Netherlands (the flag State of the Greenpeace vessel), which instead considered that such protests remain within the freedoms that UNCLOS reserves to flag States.[7]

The second phenomenon (concerning the division of jurisdiction between treaty bodies) has a fairly long history in the practice of UNCLOS, and has arisen most clearly in the relationship between the International Tribunal for the Law of the Sea (ITLOS) and the Commission on the Limits of the Continental Shelf (CLCS). Whereas ITLOS is a judicial body with expertise in delimiting maritime boundaries between coastal States, the CLCS is a technical body composed of scientists with expertise in delineating between the outer limits of individual States' continental shelves and the International Seabed Area (which belongs to 'the common heritage of mankind').[8] Under UNCLOS, all coastal States have an automatic entitlement of up to 200 nautical miles (nm) of continental shelf from their respective coasts, while entitlement to a more extensive continental shelf requires submitting substantial geological and geomorphological data for CLCS review.[9]

The question of the relationship between these institutions first came to a head during the *Bay of Bengal* dispute between Bangladesh and Myanmar. In that case, the Tribunal needed to determine whether it could proceed to delimit the maritime boundary between the two parties beyond 200 nm, despite the fact that the CLCS had yet to adopt a formal recommendation as to the extent of the parties' continental shelves. Indeed, it was prohibited from doing so, as UNCLOS makes clear that it can take no formal action if a State protests that the shelf in question is the subject of a territorial dispute.[10]

6 International Seabed Authority, *The Secretary-General of the ISA Takes Immediate Measures in Response to Nori D Area Incident* (International Seabed Authority, 2024), available at <https://www.isa.org.jm/news/the-secretary-general-of-the-isa-takes-immediate-measures-in-response-to-nori-d-area-incident/>.

7 See Arron N. Honniball and Pham Ngoc Minh Trang, "On Whose Authority? Freedom of Navigation and Protests in the 2023 NORI-D Area Incident", at *EJILtalk* (Blog of the *European Journal of International Law*), 9 May 2024, available at <https://www.ejiltalk.org/on-whose-authority-freedom-of-navigation-nori-d-incident/>.

8 United Nations Convention on the Law of the Sea (signed 10 December 1982, entered into force 16 November 1994), 1833 *UNTS* 3, preamble and Art. 136.

9 See UNCLOS, Part VI and Annex II.

10 See CLCS Rules of Procedure, Annex I, CLCS/40/Rev.1 (17 April 2008).

Viewed as such, the core issue in such situations is whether ITLOS – or any international court or tribunal, for that matter – exceeds its judicial function by drawing a hypothetical boundary where neither State has demonstrated entitlement to the disputed area. In the *Bay of Bengal* case, the Tribunal resolved this impasse by turning the issue on its head. Rather than ask whether delimiting beyond 200 nm would exceed its competence, it considered in this instance that *not* delimiting would constitute a failure to uphold its institutional mandate, and would stymy the intent of the States Parties to UNCLOS. In the Tribunal's words,

> [i]naction in the present case, by the Commission and the Tribunal, two organs created by the Convention to ensure the effective implementation of its provisions, would leave the Parties in a position where they may be unable to benefit fully from their rights over the continental shelf.[11]

Yet this decision was made much easier by the unique circumstances of the Bay of Bengal, where the existence of a continental shelf beyond 200 nm from the coast had been made well-known during the negotiation of UNCLOS at the Third UN Conference on the Law of the Sea.[12] The situation becomes more contentious when the existence of entitlement to the area in question has not been publicly vetted and scientifically reviewed, as some judges noted in the subsequent case of *Somalia v. Kenya* before the International Court of Justice (ICJ).[13] The issue more recently took on new aspects in the ITLOS case of *Mauritius/Maldives*, in which the present author acted as Counsel for the Maldives at the merits stage. In its final judgment, the Tribunal not only refused to delimit beyond 200 nm for lack of evidence of Mauritius' entitlement to an extended continental shelf, but also declined Mauritius' request to appoint an expert to perform the delineation task that UNCLOS States Parties

11 ITLOS, *Delimitation of the maritime boundary in the Bay of Bengal* (*Bangladesh/Myanmar*), Judgment, ITLOS Reports 2012, para. 392.

12 *Ibidem*, para. 444. See also Dissenting Opinion of Judge Lucky, p. 290.

13 See, e.g., ICJ, *Maritime Delimitation in the Indian Ocean* (*Somalia v. Kenya*), Dissenting Opinion of Judge Robinson, [2021] ICJ Reports, p. 206, para. 14.

had arguably reserved to the CLCS.[14] Such instances shed light on the otherwise 'extensive jurisdiction'[15] that has characterized the envisaged role of ITLOS.

3 Sources of Applicable Law

As noted above, UNCLOS does not prescribe specific rules for the resolution of some of the most sensitive disputes concerning ocean governance.[16] Where the Convention does attempt to define the scope of law applicable to relations between the States Parties, it takes a potentially expansive approach in practice,[17] as seen in Article 293's vague inclusion of "other rules of international law not incompatible with this Convention".[18] This phenomenon, in turn, metastasizes through the codification of related conventions that incorporate similar text.[19] The phenomenon is particularly evident in the context of dispute settlement, and illustrates the autonomy which States Parties retain in determining the legal sources which may be invoked before UNCLOS bodies.[20]

---

14 ITLOS, *Delimitation of the Maritime Boundary in the Indian Ocean (Mauritius/Maldives)*, Judgment, ITLOS Reports 2022–2023, paras. 454–455. See further Makane M. Mbengue and Brian McGarry, "From 'Rigour and Scrutiny' to 'Significant Uncertainty': Threshold and Procedural Questions in the Merits Phase of Mauritius/Maldives", in Tomas Heidar, Naomi Burke and Hyun-Jung Kim (eds.), *The Judicial Work of the International Tribunal for the Law of the Sea: Progress and Challenges – Liber Amicorum Judge Jin-Hyun Paik* (Routledge, forthcoming).

15 Schermers and Blokker (*supra* note 5), p. 466.

16 See, e.g., the requirement of an 'equitable result' (without specifying the means for achieving this) in maritime boundary delimitation under Arts. 74 and 83 of the Convention.

17 See, e.g., ITLOS, *The M/V 'Saiga' (No. 2) Case (Saint Vincent and the Grenadines v. Guinea)*, Judgment, ITLOS Reports 1999, paras. 98, 155; ITLOS Seabed Disputes Chamber, *Responsibilities and Obligations of States with respect to Activities in the Area*, Advisory Opinion, ITLOS Reports 2011, paras. 125–129, 135; Permanent Court of Arbitration, *South China Sea Arbitration (Philippines v. China)*, Case No. 2013–19, Award, 12 July 2016, para. 941.

18 See further Report of the Study Group of the International Law Commission: *Fragmentation of International Law: Difficulties Arising from the Diversification and Expansion of International Law*, UN Doc. A/CN.4/L.682 (2006), para. 172.

19 See Agreement for the Implementation of the Provisions of the United Nations Convention on the Law of the Sea of 10 December 1982 Relating to the Conservation and Management of Straddling Fish Stocks and Highly Migratory Fish Stocks (adopted 4 August 1995, entered into force 11 December 2001), 2167 *UNTS* 3, Art. 35.

20 See ITLOS, *Dispute Concerning Delimitation of the Maritime Boundary Between Ghana and Côte d'Ivoire in the Atlantic Ocean (Ghana/Côte d'Ivoire)*, Judgment, ITLOS Reports 2017, para. 87 (applying the law of State responsibility in a dispute which the parties' special

A more peculiar aspect of this approach to legal sources concerns the extent to which the work of UN bodies finds cross-fertilization and application in disputes arising under UNCLOS. This too has been treated quite expansively in practice. In *Mauritius/Maldives*, for example, a Special Chamber of ITLOS treated the ICJ's *Chagos* advisory opinion – an ostensibly non-binding decision – as having extinguished jurisdictional objections raised by the Maldives (a non-party to the Chagos dispute and non-participant in the ICJ's proceedings).[21] The same case also raised, but did not directly resolve, a question of the legal force of UN Secretariat publications, as Mauritius sought to rely upon the depiction of its CLCS filings on the website of the UN Division for Ocean Affairs and the Law of the Sea. While the contention seems quite dubious in this specific instance,[22] there may be broader precedent in ICJ cases such as *Nicaragua v. United States* for imbuing similarly administrative publications with legal force,[23] and little reason to question the compatibility of such sources with UNCLOS.

4 Exercise of Implied Powers

According to the principle of attribution, international organizations require a legal basis for their activities. However, constitutive treaty instruments often do not include an exhaustive list of powers, particularly where unpredictable developments are likely in practice.[24] As a result, international organizations

agreement had circumscribed as concerning only boundary delimitation, on the basis that that they had subsequently argued on this point before the Tribunal). Notably, the same point could have been determined under Art. 293 by an UNCLOS arbitral tribunal in a unilaterally filed case, without the confines of a special agreement – a symptom of institutional proliferation under the Convention.

21 Finding that the UK was not an indispensable party, see ITLOS, *Dispute Concerning Delimitation of the Maritime Boundary between Mauritius and Maldives in the Indian Ocean* (*Mauritius/Maldives*), Preliminary Objections, Judgment, ITLOS Reports 2020–2021, paras. 82, 203, 243, 246.

22 See the argument of the Maldives in Verbatim Record, *Delimitation of the Maritime Boundary in the Indian Ocean* (*Mauritius/Maldives*), ITLOS/PV.22/C28/4/Rev.1, p. 42 [Mbengue].

23 Resolving a jurisdictional objection by reference to publications of the UN Secretariat, see ICJ, *Military and Paramilitary Activities in and against Nicaragua* (*Nicaragua v. United States*), Jurisdiction and Admissibility, Judgment, [1984] ICJ Reports, para. 36.

24 See Niels Blokker, "International Organizations or Institutions, Implied Powers", in Anne Peters and Rüdiger Wolfrum (eds.), *Max Planck Encyclopedia of Public International Law* (Oxford UP, 2009, last updated in December 2021); Niels Blokker, "Beyond 'Dili': On the

at times invoke 'implied' powers, when such unstated powers are deemed necessary to fulfil their stated mandates.[25]

While UNCLOS includes a provision on the advisory function of the Seabed Disputes Chamber of ITLOS,[26] it does not explicitly address the same for ITLOS sitting as a full tribunal. As a result, the legal foundation for ITLOS's advisory jurisdiction is not obvious. Given that the competence and powers of an international court or tribunal derive from the consent of treaty parties, the issue arises as to whether the drafters of UNCLOS intended to grant advisory jurisdiction to ITLOS. In the *SRFC* advisory proceedings, it was argued that the Tribunal lacked any implied powers of advisory jurisdiction.[27] Furthermore, it was contested that Article 138 of the ITLOS Rules (concerning advisory proceedings) "purports to confer a power upon the Tribunal to give advisory opinions, which has no basis in the Convention or its Annexes".[28] The Tribunal dismissed these arguments through a rather specific exercise of terminological interpretation,[29] and thus did not rely on the doctrine of implied powers in this instance.

Nevertheless, the Tribunal could face greater pressure to invoke this doctrine when addressing the potential revision of a final judgment. While ITLOS explicitly recognizes the power to revise its own judgments in its Rules, there appears to be no clear textual basis for this power in UNCLOS. This raises important questions about the source of such authority and whether ITLOS could, if challenged, justify revision on the basis of implied (or 'inherent') powers.[30]

Powers and Practice of International Organizations", in Gerard Kreijen a.o. (eds.), *State, Sovereignty, and International Governance* (Oxford UP, 2002).

25 See ICJ, *Certain Expenses of the United Nations (Article 17, paragraph 2, of the Charter)*, Advisory Opinion, [1962] ICJ Reports, p. 151.

26 UNCLOS, Art. 191.

27 ITLOS, *Request for an Advisory Opinion submitted by the Sub-Regional Fisheries Commission*, Advisory Opinion, ITLOS Reports 2015, para. 41.

28 *Written Statement of the United Kingdom of Great Britain and Northern Ireland* (SRFC Advisory Opinion, ITLOS, 2014), para. 10.

29 ITLOS, *SRFC Advisory Opinion* (*supra* note 27), paras. 53, 58. See also ITLOS, *Request for an Advisory Opinion submitted by the Commission of Small Island States on Climate Change and International Law*, Advisory Opinion, ITLOS Reports 2024–2025, para. 89.

30 For a theoretical distinction between these concepts, see Brian McGarry and Nasim Zargarinejad, "Tracing the Powers of WTO MPIA Arbitrators", in *McGill Journal of Dispute Resolution*, vol. 8(2) (2022), pp 6–8. Addressing the issue in the context of revision, see Iran-United States Claims Tribunal, *Decision No. DEC 133-485-1* (17 November, 2004), para. 43.

On the other hand, the argument could be made that the power of ITLOS to revise its judgments has been tacitly accepted by Member States through acquiescence. For example, in the *SRFC* advisory opinion, Judge Cot suggested that the mere publication of the Tribunal's procedural rules, without formal objection from States, could be seen as a form of implicit consent to those rules.[31] This reasoning arguably aligns with broader principles in international law, such as the absence of protest by States being taken as consent (as seen in the aforementioned ICJ case of *Nicaragua v. United States*, as well as its advisory opinion in *Namibia*).[32] However, it is unclear whether such an argument of tacit amendment may be properly applied to a treaty such as UNCLOS, as it includes formal amendment mechanisms[33] and, as noted above, appears to provide no specific textual basis on which a power of revision might be plausibly founded. The question of implied powers is thus likely to re-emerge in the future practice of the Convention.

5 Independence and Neutrality

The independence of the international civil service is widely recognized as a cornerstone of international organizations.[34] In its advisory opinion in *Reparation for Injuries*, the ICJ emphasized that the independence of agents of the UN is essential to the effective operation of the organization itself.[35] In the *Immunity from Legal Process of a Special Rapporteur* advisory opinion, the ICJ reaffirmed that the independence granted to UN officials is not for their personal advantage, but rather to enable them to effectively carry out the responsibilities bestowed by the organization.[36]

Institutions such as the ISA rely on the impartiality and integrity of their officers to maintain legitimacy and trust in the international arena. There is thus a connection between this operational independence and the neutrality

31 Declaration of Judge Cot in ITLOS, *SRFC Advisory Opinion* (*supra* note 27), para. 4.

32 Interpreting Art. 27 of the UN Charter, see ICJ, *Legal Consequences for States of the Continued Presence of South Africa in Namibia (South West Africa) notwithstanding Security Council Resolution 276 (1970)*, Advisory Opinion, [1971] ICJ Reports, p. 16.

33 See UNCLOS, Arts. 312–316.

34 Schermers and Blokker (*supra* note 5), p. 387.

35 ICJ, *Reparation for injuries suffered in the services of the United Nations*, Advisory Opinion, [1949] ICJ Reports, p. 183.

36 ICJ, *Difference Relating to Immunity from Legal Process of a Special Rapporteur of the Commission on Human Rights*, Advisory Opinion, [1999] ICJ Reports, p. 62, para. 51.

of the organization itself. However, neutrality must not be confused with passive indifference. This idea was articulated by the then UN Secretary-General Dag Hammarskjöld, who emphasized that neutrality means upholding the law and the common values of the organization.[37] Hammarskjöld further observed that "the international civil servant cannot be accused of lack of neutrality simply for taking a stand on a controversial issue when this is his duty and cannot be avoided".[38]

In practice, certain tensions can arise between independence and perceived partiality. In an illustrative case, Michael Lodge, the outgoing Secretary-General of the ISA, was recently accused of favouring corporate interests, specifically in relation to the aforementioned situation of NORI's application for mining contracts in the deep seabed.[39] Following protests by Greenpeace International, Secretary-General Lodge issued a letter calling for an end to the demonstrations, and urging the Netherlands (as the flag state of the Greenpeace vessel) to take measures against the protestors.[40] Several civil society organizations and some Member States expressed concerns that the Secretary-General's leadership may be influenced by NORI's corporate interests,[41] citing his participation in commercial advertisements promoting seabed mining activities[42] and statements endorsing the institution of industrial-scale mining in the Pacific Ocean.[43]

In this context, the principle outlined by Hammarskjöld becomes particularly relevant. If Lodge's actions are viewed as grounded in the ISA's mandate and the principles of UNCLOS – an entirely plausible view in light of the extensive

37 Mona Ali Khalil, "The Quintessential Attribute of the UN's Moral Authority in Ukraine" (1 November 2022), available at <https://untoday.org/the-un-must-be-impartial-to-the-parties-but-not-neutral-to-the-law/>.

38 Dag Hammarskjöld Foundation, *Oxford Speech*, available at <https://www.daghammarskjold.se/wp-content/uploads/2019/10/ics_100_no_4_oxfordspeech.pdf>.

39 DSM Campaign, *Why the Rush?* (2022), available at <https://dsm-campaign.org/wp-content/uploads/2022/07/Why-the-Rush_WEB.pdf>.

40 International Seabed Authority (*supra* note 6).

41 See the views of Germany's Minister for Economic Affairs and Climate Action in Franziska Brantner, *Letter to Michael Lodge, Secretary-General of the International Seabed Authority, and Tomasz Abramowski, President of the Council of the International Seabed Authority* (16 March 2023), available at <https://uploads.guim.co.uk/2023/03/20/full.pdf>.

42 Los Angeles Times, *Seabed mining company promo* (19 April 2022), available at <https://www.latimes.com/00000180-0150-dd9c-a5ca-ff75c88e0000-123>.

43 New York Times, *Leader of international seabed mining agency admonished by diplomats* (8 March 2023), available at <https://www.nytimes.com/2023/03/19/us/politics/seabed-mining-metals-united-nations.html>.

negotiation (and renegotiation)[44] of UNCLOS Part XI – then the aforementioned facts might be seen instead as a reflection of his commitment to the purpose of this legal framework, rather than evidence of improper influence. In this light, uncertainty concerning the future direction of UNCLOS institutions underscores the continuing relevance of Hammarskjöld's conceptualization of independence and neutrality in the practice of international organizations.

6 Legal Status and Personality

As the ICJ observed in its landmark advisory opinion on *Reparation for Injuries*, an international organization may be defined as "an entity possessing objective international personality, and not merely personality recognized by [its Member States] alone, together with capacity to bring international claims".[45] This most fundamental of questions in international institutional law has recently attached not to any institutions established by UNCLOS, but rather to the legal character of an entity which sought to make use of these institutions.

The Commission of Small Island States on Climate Change and International Law (COSIS) was established in 2021 by two States, Antigua and Barbuda on the one hand, and Tuvalu on the other. One of the few purposes stated in its constitutive treaty is to request advisory opinions from ITLOS in relation to climate change.[46] After it sought an advisory opinion clarifying the link between greenhouse gas emissions and UNCLOS obligations to protect and not pollute the marine environment,[47] some UNCLOS States Parties raised jurisdictional objections or concerns on the basis that they did not consider COSIS to be a genuine international organization.[48] The general tenor of these protests was that COSIS had exploited the Tribunal's advisory competence – and the

44 See Agreement relating to the Implementation of Part XI of the United Nations Convention on the Law of the Sea of 10 December 1982, 1836 *UNTS* 3 (New York, 28 July 1994).

45 ICJ, *Reparation for Injuries* (*supra* note 35), pp. 174, 185.

46 Agreement for the Establishment of the Commission of Small Island States on Climate Change and International Law (adopted 31 October 2021), Art. 2(2).

47 ITLOS, *Request for an Advisory Opinion submitted by the Commission of Small Island States on Climate Change and International Law*, Order of 16 December 2022, ITLOS Reports 2022–2023, p. 191.

48 See, e.g., *Written Statement of the United Kingdom of Great Britain and Northern Ireland* (16 June 2023), para. 18. See further Separate Opinion of Judge Kittichaisaree in ITLOS, *COSIS Advisory Opinion* (*supra* note 29), para. 6.

requirement that such requests be filed by an international organization[49] – in the manner of an *abus de droit*.

Following proceedings in which the present author acted as Counsel and Advocate for COSIS, however, ITLOS found in its 2024 advisory opinion that COSIS had been established as an intergovernmental organization and imbued with international legal personality.[50] What is particularly notable about COSIS's arguments on this point is that it provided evidence of its 'legitimacy' by utilizing an entirely separate institutional channel: a request to participate in the ICJ's own advisory proceedings regarding climate change, which is open only to States and international organizations.[51] The ICJ's acceptance of this request was invoked by COSIS at the ITLOS hearings a few short months later.[52] This suggests the potential for shaping the recognition and perceived legitimacy of international organizations not only on the basis of their internal features, but also through the cross-fertilization of acceptance in the broader international legal community – including through strategic, multi-forum litigation.

7 Untested Questions

Since the adoption of UNCLOS in 1982, the gradual establishment of key structures in ocean governance has continued to raise novel questions. This evolutionary process is particularly evident in the Enterprise, one of the most complex – and as-yet untested – institutional designs in the UNCLOS framework. The Enterprise is not only a treaty body but also a commercial entity, and is ultimately responsible for the effective implementation of the principle of the common heritage of mankind in the deep seabed (i.e., through the equitable distribution of the proceeds of mining in this area, once exploitation of these mineral resources has begun).[53]

49 See ITLOS, Rules of the Tribunal (adopted 28 October 1997, amended 17 March 2009), para. 138. See further Tafsir Malick Ndiaye, "The Advisory Function of the International Tribunal for the Law of the Sea", in *Chinese Journal of International Law*, vol. 9 (2010), pp. 565–588.

50 ITLOS, *COSIS Advisory Opinion* (*supra* note 29), paras. 99–100.

51 ICJ, *The Court Authorizes the Commission of Small Island States on Climate Change and International Law to Participate in the Proceedings* (Press Release, 22 June 2023).

52 See Verbatim Record, *Request for an Advisory Opinion submitted by the Commission of Small Island States on Climate Change and International Law*, 12 September 2023, ITLOS/PV.23/C31/3/Rev.1, p. 4 [McGarry].

53 See UNCLOS Art. 153(2)(a); Art. 3 of Annexes III and IV; and section 2(2) of the Annex to the 1994 Implementing Agreement. See also International Seabed Authority,

The Enterprise is currently run by an interim director, but does not operate independently.[54] As of 2024, the Secretariat of the ISA continues performing the functions of the Enterprise during this interim period.[55] Criticisms of the Enterprise's mandate and functionality have been voiced since the negotiation of UNCLOS itself, and reflect entrenched divisions between the Global South and North on the management of the common heritage of mankind. As with the examples discussed above, these criticisms are likely to manifest in myriad institutional questions once the system for resource exploitation outlined in UNCLOS Part XI is ultimately tested.

Looking beyond UNCLOS, it is notable that the 2023 UN Agreement on the Conservation and Sustainable Use of Marine Biological Diversity of Areas beyond National Jurisdiction (BBNJ Agreement) introduces several institutional mechanisms to ensure the protection and sustainable use of biodiversity in the high seas. These include a Conference of Parties,[56] a Clearing-House Mechanism,[57] and a funding system,[58] which collectively aim to coordinate international efforts regarding marine biodiversity.

Among the many principles stipulated in the BBNJ Agreement, two are of particular note in the present context. First, this treaty recognizes the special circumstances of small island developing States and least developed countries, acknowledging their vulnerability and need for additional support in marine conservation efforts.[59] Second, it incorporates the principle of equity, ensuring the fair and equitable sharing of benefits derived from the use of marine biological resources.[60] Balancing these treaty principles with the operational mechanisms established therein is all but certain to raise institutional questions and challenges in practice.

Operationalization of the Enterprise (2022), available at <https://www.isa.org.jm/wp-content/uploads/2022/06/Operationalization_of_the_Enterprise.pdf>.

54 International Seabed Authority, *The Enterprise*, available at <https://www.isa.org.jm/organs/the-enterprise/>.

55 *Ibidem.*

56 United Nations, Text of the Agreement under the United Nations Convention on the Law of the Sea on the Conservation and Sustainable Use of Marine Biological Diversity of Areas Beyond National Jurisdiction (2024), available at <https://www.un.org/bbnjagreement/sites/default/files/2024-08/Text%20of%20the%20Agreement%20in%20English.pdf>.

57 *Ibidem*, Art. 51.

58 *Ibidem*, Art. 52.

59 *Ibidem*, Art. 9(b).

60 *Ibidem*, Art. 14.

8 Conclusion

The law of the sea has been praised for maintaining momentum in international law-making, even as other areas of multilateral negotiation have faced significant decline. UNCLOS and related treaties have achieved this, in part, by delegating many of the more complex, contentious, and unresolved issues to the institutions they establish. By leaving the thorniest questions to be addressed over time by these institutions, the Convention has allowed for continuous development and adaptation, even when foundational disagreements arise over their roles and functions. Treatymakers in this field thus have the unenviable task of codifying an agreed approach to the sensitive, contentious, and evolving issues that characterise ocean governance. This framework moreover prioritizes the development of flexible institutional mechanisms, further heightening the challenges of this field.

Yet in the present author's view, perhaps the greatest challenges that distinguish law-making in the world's ocean is the fact that effective and efficient legal implementation requires a perfect storm of (i) comprehensive coverage across a broad range of subject-matter, (ii) widespread ratification, and (iii) a 'package deal' approach that prohibits customized reservations.[61] Striving for these ideals enhances the coherence of the law of the sea and the object and purpose of its underlying conventions, but makes consensus impracticable without robust institution-building and gap-filling. In this unique setting, dormant disagreements eventually give bloom to an extraordinary array of questions that remain central to the law and practice of international organizations.

While the rhythm of this field's development is tempestuous, this has not given way to legal fragmentation or a precipitous decline in the will of States to cooperate toward greater institutionalisation of ocean governance. For all its halting movements and swaying modulations, the institutional framework of the law of the sea is thus more symphony than siren song. Indeed, the ebb and flow of this composition bears the hallmarks of Professor Blokker's variations on a musical theme, and recalls the 'unity within diversity' for which he will remain celebrated.

61 See further Tommy Koh, "Negotiating the UN Convention on the Law of the Sea: a practitioner's reflection", in Simon Chesterman, David M. Malone and Santiago Villalpando (eds.), *The Oxford Handbook of United Nations Treaties* (Oxford UP, 2019), pp. 539–542.

CHAPTER 11

The Quadripartite: Building Alliances between the WHO, the FAO, WOAH and UNEP

*André Nollkaemper**

1 Introduction

This contribution is written in honour of the work and legacy of Niels Blokker. Throughout his career, he has made significant contributions to the knowledge and understanding of the law and practice of international institutions. The field of international institutions is ever evolving to keep pace with the development of shared interests of states and the wider international community. The emergence of the little known Quadripartite, discussed in this contribution, is yet another example of the evolution.

Yuval Noah Harari observed that "modern industrial agriculture might well be the greatest crime in history".[1] Every year, billions of animals are born, live and die in industrialised farms where they are subjected to industrial management practices, with the aim of achieving maximum yields of output per animal.[2] Cattle, pigs, poultry, and sheep live and die together in overcrowded spaces or alone in narrow cages, leading to stress, aggression and inability to display natural behaviour, and experience additional suffering during transport and slaughter.

* The author is University Professor of International Law and Sustainability, University of Amsterdam.

1 Yuval Noah Harari, "Industrial Farming Is One of the Worst Crimes in History", in *The Guardian* of 25 September 2015.

2 Heinrich Böll Stiftung, *Meat Atlas 2021: Facts and Figures about the Animals We Eat*, available at <https://eu.boell.org/en/MeatAtlas>, accessed 25 December 2021; Marco Liverani a.o., "Understanding and Managing Zoonotic Risk in the New Livestock Industries", in *Environmental Health Perspectives* (2013), p. 873; James M. MacDonald, "CAFOs: Farm Animals and Industrialized Livestock Production", in Richard W. Hazlett (ed.), *The Oxford Encyclopedia of Agriculture and the Environment* (Oxford UP, 2020); William Gilbert a.o., "Review: Mitigating the Risks Posed by Intensification in Livestock Production: The Examples of Antimicrobial Resistance and Zoonoses", in *Animal: An International Journal of Animal Bioscience* vol. 15 (2021), pp. 100–123; G.M. Cronin a.o. "Lessons Learned from Past Experience with Intensive Livestock Management Systems", in *Revue scientifique et technique* (published by OIE) vol. 33 (2014), p. 139.

 | DOI:10.1163/9789004699939_013

While initially international law supported this process with a view to meet the nutritional needs of a growing population, in the past decades states and international institutions have sought to address the worst excesses of this situation. They allowed the World Organization for Animal Health (WOAH)[3] to transition from an organization solely focused on animal health problems that created risks for humans, to an organization that professes to protect animal welfare world-wide.[4] In 2005 it incorporated animal welfare standards in the Terrestrial Animal Health Code (TAHC),[5] a comprehensive international set of standards for the protection of farm animals, signalling that animal welfare "had become an issue for official attention at a global level".[6]

Although WOAH has achieved remarkable progress in the past two decades, its regime is limited in fundamental respects. The TAHC is not legally binding, it lacks concrete indicators of animal welfare, and its scope is limited. For the most part, it addresses conditions *inside* intensive animal farms. It does not provide regulations that may reduce the scale of industrial farming, by targeting the supply-side (e.g. reducing subsidies for intensive livestock farming, granting subsidies for organic farming, providing support for plant-based options and cultured meat) and/or the demand side (e.g. higher taxes on meat, labelling and information campaigns, supporting non-meat consumption in public catering, or financial support to help low-income households purchase food produced in an environmentally friendly manner).[7] Developing a regulatory approach that includes such supply and demand measures presents a huge challenge at the national and regional levels (where the EU is a frontrunner

3 In 1924, the WOAH was set up as the International Agreement for the Creation of an Office International des Épizooties (OIE). The organization used the name OIE – also in English language documents – until May 2022, when the organization started to use the new name and acronym to provide more clarity to its mandate; see *The World Organisation for Animal Health launches its refreshed brand identity.* <https://www.woah.org/en/the-world-organisation-for-animal-health-launches-its-refreshed-brand-identity/>. In this article I will use the name WOAH, but I still will refer to OIE for older documents that used the initial name. See on the WOAH also the contribution by Klabbers elsewhere in this volume.

4 OIE – World Organisation for Animal Health, *Strategy*, available at <https://www.oie.int/en/who-we-are/strategy/>, accessed 13 March 2022.

5 *Terrestrial Animal Health Code* (as amended in May 2021 by the World Assembly of Delegates of the OIE), Art. 7.1.1. WOAH published the first edition in 1968; this edition as well as all later editions until 2004 were only concerned with animal health. For a rare discussion, see Anne Peters, *Animals in International Law* (2021), pp. 85–97.

6 David Fraser, "Toward a Global Perspective on Farm Animal Welfare", in *Applied Animal Behaviour Science* vol. 113 (2008), pp. 330, 331.

7 Céline Bonnet a.o., "Viewpoint: Regulating Meat Consumption to Improve Health, the Environment and Animal Welfare", in *Food Policy* vol. 97 (2020), pp. 101847.

with its 'Farm to Fork' strategy),[8] and much more so at the global level. WOAH is not well positioned to push this agenda. Given world-wide differences in cultures, socio-economic situations, cultural values, consumer preferences and perspectives on animal welfare, states are unlikely to support a more demanding WOAH regime that is based on the intrinsic value of animal welfare.

In this situation, the activities of other international institutions are critical. Industrial animal farming does not only harm animals but also humans. A variety of international institutions have acted to address such impacts, in particular in relation to the global economy, human health and climate change. These institutions, that together form a regime complex for meat production,[9] include the World Health Organization (WHO), that has recognized the close connections between animal welfare and human health,[10] the Conferences of the Parties to the UN Climate Change Convention that could reduce the scale of the livestock industry to curtail climate change,[11] and the United Nations Environment Programme (UNEP) that aspires to reduce nitrogen pollution, which could require reductions in the scale of intensive farming.[12] The prospect for improved legal protection of the welfare of farm animals does not only depend on WOAH's own practices but also on the ability of WOAH to engage in alliances with these 'human-centred' international institutions.

In this paper, I will focus on one particular type of alliance. In 2010, FAO, OIE (now WOAH), and WHO formed the Tripartite to implement connected strategies.[13] In 2022, the Tripartite organizations partnered with the UNEP,

8 European Commission, *Communication from the Commission to the European Parliament, the Council, the European Economic and Social Committee and the Committee of the Regions: A Farm to Fork Strategy for a Fair, Healthy and Environmentally-Friendly Food System*, (2020) COM/2020/381 final.

9 For the concept of regime complexity, see Karen J. Alter and Sophie Meunier, "The Politics of International Regime Complexity", in *Perspectives on Politics* vol. 7 (2009), p. 13; Thomas Gehring and Benjamin Faude, "The Dynamics of Regime Complexes: Microfoundations and Systemic Effects", in *Global Governance* vol. 19 (2013), p. 119.

10 Colin Kinniburgh, "Covid-19: How the Meat Industry Became a Global Health Liability", at *France 24*, 24 May 2020.

11 Zoran Petrovic a.o., "Meat Production and Consumption: Environmental Consequences", in *Procedia Food Science* vol. 5 (2015), p. 235; Quirin Schiermeier, "Eat Less Meat: UN Climate-Change Report Calls for Change to Human Diet", in *Nature* (2019), p. 291.

12 Susan J. Kraham, "Environmental Impacts of Industrial Livestock Production", in Gabriela Steier and Kiran K. Patel (eds.), *International Farm Animal, Wildlife and Food Safety Law* (Springer, 2017), available at <https://doi.org/10.1007/978-3-319-18002-1_1>, accessed 22 April 2022.

13 See *The FAO-OIE-WHO Collaboration. Sharing Responsibilities and Coordinating Global Activities to Address Health Risks at the Animal-Human-Ecosystems Interfaces. A Tripartite Concept Note* (2010).

turning the Tripartite into a Quadripartite.[14] I will assess how WOAH, through its alliances with other international institutions, notably in the Quadripartite, has attempted to advance the goals of animal welfare and assess what lessons we can draw from this collaboration for cooperation between international institutions.

2 Framework for Understanding Alliances between International Institutions

To analyse WOAH's animal welfare alliances, I will draw on the conceptual framework and theoretical insights developed in research on regime complexes,[15] governance by 'orchestration'[16] and diffusion of norms.[17] From this literature, we can infer that international organizations will engage in alliances with other international organizations (and sometimes NGOs or other actors) when they have ambitious governance goals but only moderate governance capacity and when they are nested in a regime complex with other institutions with (wholly or partly) overlapping goals and relevant capabilities.[18] Engaging in such alliances can then help an organization pursue its goals.[19]

For international institutions, alliances are an indirect form of governance. While most organizations eventually seek to achieve their objectives by impacting directly on the practices of states or private actors ('target actors') that are material to the goals of the organization, in an alliance, an international organization does not target such actors directly; but rather works with 'intermediary actors'. Such intermediaries bring capabilities (e.g., rulemaking power, expertise, political support) to the table that the organization itself does not have to strengthen its ability to impact the practice of target actors.[20]

14 See *UN Environment Programme Joins Alliance to Implement One Health Approach* (World Health Organization, 18 March 2022).

15 For the concept of regime complexity, see the sources mentioned *supra* note 9.

16 The term orchestration is somewhat misleading. It has a connotation of one-directedness, whereas in most cases one cannot really speak of one organization 'orchestrating' another organization, but rather of collaboration between two or more international organizations that seek shared or overlapping goals.

17 Michael Zürn, André Nollkaemper and Randall Peerenboom, "Introduction: Rule of Law Dynamics in an Era of International and Transnational Governance", in Zürn, Nollkaemper and Peerenboom (eds.), *Rule of law dynamics in an era of international and transnational governance* (Cambridge UP 2012).

18 Kenneth W. Abbott a.o., "Orchestrating Global Governance: From Empirical Findings to Theoretical Implications", in *APSA 2014 Annual Meeting Paper*.

19 *Ibidem*.

20 Jaye Ellis, "Calculative Practices in International Environmental Governance: In (Partial) Defence of Indicators", in *Transnational Environmental Law* vol. 9 (2020), p. 297; Thomas

Such indirect governance is relevant to WOAH, which has high ambitions to protect animal welfare in the meat industry but whose ability to induce change in policies and practices of states and corporations is constrained by its restrictive mandate and limited financial and administrative resources. WOAH therefore has engaged in alliances with a variety of other organizations (at global level WHO, FAO, and UNEP but also regional and non-governmental organizations), which give it access to governance capabilities that WOAH itself lacks – such as different regulatory instruments, technical expertise, enforcement capacity, material resources, legitimacy and direct access to target actors.[21]

For identifying, describing and evaluating the practices of alliances in the field of animal welfare, this paper will use three theoretical propositions developed in prior scholarship. First, alliances are more likely to contribute to the goals of an international organization when the intermediaries, with whom it forms the alliance, have correlated goals. Conversely, the intermediary's willingness to participate in an alliance depends on whether its goals are aligned or compatible with those of the 'orchestrator'. Aligned goals may derive from shared norms, values or principles laid down in the constituting treaties or mandates of the relevant actors. They also may be socially constructed through diffusion of norms, influenced by international organizations. On this point, the insights of the literature on norm diffusion are relevant.[22] Alliances also may lead to an adjustment of goals or the articulation of new ones.[23] However, correlating goals do not necessarily imply harmony. Goals may overlap in part and conflict in other respects; intermediaries may have different substantive or organizational priorities that clash with the orchestrator's goals.

Second, the possibility that an organization will be successful in engaging in alliances that help it to pursue its goals, depend on whether it has something to offer to the other partners in the alliance. An organization will be more successful if it can offer support, or added capabilities, to intermediaries in an alliance. For instance, it can offer normative guidance on governance issues and

---

Gehring and Sebastian Oberthür, "The Causal Mechanisms of Interaction between International Institutions", in *European Journal of International Relations* vol. 15 (2009), p. 125; Thomas Gehring and Sebastian Oberthür, "Exploring Regime Interaction", in Arild Underdal and Oran R Young (eds.), *Regime Consequences: Methodological Challenges and Research Strategies* (Springer, 2004); Ellen Hey and Federica Violi, "The Hard Work of Regime Interaction: Climate Change and Human Rights", *Preadvies Koninklijke Nederlandse Vereniging voor Internationaal Recht* [Conference Paper, Royal Netherlands Society of International Law] (2018); Olav Schram Stokke, *The Interplay of International Regimes: Putting Effectiveness Theory to Work* (Fridtjof Nansen Institute, 2001).

21 Jeffrey L. Dunoff, "A New Approach to Regime Interaction", in Margaret A. Young (ed.), *Regime Interaction in International Law: Facing Fragmentation* (Cambridge UP, 2012).

22 Zürn a.o. (*supra* note 17).

23 Dunoff (*supra* note 21); Hey and Violi (*supra* note 20).

plausible policy solutions for such issues; such guidance may influence priorities of intermediaries and help them define their strategies. Organizations also may provide material support, such as financial or administrative assistance or technical expertise; thereby, they can strengthen intermediaries' operational capacities to pursue shared objectives. International organizations can also empower intermediaries by endorsing them as competent and legitimate and by formally recognizing their activities. They can also increase the impact of intermediaries by coordinating their activities; this may both serve the orchestrator's goals and enhance the intermediaries' effectiveness.[24]

Third, alliances are more likely to contribute to the goals of an international organization when intermediary organizations have capabilities that can compensate for capabilities that the organization lacks. When an organization lacks elements of regulatory competence, operational capacity, and/or legitimacy to unilaterally achieve its objectives vis-à-vis target actors, intermediaries can provide such missing capabilities. Alliances may also help an organization develop its capabilities and expand its authority beyond its initial powers. They may allow the organization to enhance its expertise and legitimacy and pursue more demanding governance modes or to expand into areas it was not previously capable of addressing.[25]

Each of these theoretical insights is relevant for analysing and evaluating the practice of collaboration between organizations in the global animal welfare regime. In the following sections, I will explore how these benefits have actually materialized.

3 WOAH's Animal Welfare Standards

From the perspective of animal welfare, the animal welfare standards adopted by WOAH lie at the heart of the strategic alliances in the Quadripartite. In the early part of the 20th century, states recognized the risks of an unrestrained transnational process of meat production. As animal diseases spread to humans and crossed boundaries, states tried to curtail such risks by imposing trade restrictions.[26] In 1924 twenty-eight states established what is now WOAH and agreed that traded meat products had to be accompanied by sanitary

24 Abbott a.o. (*supra* note 18).

25 Cornis van der Lugt and Klaus Dingwerth, "Governing Where Focality Is Low: UNEP and the Principles for Responsible Investment", in Kenneth Abbott a.o. (eds.), *International Organizations as Orchestrators* (Cambridge UP, 2015).

26 Sylvain Kahn, "Animal Welfare in the Context of World Trade Organization Dispute Settlement", in *Revue scientifique et technique* vol. 39 (2020), p. 69.

documents provided by properly organized veterinary services; only such documents could sufficiently guarantee food safety.[27]

While initially WOAH's role was limited to contagious animal diseases,[28] eighty years after its establishment WOAH has assumed a central role in the global regime for the protection of the welfare of animals.[29] Considerations that drove this change appeared to be that animal health and animal welfare were inextricably linked and the need for guidance to assist states in international trade and bilateral negotiations.[30] In its 2001–2005 Strategic Plan, the Member Countries prioritised animal welfare and agreed that the WOAH must provide international leadership.[31] In 2002, the organization formally adopted an animal welfare mandate.[32]

The TAHC is the primary normative instrument by which WOAH has given substance to its leadership role;[33] it is the single most authoritative global instrument for protecting farm animals. Based on a broad definition of animal welfare,[34] it articulates standards for production systems for beef cattle,[35] chicken,[36] and pigs.[37] Given differences in socio-economic situations, cultural

27 International Agreement for the Creation of an Office International des Epizooties in Paris (25 Jan. 1924), 57 LNTS 135.

28 Organic Statutes of the OEI (adopted 25 Jan. 1924, 57 LNTS 135, hereafter Organic Statues), Art. 4.

29 Gardner Murray, Katherine Ashley and Rasto Kolesar, "Drivers for Animal Welfare Policies in Asia, the Far East and Oceania", in *Revue scientifique et technique* vol. 33 (2014), pp. 77, 78.

30 A. Petrini and D. Wilson, "Philosophy, Policy and Procedures of the World Organisation for Animal Health for the Development of Standards in Animal Welfare", in *Revue scientifique et technique* vol. 24 (2005), pp. 665, 666.

31 *Ibidem.*

32 OIE, Res. XIV on the Animal Welfare Mandate of the OIE, 70th Gen. Sess., OIE Doc. 70GS/FR (May 26–31, 2002), at pp. 31–33. See Peters (*supra* note 5), pp. 86–89.

33 TAHC, *supra* note 5.

34 An animal experiences good welfare if it is "healthy, comfortable, well nourished, safe, is not suffering from unpleasant states such as pain, fear and distress, and is able to express behaviors that are important for its physical and mental state"; and good animal welfare requires "disease prevention and appropriate veterinary care, shelter, management and nutrition, a stimulating and safe environment, humane handling and humane slaughter or killing"; *ibidem*, Article 7.1.1. See also David Fraser, "Understanding Animal Welfare", in *Assessment of Animal Welfare Collection* (2008). And see Caroline J. Hewson, "What Is Animal Welfare? Common Definitions and Their Practical Consequences", in *The Canadian Veterinary Journal* vol. 44 (2003), pp. 496, 496, defining animal welfare as comprising "the state of the animal's body and mind, and the extent to which its nature (genetic traits manifest in breed and temperament) is satisfied".

35 TAHC, *supra* note 5.

36 *Ibidem*, at Chapter 7.10.

37 *Ibidem*, at Chapter 7.13.

values and consumer preferences across the world, the fact that the WOAH succeeded in getting these standards adopted by representatives of (now) 182 states in the WOAH's World Assembly of Delegates was a remarkable achievement.

The TAHC, and its contribution to the protection of farm animals is limited in three respects, however. First, like all normative instruments adopted by WOAH, the TAHC is not a legally binding document.[38] States remain free to engage in meat production processes causing great suffering to animals, without facing legal consequences.

Second, the TAHC has a narrow scope in addressing the causes of animal suffering. It mainly regulates production systems for farm animals, addressing such matters as animal health management, temperature, lighting, air quality, nutrition, stocking density, resting areas, castration, tail docking, transport (for instance, addressing the time animals should spend on a journey, the competency of animal handlers, the availability of water and feed, and inspection)[39] and slaughter (e.g. stunning practices).[40] It does not include measures that address supply or demand side for meat, that may be required for addressing structural causes of suffering of farm animals. WOAH appears to have accepted intensive livestock farming as a given or has found reform of industrial farming beyond its mandate, and on that basis has addressed specific welfare threats within that practice such as space, animal feed and conditions of transport and slaughter.

Third, the definition of animal welfare in the THAC and the standards that it incorporates are formulated in general terms, which may be interpreted differently by different actors in different regions.[41] Most standards lack concrete indicators that would make it possible to determine whether or not a particular standard is actually complied with, and producers, veterinarians and other actors have leeway to make choices that fit the local context.[42] This is not to suggest that in 2005 more could have been done, given diversity on this topic, but it is a dominant feature that limits the ability to rely on the standards to push for a change in animal welfare practices.

Within these three limitations, WOAH faces the challenge of getting these standards accepted and implemented by the relevant actors, in particular

38 The only legal obligation stemming from the Organic Statutes of the OEI is that member states must notify disease status and disease control measures to the OIE; see Organic Statues, Art.5. This legal obligation does not pertain to the TAHC.

39 TAHC (*supra* note 5), at Chapter 7.3.

40 *Ibidem*, at Art. 7.5.10.

41 Bonnet a.o. (*supra* note 7).

42 Peters (*supra* note 5), pp. 89–90.

states, meat-producing corporations, and veterinarians. However, the ability of WOAH to support the implementation of the TAHC by these actors is limited by the resources that its members and other parties have given it. Its budget is just over 42,5M USD,[43] compared to about 195M USD for the World Trade Organization (WTO),[44] USD 872M for UNEP,[45] USD 3.25 billion for the FAO[46] and USD 6,72 billion for the WHO.[47] These differences give some idea of the differences in political weight attached to animal welfare as compared to other public policy issues. They also highlight the fact that WOAH cannot operate alone, but depends on cooperation with other international institutions.

4 WOAH and the WHO

WOAH has found some allies in institutions engaged with the protection of human health from the adverse consequences of meat production and consumption. In response to such adverse effects (the FAO observed that "livestock health is the weakest link in our *global health chain*"[48]), WOAH has engaged in alliances in relation to antimicrobial resistance and infectious diseases.[49]

The practice of providing large doses of antimicrobials to cattle contributes to antimicrobial resistance (AMR) and related health problems for humans.[50]

43 WOAH, *OIE 88th General Session Financial Summary Report* (2020), available at <https://web.oie.int/downld/SG/2021/A_88SG_OIE_Financial_Summary.pdf>, at p. 3.

44 WTO, *WTO Annual Report* 2022, available at <https://www.wto.org/english/res_e/booksp_e/anrep_e/ar22_e.pdf>, at p. 208.

45 UNEP, *Programme of work and budget for 2022–2023*, UNEP/EA.5/3/Add.1, Dec. 2022, § 48, at p. 37.

46 FAO, *Adjustments to the Programme of Work and Budget 2022–23*, CL 168/3, Oct. 2021, at p. 15.

47 WHO budget, available at <https://www.who.int/about/accountability/budget>.

48 FAO, *World Livestock 2013. Changing Disease Landscapes* (2013); Evelyne Battaglia Richi a.o., "Health Risks Associated with Meat Consumption: A Review of Epidemiological Studies", in *International Journal for Vitamin and Nutrition Research* (2015), p. 70; Charles H.J. Godfray a.o., "Meat Consumption, Health, and the Environment", in *Science* (2018); Leo Horrigan, Robert S. Lawrence and Polly Walker, "How Sustainable Agriculture Can Address the Environmental and Human Health Harms of Industrial Agriculture", in *Environmental Health Perspectives* (2002), p. 445.

49 There are also examples of alliance without WOAH involvement, e.g. in relation to the international food standards of the Codex Alimentarius of the FAO and the WHO; see FAO/WHO, *Codex Alimentarius – Code of Practice to Minimize and Contain Antimicrobial Resistance* (2005) CXC 61–2005.

50 The World Bank estimated that low-income countries will experience larger declines in economic growth, thereby further increasing economic inequality and potentially driving an additional 24 million people into extreme poverty by 2030 and that by 2050, global

Initiatives to curtail the use of antibiotics with a view to protect human health, may benefit farm animals.[51] Given that the entire architecture of industrialised meat production was in large premised on antibiotics;[52] substantial reductions in the use of antibiotics may spur alternative, less intensive ways of farming.

Based on the partly overlapping goals, WOAH brings something to the table in the alliance that can benefit the WHO and the other institutions. WOAH has direct access to the meat production sector, which the WHO lacks. It incorporated standards for the use of antibiotics for animals in the TAHC[53] and adopted a list of Antimicrobial Agents of Veterinary Importance that indicates when providing a particular antimicrobial agent is compatible with the principle of responsible and prudent use.[54] Some of this is expressly aimed at protecting human health. For instance, the WOAH Working Group on Antimicrobial Resistance has been given the mandate to "maintain a global perspective and foresight on antimicrobial resistance regarding animal health and the interface *with human health*, food production and the environment".[55]

Conversely, the WHO has the expertise that adds capabilities to WOAH, and that can benefit WOAH's goals to reduce antibiotics in animals with a view to protecting animal welfare. Examples are the WHO's List of Critically Important Antimicrobials for Human Medicine and the WHO Guidelines on Antimicrobials, which attribute weight to the need to protect animal welfare by ensuring the availability of antimicrobials to treat sick animals.[56] The collaboration between the institutions also led to the joint recommendation to

increases in health-care costs could range from $300 billion to more than $1 trillion per year and a decline in global livestock production could range from 2.6 per cent to 7.5 per cent per year. See Report of the Secretary-General, *Follow-up to the Political Declaration of the High-Level Meeting of the General Assembly on Antimicrobial Resistance* (2019), UN Doc A/73/869.

51 Claas Kirchhelle, "Pharming Animals: A Global History of Antibiotics in Food Production (1935–2017)", in *Palgrave Communications* vol. 4 (2018), p. 1, noting that "regulating these supply chains and reducing antibiotic consumption will require global solutions".

52 Ignacio R. Castanon, "History of the Use of Antibiotic as Growth Promoters in European Poultry Feeds", in *Poultry Science* (2007), p. 2466.

53 TAHC (*supra* note 5), at par. 6.10.2.

54 See *List of Antimicrobial Agents of Veterinary Importance Adopted by WOAH* (Res. No. XXVIII, May 2007).

55 OIE Working Group on Antimicrobial Resistance, Terms of Reference.

56 *Ibidem*. See also Lawrence O. Gostin, Mary Clare DeBartolo and Rebecca Katz, "The Global Health Law Trilogy: Towards a Safer, Healthier, and Fairer World", in *The Lancet* (2017), pp. 1918, 1921–1922, suggesting that the International Health Regulations should address the integral connections existing between the health of people, animals, and the environment, and the WHO should therefore embody the One Health concept in these regulations as a legal basis for working with complementary organizations.

reduce the use of antimicrobials when not needed for the treatment of diseases of individual animals.[57] These instruments, if properly implemented, can help to protect both human health and animal welfare. Based on the 2022 Strategy, the alliance also aims to strengthen the capacity of states to implement 'one-health responses' to AMR by aligning legislation and regulations with international standards[58] – an example where the alliance will be able to do much more than what WOAH could do alone.

Another potential lead to reform industrial farming is the risk that such farming may cause infectious diseases. A recent study found that agricultural practices have been associated with more than 50 percent of zoonotic infectious diseases that have emerged in humans, and that this number is likely to increase as agriculture expands and intensifies.[59] While in relation to COVID-19 much attention has focused on the interaction between humans and wild animals, also industrialized meat production creates risks of infectious diseases[60] and indeed can create pandemic risks.[61] Drivers are the increased scale of disease impact, the immunosuppression of intensively farmed animals, and the risks associated with transportation.[62]

In some situations regulation of meat production to protect human health may have beneficial impact on animal welfare, in particular when they would lead to reduction of production and consumption.[63] It is here where the agendas of WOAH and the WHO intersect. The One Health Strategy that WOAH,

57 Ad hoc Interagency Coordination Group (IACG) on Antimicrobial Resistance. This aim was included in the 2013 Chennai Declaration, that recommends 80% compliance with the rule that antibiotics used for human treatment will not be used for growth promotion in food animals; see *Indian Journal of Medical Microbiology* vol. 32 (2014), p. 221.

58 Strategic Framework for Collaboration on Antimicrobial Resistance – Together for One Health – WOAH – World Organisation for Animal Health.

59 Jason R. Rohr a.o., "Emerging Human Infectious Diseases and the Links to Global Food Production" in *Nature Sustainability* vol. 2 (2019), p. 445.

60 Richard Coker a.o., "Towards a Conceptual Framework to Support One-Health Research for Policy on Emerging Zoonoses", in *The Lancet* (2011), p. 11; Leah Garcés, "COVID-19 Exposes Animal Agriculture's Vulnerability", in *Agriculture and Human Values* (2020); Courtney G. Lee, "Industrial Animal Agriculture in the Pandemic Spotlight" (SSRN Scholarly Paper ID 3810976); Romain Espinosa, Damian Tago and Nicolas Treich, "Infectious Diseases and Meat Production", in *Environmental & Resource Economics* (2020); Liverani a.o. (*supra* note 2).

61 UNEP and International Livestock Research Institute, *Preventing the next Pandemic: Zoonotic Diseases and How to Break the Chain of Transmission* (2020); Espinosa a.o. (*supra* note 60); Peter Daszak and others, *IPBES Workshop Report on Biodiversity and Pandemics* (Intergovernmental Platform on Biodiversity and Ecosystem Services, 2020).

62 Coker a.o. (*supra* note 60); Espinosa a.o. (*supra* note 60).

63 Moreno Di Marco a.o., "Opinion: Sustainable Development Must Account for Pandemic Risk", *Proceedings of the National Academy of Sciences of the United States of America* vol. 117 (2020), p. 3888; Espinosa a.o. (*supra* note 60).

the WHO, the FAO and UNEP adopted in 2022 expressly recognized farming as a potential driver of pandemics and recognized the need for regulation of farming as a risk mitigation measure,[64] and thus provides for correlating goals. This alliance can be beneficial for both institutions. WOAH brings expertise and direct access to practices of veterinarians and other actors involved in animal farming; WHO brings expertise on human health risks and, potentially, a more developed institutional machinery and much larger resources. On this basis, the alliance could give concrete meaning to the general obligation of preventing pandemics as recognized by the 2021 resolution of the *Institut de Droit International* (IDI), for instance, by requiring states to improve regulation of the production of meat and reduce its consumption.[65]

However, concrete initiatives have yet to emerge to regulate farming as a risk mitigation strategy. This certainly is not on the agenda of the WHO; even though the WHO mandate extends to diseases and risks stemming from industrial meat production, the treatment of animals and reform of the intensive farming sector is outside the agenda of the WHO. The ongoing revisions of the International Health Regulations do not move in that direction.[66] The same is true for the global pandemic prevention, preparedness, and response instrument.[67] WOAH does not appear to have been a relevant participant in this process.

It follows that while the risks that intensive meat production poses for human health have allowed WOAH to work with other organizations to address such risks, these alliances have not resulted in regulatory strategies to address the root causes of such risks beyond the animal health and welfare standards

64 *One Health Joint Plan of Action Launched to Address Health Threats to Humans, Animals, Plants and Environment* (WOAH – World Organisation for Animal Health, 17 October 2022), p. 27, available at <https://www.woah.org/en/one-health-joint-plan-of-action-launched-to-address-health-threats-to-humans-animals-plants-and-environment/>, accessed 22 October 2022.

65 Espinosa a.o. (*supra* note 60); *Meat Atlas 2021* (*supra* note 2), p. 47; Lawrence Gostin, "Strengthening International Legal Authorities to Advance Global Health Security", in *Bill of Health*, 29 Sept. 2021, available at <http://blog.petrieflom.law.harvard.edu/2021/09/29/pandemic-treaty-health-security/>, accessed 15 July 2022.

66 Nasiya Daminova, "The First Working Draft of the WHO's 'Pandemic Treaty': Attempting to Cover Normative Gaps Indicated by the COVID-19 Pandemic?", in *EJIL:Talk!* (13 October 2022), available at <https://www.ejiltalk.org/the-first-working-draft-of-the-whos-pandemic-treaty-attempting-to-cover-normative-gaps-indicated-by-the-covid-19-pandemic/>, accessed 22 October 2022.

67 WHO, *First Meeting of the Intergovernmental Negotiating Body to Draft and Negotiate a WHO Convention, Agreement or Other Instrument on Pandemic Prevention, Preparedness and Response*, UN Doc A/INB/1/10 (1 June 2022).

of WOAH that currently are in place. It remains to be seen whether the risks are given sufficient weight to allow WOAH, the WHO, and other actors to articulate an evidence-based strategy to assess the risks of intensive meat production.[68]

5 WOAH and UNEP

WOAH can find a separate set of allies for its animal welfare agenda in institutions seeking to address meat production's adverse environmental effects. Intensive livestock production has resulted in a range of other environmental problems,[69] and regulations that aim for environmental protection from meat production may need to lead to restrictions on intensive farming.

For instance, intensive livestock production is a significant source of nitrogen emissions. Application of synthetic nitrogen fertiliser and manure to cropland and grassland and the management, accumulation and transport of manure result in risks for both ecosystems and humans in the form of air pollution, pollution of freshwater and coastal areas, and loss of biodiversity.[70] There is good authority for the proposition that "a reduction in the production and consumption of livestock products is probably necessary to keep global [nitrogen] emissions within planetary boundaries".[71]

Comparable to climate change policies, international regulatory policies addressing such environmental effects can benefit animal welfare. In the Netherlands, concerns over nitrate pollution have led to initiatives to introduce a subsidy programme for farms that go out of the business of intensive livestock farming and a scheme to reduce the number of dairy cows and young cattle.[72] Apart from reducing the size of livestock production, measures to

68 See, e.g., Gostin a.o. (*supra* note 56), pp. 1921–1922.

69 FAO, *Livestock's Long Shadow. Environmental Issues and Options*; Kraham (*supra* note 12); Thomas Banhazi, Andres Aland and Jörg Hartung, *Air Quality and Livestock Farming* (CRC Press, 2018); Brian Machovina, Kenneth J. Feeley and William J. Ripple, "Biodiversity Conservation: The Key Is Reducing Meat Consumption", in *Science of The Total Environment* vol. 536 (2015), p. 419.

70 Aimable Uwizeye a.o., "Nitrogen Emissions along Global Livestock Supply Chains", in *Nature Food* vol. 1 (2020), p. 437.

71 Joseph Poore and Thomas Nemecek, *Reducing Food's Environmental Impacts through Producers and Consumers* (2018), p. 987; Marco Springmann a.o., "Options for Keeping the Food System within Environmental Limits", in *Nature* (2018), p. 519; Uwizeye a.o. (*supra* note 70), p. 443.

72 NL Times, "More Nitrogen Polluters to Be Targeted; Most Farmers Claim No Negative Influence on Environment", available at <https://nltimes.nl/2022/10/22/nitrogen-polluters-targeted-farmers-claim-negative-influence-environment>, accessed 22 October 2022.

address nitrogen pollution include breeding, feeding and manure management in large-scale livestock farms[73] and distribution of livestock production.[74] While not all of such measures benefit animals (distribution just means suffering in different places; and in China, such measures aim to realize more livestock protein with fewer animals and less total pollution impact), policies aimed to reduce environmental advise effects of nitrogen on the environment and humans may well benefit animal welfare.

Also, in this field, we can identify a correlation between the goals of various international institutions. These include WOAH, FAO and UNEP, but the problem of nitrogen pollution is also on the agenda of the states parties to the Convention on Biological Diversity (CBD)[75] (that adopted the Aichi Biodiversity Targets, requiring that by 2020 pollution from excess nutrients be brought to levels that are not detrimental to ecosystem function and biodiversity),[76] the states parties to the Convention for the Protection of the Marine Environment of the North-East Atlantic (OSPAR Convention)[77] (which have called for the reduction of input from agriculture),[78] and the states parties to the Convention on Long-Range Transboundary Air Pollution (CLRTAP).[79]

Compared to the human health agenda, WOAH and FAO play a modest role here. The problem of nitrogen pollution was not addressed in the 2022 One Health Action Plan. However, FAO has engaged in a widespread programme to develop information on livestock and the environment[80] and has set up a

---

73 Zhiping Zhu a.o., "Integrated Livestock Sector Nitrogen Pollution Abatement Measures Could Generate Net Benefits for Human and Ecosystem Health in China", in *Nature Food* vol. 3 (2022), p. 161; J. Dijkstra, O. Oenema and A. Bannink, "Dietary Strategies to Reducing N Excretion from Cattle: Implications for Methane Emissions", in *Current Opinion in Environmental Sustainability* vol. 3 (2011), p. 414.

74 Zhaohai Bai a.o., "Relocate 10 Billion Livestock to Reduce Harmful Nitrogen Pollution Exposure for 90% of China's Population", in *Nature Food* vol. 3 (2022), p. 152.

75 Convention on Biological Diversity (CBD) of 5 June 1992, 1760 *UNTS* 79.

76 CBD, Key Elements of the Strategic Plan 2011–2020, Including Aichi Biodiversity Targets (2018).

77 Convention for the Protection of the Marine Environment of the North-East Atlantic (OSPAR Convention) of 22 September 1992, 2354 *UNTS* 67.

78 OSPAR Commission, *Nutrients in the Convention Area Inputs of Nutrients into the Convention Area Implementation of PARCOM Recommendations 88/2 and 89/4*.

79 Convention on Long-Range Transboundary Air Pollution (CLRTAP) of 12 November 1979, 1302 *UNTS* 217. On the application of this convention to nitrogen; see *Report of the First E-Briefing for the Nitrogen Working Group of the United Nations Environment Programme: Implementation of the UNEA-4 Resolution on Sustainable Nitrogen Management*, par. 42.

80 *Livestock and the Environment* (*LivestockEnv*), available at <http://www.fao.org/livestock-environment/en>, accessed 19 November 2022.

'Livestock Environmental Assessment and Performance Partnership', in which WOAH participates.[81]

As yet, none of this has led to regulation at the global level. In 2019, the UNEP Assembly set in motion a process to establish an inter-governmental mechanism to coordinate nitrogen policies.[82] After initial discussions indicated little support for a global convention,[83] the process is now expected to bring into existence a mechanism for inter-convention nitrogen coordination[84] among various conventions relevant to nitrogen emissions, including the CBD, the United Nations Framework Convention on Climate Change (UNFCCC),[85] CLRTAP, and the Global Programme for Action on the Protection of the Marine Environment from Land-based Activities (GPA), to enhance the consistency of actions taken by and the sharing of solutions among member states.[86] FAO and WOAH do not appear to be involved in this process.

The overall picture is that of a patchwork of international agreements that have articulated requirements for the livestock sector to reduce nitrogen emissions in varying degrees of detail but invariably stop short of legally binding restrictions on intensive animal farming. There are few indications that states see the threats of nitrogen emissions to the environment and human health as sufficiently serious to allow the UNEP-driven initiatives at the global level to lead to legal restrictions on intensive livestock production.

6 The Quadripartite

It appears from the above that institutional governance of animal welfare, food production, human health, and environmental protection has close connections. However, institutional fragmentation has hampered the effective addressing of these links. To address this problem, in 2010, FAO, OIE (now

81 'Partners | Livestock Environmental Assessment and Performance (LEAP) Partnership | Food and Agriculture Organization of the United Nations' <https://www.fao.org/partnerships/leap/partners/en/> accessed 19 November 2022.

82 UNEP, UN Environment Assembly, *Sustainable Nitrogen Management*, doc. Res. UNEP/EA.4/L.16 (28 March 2019).

83 Fourth Meeting of the International Nitrogen Management System (INMS-4). Summary of the High-Level Segment (2019).

84 Report of the First E-Briefing (*supra* note 79).

85 United Nations Framework Convention on Climate Change (UNFCCC) of 9 May 1992, 1771 *UNTS* 107.

86 Report of the First E-Briefing (*supra* note 79), at par. 56.

WOAH), and WHO formed the Tripartite, which was extended through a partnership with UNEP into the Quadripartite.

The Quadripartite is now the main governance forum for addressing the combined problems of animal welfare, food production, global health, and protection of the environment. This alliance between the four institutions is based on partly overlapping goals. For instance, a reduction in the use of antibiotics is suitable for animal welfare and human health alike. These overlapping goals are brought together in the overarching concept of One Health,[87] which is premised on the idea that the health of people, animals, and the wider environment are intertwined and must be addressed in a coordinated manner.[88] In 2022, the Quadripartite adopted a five-year action plan for One Health to provide for such coordinated policies.[89] The alliance also provided several policy documents relating to AMR, culminating in the 2022 joint WAOH, WHO, FAO and UNEP strategy.[90]

Potentially, the Quadripartite can provide each of the benefits of international institutional alliances identified in section 2. The alliance can contribute to the goals of each of the organizations since they, to some extent, have correlated goals derived from the constituting treaties and mandates of the four participating institutions.

The Quadripartite can also help pursue the individual organizations' goals. For instance, it can offer normative guidance on governance issues and plausible policy solutions for such issues. The institutions can also pool financial or administrative assistance or technical expertise, thereby strengthening their individual operational capacity objectives. It can contribute to the goals of individual institutions by providing capabilities that compensate for each organization's capabilities. For instance, in theory, WHO and UNEP can address other stakeholders other than WOAH and vice versa.

The results have been mixed in the few years since the initiation of the Quadripartite. Regarding goals, the animal welfare goals of WOAH only partly correlate to and may be furthered by, or undermined by, the human-centred

87 UNEP, UN Environment Assembly, *Animal Welfare – Environment– Sustainable Development Nexus*, Res. UNEP/EA.5/Res.1 (2 March 2022).

88 Ad hoc Interagency Coordination Group (IACG) on Antimicrobial Resistance, *No Time to Wait: Securing the Future from Drug-Resistant Infections* (2019).

89 One Health Joint Plan of Action (2022–2026) *Working Together for the Health of Humans, Animals, Plants and the Environment* (WOAH, 2022).

90 Strategic Framework for Collaboration on Antimicrobial Resistance – Together for One Health – WOAH, available at <https://www.woah.org/en/document/strategic-framework-for-collaboration-on-antimicrobial-resistance-together-for-one-health/>, accessed 9 October 2022.

goals of organizations like WHO and FAO. An illustration of the non-parallelism of the goals is the situations where to avoid the risk of human contamination, all animals at farms located in zones at high risk of a spread of disease were culled once a case was detected.[91] For instance, the African Swine Fever led to a contraction of more than 40 per cent of China's swine inventory (which represents almost a quarter of the global swine herd) within the first year.[92] Also, recent bird flu outbreaks have led to calls to shut down free-range chicken production, leading to another tension between human health and animal welfare.[93]

When combined under the One Health umbrella, the organizations' goals do not appear to be identical.[94] For instance, the respective policy documents of the organizations show that they define the AMR problem differently.[95] A survey among human and animal health practitioners revealed disagreements concerning prioritising human health, animal health, and economic considerations.[96] Indeed, One Health policy documents often frame the causality of human-animal relations as one-directional. Humans suffer from AMR, "while animals are presented mainly as potential risk factors for human health".[97] This framing entails that the values of the human health sector prevail above those of other non-human sectors.

As regards the benefits that WOAH may bring to the other partners in the Quadripartite, it appears that WOAH can, in particular, bring expertise and a network of stakeholders to the table, which may make it for the WHO, FAO and UNEP worthwhile to engage in an alliance with WOAH and work towards common goals. Conversely, WHO, FAO, and UNEP each bring their expertise and

91 Espinosa a.o. (*supra* note 60).

92 *Ibidem*. Another example is the decision of the Danish Government to cull 17 million minks after the report of mink-specific mutations of severe acute respiratory syndrome coronavirus 2 in humans; see Roger Frutos and Christian A Devaux, "Mass Culling of Minks to Protect the COVID-19 Vaccines: Is It Rational?", in *New Microbes and New Infections* vol. 38 (2020), 100816.

93 Tom Levitt, "The Birds Are All Back inside: Could This Be the End for Free-Range Eggs in the UK?", in *The Guardian* of 21 October 2022.

94 Steve Hinchliffe, "More than One World, More than One Health: Re-Configuring Interspecies Health", in Social Science & Medicine (2015), p. 129; Alena Kamenshchikova a.o., "Anthropocentric Framings of One Health: An Analysis of International Antimicrobial Resistance Policy Documents", in *Critical Public Health* vol. 31 (2021), p. 306.

95 *Ibidem*.

96 *Ibidem*, stating that while human health professionals gave greater weight to the emotional well-being of people, those from the animal health sector gave greater weight to animal health and economic concerns.

97 *Ibidem*.

networks to the collaboration. However, it seems that neither of these institutions can expand capabilities for regulation or oversight of state and private actors and expand the focus of regulation from conditions inside industrial farming to more fundamental causes of supply and demand of meat.

It is noteworthy that the 2022 joint One Health agenda also does not consider the broader and more fundamental risks that human practices – above all industrialised meat production – can pose to animals.[98] The Quadripartite's 2022 One Health Action Plan only contains a single reference to the problems of intensive livestock farming as a cause of problems of animal welfare, human health, climate change and environmental pollution[99] None of the action tracks provided for the Action Plan sets out to provide such attention and integrated policies.

7 Conclusions

The above assessment does indicate that in the past two decades, we have witnessed a substantial development of the global regime for the protection of the welfare of farm animals. WOAH's adoption of the TAHC and its alliances with the WHO, the FAO and UNEP has strengthened the position of animal welfare in the regime complex for meat production, even though, to a large extent, these agendas for now are stuck in strategies and policies rather than actual regulation that concretely will benefit farm animals.

Beyond the activities of WOAH and the Quadripartite, protection of farm animals may be strengthened by autonomous policies and practices on institutions; these include self-regulation of meat-producing corporations, the CFS with its Principles for Responsible Investment in Agriculture and Food Systems, the WTO's Appellate Body with its series of somewhat animal welfare friendly rulings, the FAO and so on – these practices indicate that animal welfare has become an interest that many institutions can (for a variety of reasons) no longer disregard.

98 *Ibidem.*

99 *One Health Joint Plan of Action Launched to Address Health Threats to Humans, Animals, Plants and Environment*, at p. 9, stating that "Healthy and sustainable agrifood systems are an integral part of the One Health vision for a better future. Livestock and fish food systems require targeted attention and integrated policies given the multiple effects that the growing demand for protein has on the animal production sector and associated systems (for example, deforestation for the production of animal feed, the increasing scale and density of animals, disease emergence and land-use change".

Even though much progress has been made in the past decades, the institutional architecture and regulations that apply to intensive meat production seem inadequate for realizing a structural improvement in the protection of farm animals. Given the projected trends in meat consumption and production, the magnitude of animal suffering worldwide, and the adverse effects of industrial meat production on human health and climate change, the highly fragmented and legally undeveloped regime for animal welfare protection will not be fit for purpose.

While WOAH has formulated relatively demanding standards that aim to protect the welfare of animals within intensive livestock farming, at the global level, no policies are on the agenda that would more fundamentally curb the scale of intensive livestock farming in a way that the EU Farm to Form agenda has done this.

The story of the emergence of WOAH as a global actor in the protection of animal welfare certainly cannot be seen as a story of institutional and normative development that led to a decisive improvement in the welfare of farm animals. However, it is a story of a slow transformation of a regime that for the most of history has aimed to stimulate growth in meat production with direct consequences for animal suffering to a regime that recognizes the interest of animals and that slowly builds instruments that can be used for the protection of animal welfare. It is also a story that indicates that such a massive task cannot be undertaken by any organization alone but rather depends on alliances that are premised on correlating goals and do expand capabilities in pursuit of a partly joint agenda. The Quadripartite is an innovative experiment to shape such alliances. It provides another example of how states and international institutions pursue global problems that transcend the mandates of individual institutions.

The Quadripartite is an interesting new form of institutional cooperation between independent international institutions that have their own goals but cannot achieve them without the other institutions. However, such institutional cooperation eventually is limited by the mandates, powers, and capabilities of the participating institutions – individually and combined. Critically, informal cooperation in a forum like the Quadripartite, cannot create mandates or legal powers where none exist. Decisive international responses to the fundamental problems raised by global industrialized meat production can use and build on the machinery of the Quadripartite but will require more than that.

CHAPTER 12

The International Tribunal for the Law of the Sea and the Meeting of States Parties to the 1982 UN Convention on the Law of the Sea

Mare Ignotum *for the Law of International Organizations?*

*Meagan S. Wong**

1 Introduction

To honour one's *Doktorvater* in a *Liber Amicorum* is a task that brings profound joy and careful consideration of a subject for inquiry. Upon reflection, thinking of many conversations with Niels Blokker over coffee (and more recently, a smoothie),[1] I cannot resist but engage with an inquiry that persisted throughout the course of our meetings in recent years: the law and practice of treaty bodies. Of note, and particular interest, is the law and practice of treaty bodies that Niels Blokker calls *in*ternational *ju*dicial *go*vernance *ins*titutions – or 'INJUGOVINS',[2] which relate to the governance of international courts and tribunals. Whilst the law and practice of international courts and tribunals is not a subject of a new enquiry, Niels Blokker has pointed out that INJUGOVINS have received significantly less attention:

> The role and functioning of international judicial governance institutions is to some extent a *terra incognita*.[3]

This contribution selects a specific individual institution as the subject of inquiry: the Meeting of States Parties to the 1982 United Nations Convention

* The author is Lecturer in Law, Essex Law School, University of Essex.

1 Lebkov & Sons, Leiden.

2 Niels Blokker, "Governance of the International Tribunal of the Law of the Sea: The Role of the Meeting of States Parties to the Law of the Sea Convention", in Angela Del Vecchio and Roberto Virzo (eds.), *Interpretations of the United Nations Convention on the Law of the Sea by International Courts and Tribunals* (Springer, 2019), p. 81.

3 Niels Blokker, "The Governance of International Courts and Tribunals: Organizing and Guaranteeing Independence and Accountability", in Andreas Follesdal and Geir Ulfstein (eds.), *The Judicialization of International Law: A Mixed Blessing?* (Oxford UP, 2018), p. 42.

 | DOI:10.1163/9789004699939_014

on the Law of the Sea (SPLOS), which is the INJUGOVIN to the International Tribunal for the Law of the Sea (ITLOS). Curiously, the constituent instrument of ITLOS – the United Nations Convention on the Law of the Sea (UNCLOS)[4] – only provides one line for the establishment of SPLOS. Article 319 (2)(e) of the Convention stipulates that the Secretary-General of the United Nations (UN), in addition to his (her) functions as the depository of the Convention, shall "convene necessary meetings of States Parties in accordance with this Convention". Niels Blokker observed that SPLOS developed from a "very thin basis" into a "specialized mini General Assembly" and established its own practice with the support of the UN Secretariat.[5] Thus, two institutional frameworks are at play: the practice of SPLOS and the practice of the UN since the adoption of UNCLOS. The former cannot be viewed in isolation from the latter – and yet, both UNCLOS and the United Nations Charter are separate constituent instruments. How curious. Does this mean SPLOS is *mare ignotum* for the law of international organizations?

The first meeting of SPLOS was convened in 1994, following the entry into force of UNCLOS.[6] SPLOS has adopted its own Rules of Procedure[7] which, as Niels Blokker has observed, "closely follow the rules and procedure for UN Conferences and Meetings".[8] Notably, in recent SPLOS meetings, the President of the Meeting has emphasized the need to ensure gender balance with respect to its rules of procedure.[9] The mandate of SPLOS in relation to ITLOS includes electing judges of ITLOS,[10] deciding on their renumeration

4 United Nations Convention on the Law of the Sea (UNCLOS, 1982).

5 Blokker (*supra* note 2), p. 86.

6 Report of the First Meeting of States Parties, 21 and 22 November 1994, SPLOS/3 (1995).

7 Rules of Procedure for Meetings of States Parties, SPLOS/2/Rev.5 (2020).

8 Blokker (*supra* note 2), p. 84.

9 Report of the Thirty-third Meeting of States Parties, 12–16 June, SPLOS/33/15 (2023), para. 104. See also Report of the Thirty-first Meeting of Parties, 21–25 June 2021, SPLOS/31/9 (2021), para. 98.

10 UNCLOS (*supra* note 4) Annex VI, Art. 4. The present seat allocation is as follows: (a) five members from the Group of African States; (b) five members from the Group of Asian States; (c) three members from the Group of Eastern European States; (d) four members from the Group of Latin American and Caribbean States; (e) three members shall be from the Group of Western European and other States; and (f) the remaining one member of each body from among the Group of African States, the Group of Asian States and the Group of Western European and other States, Report of nineteenth meeting of SPLOS, 22–26 June 2009, SPLOS/203 (2009), para.101. The initial allocation of seats was determined in the fifth meeting of States Parties, 24 July–2 August 1996, SPLOS/L.3/Rev.1 (1996): (a) Five judges from the African Group; (b) Five judges from the Asian Group; (c) Four judges from the Latin American and Caribbean Group; (d) Four judges from the Western European and other States Group; (e) Three judges from the Eastern European Group.

(salaries, allowances, compensation),[11] the salary of the Registrar,[12] conditions under which retirement pensions may be given to judges and to the Registrar,[13] and conditions under which judges and the Registrar shall have their travelling expenses refunded.[14] As the development of practice with regard to these functions is relatively straightforward, I choose instead to address four issues: the practice of SPLOS to amend/modify UNCLOS (paragraph 2); the relationship between SPLOS and ITLOS (paragraph 3); the nature of the mandate of SPLOS pursuant to Article 319 of UNCLOS (paragraph 4) and the practice of the UN – and more specifically, the role of the General Assembly and Security Council – after the adoption of UNCLOS (paragraph 5).

2 The Practice of SPLOS to Amend/Modify UNCLOS

UNCLOS, heralded as the "constitution" of the seas,[15] with 304 provisions and 9 Annexes, establishes a legal order for the seas and oceans, and provides for the codification and progressive development of the law of the sea. As such, the Convention does not establish an international organization, but rather creates rights and obligations for States Parties *inter se* and serves as a framework convention with respect to a broad range of areas, e.g., conservation and management of marine living resources,[16] protection and preservation of marine environment,[17] marine scientific research.[18] The Convention establishes three institutions: the International Seabed Authority;[19] a Commission on the Limits of the Continental Shelf (CLCS);[20] and ITLOS (Article 1, Annex VI).[21] Notably, the function of ITLOS is to settle disputes concerning the interpretation or

See also Report of the Seventeenth Meeting of States Parties 14–22 June 2007, SPLOS/164, paras. 93–96. On the issue of mechanisms to ensure that the best qualified candidates are elected, see Blokker (*supra* note 3), pp. 87–88.

11 *Ibidem*, Annex VI, Art. 4(2); Art. 18 (5).

12 *Ibidem*, Annex VI, Art. 18 (6).

13 *Ibidem*, Annex VI, Art. 18 (7).

14 *Ibidem.*

15 In the Thirty-third Meeting of States Parties (*supra* note 9, at para. 77), many delegations reaffirmed that UNCLOS is a "constitution for the oceans". Yoshifumi Tanaka, *The International Law of the Sea* (4th ed., Cambridge UP, 2023), p. 40.

16 UNCLOS (*supra* note 4), Artt. 61–68.

17 *Ibidem*, Part XII.

18 *Ibidem*, Part XIII.A.

19 *Ibidem*, Art. 156.

20 *Ibidem*, Annex II, Art. 1.

21 *Ibidem*, Annex VI, Art. 1.

application of UNCLOS.[22] SPLOS, accordingly, is conferred decision-making powers with respect to the election of judges and financial expenses of the Tribunal.[23]

SPLOS, however, has amended UNCLOS without a formal amendment process.[24] Three occasions come to mind. The first meeting of SPLOS decided by consensus to postpone the first election of ITLOS from 16 May 1995 (which was the last date compatible with Article 4(3) of Annex VI to UNCLOS) to 1 August 1996.[25] The fifth meeting of SPLOS decided to postpone the date of the first election of the CLCS by a year (which according to Article 2(2) of Annex II was to be held within 18 months after the date of entry into force of UNCLOS).[26] The third instance of SPLOS practice in amending UNCLOS is not so clear with respect to whether this amendment is only procedural or substantive in nature, thereby affecting the rights and obligations of States Parties.[27] This was the tenth meeting of SPLOS, when developing States voiced concerns regarding the difficulty of complying with the time limit in Article 4 of Annex II to UNCLOS.[28] This provision stipulated that a coastal State intending to establish the outer limits to its continental shelf beyond 200 nautical miles is obligated to submit particulars of such limits to the Commission on the Limits of the Continental Shelf along with supporting scientific and technical data as soon as possible, but in any case within 10 years of the entry into force of the Convention for that State.[29] When considering the issue of Article 4 of Annex II to UNCLOS, in the eleventh meeting of SPLOS, States

22 *Ibidem*, Art. 287.

23 *Ibidem*, Art. 4(2); Art. 18(5), 18(6), 18(7); Art. 19.

24 Malgosia Fitzmaurice and Panos Merkouris, "Re-Shaping Treaties While Balancing Interests of Stability and Change: Critical Issues in the Amendment/Modification/Revision of Treaties", in *Austrian Review of International and European Law* vol. 20 (2015), pp. 41, 61–65; Georg Nolte, *Treaties and Subsequent Practice* (Oxford UP, 2013), pp. 364–365.

25 Report of the First Meeting of States Parties, 21 and 22 November 1994 (*supra* note 6), para.16(a): "one-time deferment"; para. 61(c). See also Tullio Treves, "The General Assembly and the Meeting of States Parties in the Implementation of the LOS Convention", in Alex G. Oude Elferink (ed.), *Stability and Change in the Law of the Sea: The Role of the LOS Convention* (Brill 2004), pp. 69–70; Blokker (*supra* note 2), p. 86.

26 Report of the Fifth Meeting of States Parties, 24 July–2 August 1996, SPLOS/14 (1996), paras. 41–42.

27 Treves (*supra* note 25), p. 72. See also Irini Buga, "Between Stability and Change in the Law of the Sea Convention: Subsequent Practice, Treaty Modification, and Regime Interaction", in Donald Rothwell and others (eds.), *The Oxford Handbook of the Law of the Sea* (Oxford UP, 2015), p. 57.

28 Report of the Tenth Meeting of States Parties 22–26 May 2000, SPLOS/60 (2000), paras. 61–62.

29 UNCLOS (*supra* note 4) Annex II, Art. 4.

Parties discussed how to give effect to any decision extending the ten-year time period and put forward four possible procedures:

(a) An amendment in accordance with article 312 of the Convention;

(b) An amendment by means of the simplified procedure provided for in article 313;

(c) An agreement relating to the implementation of article 4 of annex II to the Convention;

(d) A decision by the Meeting of States Parties along the lines of the procedure used by the Meeting regarding the postponement of the election of the members of the Tribunal and of the members of the Commission on the Limits of the Continental Shelf.[30]

It can be inferred that States Parties were aware that the intended modification to the ten-year time period would be an amendment to UNCLOS of sorts.[31] Notably, in the Meeting of Parties, it was decided:

> In the case of a State Party for which the Convention entered into force before 13 May 1999, it is understood that the ten-year time period referred to in article 4 of Annex II to the Convention shall be taken to have commenced on 13 May 1999.[32]

Thus, the ten-year period pursuant to UNCLOS was amended by a decision of the Meeting of Parties – indicative that the practice of SPLOS has developed whereby States Parties may make amendments or modification to the Convention.[33] Subsequently, a combination of factors – discussions regarding the ability of States, particularly developing States, to fulfil the requirements of article 4 of annex II to the United Nations Convention on the Law of the Sea; the decision contained in SPLOS/72, paragraph (a); and the workload of the Commission on the Limits of the Continental Shelf – led to the eighteenth meeting of SPLOS to decide *inter alia*:

> It is understood that the time period referred to in article 4 of annex II to the Convention and the decision contained in SPLOS/72, paragraph (a), may be satisfied by submitting to the Secretary-General preliminary information indicative of the outer limits of the continental shelf beyond

30 Report of the Eleventh Meeting of States Parties, 14–18 May 2001, SPLOS/73 (2001), para. 78.

31 Buga (*supra* note 27), p. 57.

32 Decision regarding the date of commencement of the ten-year period for making submissions to the Commission on the Limits of the Continental Shelf set out in Art. 4 of Annex II to the United Nations Convention on the Law of the Sea, 29 May 2001, SPLOS/72 (2001), para. (a).

33 Fitzmaurice and Merkouris (*supra* note 24), pp. 63–64; Nolte (*supra* note 24), p. 386; Buga (*supra* note 27), pp. 55–57.

> 200 nautical miles and a description of the status of preparation and intended date of making a submission in accordance with the requirements of article 76 of the Convention and with the Rules of Procedure and the Scientific and Technical Guidelines of the Commission on the Limits of the Continental Shelf.[34]

From a law of treaties perspective, a question arises whether this decision may be read as a modification to article 4 of Annex II to UNCLOS, and SPLOS/72, paragraph (a) – or a subsequent agreement between the parties regarding the interpretation of the Convention.[35] Whilst this question exceeds the compass of the present discussion, it nevertheless prompts reflection whether an INJUGOVIN, which is comprised of States Parties to a multilateral treaty, may interpret or modify the constituent instrument of the relevant international court or tribunal.[36]

3 The Relationship between SPLOS and ITLOS

Whilst there are no established criteria for the role of INJUGOVINS, Niels Blokker has pointed out two minimum requirements as desirable – and fulfilled by SPLOS: "First, SPLOS is the main forum to which ITLOS is accountable, so it must provide a stable and reliable context where ITLOS can explain its performance. Second, SPLOS must fully respect the independence of ITLOS".[37]

The President of ITLOS presents an annual report comprising an overview of its activities for the period of a year, and information on recent developments regarding the work of the Tribunal,[38] which includes *inter alia* judicial matters,[39] caseload,[40] various activities undertaken by the Tribunal to enhance capacity in the law of the sea and increase awareness of its role in the settlement of disputes. The Report of the Tribunal is an agenda item on the Meeting

34 Decision regarding the workload of the Commission on the Limits of the Continental Shelf and the ability of States, particularly developing States, to fulfil the requirements of Art. 4 of annex II to the United Nations Convention on the Law of the Sea, as well as the decision contained in SPLOS/72, paragraph (a) SPLOS/183 (2008), para. 1(a).

35 Vienna Convention on the Law of Treaties 1969 (VCLT), Art. 31(3)(a).

36 Meagan S. Wong, "The Activation of the International Criminal Court's Jurisdiction over the Crime of Aggression: International Institutional Law and Dispute Settlement Perspectives", in *International Community Law Review* vol. 22 (2020), pp. 197, 211–214; Fitzmaurice and Merkouris (*supra* note 24), pp. 61–65.

37 Blokker (*supra* note 2), p. 87.

38 Most recent Annual Report of the Tribunal for 2022, SPLOS/33/2 (2023).

39 Report of the Thirty-third Meeting of States Parties (*supra* note 9), para. 14.

40 *Ibidem*, para. 15.

of Parties, whereby the Meeting "takes note" of the report,[41] and States present their views and comments. In a recent meeting of SPLOS, many delegations, including one group of States, showed their full support for the Tribunal and "highlighted its important contribution to the peaceful settlement of disputes and the development of jurisprudence".[42] Furthermore, many delegations and a group of States expressed appreciation for the Tribunal's capacity-building activities.[43] Notably, many delegations welcomed the Request for an Advisory Opinion Submitted by the Commission on Small Island States on Climate Change and International Law; with some delegations even expressing their intention to submit written statements relating to the case.[44] Thus, States have a setting in SPLOS in which they may express their views on the activities and work of the Tribunal.

Whilst States Parties are generally positive with respect to the Tribunal, there have been occasions where non-State Parties are not so complimentary. For instance, an observer delegation has expressed the view that UNCLOS, including the Statute of the Tribunal contained in annex VI, "did not expressly provide for any advisory jurisdiction beyond that bestowed upon the Seabed Disputes Chamber".[45] Be that as it may, the Meeting provides an item on the agenda whereby non-State Parties, as observer delegations, are also able to participate in the discussion on the work of ITLOS. It should also be noted that States have also presented their positions in relation to judgements of the Tribunal under the agenda of the Report of the Secretary-General under article 319 of UNCLOS;[46] as such, they are responding to the Secretary-General's Report and therefore acting within the institutional practice of SPLOS.

As aptly pointed out by Niels Blokker, "an acceptable balance is found between the need for the Tribunal to explain what and how it is doing, and the wish of states parties and observers to give their views on the work of the Tribunal without affecting its independence";[47] and that fundamentally, "an atmosphere of trust has prevailed in the relationship between ITLOS and SPLOS".[48]

41 *Ibidem*, para. 18.

42 *Ibidem*, para. 20.

43 *Ibidem.*

44 *Ibidem*, para. 21.

45 Report of the Twenty-sixth Meeting of States Parties, 20–24 June 2026, SPLOS/303 (2016), para. 25.

46 Report of the Thirty-first Meeting of States Parties (*supra* note 9), para. 81: A delegation drew attention to the recent judgment of the Special Chamber of the Tribunal concerning delimitation of the maritime boundary between Mauritius and Maldives in the Indian Ocean.

47 Blokker (*supra* note 2), p. 90.

48 *Ibidem.*

4 The Nature of the Mandate of SPLOS Pursuant to Article 319 UNCLOS

Is the mandate of SPLOS pursuant to Article 319 of UNCLOS restricted to administrative, financial, and procedural functions – or does the Meeting of Parties also have broader powers to hold substantive discussions? Since 1997, this topic has served as a divisive theme in meetings of SPLOS.[49] Recall the nature of ITLOS as an international tribunal – it does not create rights and obligations for States Parties, but rather its role is to settle disputes on the application and interpretation of UNCLOS. This issue thus speaks to the role of SPLOS as a Meeting of Parties rather than its role as an INJUGOVIN to ITLOS. Indeed, treaties typically establish mechanisms to oversee their review and implementation – which is absent in UNCLOS.[50] The absence thereof raises questions pertaining to the mandate of SPLOS pursuant to Article 319 (2)(e) of UNCLOS – whether "necessary meetings" include meetings that speak on substance of the Convention.[51]

The discussion first arose at the sixth meeting of SPLOS, where the Meeting decided to include "the role of the Meeting of States Parties in reviewing ocean and law of the sea issues" in the agenda of the next meeting.[52] At the tenth meeting of SPLOS, Chile submitted a proposal to include a new item in the agenda of the next SPLOS meeting, entitled either "Implementation of the United Nations Convention on the Law of the Sea" or "Issues of a general nature related to the United Nations Convention on the Law of the Sea".[53] Notably, the

49 See Report of the Sixth Meeting of States Parties, 10–14 March 1997, SPLOS/20 (1997); Report of the Seventh Meeting of States Parties, 19–23 May 1997, SPLOS/24 (1997); Report of the Eighth meeting of States Parties, 18–22 May 1998, SPLOS/31; Report of the Ninth meeting of States Parties, 19–28 May 1999, SPLOS/48 (1999); Report of Tenth meeting of States Parties (*supra* note 28); Report of Eleventh Meeting of States Parties (*supra* note 30); Report of Twelfth Meeting of States Parties, 16–26 April 2002, SPLOS/91 (2002); Report of Thirteenth Meeting of States Parties, 9–13 June 2003, SPLOS/103; Report of Fourteenth Meeting of States Parties, 14–18 June 2004, SPLOS/119 (2004).

50 Alex G. Oude Elferink, "Reviewing the Implementation of the LOS Convention: The Role of the United Nations General Assembly and the Meeting of States Parties", in Alex G. Oude Elferink and Donald Rothwell (eds.), *Ocean Management in the 21st Century: Institutional Frameworks and Responses* (2004), p. 302.

51 Liesbeth Lijnzaad, "Formal and Informal Processes in the Contemporary Law of the Sea at the United Nations, a Practitioner's View", in *German Yearbook of International Law* vol. 57 (2014), pp. 111, 114.

52 Report of the Sixth Meeting of States Parties (*supra* note 49), para. 36(e). Report at the Seventh Meeting of States Parties (*supra* note 49), paras. 38–41. See also Report of the Ninth Meeting of States Parties (*supra* note 49), paras. 49–53.

53 Report of the Tenth Meeting of States Parties (*supra* note 28), para. 73: Chile proposed, *inter alia*, "that the Parties to the Convention should consider the implementation of the

proposal revisited Article 319 (2)(a) to suggest *inter alia* that the Meeting of States Parties would receive a report from the Secretary-General of the UN every year on issues of a general nature that had arisen with respect to the Convention.[54] This was met with different views between States.[55] Of note, some delegations "expressed the view that an expansion of the mandate of the Meeting of States Parties beyond budgetary and administrative matters, as proposed by Chile and other delegations, was not provided for in the Convention".[56] In view of the divergent views expressed, the Meeting agreed to include in the agenda of the next Meeting an item entitled "Matters related to Article 319 of UNCLOS".[57] This item remained on the agenda until the Fourteenth Meeting, where it continued to be met with opposing views.[58] Delegations in support of a more substantive role for the Meetings of Parties advanced a proposal that referred to the reporting function of the Secretary-General under Article 319 (2)(a) of UNCLOS.[59] Accordingly, the Secretary-General would report to the Meeting on issues of a general nature that had arisen with respected to the Convention. This report would facilitate substantive discussions by the Meeting.[60]

Extensive deliberations were put forward, and ultimately the Meeting approved the adoption of the proposal that "the annual report of the Secretary-General on oceans and the law of the sea presented before the General Assembly should make reference to the fact that it is also presented to States Parties pursuant to article 319 of the Convention".[61] This proposal also included a new item, entitled "Report of the Secretary-General under article 319 for the information of States Parties on issues of a general nature relevant to States Parties that have arisen with respect to the UN Convention on the Law of the Sea" to be included in the agenda of the next Meeting.[62] The item has retained on the agenda of SPLOS to date,[63] allowing States Parties in SPLOS meetings to be provided information on substantive issues with respect to UNCLOS and

Convention. To that end, the Meeting of States Parties would receive a report from the Secretary-General of the United Nations every year on issues of a general nature that had arisen with respect to the Convention, as provided for in Art. 319 of the Convention [...]".

54 *Ibidem.*

55 *Ibidem*, para. 74 (for views in support); para. 75 (for views against).

56 *Ibidem*, para. 75.

57 *Ibidem*, para. 78.

58 Report of the Fourteenth Meeting of States Parties (*supra* note 49), para.79.

59 *Ibidem*, para. 82.

60 *Ibidem.* Note that some delegations reiterated their opposition to the consideration of issues of implementation of the Convention by the Meeting of States Parties.

61 *Ibidem*, para. 85.

62 *Ibidem.*

63 Report of the Thirty-third Meeting of States Parties (*supra* note 9), paras. 76–95.

to communicate their views. The Meeting takes "note" of the reports of the Secretary-General under article 319 and the views expressed by the delegations under that agenda item.[64]

Recently, views expressed by delegations under the agenda item "Reports of the Secretary-General under article 319 of the Convention" have included *inter alia* welcoming the ratification by Rwanda of UNCLOS;[65] noting the progress in the negotiations on a legally binding agreement on plastic pollution and underscoring the importance of addressing plastic pollution to advance ocean sustainability;[66] reaffirming commitment to achieving the ocean-related targets set out in the 2030 Agenda for Sustainable Development;[67] drawing attention to the human dimension of the ocean and vulnerable groups that depend on the ocean and its resources for food security and livelihoods, including women and girls, migrants at sea and seafarers, many of whom continued to suffer from the impacts of the COVID-19 pandemic as well as natural disasters linked to the oceans;[68] the impact of human activities on the ocean;[69] taking note of the request by the General Assembly to the ICJ to render an advisory opinion on the obligations of States in respect of climate change, as well as the request for an advisory opinion submitted by the Commission of Small Island States on Climate Change and International Law to the Tribunal;[70] particular challenges posed by sea level rise and the potential impacts on maritime zones, the Declaration on Preserving Maritime Zones in the Face of Climate-Change-related Sea-Level Rise which was issued by the Pacific Island Forum member countries in 2021 and noting the work of the International Law Commission;[71] the issue of overexploitation of living resources and overfishing;[72] serious concern about the planned release by Japan of treated water from the Fukushima Daiichi nuclear power station into the sea;[73] the issue of the South China Sea;[74] concern about reports of an increased number of incidents in the Straits of Malacca and Singapore, as well as the illegal activities of flag State vessels in the Gulf of Guinea.[75]

64 *Ibidem*, para. 95.
65 *Ibidem*, para. 78.
66 *Ibidem*, para. 80.
67 *Ibidem*, para. 81.
68 *Ibidem*, para. 83.
69 *Ibidem*, para. 87.
70 *Ibidem*, para. 88.
71 *Ibidem*, para. 89.
72 *Ibidem*, para. 90.
73 *Ibidem*, para. 91.
74 *Ibidem*, para. 92.
75 *Ibidem*, para. 93.

It would, thus, appear that the States Parties to the Meeting are able to engage on issues beyond the administrative and financial governance of ITLOS, and that the Meeting takes note of their views along with the Secretary-General's Reports under article 319.[76] Notably, an observer delegation has reiterated in a recent meeting of SPLOS that "the focus of the Meeting of States Parties should be on administrative, procedural and financial issues and that it should not engage in a broad review of the application or interpretation of the Convention".[77] Perhaps it can be inferred that a non-State Party to UNCLOS may have a preference for substantive issues on the law of the sea to be discussed in the General Assembly. The political sub-text exceeds the compass of this inquiry.[78] Instead, the inquiry poses an international institutional law question, which is whether SPLOS has a substantive role in reviewing law of the sea issues – or whether this role falls within the mandate of the General Assembly pursuant to its resolutions 49/28 of 6 January 1994 and 54/33 of November 1999.[79] The latter is a definite yes; as it will be discussed further below. With respect to the former, the issue remains an open question as UNCLOS does not confer express powers to the Meeting of Parties to make decisions pertaining to substantive issues on the law of the sea. Be that as it may, the Meetings nevertheless provide a multilateral setting where States Parties and observer States can communicate their views in response to the Secretary-General's reports under Article 319 of UNCLOS and, in so doing, put forward their position on matters relating to the law of the sea and more.

5 The Practice of the United Nations since the Adoption of UNCLOS

UNCLOS is mostly silent with respect to the General Assembly.[80] Nevertheless, since the adoption of UNCLOS in 1982, the General Assembly *decided* to undertake an annual review and evaluation of the implementation of UNCLOS, and other developments related to the law of the sea.[81] Notably, the General Assembly entrusted itself with this role. Whilst this role is generally assumed by the Meeting of Parties/Conference of Parties in multilateral treaties,[82] UNCLOS itself is silent on this role. As such, the General Assembly assumed this role. This is in line with its long-standing involvement with the law of the

76 *Ibidem*, para. 95.
77 *Ibidem*, para. 94.
78 Lijnzaad (*supra* note 51), pp. 116–117; Treves (*supra* note 25), pp. 61–63.
79 A/RES/49/28 (1994) and A/RES/54/33 (1996).
80 Treves (*supra* note 25), p. 57.
81 GA Resolution A/Res49/28 (1994), para. 12.
82 Oude Elferink (*supra* note 50), p. 304.

sea, which had commenced even before the adoption of UNCLOS.[83] To date, the General Assembly considers the agenda item "Oceans and the law of the sea" every year. In 1996, the General Assembly granted observer status to ITLOS, enabling the Tribunal to participate in the meetings and work of the General Assembly when matters of relevance to the Tribunal are considered,[84] and for the President of ITLOS to address the General Assembly during the agenda item on Oceans and law of the sea.

In 1999, the UN Open-ended Informal Consultative Process on Oceans and the Law of the Sea ("UN Process") was established pursuant to UNCLOS and the goals of chapter 17 of Agenda 2:

> in order to facilitate the annual review by the General Assembly, in an effective and constructive manner, of developments in ocean affairs by considering the Secretary-General's report on oceans and the law of the sea and by suggesting particular issues to be considered by it, with an emphasis on identifying areas where coordination and cooperation at the intergovernmental and inter-agency levels should be enhanced.[85]

The UN Process is open to member States, members of UN specialized agencies, parties to the Convention, invited entities, and competent international organizations.[86] From a multilateralism perspective, the General Assembly is indeed uniquely placed to further coherence of oceans law and policy – and to facilitate new-law making efforts by convening intergovernmental conferences for the negotiation and adoption of internationally binding instruments, e.g., an international legally binding instrument under UNCLOS on the conservation and sustainable use of marine biological diversity of areas beyond national jurisdiction.[87]

---

83 For example, GA Resolution 1105(XI) 1957 (decides to convene the United Nations Conference on the Law of the Sea in Geneva from 24 February to 27 April 1958); GA Resolution 1307 (XIII) 1960 (convening a second United Nations conference on the law of the sea); GA Resolution 2750 C (XXV) (decides to convene a third conference on the law of the sea in 1973).

84 GA Resolution A/Res/51/204, 17 December 1996.

85 GA Resolution A/Res/54/33 (2000), para.2.

86 *Ibidem*, para.3(d): the meetings should, in identifying areas where coordination and cooperation are to be enhanced, bear in mind the differing characteristics and needs of the different regions of the world and should not pursue legal or juridical coordination among the different legal instruments. See Treves (*supra* note 25), p. 67.

87 General Assembly Resolution 72/249 (2017). On 19 June 2003, the Conference adopted, by consensus, the Agreement under UNCLOS on the conservation and sustainable use of marine biological diversity of areas beyond national jurisdiction (A/CONF.232/2023/4).

The inquiry now shifts towards examining the practice of the Secretary-General after the adoption of UNCLOS. The responsibilities of the Secretary-General under UNCLOS were specified through the adoption, in 1982, by the General Assembly of Resolution 37/66, which recognized the "need for the Secretary-General to be authorized to assume his functions under the Convention and the related resolutions, including in particular the provision of the secretariat services required by the Preparatory Commission for its effective and expeditious functioning";[88] and approved "the assumption by the Secretary-General of the responsibilities entrusted to him under the Convention".[89] The General Assembly also requested *inter alia* that the Secretary-General should continue to carry out the responsibilities entrusted to him upon the adoption of the Convention, which included "preparing for and convening the Meetings of States Parties to the Convention and providing the necessary services for such meetings, in accordance with the Convention".[90]

Indeed, the entry into force of UNCLOS triggered a series of actions undertaken by the Secretariat, and the Secretary-General as mandated by the Convention, and resolutions of the General Assembly.[91] The Office of Legal Affairs, as a department of the Secretariat, established a Division for Ocean Affairs and the Law of the Sea (DOALAS) after the adoption of UNCLOS. Its core functions include inter alia: (a) promoting better understanding and wider appreciation of UNCLOS [...]; (b) discharging depository responsibilities of the Secretary-General under the Convention other than treaty depository functions [...]; (c) providing substantive servicing to the Meeting of States Parties to the Convention.[92] The Secretariat of SPLOS is DOALAS, thereby providing a "UN flavour" to the Meeting of Parties as coined by Liesbeth Lijnzaad.[93]

The first Report of the Secretary-General under article 319(a) of UNCLOS was reported to the Fifth Meeting of Parties in 1996.[94] Subsequently, no reports had been submitted to the Meeting of SPLOS under Article 319 (2)(a).[95] The matter received attention in the Tenth Meeting of SPLOS, pursuant to Chile's proposal

88 GA Resolution 37/66 (1982), preamble.

89 *Ibidem*, para. 7.

90 GA Resolution 49/28 1994, para. 15(g); GA Resolution 52/26 1998, para. 11(g).

91 A/49/631 1994, para. 16. See also A/50/713 1995; A/51/645 1 November 1996.

92 Organization of the Office of Legal Affairs 18 January 2021, ST/SGB/2021/1, Section 9, Division for Ocean Affairs and the Law of the Sea.

93 Lijnzaad (*supra* note 51), p. 113.

94 Report of the Secretary-General under Art. 319 of the United Nations Convention on the Law of the Sea, SPLOS/6 (1996), para. 55; Report of the Fifth Meeting of States Parties, 24 July–2 August 1996, SPLOS/14 (1996), para. 4.

95 See Report of the Fourteenth Meeting of States Parties (*supra* note 49), para. 83.

that the Meeting should receive an annual report from the Secretary-General on issues of a general nature that had arisen with respect to the Convention.[96] The issue was addressed again at the Eleventh Meeting of States Parties, where the Under-Secretary-General for Legal Affairs made a statement on the mandate given to the Secretary-General by the Assembly with regard to the preparation of comprehensive reports on developments relating to the implementation of the Convention, the law of the sea and ocean affairs.[97] As already discussed above, States Parties approved in the Fourteenth Meeting of SPLOS that "the annual report of the Secretary-General on oceans and the law of the sea presented before the General Assembly should make reference to the fact that it is also presented to States Parties pursuant to article 319 of the Convention".[98] Accordingly, the Secretary-General's report to the General-Assembly in 2004 included a reference to States Parties pursuant to Article 319;[99] and this practice has continued to ensue in all Secretary-General's reports to the General Assembly on Oceans and the Law of the Sea.[100]

One further institutional arrangement should be mentioned briefly. ITLOS has a voluntary Trust Fund to provide States Parties to the Convention with financial assistance for expenses associated with cases which have already been submitted or which may be submitted to the Tribunal, including to the Seabed Disputes Chamber or any other chamber.[101] The Tenth Meeting of SPLOS decided to recommend to the General Assembly to consider the establishment of a trust fund, to be financed through voluntary contributions, for the purpose of providing financial assistance to States in order to help them in proceedings before the Tribunal.[102] Consequently, the General Assembly requested the Secretary-General to establish a voluntary trust fund to assist States in the settlement of disputes through the Tribunal and to report annually to the Meeting of States Parties to the Convention on the status of the fund on Cooperation.[103] In 2000, the Secretary-General established the Truth

96 Report of the Tenth Meeting of States Parties (*supra* note 28), para. 73.

97 Report of the Eleventh Meeting of States Parties (*supra* note 30), para. 86.

98 Report of the Fourteenth Meeting of States Parties (*supra* note 49), para. 85. Note that the Director of the Division for Ocean Affairs and the Law of the Sea provided information on the obligations of the Secretary-General under Art. 319(2)(a) at para. 83.

99 Addendum to the annual report of the Secretary-General, 18 August 2004, A/59/52/Add.1.

100 Most recently, Report of the Secretary General, 1 September 2023, A/78/339.

101 GA Resolution A/Res/55/7 (2001) Annex 1, para. 4.

102 Decision regarding the establishment of a trust fund for assisting States in proceedings before the International Tribunal for the Law of the Sea, SPLOS/57 (2000); Report of the Tenth Meeting of States Parties (*supra* note 28); SPLOS/60 (2000), paras. 41–47.

103 GA Resolution A/Res/55/7 (2001), para. 9.

Fund in accordance with GA Resolution 55/7 and pursuant to the Agreement on Cooperation and Relationship between the UN and ITLOS.[104] This institutional arrangement is indicative that the practice of SPLOS cannot be viewed in isolation from the practice of the United Nations.

6 *Mare Ignotum?*

The present contribution to this *Liber Amicorum* has adopted an international institutional law analytical framework to engage with the *sui generis* nature of SPLOS. Accordingly, States Parties to UNCLOS as the 'masters of the treaty' have the power to modify/amend the Convention, and to develop the practice of the Meeting of Parties to the Convention. The seemingly 'very thin basis' in UNCLOS that led to the establishment, and practice of SPLOS, was given effect by the existing institutional framework of the UN: the General Assembly approved the assumption of the Secretary-General of the responsibilities entrusted to him (her) upon the adoption of UNCLOS. The Secretariat of the UN established DOALAS under the Office of Legal Affairs to act as the Secretariat for SPLOS and service the Meeting of Parties.

The practice of SPLOS has developed in a way where both States Parties and non-states Parties may present their views in the Meetings in response to the Report presented by the President of ITLOS and the Secretary-General's report under Article 319. Thus, it appears that SPLOS has developed into a forum where States can comment broadly upon matters relating to the law of the sea and, more generally, ocean governance. Specific competences of SPLOS can be explained by delving into the institutional law and practice of the UN. For instance, its role with respect to substantive issues in UNCLOS is aligned with the role entrusted to the Secretary-General by the Convention in Article 319 (2)(a) – and as approved by the General Assembly. In a similar vein, SPLOS provides a setting for States Parties to make recommendations to the General Assembly, e.g., on the establishment of the Trust Fund for ITLOS. There is notably a relationship between SPLOS and the UN, as well as a clear institutional arrangement between the respective competences with regard to the law of the sea. On this note, perhaps SPLOS, the INJUGOVINS of ITLOS, may not be *mare ignotum* after all.

104 *Ibidem*, and GA Resolution A/Res/52/521 (1998).

PART 3

Preserving Justice

CHAPTER 13

The Contribution of International Organizations to the Settlement of International Disputes

*Eric De Brabandere and Jason Rudall**

1 Introduction

In their seminal book, Henry Schermers and Niels Blokker observed that there has been a "formidable increase in the number of international courts and tribunals since the 1990s".[1] Indeed, in recent decades the number of legal dispute settlement mechanisms charged with settling disputes based on international law has significantly increased. What is more, the role and involvement of non-state actors in these 'new' and existing dispute settlement mechanisms is multifaceted.[2] This chapter focuses on one specific actor, namely international organizations, and will map the various ways that international organizations have contributed to the settlement of international disputes.

The obligation to settle disputes peacefully is expressed in Article 1(1) and Article 2(3) of the United Nations (UN) Charter. Much has been written on the range of dispute settlement means available, such as those indicated in Article 33 of the UN Charter,[3] on specific types of dispute settlement mechanism, such as judicial or diplomatic means of settlement,[4] and on the forms of dispute settlement that have become predominant in certain specialized fields of international law, such as human rights law, international trade law or

* Grotius Centre for International Legal Studies, Leiden University.

1 Henry G. Schermers and Niels M. Blokker, *International Institutional Law* (6th ed., Brill, 2018), p. 1273.

2 See Eric de Brabandere, "Non-State Actors and the Individualization and Proliferation of International Dispute Settlement", in B. Reinalda (ed), *The Ashgate Research Companion to Non-State Actors* (Ashgate, 2011), pp. 347–59.

3 See, e.g., John Merrills and Eric de Brabandere, *Merrills' International Dispute Settlement* (7th ed., Cambridge UP, 2022); John Collier and Vaughan Lowe, *The Settlement of Disputes in International Law* (Oxford UP, 1999).

4 See, e.g., Merrills and De Brabandere (note 3); Thomas Schultz and Federica Ortino (eds.), *The Oxford Handbook of International Arbitration* (Oxford UP, 2020); Cesare Romano, Karen Alter and Yuval Shany (eds.), *The Oxford Handbook of International Adjudication* (Oxford UP, 2013); Laurence Boisson de Chazournes, Marcelo Kohen and Jorge Viñuales (eds.), *Diplomatic and Judicial Means of Dispute Settlement* (Brill, 2013).

 | DOI:10.1163/9789004699939_015

investor-state dispute settlement.[5] But little scholarship has been dedicated to the full panoply of contributions that international organizations have made to and their role within the settlement of international disputes.[6] This chapter seeks to fill that gap.

We identify three broad frames within which international organizations have contributed to the settlement of international disputes. First, international organizations can play a role in the creation of dispute settlement mechanisms, providing the institutional context, machinery and constraints for the settlement of disputes that arise within the mandate of the international organization. We call this their architectural contribution. Second, international organizations can play a role, often diplomatic in nature, at various stages of specific disputes between other actors, either at the initiation of a dispute, during the proceedings or after a dispute has been decided by a judicial mechanism, all generally with the purpose of facilitating the final settlement of a dispute. As such, we characterize this contribution as one of facilitation. Third, international organizations can be parties to disputes themselves. We call this frame participation.

2 Architectural: International Organizations and the Creation of Dispute Settlement Mechanisms

An important function of international organizations in international dispute settlement is their role in the creation of dispute settlement mechanisms, mostly for disputes involving parties other than the organization itself. While the creation of new international organizations may not automatically lead to the formation of new dispute settlement mechanisms, it is often the case that an arbitral forum, international court or tribunal, or accountability mechanism

---

5 See, e.g., Charles Jalloh, Kamari Clarke and Vincent Nmehielle (eds.), *The African Court of Justice and Human and Peoples' Rights in Context: Development and Challenges* (Cambridge UP, 2019); Philip Leach, *Taking a Case to the European Court of Human Rights* (2nd ed., Oxford UP, 2005); Laurence Burgorgue-Larsen and Amaya Úbeda de Torres, *The Inter-American Court of Human Rights. Case Law and Commentary* (Oxford UP, 2011); Tim Stephens, *International Courts and Environmental Protection* (Cambridge UP, 2009); David Palmeter and Petros Mavroidis, *Dispute Settlement in the World Trade Organization: Practice and Procedure* (3rd ed., Cambridge UP, 2022); Taylor St. John, *The Rise of Investor-State Arbitration: Politics, Law and Unintended Consequences* (Oxford UP, 2018).

6 For one older contribution, see Laurence Boisson de Chazournes, Cesare Romano and Ruth Mackenzie (eds.), *International Organizations and International Dispute Settlement: Trends and Prospects* (Brill, 2002).

is linked to the international organization in some form. This could either be because these have been established under the auspices of an international organization or through its active implication, or because such a mechanism has been created as an organ of an international organization. The architectural contribution of international organizations to dispute settlement, then, is mostly visible through the establishment of legal methods of settlement, i.e. those which result in a binding outcome through arbitration or adjudication, but also through other methods of settlement such as conciliation and fact-finding.

A first type of dispute settlement mechanism, in particular courts and tribunals, have been established as organs of an international organization. In those cases, international organizations have created these mechanisms to settle disputes between their member states, and/or to interpret the constitution of the organization and to settle disputes in respect of the organization's functioning.

A well-known example can of course be given with the International Court of Justice (ICJ), the principal judicial organ of the UN. The primary function of the ICJ is to settle legal disputes between states and to give advisory opinions on legal questions referred to it by the UN General Assembly, the UN Security Council, and other specialized UN agencies and related organizations. This in and of itself provides an insight as to the interaction between an international organization and a judicial dispute settlement mechanism. But the ICJ is unique, as the establishment of the ICJ within the framework of the UN does not necessarily imply that the Court's competence is limited to disputes arising out of the Charter obligations of its members, or disputes relating to the organization's functioning. The ICJ has no compulsory jurisdiction over states' obligations under the UN Charter or towards the organization. Instead, the ICJ has an optional general competence for the settlement of international disputes. That the ICJ is a UN organ is first and foremost observable from the Court's jurisdiction in advisory proceedings.

There are many examples of other international organizations that have created a dispute settlement mechanism to deal principally with disputes relating to the obligations of states arising under the constitution of the organization or related treaties or to interpret the constitution of the organization. The World Trade Organization (WTO), for example, has a dispute settlement mechanism that allows member states to bring trade-related disputes for settlement under the various agreements which are part of the WTO Agreement.[7]

7 Surya P. Subedi, "The WTO Dispute Settlement Mechanism as a New Technique for Settling Disputes in International Law", in Duncan French, Matthew Saul and Nigel D. White (eds.), *International Law and Dispute Settlement: New Problems and Techniques* (Hart, 2010), pp. 173–190.

The WTO Dispute Settlement Understanding (DSU) has created a multi-tiered dispute settlement system which has jurisdiction over disputes between Members concerning their rights and obligations under the WTO Agreement (Art. 1 DSU). This dispute settlement mechanism had once been lauded as a particularly effective one among international courts and tribunals. However, the WTO's Appellate Body has ceased to function in recent years, exposing the weaknesses of dispute settlement bodies tied to political institutions. Due to the blocking of appointments of members, the Appellate Body eventually failed to have the minimum three members required to form a quorum and hear cases.

Another example is the EU's Court of Justice, which probably provides the best example of an all-inclusive international judicial dispute settlement mechanism integrated in an international organization since it is competent to interpret the constitution of the international organization, to settle disputes in respect of its functioning (including the review of judicial acts of its organs), and to settle disputes in respect of the obligations of states under the international organization's constitutional treaty.[8] This type of institutional dispute settlement is unique because the EU is an organization with a high level of integration.

Sometimes international organizations play a less involved role in the settlement of disputes, while still establishing the institutional forum within which disputes are settled. International organizations then have contributed to the creation of mechanisms which are formally outside the structure of an international organization. Such judicial bodies may themselves be independent international organizations but are, strictly speaking, not organs of a specific international organization. This is the case for the International Tribunal for the Law of the Sea (ITLOS).[9] Another example is the World Bank, which serves as the host and administrative body of the International Centre for the Settlement of Investment Disputes (ICSID), providing facilities for dispute resolution and acting as a secretariat for ICSID arbitration.[10] ICSID is an autonomous institution, and its dispute settlement function is distinct from the World Bank's operations. But the World Bank acts as the depository of the ICSID Convention, which establishes the legal framework for the resolution of investment disputes in this context.

8 Frank Hoffmeister, "The European Union and the Peaceful Settlement of International Disputes", in *Chinese J Intl L* vol. 11 (2012), p. 77.

9 See De Brabandere (*supra* note 2), pp. 347–359.

10 See Antonio R. Parra, *ICSID: An Introduction to the Convention and Centre* (Oxford UP, 2020), in particular Chapter 1.

International organizations can also play an important role in settling disputes that arise in particular regions or over specific types of disputes, such as shared resources. The regional and targeted dispute settlement mechanisms, however, are mostly a combination of various forms of diplomatic settlement, such as providing facilities for negotiation, mediation, and conciliation, but they do sometimes institutionalize a dispute settlement mechanism that goes beyond facilitation. For instance, in the context of freshwater governance, certain basin organizations have a clearly articulated dispute settlement mechanism envisaged in their constitutive instruments. The Administrative Commission of the River Uruguay (CARU), constituted under the 1975 Statute on the River Uruguay, has a part to play in the settlement of disputes, for example. As the ICJ highlighted in the *Pulp Mills* case, the 1975 Statute provides that "the Commission can act as a conciliation body in any dispute which may arise between the parties".[11] Under the Lake Chad Basin Commission's Statute of 1964, this Commission is endowed with the power to resolve disputes[12] while the Water Charter for the Lake Chad Basin of 2012, which provides the broader legal framework governing the basin, sets out in Article 87 that "[i]f the parties fail to come to an agreement after negotiation, any party thereto shall bring the case to the Commission, which shall conduct good offices or mediation procedure in attempt to reach a settlement".

What might be characterized as less direct forms of dispute settlement can be highlighted in the form of the role that international organizations and their representatives play in settling disputes, often through the establishment of an *ad hoc* method of settlement. Good examples are commissions of inquiry that are often created by and operate under the auspices of an international organization. International commissions of inquiry represent a form of independent expert investigation and provide a form of remedial action for victims of damage. Such missions are often established by international organizations or agencies and are mostly set up to investigate situations or conflicts, rather than to settle disputes in the legal-technical sense. We might point to the Report of the Independent Inquiry into the Actions of the United Nations during the 1994 Genocide in Rwanda,[13] the Report of the Secretary-General Pursuant to General Assembly Resolution 53/35 into the Fall of Srebrenica,[14] or the report

11 ICJ, *Pulp Mills on the River Uruguay* (*Argentina v. Uruguay*), [2010] ICJ Reports 14 [92].

12 Convention and Statutes Relating to the Development of the Chad Basin (adopted 22 May 1964, entered into force 22 May 1964), 61 *FAO Legislative Series* (FAO, 1997), art 9(h).

13 UNSC, *Report of the Independent Inquiry into the Actions of the United Nations during the 1994 Genocide in Rwanda* (16 December 1999), UN Doc S/1999/1257.

14 UNGA, *Report of the Secretary-General pursuant to General Assembly resolution 53/35: The fall of Srebrenica* (15 November 1999), UN Doc A/54/549.

issued by a commission of inquiry set up by the UN Secretary-General in the *Mavi Marmara* incident of 2010 to "examine and identify the facts, circumstances and context of the incident; and consider and recommend ways of avoiding similar incidents in the future".[15]

Despite the proliferation of dispute settlement mechanisms set up by or as part of an international organization, it is important to highlight that recent years have witnessed a 'backlash' against international organizations as well as their dispute settlement procedures.[16] One may think of withdrawal and other challenges faced by the International Criminal Court, the WTO and in particular its Appellate Body, the Court of Justice of the European Union and the European Court of Human Rights, as well as ICSID.[17] But international organizations nevertheless continue to play an important role in dispute settlement, not least in facilitating the resolution of specific disputes throughout dispute settlement processes, to which the next section turns.

3 Facilitation: The Role of International Organizations Before, During and After Specific Disputes

Aside from their architectural function in the creation and hosting of dispute settlement mechanisms, international organizations also play an important role in the settlement of specific disputes that arise. This role can take place before, during and after a given dispute, and can take various forms, such as the use by international organizations of diplomatic means of settlement, or the role international organizations have before, during or after a judicial mechanism has been seized of a particular dispute.

In the first instance, international organizations often engage in conflict prevention and early warning activities to identify potential sources of tension and conflict before they escalate. Through diplomatic channels and monitoring mechanisms, they can work to address underlying issues and prevent disputes from turning into open conflicts. Many international organizations actively try to bring parties together, facilitating dialogue, and proposing solutions that can lead to peaceful settlements. Some of these methods are indicated by

15 See United Nations, *Report of the Secretary-General's Panel of Inquiry on the 31 May 2010 Flotilla Incident* (September 2011), available at <www.unispal.un.org/pdfs/GazaFlotillaPanelReport.pdf>, accessed 17 January 2024.

16 Joost Pauwelyn and Rebecca Hamilton, "Exit from International Tribunals", in *J Intl Dispute Settlement* vol. 9 (2018), p. 679.

17 *Ibidem*, pp. 679–80.

Article 33 UN Charter, located in Chapter VI of the UN Charter entitled 'Pacific Settlement of Disputes', and include negotiation, enquiry, mediation, or conciliation. In fact, international organizations have very often provided good offices that have aided in the resolution of disputes. In the context of the UN, the Secretary-General has played an important role in that respect, aside from this formal role under the UN Charter. As noted by the Security Council, "the work of the Council regarding conflict prevention and the peaceful settlement of disputes has, however, required the involvement of the Secretary-General in all relevant aspects of that agenda".[18] This involvement mostly relates to "the good offices work of the Secretary-General, as well as that of his special representatives and envoys, in support of efforts to end violent conflict, of peace and reconciliation processes, and the resolution of outstanding disputes".[19] In the recent war between Russia and Ukraine, offers of good offices in relation to that conflict have been made by the UN Secretary-General, amongst others,[20] and the agreement relating to the resumption of the export of grain and fertilizers, the so-called 'Black Sea Grain Initiative',[21] was the result of mediation by Turkey and the UN Secretary-General. In 2018, several Security Council Member States have, moreover, "encouraged the Secretary-General to fully exercise his power under Article 99 and to strengthen the effectiveness of his good offices".[22] While the UN has a long history of mediating conflicts in different regions, regional organizations, such as the EU and the Organization of American States (OAS), similarly facilitate dialogue and cooperation among their members.

Secondly, the exercise of diplomatic means within an international organization can play a significant role before, during or after a judicial mechanism has been seized of a particular dispute. A first role consists of recommending specific methods of settlement to the disputing parties. Article 36 of the UN Charter, for example, provides that the "Security Council may, at any stage of a dispute of the nature referred to in Article 33 or of a situation of like nature,

18 United Nations, *Repertoire of the Practice of the Security Council: Supplement 2019* (2021) UN Doc ST/PSCA/1/Add.22, 43.

19 *Ibidem.*

20 See EEAS Press Team, *Ukraine: Statement by High Representative/Vice-President Josep Borrell at the UN General Assembly Emergency Session* (New York, 22 February 2023), available at <www.eeas.europa.eu/eeas/ukraine-statement-high-representativevice-president-josep-borrell-un-general-assembly_en>, accessed 17 January 2024.

21 'Beacon on the Black Sea' (*United Nations*), available at www.un.org/en/black-sea-grain-initiative, accessed 17 January 2024.

22 United Nations, *Repertoire of the Practice of the Security Council: Supplement 2018* (2020) UN Doc ST/PSCA/1/Add.21, 313.

recommend appropriate procedures or methods of adjustment" but that it should consider any procedures for dispute settlement already pursued by the parties and that "as a general rule" disputes should "be referred by the parties to the International Court of Justice". That international organizations can recommend disputes to be referred to international courts or tribunals was evident in the very first case heard by the ICJ. Through its Resolution 22 of 1947, the UN Security Council advised that Albania and the United Kingdom submit their dispute concerning the mining of the Corfu Channel to the ICJ.[23] Outside of the UN, the Council of the OAS acting provisionally as an Organ of Consultation advised Nicaragua and Honduras that their dispute over the *Arbitral Award made by the King of Spain* be submitted by special agreement to the ICJ.[24]

Once a dispute has been initiated before a judicial mechanism, there can be various ways that an international organization and the dispute settlement mechanism interact. One such example can be found under Article 41(2) of the ICJ Statute, according to which the ICJ informs the Security Council of provisional measures it has indicated. International organizations might also play a role in providing evidence for the court or tribunal, often from prior fact-finding missions that may have been conducted.[25]

And international organizations regularly play a role after a decision has been handed down by a dispute settlement mechanism. International organizations are often the forum in which diplomatic means of dispute settlement complement judicial means of dispute settlement. Indeed, international organizations can provide a helpful framework for negotiation, cooperation and support for states as they implement the findings of a judicial dispute settlement process.[26] As Judge Sepúlveda Amor put it, "in a world of sovereign states characterized by the absence of centralised enforcement mechanisms, diplomatic

23 UNSC Res 22 (9 April 1947), UN Doc S/RES/22.

24 See Resolution of the Council of the Organization of American States of 5 July 1957, OAS Doc C-sa-254; *Arbitral Award made by the King of Spain* (*Honduras v. Nicaragua*), [1960] ICJ Reports 162.

25 For example, the reports of the UN Independent International Fact-Finding Mission on Myanmar, established by the UN Human Rights Council in 2017, played a role in *Application of the Convention on the Prevention and Punishment of the Crime of Genocide* (*The Gambia v. Myanmar*) (Preliminary Objections), [2022] ICJ Reports 477, [66], [68]–[69], [72]–[74], [76].

26 Laurence Boisson de Chazournes and Antonella Angelini, "Between Saying and Doing: The Diplomatic Means to Implement the International Court of Justice's Iuris Dictum", in Boisson de Chazournes a.o. (*supra* note 4), p. 168.

means remain, for better or for worse, the last resort to guarantee the outcome of third-party adjudication".[27]

Following the ICJ's decision in the *Land and Maritime Boundary* (*Cameroon v. Nigeria*) case, for example, the UN Secretary-General assisted with the creation of a Mixed Commission to overcome several outstanding issues that would otherwise have prevented the implementation of the Court's judgment.[28] Another example is the role played by the UN observer mission UNASOG in the aftermath of the ICJ's decision in *Frontier Dispute* (*Burkina Faso/Mali*). There, the UN oversaw the withdrawal of Libyan troops.[29] Following the *Arbitral Award made by the King of Spain* the OAS' Inter-American Peace Committee assisted with issues around nationality and acquired rights that had been particular obstacles in implementing the decision of the ICJ.[30]

Finally, international organizations can also assist with the enforcement of judicial decisions. Article 94(2) of the UN Charter provides that "[i]f a party to a case [at the ICJ] fails to perform the obligations incumbent upon it under a judgment rendered by the Court, the other party may have recourse to the Security Council, which may, if it deems necessary, make recommendations or decide upon measures to be taken to give effect to the judgment". In practice, the recourse to and operation of this provision has been both rare and problematic, revealing the weaknesses of international organizations as fora in which judicial decisions are enforced. The *Nicaragua* decision provides a good example.[31] There, a Security Council resolution pursuant to Article 94(2) of the UN Charter was vetoed by the United States. This provision was also pursued by Honduras in the context of the *Land and Maritime Dispute* (*El Salvador/Honduras*), but to no avail.[32] The limited use and practical effect of this provision has prompted scholarly critique.[33] That said, the Security

27 Bernardo Sepúlveda Amor, "Opening Remarks", in Boisson de Chazournes a.o. (*supra* note 4), p. 9.

28 See 'Cameroon-Nigeria Mixed Commission' (*UNOWAS*) <https://unowas.unmissions.org/cameroon-nigeria-mixed-commission>, accessed 17 January 2024; *Land and Maritime Boundary Between Cameroon and Nigeria* (*Cameroon v. Nigeria, Equatorial Guinea intervening*), [2002] ICJ Reports 303.

29 UNSC Res 915 (4 May 1994), UN Doc S/RES/915.

30 Constanze Schulte, *Compliance with Decisions of the International Court of Justice* (Oxford UP, 2004), pp. 129–132.

31 ICJ, *Military and Paramilitary Activities in and against Nicaragua* (*Nicaragua v. USA*) (Merits), [1986] ICJ Reports 14.

32 See United Nations, *Article 94: Repertory of Practice of United Nations Organs, Supplement No. 10 (2000–2009)* [13].

33 See, for example, Aloysius Llamzon, "Jurisdiction and Compliance in Recent Decisions of the International Court of Justice", in *EJIL* vol. 18 (2007), pp. 815, 846–848.

Council has played a more prominent role in the settlement of disputes following their adjudication by the ICJ outside of the context of Article 94(2).[34]

Contrary to the example of the ICJ, which as noted has strong connections with the UN as its principal judicial organ but also has, in the context of its jurisdiction, fewer connections with the obligations of UN member states under the Charter, there seems to be more engagement with the enforcement of decisions when courts and tribunals are part of the architecture of an international organization. For example, in the context of the multilateral trade system – notwithstanding the present difficulties – the wider institution of the WTO plays an important role at various stages in the dispute settlement process, including enforcement. Notably, the General Council convening as the Dispute Settlement Body (DSB) exercises surveillance over the implementation of recommendations and rulings that have been set out in reports and authorize the suspension of concessions where a WTO member does not comply with recommendations and rulings made during the dispute settlement process.

Another example is the Committee of Ministers of the Council of Europe which supervises the execution of judgments of the European Court of Human Rights, adopts resolutions and action plans to help member states comply with findings, and can exercise diplomatic pressure or even infringement proceedings where states fail to comply. The African Union (AU) Assembly too plays a significant role in the enforcement of African Court on Human and Peoples' Rights decisions. The AU Assembly receives reports from the Court and is responsible for overseeing the implementation of judgments. And the enforcement of judgments of the Inter-American Court of Human Rights involves a cooperative process between the Court, the Inter-American Commission on Human Rights (IACtHR), and the member states of the OAS.

While many other examples could be given, it is evident that international organizations make a significant contribution in various ways to facilitating the resolution of specific international disputes between different actors, be it through specific mechanisms within the international organization itself, the role of the organization and its officials in diplomatic means of settlement, or by interacting with judicial means.

34 See, e.g., *Right of Passage over Indian Territory* (*Portugal v. India*) (Merits), [1960] ICJ Reports 6; *United States Diplomatic and Consular Staff in Tehran* (*USA v. Iran*), [1980] ICJ Reports 3; *Application of the Convention on the Prevention and Punishment of the Crime of Genocide* (Preliminary Objections), [1996] ICJ Reports 595.

4 Participation: International Organizations as Parties to a Dispute

International organizations can also be parties to a dispute. However, their participation as litigants in dispute settlement processes has significant limitations, usually either because international organizations do not have standing before particular tribunals or because of the doctrine of immunities.

International organizations cannot, for example, be parties to contentious disputes before the ICJ in light of the rule expressed in Article 34(1) of the Statute of the ICJ that "[o]nly States may be parties in cases before the Court". They may, however, be parties in disputes before other fora, such as ITLOS, the WTO's Dispute Settlement Body and certain arbitral proceedings. Allowing international organizations to be party to disputes before international courts and tribunals can be particularly important where that organization has been transferred certain competences (sometimes exclusive competence) by member states. One may think of the EU with respect to trade, investment, and fisheries, among others. And the EU has been involved in a range of cases before the WTO and ITLOS with respect to disputes in these issue-areas. Pursuant to Article 20(1) of the Statute of ITLOS, the Tribunal is "open to States Parties". "States Parties" in this context can also mean international organizations that are party to UNCLOS.[35] The EU is such a party to UNCLOS and thus can be a party to disputes before ITLOS. The EU has also been involved as respondent in arbitral proceedings brought under the Energy Charter Treaty, of which it is a member. But overall, the practice shows that international organizations are only very rarely involved as parties before international courts and tribunals. The examples of the EU are very much the exception and particular to the EU.

There are also situations where an international organization can be party to disputes before courts, tribunals or other mechanisms that might be governed by domestic law. Indeed, international organizations often have legal personality under national law and can be parties to disputes before national courts.[36] A significant barrier in this context, however, is the doctrine of immunities of international organizations. To provide an example of the legal framework in this context, the UN enjoys certain immunities as an international organization.[37] Article 105(1) of the UN Charter provides that "[t]he Organization shall enjoy in the territory of each of its members such privileges

35 See United Nations Convention on the Law of the Sea (adopted 10 December 1982, entered into force 16 November 1994) 1833 *UNTS* 3 (UNCLOS) art 1(2), 305(1)(f), annex IX.

36 See August Reinisch, *International Organizations Before National Courts* (Cambridge UP, 2000), pp. 37–70, 175–177.

37 See Schermers and Blokker (*supra* note 1), pp. 267, 1076.

and immunities as are necessary for the fulfilment of its purposes". This basic provision set out under the UN Charter has been supplemented by other general, bilateral, headquarters and host agreements. Many domestic and regional courts and tribunals have encountered the issue of the immunity of international organizations and have generally interpreted this doctrine in a strict way, though some erosion of the absolute principle of immunity is evident.[38]

The issue of immunity has led some to argue that international organizations enjoy a 'lack of accountability'.[39] Indeed, the International Law Association (ILA) has expressed this view, which it warned could amount to a denial of justice where no alternative was available for aggrieved individuals.[40] It should be noted that there might be situations where immunity is waived, such as by the executive head of an international organization, though this is of course discretionary.[41]

The International Law Commission (ILC) is presently considering the topic of '[t]he settlement of international disputes to which international organizations are parties', which was originally proposed in 2016.[42] The topic is concerned with disputes that might arise between international organizations and states and between international organizations themselves. However, it does not presently extend to third-party disputes against organizations, and it is not envisaged that the work will encompass the immunity of international organizations. As such, the law of the immunity of international organizations is likely to hinge upon the position taken in different jurisdictions by domestic courts and there remains a significant accountability gap that has been exposed by the doctrine. The ILA has suggested that the accountability gap in this context ought to be overcome by the creation of alternative remedial mechanisms within international organizations themselves.[43]

---

38 See *Menandro v. World Bank* 717 F 2d 610 (1983), 615–17; *Iran-US Claims Tribunal v. AS* (1984) 94 ILR 321, 329; *Eckhardt v. European Organization for the Safety of Air Navigation (Eurocontrol) No. 2*, (1987) 94 ILR 331, 337–38; *Waite and Kennedy v. Germany* (Merits) [1999] 118 ILR 121; *Behrami v. France* (2007) 46 ILM 746; *Jam v. International Finance Corporation* 139 S Ct 759 (2019).

39 Niels Blokker, "International Organizations", in Cecily Rose (ed.), *An Introduction to Public International Law* (Cambridge UP, 2022) p. 159.

40 Committee on Accountability of International Organizations, "Accountability of International Organisations: Final Report", in International Law Association, Berlin 2004, p. 41.

41 *Ibidem*.

42 ILC, "The Settlement of International Disputes to which International Organizations are Parties", in *Annual Report of the Commission on the Work of its Sixty-Eighth Session* (2 May–10 June and 4 July–12 August 2016) UN Doc A/71/10.

43 Committee on Accountability of International Organisations (*supra* note 40), p. 41.

In this context, accountability mechanisms have become increasingly important as an alternative conduit through which redress can be sought for wrongs committed by international organizations and disputes can be settled between international organizations and third parties.[44] Developments in this respect have been more prominent in some international organizations, such as the Bretton Woods institutions (with the World Bank's Inspection Panel serving as a pioneering example), than in others, such as the UN.[45] Other forms of accountability mechanism, like the UN, World Bank or International Labour Organization (ILO) Administrative Tribunals also exist and are intended to adjudicate disputes between the relevant international organizations and their staff.[46] Overall, these emerging accountability mechanisms are important for resolving disputes and providing remedies in the context of international organization decision-making and damage.[47]

Finally, international organizations may be party to disputes that concern private law. These are often cases involving a contractual dispute. Such disputes are usually submitted to arbitration under specific clauses provided for in the relevant instrument rather than domestic courts, to avoid obstacles posed by the doctrine of immunities. Recently, for example, several cases have been initiated by private parties against the Food and Agriculture Organization (FAO) for disputes relating to contracts between them and the FAO.[48]

5 Conclusions

In this chapter we have sought to map the contribution of international organizations to the settlement of international disputes. Our study has revealed three major types of contribution. First, international organizations can play an architectural role in the creation and operation of dispute settlement mechanisms. Second, international organizations facilitate the settlement of

44 Günther Handl, "The Integration of Environmental Principles into the Policy and Practice of Multilateral Development Banks", in Michael Faure (ed.) *Elgar Encyclopedia of Environmental Law* (Edward Elgar, 2023), p. 639.

45 Eisuke Suzuki and Suresh Nanwani, "Responsibility of International Organizations: The Accountability Mechanisms of Multilateral Development Banks", in *Michigan J Intl L* vol. 27 (2005), pp. 177, 182–183.

46 Tullio Treves, "International Organizations as Parties to Contentious Cases: Selected Aspects", in Boisson de Chazournes a.o. (*supra* note 6), pp. 44–45.

47 Suzuki and Nanwani (*supra* note 45), pp. 204–206.

48 *Saboor Chicks v. UN Food and Agriculture Organization*, PCA Case No 2023-25; *Surivit and Wi! Uma Fu Sranan v. UN Food and Agriculture Organization*, PCA Case No 2023-59.

particular disputes, either at the initiation of a dispute, during the proceedings or after a dispute has been decided by a judicial mechanism. Third, international organizations can participate in disputes themselves as parties. Within each of these broad frames, we have shown that international organizations play a myriad of different roles in dispute settlement. However, there remain fundamental shortcomings within each frame, whether this be the political nature of international organizations themselves, weaknesses in the institutional machinery or the doctrine of immunities, amongst many other reasons. Nevertheless, it is clear that international organizations have made an important contribution to the settlement of international disputes and have done so in increasingly creative ways.

CHAPTER 14

The EU's Foreign and Security Policy and Legal Remedies

Three Remarkable Cases before the EU Courts

*Mielle Bulterman and Larissa van den Herik**

1 Introduction

As the world is heating up, not only through climate change but also as a result of increased military conflict and geopolitical tensions, domestic courts are being called upon to adjudicate an ever-greater variety of governmental decisions made in the realm of foreign policy.[1] The European Court of Justice (ECJ) and the General Court – which together make up the Court of Justice of the European Union (CJEU) – are also confronted with this dynamic, as these courts have jurisdiction to review matters related to the EU's Common Foreign and Security Policy (CFSP). In this chapter, we will discuss three cases related to the CFSP. We have selected these cases not only because of their innovative features and precedential value, but also because in these cases the field of expertise of Niels Blokker, in whose honour this contribution is written, meets with the terrain of study of the two authors of this chapter, namely EU law and international law respectively. The three cases obviously are about EU law, yet they also concern broader questions of international institutional law, and they involve issues of peace and security and human rights. Moreover, the cases are situated at the crossroads of law and diplomacy, which is a site very familiar to professor Blokker. As an academic Niels Blokker has always taken a great interest in the functioning of the rules of international law in practice

* Mielle Bulterman is head of the EU law division at the Dutch Ministry of Foreign Affairs. This article is written in her personal capacity. Larissa van den Herik is professor of public international law at Leiden University.

1 For two recent examples relating to the hostilities between Israel and Hamas, see *Stichting Oxfam Novib, PAX and The Rights Forum v. The Netherlands*, District Court of The Hague, 15 December 2023, ECLI:NL: RBDHA:2023:19744, and Court of Appeal of The Hague, 12 February 2024, ECLI:NL:GHDHA:2024:191. See also *Defense For Children International – Palestine a.o. (Plaintiffs) v. Joseph R. Biden, Jr., President Of The United States a.o. (Defendants)*, US District Court for the Northern District of California, Case No.: 23-cv-05829.

 | DOI:10.1163/9789004699939_016

and he has always used the practical experience gained as an international lawyer at the Ministry of Foreign Affairs for the benefit of his students.

The first two cases are direct actions against EU sanctions in which the CJEU's jurisdiction is undisputed. While the CJEU's role in the area of the EU's Common Foreign and Security Policy is limited, it does have jurisdiction to review the legality of CFSP decisions providing for restrictive measures against natural or legal persons, pursuant to Article 275 of the Treaty on the Functioning of the EU (TFEU). In addition, the CJEU has full jurisdiction with respect to EU measures implementing CFSP decisions adopted on the basis of the TFEU (mostly regulations).[2]

The first case that is discussed concerns the sanctions packages against Russia after the full-scale invasion of Ukraine in 2022, and one type of sanction in particular, namely sanctions imposed on media outlets. As an important player in the sanctions-domain generally and specifically also in relation to Russia, the EU has taken the lead in exploring and adopting new sanction instruments such as a ban on Kremlin-backed media outlets including Russia Today. This ban has been vigorously contested by one of the affected media outlets, Russia Today France. Freedom of expression and information as guaranteed by Article 11 of the EU Charter of Fundamental Rights (the Charter), which corresponds to Article 10 of the European Convention on Human Rights (ECHR), was an animating concern here.

The second case that is discussed involves the standing of third states to challenge EU sanctions under Article 263 TFEU before the EU courts. This question came up when Venezuela brought a case in 2018, after sanctions had been imposed by the EU in relation to the situation in Venezuela as it emerged in the preceding year.

The third case does not concern an action for annulment of sanctions under Article 263 TFEU. It rather concerns a claim for damages (Article 268 TFEU) against the EU with respect to the functioning of the EU Rule of Law Mission in Kosovo (Eulex Kosovo), and specifically its responsibilities regarding the investigation of disappearance and killings that occurred during the 1999 Kosovo conflict. This case raises fundamental questions concerning the scope of the limitation to the EU Court's jurisdiction under the CFSP. These questions are not only important from the perspective of the EU system of fundamental rights protection. The outcome of the case may also be of direct relevance for finding a solution to the so-called "CFSP-issue" identified by the ECJ in Opinion 2/13 on the EU accession to the ECHR.

2 As confirmed by the ECJ in its judgment of 28 March 2017, *Rosneft*, C-72/15, EU:C:2017:236, para. 106.

The three cases are discussed in turn. We will conclude with some overarching reflections on the role of the EU courts in relation to foreign policy and security matters.

2 Media Sanctions and the Freedom of Expression

Sanctions adopted outside the United Nations (UN) system of collective security are proliferating. The EU is an active sanctions-sender, especially since the Russian invasion of Ukraine.[3] While non-UN or autonomous sanctions were, for long, a tool imposed predominantly by Western powers, other states are stepping up their game. With such omni-presence of autonomous sanctions, the question of legality and legal protection also takes centre stage. The unique feature of EU sanctions is that they are adopted in a multilateral setting with a special role for the EU courts. And through its compelling case law the EU court has produced standard-setting guidance on the legality of sanctions and specifically the issue of legal protection.

Sanctions litigation before the EU courts has metastasized in recent years. It generally evolves around procedural and evidentiary issues.[4] Yet, as novel types of sanctions emerge, new legal questions arise as well. One new type of sanctions that was imposed in the context of the Russia sanctions packages were the so-called media sanctions. While certain Eastern European states and particularly Baltic states, as well as the US, had already imposed such sanctions and prohibitions before,[5] the EU targeted the media via sanctions for the first time in the context of the sanctions against Russia. Recognizing the hybrid threats coming from Russia and the "international campaign of media manipulation and distortion of facts" with a view to destabilising neighbouring states and the EU as such, and specifically the propaganda action to support and justify its aggression, the EU decided to prohibit broadcasting activities within the EU of Russia Today subsidiaries and of Sputnik on 2 March 2022.[6]

---

3 For an analysis of the Russia sanctions specifically, see Larissa van den Herik and Peter A.G. van Bergeijk, "Legal, Economic, and Political Perspectives On Sanctions Against Russia; an Intermediate Assessment", in *Security and Human Rights Monitor*, 2023.

4 Christina Eckes, "The law and practice of EU sanctions", in Steven Blockmans and Panos Koutrakos (eds.), *Research Handbook on the EU's Common Foreign and Security Policy* (Elgar, 2018).

5 F.J. Cabrera Blázquez, *The implementation of EU sanctions against RT and Sputnik* (European Audiovisual Observatory, Strasbourg, 2022).

6 Council Decision (CFSP) 2022/351 of 1 March 2022 amending Decision 2014/512/CFSP concerning restrictive measures in view of Russia's actions destabilising the situation in

The lawfulness of this prohibition was quickly – and unsuccessfully – challenged by RT France before the General Court. The case was adjudicated within 4.5 months under the expedited procedure by the Grand Chamber of the General Court.[7] RT France claimed *i.a.* that the media sanctions infringed on the freedom of expression as guaranteed by Article 11 of the Charter. The General Court rejected this plea, ruling that the conditions for justifiably limiting the freedom of expression under EU law were met. A crucial element in this assessment is the fact that that the media sanctions are temporary and reversible, and do not prevent RT France from carrying out other activities in the EU than broadcasting. For this reason, the Court ruled that the essence of freedom of expression is complied with.[8] Furthermore, the proportionality of the measures was examined by the Court elaborately.[9] In that context, the Court underlined *i.a.* the temporary character of the measures as well as the fact that this particular sanction measure was part of a broader package that responded to the aggression that was condemned by the UN General Assembly and that constituted a violation of the *erga omnes* obligations imposed by international law. The Court also found that it had been established that the media organization concerned was under the "permanent direct or indirect control of the leadership of the Russian Federation", and the judgment illustrated at length that the applicant of the case had broadcast the official Russian position and used similar wording as Russian authorities with a view to justifying and supporting the Russian aggression and influencing European civil society.[10] This elaborate examination of the proportionality makes it clear that this specific type of sanction cannot be adopted lightly. As such, the Court, while confirming the lawfulness of the challenged measures, clearly does not give the Council

Ukraine (*OJ* 2022 L 65, p. 5, 'the contested decision') and Council Regulation (EU) 2022/350 of 1 March 2022 amending Regulation (EU) No 833/2014 concerning restrictive measures in view of Russia's actions destabilising the situation in Ukraine (*OJ* 2022 L 65, p. 1, 'the contested regulation').

7 *RT France v Council of the European Union*, Judgment of the General Court of 27 July 2022, Case T-125/22, ECLI:EU:T:2022:483. For an analysis of this case, see also V. Szép, and R.A. Wessel, "Balancing restrictive measures and media freedom: *RT France v. Council*, Case note on General Court (Grand Chamber), 27/07/2022, T–125/22", in *Common Market Law Review* vol. 60 (2023), pp. 1383–1396.

8 *RT France* (*supra* note 7), paras. 153–159.

9 Namely, whether the restrictive measures at issue are provided for by law, comply with the essence of freedom of expression, pursue an objective of general interest and are not disproportionate (para. 148).

10 *RT France* (*supra* note 7), paras. 127, 142, 143, 154, 159, 164, 165, 172–174, 177–191, 209.

a *carte blanche* to include new tools in the EU sanctions toolbox, despite calls for a wider use of sanctions to combat foreign influence operations.[11]

On 17 May 2024 the Council did add four media outlets to its sanctions list, namely Voice of Europe, RIA Novosti, Izvestia and Rossiyskaya Gazeta. The four were considered to be "under permanent direct or indirect control of the leadership of the Russian Federation, and have been essential and instrumental in bringing forward and supporting Russia's war of aggression against Ukraine, and for the destabilisation of its neighbouring countries".[12]

In this regard it is notable that Norway, which generally aligns with EU sanctions, chose not to implement the sanctions against Russia state-controlled media, pursuant to a constitutional assessment. The Norwegian government considered that the high media literacy of its population and a culture of strong editorial opinion was sufficient to resist manipulation.[13] This reflects a preference to deal with disinformation via other tools than sanctions; a similar position may have inspired the cautious way in which the Court considered this case.

3 The Legal Standing of Third States to Challenge EU Sanctions before EU Courts

Under Article 263, fourth paragraph, of the TFEU any natural or legal person can bring an action for annulment against an EU regulatory act that is of direct concern to him and does not require implementing measures. In the context of the sanctions imposed by the EU against Venezuela, the question arose as to whether these admissibility requirements can be fulfilled when a third state challenges EU sanctions before the EU courts.

3.1 *Sanctions against Venezuela*

The EU imposed sanctions against Venezuela in November 2017, citing the irregularities and non-recognition by the opposition of the Gubernatorial

---

11 Council conclusions on a Framework for a coordinated EU response to hybrid campaigns, 21 June 2022, ST 10016/22, para. 14.

12 Council of the EU, *Press release, Russia's war of aggression against Ukraine: Council bans broadcasting activities in the European Union of four more Russia-associated media outlets*, 17 May 2024, available at <https://www.consilium.europa.eu/en/press/press-releases/2024/05/17/russia-s-war-of-aggression-against-ukraine-council-bans-broadcasting-activities-in-the-european-union-of-four-more-russia-associated-media-outlets/>.

13 European Audiovisual Observatory, *Sanctions on RT and Sputnik not to be adopted in Norway*, IRIS Merlin 2022–5:1/5.

elections of October 2017. The measures were imposed in addition to political and diplomatic efforts, with a view to supporting “a peaceful negotiated way out of the political crisis”.[14] The CFSP Decision adopted on 13 November provided for an embargo on arms and on related material that might be used for internal repression, as well as for travel bans and assets freezes that would target those involved in the non-respect of democratic principles or the rule of law and the violation of human rights. Right at the adoption of those measures, it was specified that the sanctions would be reversible.[15] Elements that were relevant in this respect included the holding of credible and meaningful negotiations, the respect for democratic institutions, the adoption of a full electoral calendar and the liberation of all political prisoners.[16] Gradually individuals were added to the list of targeted persons, including state officials and members of the armed forces,[17] as well as members of the security and intelligence forces.[18] Reasons for being listed included involvement in torture, and specifically also the death of Captain Acosta Arévalo, as well as acts related to the democratic process such as the stripping of parliamentary immunity of members of the opposition, including the President of the National Assembly Juan Guaidó.[19]

14 Council of the EU, *Press release, Venezuela: EU adopts conclusions and targeted sanctions*, 13 November 2017, para. 5, available at <https://www.consilium.europa.eu/en/press/press-releases/2017/11/13/venezuela-eu-adopts-conclusions-and-targeted-sanctions/>.

15 Council Decision (CFSP) 2017/2074 of 13 November 2017 concerning restrictive measures in view of the situation in Venezuela, *OJ* 2017, L 295, pp. 60–68. Council Regulation (EU) 2017/2063 of 13 November 2017 concerning restrictive measures in view of the situation in Venezuela, *OJ* 2017, L 95, p. 21–37.

16 *Press release, Venezuela* (*supra* note 14), para. 4.

17 Council Decision (CFSP) 2018/901 of 25 June 2018 amending Decision (CFSP) 2017/2074 concerning restrictive measures in view of the situation in Venezuela, *OJ* L 160 I/12. And Council Implementing Regulation (EU) 2021/275 of 22 February 2021 implementing Regulation (EU) 2017/2063 concerning restrictive measures in view of the situation in Venezuela, *OJ* L 60I, and Council Decision (CFSP) 2021/276 of 22 February 2021 amending Decision (CFSP) 2017/2074 concerning restrictive measures in view of the situation in Venezuela, *OJ L 60I.*

18 Council Implementing Regulation (EU) 2019/1586 of 26 September 2019 implementing Regulation (EU) 2017/2063 concerning restrictive measures in view of the situation in Venezuela, *OJ* L 248/1, and Council Decision (CFSP) 2019/1596 of 26 September 2019 amending Decision (CFSP) 2017/2074 concerning restrictive measures in view of the situation in Venezuela, *OJ* 248 L74.

19 Council Implementing Regulation (EU) 2020/897 of 29 June 2020 implementing Regulation (EU) 2017/2063 concerning restrictive measures in view of the situation in Venezuela, *OJ* L 205 I/1, and Council Decision (CFSP) 2020/898 of 29 June 2020 amending Decision (CFSP) 2017/2074 concerning restrictive measures in view of the situation in Venezuela, *OJ* 205 I/6.

The sanctions were renewed on a yearly basis until November 2023, when they were renewed for a six month period only.

Parallel to the EU sanctions, or in fact prior to them, the United States (US) also adopted sanctions in relation to the unfolding situation in Venezuela. The US first adopted democracy and human rights-related sanctions in relation to Venezuela in 2015.[20] The US sanctions net widened over the years, and started to prohibit access to US financial markets by the Venezuelan government, including state energy company Petróleos de Venezuela, S.A. (PdVSA), with certain exceptions intended to minimize the impact on the Venezuelan people and US interests.[21] In January 2019 PdVSA became a direct subject to US sanctions, and all of its property and interests in property that were subject to US jurisdiction were frozen; US persons, companies and individuals alike, were prohibited from engaging in transactions with the company. Venezuela's Central Bank, the National Development Bank, and the state-owned gold company, Minerven, were equally sanctioned,[22] and somewhat later in the year the assets of the Maduro government were frozen.[23] In contrast to the EU sanctions, President Maduro, his wife and son, the Venezuelan Vice-President and the Minister of Defence were also listed. The US sanctions were thus significantly more comprehensive in scope than the EU sanctions. The aim of the US sanctions was also more explicit in its targeting of Maduro's "usurpation of power", and his ongoing attempts to undermine Interim President Juan Guaido and the Venezuelan National Assembly's exercise of legitimate authority,[24] leading to allegations that their aim was regime change.

With a view to challenging the sanctions, Venezuela made a referral under Article 14 of the Statute of the international Criminal Court (ICC), requesting the Prosecutor to investigate crimes against humanity committed on its own territory.[25] According to Venezuela, the sanctions had significantly raised mortality rates, including of children, and negatively affected the enjoyment of

20 US Executive Order 13692 of 8 March 2015, Blocking Property and Suspending Entry of Certain Persons Contributing to the Situation in Venezuela.

21 US Executive Order 13808 of August 24, 2017, Imposing Additional Sanctions with Respect to the Situation in Venezuela.

22 Designations on 28 January 2019 pursuant to US Executive Order 13850 of 1 November 2018, Blocking Property of Additional Persons Contributing to the Situation in Venezuela.

23 US Executive Order 13884 of 5 August 2019, Blocking Property of the Government of Venezuela.

24 *Ibidem.*

25 Prior to this self-referral, the situation in Venezuela had been referred to the ICC Prosecutor in 2018 by Argentina, Canada, Chile, Colombia, Paraguay and Peru (Venezuela I). A decision to conclude preliminary examination and proceed to investigations was made on 3 November 2021.

human rights, such as particularly the right to food, education, medical care, and this had resulted in large-scale emigration which further affected Venezuela.[26] While Venezuela's complaint "primarily" regards the US sanctions,[27] its referral does not exclude the EU sanctions explicitly. For a specific challenge of the EU sanctions, however, Venezuela turned elsewhere: the EU courts.

3.2 *Venezuela before the EU Courts*

Venezuela brought an action under Article 263 TFEU to annul the sanctions in February 2018. The Council put forward three grounds of inadmissibility, namely that Venezuela had no legal interest, that it was not directly concerned, and that it was not a natural or legal person in the sense of Article 263, fourth paragraph, TFEU.[28] The General Court only addressed the second ground of inadmissibility raised by the Council. It dismissed the case on the ground that no sanctions were imposed on Venezuela as a state. It held,

> At most, the contested provisions are likely to have indirect effects on the Bolivarian Republic of Venezuela, in so far as the prohibitions imposed on natural persons who are nationals of a Member State and on legal persons constituted under the law of one of them could have the effect of limiting the sources from which the Bolivarian Republic of Venezuela can obtain the goods and services in question.[29]

Venezuela appealed this decision before the ECJ. On appeal,[30] the ECJ decided to raise of its own motion a question that was not addressed in the judgment of the General Court, namely whether Venezuela is a "legal person" in the sense of Article 263, fourth paragraph, TFEU. The parties to the appeal (Venezuela and the Council), as well as the Commission and all Member States, were invited to take a position on that issue.[31] Referring to the EU's founding value of respect for the rule of law, the ECJ held that the notion of legal person of Article 263,

26 ICC, Referral pursuant to Article 14 of the Rome Statute to the Prosecutor of the International Criminal Court submitted by the Bolivarian Government of Venezuela with respect to Unilateral Coercive Measures, 13 February 2020 (Venezuela II).

27 The word "primarily" is explicitly used by Venezuela in its referral, see doc. ICC-01/20-4-AnxI of 4 March 2020, p. 2.

28 GC, judgment of 20 September 2019, *Venezuela v. Council*, T-65/18, para. 23.

29 *Ibidem*, para. 34.

30 ECJ, judgment of 22 June 2021, *Venezuela v. Council*, C-872/19 P.

31 Observations on that question were submitted by the parties to the appeal, i.e. Belgium, Bulgaria, Estonia, Germany, Greece, Lithuania, the Netherlands, Poland, Slovenia, Slovakia, Sweden and the Commission.

fourth paragraph, should be interpreted widely as including third states, such as Venezuela. It also held that the Union's obligations to ensure respect for the rule of law cannot be made subject to a condition of reciprocity.[32] It concluded that a legal person governed by public international law "is equally likely as any another person or entity to have its rights or interests adversely affected by an act of the European Union and must therefore be able, in compliance with those conditions, to seek the annulment of that act".[33]

Having established that Venezuela is to be regarded as a "legal person" under Article 263, fourth paragraph, TFEU, the ECJ examined Venezuela's ground for appeal, namely that the General Court had wrongly interpreted the "direct concern" requirement. The ECJ found that the provisions in Regulation 2017/2063 prevented the state of Venezuela from obtaining the sanctioned goods and services. These provisions thus directly affect he legal situation of Venezuela. The Court also concurred with the Advocate-General that the reference in the prohibitions "to any natural or legal person, entity, body in, or for use in, Venezuela" includes the Venezuelan government.[34] Hence, the Court decided to uphold the ground of appeal of Venezuela and set aside the judgment of the General Court. It furthermore considered that it was able to give final judgment on the admissibility of the action of Venezuela. It rejected the first ground of admissibility put forward by the Council, claiming a lack of interest in bringing proceedings. The ECJ held that, as the prohibitions introduced by Regulation 2017/2063 were liable to harm the interests of Venezuela, their annulment was, by itself, capable of procuring an advantage for it.[35] With respect to the second ground of inadmissibility, it held that the provisions of Regulation 2017/2063 do not entail implementing measures. It concluded that Venezuela had standing to bring proceedings under Article 263, fourth paragraph,[36] and referred the case back to the General Court for a judgment on the merits.

On the merits, the General Court subsequently rejected all pleas in law put forward by Venezuela and thus dismissed the action.[37] It ruled that the right to be heard, as invoked by Venezuela, was of paramount importance in the context of sanctions targeted against specific (legal or natural) persons, but could not be relied upon in the context of restrictive measures of general

32 ECJ, judgment of 22 June 2021, *Venezuela v. Council*, C-872/19 P, paras. 20–53.

33 *Ibidem*, para. 50.

34 *Ibidem*, para. 69.

35 *Ibidem*, para. 83.

36 *Ibidem*, para. 92.

37 GC, judgment of 13 September 2023, *Venezuela v. Council*, T-65/18 RENV. As no appeal has been lodged against this judgment, it has become final.

application, such as measures interrupting the economic relations with a third country in relation to certain goods and services. Furthermore, an obligation to hear Venezuela before the adoption of the sanctions, would in essence oblige the Council to engage in international negotiations. This would undermine the effectiveness of sanctions as a tool available to the EU.[38] The General Court also dismissed Venezuela's plea in relation to the obligation to state reasons. It held that Venezuela should have been able to identify and understand the reasons why the measures had been imposed as these had been clearly set out in respective Council decisions.[39] As to Venezuela's plea concerning inaccuracy of the facts relied upon by the Council, as well as of the Council's assessment of the political situation in Venezuela, the General Court indicated that, according to settled case-law, it could only set aside the sanctions if there had been a manifest error by the Council in assessing the political situation in Venezuela. Referring to reports of Human Rights Watch, the Inter-American Commission of Human Rights, and the Organization of American States the Court rejected Venezuela's arguments that there had been such manifest errors.[40] In relation to Venezuela's plea that the measures constitute unlawful countermeasures, the Court agreed with the Council's submission that the restrictive measures had not been presented as countermeasures at all. The Court also agreed with the Council that there was no requirement under customary international law that such measures could only be imposed with prior authorization of the UN Security Council. It also found the measures to be proportional. In the latter respect, it points specifically to the "reasonable relationship between, on the one hand, the restrictive measures consisting in a prohibition on the sale, supply, transfer or export of equipment which might be used for internal repression and services related to that equipment and to military equipment, and, on the other, the objective pursued, which is to prevent the risk of further violence, excessive use of force and violations or abuses of human rights".[41]

The decision of the ECJ on the interpretation of the notion "legal person" under Article 263, fourth paragraph, TFEU has been criticized for being too generous by scholars who argue that only individuals including foreign state officials should have been able to turn to the EU courts in this case, and not the state of Venezuela as such. Others have rather welcomed the judgment, seeing it as a sign of the EU's confidence in the robustness of its legal order. The fact that the General Court has been able to review Venezuela's action for

38 *Ibidem*, paras. 36–45.
39 *Ibidem*, paras. 46–58.
40 *Ibidem*, paras. 59–82.
41 *Ibidem*, paras. 83–120.

annulment on the merits of the case and ruled that this action should be dismissed strengthens the legitimacy of the EU external action.

4 Claim for Damages for Human Rights Violations and CFSP Action

The main issue in the final case that will be explored in this contribution concerns the scope of the limitation to the EU Court's jurisdiction under the CFSP. Article 24 TEU provides that the CJEU does not have jurisdiction with respect to the CFSP provisions of the EU Treaty, with two important exceptions: the jurisdiction to monitor compliance with Article 40 TEU (on the demarcation between the CFSP and the EU competences under the TFEU) and the jurisdiction to rule on the lawfulness of restrictive measures against natural or legal persons (Article 275, second paragraph, TFEU). This limited jurisdiction of the EU Court under the CFSP gives rise to the question as to whether there could be a lacuna in judicial protection within the EU legal order. Obviously, to accept that such a lacuna exists would be difficult to reconcile with the importance of effective judicial protection as an essential feature of the EU legal order.

4.1 *The CFSP Issue and EU Accession to the ECHR*

In 2013, the Commission requested an Opinion of the ECJ under Article 218, eleventh paragraph, TFEU on the draft agreement that had been negotiated to enable the EU to accede to the European Convention on Human Rights. In its Opinion, the ECJ identified the ECJ's limited jurisdiction with respect to the CFSP as one of several problematic elements of the draft accession agreement from the perspective of EU Treaties.[42] It noted that it did not have the opportunity yet to clarify the scope of the limitation to its jurisdiction under the CFSP. It then remarked that, as EU law stood at the moment of its Opinion, certain CFSP acts fell outside the scope of its jurisdiction. It also ruled that it would be incompatible with the EU legal order to accept that the European Court of Human Rights (ECtHR) would be empowered to rule on the compatibility with the ECHR of CFSP action whose legality the ECJ could not review in the light of fundamental rights.[43]

In order to find a solution to the features of the accession agreement that were identified as problematic by the ECJ in Opinion 2/13, renegotiations took place since 2019 within an hoc group of the Council of Europe's Steering Committee for Human Rights (CDDH), composed of the Member States

42 Opinion of 18 December 2014, Opinion 2/13.

43 *Ibidem*, paras. 249–258.

of the Council of Europe and a representative of the European Union.[44] In March 2023, the ad hoc group concluded that provisional agreement had been attained on all issues raised by Opinion 2/13. With respect to the CFSP issue, it was agreed that the EU would aim to resolve this internally.[45] The possible avenues for finding an internal solution, to a large extent depend on the EU Court's view on its jurisdiction under the CFSP.

4.2 *Strict Interpretation of the Exclusion of Jurisdiction under the CFSP*

In several recent cases, the EU Court has been able to clarify the scope of the exclusion of its jurisdiction under the CFSP. For instance, in *Rosneft* the ECJ held that while Article 47 of the Charter cannot create jurisdiction for the ECJ where this is explicitly excluded by the Treaty, the principle of effective judicial protection requires that this exclusion should be interpreted strictly.[46] For this reason, it held that it may review restrictive measures not only in direct action cases (as is explicitly stated in Article 275, second paragraph, TFEU), but also in preliminary ruling proceedings.[47] In the same vein, the ECJ held that it has jurisdiction in claims for damages (Article 268 TFEU) allegedly caused by restrictive measures contained in a CFSP decision, even though this is not explicitly stated in Article 275, second paragraph, TFEU.[48] Furthermore, with respect to the action of EU missions established under the CFSP, the ECJ has made it clear that it has jurisdiction with respect to actions and measures of such missions that do not really concern CFSP matters. Thus, the ECJ held it has jurisdiction in a staff case of an EU civilian mission[49] and in a case concerning a public contract for helicopter services of the EU mission in Kosovo, called Eulex Kosovo.[50]

4.3 *Claim for Damages Caused by CFSP Action Allegedly Violating Fundamental Rights*

In the cases mentioned so far, the ECJ has always managed to prevent that the exclusion of its jurisdiction under the CFSP would entail a lacuna in EU system

44 See the information available at <https://www.coe.int/en/web/human-rights-intergovernmental-cooperation/accession-of-the-european-union-to-the-european-convention-on-human-rights>.

45 Meeting Report of the 18th Meeting of the CDDH Ad Hoc Negotiation group ("46+1") on the accession of the European Union to the ECHR, 46+1(2023)R18, para. 7.

46 ECJ, judgment of 28 March 2017, *Rosneft*, C-72/15, para.74.

47 *Ibidem*, paras. 64–81.

48 ECJ, judgment of 6 October 2020, *Bank Refah Kargaran v. Council*, C-134/19 P, paras. 23–52.

49 ECJ, judgment of 19 July 2016, *H v. Council and Others*, C-455/14 P, EU:C:2016:569.

50 ECJ, judgment of 12 November 2015, *Elitaliana v. Eulex Kosovo*, C-439/13 P, EU:C:2015:753.

of legal protection. But due to the specificities of these cases, this case-law does not yet enable us to conclude that such lacunas do not exist. This could change with the judgment of the ECJ in the claim for damages brought before it by KS and KD ("the applicants"). They are family members of persons who were murdered or have disappeared in the aftermath of the Kosovo conflict. The applicants claimed that Eulex Kosovo's failure to properly investigate these disappearances and killings amounted to a breach of their fundamental rights as protected under EU law. The General Court dismissed their action, as it held that it manifestly lacked jurisdiction to hear and determine it.[51]

Both the Commission and the applicants lodged an appeal before the ECJ. In her Opinion, Advocate General Capeta argued that by dismissing the action, the General Court failed to recognize that the limitation to its jurisdiction under the CFSP is an exception, and thus should be interpreted narrowly.[52] In her view, in order to determine the scope of the exclusion of the CJEU's jurisdiction in the field of CFSP, it is important to take into account the purpose of this exclusion.[53] This purpose is to prevent the EU courts from adjudicating the policy choices that are made in the area of foreign relations.[54] However, this should not prevent the CJEU from adjudicating alleged breaches of fundamental rights: "[I]n constitutional democracies, policy choices are not unlimited. In a Union based on the rule of law, it could not have been the intention of the authors of the Treaties to allow for breaches of fundamental rights in the CFSP. As the breach of a fundamental right cannot be a policy choice, the EU Courts must be able to control whether that limit was crossed".[55] The Advocate General thus concluded that the CJEU has jurisdiction to review any CFSP measure, including a political or strategic one, in order to ensure its conformity with fundamental rights.

The ECJ delivered its judgment on 10 September 2024. In the ECJ's reasoning, not the proclaimed impact on fundamental rights, but the nature of act or omission is the decisive element to determine whether the CJEU has jurisdiction. It is apparent from its earlier case-law, the ECJ ruled, that the jurisdiction of the CJEU may be based on "the fact that the acts and omissions at issue are not directly related to the political or strategic choices made by the

51 GC, judgment of 10 November 2021, *KS and KD v. Council and Others*, T-771/20, EU:T:2021:798.

52 Opinion of 23 November 2023, *KS and KD v. Council and Others*, Joined case C-29/22 P and C-44/22 P, para. 92.

53 *Ibidem*, para. 111.

54 *Ibidem*, para. 112.

55 *Ibidem*, para. 115.

institutions, bodies, offices and agencies of the Union in the context of the CFSP, and in particular the CSDP".

In view of the timing of the ECJ's judgment (or rather the deadline for submitting this article) we are only in a position to give some brief and tentative reflections. The ECJ's judgment evidently deviated on a crucial point from the Advocate General's approach, as the ECJ explicitly ruled that the mere claim that a CFSP act infringes upon an individual's fundamental rights is not in itself sufficient for the CJEU to rule that it has jurisdiction.[56] At the same time, the ECJ's judgment clearly echoes the Advocate General's observations on the importance of the rule of law and fundamental rights as basic principles of the EU legal order, including the CFSP.[57] The question as to whether this difference in approach also entails a fundamental different outcome when determining whether the ECJ has jurisdiction in CFSP related cases, is yet still open for debate.[58]

5 Conclusion

The cases discussed in this contribution illustrate the importance of effective legal protection as a fundamental element of the EU legal order. The comparatively generous admissibility requirements enable individuals as well as states to challenge EU sanctions before the EU courts. In these cases, the CJEU does not shy away from putting human rights and the rule of law centre stage, also when it comes to foreign policy. While the CJEU's human rights scrutiny is strict, at the same time it is careful to preserve the Council's need for policy space. Also, the CJEU needs to take into account the boundaries to its jurisdiction as they follow from the Treaties. So far, the CJEU has been actually very capable of balancing the different interests involved in a meaningful way, respecting political priorities and urgencies while still delivering on its mandate. In doing so, the CJEU is making an immensely valuable contribution to the standard-setting of legal requirements for the use of sanctions as an instrument to respond to violations of international law by states. And thus it

56 ECJ, judgement of 10 September 2024, *KS and KD v. Council and Others*, Joined case C-29/22 P and C-44/22 P, para 73.

57 *Ibidem*, para 68.

58 For two opposite perspectives, see Daniel Sarmiento and Sara Iglesias Sánchez, "KS and Neves 77: Paving the Way to the EU's Accession to the ECHR", at *EU Law Live*, 12 September 2024, and Thomas Verellen, "KS and KD, on the Jurisdiction of the CJEU within the CFSP: Taking Conferral Seriously?", available at <www.thomasverellen.com>.

contributes to the preservation and development of international law in this domain.

We believe this role of the CJEU is of great importance, especially in times to come. On 25 April 2024, President Macron warned that the European Union is mortal and could die, unless the right choices were made to avert the risks of an ever more dangerous world.[59] Macron's previous claim of 2019 that NATO had become "braindead" contributed to a strategic rethinking of that organization, reinforced also by other geopolitical developments. The European Union will likely also embark on a reorientation, but it has to do so against the background of the rise of far-right political parties in several member states. In such a volatile setting, the reflex could be to minimize legal scrutiny when it comes to foreign policy and to allow political organs unfettered rein.

The question therefore arises as to whether the EU courts will be able to remain steadfast and to hold on to their approach as the rules of the game of international politics change and as the EU will have to adjust to new internal and geopolitical dynamics. Evidently, in these challenging circumstances times, the role of the CJEU to serve as a beacon of the rule of law and to uphold the EU's unique commitment to values is of crucial importance.

In view of the challenges ahead, we expect new fascinating judgments in the realm of foreign policy to be issued in years to come. When discussing and analysing those judgments, questioning whether they manage to find the right balance, we will draw on professor Blokker's writings and insights. Yet, we will miss his wise and calm demeanour, and his rich practical and academic experience.

---

59 Speech of President Macron at Sorbonne university, 25 April 2024.

CHAPTER 15

Statement Decisions as Institutional Authority

*Jacob Katz Cogan**

1 Introduction

In legal systems where decision authority and decision enforcement are separated, the functions of decision-making and decision implementation are distinct, yet the likelihood of the latter is typically not without relevance to the processes of the former.[1] Decisionmakers care about whether their edicts will be enforced, regardless of whether they are legislative or judicial bodies, as they care – and need to care – about whether their work has – and is seen to have – real consequences and meaning. While in sophisticated domestic systems, decisionmakers can in the normal course count on implementation, and hence they can make decisions largely without concern for whether their decrees will become nullities, in the international system, with no centralized enforcement mechanism, decisionmakers must be especially attuned to the possibility that their pronouncements will go unheeded, lest their acts lack import and therefore their role within the system be undercut and ignored. As nonstate entities, international institutions, and particularly international courts, are especially sensitive to this dynamic since they are entirely dependent on other actors to apply their decisions, and no assumptions can be made that implementation will naturally ensue.

Accordingly, as they consider cases, international tribunals will generally take into account the risk that the respondent state (or, with advisory opinions, the states and international organizations whose duties are implicated) will not comply with an order or judgment (or heed an opinion) that requires some action or inaction, and so they adapt their decisions accordingly. Sometimes they decline jurisdiction, sometimes they declare a matter inadmissible, sometimes they attune their analysis of the merits, sometimes they adjust the

* The author is Judge Joseph P. Kinneary Professor of Law, College of Law, and Affiliate Faculty, Department of History, University of Cincinnati. An earlier version of this paper was presented at a workshop at Temple Law School.

1 For a discussion of the themes in this paragraph, see W. Michael Reisman and Mahnoush H. Arsanjani, "Legal Decisions and Their Implementation in International Law", in James Crawford a.o. (eds.), *The International Legal Order: Current Needs and Possible Responses – Essays in Honour of Djamchid Momtaz* (Brill Nijhoff, 2017), p. 149.

 | DOI:10.1163/9789004699939_017

remedies they award, and sometimes they combine some or all of these techniques as they fashion an interim or final decision.[2]

There are rare cases, however, in which the tribunal, paradoxically, appears to come to a decision without regard to the likelihood of its implementation – or even knowing that implementation is highly unlikely in the foreseeable future. These are "statement decisions" – decisions that assert what the law is – that make a statement regarding important legal principles and their consequences – independent of enforcement considerations. The International Court of Justice (ICJ), in a series of advisory opinions dating back decades, including recent ones pertaining to Israel and the United Kingdom's control of the Chagos Islands,[3] as well as occasionally in judgments and provisional measures orders in contentious cases, such as in the recent cases brought by Ukraine against Russia and by South Africa against Israel,[4] provide examples. Remarkably, the Court issued these opinions, judgments, and orders apparently without concern for whether the states that are the primary subjects of the decisions would abide by the Court's directives. Indeed, it appears likely that the ICJ went ahead knowing full well that Israel, the United Kingdom, and Russia would ignore its legal conclusions and findings. Approving the Court's approach in the *Chagos* matter, Phillipe Sands, who was an advocate in that proceeding, wrote: "[T]he real-world consequences of a ruling … can take time

---

2 See, e.g., ICJ, *Oil Platforms* (*Iran v. U.S.*), Judgment of 6 Nov. 2003, concluding that the military actions taken by the US were not measures necessary to protect its essential security interests but at the same time dismissing the claim of Iran against the US under the Treaty of Amity. All ICJ decisions referred to can be found on the Court's website, www.icj-cij.org.

3 See ICJ, *Legal Consequences for States of the Continued Presence of South Africa in Namibia* (*South West Africa*) *notwithstanding Security Council Resolution 276* (*1970*), Advisory Opinion of 21 June 1971 [hereinafter *Namibia* Advisory Opinion]; *Legal Consequences of the Separation of the Chagos Archipelago from Mauritius in 1965*, Advisory Opinion of 25 Feb. 2019 [hereinafter *Chagos* Advisory Opinion]; *Legal Consequences of the Construction of a Wall in the Occupied Palestinian Territory*, Advisory Opinion of 9 July 2004 [hereinafter *Wall* Advisory Opinion]; *Legal Consequences Arising from the Policies and Practices of Israel in the Occupied Palestinian Territory, Including East Jerusalem*, Advisory Opinion of 19 July 2024 [hereinafter *OPT* Advisory Opinion].

4 See, e.g., ICJ, *Case Concerning Military and Paramilitary Activities in and Against Nicaragua* (*Nicaragua v. U.S.*), Judgment (Merits) of 27 June 1986 [hereinafter *Nicaragua* Judgment]; *Allegations of Genocide under the Convention on the Prevention and Punishment of the Crime of Genocide* (*Ukraine v. Russian Federation*), Order of 16 March 2022 [hereinafter *Russia* Provisional Measures Order]; *Application of the Convention on the Prevention and Punishment of the Crime of Genocide in the Gaza Strip* (*South Africa. v. Israel*), Order of 24 May 2024 [hereinafter Modified Provisional Measures Order].

to work their magic".[5] Delays in compliance, though, typically incur reputational costs for tribunals, and courts usually don't issue rulings on the assumption that their words will have bite at some indeterminate time in the future. Why has the Court chosen to accept the costs of non-implementation in these instances but not in others?

By examining the ICJ's opinions in these cases, as well as its decisions in a few other matters, we can explore under what circumstances statement decisions arise and the reasons for their use by international tribunals. Though those who agree with their results see the operation of the rule of law in the outcome of these cases, the decisions show that the International Court of Justice is an adept institutional actor, with the concerns and inclinations that are typical of international bodies that continually seek to retain and maintain their position as times change. In this way, statement decisions are one technique international tribunals use to ensure their institutional authority.

This chapter pays tribute to Niels Blokker, whose authoritative scholarship – through its nuanced and careful analysis of the practice of international organizations – and dedicated institution-building – through the *International Organizations Law Review* – have "contribute[d] to a better understanding of international institutional law".[6]

2 The *Chagos* Advisory Opinion as a Statement Decision

Of the three international cases pertaining to Chagos, the ICJ's advisory opinion is the only one that deals directly with the issue of Mauritius's sovereignty over the Chagos Archipelago. While the two other decisions are both interesting and consequential in their own ways – in the case brought by Mauritius against the United Kingdom, the Annex VII arbitral tribunal found that the undertakings made by the United Kingdom to Mauritius in 1965 were binding and in consequence certain obligations of the Law of the Sea Convention were breached by the Marine Protected Area that was established by the United Kingdom in 2010,[7] and in the case brought by Mauritius against Maldives,

5 Philippe Sands, *The Last Colony: A Tale of Exile, Justice, and Britain's Colony Legacy* (Weidenfeld & Nicolson, 2022), p. 98.

6 Henry G. Schermers & Niels M. Blokker, *International Institutional Law* (6th rev. ed.; Brill Nijhoff, 2018), p. 9.

7 Arbitral tribunal constituted under Annex VII of the UN Convention on the Law of the Sea, *Matter of the Chagos Marine Protected Area Arbitration* (*Mauritius v. UK*), Award of 18 Mar. 2015), available at <https://files.pca-cpa.org/pcadocs/MU-UK%2020150318%20Award.pdf> [hereinafter PCA Award].

the International Tribunal for the Law of the Sea (ITLOS) special chamber decided that it had jurisdiction to delimit the maritime boundary between the two countries on the assumption that Chagos belongs to Mauritius (and not the United Kingdom)[8] – neither one takes on itself the central question. The first tribunal decided it did not have jurisdiction over the issue of sovereignty, and the second deferred to – and consequently applied – the ICJ's legal conclusions.[9] Both decisions are good examples of judicial avoidance, and neither risked noncompliance by the United Kingdom.[10] Neither tribunal, in other words, issued statement decisions.

Only the ICJ's advisory opinion issued a clear statement concerning the fundamental principle of international law at stake in the dispute between Mauritius and the United Kingdom. The Court's conclusions regarding the law of decolonization, and particularly the law pertaining to territorial integrity during that process, were plainly stated. The Court found that "States have consistently emphasized that respect for the territorial integrity of a non-self- governing territory is a key element of the exercise of the right to self-determination under international law".[11] Thus, the Court "consider[ed] that the peoples of non-self-governing territories are entitled to exercise their right to self-determination in relation to their territory as a whole, the integrity of which must be respected by the administering Power".[12] Consequently, "any detachment by the administering Power of part of a non-self-governing territory, unless based on the freely expressed and genuine will of the people of the territory concerned, is contrary to the right to self-determination".[13] The Court went on to find, on the facts, that the "agree[ment] in principle [by the Council of Ministers of the Colony of Mauritius] to the detachment of the Chagos Archipelago ... was not based on the free and genuine expression of the will of the people concerned".[14] In its operative clause, the Court was of the opinion "that, having regard to international law, the process of decolonization

8 ITLOS, *Dispute Concerning Delimitation of the Maritime Boundary Between Mauritius and Maldives in the Indian Ocean* (*Mauritius v. Maldives*), Judgment of 28 Jan. 2021, available at <https://www.itlos.org/fileadmin/itlos/documents/cases/28/preliminary_objections/C28_Judgment_prelimobj_28.01.2021_orig.pdf> [hereinafter ITLOS Judgment].

9 PCA Award (*supra* note 7), para. 547(1); ITLOS Judgment (*supra* note 8), para. 205 ("The Special Chamber considers that [the ICJ's] determinations do have legal effect").

10 The ITLOS case created no obligations for the United Kingdom, only for Maldives and Mauritius.

11 *Chagos* Advisory Opinion (*supra* note 3), para. 160.

12 *Ibidem.*

13 *Ibidem.*

14 *Ibidem*, para. 172.

of Mauritius was not lawfully completed when that country acceded to independence in 1968, following the separation of the Chagos Archipelago" and as a result "that the United Kingdom [was] under an obligation to bring to an end its administration of the Chagos Archipelago as rapidly as possible".[15]

While the *Chagos* Advisory Opinion did not create binding obligations on the United Kingdom as such (since it was not a contentious case), the ICJ's statement was also not mere dicta.[16] But regardless of how we might view the formal legal consequences of the opinion, the Court clearly characterized the actions of the United Kingdom as a violation of international law and clearly indicated that that state and other UN member states had an obligation to take actions to remedy that violation and "to complete the decolonization of Mauritius".[17] Consequently, the absence of a formal legal obligation to comply with the advisory opinion should not have reduced the ICJ's concern regarding the likelihood of the United Kingdom's noncompliance. The ICJ stated the law and found on the facts a violation, and statements of law and conclusions therefrom need to be adhered to if a tribunal's decisions are to be considered more than just wishes and abstractions that are of no consequence. A tribunal, like the ICJ, which is dependent on states opting in to its jurisdiction and requesting advisory opinions and which issues decisions that are ignored, can quickly become a tribunal that hears no cases because its rulings will be considered meaningless.

But evidently the ICJ was not concerned. At no point would a realistic observer have expected the United Kingdom to leave the Chagos Archipelago in the near future just because the ICJ so ruled. Indeed, noncompliance was entirely to be expected if the United Kingdom was found by the Court to be in violation of international law – and the actions and statements of the United Kingdom subsequent to the advisory opinion (in which it referred to the opinion as nonbinding) did not disappoint in this regard. In a statement in the UN General Assembly made during the debate on a resolution that "welcome[d]" the advisory opinion and "[d]emand[ed] that the United Kingdom … withdraw its colonial administration from the Chagos Archipelago unconditionally within a period of no more than six months from the adoption of the present resolution,"[18] the representative of the United Kingdom said dismissively: "The

15 *Ibidem*, para. 183(3), (4).
16 This is different from judicial dicta. For a discussion, see for example Pierre N. Leval, "Judging Under the Constitution: Dicta About Dicta", in *NYU Law Review* vol. 98 (2006), p. 1249.
17 *Chagos* Advisory Opinion (*supra* note 3), para. 183(5).
18 Adopted as A/RES/73/295 (May 22, 2019).

specific advisory opinion before us does not, we believe, give sufficient regard to a number of legal and material factual issues".[19] Why did the ICJ, which otherwise should have cared deeply about the implementation of its ruling, apparently not worry about compliance with this decision? Why was it apparently happy to make a statement decision?

3 Additional Examples of Statement Decisions

The *Chagos* opinion was not the first time that the ICJ has issued a statement decision. Three others issued prior to *Chagos* are familiar: the advisory opinion on the "Legal Consequences for States of the Continued Presence of South Africa in Namibia (South West Africa)" (*Namibia*),[20] the *Nicaragua* case,[21] and the advisory opinion on "Legal Consequences of the Construction of a Wall in the Occupied Palestinian Territory" (*Wall*).[22] And more recent decisions concerning Israel – the advisory opinion on "Legal Consequences arising from the Policies and Practices of Israel in the Occupied Palestinian Territory, including East Jerusalem" (*Occupied Palestinian Territory*) and the provisional measures orders in the case brought by South Africa regarding the Genocide Convention – as well as Russia – which was accused by Ukraine of breaches of the Genocide Convention – are in the same tradition.[23]

In all these matters, the Court knew, or should have known, that its decisions would not be implemented. Yet, it went ahead nonetheless and reached clear conclusions that the states concerned violated the law (in all but the provisional measures orders) and issued specific obligations of conduct on states. In the *Namibia* advisory opinion, the Court declared that South Africa's "continued presence" in Namibia was "illegal," and consequently "South Africa [was] under [an] obligation to withdraw its administration from Namibia immediately and thus put an end to its occupation of the Territory."[24] In *Nicaragua*, in the absence of U.S. participation during the merits stage of the proceedings, the Court famously expounded its views on self-defense and decided that the United States was under an obligation to make reparation for its breaches

19 See, e.g., UN Doc. A/73/PV.83, at 11 (May 22, 2019) (statement of the representative of the United Kingdom); see also Sands (*supra* note 5), at p. 136.

20 *Namibia* Advisory Opinion (*supra* note 3).

21 *Nicaragua* Judgment (*supra* note 4).

22 *Wall* Advisory Opinion (*supra* note 3).

23 OPT Advisory Opinion (*supra* note 3); Modified Provisional Measures Order (*supra* note 4); *Russia* Provisional Measures Order (*supra* note 4).

24 *Namibia* Advisory Opinion (*supra* note 3), para. 133(1).

of customary international law.[25] In the *Wall* advisory opinion, Court provided extensive discussion of the law of occupation and found that Israel had to terminate its breaches of its obligations under international law and dismantle the wall that it was building.[26] In the case brought by Ukraine against Russia, the provisional measures order required Russia to "immediately suspend the military operations that it commenced on 24 February 2022 in the territory of Ukraine".[27] In the case brought by South Africa against Israel, the Court's modified provisional measures order required Israel to "[i]mmediately halt its military offensive, and any other action in the Rafah Governorate, which may inflict on the Palestinian group in Gaza conditions of life that could bring about its physical destruction in whole or in part".[28] And in the *Occupied Palestinian Territory* opinion, the Court decided that "Israel's continued presence in the Occupied Palestinian Territory is unlawful," that "Israel is under an obligation to bring to an end its unlawful presence in the Occupied Palestinian Territory as rapidly as possible," and that "Israel is under an obligation to cease immediately all new settlement activities, and to evacuate all settlers from the Occupied Palestinian Territory".[29]

In all these examples, as with *Chagos*, to no one's surprise and everyone's expectation, noncompliance followed. South Africa did not agree to Namibia's independence until 1988.[30] The United States vetoed an attempt to enforce the *Nicaragua* judgment at the Security Council and never provided reparation to Nicaragua.[31] Israel's construction of the wall continued unabated, and it remains in place to this day. Israel did not comply with the provisional measures order that required it to halt its offensive in Gaza issued in the case brought against it by South Africa, and it is also clear that its occupation will not be affected by the ICJ's advisory opinion.[32] Russia, of course, did not suspend its military operations in Ukraine.

---

25 *Nicaragua* Judgment (*supra* note 4), para. 292.

26 *Wall* Advisory Opinion (*supra* note 3), para. 163.

27 *Russia* Provisional Measures Order (*supra* note 4), para. 86(1).

28 Modified Provisional Measures Order (*supra* note 4), para. 57(2)(a).

29 *OPT* Advisory Opinion (*supra* note 3), para. 285.

30 *See* Christopher S. Wren, "Namibian Assembly Sets a Date for Independence", in *New York Times* (1 Feb. 1990), available at <https://www.nytimes.com/1990/02/01/world/namibian-assembly-sets-a-date-for-independence.html>.

31 See Constanze Schulte, *Compliance with Decisions of the International Court of Justice* (Oxford UP, 2004), pp. 199–205; Colter Paulson, "Compliance with Final Judgments of the International Court of Justice Since 1987", in *American Journal of International Law* vol. 98 (2004), p. 434.

32 *See* Loveday Morris, "Israel Should Evacuate Settlements, Pay Reparations, ICJ Says", in *Washington Post* (19 July 2024), at <https://www.washingtonpost.com/world/2024/07/19/israel-icj-occupation-palestinian-territory>.

4 Implementation and Reception as Judicial Goals

The ICJ's decisions in these cases might tempt some to conclude that international courts generally act – or should act – without regard to whether their rulings will be followed. That, though, would be an incomplete reading. Tribunals care about implementation – that is, whether those they call upon to act will actually comply – because they and those that initiate proceedings want their cases to have real effects. If a court's judgments don't have real effect, why would potential litigants bring to the court their disputes? But tribunals also care about how their decisions will be evaluated by audiences beyond the particular states whose actions are at issue – that is, they care about the international reception of their decisions. Courts are dependent in various ways on the good opinion of states and others who have nothing directly at stake in a particular case. It is well-known that the ICJ's refusal to declare that South Africa was in breach of its mandate for South West Africa led to a boycott of the Court.[33] Reception and implementation are separate considerations that are balanced by tribunals, and sometimes, if the two are not aligned, reception is prioritized over implementation. In those circumstances, statement decisions result.

For cases at the core of the Court's docket – those pertaining to maritime and territorial disputes – reception and implementation coincide. In these cases, the Court does not make broad statements elaborating the law. It seeks, instead, to issue technical and well-reasoned judgments that adhere predictably to the Court's jurisprudence. It does so because the states want the Court to issue such rulings because those types of judgments lead to implementation, which is what the Court's audience – states that choose to litigate boundary disputes before the Court – desires. The Court's sensitivity to reception in these types of cases is particularly strong because of the competition for litigants between the Court and other fora that could hear these disputes.[34] If the Court wishes to maintain this part of its docket, which is based on state consent, it must avoid statement decisions. It must issue – and hence craft – decisions that will be followed.

The inclination to avoid making statement decisions arises as well when there is no clear "side" to take between recognition and reception and when there is a balance between the two. In these circumstances the default preference – implementation – will take priority for the Court.

---

33 ICJ, *South West Africa (Liberia v. South Africa; Ethiopia v. South Africa)*, Judgement (Second Phase) of 18 July 1966.

34 *See* Jacob Katz Cogan, "Competition and Control in International Adjudication", in *Virginia Journal of International Law* vol. 48 (2008), p. 411.

In statement decisions, such as *Nicaragua*, *Wall*, and *Chagos*, the Court trades implementation for reception. That is not a comment upon the correctness of these decisions as a matter of law. It is instead a candid understanding of the choices made and the strategies undertaken by an international institution – the ICJ – that, like any other, needs to be sensitive to its position in the international public order if it wishes to maintain its pride of place within it. In the *Nicaragua* case and in the *Namibia*, *Wall*, and *Occupied Palestinian Territory* opinions, it would seem that the Court made the correct assessment of its audience and the benefits of playing to it even at the cost of having its decisions ignored by the states to which those decisions were primarily directed. It is likely that the Court made the right choice in *Chagos* as well from this institutionalist perspective. We know this because of the overwhelmingly favorable reception given to these decisions by the General Assembly.[35] It is likely that a different outcome would have had serious negative repercussions for the Court. But we shouldn't confuse organizational self-preservation with effectiveness.

5 The Need for Institutional Authority

It is tempting – particularly for those who agree with the reasoning and results of statement decisions – to attribute their outcomes to the law. This predilection assumes that the results were doctrinally correct, and so the outcome in these cases simply reflects the inevitable consequence of good legal reasoning and the triumph of the rule of law. According to this account, the Court had no choice under the law, and the Court must follow the law no matter where it leads – indeed, even if it results in noncompliance. Courts are responsible only to the law, and so failing to adhere to the law would be an abdication of judicial responsibility. Between the two, implementation of decisions is not as critical as decisions getting the law right.

But there is often also a concomitant belief of those who take this approach that, if not at first, eventually the law will win out and that at some time in the future the decision will be enforced. The "real world consequences," to use Philippe Sands's words, will eventually "work their magic."[36] Law will always prevail in the long term. So, in the end, in this optimistic view, we will have the best of both worlds: a correct decision and that decision's implementation.

35 See A/RES/73/295 (2019); see also A/ES-10/L.31/Rev.1 (2024); A/ES-10/L.18/Rev.1 (2004) (welcoming the ICJ's *Wall* and *Occupied Palestinian Territory* advisory opinions).

36 See text at note 5 *supra*.

While (as in *Chagos*) implementation of statement decisions can occur after a delay,[37] such a framing ignores the institutional aspects of international decision-making. International institutions, including courts and tribunals such as the International Court of Justice, cannot take their authority and relevance for granted. Their position and standing are, in fact, highly contingent. They are dependent on others: for their cases, for their funding, for their effectiveness, and for their reputation. Consequently, they must be attuned to and responsive to their audiences – those who provide them with authority and make them relevant.

There are many bases of institutional authority for international tribunals. Sometimes that authority stems from the confidence that the court will issue decisions that will be implemented. Legal correctness matters, of course, yet it is not the sole consideration. The parties must believe that the outcome is right and be willing to apply the result, and so the tribunal is constrained, and indeed it may issue a compromise decision as a result. Authority here is a function of compliance. But institutional authority for international tribunals is not just about implementation. It is also sometimes about belief in the legal correctness of the outcome regardless of the likelihood of implementation. Whereas the audience for implementation is the specific litigants in a case, the audience for correctness is all states and the public beyond. Correctness not in any objective sense. Rather, correctness as what the broader audience considers to be the right result. If this wider audience considers the outcome correct, then the Court will maintain its position regardless of compliance with the result.

Statement decisions are thus techniques for accumulating institutional authority. They are methods that courts use to ensure their position going forward in a world in which their relevance and continued use is not guaranteed. International tribunals are in this way like all international organizations: politically sensitive and, if successful, politically adept.[38]

---

37 See Haroon Siddique, Diane Taylor & Patrick Wintour, "Britain to Return Chagos Islands to Mauritius Ending Years of Dispute", in *Guardian* (3 October 2024).

38 Though the discussion in this contribution has focused on the International Court of Justice, its conclusions apply to other international tribunals as well. The European Court of Human Rights, for example, has gone ahead with hundreds of cases against Russia even though it is doubtful that Russia will comply with the rulings following its expulsion from the Council of Europe. See, e.g., Lynsey Chutel, "Russia Committed Human Rights Violations in Crimea, European Court Finds", in *New York Times* (25 June 2024), at <https://www.nytimes.com/2024/06/25/world/europe/russia-crimea-european-human-rights-court.html>.

CHAPTER 16

The International Court of Justice in Conflict

Reflections on the Role and Impact of the Palestine Litigation

*Helen Duffy and Giulia Pinzauti**

1 Introduction

The multi-faceted engagement of the International Court of Justice (ICJ) with the conflict in Palestine has drawn unprecedented attention to the Court, and raised questions and controversies regarding its role in armed conflict situations. Reactions have ranged from exhorting the ICJ as embodying the one remaining source of hope for victims, to condemning the instrumentalization of the Court and questioning the appropriateness of adjudicating complex political situations.

This chapter explores the role of the ICJ in recent proceedings concerning the Occupied Palestinian Territory (OPT), against the backdrop of its role in situations of armed conflict more broadly, before reflecting on the implications and limitations of this role through the lens of strategic human rights litigation. We see the role of the principal judicial organ of the UN in addressing key rule of law challenges of our time, its impact on and relationship with the political organs, as a crucial institutional and rule of law issue – the subject-matter of a life's work of scholarship by Niels Blokker. It is also a subject that sits at the intersection of academia and practice, reflecting Niels' career and approach, and our own, having benefitted from his inspiration and support.

Section 2 outlines the Palestine cases, and some of their remarkable features – including the scope and import of the issues before the Court and the engagement of contentious and advisory jurisdictions to address the responsibility of various states (Israel, cooperating states, and other third states). Section 3 contextualises this litigation against the backdrop of the Court's (considerable) practice in armed conflict situations. Section 4 reflects on the ICJ Palestine litigation in the context of the growing global phenomenon of strategic litigation, including in relation to armed conflicts violations. Considered through

* Grotius Centre for International Legal Studies, Leiden University. The authors wish to thank Cara Fanning, Robbert Thierens, Emile Tournoy and Natalia Venegas Arango for their research assistance.

 | DOI:10.1163/9789004699939_018

the lens of strategic litigation analysis, it offers preliminary reflections on the significance, impact and limitations of the Court's engagement.

2 Palestine and the ICJ

ICJ cases are shaped by the Court's jurisdictional constraints. These concern both access to the Court and its jurisdiction *ratione materiae*. First, the Court is only open to states that are parties to its Statute[1] – which Palestine is not without full UN membership – and cannot pronounce on the responsibility of armed groups. This is a significant limit, as nowadays non-international armed conflicts are prevalent. Second, the Court's contentious jurisdiction is based on consent, which can be expressed through a treaty or through matching optional clause declarations.[2] These jurisdictional rules (which ultimately reflect state choices) limit the claims that are brought in a conflict and how they are framed. Contrarily, the Court's advisory jurisdiction is not subject to the same limits, thereby representing a flexible and attractive avenue for bringing contentious matters before the Court.[3]

In relation to the situation in Palestine, the Court has been called upon by distinct actors to exercise both advisory and contentious jurisdiction. To date, it has issued two advisory opinions and multiple orders in two contentious cases, which are discussed below. The sheer level of engagement is noteworthy in itself, paralleled only by the four advisory opinions[4] and one contentious case concerning South West Africa/Namibia.[5]

1 Art 34(1) ICJ Statute.

2 Art 36(1) and (2) ICJ Statute. A third way of expressing consent to ICJ jurisdiction is the so-called *forum prorogatum*, consisting in the subsequent acceptance of the Court's jurisdiction.

3 Giulia Pinzauti, "Should the ICJ Answer the General Assembly's Request for an Advisory Opinion on the Legality of Israel's Occupation?", in *Opinio Juris*, 28 February 2023, available at <http://opiniojuris.org/2023/02/28/should-the-icj-answer-the-general-assemblys-request-for-an-advisory-opinion-on-the-legality-of-israels-occupation/>.

4 ICJ, *International Status of South West Africa* (Advisory Opinion), [1950] ICJ Reports, p. 128; *South West Africa – Voting Procedure* (Advisory Opinion), [1955] ICJ Reports, p. 67; *Admissibility of Hearings of Petitioners by the Committee on South West Africa* (Advisory Opinion), [1956] ICJ Reports, p. 23; *Legal Consequences for States of the Continued Presence of South Africa in Namibia (South West Africa) notwithstanding Security Council Resolution 276 (1970)* (Advisory Opinion), [1971] ICJ Reports, p. 16.

5 ICJ, *South West Africa (Ethiopia v South Africa; Liberia v South Africa) Second Phase,* [1966] ICJ Reports, p. 6.

2.1 *Advisory Proceedings*

For over 50 years, since the start of the occupation in 1967, the Court's jurisdictional requirements seemed to preclude the possibility of initiating a contentious case against Israel. Thus the Court's only engagement with the situation in Palestine was through advisory proceedings.

First, in the 2004 *Wall* Advisory Opinion, the Court addressed the legal consequences arising from the construction by Israel of a separation barrier in the OPT, including in and around East Jerusalem. The Court dismissed objections that its decision would interfere with political negotiations.[6] It concluded by a large majority that "the construction of the wall … and its associated régime, are contrary to international law".[7] It spelled out both Israel's obligations to terminate its breaches of international law and to make reparation for the damage caused. Significantly, it underscored the obligations of third states and the UN not to recognise the illegal situation or to render aid and assistance to maintain it, and to cooperate to ensure that any impediment to the right of self-determination resulting from the Wall be brought to an end.[8] The Advisory Opinion alerted the international community that if the Wall and its associated regime became a permanent fact, this would be tantamount to unlawful annexation. While the Advisory Opinion had various implications and reverberations,[9] the Court's call ultimately remained unheeded as the Wall still stands and violations in Palestine continued to expand.

In December 2022, the UNGA requested the Court to render an opinion of much broader scope, concerning: (a) the legal consequences of Israel's violations of the law of occupation in "the Palestinian territory occupied since 1967"; and (b) their impact on the legal status of the occupation, and the legal consequences arising therefrom for all states and the United Nations.[10] Engagement with these proceedings was unprecedented, and oral hearings, which took place in February 2024 while Israel's offensive in Gaza was ongoing, saw the participation of 50 states, including Palestine, and three international organizations. Israel presented written memoranda but did not participate in the hearings.[11]

---

6 ICJ, *Legal Consequences of the Construction of a Wall in the Occupied Palestinian Territory* (Advisory Opinion), [2004] ICJ Reports, p. 136, para. 51.

7 *Ibidem*, para. 163 (Judge Buergenthal dissenting).

8 *Ibidem*, para. 163.

9 For discussion of impact, see Helen Duffy, *Strategic Human Rights Litigation: Understanding and Maximising Impact* (Hart, 2018), pp. 223–229, and section 4.

10 UNGA Res. 77/247 (30 December 2022).

11 ICJ press release 2024/17 (26 February 2024).

In July 2024 the Court issued wide-reaching findings described as "path-breaking" or "seismic" in significance and scope.[12] A decisive majority concluded that Israel's occupation of and its continued presence in the OPT, encompassing the West Bank, East Jerusalem and the Gaza Strip, is unlawful.[13] The settlements established or maintained with Israel's support, confiscation of land, exploitation of natural resources, extension of Israeli laws, forced displacement and violence against Palestinian population, all violate international humanitarian law and in some cases international human rights law. Israel's unlawful policies and practices breach the right of the Palestinian people to self-determination[14] and amount to annexation.[15] The Court addressed the consequences for Israel, which must withdraw from the OPT and afford reparation, and for third states and the UN, in view of the serious breaches of obligations *erga omnes* under international law. These include duties of 'non-recognition' of the unlawful acts and duties to co-operate with the UN to put modalities into effect to protect the rights of the Palestinian people.[16]

Multiple concurring and dissenting opinions fleshed out considerations and tensions. For example, Judge Charlesworth noted that the occupied owe no allegiance to the occupier, of relevance to the much debated right to resist,[17] while others expressed discomfort with the role of the Court in the context of "complexity", "conflict" and "security" concerns, and emphasised the role of negotiations over adjudication.[18]

2.2 *Contentious Cases*

Following the 7th of October violent attack and hostage taking by Hamas in Southern Israel, the massive military offensive launched by Israel in Gaza prompted the initiation of contentious cases against Israel and one of its closest allies for their role in the conflict. The ICJ was therefore called upon to engage in real time in a conflict that has, at time of writing, taken the lives of

12 "Episode 28: Unlawful Occupation, Annexation and Segregation: The ICJ's Advisory Opinion on Palestine", at *EJIL: The Podcast!*, 17 September 2024, available at <https://www.ejiltalk.org/ejil-the-podcast-episode-28-unlawful-occupation-annexation-and-segregation-the-icjs-advisory-opinion-on-palestine/>.

13 ICJ, *Legal Consequences Arising from the Policies and Practices of Israel in the Occupied Palestinian Territory, Including East Jerusalem* (Advisory Opinion) (19 July 2024), available at <https://www.icj-cij.org/case/186>, paras. 72–83.

14 *Ibidem*, paras. 230–243.

15 *Ibidem*, para. 173.

16 The obligation of non-recognition applied also to the UN.

17 ICJ, *Policies and Practices* (*supra* note 13), Declaration Judge Charlesworth, para. 23.

18 *Ibidem*, Dissenting Opinion Judge Sebutinde, paras. 90–92; Joint Opinion of Judges Tomka, Abraham and Aurescu.

nearly 42,000 in Gaza, injured hundreds of thousands others, and devastated civilian infrastructure.

The first case was brought by South Africa against Israel under Article IX of the Genocide Convention. South Africa's case at its core is that Israel has breached the Genocide Convention in three ways: (i) by committing genocide against Palestinians in Gaza, (ii) by failing to prevent it; (iii) by failing to hold senior Israeli officials and others accountable for their direct and public incitement to commit genocide. While the case may take several years to reach a ruling on the merits, it highlights the role that the preliminary exercise of ICJ jurisdiction can have. South Africa asked the Court to indicate provisional measures to protect the rights of the Palestinian people in Gaza from the risk of genocide and to ensure the preservation of evidence on four occasions, and the Court indicated provisional measures three times.

In a landmark order issued on 26 January 2024, the Court recognised a plausible case of genocide for Israel to answer[19] and the urgency of addressing a catastrophic humanitarian situation on the ground. By a large majority, it ordered Israel to take six measures to prevent the commission of genocidal acts, prevent and punish the direct and public incitement to commit genocide, enable the provision of urgently needed basic services and humanitarian assistance to Gaza's besieged population, and to ensure the preservation of evidence.[20] These measures were widely acclaimed, but also criticised by some for falling short in specificity and for failing to order a ceasefire.[21]

Making broad demands in a provisional measures order is not at all unusual for the Court, which has repeatedly ordered states involved in conflict, for example, to "take all measures necessary to comply with all of their obligations under international law",[22] or to "refrain from any action … which might aggravate or extend the dispute before the Court or make it more difficult to resolve".[23]

19 ICJ, *Application of the Convention on the Prevention and Punishment of the Crime of Genocide in the Gaza Strip (South Africa v Israel)* (Order of 26 January 2024) <https://www.icj-cij.org/sites/default/files/case-related/192/192-20240126-ord-01-00-en.pdf>, para. 54.

20 *Ibidem.*

21 Nico Krisch, "Speaking the Law, Plausibly: The International Court of Justice on Gaza", at *EJIL:Talk!* 2024, available at <https://www.ejiltalk.org/speaking-the-law-plausibly-the-international-court-of-justice-on-gaza/>.

22 ICJ, *Armed Activities on the Territory of the Congo (Democratic Republic of the Congo v. Uganda)*, [2005] ICJ Reports, p. 168, para. 129.

23 ICJ, *Application of the Convention on the Prevention and Punishment of the Crime of Genocide (Bosnia v Serbia)* (Order of 8 April 1993), [1993] ICJ Reports p. 3, para. 24; *Temple of Preah Vihear (Cambodia v Thailand)* (Interpretation) (Order of 18 July 2011), [2011] ICJ Reports p. 537; *Allegations of Genocide under the Convention on the Prevention and*

Vagueness or openness in the orders may be the price of consensus-building within the bench, or the effort to afford states the flexibility to determine the most appropriate and effective ways of meeting orders, which is not unusual in international legal practice.[24]

Just a few weeks thereafter, when Israel's offensive on Rafah seemed imminent, South Africa called upon the Court to exercise its powers to modify *proprio motu* the provisional measures it had previously indicated and order Israel to suspend its military operations. The Court demanded immediate and effective implementation of the earlier measures but declined to indicate new ones.[25]

Faced with a further deterioration of the humanitarian situation and the spread of famine, South Africa made a third request for provisional measures in March 2024. The Court found that the spread of famine constituted an "exceptionally grave" development warranting new measures.[26] This time, the Court ordered Israel to take more specific measures to ensure the provision of humanitarian aid including food, water, electricity, fuel, shelter, clothing, hygiene and sanitation requirements, as well as medical supplies and medical care. The Court unanimously ordered Israel to increase the capacity and number of land crossing points and maintain them open for as long as necessary.[27] It also specified that Israel should ensure that its military does not prevent the delivery of humanitarian assistance.[28] Once again, the Court did not explicitly order Israel to suspend its military operations, although there was wide consensus within the bench that the only way for Israel to comply with the Court-ordered measures was to bring its offensive to an end.[29]

Neither mounting international pressure, nor the Court's order, averted the incursion of the Israeli military into Rafah in May 2024. The Court responded with a third set of provisional measures that indicate its incrementally more robust and specific engagement with the situation. The "disastrous" conditions

---

Punishment of the Crime of Genocide (*Ukraine v Russia*) (Order of 16 March 2022), [2022] ICJ Reports p. 211, para. 231.

24 See e.g. the practice of the European Court of Human Rights which often leaves it to the state, subject to ongoing Council of Europe oversight, to determine appropriate measures.

25 ICJ Press Release 2024/16 (16 February 2024).

26 ICJ, *Gazan Genocide* (Order of 28 March 2024), available at <https://www.icj-cij.org/sites/default/files/case-related/192/192-20240328-ord-01-00-en.pdf>, para. 22.

27 *Ibidem*, para. 51(2)(a).

28 *Ibidem*, para. 51(2)(b).

29 *Ibidem*, Declaration of President Salam, para. 11; Declaration of Judge Yusuf, para. 7; Joint Declaration of Judges Xue, Brant, Gómez-Robledo and Tladi, paras. 7–8; Declaration of Judge Charlesworth, para. 7.

of life in Gaza prompted the Court to order new measures, including: (1) the suspension of Israel's offensive in Rafah Governorate; (2) the opening of the Rafah crossing; and (3) the unimpeded access to the Strip by UN investigative bodies.[30] By a 13–2 majority, the Order sent a strong message to Israel, its allies and the international community. While once again Israel did not comply, or purport to, the Order provided benchmarks for engagement with the unfolding humanitarian disaster.

The second contentious case was initiated by Nicaragua against Germany concerning alleged breaches of the Genocide Convention and the Geneva Conventions in respect of the OPT. The Application contained a request for the indication of provisional measures to "stop aid" – in particular military assistance – to Israel, to ensure that weapons and other military equipment already delivered by Germany to Israel would not be used to commit or to facilitate serious violations of international law, and to enjoin Germany to resume its financial support for the United Nations Relief and Works Agency for Palestine Refugees in the Near East (UNRWA).[31]

On the facts and legal arguments presented by the parties, the Court concluded that the circumstances did not justify the indication of provisional measures at that point. As others have noted, the decision is firmly based on the facts rather than on a discussion of the criteria for indicating provisional measures.[32] Moreover, the Court did not throw the case out, as requested by Germany.[33] It remained seized of the case, and took the opportunity to reiterate its deep concerns regarding the humanitarian situation in Gaza and to underscore the preventive protective obligations of all states under Article 1 of the Geneva Conventions and the Genocide Convention. Such obligations in the context of military assistance necessarily impose a duty on states parties to be proactive in ascertaining and avoiding "the risk that such arms might be used to violate the … Conventions".[34]

30 ICJ, *Gazan Genocide* (Order of 24 May 2024), available at <https://www.icj-cij.org/sites/default/files/case-related/192/192-20240524-ord-01-00-en.pdf>, para. 57.

31 ICJ, *Alleged Breaches of Certain International Obligations in respect of the Occupied Palestinian Territory (Nicaragua v Germany)* (Provisional Measures: Order of 30 April 2024), available at <https://www.icj-cij.org/sites/default/files/case-related/193/193-20240430-ord-01-00-en.pdf>, para. 11.

32 Michael A. Becker, "Nicaragua Comes Up Empty: Provisional Measures in *Nicaragua v Germany* at the ICJ", at *Verfassungsblog* 2024, available at <https://verfassungsblog.de/nicaragua-comes-up-empty/>.

33 *Nicaragua v Germany* (*supra* note 31), para. 21.

34 *Ibidem*, para. 24.

3 The ICJ and Armed Conflict: Contextualising the Palestine Litigation

While litigation in the Palestine cases was ongoing, some commentators suggested that the Court, as the principal *judicial* organ of the UN, had "no role to play" in the settlement of the situation in Gaza, which should be "politically resolved".[35] Similar considerations resonated with some members of the Court.[36]

We argue that the Court's engagement with the situation in Gaza, and the OPT more generally, is consistent with its longstanding practice in conflict scenarios, and particularly with the Court's reinvigorated role in recent years. While of course one cannot expect courts to solve conflicts – at the end of the day, as Judge Tladi put it, "the Court is only a court!"[37] – the suggestion that they have no role to play views them as alternative or even antithetical to the role of political actors, and is at odds with the longstanding practice of the Court.

In fact, the Court has actively engaged in conflict scenarios since its establishment, addressing a broad array of issues, ranging from allegations of genocide and racial discrimination, *jus ad bellum*, occupation, frontier disputes at the heart of conflict, and the legality of nuclear weapons.[38] The nature of the Court's involvement has evolved quantitatively and qualitatively over time. In the last five years (2020–2024), there has been a quantitative growth spurt in the number of cases before the Court generally, and those concerning conflict specifically, with seven such cases currently pending. Qualitatively, many such cases address the conduct of belligerents and states in ongoing conflicts, not only accountability for past violations.[39] Other features during this phase have

35 Stefan Talmon on X (9 April 2024), available at <https://x.com/StefanTalmon>.

36 See e.g. *Gazan Genocide* (Order of 26 January 2024) (*supra* note 19), Dissenting Opinion Judge Sebutinde.

37 *Gazan Genocide* (Order of 24 May 2024) (*supra* note 30), Declaration Judge Tladi, para. 19.

38 To date the Court has rendered seven advisory opinions, seven merits decisions, one judgment on a request for interpretation, one judgment on reparation for wartime damage and a remarkable 33 decisions on provisional measures. Many more cases ended at the preliminary objections stage or were discontinued.

39 ICJ, *Application of the Convention on the Prevention and Punishment of the Crime of Genocide (The Gambia v. Myanmar)*; *Application of the Convention against Torture and Other Cruel, Inhuman or Degrading Treatment or Punishment (Canada and the Netherlands v Syrian Arab Republic*; *Ukraine v Russia* (*supra* note 23); *Application of the International Convention on the Elimination of All Forms of Racial Discrimination (Azerbaijan v Armenia); Application of the International Convention on the Elimination of All Forms of Racial Discrimination (Armenia v Azerbaijan)*; *Gazan Genocide* (*supra* note 19); *Nicaragua v Germany* (*supra* note 31); *Policies and Practices* (*supra* note 13).

included increased third-party interventions, and a rise in strategic or public interest litigation: states not directly affected by the internationally wrongful act bringing claims on the basis of their shared interest in the fulfilment of obligations *erga omnes partes*, such as those enshrined in the Genocide Convention or the Convention against Torture.

The Palestine litigation thus appears to be part of a broader trend of resort to the Court in conflict situations. Simply put, there is nothing exceptional about it. Questions may legitimately be asked about the effectiveness or impact of that litigation in practice (which we address in the next section). But that is a different question from *a priori* discarding the Court's ability to play a role in a complex armed conflict situation.

4 The Palestine Litigation through a Strategic Litigation Lens

There can be little doubt that in an increasingly desperate situation, where political solutions have long proved elusive, many look to the Court to exert decisive influence. For some, concerns certainly arise as to expectations, which at times appear inflated and unrealistic. For others, the flagrant non-implementation of opinions and orders represent the futility of the ICJ and even the failure of international law. In this context, understanding the significance and limitations of the ICJ's role, and of courts in the enforcement of international law more broadly, is essential.

Discussions of the impact of litigation often focus on the content of judicial decisions, and this undoubtedly matters, particularly from a court with the role and standing of the ICJ. The ICJ's acceptance of the plausibility of a genocide claim is a powerful indictment of unfolding events, irrespective of how the Court will address responsibility on the merits. The binding orders signal essential steps to be taken by the warring parties and third states, incrementally expanding these over time, and to some extent providing benchmarks for future action. The latest Advisory Opinion, even if not binding, provides an unequivocal and authoritative statement of the illegality of Israel's presence in the OPT and many of its policies and practices impacting Palestinian lives. The statement that Israel must end the occupation, dismantle the settlements in the OPT and make reparation for damage caused has significant implications.

It now falls on states (Israel, its allies and third states) and international organizations to implement the Court's rulings. This is crucial to give full effect to the ICJ's judgments and opinions. Non-compliance is a challenge to the authority of the Court and its ability to uphold international law in conflict scenarios. While non-implementation is a key challenge across international litigation that must be addressed, it is not the whole story.

Experience from strategic human rights litigation practice and impact analysis[40] suggests that, beyond judgments or orders, the power of the *process*, as it unfolds inside and outside the courtroom, can be as powerful as any judicial 'outcome' or 'result'. Likewise, implementation and impact are not coterminous. Moreover, experience suggests that litigation itself rarely resolves problems, still less complex systemic inter-generational ones, and we must not inflate or mythologise the power of the courts. But that does not detract from their role in contributing in diverse ways to solutions, directly and indirectly, immediately and in the longer term.

4.1 *Platform for Facts, Evidence and Historical Record*

There are limits to truth telling in legal fora, including who is given a voice (at the ICJ, states) and the necessarily limited issues addressed (depending on how claims are framed and jurisdiction *ratione materiae*). Often judicial contexts are alienating or exclusionary for those most affected and off-putting for the media. However, the provisional measures hearings in the *Gazan Genocide* case showcase the enormous potential, as Goldston has noted, for international courts to fulfil Arendt's vision of courts as "'arenas' for public debate about 'moral and political' issues," and for "public shaming."[41]

The ICJ provided a remarkable platform for the presentation, to the court and to the world, of detailed factual evidence regarding the conflict in Gaza and its devastating effects on the ground. The Court became a "front-page forum for a genuinely global discussion about the most pressing issue of the day."[42] The evidence presented in open court, as well as the readings of the ICJ orders, conveyed powerful messages regarding the urgency, and the importance, of the situation. The proceedings played a role in setting down a historical record of the conflict, even at this very preliminary stage, which may be one of the most impactful and enduring aspects of the case.[43]

Massive media coverage, unprecedented for the ICJ at least, if not for rights-related litigation more broadly, and a packed Peace Palace spilling onto

---

40 See, e.g., Duffy (*supra* note 9), noting a growing body of impact analysis and literature.

41 James Goldston, "Strategic Litigation Takes the International Stage: *South Africa v Israel* in Its Broader Context", in *Just Security* 2024, available at <https://www.justsecurity.org/91688/strategic-litigation-takes-the-international-stage-south-africa-v-israel-in-its-broader-context/>.

42 *Ibidem.*

43 Krisch (*supra* note 21).

Churchillplein where massive screens broadcast legal proceedings live to crowds, ensured that the evidence and arguments had expansive reach, with reverberations long before any order was issued.

The Advisory Opinion proceedings broadened out the evidence to include the context of racial discrimination, apartheid, land dispossession, settlements, plunder of natural resources. While some questioned the scope of the Advisory Opinion (considering the occupation from 1967 not 1948), there can be little doubt that the records of the proceedings played a role as "the great library of the occupation".[44]

The extent of participation in the proceedings itself[45] signalled that Palestine is, or must be, a matter of urgent of concern to the international community.

4.2 *Framing Violations*

The framing of disputed facts as legal arguments often has a powerful expressive value, as well as potential catalytic effect. In the *Gazan Genocide* case, centring the claim around the Genocide Convention was almost certainly prompted by a desire to engage the Court's jurisdiction rather than by strategic choices. It was undoubtedly deeply contested by many.[46] However, the genocide framing brought into sharp public focus 'the group' targeted, the risk of its destruction in whole or in part and the 'intent' of the state, all of which underscored the extreme gravity of facts and their potential implications. While controversial and arguably polarising, genocide allegations spoke to the systemic and long-lasting nature of the allegations in a way that war crimes, however important and egregious, may not.

Likewise, the ICJ's endorsement of Israel's discriminatory policies and practices as racial segregation or apartheid were among the important findings in its July 2024 Advisory Opinion.[47] Both genocide and apartheid have particular public resonance, due to the notoriety and gravity of crimes of the Nazi holocaust and the South African apartheid regime. The nature of the parties contributed to the symbolic force of these allegations. The voice of South Africa,

44 A. Feldman, "Which Side Are You On, Grandpa Weinstein?", in *Haaretz* of 25 July 2013, cited in Duffy (*supra* note 9), p. 215.

45 *Supra* note 11.

46 See, e.g., US Secretary of State Blinken on the "meritless" nature of the claim: <https://www.haaretz.com/us-news/2024-01-09/ty-article/.premium/blinken-genocide-charge-against-israel-meritless-palestinians-must-be-allowed-return/0000018c-ef8f-da6b-abdd-ffcf48d60000>.

47 *Policies and Practices* (*supra* note 13), para. 229. The Court concluded that Israel's policies and practices breached Art. 3 CERD, without determining whether they amounted to racial discrimination or apartheid.

given its experience of exclusion, discrimination and settler-colonial violations, had symbolic significance and global resonance.

In sum, this litigation illustrates how the legal framing of allegations in the contentious and advisory proceedings, running in parallel, can be significant in shaping legal discourse and breathing life into legal and policy debates.

4.3 *Legal and Political Impact on Third States?*

Strategic human rights litigation has often contributed to normative development, including in relation to human rights in armed conflicts.[48] The ICJ itself has developed or clarified many issues related to applicable law, including on co-applicability of international humanitarian law and international human rights law,[49] conflict classification,[50] the legality of nuclear weapons,[51] the requirement of effective control (and irrelevance of physical presence) for belligerent occupation,[52] and on the use of force in occupied territory.[53] The Advisory Opinion on the legality of the occupation is remarkable for clarifying for example that belligerent occupation can become unlawful if it amounts to territorial acquisition by force and/or infringes the right to self-determination of the occupied people.[54]

One of the most noteworthy aspects of the Palestine litigation as a whole relates to its implications for third states. At a normative level, the ICJ reaffirmed and clarified the obligations of third states under international humanitarian law, under the Genocide Convention, and in the face of serious breaches of *erga omnes* obligations. Despite their significance, such obligations have rarely been litigated, precisely on account of the Court's jurisdictional limitations.

The military, economic and political implications are potentially profound, impelling states to consider the implications of their cooperation and assistance to states accused of certain violations.[55] As many scholars noted, the

---

48 Helen Duffy, "Trials and Tribulations", in Ziv Bohrer, Janina Dill and Helen Duffy, *Law Applicable to Armed Conflict* (Cambridge UP 2020), Chapter 3.

49 ICJ, *Legality of the Threat or Use of Nuclear Weapons,* [1996] ICJ Reports p. 226, para. 25; *Wall* (*supra* note 6), para. 106; *Armed Activities* (*supra* note 22), para. 216.

50 *Military and Paramilitary Activities in and against Nicaragua* (*Nicaragua v US*) [1986] ICJ Rep p. 14, para. 219.

51 *Nuclear Weapons* (*supra* note 49).

52 *Policies and Practices* (*supra* note 13), paras. 90–93.

53 *Wall* (*supra* note 6), para. 139.

54 *Policies and Practices* (*supra* note 13), paras. 251–257, 261–264 (even if the ICJ did not dispel all doubts on the relationship between *ius ad bellum* and *ius in bello*).

55 Cf. Nora Salem, "The Legal Limits of Supporting Israel", at *Verfassungsblog,* 2024, available at <https://verfassungsblog.de/the-legal-limits-of-supporting-israel/>; Jinan Bastaki, "The 'Capacity to Influence' – State Responsibility, and the Obligation to Prevent

decisions in *South Africa v Israel* put third States on notice of their own obligations under the Genocide Convention – not to cooperate, aid and assist internationally wrongful acts, and of preventing genocide.[56]

What difference this has made in practice, and the causal connections between litigation and policy and practice, are extremely difficult to assess, and any such effort would need a longer time to lapse. It appears, however, that the litigation has already elicited reactions from states. For example, despite there being no findings against Germany and no provisional measures granted in *Nicaragua v. Germany*, Germany made assurances regarding its evolving policy on arms transfers during proceedings that may make it difficult to resume large scale exports in military aid to Israel.[57] More broadly, the messaging to Germany and third states from the Court in that case alone was that, while provisional measures were not granted on the facts (showing that Germany had *not* transferred to Israel since October 2023), the Court's approach may change if facts change. Judge Cleveland suggested states should be attentive to the detail and operation of their legal and policy frameworks, by drawing a distinction between Germany's legal framework for military assistance and the Netherlands', which she noted is being examined in the recent case concerning the transfer of F35 fighter jets parts.[58]

Important questions also arise as to the diplomatic, political and practical ramifications beyond directly cooperating states. States' responses to the initial order certainly varied. However, even Israel's staunch supporters such as Germany, Canada and Australia made clear that ICJ provisional measures were binding.[59] France, which had earlier voiced its scepticism about South Africa's case, affirmed its confidence in, and support for, the ICJ.[60] It has been suggested that the ICJ proceedings may have contributed, albeit within a much broader landscape, to an "unprecedented" erosion of political support for

Genocide", in *Opinio Juris,* 2024, available at <http://opiniojuris.org/2024/03/30/the-capacity-to-influence-state-responsibility-and-the-obligation-to-prevent-genocide/>.

56 Janina Dill, "Top Experts' Views of Int'l Court of Justice Ruling on Israel Gaza Operations (South Africa v Israel, Genocide Convention Case)", in *Just Security,* 2024, available at <https://www.justsecurity.org/91457/top-experts-views-of-intl-court-of-justice-ruling-on-israel-gaza-operations-south-africa-v-israel-genocide-convention-case/>.

57 Becker (*supra* note 32).

58 Declaration of Judge Cleveland, available at <https://www.icj-cij.org/sites/default/files/case-related/193/193-20240430-ord-01-03-en.pdf>, para. 14.

59 Thomas Obel Hansen, "Not all Scripts with One Voice: Variations in State Responses to South Africa v Israel", at *EJIL:Talk,* 2024, available at <https://www.ejiltalk.org/not-all-scripts-come-with-one-voice-variations-in-state-responses-to-south-africa-v-israel/>.

60 *Ibidem.*

Israeli military operations.[61] Some countries recalled their ambassador or cut diplomatic ties altogether, citing the facts or allegations underpinning ICJ proceedings. In some cases, diplomatic moves preceded (Turkey) or immediately followed (Colombia) interventions in South Africa's case.[62]

This was coupled with significant, historic shifts towards recognition of and support for Palestine, such as the UNGA vote in favour of statehood and full UN membership, adopted by an overwhelming 143 to 9 votes.[63] An additional 10 states in the Caribbean and Western Europe recognised Palestine in April–June 2024.[64] UNGA debates and statements on the humanitarian situation in Gaza are replete with references to the ICJ provisional measures.[65] A resounding vote of the General Assembly followed the adoption of the latest Advisory Opinion. While ICJ was at times explicitly referenced, even where it was not these stark shifts in policy and practice may have at least been informed or emboldened by the proceedings illuminating the nature of Israel's violations and the grave risks for the Palestinian people.

4.4 *Accountability Catalyst?*

While the suggestions that the "[t]he Court's ruling is the end of impunity for the Israeli occupation"[66] is hyperbolic, the proceedings may be seen as offering at least a degree of transparency, oversight and hence accountability. The ICJ's high profile and robust engagement may also have played a role in catalysing other accountability actors, including the ICC or national jurisdictions focused on individual accountability.

61 Peter Beaumont, "Israel's isolation grows over war in Gaza and rise in settler violence", in *The Guardian* of 10 May 2024.

62 Turkey cut trade relations with Israel in May 2024 and filed its declaration of intervention in August 2024. Aoife Walsh, "Turkey halts trade with Israel over 'humanitarian tragedy' in Gaza", at BBC News of 3 May 2024, available at <https://www.bbc.com/news/world-middle-east-68945380>. Colombia filed its declaration of intervention in April and severed diplomatic relations in May 2024. "Colombia president cuts ties with Israel over war on Gaza", at *Aljazeera* of 2 May 2024, available at <https://www.aljazeera.com/program/newsfeed/2024/5/2/colombia-president-cuts-ties-with-israel-over-war-on-gaz>.

63 UNGA res 10/23 (10 May 2024) adopted with 25 abstentions and 16 non-voting states.

64 Barbados, Jamaica, Trinidad and Tobago, the Bahamas, Spain, Ireland, Norway, Slovenia and Armenia. Statement by the Permanent Observer for the State of Palestine at the UNGA (26 June 2024), available at <https://press.un.org/en/2024/gapal1469.doc.htm>.

65 E.g. the UNGA debates on 4 March 2024 on the humanitarian situation in Gaza and the US veto on the draft UNSC resolution calling for a ceasefire, available at <https://news.un.org/en/story/2024/03/1147202>.

66 Statement by Algeria, available at <https://www.trtworld.com/middle-east/global-reactions-to-icj-ruling-on-gaza-genocide-case-against-israel-16783508>.

As is well known, in May 2024, the ICC Prosecutor filed an application for arrest warrants against Israel's Prime Minister Netanyahu and Defence Minister Gallant, together with three Hamas leaders, for war crimes and crimes against humanity.[67] It remains to be seen whether the ICJ's vindication of facts and framing of violations may shape the focus of other judicial processes. As regards national litigation, it was also noteworthy that just five days after the ICJ handed down its first order, this was already referred to in legal proceedings in the US. In *Defense for Children International – Palestine v Biden*, the plaintiffs alleged that the US President, Secretary of State and Defence Secretary are failing to prevent the unfolding genocide in Gaza and "actively abetting" its development. Although this case was thrown out pursuant to jurisdictional rules that precluded national courts' adjudication of political issues, the decision is remarkable for noting that there is a plausible genocide case, and extensively quoting the ICJ orders in reaching that conclusion.[68] Undoubtedly the ICJ will continue to be relied upon as an authoritative statement of law and fact in other domestic proceedings around the globe.

4.5 *Mobilisation, Resistance and Hope*

UN Special Rapporteurs described the ICJ orders in *Gazan Genocide* as offering "hope" for the protection of "civilians enduring apocalyptic conditions in Gaza".[69] Whether that hope translates into concrete action and contributes to protecting Palestinian victims depends on the actions of third states and IOs. One Palestinian commentator noted that when the ICJ cases were heard, she felt "seen" and "heard" for the first time, even if the Court's rulings fail to fully capture the suffering of the Palestinian people.[70] One survivor described

67 *Statement of ICC Prosecutor Karim A.A. Khan KC: Applications for arrest warrants in the situation in the State of Palestine* (20 May 2024), available at <https://www.icc-cpi.int/news/statement-icc-prosecutor-karim-aa-khan-kc-applications-arrest-warrants-situation-state>.

68 The judge found strong evidence that Israel's "military siege in Gaza is intended to eradicate a whole people and therefore plausibly falls within the international prohibition against genocide" and noted that "the undisputed evidence before this Court comports with the finding of the ICJ and indicates that the current treatment of the Palestinians in the Gaza Strip by the Israeli military may plausibly constitute a genocide in violation of international law" (*Defense for Children International – Palestine v Biden*, US Northern District of California (31 January 2024, no. 23-cv-05829-JSW 4).

69 "Gaza: ICJ ruling offers hope for protection of civilians enduring apocalyptic conditions, say UN experts" (31 January 2024), available at <https://www.ohchr.org/en/press-releases/2024/01/gaza-icj-ruling-offers-hope-protection-civilians-enduring-apocalyptic?utm_source=miragenews&utm_medium=miragenews&utm_campaign=news>.

70 Diana Buttu (*supra* note 12), at 33:57.

the importance of the assembly outside the Peace Palace as forum for solidarity, support and resistance.[71] Litigation is not the only or necessarily the most effective form of legal and social action, but as this litigation and many other examples show, it can complement, catalyse and energise other forms of lawful resistance.

5 Conclusions

In recent years, there has been a *quantitative* and *qualitative* increase in ICJ engagement with armed conflict. Many pending cases concern alleged violations of international law during conflict, and the conduct of belligerents on the battlefield. These proceedings are often politically contentious, and used strategically by political entities (states) for various reasons – seeking accountability for international law violations and justice for victims, reaffirming the obligations breached, guiding the conduct of belligerents on the battlefield, and also, inevitably, their own political considerations. This is neither surprising nor inherently problematic. What is essential is that the Court acts with independence and impartiality. This does not mean avoiding political controversy, which would rule out most cases before the Court and render international legal process obsolete. Nor does it imply that the Court will entirely ignore political context and considerations, and the ICJ's reference to the obligations of Hamas and other armed groups in its decisions, despite limitations in its jurisdiction, may be one illustration.[72] As Niels Blokker put it, in considering the "constitutional" role of the ICJ within the UN system, the Court has "fully played its role as a judicial body, a court of law, while also taking into account political sensitivities, not being deaf to political reality".[73]

The Palestine litigation shows the role an increasingly engaged ICJ can play in reasserting the role and relevance of international law, diverse areas of which indisputably apply in armed conflicts.[74] This litigation provides a rare example of how multiple, distinct but overlapping pluri-centric legal controversies can be considered through the prism of the Court's jurisdiction. No-one

71 <https://www.ohchr.org/en/press-releasese/2024/01/gaza-icj-ruling-offers-hope-protection-civilians-enduring-apocalyptic>.

72 *Gazan Genocide* (Order of 26 January 2024) (*supra* note 19), para. 85, reiterated in Order of 28 March 2024 (*supra* note 26), para. 50.

73 Niels Blokker, "The Constitutional role of the ICJ within the UN System", in S. van Hoogstraten (ed.), *New Challenges to International Law. A View from The Hague* (Brill Nijhoff, 2018), p. 26.

74 Helen Duffy and Philip Leach, *Strategic Litigation in Armed Conflict* (forthcoming 2024).

acquainted with the realities of international legal process would look to the ICJ, or indeed any court, to solve complex intergenerational problems such as the situation in Palestine. As the practice of strategic human rights litigation attests, courts rarely solve problems in themselves, but they can make essential contributions towards such solutions, playing a role that is complementary not alternative to that of political actors.

That role takes many forms, some of which have been flagged. At a minimum, the Palestine litigation has made suffering visible, gathered and lent weight to evidence, provided a degree of recognition, influenced discourse and underscored the urgency of fuller engagement and accountability. International norms have been clarified as they apply to Gaza and the occupation more broadly, and given greater meaning and relevance in the real world. The ICJ has been lauded for speaking law to power. Ultimately, it contributes tools in the protection and restoration of the rule of law, and the significance of the litigation will depend on how they are used. At a minimum, the Palestine proceedings assert the relevance of international law to events, the practice of states and the relationships between them. They make resoundingly clear that even in the midst of conflict 'laws are not silent' and victims will not go unseen.

CHAPTER 17

The United Nations Criminal Tribunals: Terminable Yet Independent?

*Huw Llewellyn**

1 Introduction

The author's 2019 Leiden University PhD dissertation, under the insightful supervision, encouragement and enthusiasm of professors Niels Blokker and Larissa van den Herik, assessed the five United Nations (UN) criminal tribunals from an institutional law perspective. In particular, it considered how the tribunals' independence is protected in the close one-to-one relationships with powerful UN organs and committees of major donor States that characterise their oversight arrangements. Five years on, and shortly after the abrupt closure of the Special Tribunal for Lebanon (STL), at the end of 2023, before it had completed all ongoing judicial proceedings, it is timely to take a fresh look at the inherent tensions present in these arrangements. The temporary nature of the UN criminal tribunals, and the consequent need for their oversight bodies at some point to determine when they should close, has been described as the "paradox" inherent in independent yet terminable tribunals.[1]

The five UN criminal tribunals are:[2] the International Criminal Tribunal for the Former Yugoslavia (ICTY),[3] the International Criminal Tribunal for

* The views expressed in this chapter are personal to the author and do not necessarily represent the views of the United Nations. The Chapter is based on the author's PhD dissertation, defended at Leiden University in September 2019.

1 Laura Bingham, "Strategy or Process? Closing the International Criminal Tribunals for the Former Yugoslavia and Rwanda", in *Berkeley Journal of International Law* vol. 24 (2006), p. 691.

2 The term 'UN criminal tribunals' is preferred to 'UN international criminal tribunals' because the ECCC was established as a national court of Cambodia, not as an international tribunal.

3 The ICTY was established by UN Security Council resolution 808, 22 February 1993, UN Doc S/RES/808 and UN Security Council resolution 827, 25 May 1993, UN Doc S/RES/827, which approved the 1993 report of the Secretary-General: *Report of the Secretary-General Pursuant to Paragraph 2 of Security Council Resolution 808 (1993)*, 3 May 1993, UN Doc S/25704 and annex containing the ICTY Statute.

 | DOI:10.1163/9789004699939_019

Rwanda (ICTR),[4] the Special Court for Sierra Leone (SCSL),[5] the Extraordinary Chambers in the Courts of Cambodia (ECCC),[6] and the STL.[7] Establishment of each of these tribunals was mandated by a principal organ of the UN – the Security Council in the case of the ICTY, the ICTR, the SCSL and the STL, and the General Assembly for the ECCC.

As temporary tribunals with finite mandates, each of the UN criminal tribunals has an establishing and terminating body (the 'parent' body) and a body charged with overseeing its functioning, responsible for its external financial and administrative management, and shepherding it to carry out and complete its mandate in the most efficient and cost-effective manner possible (the 'oversight' body).[8] Establishing and overseeing international criminal tribunals has proven to be an expensive and long-term undertaking. The oversight bodies have an inevitable interest in trying to control their cost and duration, which triggers inherent tensions between these needs and the imperative that the tribunals, as judicial bodies, function independently. The constituent instruments within which the tribunals and their oversight bodies operate and interact therefore have to be sufficiently robust that the integrity and independence of the judicial process is protected.

The UN criminal tribunals were established at 'Nuremberg moments'[9] – when there was sufficient political and financial will among UN Member States to embark on the lengthy and expensive business of initiating and sustaining international or internationalised criminal tribunals. Nuremberg moments are

4 The ICTR was established by UN Security Council resolution 955, 8 November 1994, UN Doc S/RES/955.

5 Agreement between the United Nations and the Government of Sierra Leone on the Establishment of a Special Court for Sierra Leone, with annexed Statute, signed 16 January 2002, entered into force 12 April 2002, 2178 UNTS 137.

6 Although 2003 is commonly stated as the year of establishment, the ECCC was in fact first established by the Law on the Establishment of the Extraordinary Chambers in the Courts of Cambodia, 10 August 2001, which is Cambodian national legislation. This was subsequently amended by the Law to Amend the 2001 Law on the Establishment of the Extraordinary Chambers in the Courts of Cambodia, 27 October 2004. Both pieces of Cambodian national legislation are set out on the ECCC website at <www.eccc.gov.kh/en/document/legal/law-on-eccc>. 2003 is the year commonly referred to because the Agreement between the UN and the Government of Cambodia concerning the Prosecution under Cambodian Law of Crimes Committed during the Period of Democratic Kampuchea was signed on 6 June 2003, 2329 *UNTS* 117.

7 UN Security Council resolution 1757, 30 May 2007, UN Doc S/RES/1757, with annexed draft Agreement and draft Statute.

8 The parent and oversight bodies are the 'international judicial governance institutions' (INJUGOVINS), a term coined by professor Blokker.

9 Bingham (*supra* note 1), pp. 687 and 691.

fleeting. Growing concerns in the late 1990s about the slow pace of proceedings and high costs of the ICTY and the ICTR, which had been established within the UN Organization as subsidiary organs of the Security Council, funded by assessed contributions, led to changed institutional forms, funding and oversight arrangements for the SCSL, the ECCC, and the STL. These tribunals were based primarily on voluntary funding with oversight placed in the hands of small committees of the most interested States, primarily the major donors, to oversee their non-judicial functions and to act as their budgetary authorities.

The closure of the STL at the end of 2023 for lack of financing before all of its ongoing judicial proceedings had been completed is a wake-up call. It calls into question not only the viability of voluntary-funding as a suitable basis for the functioning of international criminal tribunals, but also the new form of oversight arrangements that the major donors themselves were instrumental in designing.

2 The Imperative of Independence

It is, of course, imperative that international criminal tribunals, particularly those created by the UN, function as judicial bodies independently of the organization, organ or State that created them and which oversee their functions. The right of defendants to trial by an independent and impartial tribunal established by law is enshrined in Article 10 of the Universal Declaration of Human Rights and Article 14(1) of the 1966 International Covenant on Civil and Political Rights. It is further elaborated in the jurisprudence of the UN Human Rights Committee, in regional human rights treaties and jurisprudence, in the case law of international criminal tribunals, and in relevant non-binding international principles and guidelines.[10] It is embedded in all major international

10 See Universal Declaration of Human Rights, 10 December 1948, UN General Assembly resolution 217 A(III), Art. 10; UN Basic Principles on the Independence of the Judiciary, adopted by the Seventh UN Congress on the Prevention of Crime and the Treatment of Offenders held at Milan from 26 August to 6 September 1985 and endorsed by UN General Assembly resolution 40/32, 29 November 1985, UN Doc A/RES/40/32 and UN General Assembly resolution 40/146, 13 December 1985, UN Doc A/RES 40/146; Judicial Group on Strengthening Judicial Integrity, The Bangalore Principles of Judicial Conduct, as revised at the Round Table Meeting of Chief Justices held at the Peace Palace, The Hague, November 25–26, 2002; and the Burgh House Principles on the Independence of the International Judiciary, adopted in 2004 by the Study Group of the International Law Association on the Practice and Procedure of International Courts and Tribunals, in association with the Project on International Courts and Tribunals.

human rights instruments, both universal and regional,[11] and in international humanitarian law instruments.[12] It is safe to conclude that the right is a rule of customary international law.[13]

As the UN is not itself a party to the relevant international legal instruments, the status of the right to a competent, independent, and impartial tribunal established by law as a rule of customary international law is key to its applicability to the UN criminal tribunals. The UN Human Rights Committee considers that the "fundamental principles of fair trial" form part of customary international law and that they are peremptory norms of international law,

11 Universal Declaration of Human Rights, ibidem, Art. 10; International Covenant on Civil and Political Rights, *ibidem*, Art. 14(1); American Convention of Human Rights, adopted on 22 November 1969, entered into force 18 July 1978, 1144 UNTS 123, Art. 8(1); European Convention on Human Rights, adopted 4 November 1950, entered into force 3 September 1953, 213 UNTS 221, Art. 6(1); African Charter on Human and Peoples' Rights, adopted 27 June 1981, entered into force 21 October 1986, 1520 UNTS 217, Art. 7(1); Revised Arab Charter on Human Rights, adopted 22 May 2004, entered into force 2008, 12 IHRR 893, Art. 13; and ASEAN Human Rights Declaration adopted 18 November 2012, Art. 20; The essential elements are common to all of these instruments. The requirement that the tribunal be "competent" is interpreted under the ECHR as being included in the term "established by law".

12 Geneva Convention (III) Relative to the Treatment of Prisoners of War, adopted 12 August 1949, entered into force 21 October 1950, 75 UNTS 135, Arts. 84–87 and 99–108; Geneva Convention (IV) Relative to the Protection of Civilians, adopted 12 August 1949, entered into force 21 October 1950, 75 UNTS 287, Arts. 5 and 64–76; Protocol Additional to the 1949 Geneva Conventions and Relating to the Protection of Victims of International Armed Conflicts (1979) 1125 UNTS 3, Art. 75; Protocol Additional to the 1949 Geneva Conventions and Relating to the Protection of Victims of Non-International Armed Conflicts (1979) 1125 UNTS 609, Art. 6.

13 For a detailed survey of the extent to which the Universal Declaration of Human Rights reflects customary international law and general principles of law, see Hurst Hannum, "The Status of the Universal Declaration of Human Rights in National and International Law", in *Georgia Journal of International and Comparative Law* vol. 25 (1995/1996) p. 287. See also *Human Rights in the Administration of Justice, A Manual on Human Rights for Judges, Prosecutors and Lawyers* (OHCHR and International Bar Association, 2003), p. 118, available at <www.ohchr.org/Documents/Publications/training9chapter4en.pdf>. See also Michael O'Boyle and Michelle Lafferty, "General Principles and Constitutions as Sources of Human Rights Law" in Dinah Shelton (ed.), *The Oxford Handbook of International Human Rights Law* (Oxford UP, 2013), p. 194; Bertrand G. Ramcharan, "The Law-Making Process: From Declaration to Treaty to Custom to Prevention", *ibidem*, p. 499. See also, for example, Patrick Robinson, "The Right to a Fair Trial in International Law with Specific Reference to the Work of the ICTY", in *Berkeley Journal of International Law* vol. 3 (2009), p. 5; and the UN Counter-Terrorism Implementation Task Force Basic Human Rights Reference Guide, *Right to a Fair Trial and Due Process in the Context of Countering Terrorism* (2014), para. 10, available at <http://www.ohchr.org/EN/newyork/Documents/FairTrial.pdf>.

i.e. rules of international law from which no derogation is permissible.[14] The Burgh House principles, which are not legally binding, are a source of guidance that confirms the necessary separation of powers between international tribunals and organs of the international organizations under whose auspices they were created.[15] The case law of the UN criminal tribunals themselves also supports the applicability of the right of the accused to the fundamentals of a fair trial, including the Appeals Chamber in the ICTY *Tadić* case,[16] the ICTR Trial Chamber in the *Kanyabashi* case,[17] the SCSL Appeals Chamber in the *Kallon* case[18] and the STL Appeals Chamber in the *Ayyash* case.[19]

3 The Unique Context in Which International Criminal Tribunals Operate

The challenges facing the independent functioning of the UN criminal tribunals is entirely different to those faced by national courts. National courts are not temporary, they operate within an established constitutional setting and enjoy extensive support networks of existing national law enforcement and criminal justice institutions that provide access to crime sites, ensure the availability and participation of witnesses, execute arrest warrants and enforce prison sentences. In national criminal justice systems, the judicial, investigative, prosecutorial, defence, and administration functions are each separately constituted, with the judicial and prosecutorial functions, in particular, being distinct and supported by their own administrations.

By contrast, the UN criminal tribunals were created individually and temporarily, on the basis of *ad hoc* legal instruments negotiated and concluded specifically for this purpose. Each is a singular entity, not part of a system of courts with a network of supporting criminal justice institutions, and each sits

14 UN Human Rights Committee, *General Comment No. 29*, 31 August 2001, UN Doc CCPR/C/21/Rev.1/Add.11, para. 11.

15 See the Burgh House Principles (*supra* note 10), Principle 1.2.

16 *Decision on the defence motion for interlocutory appeal on jurisdiction, Prosecutor v. Tadić*, IT-94-1-AR72, AC, ICTY, 2 October 1995, paras. 42 and 45.

17 *Decision on the Defence Motion on Jurisdiction, Prosecutor v. Kanyabashi*, ICTR-96-15-T, TC, ICTR, 18 June 1997, paras. 37–44.

18 *Decision on Constitutionality and Lack of Jurisdiction, Prosecutor v. Kallon et al.*, SCSL-2004-15-AR72(E), AC, SCSL, 13 March 2004, paras. 54–56.

19 *Decision on the Defence Appeals against the Trial Chamber's Decision on the Defence Challenges to the Jurisdiction and Legality of the Tribunal, Prosecutor v. Ayyash et al.*, STL-11-01/PT/AC/AR90.1, AC, STL, 24 October 2012, para. 44.

in a direct bilateral relationship with the State(s) and/or UN organ that created it and which oversee it. The lack of a support network of law-enforcement and criminal justice institutions places the tribunals in a situation of dependence on third parties, usually States and international organizations, for these and other essential aspects of cooperation. They also depend on their oversight bodies playing an active role to encourage and enable such cooperation from third parties.

The tribunals' creation as single entities requires an internal structure of separate organs to maintain the critical separation and independence of the judicial, prosecutorial and administrative functions. In relation to external actors, despite the above aspects of dependence for essential cooperation and support, it must of course remain the case that these relationships, including crucially with the oversight body, respect the integrity and independence of the tribunals' judicial process.

4 The Institutional Architecture of the UN Criminal Tribunals

There are two essential aspects to the institutional architecture within which the UN criminal tribunals function: the legal basis and institutional form of the tribunal itself; and the oversight arrangements within which the tribunal and its parent and oversight bodies interact. This section focuses on the form of oversight arrangement developed for the voluntarily-funded UN criminal tribunals, and in particular, the legal 'disconnect' between these tribunals and their oversight bodies.

4.1 *The Institutional Forms of the UN Criminal Tribunals*

The ICTY and ICTR were established by the Security Council under Chapter VII of the UN Charter as subsidiary organs of the Council.[20] They thus formed part of the UN Organization and were financed from UN assessed contributions which, in accordance with Article 17 of the UN Charter, fall to the Assembly to determine. The establishment of UN criminal tribunals directly by the Security Council as subsidiary organs within the UN Organization was not repeated after 1994.

20 This was not expressly stated in Security Council resolution 827 (1993), but in the Secretary-General's 1993 report that underpinned the ICTY's establishment, endorsed in its entirety by the Council (*supra* note 3). The establishment of the ICTR in 1994 replicated the institutional form of the ICTY.

The SCSL was the first of the new model of UN criminal tribunal established in the light of the experience of the first few years of operation of the ICTY and ICTR. The armed conflict in Sierra Leone lasted from 1991 to 2002. 50,000 people died and large-scale crimes were committed, including the severing of limbs, mass rapes and other sexual violence and enslavement, and the use of child soldiers. The SCSL was established by a 2002 treaty between the United Nations and the Government of Sierra Leone to which the SCSL Statute was annexed.[21] The negotiation of the treaty with the Government had been mandated by the Security Council,[22] and conducted by the UN Office of Legal Affairs (OLA) on behalf of the Secretary-General. The SCSL sat outside the UN Organization and, as confirmed by the SCSL Appeals Chamber, was an international organization in its own right.[23] It was financed from voluntary contributions.

The ECCC was established to prosecute the shocking and wide-scale crimes committed during the period of the Khmer Rouge regime, which held power in Cambodia from April 1975 to January 1979. It was established as a national court of Cambodia under domestic legislation in 2001,[24] which was subsequently amended in 2004 following the conclusion of an Agreement between the UN and the Government of Cambodia in 2003 that governed the functioning of the ECCC.[25] It was also primarily dependent on voluntary funding. The General Assembly had asked the Secretary-General to examine Cambodia's request for a tribunal,[26] which led to OLA conducting the negotiations with the Government that led to the ECCC Agreement, which the Assembly approved.[27] The UN Secretary-General and the Legal Counsel expressed serious misgivings about the Agreement, which they considered would not ensure an

21 SCSL Agreement and SCSL Statute (*supra* note 5).

22 UN Security Council resolution 1315, 14 August 2000, UN Doc S/RES/1315.

23 *Decision on Preliminary Motion on Lack of Jurisdiction Materiae: Illegal Delegation of Powers by the United Nations, Prosecutor v. Moinina Fofana*, SCSL-2004-14-AR72(E), AC, SCSL, 25 May 2004.

24 The Law on the Establishment of the Extraordinary Chambers in the Courts of Cambodia, 10 August 2001, subsequently amended by the Law to Amend the 2001 law on the Establishment of the Extraordinary Chambers in the Courts of Cambodia (27 October 2004), *supra* note 6, available at <www.eccc.gov.kh/en/documents/legal/law-establishment-extraordinary-chambers-amended>.

25 ECCC Agreement (*supra* note 6).

26 UN General Assembly resolution 52/135, 27 February 1998, UN Doc A/RES/52/135.

27 UN General Assembly resolution 228 B, 22 May 2003, UN Doc A/RES/57/228B.

independent and impartial process given the "… precarious state of the judiciary in Cambodia".[28]

The STL was established to prosecute those responsible for the attack of 14 February 2005 in Beirut that killed 22 people, including the former Lebanese Prime Minister, Rafiq Hariri, and also related attacks. At the request of the Security Council, the draft Agreement to establish the STL and draft Statute were negotiated by the UN Legal Counsel with the Government of Lebanon, reaching a successful conclusion in November 2006.[29] In Lebanon, the question of a tribunal led to a constitutional crisis.[30] The Lebanese Parliament was unable to ratify the Agreement, which could not therefore enter into force in accordance with its terms. The Prime Minister nevertheless wrote to the Secretary-General to ask that the Security Council bring the STL into effect.[31] The Security Council adopted resolution 1757 (2007) in May 2007 under Chapter VII of the UN Charter.[32] It was drafted to bring "the provisions of" the draft STL Agreement and its annexed draft STL Statute into effect. In other words, the intention of the drafters was that the Council would give mandatory force under Chapter VII to the words contained in the draft documents, not bring the Agreement as such into force as a treaty between the UN and Lebanon.[33]

The STL Appeals Chamber later determined in a 2012 decision that "[t]he Tribunal is purely a creature of a Security Council resolution" and that resolution 1757 (2007) was the sole legal basis of the STL's establishment. The Agreement that had been negotiated with the Government of Lebanon was not the legal basis of the STL.[34] Despite the Chapter VII legal basis of the STL, the practice of the Security Council, the General Assembly, Member States,

28 *Report of the Secretary-General on the Khmer Rouge Trials*, 31 March 2003, UN Doc A/57/769, para. 79.

29 *Report of the Secretary-General on the establishment of a special tribunal for Lebanon*, 15 November 2006, UN Doc S/2006/893.

30 See Nadim Shehadi and Elizabeth Wilmshurst, *The Special Tribunal for Lebanon: The UN on Trial?* (Chatham House, Middle East International Law Briefing Paper, 1 July 2007), pp. 4 and 6, available at <https://www.chathamhouse.org/sites/default/files/public/Research/Middle%20East/bp0707lebanon.pdf>.

31 Letter of 14 May 2007 from the Prime Minister of Lebanon to the Secretary-General, annexed to the letter of 15 May 2007 from the Secretary-General to the President of the Security Council (2007), UN Doc S/2007/281.

32 UN Security Council resolution 1757 (2007), *supra* note 7.

33 See UN Security Council Verbatim Record of the 5685th meeting, 30 May 2007, UN Doc S/PV.5685, in particular the statement of the Permanent Representative of France.

34 *Decision on the Defence Appeals against the Trial Chamber's Decision on the Defence Challenges to the Jurisdiction and Legality of the Tribunal, Prosecutor v. Ayyash et al.*, STL-11-01, AC, STL, 24 October 2012, paras. 46 and 53.

and the UN Secretariat since the adoption of resolution 1757 (2007) indicates that it has not been regarded as a subsidiary organ of the Council, but in all respects as a free-standing international organization outside the UN Organization, similar to the SCSL. In particular, the STL did not report to the Council,[35] its financing did not come from UN assessed contributions,[36] its staff were not UN staff members,[37] the tribunal was accepted into the UN Joint Staff Pension Fund on the basis of being an international organization,[38] and budgetary and administrative decision-making lay not in the hands of the Fifth Committee of the General Assembly, but with the Management Committee of the STL.[39] Furthermore, under Article 7 of the draft STL Agreement, the STL had the juridical capacity to enter into treaties with States within the sphere of its competence. All of these factors point toward the STL being regarded in the practice of the UN and its Member States as an international organization in its own right, not a subsidiary organ of the Council.

4.2 *Oversight Arrangements for the SCSL, ECCC and STL: a Legal Disconnect*

The oversight of the ICTY and ICTR was conducted by the Security Council and the General Assembly.[40] It was periodic in nature, unspecific as to its substantive content, and non-dedicated, in the sense that it was entrusted to UN organs with considerable other responsibilities. The process of budgetary and administrative consideration, entrusted to the Fifth Committee of the Assembly, was already well-established prior to the creation of the two tribunals.[41] The meetings of the Security Council and the General Assembly, in their capacity as the oversight bodies, took place in public, and their decisions were a matter of public record.[42] Over time, these meetings developed into six-monthly written and oral reports to the Council by the Presidents and

35 In accordance with Art. 10(2) STL Agreement annexed to UNSC Res 1757 (2007, *supra* note 7), the President of the STL reports annually to the "parties", the Secretary-General, and the Government of Lebanon.

36 *Ibidem*, Art. 5.

37 Confirmed on the STL website at <www.stl-tsl.org/fr/jobs/647-information>.

38 *Ibidem.*

39 The Management Committee is mentioned in the STL Agreement annexed to UN Security Council resolution 1757 (2007, *supra* note 7), Art. 6.

40 Statute of the ICTY (*supra* note 3), Art. 34; Statute of the ICTR (*supra* note 4), Art. 32.

41 The Fifth Committee of the General Assembly is one of the main committees established in Rule 98 of the Rules of Procedure of the General Assembly, 18 September 2016, UN Doc A/520/Rev.

42 The Council's Informal Working Group on International Tribunals, consisting of the legal officers of the fifteen Council members, meets in private to discuss tribunals matters, but the fruits of its labour come to the Council for adoption.

Prosecutors, primarily concerned with progress in meeting the completion strategies.[43]

The ICTY was the first international criminal tribunal established since the Nuremberg and Tokyo International Military Tribunals. The latter had been criticised for being established by a small group of States representing 'victors' justice'.[44] In this sense, the UN, with close to universal membership, was the natural vehicle through which truly international criminal tribunals could be established. Although the establishment of the voluntarily-funded UN criminal tribunals described above was mandated by UN principal organs – the Security Council for the SCSL and the STL, and the General Assembly for the ECCC – their oversight was, in practice, outsourced to small groups of States (management committees) comprised primarily of the major donors.

The establishment of the SCSL Management Committee, the first such oversight arrangement outside the UN Organization, set the pattern in this regard. The proposal to establish it was made by the President of the Security Council in December 2000[45] to address the Secretary-General's opposition to an international criminal tribunal functioning on the basis of voluntary contributions.[46] The UN Legal Counsel discussed the proposal with a broad

43 Security Council resolution 1503 (2003) of 28 August 2003, UN Doc. S/RES/1503 (2003). See the six-monthly completion strategy reports of the President and Prosecutor of the ICTY to the Security Council at <www.icty.org/en/documents/completion-strategy-and-mict>, and the annual reports of the ICTY President to the Security Council and the General Assembly at <www.icty.org/en/documents/annual-reports>. See the six-monthly completion strategy reports of the President and Prosecutor of the ICTR to the Security Council at <http://unictr.unmict.org/en/documents/completion-strategy-reports>, and the annual reports of the ICTR President to the Security Council and the General Assembly at <http://unictr.unmict.org/en/documents/annual-reports>.

44 For an account of the contemporaneous and modern criticisms, see G. Mettraux (ed.), *Perspectives on the Nuremberg Trial* (Oxford UP, 2008), with contributions by N. Birkett, "International Legal Theories Evolved at Nuremberg (1947)" at p. 307, and H. Wechsler, "The Issues of the Nuremberg Trial, (1947)", at p. 319; N. Bolster and R. Cryer, *The Tokyo International Military Tribunal: A Reappraisal* (Oxford UP, 2008); B. Meltzer, "A Note on Some Aspects of the Nuremberg Debate", in *University of Chicago Law Review* vol. 14 (1947), p. 455, at p. 469.

45 *Letter from the President of the Security Council addressed to the Secretary-General*, 22 December 2000, UN Doc. S/2000/1234. Such exchanges of letters between the President of the Security Council and the Secretary-General are relatively common. The President of the Council sends the letter after consulting the members of the Council and receiving their approval for the terms of his proposed reply. In other words, consensus, or at least lack of opposition, is required among the Council members.

46 *Report of the Secretary-General on the establishment of a Special Court for Sierra Leone*, 4 October 2000, UN Doc S/2000/915.

group of thirty or so States (the SCSL group of interested States),[47] which included many potential donors.[48] The terms of reference, finalised in August 2001,[49] were sent in the form of a letter from the Permanent Representative of Canada to the Legal Counsel, not incorporated into an agreement or other legal instrument.[50] The letter stated that agreement had been reached among the member States of the SCSL group of interested States. It did not ask for a reply or confirmation of agreement on the part of the UN, and it requested that the text be brought to the attention of the Secretary-General "for his information". It stated expressly that the SCSL Management Committee was to be an informal arrangement. Article 7 of the SCSL Agreement, which was under negotiation by the UN with the Government of Sierra Leone at the time, referred to "the understanding of the Parties that interested States will establish a management committee to assist the Secretary-General".[51] That provision did not itself establish the Committee.

The new form of oversight that emerged for the SCSL therefore combined, in effect, the oversight roles played by the Security Council and the General Assembly for the *ad hoc* tribunals into one dedicated oversight body that could meet as frequently as necessary. Although lacking any formal legal basis for doing so, and although the SCSL Agreement and the terms of reference had described its role as assisting the Secretary-General, the Management Committee in fact acted as the budgetary and administrative authority of

47 The existence and original size of this group of interested States is referred to in the *First annual report of the President of the Special Court for Sierra Leone, 2 December 2002–1 December 2003*, available at <www.rscsl.org/Documents/AnRpt1.pdf>, at p. 29.

48 See the account in G. Tortora, "The Financing of the Special Tribunals for Sierra Leone, Cambodia and Lebanon", in *International Criminal Law Review* vol. 13 (2013), pp. 93, 104–106.

49 For a detailed account of the negotiations, see P. Mochochoko and G.Tortora, "The Management Committee for the Special Court for Sierra Leone", in C. Romano, A. Nollkaemper and J.K. Kleffner (eds.), *Internationalised Criminal Courts and Tribunals* (Oxford UP, 2004), pp. 141–156.

50 *Letter dated 21 August 2001 from the Permanent Representative of Canada to the United Nations in New York to the UN Legal Counsel*, appended to the letter dated 8 March 2002 from the Secretary-General to the President of the Security Council, Report of the Planning Mission on the Establishment of the Special Court for Sierra Leone, 8 March 2002, UN Doc S/2002/246.

51 SCSL Agreement (*supra* note 5), Art. 7. In November 2001, the SCSL group of interested States selected the following Management Committee members: Canada, Lesotho, the Netherlands, Nigeria, the UK, and the US. Lesotho and Nigeria were selected as African States to provide regional support. Canada, the Netherlands, the UK, and the US became the major donors, providing approximately 75% of the tribunal's financing over its lifetime. See the account in Tortora (*supra* note 48), pp. 102, 104–106. In practice, Lesotho and Nigeria were not frequent attenders of Management Committee meetings.

the tribunal.[52] Through the Management Committee, the States most closely interested and invested in the success of the SCSL were directly and continuously connected with it, and in a strong position to determine its efficiency and cost-effectiveness.

This new form of oversight body, however, lacked a legal basis. It also lacked transparency (decisions were taken behind closed doors) and accountability to any broader representative group of UN Member States.[53] The UN and the Government of Sierra Leone, as the parents of the SCSL and the parties to the SCSL Agreement, were responsible for ensuring the tribunal's independent and impartial functioning in accordance with the SCSL Agreement and Statute. Through the financing and oversight arrangements, however, they did not have effective control over the means to fulfil these obligations – in particular, in respect of the funding of the tribunal and decision-making authority over its budgetary and administrative management. Conversely, the Management Committee and its member States had control over these matters, but no corresponding obligations under the SCSL Agreement, to which they were not party.

Although the details differ, the oversight bodies established for the ECCC and the STL essentially followed the model established for the SCSL.[54] Budgetary authority and close oversight lay in the hands of small committees of States, without a treaty or other formal legal basis for their authority, which met and took decisions behind closed doors, and whose member States had no legal obligations in relation to these tribunals through their constituent instruments, to which they were not parties. The legal 'disconnect' between the tribunals and their oversight bodies that had been established for the SCSL was replicated for the ECCC and the STL.

Article 6 of the draft STL Agreement, annexed to, and brought into effect by Security Council resolution 1757 (2007), stated that "[t]he parties shall consult concerning the establishment of a Management Committee".[55] That provision did not establish the Committee, as such, but required consultations with a view to its establishment. The process that led to its establishment demonstrates that, as was the case with the SCSL Management Committee, the STL Management Committee was not established on the basis of an agreement or other

52 This is apparent from the various annual reports of the SCSL President available on the website of the Residual SCSL at <www.rscsl.org/documents.html>.

53 In the author's experience, no briefings to the SCSL group of interested States took place during the period from 2004 to the tribunal's closure at the end of 2013.

54 For a detailed account of the establishment of each of these oversight bodies, see H. Llewellyn, *An Institutional Perspective on the United Nations Criminal Tribunals: Governance, Independence and Impartiality* (Brill, 2021).

55 STL Agreement, annexed to UNSC Res 1757 (2007, *supra* note 7), Art. 6.

legal instrument concluded between the UN and the Government of Lebanon, nor was it an organ of the UN or the STL.

The terms of reference of the Management Committee were finalised by the Secretary-General in February 2008 after consulting the Government of Lebanon and a broad group of interested States, including the main donors.[56] The terms of reference were not formalised with these various governments, for example in an exchange of letters or a memorandum of understanding. They stated that the Management Committee was an informal body,[57] yet like the SCSL Management Committee, it had authority over budgetary, financial and administrative matters. It determined, for example, the terms and conditions under which the judges, other senior officials and all staff served, although the terms of reference were silent on these matters.[58]

The Management Committee was not accountable to the Council nor any other UN organ.[59] Its meetings took place behind closed doors and its decisions, apart from the determination of the annual budget, were not made publicly available. There was thus a legal 'disconnect' between the STL and its Management Committee in the same manner as the SCSL and its Management Committee. There was no treaty or other legal instrument that provided a basis for the Committee's exercise of its considerable authorities, nor which placed

56 Terms of Reference of the Management Committee for the Special Tribunal for Lebanon, approved on 29 February 2008, as amended on 11 October 2013, available at <www.stl-tsl.org/sites/default/files/documents/Terms-of-Reference-for-the-Management-Committee.pdf>. Establishment of the Committee by the UN Secretary-General (acting alone) was in accordance with para. 29 of the report of the Secretary-General pursuant to UNSC Res 1757 (2007).

57 They identified the members as Lebanon, the Netherlands (both as the host country and as a major donor), France, Germany, the UK, and the US. Canada, Italy, and Japan joined subsequently. They stated further that a representative of the Secretary-General would participate in the Committee's meetings *ex officio*. In practice, this was a legal officer of the UN Office of the Legal Counsel.

58 See the conditions of service of staff at <www.stl-tsl.org/en/jobs/vacancies/professional/175-conditions-of-service-professionals-and-higher>. See STL Financial Regulations and Rules, approved on 5 June 2008, as last amended on 22 April 2015, available at <https://www.stl-tsl.org/sites/default/files/documents/administrative-documents/20150422_STL_Financial_Rules_and_Regulations.pdf>; Staff Regulations and Rules of the STL, STL/RB/1/Rev. 5, 18 December 2017, available at <www.stl-tsl.org/sites/default/files/documents/administrative-documents/20171218_Staff%20Regulations%20and%20Rules%20of%20the%20STL_STL-RB-1-Rev5.pdf>; and the Code of Conduct for the Staff Members of the STL, STL/RB/2, 26 March 2009, available at <www.stl-tsl.org/sites/default/files/documents/administrative-documents/090329_Code_of_Conduct_for_Staff_Members_of_the_STL.pdf>.

59 It did, though, hold briefing meetings with a broad STL 'group of interested states' roughly twice per year. This information was provided by the UK Chair of the STL Management Committee.

obligations on the Committee and its member States in relation to the functioning of the STL. Under the terms of resolution 1757 (2007) and its annexed documents, the UN and the Government of Lebanon carried legal obligations in respect of the functioning of the STL. These included the Government's obligation to provide 49% of the budgeted financial resources. The UN and the Government were dependent, for the remaining 51% of voluntary financing, on States that were not subject to any legal obligation to provide these resources, nor indeed any other legal obligation in relation to the tribunal.

5 Tensions in the New Oversight Arrangements

Each of the UN criminal tribunals has experienced completion strategies or other forms of close oversight attention to the timeline needed to complete the judicial work, and the costs involved in doing so.

The early phase of the SCSL, for example, demonstrated that lessons had been learned from the costly ICTY and ICTR experiences, but also that new challenges faced this smaller, cheaper form of tribunal based on voluntary funding by States and close oversight by its major donors. The major donors rejected the UN Legal Counsel's estimates based on ICTY/ICTR-type costing and approved instead a three-year total estimate for the anticipated lifespan of the SCSL and a total budget of $56.8 million.[60] Both the time and the cost estimate proved to be unrealistic,[61] placing the tribunal, in particular its Registrar, under intense pressure. Significant time and energy had to be spent in fundraising. Audits conducted during this period found that the SCSL faced a "precarious funding position".[62] The President reported that expectations had surrounded the tribunal's establishment, yet resources were extremely limited and unpredictable, forcing short term planning and inefficiencies.[63]

The STL provides a recent and stark example where such time and cost pressures terminated the judicial process. The STL Registrar announced on 2 June 2022 that the tribunal faced an unprecedented financial shortage due to the COVID-19 pandemic and the economic crisis in Lebanon, and would not be able to operate beyond July 2022.[64] The STL completed the

60 Tortora (*supra* note 48), p. 93, at pp. 104–106.

61 *First annual report of the President of the SCSL*, 2 December 2002–1 December 2003, available at <www.rscsl.org/Documents/AnRpt1.pdf>, at p. 29.

62 *Ibidem*, p. 29.

63 *Ibidem*, pp. 30–31.

64 See STL press release, *Severe financial crisis threatens the STL's ability to fulfil its mandate*, 2 June 2021, available at <www.stl-tsl.org/en/media/press-releases/severe-financial-crisis-threatens-the-stls-ability-to-fulfil-its-mandate>.

appeal proceedings *in absentia* in the *Ayyash et al.* (Hariri bombing) case on 16 June 2022, and two weeks later, on 1 July 2022, it entered a residual phase.[65] The Members of the STL Management Committee (the major donor States) did not make up the financial shortfall nor seek a further subvention from the UN General Assembly, and accordingly, all proceedings in the *Ayyash case* – the trial of the 'connected cases' concerning three car bombings carried out in a manner similar to that in the Hariri assassination – were suspended. The trial in that case had been due to begin in June 2022. The Secretary-General extended the mandate of the STL for the last time from 1 March 2023 to 31 December 2023 for the limited purpose of completion of the STL's non-judicial residual functions and for its orderly closure.[66] The STL closed on 31 December 2023 with the judicial proceedings in the *Ayyash case* suspended.

6 Concluding Remarks

Driven by considerations of cost and length of the judicial proceedings, the legal construction of the UN criminal tribunals changed in institutional form from their ICTY and ICTR beginnings as Security Council subsidiary organs with UN regular budget funding. The new institutional forms and oversight arrangements that emerged for the voluntarily-funded tribunals, the SCSL, the ECCC and the STL, may have had advantages for the major donors in terms of their increased control over costs, but also brought challenges for the tribunals through downward pressure on their budgets and timelines, including precarious funding situations, instability, short-term planning and inefficiencies.[67] As is demonstrated by the STL's abrupt closure, the ability of a voluntarily-funded tribunal to survive such challenges and to complete all mandated judicial proceedings depends ultimately on the financial and political will of the major donor States in its management committee – States that have no legal obligations toward the tribunal. Long after the 'Nuremberg moment' of creation has passed, such financial and political will cannot necessarily be relied on.

Successive UN Secretaries-General have warned that voluntary funding is not a sufficiently stable basis upon which international criminal tribunals can

65 See the website of the STL at <www.stl-tsl.org/en/home/donor>.

66 *Press release on behalf of the UN Secretary-General commending the work of the Special Tribunal for Lebanon*, UN Doc. SG/SM/21654 of 12 January 2023, and *Statement attributable to the Spokesperson for the UN Secretary-General on the Special Tribunal for Lebanon*, 12 January 2023, available at <www.un.org/sg/en/content/sg/statement/2023-01-12/statement-attributable-the-spokesperson-for-the-secretary-general-%E2%80%93-the-special-tribunal-for-lebanon>.

67 Tortora (*supra* note 48), pp. 29–31.

function.[68] This has been borne out, but the challenges also run deeper and include the new form of oversight arrangements for the UN criminal tribunals. Whatever the advantages of this new form of oversight, the STL experience demonstrates that conferring considerable authority and control over budgetary and administrative matters to a small group of major donor States, but leaving their relationship with the tribunal on an informal footing with no corresponding legal obligations to sustain the judicial proceedings until complete, may render the tribunal's survival precarious.

The era of UN criminal tribunals triggered by the Security Council in 1993 with the establishment of the ICTY, the first international criminal tribunal since Nuremberg, was an innovative moment that demonstrated that the UN, with near universal membership, was the natural vehicle to establish a truly international criminal jurisdiction that moved away from any notion of 'victors' justice' or ownership by a small group of States. The new form of oversight developed for the voluntarily-funded tribunals, however, returns us to a situation where a small committee of donor States is closely connected with each tribunal's functioning, is not accountable to the broader UN membership, and ultimately is not a guarantor against termination of the judicial process for financial reasons.

It is unclear whether the era of establishing UN criminal tribunals has come to an end[69] or whether, for example, a tribunal as called for by a 'core group' of Member States to prosecute senior leaders of the Russian Federation for the crime of aggression concerning Russia's invasion of Ukraine may be established.[70] If the establishment of any further UN criminal tribunals is to be contemplated, it would be wise to recall the above historical context. The STL experience would suggest not only that dependence on voluntary funding should be avoided, but also that the institutional form and legal construction of any future tribunals should be such that the oversight body is itself placed on a firm legal footing, accountable to the broader UN membership.

---

68 See, for example, *Report of the Secretary-General on the establishment of a Special Court for Sierra Leone*, 4 October 2000, UN Doc. S/2000/915.

69 The most recent was the STL, established in 2007. Since then, there has been a tendency toward the establishment of investigative mechanisms that are not themselves tribunals, including those for Syria and Myanmar.

70 See reference, for example, to an online summit of this core group, available at <www.coe.int/en/web/secretary-general/-/online-summit-of-the-leaders-of-the-member-states-of-the-coalition-core-group-on-the-creation-of-a-special-tribunal-on-the-crime-of-aggression-against-ukraine>.

CHAPTER 18

When the Whole Becomes More than the Sum of Its Parts

How the ICC Re-Invented Itself through Complementarity

*Carsten Stahn**

1 Introduction

As part of his professional career, Niels Blokker has devoted significant time to the emergence and review of the practices of the International Criminal Court (ICC). Before becoming close colleagues at Leiden, we met in the context of the negotiation of the Headquarters Agreement of the ICC, where Niels was part of the Dutch delegation and explained the position of the host state on core issues. We met again in the framework of the Princeton meetings on the crime of aggression, where Niels was a key player in the negotiations. At Leiden, we have shared many fond memories as part of the Advanced LL.M. programme in Public International Law, the Management Team of the Grotius Centre, or the graduation of PhD students. In light of this journey, it is only logical to devote this essay to a topic which has formed a mutual bond between us for decades: the ICC.

As Niels has argued in his work, "international organizations themselves need to change, to adapt to the changing international milieu" in order to "be able to perform their functions".[1] This is often done without burdensome amendment of statutory instruments and through alternative legal techniques, such as the invocation of 'implied powers', 'notions of practice' and 'various methods of interpretation'.[2] The same is true with respect to international courts and tribunals, such as the ICC. The evolution of the Court's approach towards complementarity is a case in point. The way in which complementarity has evolved over time shows how the Court re-configured itself as broader justice institution in the face of different phases of its institutional

* The author is Professor of International Criminal Law and Global Justice, Leiden & Queen's University Belfast.

1 See Niels Blokker, "NATO as an International Organization: Ten Brief Observations", in *Emory International Law Review*, vol. 34 (2019), pp. 29–36, 30.

2 *Ibidem*, p. 30.

 DOI:10.1163/9789004699939_020

history: Statute negotiations, the set-up and operationalization of the Court, its response to backlash and pushback, and its changing space in the accountability landscape.

Complementarity is not only a technical-legal admissibility concept, but a structural principle of the Court. It is closely linked to broader governance aspects of the institutions, which Niels has addressed in his writings and project on international judicial governance institutions ('injugovin'),[3] together with Sergey Vasilev.[4]

In this contribution, I wish to illustrate how dominant understandings of complementarity have shifted and evolved through practices and policies of the ICC and the Assembly of States Parties (ASP), without formal amendment or supplement of key legal instruments.[5] I argue that complementarity has moved towards a new *terra incognita*[6] (as Niels has stated in a different context) and become more than the sum of its parts. It has taken on at least five different faces, through a mix of Court and governance practices: (i) complementarity as preservation of sovereignty, (ii) 'positive complementarity',[7] (iii) complementarity as *quasi* primacy,[8] based on the strict interpretation of the same person, same conduct' test,[9] (iv) 'positive complementarity 2.0',[10]

---

3 See Niels Blokker, "The Governance of International Courts and Tribunals: Organizing and Guaranteeing Independence and Accountability", in Andreas Follesdal, and Geir Ulfstein (eds), *The Judicialization of International Law: A Mixed Blessing?* (Oxford UP, 2018), pp. 26–42.

4 The project goes back to a Conference on Governance of International Courts and Tribunals, held in Leiden in September 2019, and is followed by an edited volume with Oxford University Press.

5 See generally Carsten Stahn, "The ICC in Its Third Decade: Setting the Scene", in C. Stahn (ed.), *The International Criminal Court in its Third Decade* (Brill Nijhoff, 2024), pp. 4–40.

6 Blokker (*supra* note 3), p. 41.

7 See Carsten Stahn, "Complementarity: A Tale of Two Notions", in *Criminal Law Forum*, vol. 19 (2008), pp. 87–113.

8 For critiques, see Kevin Jon Heller, "Radical Complementarity", in *Journal of International Criminal Justice*, vol. 14 (2016), pp. 637–665; Sarah M.H. Nouwen, *Complementarity in the Line of Fire: The Catalysing Effect of the International Criminal Court in Uganda and Sudan* (Cambridge UP, 2013); Christian De Vos, *Complementarity, Catalysts, Compliance: The International Criminal Court in Uganda, Kenya, and the Democratic Republic of Congo* (Cambridge UP, 2020), pp. 68–103; Marieke Wierda, *The Local Impact of the International Criminal Court: From Law to Justice* (Cambridge UP, 2023), pp. 50–82; Patryk I. Labuda, *International Criminal Tribunals and Domestic Accountability* (Oxford UP, 2023).

9 Rod Rastan, "What is 'Substantially the Same Conduct'? Unpacking the ICC's 'First Limb' Complementarity Jurisprudence", in *Journal of International Criminal Justice*, vol. 15 (2017), pp. 1–29.

10 ICC, Office of the Prosecutor, *Policy on Complementarity and Cooperation*, April 2024, available at <https://www.icc-cpi.int/sites/default/files/2024-04/2024-comp-policy-eng.pdf>.

adopted as a follow up of the Independent Expert review,[11] and (v) 'regional complementarity'[12] which re-defines the ICC's relationship to other international institutions, including regional justice mechanism. These faces emerged gradually in the course of the ICC's institutional history, but continue to co-exist simultaneously. This diversification extended the meaning of complementarity beyond its original statist conceptions. The 2024 *Policy on Complementarity and Cooperation* of the Office of the Prosecutor (OTP) reflects a locally centered understanding of complementarity:

> the primary responsibility of domestic jurisdictions under the Rome Statute is not only an expression of national sovereignty but a reflection of the fact that accountability processes work best when those affected by atrocities can engage, can be empowered to come forward with their accounts and can see that justice is rendered locally.[13]

It also marks a turn towards a polycentric justice model, which integrates interaction with regional entities (e.g., through cooperative justice).

2 Face #1: Complementarity as Preservation of Sovereignty

Let us first go back to the beginnings. In the drafting history, complementarity was strongly associated with the preservation of domestic jurisdiction and non-interference with domestic sovereignty. The key idea was to provide assurance to states that the ICC would not override domestic jurisdiction or pass judgment on domestic justice.[14] This state-sovereignty based understanding of complementarity was partly a reaction to the strong focus on primacy over national courts at the *ad hoc* tribunals, which was promoted by the 1995 *Tadiç*

11 ICC, Independent Expert Review of the International Criminal Court and the Rome Statute System, Final Report, 30 September 2020.

12 See Miles Jackson, "Regional Complementarity: The Rome Statute and Public International Law", in *Journal of International Criminal Justice*, vol. 14 (2016), pp. 1061–1072; Seun Bakare, *Regional Complementarity: Making Sense of the Four-Tiered Justice Paradigm* (PhD Leiden, 2024).

13 OTP Policy (*supra* note 10), para. 73.

14 See Mohamed El Zeidy, *The Principle of Complementarity in International Criminal Law* (Brill, 2008); Federica Gioia, "State Sovereignty, Jurisdiction, and 'Modern' International Law: The Principle of Complementarity in the International Criminal Court", in *Leiden Journal of International Law*, vol. 19 (2006), pp. 1095–1123.

Interlocutory Appeal[15] and concerns regarding the independent *proprio motu* powers of the Prosecutor. This vision of complementarity was based on the idea that the ICC marks a threat to domestic jurisdiction, based on its "intrusive powers"[16] ("if a national judicial system functions properly, there is no reason for the ICC to assume jurisdiction"[17]). It views the ICC as competitor to domestic jurisdiction.

This approach has some shortcomings from a theoretical perspective. It implies that the exercise of ICC jurisdiction is undermining state authority, rather than helping states to assert their responsibilities. It theorizes sovereignty predominantly through the veil of state interests, rather than the people and individuals behind it. However, it continues to be invoked in practice in specific contexts. It is repeated as a legal argument whenever the ICC is attacked by states, which use political or extra-legal strategies to contest ICC jurisdiction.[18] It also gains relevance whenever the Court seeks to demarcate its limits as a criminal court, as opposed to a human rights court.

The idea of complementarity as shield against ICC interference has also served as a foundation for a preventive, rather than a reactive understanding of complementarity. It supports a 'carrot and stick' logic, which has been used to develop the idea that the ICC serves as a catalyst for compliance.[19] It involves the power of the ICC to remind states of their statutory responsibility to investigate and prosecute. It promotes the continuing efforts of states, including non-state parties,[20] to investigate and prosecute themselves, and

15 ICTY, *Prosecutor v. Tadić*, Decision on the Defence Motion for Interlocutory Appeal on Jurisdiction, IT-94-1, 2 October 1995, para. 58 ("when an international tribunal such as the present one is created, it must be endowed with primacy over national courts").

16 John. T. Holmes, "Complementarity: National Courts versus the ICC", in Antonio Cassese a.o. (eds.), *The Rome Statute of the International Criminal Court: A Commentary* (Oxford UP, 2002), pp. 667–685, at 668.

17 Philippe Kirsch, "The International Criminal Court: Consensus and Debate on the International Adjudication of Genocide, Crimes Against Humanity, War Crimes, and Aggression", in *Cornell International Law Journal* vol. 32 (1999), pp. 437–442, 438.

18 Complementarity serves a means to encourage states such as the U.S. or Israel to challenge decisions of the ICC through legal, rather than political channels or sanctions. See e.g. ASIL, Expert Report, "ASIL Task Force on Policy Options for U.S. Engagement with the ICC" (2021), available at <https://www.asil-us-icc-task-force.org/uploads/2021-ASIL-Task-Force-Report-on-US-ICC-Engagement-FINAL.pdf>.

19 Jann Kleffner, *Complementarity in the Rome Statute and National Criminal Jurisdictions* (Oxford UP, 2008), pp. 309–340.

20 It is reported that Israel gathered intelligence to enable the domestic military system to "open investigations retroactively" into cases of violence against Palestinians, in order to use the "principle of complementarity" to its advantage. See Yuval Abraham and Meron Rapoport, "Surveillance and interference: Israel's covert war on the ICC exposed",

encourages states parties to implement the Statute into domestic legislation or to extend their own jurisdiction over international crimes.[21] The new 2024 *Policy on Complementarity and Cooperation* extends this idea from domestication of crimes to harmonisation of procedure for evidence collection.[22]

In practice, it has become evident that the promised catalytic effect of complementarity does not occur automatically, but is dependent on various intermediate factors. Complementarity only serves as a 'carrot and stick' if there is sufficient transparency on ICC policies, including regular and transparent reporting of preliminary examinations and investigations, and adequate monitoring structures for continuing complementarity assessment.[23] Moreover, mere implementation of the Statute does not mean that States will in effect carry out international crime investigations and prosecutions. In many contexts, they have still relied on 'ordinary' crime prosecutions or national counter-terrorism framework to respond to atrocity crimes.[24]

3 Face #2: the Turn to Positive Complementarity

A second face of complementarity, namely 'positive complementarity', emerged as part of the operationalization of the Court. It was promoted in the pioneering phase when the ICC sought to attract cases. It shows a different side of complementarity. It is based on the premise that the ICC and states are not necessarily in competition with each other, but pursue common goals in an interconnected way. It represents the 'gentle side of the Court'. It integrated ideas of sharing of labour and support to domestic jurisdictions into ICC complementarity policies and practice and became an argument to structure

+972 *Magazine*, 28 May 2024, available at <https://www.972mag.com/icc-israel-surveillance-investigation/>.

21 See Olympia Bekou, "National Implementation of the Rome Statute as a Critical Precondition for Complementarity and Cooperation", in Stahn (*supra* note 5), pp. 338–352.

22 OTP Policy (*supra* note 10), para. 112.

23 Elisabeth Evenson, "ICC Preliminary Examinations and National Justice: Opportunities and Challenges for Catalysing Domestic Prosecutions", in Morten Bergsmo and Carsten Stahn (eds.), *Quality Control in Preliminary Examination* vol. 2 (Torkel Opsahl Academic EPublisher, 2018), pp. 711–730.

24 For instance, many of the 'foreign fighters' involved in ISIL atrocity have been prosecuted for terrorist offences, including membership of a terrorist organization, instead of core crimes. See Tanya Mehra, "Improving the prospects of prosecuting 'terrorists' for core international crimes committed in the context of the conflict in Syria and Iraq", ICCT Report, October 2023, available at <https://www.icct.nl/sites/default/files/2023-10/Improving%20prospects%20of%20prosecuting%20terrorists.pdf>.

prosecutorial discretion and justify prosecutorial choices regarding situation and case selection. It was developed in 2003 in the *Informal Expert Paper on Complementarity in Practice,* which stated:

> the Prosecutor's objective is not to 'compete' with States for jurisdiction, but to help ensure that the most serious international crimes do not go unpunished and thereby to put an end to impunity. The complementarity regime serves as a mechanism to encourage and facilitate the compliance of States with their primary responsibility to investigate and prosecute core crimes.[25]

In the initial phase, the concept served to build a constructive relation of partnership and trust between the ICC and states. It promoted consensual practices, such as self-referrals or voluntary state cooperation. It helped the OTP to explain the inherent weaknesses of the ICC and to justify situational engagement through state consent. It gained a central role in the Stocktaking Exercise of the ASP during the 2010 Review Conference in Kampala.[26] When the ICC docket grew, it became an instrument to develop a closure strategy for situations,[27] In this context, it became a means to deal with the Court's own capacity limits and resource constraints.

The turn to positive complementarity opened new avenues for a more systemic understanding of the Statute and the close interplay between complementarity and cooperation. But it has been criticized from multiple fronts. Some have criticized positive complementarity from a political economy perspective: the focus on cooperation and assistance to states would detract the ICC from its core mandate or turn it into a development agency. Other critiques have emphasized conflicts between dependency on state consent and the impartiality and independence of the Court. The most forceful critique is that the turn to positive complementarity creates risk of manipulation and selective or one-sided justice.

For instance, Amnesty International has cautioned in its submission to the ICC-OTP Consultation on Complementarity and Cooperation Policy

---

25 OTP, "*The principle of complementarity in practice*" (Informal expert paper, 2003), available at <https://www.icc-cpi.int/sites/default/files/RelatedRecords/CR2009_02250.PDF>.

26 See Report of the Bureau on stocktaking: Complementarity, Review Conference, Resolution ICC-ASP/8/Res.9, adopted at the 10th plenary meeting (2010), by consensus, Appendix, pp. 14–22.

27 In 2021, the OTP adopted a policy on situation completion, see OTP, *Policy on Situation Completion* (2021), available at <https://www.icc-cpi.int/sites/default/files/itemsDocuments/20210615-Situation-Completion-Policy-eng.pdf>.

that positive complementarity may provide a pretext for a mere "veneer of accountability".[28] It enables states to present themselves as law-abiding States through constructive dialogue and cooperation with the Court, while pursuing "incomplete, low-level, or one-sided investigations" or focusing exclusively on non-state actors.[29] In some contexts, victims and survivors or civil society organizations have come to perceive the ICC as a prolonged arm of governments supporting investigations and prosecutions. Another fear is that practices of reverse cooperation or evidence-sharing may make the ICC complicit in a potential violation of fair trial standards at the domestic level. The ICC requires thus a due diligence policy in relation to the application of positive complementarity.

4 Face #3: Technical-Legal Complementarity as *Quasi* Primacy

The wide understanding of complementarity as policy concept contrasts with a third face of complementarity, namely its narrow reading in the context of admissibility challenges.

This face of complementarity became more visible in contexts where the ICC acted without consent of domestic jurisdictions. In these contexts, complementarity was more antagonistic. Both the OTP and Chambers have adopted a strict legalistic reading of complementarity, which focuses more on the text of the Statute, rather than its object or purpose or context. The Court has interpreted Article 17 to require domestic jurisdictions to model their action after that of the Court, in order to be able to challenge complementarity. This approach has been grounded in a literal and systemic reading of the Statute. The Statute links the possibility of states to challenge admissibility to cases before the ICC. If a state seeks to investigate or prosecute a 'different case', for instance different conduct of the same person or other persons, the Statute promotes cooperation and consultations to allow both cases to proceed.[30]

The required degree of symmetry between ICC action and domestic action is not strictly defined by the Statute. In the situation concerning the Philippines, the ICC Appeals Chamber has specified that "domestic criminal proceedings

28 Amnesty International, *Submission to ICC-OTP Consultation on Complementarity and Cooperation Policy* (2023), available at <https://hrij.amnesty.nl/submission-icc-otp-complementarity-and-cooperation-policy-amnesty/>.

29 *Ibidem.*

30 Part 9 of the Statute envisages cooperation, allowing both cases to proceed, either concurrently (see Arts. 94, 93(10)), or in sequence (Art. 89(4), Rule 183 of the Rules of Procedure and Evidence).

must sufficiently mirror the scope of the Prosecutor's intended investigation", in order to justify a deferral of a Prosecutor's investigation under Article 18 (2) of the Statute.[31] It required "an advancing process of domestic investigations and prosecutions of the same groups or categories of individuals in relation to the relevant criminality, including the patterns and forms of criminality, within a situation".[32] In the context of admissibility challenges regarding cases under Article 19, the Appeals Chamber has adopted a strict approach. For instance, in the *Simone Gbagbo* case, the Appeals Chamber noted that the "presumption in favour of domestic jurisdiction only applies where it has been shown that there are (or have been) investigations and/or prosecutions at the national level".[33] The state must demonstrate tangible, concrete, progressive investigative steps in its investigations and proceedings.

The existing test is strict in light of three elements: (i) the fact that the challenge fails in case of inaction: states need to show concrete investigative steps; (ii) the timing requirement, which requires admissibility to be assessed at the time of the Court's determination on admissibility; and (iii) the standard of review, namely the 'substantially the same conduct test' which has been interpreted to require "overlap between incidents being investigated by the Prosecutor and those being investigated by a State".[34] This is a relatively demanding standard,[35] since domestic justice investigations have to constantly catch up to ICC investigations and replicate their focus.

It seeks to accommodate the risk that "any one national case" could "block" an "entire situation before the ICC".[36] But it made complementarity more ICC-centric (*de facto* primacy), than state-centred.

---

31 ICC, *Situation in the Philippines*, Judgment on the appeal of the Republic of the Philippines against Pre-Trial Chamber I's "Authorisation pursuant to article 18(2) of the Statute to resume the investigation", ICC-01/21 OA, 18 July 2023, para. 2.

32 *Ibidem*, para. 106.

33 ICC, Situation in the Republic of Côte d'Ivoire, *The Prosecutor v. Simone Gbagbo*, Appeals Chamber, Judgment on the appeal of Côte d'Ivoire against the decision of Pre-Trial Chamber I of 11 December 2014 entitled "Decision on Côte d'Ivoire's challenge to the admissibility of the case against Simone Gbagbo", 27 May 2015, ICC-02/11-01/12-75-Red, para. 59.

34 ICC, Situation in Libya, *The Prosecutor v. Saif Al-Islam Gaddafi*, Appeals Chamber, Judgment on the appeal of Libya against the decision of Pre-Trial Chamber I of 31 May 2013 entitled "Decision on the admissibility of the case against Saif Al-Islam Gaddafi", 21 May 2014, ICC-01/11-01/11-547-Red, para. 72.

35 It is not based on the comparative seriousness of the conduct, prospects of a genuine proceeding at the domestic level or the desirability of national proceedings.

36 Rastan (*supra* note 9), p. 23.

This interpretation has encountered critiques from multiple sides. Some judges (e.g. Judges Song and Ušacka) have criticized the narrow interpretation of the 'same conduct test' in the Libya jurisprudence.[37] Defence teams and states making challenges under Article 19 have questioned the premises of the test since it offers only remote chances of success.[38] The Libyan cases have shown that it is very difficult for countries in transition from armed conflict to peace to challenge admissibility,[39] if they are willing but unable to cover the same acts or incidents. In the Palestine situation, similar timing concerns have been raised in relation to the ability of the Israeli domestic legal system to investigate and prosecute its high-level political and military leadership for the same conduct "in the midst of a difficult war".[40]

Requiring a national investigation to cover exactly the same acts makes the national investigators' task nearly impossible. It creates a race to open investigations that mirror those of the ICC if a state wants to prosecute a case itself. As Marieke Wierda[41] and Phil Clark[42] have shown, existing admissibility practices have created paradoxical situations in which domestic courts and the ICC have chased the same cases and mirrored each other's weaknesses, rather than complementing each other. This result conflicts with the idea that "the Court and States should work in unison – complementing each other – in reaching the Statute's overall goal".[43]

There are a number of ways to address these dilemmas. The Statute requires the ICC to recognize legitimate differences between the ICC and domestic jurisdictions.[44] A greater focus on context would enable a more flexible reading of the 'substantially the same case' jurisprudence. For instance, in the

37 ICC, Situation in Libya, *The Prosecutor v. Saif Al-Islam Gaddafi*, Appeals Chamber, Dissenting opinion of Judge Anita Ušacka, 29 August 2014, ICC-01/11-01/11-547-Anx2, paras. 52 ff.

38 ICC, Situation in the Central African Republic II, *The Prosecutor v. Alfred Yekatom and Patrice-Edouard Ngaïssona*, Yekatom Defence Appeal Brief – Admissibility, 19 May 2020, ICC-01/14-01/18-523, paras. 32 et seq.

39 Payam Akhavan, "Complementarity Conundrums: The ICC Clock in Transitional Times", in *Journal of International Criminal Justice*, vol. 14 (2016), pp. 1043–1059, 1044.

40 Yuval Shany and Amichai Cohen, "The Prosecutor's Circumvention of Article 18 Complementarity? A Flaw in the ICC's Palestine Investigation", in *Just Security*, 1 June 2024, available at <https://www.justsecurity.org/96296/icc-article-18-complementarity/>.

41 See Wierda (*supra* note 8), pp. 50–82.

42 Phil Clark, "Chasing Cases: The Politics of State Referral", in Carsten Stahn and Mohamed M. El. Zeidy (eds.), *The International Criminal Court and Complementarity* (Cambridge UP, 2010), pp. 1180–1203.

43 Yekatom Defence Appeal Brief (*supra* note 38), para. 36.

44 Carsten Stahn, *A Critical Introduction to International Criminal Law* (Cambridge UP, 2019), p. 225.

comparison of charges, the incident-related requirement might easily be dropped. The main test would be whether domestic charges capture the essence of criminality, rather than the same incidents. The Yekatom Appeals Brief has suggested the fair opportunity principle as a potential remedy: national jurisdictions "should be given a fair opportunity to exercise jurisdiction".[45]

5 Face #4: Positive Complementarity 2.0 – Complementarity Agreements and Complementarity as Cooperation

The third decade has led to some course correction, and in particular a re-invention of 'positive complementarity'. The OTP developed the consent-based and cooperative features of complementarity, in order to deal with an overload of situations, break the stalemate in long-standing preliminary examinations, enhance cooperation, or provide a closure strategy for investigations and situations. This turn to 'positive complementarity 2.0' partly responds to critiques which emerged in the second decade. It deviates from the idea of ICC centricity, which has been criticized by the African Union. This change is most visibly reflected in the 'hub' idea, articulated in the 2024 *Policy on Complementarity and Cooperation*. It expressly recognizes that the Office should not be viewed "as an apex of the international criminal justice architecture", but rather "as a hub at the centre of global efforts undertaken across different criminal jurisdictions".[46] This re-definition operates on the premise that the OTP may be most effective on a global scale, if assists or complements other accountability initiatives.

In terms of complementarity strategies, two changes stand out: the greater use of complementarity agreements to carve out a division of labour and new practices of cooperation. Both approaches carry promise, but also risks.

As part of his new policies, Prosecutor Khan has relied on complementarity agreements to encourage domestic investigations and prosecutions. This new approach ('contracted complementarity') has been used in different ways. In Colombia, it provided a completion strategy from a more than a decade long preliminary examination.[47] In Guinea or Venezuela, it served as window of opportunity for domestic proceedings. As Priya Pillai has argued, such

45 Yekatom Defence Appeal Brief (*supra* note 38), para. 59.

46 See OTP Policy (*supra* note 10), para. 34.

47 See Cooperation Agreement between the Office of the Prosecutor of the International Criminal Court and the Government of Colombia, 28 October 2021.

complementarity may have several beneficial effects: they may clarify state obligations and make commitments more tangible, they provide space to show greater deference to transitional justice mechanisms, and they may attenuate the perception of neo-coloniality through cooperative arrangements and assistance and support from the Court to domestic jurisdictions.[48] However, they require at the same time vigilance against abuse by domestic politics and monitoring structures.

The Colombian agreement provided a politically convenient strategy to end the preliminary examination, but has been criticized for decreasing the leverage of the Special Jurisdiction for Peace in Colombian politics.[49] It was finalized with limited input and consultation of civil society organizations and victims' associations. In Guinea, the agreement created buy-in and support for domestic investigations in trials. In Venezuela, the agreement had been used by domestic political elites to delay ICC intervention or fuel misunderstandings. For instance, Venezuelan Attorney General Tarek William Saab falsely presented it as a measure through the which the ICC has "transferred" the investigation "to Venezuela".[50] The absence of a complementarity agreement in relation to US conduct in the Afghanistan situation creates a perception of double standards in relation complementarity approaches.

It is important to understand better under what circumstances 'contracted complementarity' creates greater leverage for accountability,[51] and under what conditions it may actually contribute to accountability gaps (e.g. through delay, inaction, political games). It is also critical to create structures to apply and

---

48 Priya Pillai, "Crystallizing Complementarity: A New Gambit?" in Stahn (*supra* note 5), pp. 317–318.

49 On 27 April 2022, the International Federation for Human Rights and the Corporación Colectivo de Abogados José Alvear Restrepo requested the Pre-Trial Chamber to review and "reverse" the Prosecutor's decision to close the preliminary examination in the situation of Colombia pursuant to article 53(3)(b) of the Statute. The Chamber found that it "does not have the power to review the Prosecutor's decision to close the preliminary examination in the situation of Colombia", since the "situation in Colombia was neither referred to the Prosecutor by a State Party nor the Security Council". See ICC, PTC I, *Decision on the 'Request for review of the Prosecutor's decision of 28 October 2021 to close the preliminary examination of the situation in Colombia' and related requests'*, ICC-RoC46(3)-01/22, 22 July 2022, para. 7.

50 Orinoco Tribune, *Attorney General Saab: ICC Agreement a Victory for Venezuelan Democratic Institutions* (5 November 2021), available at <https://orinocotribune.com/attorney-general-saab-icc-agreement-a-victory-for-venezuelan-democratic-institutions/>.

51 Geoff Dancy and Florencia Montal, "Unintended Positive Complementarity: Why International Criminal Court Investigations May Increase Domestic Human Rights Prosecutions", in *American Journal of International Law*, vol. 111 (2017), pp. 689–723.

monitor complementarity agreements and review what impact these arrangements have in practical terms, for local stakeholders, and in particular affected communities. Otherwise, one element of the strategy, namely the building of support for domestic investigations and prosecutions, may be in direct conflict with another key aspect of the policy, namely the commitment to "bring justice closer to communities".[52]

The second innovation is the attempt to link complementarity more structurally to cooperation. It is in line with the broader the broader to promote the "building a community of practice".[53] Some of the strategies through which complementarity can be supported through cooperation, are spelled out in the policy. They include:

> [P]rovision of expertise and support to strengthen national capacity; information and evidence sharing with national authorities in support of genuine proceedings; joint investigative operations to reinforce efforts in increasing efforts to deliver justice; the deployment of forensic expertise for common benefit; the sharing of financial intelligence for the purpose of tracing assets and identifying financial flows; and the conduct of strategic consultations on case selection and prioritisation and burden-sharing.[54]

At first sight, this sounds promising. However, there are also darker sides. Linking complementarity to cooperation can also have counter-productive effects or unintended negative consequences.

As critics have rightly pointed out, "engaging in a concerted manner with other justice actors" may not only be "beneficial", but also "create the risk of the OTP being caught up in potentially inefficient or ineffective processes".[55] It is thus necessary to address the "negative consequences of pursuing 'joint' accountability efforts".[56]

For instance, the seconding of Western staff to the OTP, which is contemplated in the policy, is a double-edged sword. It may enhance the means of the Court in the short term but also causes vigilance or concern in the non-Western world. It is ultimately a short-cut to the resolution of the structural problems of

52 OTP Policy (*supra* note 10), paras. 72 *et seq.*

53 *Ibidem*, para. 35.

54 *Ibidem*, para. 138.

55 Amnesty International (*supra* note 28).

56 *Ibidem*.

funding, which contribute to the Court's own selectivity.[57] It may be perceived as a false signal that states can influence or 'purchase' services of the Court through voluntary contributions, even if contributions are not earmarked for a particular situation.[58]

Collaborative investigative structures, such as those applied in relation to Ukraine, need to be extended beyond the European context. Otherwise, they may reinforce ideas of Western exceptionalism.

6 Face #5: the New Frontline – Regional Complementarity

The latest incarnation of the changing conceptualization of complementarity relates to the regionalization of international criminal justice. This development is partly a reaction to the creation of regionalized hybrid courts or instruments, such as the Malabo Protocol.[59] This trend was not contemplated at the time of the drafting of the Statute. It requires a re-thinking of complementarity structures.[60] It needs to be organized along different terms than the *ne bis in idem* rule, which simply applies the 'first-come, first-serve' rule.

It can be approached in different ways. One possibility is to argue that such relations fall out of the classical frame of complementarity and ought to be regulated on a different basis, in each specific case. For instance, it is possible to determine a feasible division of labour and structures of collaboration and coordination on the basis of MOUs or agreements, in order to avoid duplication of justice efforts and detrimental impacts on witnesses, victims or defendants. This approach is in line with a polycentric vision of international criminal justice.

A second possibility is to apply complementarity, including the "unable or unwilling" test under Article 17 test, to these relations, in order to allow deference to regional justice initiatives. The wording of Article 17 does not directly address this. However, the 2024 Policy contains a step in this direction. It states:

57 See Stuart Ford, "Funding the ICC for Its Third Decade", in Stahn (*supra* note 5), pp. 368–383.

58 Chidi Anselm Odinkalu and Sharon Nakandha, "Putin Arrest Warrant: International Law and Perceptions of Double Standards", in *Opinio Juris* (27 March 2023), available at <https://opiniojuris.org/2023/03/27/putin-arrest-warrant-international-law-and-perceptions-of-double-standards/>.

59 Protocol on Amendments to the Protocol on the Statute of the African Court of Justice and Human Rights, 27 June 2014.

60 See also Jackson (*supra* note 12); Bakare (*supra* note 12).

> Although article 17 of the Statute directs its attention to whether a case is being investigated or prosecuted by a State, this *does not limit the potential application and operability of the admissibility provisions to other criminal accountability mechanisms capable of satisfying the admissibility requirements set out in the Statute*. Moreover, as a matter of discretion in matters of case selection and prioritisation, the Office can elect to defer to relevant, genuine proceedings carried out before a competent criminal accountability mechanism.[61]

In particular, the first sentence marks a possible opening towards a broader application of ICC complementarity in relation to other international justice mechanisms. It applies complementarity as a concept not only to ICC relations towards states, but also in relation to regional institutions. It carries the risk of subsuming such regional structures within the legal architecture and hierarchical power relations of the ICC system, instead of leaving space for more creative approaches towards a division of labour (e.g., based on categories of perpetrators, interconnectedness of crimes or local preferences etc.).

7 The Emperor's New Clothes – Not a Conclusion

In his 2018 article on the governance of international courts and tribunals, Niels has argued that "international judicial governance institutions are more than the sum of their members".[62] This trend is clearly visible in ICC practices on complementarity, which have been shaped through the interplay between OTP policies, admissibility rulings, ASP resolutions and practices, and input by civil society and academia. As this essay has shown, the ICC has re-invented itself through its own institutional and communicative power. It profoundly re-shaped complementarity beyond its original conceptions. This type of institutional re-invention has been necessary to avoid cumbersome treaty amendment procedures and to navigate the Court through the complex challenges and evolving structures of accountability politics.

The five different faces of complementarity are directly linked to different institutional and political challenges which the Court faced throughout different stages of its operation. They seek to address institutional gaps and

61 OTP Policy (*supra* note 10), para. 93.

62 Blokker (*supra* note 3), p. 35.

weaknesses, respond to pushback and backlash, or re-situate the Court in the changing interplay of local, national, regional and international justice.

These developments imply a partial re-invigoration of the core idea of complementarity. They mark partially a departure from classical state-centric focus of complementarity and orient the concept more towards a systemic vision, i.e. the role and relevance of the Rome Statute as a system of justice.

These developments raise intriguing questions from a governance perspective. One key challenge is coherence. Some of the rationales of the new OTP policy are in conflict with each other. For instance, the victim-centred readings of the new policy contrasts partially with the state-consent based features of positive complementarity. The OTP's de-prioritization decision in the Afghanistan situation, which relies on the prospects of hypothetical future investigations or prosecutions, is difficult to reconcile with the parallel commitment to "bring justice closer to communities". Similarly, the recognition of the decentralization of the international criminal justice system stands in tension with the potential idea to integrate regional mechanisms under the umbrella of the complementarity regime of Article 17. Moreover, the application of complementarity still faces double standards: not all situations are treated equally under this framework.

A second challenge is to what extent these developments of the treaty system through OTP policies and practices are covered by methods of evolutive treaty interpretation (Article 31 (3) of the Vienna Convention on the Law of Treaties) and state consent. Legally, the different faces of complementarity were largely developed through statutory interpretation, practice and non-binding policy instruments, which contain self-commitments by the OTP. They have been justified by certain inherent powers (e.g., prosecutorial discretion under Article 54), lesser known statutory provisions, such as the option of reverse cooperation under Article 93 (10) or the power of the OTP to conclude agreements, admissibility jurisprudence (e.g., the mirror test under Article 18 and 19), and a re-calibration of preambular rationales. The idea that complementarity is a cardinal part of the ICC as a system of justice and 'dynamic' in nature is visibly grounded in an object and purpose based interpretation of the Statute. OTP policies are subject to constant scrutiny through consultation procedures (with states and NGOs), annual discussion at the meetings of the ASP, or review processes, such as formal review conferences (e.g., Kampala) or the Independent Expert Review.

However, there are certain legal grey zones which merit greater attention. The extension of Article 17 to other international justice mechanisms beyond states is a far-reaching legal interpretation. Some key procedural issues, such as the beginning and closure of preliminary examinations, the exercise of monitoring powers after disengagement from a situation (e.g., a sort of pre-preliminary examination), or de-prioritization of situations may require further specification in amendments of the Rules of Procedure and Evidence or validation through ASP practice. Otherwise, OTP policies may become dissociated from judicial practice or turn complementarity 'on wheels'. We are thus still at the beginning of a longer and ongoing process of transformation.

CHAPTER 19

Governing International Justice: Whence the Unified Principles?

*Sergey Vasiliev**

1 Prologue

When I joined Leiden Law School as a freshly-minted assistant professor years ago, it was Niels Blokker who went out of his way to make me feel welcome in the academic community at Leiden. Although we did not get to teach a course together, his office was next door to mine. I was fortunate to interact regularly with him as we shared lunches and coffee breaks in the faculty café. Professor Blokker's unparalleled expertise on international institutional law goes coupled with an equally unsurpassed ability to pull pertinent anecdotes and trivia from the practice of international organizations out of his sleeve at any moment. I came to value greatly his approachability, tact, and authentically warm and caring personality. His genuine interest in others and his concern for the colleagues' well-being immediately won me over. A teacher by vocation, Niels has always been willing to share his vast and erudite knowledge of international law and his realist perspective thereon he gained during his years at the Ministry of Foreign Affairs, as well as excellent literature and classical music tips. A generous supplier of Dutch winged phrases, Niels' unwavering patience with a foreign colleague learning the Dutch language and culture, including the fine nuances between Leiden and Amsterdam, has been uniquely helpful and endearing.

It did not take Niels and me too long to figure out we shared a common interest in – even fascination about – the role of the institutions entrusted with the governance of international courts and tribunals (ICTs). Whereas Niels approached this theme from a broader institutional law perspective, I arrived at a similar set of questions from the critical angle on the work of the International Criminal Court's Assembly of States Parties (ICC-ASP). By the time I left Leiden, Niels and I had started co-supervising several PhD

* The author is Professor of international law, Open University of the Netherlands.

 DOI:10.1163/9789004699939_021

candidates[1] and set up a research project on international judicial governance.[2] This gave us additional reasons to keep collaborating closely ever since. In the dark weeks and months in the aftermath of the Putin Russia's full-scale invasion of Ukraine and the atrocities that ensued, Niels was there to offer moral support and exchange views on the avenues to tackle the crime of aggression in that context. These chats helped me keep my eye on the ball without falling into despair (for too long).

I offer this chapter as a token of gratitude for Niels' collegiality and mentorship over the past years. His scholarship on international institutional law and the law of international organizations is wide-ranging and field-defining.[3] Besides the issues at the interface of the law of international organizations and international peace and security,[4] Blokker has devoted a considerable attention to *in*ternational *ju*dicial *gov*ernance *in*stitutions, coining the catchy term '*injugovins*' and authoring impactful publications on the topic.[5] What are the legal constraints informing the exercise of governance vis-à-vis ICTs by these executive and political organs? This was one of the many intriguing questions we have grappled with as part of our project and forthcoming volume.[6]

1 Michael Ramsden, *The Role of the United Nations General Assembly in Advancing Accountability for Atrocity Crimes: Legal Powers and Effects* (2021); Adriana-Maria Manolescu, *Balancing Powers: Safeguarding Judicial Independence and Promoting Accountability of International Courts through Financial Governance* (expected in 2025); Kritika Sharma, *The Assembly of States Parties to the International Criminal court – A Good Governance Approach* (expected in 2025).

2 Inaugural conference *Governance of International Courts and Tribunals: Ensuring Judicial Independence and Accountability*, Leiden, 2019.

3 Among others, Henry G. Schermers and Niels M. Blokker, *International Institutional Law* (6th rev. ed., Brill Nijhoff, 2018).

4 Niels M. Blokker, *Saving Succeeding Generations from the Scourge of War: The United Nations Security Council at 75* (Brill Nijhoff, 2020).

5 Niels M. Blokker, "The Governance of International Courts and Tribunals: Organizing and Guaranteeing Independence and Accountability", in Andreas Føllesdal and Geir Ulfstein (eds.), *The Judicialization of International Law: A Mixed Blessing?* (Oxford UP, 2018); Niels M. Blokker, "Governance of the International Tribunal of the Law of the Sea: The Role of the Meeting of States Parties to the Law of the Sea Convention", in Angela del Vecchio and Roberto Virzo (eds.), *Interpretations of the United Nations Convention on the Law of the Sea by International Courts and Tribunals* (Springer 2019).

6 Sergey Vasiliev and Niels Blokker, with Armin Cuyvers and Rick Lawson (eds.), *Governance of International Courts and Tribunals: Institutions, Practices, and Norms* (Oxford UP, forthcoming).

2 International Judicial Governance: 'Unity within Diversity'?

Like their domestic counterparts, ICTs do not and cannot operate in an institutional vacuum. Except for the judicial functioning in a narrow sense – the adjudication, the election of the *primi inter pares* on the bench, and the internal management of the caseload within the chambers –, they do not govern themselves. The courts and tribunals are necessarily part of the institutional 'galaxies' or 'ecosystems' comprising also the overseeing institutions – *injugovins* – created by states and/or parent international organizations (IOs) to perform essential legislative, financial, staffing, and disciplinary aspects of governance over these judicial organs. The *injugovins*' primary functions include electing judges and other principals, adopting budgets and allocating funds, amending legal instruments (statutes and sometimes rules of procedure), management oversight, and enforcement of judgments and decisions. Judicial governance also encompasses secondary (situational and derivative) functions: providing for financial audit, expert review of institutional structures and working practices, organisational support, addressing non-cooperation, and shielding courts against politicised attacks.

The importance of effective judicial governance cannot be overstated. Whether courts would succeed in their mandate depends on how competently their *injugovins* perform their functions.[7] Misgovernance has detrimental consequences for ICTs' effectiveness and credibility. Despite *injugovins*' centrality to courts' healthy and smooth operations, the plethora of judicial governance issues have long remained the reserve of legal advisors in the embassies and foreign ministries as well as court principals and external relations officers. By contrast to the prevalent focus on ICTs, their governance arrangements were largely neglected in the literature.[8] But understanding, let alone tackling, the problems ICTs face in delivering justice is impossible unless *injugovins* are brought in the picture and receive the deserving attention. It is largely owing to Blokker's efforts that international judicial governance has shifted to the spotlight as a distinct subject of comparative and critical academic inquiry in recent years.

7 Sergey Vasiliev, "Judicial Governance Entities as Power-Holders in International Criminal Justice: A Plea for a Socio-Legal Enquiry", in Morten Bergsmo a.o. (eds.), *Power in International Criminal Justice* (Torkel Opsahl Academic E-Publisher, 2020), pp. 495–496.

8 Blokker 2018 (*supra* note 5), p. 33.

At least 30 ICTs, excluding administrative tribunals, are presently in operation, with most having been established over the past 35 years.[9] The even greater diversity of ICTs, if defunct courts are to be counted as well, is surpassed by the variation in the legal-institutional arrangements devised for their governance. Each ICT, or each family of homogenous ICTs, is overseen by its own *injugovin* or by several organs exercising (sometimes jointly), the distinct governance functions. With a few exceptions, no arrangements are identical: the 'galaxies' rarely if ever interlock.[10] The choice of a specific set of arrangements is often overdetermined by systemic or pragmatic factors, like the ICT's parentage from a certain IO or its embedding in a global or regional treaty framework. For many ICTs, the governance modalities have been developed as an afterthought in a (semi-)improvised manner, shaping up only after the courts were established.[11]

Injugovins present a wide variety in terms of status and legal capacity (if any), institutionalisation, and modalities. In Blokker's typology,[12] three models are discerned based on whether judicial governance functions are assigned to: (a) organs of a larger IO of which the court is also a part;[13] (b) a dedicated treaty organ that neither is a part of an IO nor possesses legal personality;[14] or (c) a loose gathering of states not incorporated into an IO or a treaty organ.[15] The real-life schemes often defy neat categorization and include elements of several models. The existence of a single dedicated *injugovin* responsible for

9 Schermers and Blokker (*supra* note 3), pp. 452–53. For an overview of the 34 historic and present ICTs' *injugovins*: Niels Blokker, "International Judicial Governance Institutions: Topography, Typology, and Guiding Principles", in Vasiliev and Blokker (*supra* note 6).

10 The twin tribunals (International Criminal Tribunals for the Former Yugoslavia (ICTY) and for Rwanda (ICTR)), and residual successor tribunals (Residual Special Court for Sierra Leone or the International Residual Mechanism for Criminal Tribunals (MICT) for the SCSL and the ICTY/ICTR, respectively) were subject to the same governance schemes.

11 Huw Llewellyn, *An Institutional Perspective on the United Nations Criminal Tribunals: Governance, Independence and Impartiality* (Brill Nijhoff 2021) 6.

12 Blokker 2018 (*supra* note 5), p. 34; Blokker (*supra* note 9), para. 4.2.

13 E.g. the UN General Assembly and Security Council for the International Court of Justice, ICTY/ICTR, and MICT; the Parliamentary Assembly and the Committee of Ministers (Council of Europe) for the European Court of Human Rights (ECtHR); and the Council, European Commission, and the European Parliament for the Court of Justice of the European Union (CJEU).

14 E.g. the Meeting of States Parties to the UN Convention on the Law of the Sea for the International Tribunal for the Law of the Sea; and the ICC-ASP.

15 E.g. the CJEU judges are appointed by EU member states' governments, and the judges of the Inter-American Court of Human Rights by states party to the American Convention on Human Rights at the General Assembly of the Organization of American States: Blokker 2018 (*supra* note 5), p. 34, note 44.

all governance functions is exceptional, unlike the hybrid schemes whereby several organs bear different governance responsibilities.[16] Thus, under a hybrid setup, different functions vis-à-vis the same ICT may be allocated to the relevant IO organs *and* a non-incorporated group of states.[17] Nor do said types exhaust the spectrum of possibilities: other models have also been used.[18] Think of 'direct governance', characterized by only nominal institutionalisation, employed for the International Military Tribunal at Nuremberg, or unmediated state involvement (as was the case for the UN-sponsored special criminal tribunals in part of financing and some judicial appointments). Finally, new hybrid variants could emerge in the future. One such thought experiment is the potential Special Tribunal for the Crime of Aggression in Ukraine set up under the auspices of the Council of Europe and funded partially by the EU – hence co-governed by *two* IOs.

Neither a single blueprint nor a master design of international judicial governance can be expected to emerge. But there is an extensive repository of arrangements and approaches tried and tested (or compromised and dismissed) within insulated legal-institutional regimes. Despite the irreducible diversity and hypnotic complexity of past and present governance schemes, their underlying objectives – ensuring ICTs' effective and accountable functioning without compromising judicial independence – and the recurring challenges the *injugovins* and 'their' courts face in structuring and operationalising their relationships, are comparable across the board.[19] This rich experiential 'raw material' should be dissected, juxtaposed, and analysed critically.[20] Accounting for the common features and unique nuances across different regimes can help identify the best practices and 'lessons learnt' of broader import: the *do's* and *don'ts* of international judicial governance. It is a welcome, if overdue, development that after years of neglecting *injugovins* in academic

16 *Ibidem.*

17 On the CJEU and ECtHR, Blokker (*supra* note 9), para. 4.2. Another example is the hybrid governance of the SCSL, the Extraordinary Chambers in the Court of Cambodia (ECCC), and STL, where governance functions were exercised by an organ of the UN (Secretary-General), states parties to the constituent agreement (Sierra Leone, Cambodia, and Lebanon, respectively), and the management committees as treaty-based organs (Art. 7 SCSL Agreement; Art. 6 STL Agreement) or 'groups of interested states' ('steering committee' and 'principal donors' group' for the ECCC). In detail, Llewellyn (*supra* note 11), pp. 175–192.

18 Identifying, besides the 'envelope model' (equivalent to (a)), the 'diplomatic' model (equivalent to (b)), and 'executive/managerial' model (in some variants, equivalent to (c) or (b) above), also a 'direct governance' model: Vasiliev (*supra* note 7), pp. 533–539.

19 Blokker 2018 (*supra* note 5), p. 36.

20 Blokker (*supra* note 9), para. 1.

and policy debates, full-length comparative and thematic studies have started to emerge.[21]

3 What Are the Standards? Guiding Principles, Hard Constraints

What makes international judicial governance a pertinent subject of inquiry for international lawyers? This field is kept together not only due to the shared policy objectives, similarities in institutional forms, decision-making procedures, challenges, or the know-how. ICT governance presents a single domain of law and practice because there are certain uniform fundamental *legal* standards that 'govern the governors'. These constraints on the *injugovins'* exercise of powers vis-à-vis ICTs are the unifying normative *toile de fond* of this area of law and practice. Whether effectively enforceable or not, such standards create obligations all *injugovins* must respect as a matter of law when performing their functions. These principles ought to be distinguished from aspirational good practices and advisory rules of thumb.

This leads to the question, also raised by Blokker, of what those standards are, and what are their sources and contents.[22] Judicial independence and accountability of ICTs frequently feature as the elements of the normative framework and key 'guiding principles' for *injugovins*.[23] The principle of judicial independence no doubt constitutes a valid standard limiting the reach and modalities of judicial governance.[24] On the other hand, ICTs' accountability, as a goal and function of governance, is a constraint on ICTs rather than their *injugovins* – which themselves are (should be) accountable in their operation. *Injugovins* should be accountable for misgoverning and failing to ensure an accountable functioning of ICTs under their patronage, but that would be the accountability for their own omissions. Accountability of *injugovins* themselves qualifies as another valid legal constraint on international judicial governance, even though it remains underdeveloped at present. It is not fully clear to whom such accountability is owed (member states, the court, or other

21 Llewellyn (*supra* note 11); Manolescu (*supra* note 1); Sharma (*supra* note 1).

22 Blokker (*supra* note 9), para. 5.

23 Blokker 2018 (*supra* note 5); Blokker (*supra* note 9), para. 5; Paul Mahoney, "The International Judiciary – Independence and Accountability", in *The Law and Practice of international Courts and Tribunals* vol. 7 (2008), p. 313.

24 The closely related yet distinct principle of judicial impartiality is less relevant (except for the judicial election and disciplinary functions of *injugovins*). International Commission of Jurists (ICJ), *International Principles on the Independence and Accountability of Judges, Lawyers and Prosecutors – Practitioners Guide No. 1* (2007) at pp. 21, 27–31.

constituencies?), what forms *injugovins*' responsibility should take, and how it can be invoked let alone enforced.

Finally, one finds (partially overlapping) lists of parameters of '*good* governance' in the sphere of international development and public administration beyond judicial institutions. These feature impartiality, the rule of law, transparency, accountability, participation, inclusivity, and combatting corruption (UN Human Rights Council);[25] representation, responsiveness, effectiveness and efficiency, ethical conduct, human rights, sound financial management (Council of Europe);[26] and, additionally, consensus-orientation.[27] With necessary adaptations, these principles can be transposed to ICT governance and applied as benchmarks to guide, improve, and evaluate *injugovins'* operations.[28] Despite their normative validity, however, the import of such standards as demarcation lines between the legally admissible and inadmissible judicial governance modalities is limited. Most of them are too unspecific and inconclusive to be useful. Furthermore, they set requirements beyond the bare minimum and do not impose binding obligations on *injugovins*.

The detailed treatment of all legal constraints on international judicial governance should be left for another day. The remaining sections will outline the principles of judicial independence and the rule of law as the building blocks of the emergent unified framework for the legal regulation of *injugovins*.

4 Judicial Independence

Judicial independence constitutes a cornerstone principle ordering the relationship between ICTs and *injugovins*. Recognised both in international law and across domestic jurisdictions as *sine qua non* for any adjudicatory organ, it is in the DNA of the judicial function. A court with compromised independence is not worth the name. The principle was developed for national judiciaries, but the core concept applies to ICTs, subject to requisite adjustments

25 UN Human Rights Council resolution, *The role of good governance in the promotion and protection of human rights* (2022), UN Doc A/HRC/RES/51/5, para. 13.

26 Listing 12 'European Principles of Good Democratic Governance': Committee of Ministers of the Council of Europe, *Strategy for Innovation and Good Governance at Local Level* (2008), available at <https://rm.coe.int/1680746f16>.

27 UN Economic and Social Commission for Asia and the Pacific, *What is Good Governance?* (2009), available at <https://hdl.handle.net/20.500.12870/3794>.

28 Sharma (*supra* note 1) develops the 'good governance' framework for the ICC-ASP.

due a different context.[29] Domestic courts are part of well-developed judicial systems integrated in stable constitutional orders equipped with the checks and balances flowing from the separation of powers. By contrast, ICTs do not benefit from the equivalent constitutionalisation and the *trias politica* safeguards in their relationships with *injugovins* and/or interested states.

Combined with the politically charged character of their cases, the rarefied order in which ICTs fare makes them more vulnerable to interference than their national counterparts in liberal democracies. But the protection of ICTs' independence must be robust so they retain the confidence (and the consent to their jurisdiction) of states which supply them with disputes for resolution.[30] Moreover, for tribunals determining individual responsibility, independence is rooted in an additional rationale – the right of the accused to a fair trial before a competent, independent, and impartial tribunal established by law, which must also be respected in international proceedings.[31]

ICTs' judicial independence knows two dimensions.[32] The first is the individual autonomy of adjudicators, if as members of collective bodies.[33] The second is the institutional independence, guaranteeing the insulation from undue interference by other branches of power or, at the international level, by states and other external actors.[34] The two aspects are closely linked and reinforced by the provisions in constituent agreements and statutes regarding qualifications, selection and appointment, tenure and conditions of service (including remuneration), disqualification and dismissal of judges (and prosecutors, as appropriate), and the privileges and immunities of ICTs and their officials. These guarantees draw the 'red lines' around the admissible governance interventions, regardless of ICTs' organisational form, permanent or

29 James Crawford and Joe McIntyre, "The Independence and Impartiality of the 'International Judiciary'", in Shimon Shetreet and Christopher Forsyth (eds.), *The Culture of Judicial Independence: Conceptual Foundations and Practical Challenges* (Brill Nijhoff, 2012), p. 191.

30 Kenneth J. Keith, "Challenges to the Independence of the International Judiciary: Reflections on the International Court of Justice", in *Leiden Journal of International Law* vol. 30 (2017), pp. 137, 140.

31 Art. 10 Universal Declaration of Human Rights; Art. 14 International Covenant on Civil and Political Rights; Art. 6 European Convention on Human Rights; Art. 8 American Convention of Human Rights. See e.g. *Report of the Secretary-General pursuant to paragraph 5 of Security Council resolution 955 (1994)*, UN Doc S/1995/134, para. 106.

32 ICJ (*supra* note 24), pp. 21–25; Keith (*supra* note 30), p. 139; Blokker (*supra* note 9) para. 5.

33 E.g. Art. 2 Statute of the International Court of Justice; Art. 40 (1)-(2) Rome Statute of the International Criminal Court.

34 E.g. Preamble of the Rome Statute, para. 9; *Basic Principles on the Independence of the Judiciary* (Milan, 1985; endorsed by UNGA Res. 40/32 and 40/146), para. 1.

temporary character, and their dockets. *Injugovins* must respect and protect judicial (and prosecutorial) independence whenever exercising governance over 'their' courts. The principle has transversal relevance: from appointing principals to amending legislation; from providing budgets to ordering *ad hoc* expert reviews and audits; from disciplining mismanagement to countering hostile states' unlawful coercive measures.

The risk of *injugovins* disrespecting judicial independence or upholding it insufficiently vis-à-vis offending states, has been a live issue. One notorious example of *injugovins* cowing to an unscrupulous state is the non-reappointment of MICT Judge Akay (Turkey) by the UN General Assembly and Security Council. This was preceded by their failure to meaningfully intervene since his arrest and detention by Turkish authorities on terrorism charges, which was in breach of his and MICT's independence and immunities.[35] In the same register, albeit on a different scale, lies the United States' blocking of the appointment of WTO Appellate Body members, leading to a major crisis in the WTO dispute settlement system.[36] Another incident still is ICC-ASP's consideration, upon Kenya's urgent insistence (mildly put), of an agenda item on the issue of criminal procedure that was then *sub judice*.[37] While this episode attests that crises imperilling the integrity of adjudication can be dissipated, if not averted, through diplomatic efforts within the governance body, the former two exemplify how a manipulative state can subvert the ICT's work if the *injugovin* proves unable to counter its disrespect of judicial independence.[38]

The tensions between judicial independence and the overly intrusive – or aloof – governance are real. Yet, unlike individual states and other entities, *injugovins* are not fully 'external' to the courts they govern and must be allowed and have the means necessary to ensure competent, effective, and accountable operation of ICTs. No institution should be accountability-free, and ICTs are no exception. Judicial independence does not mean splendid isolation from management, financial, disciplinary, and other oversight; nor should it be used as a trump to deflect all accountability.[39] Striking the right balance between safeguarding judicial independence and furthering governance imperatives

35 Zsuzsanna Deen-Racsmány, "Deficient Protection of the Independence of International Judges by International Judicial Governance Institutions: The Case of Judge Akay", in Vasiliev and Blokker (*supra* note 6).

36 Peter van den Bossche, "The Demise of the WTO Appellate Body: Lessons for the Governance of International Adjudication?", in Vasiliev and Blokker (*supra* note 6).

37 Vasiliev (*supra* note 7), pp. 552–557.

38 Blokker (*supra* note 9), para. 5.

39 On financial accountability, see Manolescu (*supra* note 1).

is not a straightforward task and requires taking into account each regime's specificities.

Distinguishing between the core judicial and internal justice administration aspects, on the one hand, and ICTs' operation as IOs (or organs thereof) with view to allocating issues under different reporting lines and spheres of responsibility goes some way to addressing this dilemma. The adjudication, its organisation within the chambers, and the internal justice administration are judicial matters *par excellence* and a no-go zone for *injugovins*. Such matters belong to the exclusive competence of judges and are protected by judicial independence. By contrast, courts' functioning as (organs of) IOs is properly subject to the oversight of their governance institutions.[40] Admittedly, this distinction is no silver bullet: the two dimensions interweave and impact each other in practice. Governance decisions in the organisational and management realm spill over to the intimate sphere of adjudication and may affect, if indirectly, judicial independence. Given the lack of detailed rules on *injugovins'* obligations to respect and promote it, this aspect of practice would benefit from clearer and thicker regulation tailored to ICTs. The existing soft-law instruments on the position of (international) judges, notably the Burgh House Principles,[41] provide useful starting points but are neither binding nor specific enough. The ICT/*injugovin* relationships should be fleshed out further and captured in the 'thick' rules on judicial independence considering the institutional features of specific regimes.

5 Rule of Law

Another cornerstone principle, or a set of constraints transferable and applicable to the international judicial governance domain, is the rule of law. As a multi-layered framework of requirements, its normative contents are notoriously challenging to ascertain exhaustively and unequivocally.[42] Nevertheless, the rule of law gives rise to hard standards, not mere facultative guidelines, for *injugovins*. They are fundamental, legal by character, and sufficiently directive

40 On the three-layered model of ICC governance: Independent Expert Review of the International Criminal Court and the Rome Statute System, *Final Report* (2020), ICC-ASP/19/16, paras. 31–50.

41 Study Group of the International Law Association on the Practice and Procedure of International Courts and Tribunals, *Burgh House Principles on the Independence of the International Judiciary* (2004), available at <https://www.ucl.ac.uk/international-courts/sites/international-courts/files/burgh_final_21204.pdf>.

42 Blokker (*supra* note 4), pp. 77–81.

to inform judicial governance processes. In 2004, the UN Secretary-General defined the rule of law as:

> a principle of governance in which all persons, institutions and entities … are accountable to laws that are publicly promulgated, equally enforced and independently adjudicated, and which are consistent with international human rights norms and standards. It requires, as well, measures to ensure adherence to the principles of supremacy of law, equality before the law, accountability to the law, fairness in the application of the law, separation of powers, participation in decision-making, legal certainty, avoidance of arbitrariness and procedural and legal transparency.[43]

This definition makes it clear that all entities must be subject to, and accountable under, the rule of law. This holds *a fortiori* for the institutions governing ICTs. As bodies exercising international public authority over international judiciaries, *injugovins* cannot escape complying with its tenets that are relevant to their activities. Emphasizing its legal certainty, equal treatment, and transparency demands, Blokker has stated that governance decisions vital for the successful functioning of ICTs are preferably not to be made "in an ad hoc, improvised or haphazard way, but instead to follow a more organised model, based on predetermined procedures, following past practice where applicable", i.e. "more in accordance with the rule of law".[44]

The rule of law knows competing interpretations, with some accounts limited to 'thin' formalist approaches while others foreground additional substantive 'thick' requirements such as compliance with certain levels of human rights protection.[45] Judicial independence and accountability are at times subsumed within the catch-all concept of the rule of law, although their respectable pedigree and immanent complexity warrant treating them as self-standing principles. As the facets of the rule of law (in its 'thin' variation), the supremacy of the law, legal certainty, non-arbitrariness, and transparency are opposable to *injugovins* as dictates flowing from their exercise of authority over courts. The exercise of governance powers should not be arbitrary or dictatorial but at all times be based on clear rules agreed upon in advance. If they are to pass muster, the processes by which ICTs are governed may not

43 Report of the UN Secretary-General, *The rule of law and transitional justice in conflict and post-conflict societies* (2004), UN Doc S/2004/616, para. 6.

44 Blokker (*supra* note 9), para. 4.2; also, Blokker (*supra* note 4), pp. 84–85.

45 An influential (thin) account is defended in Joseph Raz, "The Rule of Law and its Virtue", in Raz, *The Authority of Law: Essays on Law and Morality* (Oxford UP, 1979), pp. 210–29.

boil down to top-down imposition of ready-made decisions leaving no room for prior participation of, and consultation with, court representatives (e.g. on budgetary issues).

Moreover, given the public interest in effective and accountable operation of ICTs, ensuring the requisite degree of transparency in governance is more than a noble aspiration. That said, discretion is advisable in operationalising transparency, as there are legitimate reasons for some governance activities and discussions to unfold behind closed doors. It would be counterproductive to demand unqualified openness given the political sensitivities involved and the (perceived) need to allow diplomacy to take its course. Yet, the key governance decisions should rest on transparent and clear rules, not vagaries of power, and ideally be made following the agreed procedures rather than the political expediency of working towards desired outcomes those procedures ostensibly failed to deliver. The experience shows that, when it comes to amending legislation and electing judges and prosecutors, some *injugovins*' track record in terms of transparency and respecting their own protocols has been mixed at best.[46]

6 In Lieu of Conclusion

Owing to the infectiously inspiring work of Niels Blokker, the institutions governing international judiciaries have been put firmly on the map of the international law discipline. An impressive volume of the 'raw' empirical material has been gathered and more of it is there to be uncovered, especially from the less iconic and 'popular' ICTs. The inquiry into the variegated legal, institutional, and practical arrangements in different judicial governance regimes, is still in its exploratory stages. Yet, the emerging data attest incontrovertibly to the recurrence and commonality of the challenges ICTs and governing bodies are facing in their intricate relationships hovering simultaneously between interdependency and autonomy, control and trust, the rule of power and the rule of law. These opposing poles and impulses are the leitmotifs of Blokker's incisive writings on *injugovins* and other creatures of international law.

Due to the sheer multiplicity of ICTs and their disparate governance schemes, the diversity in this field of legal policy and practice is irreducible

46 Open Society Justice Initiative, *2020–2021 International Criminal Court Prosecutor Election Process: Insights and Recommendations for Future Elections* (2021), pp. 21 and 28–29; Vasiliev (*supra* note 7), pp. 524–526 (ICC-ASP bypassing the roadmap procedure for developing rule amendments).

and there to stay. There is no one super-*injugovin* to 'govern them all' to lead the charge for the harmonisation let alone unification in this area; nor are there principled reasons to pursue such unbridled ambitions. With every governance 'ecosystem' being a unit on its own, there has been too little cross-systemic communication and critical and constructive engagement. It is all the more important for international lawyers and policy makers to intensify transversal critical analyses of the experiences of various *injugovins* and ICTs, drawing actionable lessons, and articulating best practices and cautionary tales – the *do's* and *don'ts* of judicial governance applicable across the board. This inductive exercise should take account of the core legal principles of international judicial governance – the mandatory positive law standards and 'hard *don'ts*' constraining the performance of governance authority over ICTs.

The principles of judicial independence, the rule of law, and accountability of *injugovins* can be seen as the load-bearing pillars of this emergent legal framework. A normative *toile de fond* for international judicial governance as a whole, they inject regulatory coherence into this field and align the loose self-enclosed 'galaxies' – *injugovin*-ICT pairs – into a single 'universe' subject to the same laws. The next phases of this research should devote more attention to this unified framework. The normative contents and legal implications of its core principles, along with their institutional translations in specific judicial governance regimes, ought to be spelt out with greater precision and gain a thicker texture. Since such principles are abstract and set only minimum expectations, they will be insufficient to deliver the optimal governance arrangements in every setting. They must therefore be detailed in the more context-specific rules and procedures, which will vary across distinct regimes, and complemented by the 'good governance' standards, i.e. the 'rules of thumb' and recommendatory *do's* going further in their normative demands than mere minimum rules.

Circling back to this chapter's opening words, I could not have wished for a more cordial, supportive, and reliable companion than Professor Niels Blokker on our journeys in the – no longer so desolate – universe of *injugovins*, including the adventures still lying ahead. I thank him for his collegiality, sage advice, and countless lessons in kindness, humility, integrity, and in the importance of staying true to oneself along the way. I can only hope that our broodings and conversations about the dilemmas of governing international judiciaries, but also about the beauty, paradoxes, and fragility of life beyond international law, will continue long into his retirement.

PART 4

Preserving International Cooperation

CHAPTER 20

Relations between 'European Courts'

Towards Civilized Dialogue?

Laurence Boisson de Chazournes and Pieter Jan Kuijper***

1 Introduction

The 2000s and 2010s were a period during which the legal relations between international organizations, including the relations between their courts, came more and more to the fore in Europe. This was a natural consequence of the increased production of binding decisions, mostly on economic sanctions, of the UN Security Council from the 1990s onwards, of the growth of transferred powers, including (exclusive) external relations powers, simultaneously with the growth of membership, of the European Union, and of increased activities in the human rights field, both at the global and at the regional level. This in turn contributed to increased caseloads of the regional human rights courts, in particular of the European Court of Human Rights (ECtHR) and of the Court of Justice of the European Union (CJEU). Both these courts were also reformed and restructured, and human rights were made even more an integral part of EU law after a revised Charter of Fundamental Rights was given the same legal value as the Treaties in Article 6(1) of the TEU, which entered into force in December 2009.

The relation between the European Court of Justice and international courts[1] and the relations between regional and universal international organizations, including the treatment by the CJEU and the ECtHR of UN Security Council sanctions targeting companies and individuals[2] became matters of

* Laurence Boisson de Chazournes is Professor of International Law and International Organizations, University of Geneva.

** Pieter Jan Kuijper is Professor emeritus of the Law of International Organizations, University of Amsterdam.

1 Tobias Lock, *The European Court of Justice and International Courts* (Oxford UP, 2016), which deals extensively with the CJEU's monopoly on the interpretation of the EU Treaties, including the interpretation of international agreements concluded by the EU, (Chapter 3) as well as with the "special relationship" between the CJEU and the European Court of Human Rights (Chapter 4).

2 Laurence Boisson de Chazournes, *Interactions between Regional and Universal Organizations* (Brill/Nijhoff, 2017), in particular Chapter V, "Between Coercive Measures and Human Rights: Accountability in Motion among Regional and Universal Organizations".

 | DOI:10.1163/9789004699939_022

intense academic research. Niels Blokker analysed some of these problems already in a 2011 lecture in commemoration of Professor Henry Schermers.[3] The upshot of these studies was that, despite considerable tension between the Courts among themselves, and between the CJEU and the Security Council and its sub-organs charged with the implementation of the sanctions resolutions, in the end these tensions were managed, even if not fully satisfactorily, so that the resulting situation was bearable from a legal and practical point of view. It would seem the right moment to have another look at these issues and, this time, to concentrate on the relations between the three "European Courts", the CJEU, the ECtHR and the Court of the European Economic Area (EEA), the so-called EFTA Court.[4]

The CJEU, the EFTA Court and the ECtHR are all competent to hear state to state cases brought by member-states of their organizations, but these are a small minority of the cases they treat every year. Much more important are the cases brought by natural and corporate persons, but such cases have to overcome certain barriers before they reach the ECtHR, as well as the courts of the EU and the EFTA. The ECtHR still has to apply the exhaustion of local remedies "according to the generally recognized rules of international law".[5] It should be obvious to anyone somewhat familiar with EU law that the CJEU and the EFTA Court should not be seen as traditional international courts which apply and interpret international law. They are the highest administrative and constitutional courts of their international organizations and apply international law only in incidental fashion. The ECtHR, however, like other regional human rights courts, is a kind of international appeals court in the domain of human rights for their region. All three courts thus maintain a certain level of uniformity within human rights law and the law of economic integration in the European region, albeit in different geographic zones. On this basis, we will try to analyse the recent case law of these three courts focussing on the

3 N.M. Blokker, *Schermerslezing 2011: De VN Veiligheidsraad en de mogelijkheid van rechterlijke toetsing van besluiten van dit orgaan* [*Schermers lecture 2011: The UN Security Council and the appropriateness of judicial review of its decisions*], retrieved from <https://hdl.handle.net/1887/18363>.

4 This article originates in part from a contribution to the work of the ILA Study Group *The International Law of Regional Organizations*, co-chaired by S. Besson and E. Kassoti (2020–2024), of which L. Boisson de Chazournes was a member.

5 Art. 35 ECHR. However, it has been demonstrated that in practice the ECtHR has developed its own test of exhaustion that puts the accent more on the actual presence and effectiveness of local remedies. See Silvia d'Ascoli and Kathrin Maria Scherr, *The Rule of prior Exhaustion of Local Remedies in the International Law Doctrine and its Application in the Specific Context of Human Rights Protection*, EUI Working Paper, Law 2007/2.

questions linked to general international law and human rights, as well as their relations among themselves.

2 The Court of Justice of the European Union

The Court of Justice of the European Union (CJEU) consists of the EU General Court (GC) and the Court of Justice (CoJ). The first is the court of first instance and the civil service court for all the EU institutions, agencies, offices and (executive) bodies. The second is the court of (final) appeal and the supreme court.[6] The primary task of both courts is to ensure that in the application and interpretation of the EU treaties the law is observed. This broad mandate has led the CoJ, in the early years of the EU, to develop and establish an unwritten code of principles and rules of EU law. The doctrine of primacy of EU law over national law, of direct effect of certain provisions of directives, and of Member State liability for damages incurred by natural and moral persons because of State failure to implement Union law are well-known examples.

The CJEU, in particular the CoJ, is extremely jealous of "the autonomy" of EU law and the "seamless web of legal protection" that the EU Courts have construed over the years, as soon as a question of EU law may possibly come to be decided in the last instance by a non-EU court, whether national or international. This is seen as completely contrary to Article 344 TFEU[7] and more broadly to the notion of Union loyalty derived from Article 4(3) TFEU.

Turning to the CJEU's treatment of international law, it is important first of all to mention the power of the Court, assigned to the CoJ, at the request of the Parliament, the Council or the Commission, to give an opinion on the scope of the EU's competence to conclude an international agreement before its conclusion is definitive.[8] This provision has been of great importance for defining the scope of the EU's treaty-making power, especially after the entry into force of the Lisbon Treaty in December 2009, which contained a clear list of subjects

6 The division of work between the CoJ and the GC is in part laid down in the Treaties and in part in the Statute of the CJEU, see Art. 251 ff. TFEU and Art. 51 Statute of the CJEU. For the simplified procedure for modification of the Statute, see Art. 281 TFEU.

7 Art. 244 TFEU: Member States undertake not to submit a dispute concerning the interpretation or application of the Treaties to any method of settlement other than those provided for therein.

8 See Art. 218(11) TFEU. This provision has the objective to prevent embarrassment in the international relations of the EU, which could arise if an international agreement concluded between the Union and one or more States were to be annulled by the Court after it had been in force for some time.

that fall under exclusive powers which include treaty-making in these fields.[9] Lisbon also codified the parallelism between the expanding internal legislation of the Union and its treaty-making power first laid down by the Court in the so-called *AETR* case and developed in later cases.[10] Important as it may be, all this is of little use for gaining an insight into how the CJEU applies and interprets international law, to which we will now turn.

Just as many national courts, the CJEU applies and interprets international law in incidental fashion with a view to help its two courts in deciding EU cases. To this end it has recourse to two techniques habitually used by national courts, namely direct effect and harmonious interpretation.

The CoJ has become gradually more averse from recognizing the direct effect of important international agreements, such as the UN Convention on the Law of the Sea (UNCLOS) and the WTO. In addition to the well-known test whether an individual provision of the treaty is suitable for direct application by a court without further rules for implementation, the CoJ has added a preliminary test, namely a global appreciation of whether the overall structure and operation of the treaty in question indicate that it was intended to have direct effect. The WTO and UNCLOS did not get beyond this preliminary test.[11]

The two branches of the CJEU have continued the practice of harmonious interpretation in quite liberal fashion to agreements to which the EU is a party. Moreover, the two courts regularly invoke judgments of the International Court of Justice (ICJ), the UNCLOS Tribunal, and even the WTO Appellate Body to bolster their own interpretations of these and other international agreements when deciding cases before them.[12] In one particular case, such reference to particular international instruments is encouraged by the TFEU itself, namely in the field of asylum and immigration. Article 78 (1) TFEU states explicitly that the common policy on asylum and other mechanisms of protection of refugees (*non-refoulement* is explicitly mentioned) must be in accordance with the

---

9 Art. 3(1) TFEU, mentioning the customs union, the competition rules, the euro, the conservation of the biological resource of the high seas and the common fisheries policy, as well as the common commercial policy, which according to Art. 206 TFEU has come to include foreign direct investment.

10 Art. 3(2) TFEU.

11 For the GATT, see the Joined Cases 21–24/72 *International Fruit*, paras. 20–27; for the WTO, see Case 377/02, *Van Parijs v. BIRB*, para. 54; for UNCLOS, see Case C-308/06, *Intertanko et al. v. Secretary of State for Transport*, paras. 54–64.

12 See Case C-286/90, *Anklagemyndigheden v. Poulsen & Diva Navigation, para. 9*, ECLI:EU:C:1992:155 and C-245/02, *Anheuser-Busch v. Budejovicki Budvar*, paras. 49 and 67, ECLI:EU:C:2004:717.

Geneva Convention of 1951 (and the Protocol of New York 1967)[13] "and other relevant treaties." The CoJ has recently shown its willingness to be quite liberal in having recourse to the category of "other relevant treaties" with a view to bolstering its own interpretation of non-refoulement in a case concerning a woman exposed to a risk of domestic violence in her home country.[14]

Therefore, under EU primary law, the CJEU has the liberty to draw on other international agreements and the judgments of other international courts in its application or interpretation of EU law. However, on the other hand the Member States shall not be free to bring disputes involving the final interpretation of EU law to any other courts than those provided for in the Treaty.[15] Moreover, in *Opinion 2/13* the CJEU found that the draft agreement designed to allow the Union to join the European Convention on Human Rights (ECHR) would violate the "autonomy" of the EU legal order. The Court found that the "very existence of [the] possibility" that the ECtHR could interpret EU law in the last instance, "undermines the requirement set out in Article 344 TFEU".[16] The strong wording in which this veto was expressed initially caused a bit of a crisis in the relations with ECtHR. Nevertheless, the EU Courts did not stop their standing practice of referring to judgments of the ECtHR in their own judgments when human rights were at issue in cases before them. They could hardly act otherwise, as the protection guaranteed by the Charter of Fundamental Rights of the EU was supposed not to fall below the standards set in the ECHR, which included of course their interpretation by the ECtHR.[17]

Moreover, it has never been an issue for the CJEU that EU rules in the field of trade remedies (anti-dumping and subsidies) and their application have been declared contrary to the relevant WTO law by the WTO Appellate Body from time to time, when that that jurisdiction was still functioning. This is not

---

13 Convention related to the Status of Refugees, Geneva 1951, *UNTS* vol. 189, p. 150, No. 2545 (1954) and Protocol relating to the Status of Refugees, New York 1967, *UNTS* Vol. 606, p. 267, No. 8791 (1967).

14 See Case C-621/21, *WS v. Intervyuirasht organ na Darzhavna agentsia za bezhantsite pri Ministerskia savet*, ECLI:EU:C:2024:47. The CoJ had recourse to the UN Convention on the Elimination of all forms of Discrimination against Women of 1979 (CEDAW), not open to the EU, but ratified by all Member States (paras. 44–45), to the Council of Europe Convention on the preventing and combating violence against women and domestic violence (Istanbul Convention), even though it entered into force only during the court proceedings (paras. 46–47), and to the Guidelines of the High Commissioner for Refugees on International Protection relating to the Geneva Convention (paras. 56 and 69).

15 Case C-459/03, *Commission v. Ireland*, ECLI:EU:C:2006:345, *passim*.

16 Opinion 2/13, *Accession of the European Union to the European Convention for the Protection of Human Rights and Fundamental Freedoms*, ECLI:EU:C:2014:2454, para. 208.

17 See Artt. 52(3) and 53 of the Charter of Fundamental Rights of the European Union.

surprising. If the EU ventures outside its own legal order and submits to the jurisdiction of international courts, even in situations where no exhaustion of local remedies is required, as in the WTO, it is inevitable that such courts may express a "judgment" on its legislation and the interpretation thereof by "national" (i.e. EU) courts in the light of the requirements of the international agreement, even if such "national" interpretation was not final. If necessary, the international court may explain that its interpretation of the impugned legislation is a mere question of fact, and it may even hear legal experts in order to have the legislation and its interpretation by national courts fully explained. There is nothing exceptional to that; it happens all the time, for instance before investment tribunals. Given that the accession of the EU to the ECHR is prescribed in Article 6(2) TEU, the Court will have to come along to accepting the ECtHR as final arbiter in human rights cases, but since exhaustion of local remedies is a requirement in the ECHR, the accession agreement will need a watertight assurance that in EU cases the CJEU will have the last word before a case comes before the ECtHR.[18]

The strict approach to its own authority as final arbiter of EU law has also been apparent in the way the CJEU has treated arbitration tribunals. In the field of commercial arbitration, which rests entirely on agreements between private parties, the CoJ already early on has taken the position that, since such arbitration tribunals are not courts of the Member States within the meaning of Article 267 TFEU, it will not answer any preliminary questions from such tribunals.[19]

The position of the CJEU vis-a-vis investment arbitration is wholly different because that form of arbitration, though involving private complainants, is mostly based on investment agreements between two states. As the Lisbon Treaty has shifted the competence over foreign direct investment to the Union (Article 206 TFEU), such agreements in the opinion of the CoJ, when concluded between two Member States, cannot be continued under the interpretation that it has given of Article 344.[20] This is also applicable, in the CoJ's view, to the legal obligations between Member States as parties to a broader multilateral investment agreement, such as the Energy Charter Treaty (ECT), which is a mixed agreement.[21]

18 For the latest negotiations on EU accession to the ECHR, see CoE documents 46+1(2023)35 and 36.

19 Case 102/81, *Nordsee v. Reederei Mond*, ECLI:EU:C:1982:107, paras. 11–16.

20 Case C-384/16, *Slovak Republic v. Achmea*, ECLI:EU:C:2018:158, paras. 56–60.

21 Case C-741/19, *Republic of Moldova v. Komstroy*, ECLI: EU:C:2021:665, paras. 57–66.

3 The EFTA Court as Court of the European Economic Area

The EEA was created in 1994 as successor to the EFTA, consisting of the EU and its Member States and the remaining EFTA members, Iceland, Liechtenstein, and Norway, but not Switzerland, which maintains a mosaic of over a hundred agreements with the EU.

Originally the intention was to create an EEA Court, but the European Court of Justice rejected this idea in *Opinion 1/91* on the Creation of the European Economic Area.[22] Since the EEA Court would have been composed of judges of the CJEU and of the EFTA states, the CoJ decided that this would violate the autonomy of the EU legal order. Hence it was decided that the EFTA Court has jurisdiction in the EFTA pillar alone and is institutionally separate from the CJEU. In *Opinion 1/92*, the CoJ gave its approval to the newly designed agreement since the EFTA Court "will exercise its jurisdiction only within EFTA".[23]

Nevertheless, "in full deference of the [national] courts" (preamble EEA Treaty) it remains the objective of the EEA's institutions to achieve a uniform interpretation of the EU law contained in the EEA's Protocols. This should also contribute to arriving at "homogeneity" in their shared internal market law. "Homogeneity" is a recurring buzz word in the EEA Agreement.[24]

Hence, it is obvious that the EFTA Court applies virtually the same internal market law as the CJEU – albeit without the specific EU unwritten principles of supremacy and direct effect – and that it is confronted broadly with the same causes of action as the CJEU. Hence, just as the CJEU, the EFTA Court can better be compared to a national administrative court, with less constitutional traits than the CJEU. If international law questions crop up in the cases treated by the EFTA Court, the applicable international law is interpreted and applied incidentally.

The international legal rules that are referred to before the EFTA Court most often are provisions of human rights conventions, primarily the ECHR. In such cases human and/or fundamental rights are sometimes presented as an interpretative aid, but more often as a limit on EEA law, even if the EFTA Court frequently arrives at the conclusion that this limit has not been crossed by EEA law or its application. However, the EFTA Court, just as the CJEU before the

22 Opinion 1/91, ECLI:EU:C:1991:490, paras. 14–21.

23 Opinion 1/92, *Draft Agreement between the Community, on the one hand, and the Countries of the European Free Trade Association, on the other, relating to the creation of the European Economic Area*, ECLI:EU:C:1992:189.

24 Artt. 102 and 105 ff EEA Agreement. "Homogeneity" is a typical compromise word and fulfils broadly the same functions in EEA law, as terms such as "uniformity" and "consistency" do in EU law (perhaps even a weak form of "supremacy").

EU Charter of Fundamental Rights was annexed to the EU Treaties, prefers to present fundamental and human rights as simply being part of EFTA law. In two cases the EFTA Court has suggested that the national court that asked for an advisory opinion should apply specific human or fundamental rights to the facts of the case.[25] Other examples of the EFTA Court applying international law are few and far between and sometimes far-fetched. There is at least one example in which the Court relied on an ILO Convention on Dock Work, the *Holship* case,[26] to be discussed below in the section on the ECtHR.

As has been shown above the EFTA Court has a very close and deferential relationship with the CJEU, largely driven by the principle of homogeneity. Nevertheless, the EFTA Court in some cases has led the way to homogeneity. This happened when it applied the precautionary principle for the first time to "unnecessary" food additives[27] in breakfast cereals, only to be followed two years later by the CJEU in the *Danish Cranberry Juice case*, in which that court explicitly paid tribute to the EFTA Court for its role as initiator of the application of this principle.[28] On a somewhat different level, the EFTA Court has also, on occasion, given surprising judgments, in which it adopted fundamental non-written rules from the *acquis communautaire*, such as the principle of State liability for damages caused to individuals or companies by non-implementation of directives. Even in the face of the arguments of the Commission as intervener, to the effect that the principle of State liability of the EU was very closely linked to the even more fundamental notions of supremacy and direct effect, which the EFTA States had never wanted to adopt, the Court developed its own reasoning that the EFTA rested on such principles as uniformity and homogeneity and that State liability was an important cornerstone in helping to achieve these two objectives.[29] In conclusion one can say, that if the EFTA Court is bound by the EEA Treaty to be deferential to the EU Court, it is also, on occasion, sufficiently independent to be respected by the latter Court.

---

25 Sondre Torp Helmersen, "The EFTA Court and international law", *Oslo Law Review* 2021, pp. 30–46, available at <https://doi.org/10.18261/ISSN.2387-3299-2021-01-02>. Note that "an advisory opinion" requested from the EFTA Court is comparable to a preliminary question put before the CJEU.

26 Case E-14/15, *Holship Norge and Norsk Transportarbeiderforbund*, available at <https://eftacourt.int/download/14-15-judgment-2/?wpdmdl=1224>.

27 Case E-3/00, *EFTA Surveillance Authority v. Norway*, available at <https://eftacourt.int/download/3-judgment/?wpdmdl=1481>, paras. 25–32. This was an application in principle, but in the actual circumstances, the principle was not apposite.

28 Case C-192/01, *Commission v. Denmark*, ECLI:EU:C:2003:492, para. 47 ff.

29 Case E-9/97 *Eva Maria Sveinbjörnsdóttir v. Iceland*, available at <https://eftacourt.int/download/9-97-advisory-opinion/?wpdmdl=1807>, paras. 48–63.

4 The European Court of Human Rights

The European Court of Human Rights (ECtHR) was established in 1959 by the election of its judges by the Assembly of the Council of Europe. Its objective is to ensure that the human rights of Europeans in the 46 member states of the Council of Europe that have ratified the European Convention on Human Rights (ECHR) are respected. Judgments handed down by the Court will have to be executed internally by the States, and it is the Council of Ministers of the Council of Europe which will take care of this implementation.

The ECtHR applies the ECHR which has been regularly updated by adding new rights and other improvements through the adoption of additional protocols. Like the other European courts discussed here, it confronts many other rules of international law in the exercise of its judicial role and deals with those in an incidental manner.

It is well known that human rights courts all over the globe borrow from each other and influence each other's case law, but this poses no real problem. To the contrary, it normally contributes to a well-informed and better application of human rights, also in Europe.

Within Europe, the ECtHR must coexist with two other Courts that are not primarily human rights courts: the CJEU and the EFTA Court. These Courts have taken the position for a long time already that fundamental and human rights are part and parcel of the legal order of respectively the EC/EU and the EFTA. It should be recalled here that the ECtHR from early on took a very accommodating view of this situation, especially in respect of the CJEU. This was expressed clearly in the first cases on UN sanctions, which gave rise to the so-called *Bosphorus* presumption, according to which a State carrying out a binding decision of an international organization that affected a complainant's fundamental rights (in the case of *Bosphorus* airlines its property rights to a plane that had been impounded in Ireland pursuant to UN sanctions adopted by the UN Security Council, implemented in EC law and executed by the Irish authorities) could be presumed to have acted lawfully under the ECHR, as long as the international organization could be deemed to have provided equivalent human rights protection. This presumption could be rebutted, if it was demonstrated in a particular case that the protection of the ECHR was manifestly deficient. In such a case the Convention should be fully applied by the Strasbourg court.[30] Given that the CJEU had handed down its judgment in

30 ECtHR, judgment of 30 June 2005, *Bosphorus Hava Yollari Turizm Ve Ticaret Anonim Sirketi v. Ireland* (no. 45036/98), *EHRR* vol. 42 (2006), pp. 1 ff., at paras. 155–156.

Bosphorus nine years earlier,[31] the effect of the judgment was leaving that ruling of the CJEU intact. It is not our intention to follow the whole saga of EU sanctions implementation, including the *Kadi* cases,[32] here, but to show how flexible, even deferential, the Strasbourg Court initially was in relation to its Luxemburg brethren.

Continued understanding on its part is also shown by the way in which the ECtHR protects the proper recourse to preliminary questions in cases that come up from national judges, in particular from the highest national courts in the EU – and thereby also protects the full exhaustion of local remedies in its own procedure. In two cases of 2012 and 2014, the ECtHR found that the highest national courts, which were called upon to decide a preliminary question of EU law, but did not want to do so, had to follow one of the three reasons laid down by the CJEU for its so-called *acte clair* doctrine: (1) the question is irrelevant for the solution of the case; (2) the EU provision at issue has already been interpreted by the CJEU; (3) the correct application of EU law is so obvious that there can be no reasonable doubt. In one case the ECtHR found that the Belgian Constitutional Court had duly given reasons why a preliminary question was not necessary.[33] In the other case the Italian Court of Cassation had not made any reference to the case law of the CJEU nor given any reason for its rejection of a preliminary question. This amounted to a breach of the fair trial requirement of Article 6(1) of the Convention.[34]

5 The 'European Courts' and the Erosion of Tensions

As we pointed out, the EU has now acquired a Charter of Fundamental Rights that proclaims that its protection cannot fall below the level of the ECHR, and which has acquired semi-constitutional status. The EU is also still pursuing its accession to the ECHR even after stepping back from a first attempt after the CJEU's *Opinion 2/13*. How other frictions that may arise between these three courts are nowadays resolved, is best illustrated by discussing the *Holship* case.[35]

31 Case C-84/95, *Bosphorus Hava Yollari Turizm ve Ticaret AS v. Minister for Transport, Energy and Communications et al.*, ECLI:EU:C:1996:312.

32 See Boisson de Chazournes (*supra* note 2).

33 ECtHR, decision on admissibility of 10 April 2012, *Vergauwen et al. v. Belgium* (no. 4832/04), paras. 89–90.

34 ECtHR, judgment of 8 April 2014, *Dhabi v. Italy* (no. 17120/09), paras. 31–34. These two cases have been confirmed in ECtHR, judgment of 14 March 2023, *Georgiou v. Greece* (no. 57378/18), paras 23–26.

35 See note 26 above.

First of all, it is necessary to recall that in December 2007 the CoJ decided two cases, *Viking* and *Laval*,[36] in which a clash between the right of a trade union to carry out industrial action (strikes, boycotts, blockades etc.) and the freedom of non-national EC-based companies to provide services and to establish themselves across national frontiers was at issue. The CoJ recognized the right to form trade unions and to carry out industrial actions as a fundamental right and "of overriding public importance". However, that right had to be weighed up against the four fundamental freedoms of the EU treaties, in particular the right to provide services and to use posted workers to that end. In principle, these fundamental freedoms could be overridden by the right to industrial action if the industrial action could achieve the result of protection of workers' rights and would not go beyond it.[37] It was left to the national courts that had asked the preliminary questions to decide the cases in the light of this balancing test. These cases at the time led to strong critical reactions from the trade union side, in particular in Scandinavia and the UK, mainly arguing that the CoJ's balancing test might leave the trade union movement hamstrung in face of the four freedoms of the EU, which would thus largely emasculate the trade unions' right to industrial action.

In 2015 a similar case concerning industrial action in the Norwegian port of Drammen ended up before the Norwegian Supreme Court. Here the industrial action (a boycott) was aimed at forcing a new forwarding company, wholly owned by a Danish company (*Holship*), into a collective agreement between local forwarding companies and the trade union of dock workers, which shared out the available work in the port against an agreed tariff and forced Holship to give priority to the established members. The Norwegian Supreme Court requested an Advisory Opinion from the EFTA Court. The reply of the EFTA Court broadly followed the principles of *Laval* and *Viking*, leaving their application largely to the national court, while pointing in addition to Article 11 ECHR on the freedom of association and the possibility of its restriction in the light of overriding reasons of public interest and the ECtHR's case law on this point. In addition, the EFTA Court also reminded the Supreme Court of the CoJ' s doctrine to the effect that a legitimate restriction on a fundamental principle of EU law must be able to achieve the intended aim and must not go beyond the level that is sufficient to that effect. The Court concluded that the boycott at issue could discourage or prevent the establishment of companies

36 Cases C-341/05, *Laval v. Svenska Byggnadsarbetareförbundet*, ECLI:EU:C2007:809, and C-483/05, *International Transport Workers Federation et al. v. Viking Line*, ECLI:EU:C:2007:772.

37 Note that the Swedish branch of the French Laval company was driven into bankruptcy by the industrial action.

from other EEA States and thus infringed the EEA Treaty. When the Norwegian Supreme Court in its final judgment of 2017 followed the Advisory Opinion, the case was brought before the ECtHR by the Norwegian Federation of Trade Unions.

When the ECtHR finally got around to treating the case four years later, the situation had changed, as the relevant social partners had concluded a new collective agreement, which showed that the restrictions on the unions' rights of association had not prevented them from exercising their rights under Article 11 ECHR. Given the careful balancing techniques applied by the Norwegian Supreme Court pursuant to the Judgment of the EFTA Court, the ECtHR considered that there were no strong reasons any longer "to substitute its views for that of the Supreme Court" of Norway. However, the ECtHR ended with an *obiter dictum* that maintains a certain tension between the EU and EEA court systems and itself. First, it stated that the degree of risk of economic consequences of an industrial action could not by itself be decisive in the analysis of proportionality under Article 11 ECHR. The Court also rejected the idea of balancing a fundamental right such as Article 11 against a right under the EEA agreement (such as the freedom of establishment). Fundamental rights could only be balanced against other fundamental rights; a right such as the right of establishment was at best an element in the proportionality test to be applied under Article 11(2) ECHR.[38]

For the ECtHR this is a logical approach, as it has only the ECHR to work with; unlike the CoJ, it does not interpret and apply a set of treaties that next to the Charter of Fundamental rights has another text of constitutional rank to consider, namely the TFEU, which contains such fundamental rights as the four freedoms. It remains to be seen to what extent the CJEU, and in its wake the EEA Court, will be willing to give up the possibility of balancing these in some way in relation to the rights of the Charter at the say-so of the ECtHR. For the CJEU these are all fundamental rights, a reality that the ECtHR did not fully reckon with. Or does the CJEU need to arrive at the position where the Charter's fundamental rights are more fundamental than those of the TFEU? Given that all the three 'European Courts' involved, and the Norwegian Supreme Court, accepted some kind of balancing test, sufficient room for flexibility seems to exist on all sides to avoid a head-on collision.

38 ECtHR, judgment of 10 June 2021, *Norwegian Confederation of Trade Unions (LO) and Norwegian Transport Workers' Union (NTF) v. Norway* (no. 45487/17). See also Hans-Petter Graver, *The Holship Ruling of the ECtHR and the Protection of Human Rights in Europe*, at verfassungsblog.de/holship/.

6 Conclusion

As has been shown above, there is considerable overlap between the areas of jurisdiction of the three 'European Courts'. In part this overlap is expressly so organized, as between the CJEU and the EFTA Court; in part it is involuntary, but inevitable, as between these two courts and the ECtHR. The relations between the CJEU and the EFTA Court, therefore, have been relatively simple and without much friction, the latter court largely following the case law of the former as intended, although we have found at least one instance in which the former followed the latter. The relations between the CJEU and the ECtHR have been much more complicated. We have gone from so-called '*Bosphorus* presumption' of the equivalence of protection of human rights under Community law, extended by the ECtHR to the EU to the latter binding itself to the mast of *at least* equivalent protection between the EU and ECHR.[39] However, the initially failed accession of the EU to the ECtHR caused by the rejection of the terms thereof by the CJEU[40] has had a negative effect also on the relations between the two Courts. Happily, the continued simple application of the terms of Articles 52(3) and 53 of the Charter of Fundamental Rights by the CJEU in its case law has improved the atmosphere again. Another important element that contributed to this has been the approach followed by the CJEU in the *Viking* and *Laval* cases and by the EEA Court and the ECtHR in the *Holship* case. All these courts showed deference to the national courts – often the highest courts – involved in these cases by developing so-called balancing tests and suggesting which elements could legitimately play a role in such balancing by the highest national courts. In this way they also showed deference to each other and created room for continued civilized dialogue.

---

39 ECtHR, *Bosphorus* (*supra* note 30), paras. 155–165.

40 Opinion 2/13 (*supra* note 16).

CHAPTER 21

The World Intellectual Property Organization's New Strategic Direction

Serving Underserved Communities and Helping Transform IP into a Tool That Works for Building a More Sustainable Future

Edward Kwakwa and Irina Chicu***

1 Introduction to WIPO's Vision and Mission

During the thirty-second session of the Program and Budget Committee (PBC) of the World Intellectual Property Organization (WIPO), which took place on July 12–July 16, 2021, in Geneva, the recently inaugurated administration presented to the member states of the Organization a new Medium-Term Strategic Plan 2022–2026 (MTSP). This included a novel "Strategy House," which presented a comprehensive framework for WIPO's course of action over the ensuing five years. The Strategy House is comprised of a vision, mission, four strategic pillars, and a foundation.

WIPO's current vision, according to the MTSP, is to create "a world where innovation and creativity from anywhere is supported by intellectual property for the good of everyone".[1] To support this vision, WIPO established for itself a mission to lead "the development of a balanced and effective global intellectual property ecosystem to promote innovation and creativity for a better and more sustainable future".[2]

The four strategic pillars underpin WIPO's current vision and mission and represent the Organization's broad areas of action. These action areas are: reaching out worldwide to explain the potential for intellectual property (IP) to improve the lives of everyone, everywhere; bringing people together and partnering with stakeholders to shape the future of the global IP ecosystem; providing high quality IP services, knowledge and data that deliver value to users

* Edward Kwakwa is Assistant Director General, Global Challenges and Partnerships Sector, WIPO.

** Irina Chicu is Associate Program Officer, Office of the Assistant Director General, Global Challenges and Partnerships Sector, WIPO.

1 World Intellectual Property Organization, *Medium-Term Strategic Plan for WIPO for 2022–2026* (doc. WO/PBC/32/3, 2021), para. 24.

2 *Ibidem*, para. 25.

 | DOI:10.1163/9789004699939_023

around the world; and supporting governments, enterprises, communities and individuals to use IP as a tool for growth and sustainable development.[3]

Finally, the Strategy House's foundation aims to empower the WIPO staff to work effectively, collaboratively, and innovatively towards delivering the expected results by providing them with the necessary resources and training.[4]

The core elements of the MTSP Strategy House listed above reiterate WIPO's strong commitment to its traditional areas of expertise, such as its role as a neutral forum for discussing IP issues, IP norms and standards setting, as well as the provision of global IP services. At the same time, they express a novel vision in which IP serves as a potent instrument for each country to generate employment, draw investments, foster entrepreneurship, uplift communities, and ultimately cultivate dynamic economies and sustainable development.[5] These shifts in the Organization's strategic course of action happen mainly because several critical issues, such as climate change and global health, are inherently international and cannot be effectively addressed solely at the national level. In this context, as Niels Blokker rightly observed, the role and activities of international organizations, including WIPO, have expanded and adapted to global developments.[6]

Moreover, the new strategy extends beyond the technical and legal facets of IP and aims to transform IP and innovation into accessible tools for the benefit of people around the world. The Organization wants to help different stakeholders to understand how IP plays a substantive role in their creative and innovative endeavours, experiences, and daily lives. Instead of solely interacting with IP experts and technical specialists, WIPO aspires to assist all stakeholders who can benefit from its services and in particular the communities that have traditionally been underserved by the global IP system, such as the small and medium-sized enterprises (SMEs), women, youth, indigenous peoples and local communities.[7]

3 *Ibidem*, para. 27.

4 *Ibidem*, para. 27.

5 WIPO, *WIPO Member States Consider 2022/23 Biennium Program of Work and Budget* (PR/2021/879, 12 July 2021), available at <www.wipo.int/pressroom/en/articles/2021/article_0007.html>, accessed 14 February 2024.

6 "Interview with Niels Blokker, professor at the Hugo Grotius Center for International legal studies at Leiden University (Netherlands)", in *Eurasian Law Journal* vol. 9 (148) (2020), available at <https://eurasialaw-journal.ru/en/intervyu-s-professorom-czentra-mezhdunarodno-pravovyh-issledovanij-im-gugo-grocziya-v-lejdenskom-universitete-niderlandy-nilsom-blokkerom.html>, accessed 28 August 2024.

7 WIPO, *supra* note 5.

At the intersection of change and continuity, WIPO aims to maintain its traditional role as a neutral forum for member states to address IP issues, negotiate new agreements, and provide high-quality IP services, but it also keeps pace with the opportunities and challenges of the current times and develops novel strategic focus areas. These two aspects of WIPO's current course of action will be analyzed in this chapter.

2 WIPO's Historic Role as a Provider of High-Quality Services and as a Neutral Forum for Its Member States to Address IP Issues and Negotiate New Agreements

2.1 *WIPO and IP Services*

WIPO is dedicated to delivering IP services of the highest quality. This commitment extends to the generation and sharing of knowledge and data aimed at offering highest value to users from around the world.

WIPO's IP services can be divided into two groups. The first category encompasses the Global IP Protection Services, with prominent examples being the Patent Cooperation Treaty (PCT), along with international registration systems for trademarks (the Madrid System), designs (the Hague System), and geographical indications (the Lisbon System). The activities of the WIPO Arbitration and Mediation Center are also part of this category of services.[8] The second group involves diverse data and knowledge resources designed to enhance users' understanding and navigation of the IP landscape.[9]

The primary advantage of WIPO's Global IP Protection Services lies in the fact that users can secure protection for their IP rights in numerous jurisdictions worldwide by submitting a single application. It is this distinctive feature that contributes to the continuous growth of utilization of these services.

From 1995 to 2020, there was a significant increase in the number of applications submitted under the PCT, the Madrid System, and the Hague System, with growth rates of 587 percent, 225 percent, and 60 percent, respectively.[10]

These systems are effectively managing the growing influx of applications and continue to adapt to the fast changes in economic trends and the

8 On what WIPO does in practice, including its norm-setting activities, see generally Carolyn Deere Birkbeck, *The World Intellectual Property Organization* (WIPO)*: A Reference Guide* (Edward Elgar, 2016), pp. 7–31.

9 WIPO, *supra* note 1, para. 59.

10 *Ibidem*, para. 62.

IP landscape. The shifts in IP activity, now more diverse and globalized, are notably influenced by a surge in IP filings from Asia.[11]

According to the 2024 World Intellectual Property Indicators (WIPI) Report and due to the challenging macroeconomic environment, global filings for trademarks dropped in 2023. At the same time, a record amount of patent applications has been filed worldwide in 2023, reflecting a fourth consecutive year of strong growth. Also, in continuation of a longer-term trend, the majority of IP filings originate in Asia, accounting for around 70 percent of global patents, trademarks and designs filings in 2023.[12]

The Arbitration and Mediation Center remains a central component of WIPO's IP Protection Services, contributing to the promotion of a fair and efficient international IP system. Employing various alternative dispute resolution mechanisms, particularly mediation and arbitration, along with domain name dispute resolution, the center expedites the resolution of disputes related to innovation and technology among private entities in a timely and cost-effective way.[13]

The second set of IP services focuses on disseminating information and data to users globally. Following the conventional knowledge hierarchy model, raw data is gathered and refined into information, which is then analyzed to generate knowledge. WIPO is actively engaged in providing services at each tier of this information hierarchy and produces data related to the IP system, including published information on IP rights and associated assets. It also disseminates information such as statistics, indicators, curated databases, and related reports. Furthermore, WIPO provides knowledge in the form of reports on technology trends and other relevant issues.[14]

For example, the Global Innovation Index has evolved into a pivotal resource for decision-makers and other stakeholders seeking insights into innovation ecosystems across the globe.[15] The World Intellectual Property Report, released biennially, is another significant reference that provides new perspectives on the role of innovation in market economies. The 2024 release introduced a

11 *Ibidem.*

12 WIPO, *World Intellectual Property Indicators* 2024 (doc. DOI: 10.34667/tind.50133).

13 See generally Francis Gurry, "The Dispute Resolution Services of the World Intellectual Property Organization", in *Journal of International Economic Law* vol. 2 (1999), pp. 385–398.

14 WIPO, *supra* note 1, para. 63.

15 Now in its 17th edition, the Global Innovation Index has become a leading reference for measuring countries' innovation ecosystem performance. It reveals the most innovative economies in the world, ranking the innovation performance of around 132 economies while highlighting innovation strengths and weaknesses.

new data-driven methodology designed to help policymakers take informed decisions and make innovation policy work for development.[16]

WIPO's reports and statistical databases have emerged as authoritative references in the field of IP and are instrumental for policymakers worldwide who rely on them for informing their decisions. These services are continuously enhanced, with a particular emphasis on global databases for patents, trademarks, and designs.[17]

2.2 *Discussions on IP Issues*

WIPO acts as a neutral, impartial platform for discussing and sharing guidance on diverse IP issues, also enabling an efficient coordination and collaboration among the member states and other stakeholders on such issues.

Given the fast-evolving nature of the IP landscape, WIPO continuously updates its forums and discussion formats to keep up with the needs and interests of all stakeholders. Some prominent current discussions at WIPO take place in specialized committees, such as the Committee on Development and Intellectual Property (CDIP), which focuses on development and IP, and the Advisory Committee on Enforcement (ACE), which explores various issues around the topic of IP rights enforcement.

The CDIP was created by the WIPO General Assembly in 2007. Its mandate includes formulating a work program to implement the WIPO Development Agenda, which aims to ensure that development is an integral part of WIPO's work. The Committee is also tasked with monitoring, assessing, discussing, and reporting on the implementation of the 45 recommendations of the Development Agenda. Additionally, it is responsible for coordinating with pertinent WIPO bodies, addressing IP and development-related issues, and handling other matters as decided by the General Assembly.[18]

The ACE was instituted by the WIPO General Assembly in 2002 and its primary responsibility is to provide technical assistance and coordination in the IP enforcement domain. Although norm-setting is not within the ACE mandate, the Committee concentrates on collaborating with both public and private entities to address counterfeiting and piracy issues. Its efforts include

---

16 WIPO, *World Intellectual Property Report 2024* (WIPO, 2024).

17 WIPO, *supra* note 1, para. 64.

18 World Intellectual Property Organization, Committee on Development and Intellectual Property, at <www.wipo.int/policy/en/cdip/>, accessed 14 February 2024.

public education and facilitating the exchange of information on enforcement matters.[19]

Other important topics are discussed in less formal settings, such as frontier technologies (i.e., WIPO Conversation on Intellectual Property and Frontier Technologies), protection against unfair competition, future of IP, etc. The WIPO Conversation on Intellectual Property and Frontier Technologies is a broad multi-stakeholder global venue for discussing the influence of frontier technologies on IP rights. Its purpose is to bridge the existing information gap in this rapidly evolving and intricate field, which has a substantial impact on the creation, production, and distribution of economic and cultural goods and services, as well as the economy and society. The seventh session of the Conversation analyzed a wide spectrum of frontier technologies enabling the metaverse. The most recent tenth session of the Conversation, focusing on Generative AI-IP and Outputs, took place in November 2024. Over the years, almost 9,000 people from 172 countries have participated in the sessions of the Conversation, ranging from WIPO member states and academia to IP professionals and businesses.[20]

WIPO's area of work dedicated to IP and Competition Policy examines the global patterns at the intersection of IP, antitrust, and unfair competition. Its responsibilities include active engagement in international competition networks and committees, as well as collaboration with other stakeholders on competition matters associated with IP. The efforts in this area aim to improve comprehension of the relationship between IP and competition policy, foster the exchange of experiences, and encourage dialogue between IP offices and competition authorities.[21]

The Future of IP is one of WIPO's newest areas of work, focusing on issues related to the future evolution of the IP system. It conducts research, offers thought leadership, and provides policy guidance. Its primary objective is to guide WIPO's contributions to emerging global challenges, significant societal inquiries, and pressing issues in the field of IP.[22] *WIPO Pulse* is the first global IP perception survey, which was developed by the Future of IP area. This

---

19 World Intellectual Property Organization, Advisory Committee on Enforcement, at <www.wipo.int/enforcement/en/ace/>, accessed 14 February 2024.

20 WIPO, *WIPO Conversation on Intellectual Property and Frontier Technologies*, available at <www.wipo.int/about-ip/en/frontier_technologies/frontier_conversation.html>, accessed 25 November 2024.

21 WIPO, *Intellectual Property and Competition Policy*, available at <www.wipo.int/about-wipo/en/activities_by_unit/index.jsp?id=1014>, accessed 14 February 2024.

22 WIPO, *Future of Intellectual Property*, available at <www.wipo.int/about-wipo/en/activities_by_unit/index.jsp?id=1045>, accessed 14 February 2024.

novel survey determined the IP beliefs and attitudes of 25,000 people from 50 countries. Some of the most interesting findings of *WIPO Pulse* are that copyright stands out as the most widely recognized IP right globally, while individuals in Latin America and the Caribbean, Asia-Pacific, and African countries tend to perceive greater advantages from innovation and the IP system, compared to consumers in other regions.[23]

2.3 *Current Negotiations*

The meetings of WIPO's committees and decision-making bodies take place regularly and their primary objective involves negotiating changes to existing IP agreements, as well as adopting new treaties, to ensure that the IP system responds to the needs of the fast-evolving world of innovation and creativity.[24]

As of now, WIPO administers 28 treaties, including the WIPO Convention.[25] The WIPO General Assembly of 2022 decided to convene diplomatic conferences in order to conclude two international agreements no later than 2024. One of the proposed agreements refers to the protection of designs to ease cross border trade, while the other one is a pact related to IP, genetic resources (GRs) and traditional knowledge (TK) associated with genetic resources.[26]

The Diplomatic Conference on Genetic Resources and Associated Traditional Knowledge took place at WIPO's Geneva headquarters, from May 13 to 24, 2024. The New Treaty on Intellectual Property, Genetic Resources and Associated Traditional Knowledge was adopted on May 24, 2024, and it seeks to improve the effectiveness and transparency of the patent system. Its objective is to prevent the erroneous granting of patents for inventions that lack novelty or inventiveness concerning GRs and TK linked to GRs.[27]

The diplomatic conference on a design law treaty took place between November 11 and 22, 2024, in the Kingdom of Saudi Arabia. The new treaty on design law strives to simplify the industrial designs protection global system,

23 WIPO, *WIPO Pulse Global intellectual property perception survey* 2023 (WIPO, 2023), pp. 6, 7.

24 WIPO, *Decision-making and Negotiating Bodies*, available at <www.wipo.int/policy/en/>, accessed 14 February 2024.

25 WIPO, *WIPO-Administered Treaties*, available at <www.wipo.int/treaties/en/>, accessed 14 February 2024.

26 WIPO, *WIPO Member States Approve Diplomatic Conferences for Two Proposed Accords* (doc. PR/2022/893, 21 July 2022), available at <www.wipo.int/pressroom/en/articles/2022/article_0009.html>, accessed 14 February 2024.

27 WIPO, *2024 WIPO Diplomatic Conference on Genetic Resources and Associated Traditional Knowledge*, at <www.wipo.int/diplomatic-conferences/en/genetic-resources/index.html>, accessed 14 February 2024.

to make it more accessible, expeditious, and cost-effective for designers to secure protection for their works both domestically and internationally.[28]

The General Assembly decision to convene both diplomatic conferences in 2024 is a testament to the continuous relevance of multilateralism and the importance placed on IP regulation and protection by WIPO's member states.

3 Building an IP System That Works for the Good of Everyone, Everywhere, and for a More Sustainable Future

3.1 *Serving Underserved Communities*

As mentioned above, the MTSP leverages WIPO's strengths, while also introducing a new outlook and emphasis on domains where innovation and creativity, underpinned by IP, can bring positive changes in people's lives, particularly those who historically have been served less by the global IP system.[29] WIPO's objective is to ensure that stakeholders worldwide understand the relevance of IP to their daily lives. It aims to demonstrate how IP can contribute to people's aspirations, be it making a living through creativity and innovation, or contributing to the attainment of the United Nations Sustainable Development Goals (SDGs).[30]

3.1.1 Women

There are still many disparities in the utilization of the IP system among women and other social groups. According to WIPO's data, it is estimated that only 16.2 percent of inventors listed in international patent applications in 2022 were women. Although there is an upward trend in this regard, it is occurring at a very slow pace. Based on current developments, parity among male and female inventors would only be achieved by 2061. WIPO decided to address this gap and speed up the progress of integrating women in the IP and innovation ecosystem.[31]

---

28 WIPO, WIPO Member States Adopt Riyadh Design Law Treaty, available at <https://www.wipo.int/pressroom/en/articles/2024/article_0017.html?utm_source=WIPO+Newsletters&utm_campaign=0556ff4b92-NMD_PressRelease_929_DLT_DC_TREATY_EN_211124&utm_medium=email&utm_term=0_-0556ff4b92-256973098&ct=t(NMD_PressRelease_929_DLT_DC_TREATY_EN_211124)>, accessed 25 November 2024.

29 WIPO, *supra* note 1, para. 4.

30 *Ibidem*, para. 18.

31 WIPO, *Intellectual Property, Gender, and Diversity*, available at <www.wipo.int/women-and-ip/en/>, accessed 14 February 2024.

WIPO appointed a Deputy Director General as its first IP & Gender Champion in 2021.[32] Later, a Senior Advisor on IP and Gender joined the team, emphasizing the high priority attributed to the issue of gender equality by the Organization.

The inaugural IP and Gender Action Plan (IPGAP)[33] was issued in 2023, outlining a strategic roadmap for the Organization's efforts to foster and support women's involvement in IP and innovation. The initiatives outlined in IPGAP aim to raise awareness among more stakeholders regarding the enormous potential of IP and innovation to enhance the lives of women, their communities, and member states.

Some of the most prominent initiatives directed at supporting and empowering women include customized programs for women entrepreneurs around the globe, collaboration with national IP offices to amplify the integration of gender considerations in national initiatives and to promote the exchange of good practices, development of policy and legislative advice for national policymakers aimed at helping bring more women and girls into innovative and creative activities, and data collection and analysis to determine women's participation in the IP system and improve the available knowledge base.[34]

Additionally, WIPO raised awareness on women ingenuity and potential by celebrating women inventors, creators and entrepreneurs around the world during the World Intellectual Property Day (WIPD) 2023. For example, the WIPD Gallery featured talented women from around the world who made valuable contributions in their fields of expertise and are at the forefront of their fields' development. The WIPD 2023 Video Competition collected 90-second videos on why it is important that girls and women are connected to IP and how everyone can benefit from that. More than 180 entries were submitted by participants from 72 countries.[35]

These and other initiatives reflect WIPO's commitment to close the gender gap in the IP system and support women's creative and innovative potential.

---

32 WIPO, *WIPO Patents & Technology Head Appointed Organization's First IP & Gender Champion*, available at <www.wipo.int/pct/en/news/2021/news_0043.html#:~:text=Jorgenson%20will%20officially%20take%20up,Champion%20starting%20in%20October%202021.>, accessed 14 February 2024.

33 WIPO, *WIPO Intellectual Property (IP) and Gender Action Plan* (WIPO, 2023).

34 *Ibidem*, p. 4.

35 WIPO, *World Intellectual Property Day – April 26, 2023*, available at <www.wipo.int/ip-outreach/en/ipday/2023/index.html>, accessed 14 February 2024.

3.1.2 Youth

As young people constitute a substantial portion of the population in many developing nations and present considerable innovative potential, youth engagement constitutes another focus area of WIPO's MTSP. Recognizing youth as the future innovators, creators, and entrepreneurs, WIPO considers it imperative to ensure that they understand the significance and role of IP in their lives and receive the necessary assistance and encouragement to fulfil their aspirations, be it for earning a livelihood through innovation and creativity or for addressing global challenges and sustainable development.[36]

Traditionally, the information and data related to IP often lacked language and format that is easily understandable for youth, making its relevance less apparent to them. This deficiency in accessible educational materials on IP was slowing down the process of integration of young people in the IP system and their engagement in the innovative and creative economy. To address this gap, a Youth Engagement team was formed to bridge the divide between youth and the IP system.[37] More specifically, WIPO designated its first Youth Engagement Facilitator in 2022, establishing a clear pathway for youth involvement in the IP and innovation ecosystem.[38]

WIPO is undertaking various initiatives focused on igniting interest in and promoting awareness about IP among the youth. For example, WIPO dedicated the WIPD 2022 to the theme "IP and Youth: Innovating for a Better Future," marking a successful start in a series of awareness-raising events. The WIPD Youth Video Competition gathered nearly 150 entries from dozens of countries, while the WIPD Youth Gallery featured young innovators and change makers from around the world who were praised for the work they are doing to build a better and more sustainable future.[39]

Another step in the direction of youth empowerment and inclusion by WIPO is to focus on ameliorating the Organization's communication strategies, so that positive messages about IP could reach a broader audience in an impactful way. WIPO prioritizes the use of social media to engage and establish connections with the youth. This approach enables the Organization to humanize

36 WIPO, *supra* note 1, para. 18.

37 WIPO, *Youth Engagement*, available at <www.wipo.int/youth-engagement/en/>, accessed 14 February 2024.

38 WIPO, *Report on the Committee on Development and Intellectual Property (CDIP) and Review of the Implementation of the Development Agenda Recommendations* (doc. WO/GA/56/9, 2023), para. 55.

39 WIPO, *World Intellectual Property Day – April 26, 2022*, available at <www.wipo.int/ip-outreach/en/ipday/2022/index.html>, accessed 14 February 2024.

the concept of IP, share compelling narratives, unveil passion driving innovation and creativity, and illustrate the practical value of IP in everyday life.[40]

In July 2024, WIPO published its first IP Youth Empowerment Strategy, which will guide the Organization's youth empowerment efforts and will champion youth integration in the IP system.[41]

3.2 *Indigenous Peoples and Local Communities*

WIPO's interaction with indigenous peoples and local communities involves various services, programs, and information sharing platforms. The goal of the Organization in this area is to facilitate the active involvement of indigenous peoples and local communities in WIPO's initiatives, aiming to enhance their ability to engage with the IP system and derive benefits. This engagement is also designed to better safeguard TK, GRs, and traditional cultural expressions (TCEs).[42]

A notable example of such programs includes personalized training, mentorship, and matchmaking services that WIPO presently provides to female entrepreneurs from Indigenous and local communities in different regions of the world. These programs equip women with essential skills in IP, business, and life.[43]

Additionally, there is the WIPO Indigenous Fellowship Program, which allows individuals from indigenous and local communities to gain professional experience in the Traditional Knowledge Division at WIPO, addressing matters pertinent to their communities. The WIPO Photography Prize for Indigenous Peoples and Local Communities Youth promotes the creativity of young individuals from indigenous peoples and local communities and encourages them to employ photography as a tool of self-expression, conveying significant messages about their communities and identities.[44]

Finally, various mechanisms and resources are put in place to guarantee the comprehensive and meaningful engagement of representatives from indigenous peoples and local communities in the activities of the IGC. Notably, the

40 WIPO, *supra* note 1, paras. 31, 32.

41 WIPO, WIPO Launches New Youth Empowerment Strategy for Enhanced Youth Engagement, available at <https://www.wipo.int/en/web/youth-engagement/w/news/2024/wipo-launches-new-youth-empowerment-strategy-for-enhanced-youth-engagement>, accessed 25 November 2024.

42 WIPO, *Indigenous Peoples and Local Communities' Engagement*, available at <www.wipo.int/tk/en/engagement.html>, accessed 14 February 2024.

43 WIPO, *supra* note 1, para. 112.

44 WIPO, *Unveiling the Shortlisted Photographs of the 2023 WIPO Photography Prize for Indigenous Peoples and Local Communities Youth*, available at <www.wipo.int/tk/en/news/tk/2023/news_0011.html>, accessed 14 February 2024.

organization of indigenous panels offer a valuable platform for indigenous peoples and local communities' representatives to present their experiences, concerns, and aspirations related to the safeguarding, promotion, and preservation of TK, TCEs, and GRs.[45] At the same time, a WIPO Voluntary Fund supports them financially to take part in IGC and the Intersessional Working Groups (IWGs) meetings.[46]

3.2.1 Small and Medium-Sized Enterprises

SMEs make up 90 percent of the total number of companies around the world. They contribute to more than 50 percent of employment, and account for approximatively 40 percent of the national Gross Domestic Product (GDP) in emerging economies.[47] Despite their significant role, a substantial number of SMEs lack IP knowledge and awareness regarding IP's strategic importance for business expansion. WIPO's objective is to increase the SMEs involvement in the IP system and provide extensive support to this large, yet often overlooked community, guiding them in leveraging IP to bring their ideas to the market.[48]

The WIPO Academy, due to its key position in providing essential IP training and skills development globally, continues to enhance its successful franchising model for IP education. This involves fostering partnerships with national IP institutions and other organizations to extend the reach of WIPO's educational initiatives. A key focus is currently placed on enhancing practical IP application skills and commercialization, with a particular emphasis on catering to entrepreneurs and enterprises, including SMEs.[49]

Additionally, WIPO's MTSP provides for an extensive implementation of national and regional programs that assist SMEs in leveraging IP and innovation for their business expansion and success. In this regard, WIPO develops and provides tools and services, including IP diagnostics for SMEs, which are shared with IP offices, which can then reach out easier to SMEs in their countries and deploy these tools. Such initiatives facilitate an effective incorporation of IP into the SMEs business strategies. Collaboration with government bodies and other intermediaries is also a priority in the integration of IP-related support seamlessly into the existing suite of services for SMEs. For example, WIPO has developed programs such as the Inventor Assistance

---

45 WIPO, *supra* note 1, para. 112.

46 WIPO, *WIPO Voluntary Fund*, available at <www.wipo.int/tk/en/igc/participation.html#:~:text=WIPO%20Voluntary%20Fund&text=of%20the%20Voluntary%20Fund%20are,the%20success%20of%20the%20Fund.>, accessed 14 February 2024.

47 The World Bank, *Small and Medium Enterprises (SMEs) Finance*, available at <www.worldbank.org/en/topic/smefinance>, accessed 20 February 2024.

48 WIPO, *supra* note 1, para. 17.

49 *Ibidem*, paras. 98, 99.

Program and the Patent Drafting Program, which are particularly beneficial for technology-driven SMEs looking to enhance their capabilities in IP commercialization and management, enabling them to use IP more efficiently.[50]

3.3 *IP, Sustainable Development, and the Implementation of SDGs*

WIPO's vision for the future, as described in the MTSP, is shaped by, and reflects the 2030 Agenda for Sustainable Development and its 17 SDGs, aligning with the Organization's position of a United Nations (UN) agency.[51]

The SDGs serve as a roadmap for building a better future for the global community. Unlocking innovation and fostering creativity are essential elements for underpinning this roadmap and addressing global challenges such as climate change, food security, and public health. The global IP system has many potent instruments for transforming innovation and creativity into tangible outcomes, playing a pivotal role in this transformative process.[52]

On global health, for example, WIPO collaborates closely with its trilateral counterparts, the World Trade Organization (WTO) and the World Health Organization (WHO), to formulate common responses to the challenges posed by the COVID-19 pandemic and other global health issues.[53]

Regarding climate change, WIPO faces the task of improving the innovation landscape while facilitating a rapid dissemination of green technologies worldwide. WIPO Green is an interactive platform established by WIPO to foster innovation and the sharing of green technologies. This platform connects providers of green technology and services with those seeking innovative solutions, aiding global initiatives in combating climate change by leveraging the skills and technologies accessible through its network and online database.[54]

To emphasize that IP plays a key role in the achievement of the UN SDGs, WIPO co-organized with Portugal a conference on the theme "Thinking about Industrial Property, Sustainability and the Future of the Planet" in Lisbon, on May 29–30, 2023.[55] Over 350 participants from more than 85 countries joined

50 *Ibidem*, para. 107.

51 *Ibidem*, para. 25.

52 *Ibidem*, para. 54.

53 WIPO, *Global Health and IP*, available at <www.wipo.int/policy/en/global_health/>, accessed 14 February 2024.

54 WIPO, *Climate Change and Intellectual Property*, available at <www.wipo.int/policy/en/climate_change/>, accessed 14 February 2024.

55 WIPO, *Thinking about Industrial Property, Sustainability and the Future of the Planet*, available at <www.wipo.int/edocs/mdocs/mdocs/en/wipo_ip_sdgs_lis_23/wipo_ip_sdgs_lis_23_note.pdf >, accessed 14 February 2024.

the event and reflected on the potential of IP to advance social and economic development.[56]

These and many other initiatives and activities demonstrate WIPO's commitment to the implementation of the SDGs and to building a more sustainable future. The WIPD 2024 had the theme "IP & SDGs: Building our common future with innovation and creativity," and it aimed to raise the public awareness and understanding around the role of WIPO, IP, innovation, and creativity to support and encourage change-makers who are focused on addressing global challenges to make a bigger impact for the benefit of people, communities, and the entire planet.

4 Conclusion

This chapter has described some key developments in WIPO's current course of action and its vision for the future of the global IP system, as set out in the MTSP.

The Organization continues to view IP as its core area of expertise and a valuable tool for promoting innovation and creativity. In addition to that, WIPO is currently focused on simplifying and demystifying IP, supporting all stakeholders involved in grassroots-level innovation and creativity, enhancing multilateral collaboration, and promoting the use of IP as a powerful catalyst for inclusiveness and sustainable development.[57]

Many projects and initiatives have been launched to advance these objectives, and many more are in development. The key consideration of all these activities in various areas is that WIPO is engaged in a transformative journey, which aims to build a more dynamic, open, and engaging global IP system.

---

56 WIPO, *Intellectual Property Will Play Critical Role in the Achievement of UN Sustainable Development Goals* (doc. PR/2023/902, 30 May 2023), available at <www.wipo.int/pressroom/en/articles/2023/article_0005.html#:~:text=Hundreds%20of%20representatives%20from%2085,enabler%20across%20all%2017%20SDGs>, accessed 14 February 2024.

57 WIPO, *supra* note 1, para. 25.

CHAPTER 22

The New Roles of the WTO

Gabrielle Marceau and Maria George***

1 Introduction

The priorities of the international community have shifted owing to global challenges such as climate change, biodiversity loss, environmental degradation, growing populations, and the complex effects of digitalisation. The World Trade Organization (WTO) has responded to these challenges, venturing into new fields previously outside its traditional scope – most notably emerging as a driving force for sustainable development. But there is more; the WTO has also shifted away from an adjudication-focused trade system to a more governance-favoured forum. This shift showcases its evolution into a comprehensive international trade/cross border institution, assuming new functions and a broader role in today's transnational globalization.

Niels Blokker's work on international institutional Law is seminal[1] and frames our modern understanding of how international organizations function. We explore one aspect of this in the context of the WTO: how international organizations evolve. This Chapter identifies and discusses instances where the Organization has embraced new roles, responding to the needs and priorities of its Members and accepting functions beyond its traditional mandate. In 2021, starting with the response to the COVID-19 crisis, the WTO provided an essential forum for transparency, coordination, and collaboration amongst the relevant stakeholders. The Members thereafter formalised the framework for collaboration with the private sector and other actors, beyond the pandemic. In 2022, the emerging priorities of Members, and the important role of the WTO in addressing them, was explicitly recognised by its Members at the twelfth ministerial conference. More specifically, the new roles of WTO in responses to the global challenge of climate change are seen through the

* Gabrielle Marceau, PHD, is [Associate] Professor at University of Geneva. All opinions expressed are only those of the authors, who are solely responsible for any mistake.

** Maria George is a PhD candidate at the Graduate Institute of International and Development Studies, Geneva (IHEID).

1 Most notably H.G. Schermers and N.M. Blokker, *International Institutional Law: Unity within Diversity* (6th ed., Brill, 2018). See also H.G. Schermers and N.M. Blokker (eds.), *Proliferation of International Organisations: Legal Issues* (Kluwer Law International, 2001).

 DOI:10.1163/9789004699939_024

Organization's active participation and leadership at the 28th Conference of Parties of the United Nations Framework Convention of Climate Change in December 2023. Another important aspect of the new roles of the WTO relates to the innovative ways in which the Organization assists its Members, seen through establishment of new funds and linking developing countries' obligations to their capacity to implement/assistance provided. Finally, we briefly detail the discussions surrounding WTO reform, where Members themselves attempt to formalise the new roles of the Organization. Through these sections, we hope to provide evidence of how the WTO has firmly established itself as a governance-favoured forum in responding to the needs of its Members.

2 A Forum for Transparency, Coordination, and Collaboration: Moving from Individual Action to Multilateral Cooperation during COVID-19

The unprecedent scale and impact of the COVID-19 pandemic prompted protectionist tendencies in many countries, including border closures and restriction of exports on essential goods.[2] However, the global nature of the crisis demanded cooperation in our collective response. This section explores how the WTO provided an essential forum, facilitating the shift from individual action towards multilateral cooperation.

2.1 *A Forum for Information Sharing and Promoting Transparency: Basis for Future Cooperation and Mutual Assistance*

In response to the initial export restrictions, the former Director General (DG) of the WTO, Roberto Azevêdo, urged Members to inform the WTO of measures relating to COVID-19 that have an impact on trade.[3] He suggested that the Trade Policy Review Mechanism (TPRM) Secretariat create a database on the specific trade measures implemented in response to COVID-19.[4] As of 30 August 2024, Members have submitted a total of 546 notifications, with the last notification

2 For a list of such restrictive measures, see WTO, *COVID-19: Measures affecting trade in goods*, available at <www.wto.org/english/tratop_e/covid19_e/trade_related_goods_measure_e.htm>, accessed on 6. February 2024.

3 WTO, *Report of the TPRB from the Director-General on trade-related developments*, WTO doc. WT/TPR/OV/W/14 (10 July 2020), para. 1.10.

4 WTO, *Covid-19 and world trade*, available at <www.wto.org/english/tratop_e/covid19_e/covid19_e.htm#measures>, accessed on 6 February 2024.

made by Ecuador on 14 March 2024.[5] This was the first step towards cooperation and mutual assistance, establishing transparency and information sharing between the Members.

2.2 *Facilitator of Collaboration between Intergovernmental Organizations: Coordination in Global Response*

COVID-19 highlighted the inevitable intersections between trade and areas like public health, intellectual property, and investment. Given that the areas of concern were distributed across the mandate of several intergovernmental organizations, coordination of responses was necessary. The crisis also ushered in need to actively assist developing countries in their responses. The WTO acted as a facilitator, promoting collaboration between intergovernmental organizations and ensuring coordination. The following instances are noteworthy:

In June 2021, the heads of the World Bank Group, the International Monetary Fund (IMF), the World Health Organization (WHO) and the WTO established the Task Force on COVID-19 Vaccines, Therapeutics and Diagnostics for Developing Countries. The aim of this collaboration was specifically to establish a 'war room' to track, coordinate and advance delivery of COVID-19 health tools to developing countries.[6]

The WTO, WHO and World Intellectual Property Organization (WIPO) reinforced their long-standing partnership through various initiatives. Notably, a study on an integrated approach to responding to COVID-19 was launched,[7] and a platform to provide technical assistance to Members on accessing vaccines, medicines and technologies was developed.[8]

2.3 *Facilitator of Coordination with Private Sector and of Discussions between Members: Responding to Emerging Issues*

The race to develop and distribute the COVID-19 vaccine highlighted the existing inequalities between developed and developing countries. The crisis

---

5 WTO, *WTO members' notifications on COVID-19*, at <www.wto.org/english/tratop_e/covid19_e/notifications_e.htm>, accessed on 6 February 2024.

6 WTO, *World Bank, IMF, WHO, WTO heads call for urgent action to accelerate global vaccine access*, <www.wto.org/english/news_e/news21_e/covid_30jun21_e.htm>, accessed on 6 February 2024.

7 WIPO, *Promoting Access to medical Technologies and Innovation: Intersections between public health, intellectual property and trade*, at <www.wipo.int/edocs/pubdocs/en/wipo-pub-628e-insert-en-an-integrated-health-trade-and-ip-approach-to-respond-to-the-covid-19-pandemic-update-august-30-2021.pdf>, accessed on 6 February 2024.

8 WHO, *WHO-WIPO-WTO COVID-19 Technical Assistance Platform*, at <www.who-wipo-wto-trilateral.org/en>, accessed on 6 February 2024.

fuelled the tendency for countries to prioritise their citizens first for vaccine distribution, a practice dubbed as 'vaccine nationalism'.[9] However, developed countries had a significant advantage in vaccine development and manufacturing, especially due to their privileged relationship with multinational pharmaceutical companies.[10] Such inequality could be devastating for developing countries. Here as well, there was a dire need to move away from individual action, towards multilateral cooperation. The WTO and DG Ngozi Okonjo-Iweala played a pivotal role in facilitating this shift.

Upon the request of a group of Members, DG Ngozi initiated discussions with the private sector to ensure efficient use of production capacity for COVID-19 vaccines, reduce trade barriers, and facilitate licensing of COVID-19-related medical product patents.[11] The pandemic also disrupted the supply chains of most businesses, particularly micro, small and medium-sized enterprises (MSMEs). This gravely hindered the rapid and equitable distribution of vaccines and other essential products. Recognising the need, DG Ngozi organized meetings with the private sector on supply chain issues related to vaccine manufacturing. Specifically, a technical symposium on global supply chains for COVID-19 vaccines was organised to gain a better understanding of their functionality.[12] She stressed that vaccine policy is trade policy and encouraged private sector actors to ensure fair and rapid access to vaccines.[13]

Similarly, the WTO also played an important role facilitating discussions relating to the Waiver from certain provisions of the TRIPS Agreement for the Prevention, Containment and Treatment of COVID-19 (TRIPS waiver). The temporary waiver, initially proposed by South Africa and India, aimed to ensure timely access to safe, effective, and affordable quality medical products.[14] The DG and Deputy Director General (DDG) Anabel Gonzalez facilitated the difficult negotiations that led to the Ministerial Decision on the TRIPS Agreement

9 Salma Daoudi, "Vaccine Nationalism in the context of Covid-19: An obstacle to the containment of the pandemic", in Policy Center for the New South, *Policy Brief* (2020), p. 2.

10 *Ibidem*, p. 4.

11 Australia, Brazil, Canada, Chile, Colombia, Ecuador, New-Zealand, Norway and Turkey, *Enhancing the Role of the World Trade Organization in the Global Effort Toward the Production and Distribution of COVID-19 Vaccines and Other medical products*, doc. WT/GC/230/Rev.2 (12 April 2021).

12 WTO, *WTO to host technical symposium on COVID-19 vaccine supply chain, regulatory transparency*, at <www.wto.org/english/news_e/news21_e/heal_18jun21_e.htm>, accessed on 6 February 2024.

13 WTO, *DG Okonjo-Iweala: Vaccine policy key to sustainable economic and trade recovery*, at <www.wto.org/english/news_e/spno_e/spno15_e.htm>, accessed on 6 February 2024.

14 India and South Africa, *Waiver from certain provisions of the TRIPS Agreement for the Prevention, Containment and Treatment of COVID-19*, doc. IP/C/W/669 (2 October 2020).

in June 2022.[15] The Decision grants developing country Members the right to "use of the subject matter of a patent required for the production and supply of COVID-19 vaccines without the consent of the right holder to the extent necessary to address the COVID-19 pandemic".[16]

Although the protection of public health is not a function explicitly recognised by the Marrakesh Agreement Establishing the World Trade Organization, the Organization has adapted its functions and responded to the needs of its Members by providing a forum for multilateral cooperation in addressing a global health crisis.

3 Formalising Collaboration with the Private Sector and Other Actors: Beyond COVID-19

The COVID-19 crisis was the birth of the expansive role of the WTO. As seen through the next sections, these new roles were welcomed by WTO Members and were employed to address various global issues beyond the pandemic. The following examples highlight how interactions with the private sector and other non-state actors were formalised and strengthened beyond the response to the COVID-19 crisis.

3.1 *Supply and Distribution Chains*

Drawing from the work relating to global supply chains for COVID-19 vaccines, Members also requested the Organization to address supply chains more generally. Most recently, Members have proposed a draft Ministerial Statement for the 13th WTO Ministerial Conference (MC13),[17] aiming to formalise the role of the Organization in strengthening the resilience and stability of global supply chains.

DG Ngozi's desire to include the private sector more fully in discussions on the proper functioning of supply chains was supported by WTO Members.[18] Accordingly, in 2022 the WTO hosted the Global Forum on Supply Chains, where government representatives, experts and members of the private sector

15 WTO, *Ministerial Decision on the TRIPS Agreement*, doc. WT/MIN(22)/30 (17 June 2022).

16 *Ibidem*, para. 1.

17 China, Lau People's Democratic Republic, and Pakistan, *Strengthening the Resilience and Stability of Industrial and Global Supply Chains*, doc. WT/GC/W/891/Rev.2 (19 February 2024).

18 Brazil and the United States, *Proposal to formalize engagement with the private sector*, doc. G/TFA/W/42/Rev.1 (27 September 2021).

shared their experience and suggestions on supply chains.[19] The aim was to overcome the disruptions to global supply chains on post-COVID-19 economic recovery, while seeking ways to make international trade more resilient.[20]

3.2 *Textiles and FIFA*

A Memorandum of Understanding was concluded between the WTO and the Fédération Internationale de Football Association (FIFA), to facilitate exchange of views and development of joint projects/publications between the organizations.[21] In May 2023, this cooperation was implemented through a joint event on the inclusion of women in football-related value chains, in particular the clothing and cotton industries.[22]

3.3 *Civil Society and Business Advisory Groups*

Collaboration and exchanges with non-state actors were further formalised through two initiatives.[23] The Civil Society Advisory Group brings together representatives of NGOs such as World Wild Fund for Nature (WWF) and the International Trade Union Confederation. The Business Advisory Group brings together players from companies and industry associations such as the International Chamber of Commerce (ICC).

4 Integrating Non-trade Concerns and Multidimensional Challenges: the Results of the Twelfth Ministerial Conference (MC12)

The results of MC12 were an unequivocal acceptance by WTO Members that the new roles of the WTO in response to the COVID-19 were not isolated and ad hoc. WTO Members affirmed their commitment to addressing multi-dimensional

19 WTO, *Easing supply chain bottlenecks for a sustainable future*, at <www.wto.org/english/news_e/events_e/gscforum2022_e.htm>, accessed on 6 February 2023.

20 WTO, *WTO offers unique forum for dialogue on global supply chain issues – DG Okonjo-Iweala*, at <www.wto.org/english/news_e/news22_e/miwi_21mar22_e.htm>, accessed on 6 February 2024.

21 WTO, *WTO, FIFA team up to use trade and football as drivers of economic and social development*, at <www.wto.org/english/news_e/news22_e/igo_27sep22_e.htm>, accessed on 6 February 2024.

22 WTO, *WTO, FIFA event highlights role of football as a tool for trade and women's empowerment*, at <www.wto.org/english/news_e/news23_e/women_01may23_e.htm>, accessed on 6 February 2024.

23 WTO, *DG Okonjo-Iweala sets up civil society and business advisory groups*, at <www.wto.org/english/news_e/news23_e/bus_15jun23_e.htm>, accessed on 6 February 2024.

challenges facing the international community, and the role of the WTO in facilitating the same.

4.1 *Integration of New Priorities within the WTO Framework: Sustainable Development, Digitisation, and Collaboration*

MC12 gave Members an opportunity to identify their emerging priorities and global challenges through the Outcome Document. To highlight a few: Members specifically recognized global environmental challenges of climate change, natural disasters, biodiversity loss and pollution, and reaffirmed the importance of the Sustainable Development Goals (SDGs).[24] They reiterated their support to achieve sustainable development for all Members, in particular developing countries and least-developed countries (LDCs).[25] They also highlighted the importance of economic empowerment of women and the contribution of MSMEs for inclusive and sustainable growth of the multilateral trading system.[26] With respect to digitisation, Members reinvigorated discussions with the adoption of the Ministerial Decision on the Work Programme on Electronic Commerce.[27] They also agreed to maintain the customs moratorium on electronic transmissions until MC13.[28]

In clearly stating such priorities in the Outcome Document, the Members formally welcomed the new role of the WTO in addressing their new priorities and responding to contemporary challenges.[29] Additionally, Members also recognized the need for intensified collaboration with other intergovernmental organizations and external stakeholders in "restoring trust, certainty and predictability in the world economy".[30]

4.2 *WTO as a Governance Forum: Future Pandemics and Food Security*

The efforts made by WTO during the COVID-19 culminated in the adoption of the Ministerial Declaration on the WTO Response to the COVID-19 Pandemic

24 *MC12 Outcome Document* (hereafter referred to as *Outcome Document*), adopted on 17 June 2022, doc. WT/MIN(22)/24 WT/L/1135 (22 June 2022), para. 14.

25 *Ibidem*, para. 2. See also *Ministerial Decision on small economies, WTO, Work Programme on Small Economies – Ministerial Decision*, doc. WT/MIN(22)/25 (17 June 2022).

26 *Ibidem*, para. 13.

27 WTO, *Work Programme on Electronic Commerce – Ministerial Decision*, doc. WT/MIN(22)/32 (17 June 2022).

28 *Ibidem*. Members have agreed to maintain this moratorium on customs duties on electronic transmissions till the fourteenth session of the Ministerial Conference or 31 March 2026, whichever is earlier. See WTO, *Work Programme on Electronic Commerce – Ministerial Decision*, WT/MIN(24)/38 (4 March 2024).

29 *Outcome Document* (*supra* note 24), para. 1.

30 *Ibidem*, para. 12.

and Preparedness for Future Pandemics.[31] Three main tools were identified where the WTO could play a significant role: transparency, regulatory harmonisation, and capacity building for the most vulnerable Members. The declaration also aims to examine the measures taken during the COVID-19 crisis in order to develop best practices.[32]

In response to the urgent food insecurity during COVID-19, Members pledged to continue their efforts in addressing food security challenges as mentioned in the preamble of the Agreement on Agriculture.[33] At MC12, Members set out more specific commitments under the Ministerial Declaration on the Emergency Response to Food Insecurity, namely cooperation and the strengthening of the technical and financial capacities of the most vulnerable Members.[34] Additionally, Members adopted a historic Ministerial Decision not to introduce any prohibitions or restrictions on the export of food products purchased for humanitarian purposes by the World Food Programme.[35]

Subsequently, Members also approved the work program on food insecurity beyond COVID-19, addressing issues like financing concerns that prevent LDCs from achieving their national food security objectives.[36]

4.3 *Fisheries Subsidies Agreement: Evidence of Priority Given to Global Environmental Challenges and Sustainable Development*

The adoption of the Fisheries Subsidies Agreement[37] (FSA) at MC12 was revolutionary owing to its focus on sustainable development and conservation of marine biodiversity, as opposed to strictly trade concerns. It is an important step towards achieving Goal 14 of the SDGs aimed at conservation and sustainable use of the oceans, seas and marine resources.[38] FSA prohibits the granting of subsidies to illegal, unreported, and unregulated fishing,[39] and those relating

31 WTO, *Ministerial Declaration on the WTO Response to the COVID-19 Pandemic and Preparedness for Future Pandemics*, doc. WT/MIN(22)/31 (17 June 2022).

32 *Ibidem*, para. 24.

33 *Agreement on Agriculture*, 15 April 1994, 1867 *UNTS* 410 (entered into force 1 January 1995), preamble.

34 WTO, *Ministerial Declaration on the Emergency Response to Food Insecurity*, doc. WT/MIN(22)/28 (17 June 2022), paras. 3, 9 and 10.

35 WTO, *Ministerial Decision on World Food Programme Food Purchases Exemption from Export Prohibitions or Restrictions*, doc. WT/MIN(22)/29 (17 June 2022).

36 WTO, *Work Programme Pursuant to paragraph 8 of the Ministerial Declaration on the Emergency Response to Food Insecurity*, doc. G/AG/35 (23 November 2022), p. 2.

37 WTO, *Agreement on Fisheries Subsidies*, doc. WT/MIN(22)/33 (17 June 2022) (FSA).

38 UN High Level Political Forum, 4: *Goal 14, Life below water*, at <www.wto.org/english/res_e/booksp_e/omc_un_hlpf22_chap4.pdf>, accessed on 6 February 2024.

39 *FSA* (*supra* note 37), Article 3.

to overexploited stocks.[40] Members have also undertaken to continue negotiations on subsidies relating to overcapacity and overfishing, recalling that the FSA will be terminated if full disciplines are not adopted within four years of its entry into force.[41]

The continuing FSA negotiations provides a useful segue into discussions on the links between trade and working conditions, a highly controversial subject within the WTO. In the Draft text dated 10 July 2024, the use of forced labour by fishing vessels or operators has been explicitly addressed.[42] However, consensus on this issue is still pending.[43]

As seen from the above sections, there is an unprecedented increase in discussions at the WTO on non-trade concerns, both officially within Committees as well as informally in its corridors. Members are welcoming the WTO as a forum to discuss the impacts of trade on other areas like public health, the environment, food security, and even the controversial topic of labour. The next section examines this further in the context of climate change.

5 Initiating and Facilitating Action on Trade and Climate Change

The United Nations Framework Convention on Climate Change (UNFCCC) Conference of Parties (CoP28) held in December 2023 showcases the expansive role of the WTO in addressing climate change. The WTO Secretariat co-led the CoP28 Presidency Committee on Trade, bringing together the United Nations Conference on Trade and Development (UNCTAD), the International Chamber of Commerce, World Economic Forum (WEF) and the Abu Dhabi Department of Economic Development, with one day specifically devoted for trade and climate change: 'trade day'.[44]

During CoP28, the WTO Secretariat launched the *Trade Policy Tools for Climate Action* paper,[45] an operationalization of the World Trade Report 2022.[46] The paper proposes ten trade policy options that may be employed by Members to respond to climate change (for example, tariffs, government procurement,

40 *Ibidem*, Article 4.

41 *Ibidem*, Article 12.

42 *Additional Provisions on Fisheries Subsidies, Draft Text*, TN/RL/W/279 (10 July 2024), Article C.2(a).

43 *Additional Provisions on Fisheries Subsidies, Draft Text, Explanatory Note from the Chair: Addendum*, TN/RL/W/279/Add. 1 (10 July 2024), p. 1.

44 WTO, *WTO Secretariat at Climate Change CoP28*, at <www.wto.org/english/tratop_e/envir_e/wto_cop28_e.htm>, accessed on 6 February 2024.

45 WTO, *Trade Policy Tools for Climate Action* (2023) (hereafter referred to as *Toolkit*).

46 WTO, *World Trade Report 2022: Climate Change and International Trade* (2022).

agriculture policies, trade facilitation, et cetera).[47] Such measures can be incorporated into the Nationally Determined Contributions of Members under the Paris Agreement.[48]

The WTO also collaborated with other intergovernmental organizations and the private sector for several initiatives. First, a Task Force of intergovernmental organizations comprising of OECD, IMF and World Bank led by the WTO was launched to develop a common methodological approach to carbon pricing and carbon markets.[49] This is in continuation of the technical workshop organised by the WTO Secretariat in March 2023, where a new analytical framework for variable national carbon pricing (universal tax) was presented to Members, suggesting the creation of a technical assistance fund.

Second, the WTO and International Renewable Energy Agency launched the *International Trade and Green Hydrogen Report*.[50] This report outlines actions for policymakers, inter alia in addressing trade barriers along the green hydrogen supply chain, developing a sound quality infrastructure for green hydrogen trade, and fostering international cooperation on green hydrogen.

Third, the "Steel Standards Principles" were developed by the WTO in collaboration with standard setting bodies, intergovernmental organizations, and the private sector, establishing common methodologies for measuring greenhouse gases (GHG) emissions in the iron and steel sector.[51] The WTO had previously organised the Trade Forum on Decarbonization Standards in the Steel Sector, which similarly brought together Members, intergovernmental organizations, and the private sector at the WTO.[52]

As seen above, even though the WTO has previously taken steps towards bridging the gaps between the two regimes, the participation and leadership at CoP28 was crucial in reframing trade as an essential part of the solution to climate change.

---

47 *Toolkit* (*supra* note 45).

48 *Ibidem.*

49 Reuters, *WTO launching global carbon price task force – Okonjo-Iweala*, at <https://www.reuters.com/sustainability/wto-launching-global-carbon-price-task-force-okonjo-iweala-2023-10-17/>, accessed on 6 February 2024.

50 WTO and IRENA, *International trade and green hydrogen: Supporting the global transition to a low-carbon economy*, at <https://www.irena.org/Publications/2023/Dec/International-trade-and-green-hydrogen-Supporting-the-global-transition-to-a-low-carbon-economy>, accessed on 6 February 2024.

51 WTO, *Steel Standards Principles* (1 December 2023), at <https://www.wto.org/english/tratop_e/envir_e/steelstandprincippartner_e.htm>, accessed on 6 February 2024.

52 WTO, *Trade Forum for Decarbonization Standards: Promoting transparency and coherence in the iron and steel sector* (9 March 2023), at <https://www.wto.org/english/tratop_e/tbt_e/tbt_09032023_e/tbt_09032023_e.htm>, accessed on 6 February 2024.

6 Funds and Implementation Facilities: Ensuring That All Members Have the Means to Participate in International Trade

WTO has a long history of providing technical assistance and know-how to developing country and LDC Members. Recently, the WTO has expanded these efforts under newly negotiated agreements. A prime example is the creation of the WTO Fisheries Funding Mechanism, providing technical assistance and capacity-building under the FSA.[53] The mechanism has been operational since November 2022, and Japan was the first donor with a donation of just under 90 million yen.[54] Similarly, a global carbon fund with a carbon pricing scheme to support adversely affected countries from climate change has also been discussed.[55]

Even before the new FSA, the WTO Trade Facilitation Agreement Facility evidenced redoubling of efforts with respect to assistance.[56] The facility is dedicated to supporting developing countries with their notifications under the Agreement, offering capacity-building support and providing resources for trade facilitation projects.[57] A similar mechanism is proposed under the new Investment Facilitation for Development Agreement.[58]

These mechanisms also demonstrate a growing tendency to align the obligations of developing countries and LDCs with their capacities, and capacity-building measures, as outlined in Articles 13.2 and 14.1(c) of the Trade Facilitation Agreement. Overall, through such new roles the WTO seeks to ensure that all Members, including LDCs, have the resources and capacity to implement agreements.

7 WTO Reform Discussions: Recognition of Emerging New Roles

Discussions around 'WTO reform' generally involve proposals by Members to improve the functioning and effectiveness of the Organization. The MC12

53 WTO, *Fisheries Funding Mechanism*, at <www.wto.org/english/tratop_e/rulesneg_e/fish_e/fish_fund_e.htm>, accessed on accessed on 6 February 2024.

54 WTO, *Japan is first donor to WTO Fisheries Funding Mechanism*, at <www.wto.org/english/news_e/pres23_e/pr918_e.htm>, accessed on 6 February 2024.

55 WTO, *World Trade Report 2022: Climate Change and International Trade*, Chapters C and D.

56 WTO, *Trade Facilitation: IV. Technical assistance and capacity building*, at <www.wto.org/english/tratop_e/tradfa_e/tradfa_e.htm>, accessed on 6 February 2024.

57 WTO, *Trade Facilitation Agreement Facility, The Facility*, at <www.tfafacility.org/facility>, accessed on 6 February 2024.

58 *Investment Facilitation for Development Agreement*, doc. INF/IFD/RD/136 (6 July 2023), Article 39.10.

Outcome Document reiterated that Members would "work towards achieving necessary reform of the WTO".[59] As seen below, either by way of specific reform proposals, or through 'reform by doing', Members recognise some aspects of the new roles of the WTO. There is an ongoing debate regarding the scope of reform, whether it pertains solely to the WTO's operating processes and procedures or extends to changes in substantive rules, like FSA. Some differentiate between 'modernization' of substantive rules and institutional reform.[60] This section focuses specifically on the latter.

7.1 *Specific Member Proposals on WTO's Deliberative Function*

Several Members have made proposals to strengthen the WTO's deliberative function. This was already envisaged in 2018 by Canada[61] and reiterated in 2023 in a communication from the European Union (EU), which takes a broader view of the WTO's deliberative function as helping to demonstrate the Organization's relevance as "key international forum for global trade governance".[62] The proposals suggest reinforcing the role of chairpersons, improving meeting agendas including virtual entries, databases, meeting processes, time limits for interventions et cetera. The proposals also aim to improve transparency and reinforce notification requirements. In April 2023, Australia also put forward proposals to maximize the value of future Ministerial Conferences.[63]

7.2 *Reform by Doing in Committees: Integrating Institutional Reforms and Modernizing Rules*

WTO Members have proposed various ways of improving the functioning of specific Committees, for example the Council for Trade in Goods and its subsidiary bodies.[64] The US recently made recommendations to organize agendas more efficiently, giving priority to new items for discussion.[65] This has been

59 *Outcome Document* (*supra* note 24), para. 3.

60 See European Union, *Annex to the Communication by the Commission: Trade Policy Review – An Open, Sustainable and Assertive Trade Policy*, EU doc. COM(2921) 66 (18 February 2021), p. 10.

61 Canada, *Reinforcing the Deliberative Function of the WTO*, doc. JOB/GC/211 (14 December 2018).

62 European Union, *Reinforcing the Deliberative Function of the WTO to Respond to Global Trade Policy Challenges*, doc. WT/GC/W/864 (22 February 2023), para. 7.

63 Australia, *Maximising the value of WTO Ministerial Conferences*, doc. WT/GC/W/873 (27 April 2023).

64 Argentina, Colombia, Ecuador, Paraguay and Uruguay, *Functioning of the CTG and its subsidiary bodies*, doc. JOB/CTG/21/Rev.1 (22 February 2023).

65 United States and Thailand, *Improving the operation of the General Council and Heads of delegation/Trade Negotiations Committee*, doc. WT/GC/W/872/Rev.1 (24 July 2023).

termed 'reform by doing', a process of continuous innovation and evaluation of working procedures in WTO councils and committees.

With respect to the new roles of the WTO, communications on the 'development' aspect of reform highlight Member expectations regarding WTO's ideal functioning. In February 2023, India proposed the development of institutional mechanisms for information exchange and coordination between the Committee on Trade and Development (CTD) and other WTO bodies, as well as an institutional mechanism for reporting the work of the CTD to the General Council.[66]

The substantive work of the regular committees is also changing to encourage exchanges between Members on new subjects. For example, the discussions in the Committee on Trade and Environment, providing an important forum for international governance. The EU's Carbon Border Adjustment Mechanism (CBAM) has been discussed in multiple WTO committees in addition to the Committee on Trade and Environment. With the entry into force of CBAM in May 2023, discussions on this subject have intensified in the WTO Committees.[67]

The evolution of work in the regular committees demonstrates that the subject of reform has seized the entire WTO, and not just the heads of delegation or special negotiating groups.

7.3 *Reform by Doing: Joint Statement Initiatives (JSIs) and New Forms of Negotiating*

With a view to facilitating the negotiation of new rules on issues where consensus is not forthcoming, like-minded WTO Members have begun discussions in sub-groups within the framework of Joint Statement Initiatives (JSIs). Although the legality of JSIs has been challenged as incompatible with the principle of consensus,[68] the discussions are continuing. The initiatives are open to all Members and enable dynamic discussions to take place on a variable-geometry basis: specific issues are addressed in sub-groups, and subsequently become the subject of large-group discussions under the banner of consensus. Four issues are the focus of the negotiation JSIs: e-commerce, investment facilitation for development, domestic regulation of services,

66 India, *Committee on Trade and Development mandate: focal point for consideration and coordination of work on development in the WTO*, doc. WT/GC/W/865 (24 February 2023).

67 European Union, *Regulation (EU) 2023/956 of the European Parliament and Council of 10 May 2023 establishing a carbon border adjustment mechanism*, doc. JOB/130/52 (16 May 2023).

68 India and South Africa, *The legal status of 'Joint statement initiatives' and their negotiated outcomes*, doc. WT/GC/W/819 (18 February 2021), para. 7.

and MSMEs.[69] With the conclusion of the negotiations on the Investment Facilitation for Development Agreement (IFD Agreement),[70] Members are working towards how the results of the plurilateral JSIs could be incorporated into the broader multilateral architecture of the WTO, or whether they would remain confined to limited participation. At MC13, over 120 Members Parties to the IFD Agreement made a proposal requesting to incorporate the Agreement into Annex 4 of the Marrakesh Agreement Establishing the WTO.[71] Although this formal proposal could not be discussed at length in MC13, the Members Parties to the IFD resubmitted their request in the form of a Draft General Council Decision.[72] However, there was no consensus for the proposal in the last General Council meeting. The JSIs are one example of the new forms of negotiation that recently emerged at the WTO, evidencing the intention of Members to tackle emerging concerns.

The Structured Discussions on Trade and Environmental Sustainability (TESSD) are another example, providing Members an opportunity to exchange views on how to ensure a global trading system that takes the environment into account. They include four working groups on environmental goods and services, subsidies, trade-related climate measures, and the circular economy.[73] Likewise, through the Dialogue on Plastics Pollution and Environmentally Sustainable Plastics Trade, Members can come together to consider ways in which plastics trade can contribute to the fight against plastic pollution.[74] In addition, through the Fossil Fuel Subsidy Reform Initiative, Members and other stakeholders can share experience and technical expertise to limit inefficient fossil fuel subsidies.[75] Members have also set up the Informal Working Group

69 WTO, *Joint Statement Initiatives*, at <www.wto.org/english/tratop_e/jsi_e/jsi_e.htm>, accessed on 7 February 2024.

70 WTO, *Investment Facilitation for Development in the WTO*, at <www.wto.org/english/tratop_e/invfac_public_e/factsheet_ifd.pdf>, accessed on 6 February 2024.

71 WTO, *Draft Ministerial Decision on Adding the Investment Facilitation for Development Agreement to Annex 4 of the WTO Agreement*, WT/MIN(24)/W/25.

72 WTO, *Incorporation of the Investment Facilitation for Development Agreement into Annex 4 of the WTO Agreement*, Communication from the Members Parties to the Investment Facilitation for Development Agreement, WT/GC/W/927 (8 March 2024).

73 See for example Canada and Costa Rica (Coordinators), *Work Plan for 2022*, doc. INF/TE/SSD/W/17/Rev.1 (18 February 2022).

74 WTO, *Plastics pollution and environmentally sustainable plastics trade*, at <www.wto.org/english/tratop_e/ppesp_e/xppesp_e/ppesp_e.htm>, accessed on 6 February 2024.

75 WTO, *Fossil fuel subsidy reform*, at <https://www.wto.org/english/tratop_e/envir_e/fossil_fuel_e.htm>, accessed on 6 February 2024.

on Trade and Gender Equality, which focuses on the inclusion of women in international trade and their economic empowerment.[76]

These new forms of negotiation evidence recognition by Members of the new role of the WTO as a forum for discussion on emerging issues and a platform for building consensus.

8 Conclusion

If the COVID-19 crisis is conceived as the catalyst for the new roles of the WTO, the work undertaken through MC12 in June 2022 cemented Members' acceptance of this expansive mandate of the Organization. Although there is evidence of such expansive roles, the past few years have seen an increase in such functions, with the WTO responding actively to Members' needs. This article discusses the origins, evolution, and specific areas where the new roles and responsibilities of the WTO are evidenced. These functions have moved the WTO away from a purely adjudication-focused trade system to a more governance-favoured forum. This has reframed the Organization as a comprehensive international cross border institution, assuming new functions and a broader role in today's multidimensional geo-political setting.

76 Iceland and Botswana, *Interim Report following the Buenos Aires Joint Declaration on Trade and Women's Economic Empowerment*, doc. WT/L/1095/Rev.1 (25 September 2020), para. 5.

CHAPTER 23

Between Restraint and Enthusiasm

International Organizations' Participation in Advisory Proceedings before the ICJ and ITLOS

Pierre Klein[*]

1 Introduction

The last two years have seen a remarkable upshot in the institution of advisory proceedings, both before the International Tribunal for the Law of the Sea (ITLOS) and the International Court of Justice (ICJ). Three such proceedings have been initiated before the ICJ in 2023 alone – a number equivalent to that of the advisory opinions delivered by the Court over the 14 preceding years. And before both ITLOS and ICJ, recent advisory proceedings have been characterized by an unprecedented degree of participation. No less than 54 States submitted written statements in the context of the proceedings on the *Legal Consequences arising from the Policies and Practices of Israel in the Occupied Palestinian Territory*.[1] Participation in the proceedings on the *Obligations of States in respect of Climate Change* was even more significant, with a total of 82 States submitting written statements[2] and more than fifty States submitting written comments on the other participants' initial pleadings.[3]

But States are not the only actors to make their voice heard in such contexts. International organizations, too, have been very actively involved – more than ever, actually: a total of 11 organization have been authorized by the ICJ to take part in the proceedings concerning the *Obligations of States in respect of Climate Change*, while 10 submitted written statements in the context of the proceedings on climate change before ITLOS.[4] This is in sharp contrast with a number of advisory proceedings which, in the – not so distant – past, elicited

* The author is a Professor, Centre of International Law, Université libre de Bruxelles.

1 See ICJ, Press release 2023/43 of 7 August 2023.

2 See ICJ, Press release 2024/31 of 12 April 2024.

3 See ICJ, Press release 2024/61 of 16 August 2024.

4 See full list at <https://www.itlos.org/en/main/cases/list-of-cases/request-for-an-advisory-opinion-submitted-by-the-commission-of-small-island-states-on-climate-change-and-international-law-request-for-advisory-opinion-submitted-to-the-tribunal/> (last accessed on 18 January 2024).

 | DOI:10.1163/9789004699939_025

very little participation from international organizations – and sometimes none at all.[5] And this trend undoubtedly shows that a considerable amount of water appears to have flowed under the bridge since scholars observed that "in contrast to NGOs, international organizations are hardly baying at the gates of international courts and tribunals demanding a right to be heard […]".[6]

Against that background, it appears particularly timely and opportune to take a closer look at the history and modalities of participation of international organizations in advisory proceedings before the ICJ and ITLOS. We therefore propose to examine in the following pages the legal foundations and practical modalities of such participation (section 2), as well as the scope and contents of the interventions of international organizations (section 3).

2 The Legal Foundations and Practical Modalities of International Organizations' Participation in Advisory Proceedings

The possibility for international organizations to take part in advisory proceedings is envisaged in the rules of both the ICJ and ITLOS. In both cases, however, such participation is not a right;[7] it has to be authorized. According to Article 66(2) of the ICJ Statute – directly inherited from the PCIJ Statute – international organizations will be notified that the Court is prepared to receive written statements or hear oral statements if these organizations are "considered by the Court, or, should it not be sitting, by the President, as likely to furnish information on the question" submitted to the Court. Practically, the Court gives such notification at the outset to the organization from which the request for an advisory opinion emanates.[8] Other international organizations willing to take part in the proceedings have to request the permission

5 See for instance, at the ICJ, the proceedings concerning the *Accordance with International Law of the Unilateral Declaration of Independence in respect of Kosovo* (2010), the *Legality of the Threat or Use of Nuclear Weapons* (1996) or *Western Sahara* (1975).

6 Christine Chinkin and Ruth Mackenzie, "Intergovernmental Organizations as Friends of the Court", in L. Boisson de Chazournes *et al.* (eds.), *International Organizations and International Dispute Settlement: Trends and Prospects* (Brill, 2002), at p. 139.

7 In respect of the ICJ, see e.g. on this Andreas Paulus, "Commentary to Article 66", in A. Zimmerman *et al.* (eds.), *The Statute of the International Court of Justice: A Commentary* (3rd ed., Oxford UP, 2019), at p. 1429.

8 For instance the UN in *Legal Consequences of the Separation of the Chagos Archipelago from Mauritius in 1965* (Order of 14 July 2017, para. 1, [2017] ICJ Reports, at p. 283) or the WHO in *Legality of the Use by a State of Nuclear Weapons in Armed Conflict* (Order of 13 September 1993, [1993] ICJ Reports, at p. 468).

to do so[9] – and such requests have so far been systematically accepted by the Court.[10]

Article 133(2) of the Rules of ITLOS provides for a slightly different procedure, which appears in some respects to be more liberal than that of the ICJ. According to this provision, initially designed to apply to advisory proceedings before the Seabed Disputes Chamber but whose application has been extended to all such proceedings before the Tribunal in accordance with Article 138 of the Rules, "[t]he Chamber, or its President if the Chamber is not sitting, shall identify the intergovernmental organizations which are likely to be able to furnish information on the question". These organizations are then notified of the request and invited to make written or oral statements (Article 133(3)). In the *Request for an Advisory Opinion submitted by the Sub-Regional Fisheries Commission*, the Tribunal thus identified a total of more than 50 international organizations it deemed susceptible of furnishing information on the question submitted by the SRFC.[11] Of these, only six ultimately took part in the proceedings. This, in any event, does not prevent organizations which have not been identified beforehand by ITLOS to request a permission to submit written or oral statements. Such has for instance been the case of the African Union (AU), the International Seabed Authority and the Pacific Community in the climate change proceedings before the Tribunal.[12]

While ITLOS rules refer specifically to "intergovernmental organization", the language used in Article 66(2) of the ICJ Statute is more open: it mentions, in general terms, "international organizations". In theory, nothing would therefore have prevented – or would currently prevent – the Court to develop a broad interpretation of these terms, and to include non-governmental organizations in the categories of actors susceptible of furnishing information to the judges.[13] Such has however very generally not been the case and in spite of suggestions to the contrary,[14] only intergovernmental organizations have

9 See for instance the African Union's request to participate in the proceedings concerning the Chagos (Order of 17 January 2018, [2018] ICJ Reports, at p. 8).

10 In the only instance where the Court initially refused to grant such a permission (when the Organization of African Unity requested the authorization to take part in the proceedings on the *Legal Consequences for States of the Continued Presence of South Africa in Namibia notwithstanding Security Council Resolution 276* (1970), it ultimately reversed its decision and authorized the OUA's participation (see Paulus, *supra* note 7, p. 1435).

11 Order of 24 May 2013, *ITLOS Reports 2013*, p. 202.

12 See, respectively, the orders of 15 February 2023 and 30 June 2023.

13 Paulus, *supra* note 7, p. 1435.

14 *Ibidem.*

been accepted as participants in advisory proceedings before the ICJ.[15] The only significant exception in that respect so far has been the Court's decision to authorize the participation of the International Union for the Conservation of Nature (IUCN) in the climate change advisory proceedings.[16] This is in spite of the fact that States and governmental agencies comprise only 14% of IUCN's membership, the rest being composed of hundreds of NGOs, indigenous peoples organizations, academic institutions and business organizations.[17] One may assume that this decision was somehow influenced by that of ITLOS to authorize the IUCN to take part in two different advisory proceedings before the Tribunal, in 2014 and 2023.[18] Be that as it may, it certainly is not problematic in view of the open language used in Article 66(2) of the Court's Statute.

Neither is, for that matter, the ICJ decision to authorize six workers' and employers' organizations to make written contributions to the proceedings, pursuant to the demand made by the International Labour Organization's Governing Body in its request for an advisory opinion on the *Right to Strike under ILO Convention No. 87*.[19] The Court referred in that case to the "particular tripartite structure" of the ILO and to the fact that those six organizations have been granted general consultative status by the Governing Body. This decision is of course very much in line with those of the Permanent Court of International Justice which, on five occasions in the 1920s and 30s, authorized various workers' organizations to take part in advisory proceedings before that Court whenever issues concerning international labour law were at stake.[20]

It should finally be noted in that respect that participation of NGOs in advisory proceedings, be it before the ICJ or ITLOS, is not altogether excluded. At

15 See already Chinkin and Mackenzie, *supra* note 6, at p. 140.
16 See ICJ, Press release 2023/29 of 14 June 2023.
17 See Danilo B. Garrido Alves, "The Concept of International Organization in the Practice of the International Court of Justice", *EJIL Talk!*, 27 July 2023 (available at <https://www.ejiltalk.org/the-concept-of-international-organization-in-the-practice-of-the-international-court-of-justice/>, last accessed on 18 January 2024).
18 The *SRFC* and *Climate* advisory proceedings respectively.
19 Order of 16 November 2023, para. 4.
20 See *Designation of the Workers' Delegate for the Netherlands at the Third Session of the International Labour Conference* (Advisory Opinion of 31 July 1922); *Competence of the ILO in regard to the International Regulation of the Conditions of the Labour of Persons Employed in Agriculture* (Advisory Opinion of 12 August 1922); *Competence of the ILO to Examine Proposals for the Organization and Development of the Methods of Agricultural Production* (Advisory Opinion of 12 August 1922); *Competence of the ILO to Regulate Incidentally the Personal Work of the Employer* (Advisory Opinion of 23 July 1926); *Interpretation of the Convention of 1919 concerning Employment of the Women during the Night* (Advisory Opinion of 15 November 1932).

the ICJ, Practice Direction XII provides that while written statements or documents submitted by NGOs in advisory proceedings are not considered part of the case file, they may nevertheless be referred to by States or intergovernmental organizations participating in the proceedings and are kept at their disposal "in a designed location in the Peace Palace".[21] And at ITLOS, statements submitted by NGOs are made available on the Tribunal's website along those submitted by States and international organizations, even though they are identified as "not [being] part of the case file"[22] – the distinction between these various types of statements thus becoming very formal.

3 The Scope and Contents of the Interventions of International Organizations in Advisory Proceedings

As noted by Andreas Paulus in his commentary to Article 66 of the ICJ Statute, the scope and purpose of States and international organizations participation in advisory proceedings appears to have been conceived of in a rather restrictive way: "the purpose of Article 66 consists in the collection of information rather than the involvement of States and international organizations in their own right".[23] This can be seen as a reflection of the will to establish a clear distinction between contentious and advisory proceedings. In the latter, there should be – under that conception at least – no "parties" as such, but rather what may be characterized as "interested participants", willing to assist the Court by providing "information" susceptible of shedding a light on the matter submitted to the Court. The terms "furnish information" certainly are telling in that respect, hinting at a kind of "neutral" contribution to the Court's work.

Obviously, it did not take long for practice to belie this conception of the participation of States – to begin with these – in advisory proceedings. In many instances, the questions submitted to the Court reflect the existence of an – often deeply seated – underlying dispute between two or more States. And the written and oral statements made by States in such contexts go most often far beyond furnishing "information" to the Court. In many instances, they are

21 See <https://www.icj-cij.org/practice-directions>, last accessed on 19 January 2024.

22 See, for the climate change advisory proceedings, <https://www.itlos.org/en/main/cases/list-of-cases/request-for-an-advisory-opinion-submitted-by-the-commission-of-small-island-states-on-climate-change-and-international-law-request-for-advisory-opinion-submitted-to-the-tribunal/>, last accessed on 19 January 2024.

23 Paulus, *supra* note 7, p. 1429.

virtually undistinguishable from the argumentations developed in the context of contentious proceedings.[24]

What about international organizations? The picture that emerges from a detailed examination of their participation in advisory proceedings before ITLOS and the ICJ reveals a wide degree of variation. In many cases, such participation strictly remains within the confines of the relevant provisions governing the matter and is very deliberately limited to "furnishing information" to the judges. In others, participating international organizations develop full-fledged legal arguments, taking a firm legal stance on the issues concerned by the request. And one can of course also find intermediate positions between these extremes. Interestingly, practice shows that the same organization can opt for very different approaches to the substance of its participation in advisory proceedings, according to the issues at stake.

Regardless of the degree of participation in these proceedings, international organizations are very often adamant to emphasize their particular expertise in the area covered by the proceedings,[25] but are also careful to recall their strict adherence to the principle of speciality. In the *Climate* advisory proceedings before ITLOS, for instance, the International Maritime Organization emphasized that it was "in a position to provide views only within the scope of its status as a specialized agency of the UN".[26]

Maybe as I imagined Niels taking a break from academic chores on the shores of the North Sea near Leyden on a warm summer day, I was driven to an aquatic/maritime metaphor to envisage the various degrees of participation of international organizations in advisory proceedings, from "staying dry on the beach" to "diving in" …

3.1 *Staying Dry on the Beach: Furnishing Information in Strict Neutrality*

The first step of the ladder – furnishing information in strict neutrality – is probably best epitomized by the practice developed by some organizations to

---

24 Precedents such as the *Western Sahara*, *Wall*, *Kosovo* and *Chagos* advisory proceedings are certainly cases in point in that regard.

25 See for instance, in the *Climate* proceedings before ITLOS, the written statements of the Pacific Community (at para. 2), of the United Nations Environment Program (at paras 5 and 6) and of the International Seabed Authority (at p. 10), all available at <https://www.itlos.org/fileadmin/itlos/documents/cases/31/written_statements>, last accessed on 2 February 2024).

26 IMO written statement, at para. 15 (available at <https://www.itlos.org/fileadmin/itlos/documents/cases/31/written_statements/2/C31-WS-2-3-IMO.pdf>, last accessed on 2 February 2024).

provide a "dossier" comprising documents that are deemed likely to shed a light on the matter concerned by the request. This has, in particular, been a frequent practice of the United Nations in advisory proceedings before the ICJ. In the case concerning the *Chagos*, for instance, the UN Secretariate submitted close to 500 such documents covering all facets of the issue before the Court.[27] The UN did not, however, submit a written statement conveying any legal position of the organization on that issue. And when it did submit such a statement 15 years earlier in the *Wall* case, it was only to complement and update information provided in the dossier that had been submitted some time before by the Secretariate.[28]

In the same vein, when it took part on two different occasions in advisory proceedings before ITLOS, the Food and Agriculture Organization took great care to emphasize that the statement it submitted was intended to be "factual in nature", only providing "technical information aimed at assisting the Tribunal".[29] The organization clearly sees a limited role for itself in such a context, mentioning that the written statement "does not interpret provisions of treaties nor States' obligations under international law [since] [t]he authority to definitively interpret treaties and obligations thereunder lies with the Parties to those treaties".[30] Logically, in that perspective, the FAO does not propose any response to the question(s) submitted to the Tribunal and merely describes the legal instruments adopted within the organization that may be of relevance to the issue concerned. Such is also the position taken by the International Maritime Organization in the climate change proceedings before ITLOS, based on the same reasoning.[31] And such was already the position of the ILO, many decades ago, in the *Effects of Awards of Compensation*

27 See <https://www.icj-cij.org/index.php/case/169/request-advisory-opinion>, last accessed on 19 January 2024); see also the – very – bulky dossier (more than 1800 documents …) submitted by the UN in the proceedings on the *Legal Consequences arising from the Policies and Practices of Israel in the Occupied Palestinian Territory*, available at <https://www.icj-cij.org/case/186/request-advisory-opinion>, last accessed on 6 September 2024.

28 Written statement of the United Nations, 29 January 2004, available at <https://www.icj-cij.org/sites/default/files/case-related/131/1557.pdf>, last accessed on 19 January 2024).

29 Written statements of the FAO in, respectively, the *SRFC* advisory proceedings (at para. 5; available at <https://www.itlos.org/fileadmin/itlos/documents/cases/case_no.21/written_statements_round1/C21_Written_Statement_1_FAO.pdf>, last accessed on 2 February 2024) and *Climate* advisory proceedings (at para. 3; available at <https://www.itlos.org/fileadmin/itlos/documents/cases/31/written_statements/3/C31-WS-3-2-FAO.pdf>, last accessed on 2 February 2024).

30 *Ibidem* (climate change), at para. 4.

31 IMO written statement, *supra* note 26, at para. 19.

Made by the United Nations Administrative Tribunal case at the ICJ,[32] suggesting that restrictive conceptions of the role to be played by international organizations in advisory proceedings are deeply ingrained in their culture (or at least within the UN system).

On various occasions, international organizations have explained the impossibility to take a more assertive stance in the context of such proceedings by the fact that their members did not share a common position over the question referred to the court or tribunal. A prime example would be that of the World Health Organization, whose legal counsel argued in the hearings on the *Legality of the Use by a State of Nuclear Weapons in Armed Conflict* that the organization was facing a "delicate task, different from that of the other Parties", in reason of the absence of consensus among its membership over the issue before the Court.[33] The positions of its member States having sometimes been "diametrically opposed", the WHO felt bound to observe a "position of strict neutrality" in the proceedings.[34] This was already, almost word for word, the position expressed by the same organization some 15 years earlier in the case of the *Interpretation of the Agreement of 25 March 1951 between the WHO and Egypt*,[35] for identical reasons. More recently, in the *Sub-Regional Fisheries Commission* case before ITLOS, the Pacific Islands Forum Fisheries Agency similarly stated that it did not have the intention to reply to several of the questions raised in the request for an advisory opinion, "[a]s there may be a range of views within the FFA membership on these questions".[36]

Finally, it may also be noted that the limited degree of participation of a given international organization has sometimes been justified by the specific task that the organization in question was entrusted with in the context of the matter brought before the Court. Such was for instance the case for the UN in the *Interpretation of Peace Treaties with Bulgaria, Hungary and Romania* case. In his speech before the Court on behalf on the Secretary General,

32 Memorandum by the International Labour Office, *in CIJ, Mémoires, plaidoiries et documents* (*Effects of Awards of Compensation Made by the United Nations Administrative Tribunal, Advisory Opinion of 13 July 1954*), at p. 48 (available at <https://www.icj-cij.org/sites/default/files/case-related/21/9035.pdf>, last accessed on 19 January 2024).

33 Hearings of 30 October 1995, CR 95/22 (Claude-Henri Vignes), at p. 20 (our translation).

34 *Ibidem.*

35 Oral statement of Claude-Henri Vignes on behalf of the WHO, 20 October 1980, at p. 216 (available at <https://www.icj-cij.org/sites/default/files/case-related/65/065-19801021-ORA-01-00-BI.pdf; last accessed on 2 February 2024).

36 Written statement of the Pacific Islands Forum Fisheries Agency, at p. 1 (available at <https://www.itlos.org/fileadmin/itlos/documents/cases/case_no.21/written_statements_round1/C21_Response_Round_1_FFA.pdf>, last accessed on 30 January 2024).

Dr Kerno thus explained that the UN's participation in the proceedings would not go beyond a factual account of the situation that gave rise to the request.[37] This was justified by the fact that, in accordance with the treaties at stake, the Secretary General could be asked to nominate the third member of a commission for the settlement of disputes arising from the application or interpretation of those treaties. Against that background, any position taken by the UN on the questions referred to the Court could have affected the Secretary General's impartiality in the views of the parties to those treaties.[38]

In other instances, however, international organizations opted for a more active participation to advisory proceedings – without, for that matter, getting fully involved.

3.2 *A Toe in the Water: Contributing to the Debate*

The participation of some organizations in the *Climate* advisory proceedings before ITLOS is a case in point here. In its written statement, the Pacific Community (SPC) provides a – brief – analysis of the obligations of UNCLOS State parties in respect of climate change.[39] On that basis, rather than formulating responses to the questions addressed to ITLOS, the SPC "respectfully requests that the advisory opinion […] includes the aforementioned dimensions on the observed effects of climate-related ocean changes on coastal systems and communities".[40] In a similar fashion, the UN Environment Program (UNEP) identifies the relevant rules of UNCLOS and the rules of international law that must, in its opinion, be taken into account for the interpretation of the relevant provisions of UNCLOS.[41] But UNEP, too, does not suggest precise responses to the questions. It rather makes suggestions as to the way the questions should be approached by the Tribunal, submitting for instance that "in the context of considering States' obligations under [UNCLOS] to address the causes and impacts of climate change, human rights, and in particular the General Assembly's recognition of the right to a clean, healthy and sustainable environment, may be of particular relevance".[42]

Such contributions remain pretty much in line with the initial concept of international organization (and State) participation in advisory proceedings

37 Oral statement of Dr Kerno on behalf of the UN Secretary General, 20 February 1950, at p. 256 (available at https://www.icj-cij.org/sites/default/files/case-related/8/008-19500228-ORA-01-00-BI.pdf, last accessed on 30 January 2024).

38 *Ibidem.*

39 Written statement of the Pacific Community, *supra* note 25, at pp. 8–9.

40 *Ibidem*, at p. 10.

41 Written statement of UNEP, *supra* note 25, Chapter 3.

42 *Ibidem*, at para. 67.

reflected in the relevant provisions of the ICJ Statute and ITLOS Rules: they are largely aimed at "furnishing information", even if they also go slightly beyond that in suggesting a particular treatment of the question(s) addressed to the court or tribunal. But in a number of instances, international organizations have proved to be much more assertive.

3.3 *Diving in: Proposing Complete Responses to the Question(s) Addressed to the Court or Tribunal*

Just as States taking part in advisory proceedings are very often as wholeheartedly engaged as they would be in contentious cases, international organizations have sometimes emerged as very active participants in advisory contexts.

In various cases before the ICJ and ITLOS, several international organizations have submitted (sometimes very) comprehensive written statements, providing a detailed analysis of the issues at stake and developing elaborate legal arguments. Most often, they not only formulated precise responses to the questions referred to the court or tribunal, but also expressed an opinion on issues of jurisdiction and propriety – strongly pushing back, when needed, against any suggestion that the court or tribunal should decline to exercise its advisory jurisdiction.[43] And on some occasions, those organizations submitted not only written statements, but also written comments in response to arguments made in the first rounds of written pleadings by other participants in the proceedings.[44]

43 See for instance in that respect the written statements of the Caribbean Regional Fisheries Mechanism in the *SFRC* case before ITLOS (at paras. 46 ff.; available at <https://www.itlos.org/fileadmin/itlos/documents/cases/case_no.21/written_statements_round1/C21_Response_Round_1_CRFM.pdf>, last accessed on 2 February 2024), of the International Union for the Conservation of Nature (at paras. 7 ff.; available at <https://www.itlos.org/fileadmin/itlos/documents/cases/31/written_statements/2/C31-WS-2-2-IUCN.pdf>, last accessed on 2 February 2024) and of the African Union (at paras 65 ff.; available at <https://www.itlos.org/fileadmin/itlos/documents/cases/31/written_statements/2/C31-WS-2-7-African_Union.pdf>, last accessed on 2 February 2024) in the *Climate* case before ITLOS, of the League of Arab States (at paras. 2.3 ff.; available at <https://www.icj-cij.org/sites/default/files/case-related/131/1545.pdf>, last accessed on 2 February 2024) and of the Organization of the Islamic Conference (at paras. 2 ff. available at <https://www.icj-cij.org/sites/default/files/case-related/131/1589.pdf>, last accessed on 2 February 2024) in the *Wall* case before the ICJ and of the African Union in the *Chagos* case before the ICJ (paras 29 ff. available at <https://www.icj-cij.org/sites/default/files/case-related/169/169-20180301-WRI-07-00-EN.pdf>, last accessed on 2 February 2024).

44 Such was for instance the case of the African Union, which submitted written comments totaling 85 pages in the *Chagos* advisory proceedings (available at <https://www.icj-cij.org/sites/default/files/case-related/169/169-20180515-WRI-01-00-EN.pdf>, last accessed on 2 February 2024). In the *Climate* advisory proceedings before the ICJ, no less than eight

Any concern for "neutrality" or "impartiality" is then put aside – and in the *Chagos* case, the AU even recalled in some detail the active role it had played within the UN in earlier episodes that led to the adoption of the request for an advisory opinion.[45]

In contrast with the situations examined hereabove, where divisions among their members are the reason put forward by some organizations for not expressing any views on the substance of the questions referred to the court or tribunal, the organizations that engage more fully in advisory proceedings sometimes legitimize their strong and principled participation by the fact that they are acting on behalf of their member States – and sometimes even on behalf of the latter's populations. In the *Chagos* proceedings, the AU thus claims to be "representing its constituency".[46] And in the *Climate* proceedings before ITLOS, the same organization emphasizes that it is acting "on behalf [...] of the African States and peoples".[47]

References to the organization's mandate and responsibilities also emerge as a significant factor of legitimation of their action in such contexts. In the *Chagos* case, the AU thus explains that the organizations' membership "considers that the resolution of the questions asked to the Court constitute a matter of systemic importance in international law" and that it has a "direct interest in the [...] proceedings, as the situation in the Chagos archipelago has a direct and detrimental impact on one of the member States of the Union".[48] Similarly, in the proceedings concerning the *Occupied Palestinian Territory*, the Organization of Islamic Cooperation recalled that its Charter included among its objectives support for the Palestinian people in the exercise of their right to self-determination.[49] The OIC explained that it was therefore "hardly surprising that [the Organization was] particularly mindful of and profoundly concerned by the deterioration in the situation of the Palestinian people [...]."[50] Under such circumstances, participation in the advisory proceedings – and the expression of a strong position on the question(s) referred to the court or tribunal appears to be seen as a duty of the organization.

---

international organizations submitted written comments (see ICJ, Press release 2024/61 of 16 August 2024).

45 *Ibidem*, at para. 2.

46 *Ibidem*, at para. 21.

47 Written statement of the African Union, *supra* note 44, at paras. 3 and 339.

48 *Ibidem*, at paras. 9 and 11 respectively.

49 Written statement of the Organization of Islamic Cooperation, at para. 3, referring to Art. 1(8) of the OIC Charter, available at <https://www.icj-cij.org/sites/default/files/case-related/186/186-20230724-wri-13-00-en.pdf>.

50 *Ibidem*.

This is probably even better illustrated by the positions expressed by the United Nations in various proceedings where issues closely related to the core missions or functions of the organization were at stake. As early as 1949, in the *Reparation* case, the UN presented detailed legal arguments in the oral hearings before the ICJ and submitted clear and complete responses to the questions referred to the Court. This was justified by the "essential interests" of the Organization that the Secretary General saw as being at stake in these proceedings.[51] In the *Namibia* case, some twenty years later, the UN also fully engaged in the proceedings, making both written and oral statements, and expressing positions on all issues before the Court (including questions of jurisdiction and propriety). In his written statement, the Secretary General recalled that the Organization had "special responsibilities towards the people and territory of Namibia", since the territory had been endowed with an international status as of 1946, under the authority of the UN.[52] In his oral statement before the Court, the representative of the Secretary General explained that the latter felt "that it is his special duty to comment upon certain of the points raised mainly in one statement which, if accepted, would have profound, in fact possibly disastrous, effects upon the structure, functioning and constitutional practices of the United Nations [...]".[53] The same pattern was subsequently followed in the *Mazilu* and *Cumaraswamy* cases. In both, the UN submitted comprehensive arguments and proposed clear responses to all issues before the Court. In the *Mazilu* case, the UN legal counsel emphasized that the question on which an advisory opinion was requested was "of particular importance and interest to the United Nations".[54] And in the *Cumaraswamy* case, the full participation of the UN was even more evident, in view of the fact that the proceedings were akin to a contentious case, the matter having been referred to the Court in accordance with Article 30 of the Convention on the Privileges and Immunities of the UN. The UN was therefore in the same position there as any party in a bilateral dispute before the Court.

51 See the oral statement of Dr Kerno on behalf of the Secretary General (at p. 51; available at <https://www.icj-cij.org/sites/default/files/case-related/4/004-19490307-ORA-01-00-BI.pdf>, last accessed on 2 February 2024).

52 Written statement of the UN Secretary General, at para. 40 (available at <https://www.icj-cij.org/sites/default/files/case-related/53/9367.pdf>, last accessed on 2 February 2024).

53 Oral statement of Mr Stavropoulos on behalf of the Secretary General (at p. 31; available at <https://www.icj-cij.org/sites/default/files/case-related/53/053-19710127-ORA-01-00-BI.pdf>, last accessed on 2 February 2024).

54 Oral statement of the legal counsel, at p. 234 (available at <https://www.icj-cij.org/sites/default/files/case-related/81/081-19891004-ORA-01-00-BI.pdf>, last accessed on 2 February 2024).

4 Conclusion

This survey of the participation of international organizations in advisory proceedings before the ICJ and ITLOS thus evidences wide variations in their degree of involvement – not only from one organization to the other, but also over time for specific organizations (the UN certainly being a prime example). The main factor susceptible of explaining these variations appears to be the legitimacy of such participation, as it is perceived by the organization itself (here embodied by its chief administrative officer, or secretariate). Two main sources of legitimacy may be identified in the discourses of international organizations in those proceedings:

– the first one may be characterized as "technical," when detailed references are made to the mandate of the organization (clearly intersecting with the issue before the court or tribunal) and/or to the particular (often scientific) expertise developed within the organization on the question(s) referred for an advisory opinion; the discourses of organizations such as the IUCN, UNEP or the International Seabed Authority, mentioned above, provide typical examples of this type of legitimation;
– the second one may be identified as "legal/political", whenever international organizations explain that there are representing their member States (or even the latter's populations) and defending their interests (as the AU did on several occasions) and/or that they are acting for the preservation of fundamental principles and values they are tasked to protect (such as the UN in the *Namibia* case). In such a context, the participation of the organization in such proceedings may probably also be seen as an instance of self-legitimation,[55] in the sense that such participation may contribute to convincing national or regional audiences that the organization concerned is acting effectively on the international scene to ensure the defence of the interests of member States (and, in some cases, their populations).

Whether based on one or the other (or a combination) of these factors of legitimacy, a more engaged participation of international organizations in such proceedings appears possible only when a sufficient degree of consensus can be achieved among member States. This is clearly confirmed by the examples of the WHO, and of the UN in more recent proceedings where the issue referred to the ICJ gave rise to controversies and divisions within the organization.

55 See generally on this concept Henning Schmidtke and Tobias Lenz, "Expanding or defending legitimacy? Why international organizations intensify self-legitimation", in *The Review of International Organizations* (2023), available at <https://link.springer.com/article/10.1007/s11558-023-09498-0>, last accessed on 2 February 2024.

Such restraint, on the part of the UN in particular, nevertheless appears somehow paradoxical. It may indeed safely be said that the principles at stake in the *Wall, Chagos, Occupied Palestinian Territory* and *Climate* cases are no less fundamental than those which the Organization claimed to be upholding in the *Namibia* case. The political organs of the UN – the General Assembly in particular – have repeatedly and very clearly expressed their views on these situations. The Secretary General himself does not appear to see his role as limited by constraints of strict neutrality and impartiality, as the various statements he has made in the context of the war in Gaza in 2023–2024 or on the issue of climate change make clear. It is therefore difficult to understand why this does not translate in a more active – and principled – participation of the UN in advisory proceedings before the ICJ or ITLOS. This would make even more sense in a context where "[a]t a time of increased interdependence and complexity in the management of public affairs, the advisory function of the international court [can] play an important role for furthering the common interest of humankind".[56]

---

56 Laurence Boisson de Chazournes, "Advisory Opinions and the Furtherance of the Common Interest of Humankind", in Boisson de Chazournes (*supra* note 6), at p. 108.

CHAPTER 24

Anticipation, or the People That Make the Law of the Sea Convention Work

*Liesbeth Lijnzaad**

1 Introduction

When drafting a broad treaty like the United Nations Convention on the Law of the Sea (UNCLOS)[1] and setting up the bodies and organs necessary to implement the Convention, choices must be made regarding their composition. There are several issues to be addressed: the number of members of these bodies, the required qualifications future members should bring, and various matters concerning representativeness and diversity: the representation of the main legal systems of the world, the geographic distribution of the membership and (increasingly) gender parity. Some of these criteria are general and go to the whole composition of the body, others are specific to the profile of the individual member.

This contribution will address the composition of organs and bodies that consist of individual members in their personal capacity and make the Law of the Sea Convention work. Niels Blokker has always had a keen interest in the unusual and the quirky in the law of international organizations, and the unexpected interpretations of rules that may occur in practice. We expect negotiators to make considered and rational choices, yet it is not clear how this takes place in practice. What if it turns out that ideas and predictions about future work prove to be incorrect as work develops, or when thoughts about the composition of organs prove to have been based on ideas that may have changed? When there is a mismatch between the formal rules on membership and the work to be done?[2] What if the anticipation about future work proves to be incorrect?

* Liesbeth Lijnzaad is a judge at the International Tribunal for the Law of the Sea, and endowed professor of the Practice of International Law at Maastricht University.

1 United Nations Convention on the Law of the Sea, 10 December 1982, 1833 UNTS 397.

2 It has not been investigated, for the purpose of the present contribution, if or how this type of development has taken place elsewhere as well.

© KONINKLIJKE BRILL BV, LEIDEN, 2025 | DOI:10.1163/9789004699939_026

2 Anticipation, or Looking for Relevant Examples?

Even if negotiators complain about tedious negotiations, the slowness of the drafting process, the repetition of arguments or the lack of sleep during complex negotiations, some aspects can be exhilarating: the drafting of institutional structures which will be used during the treaty's life is one such example. This is what negotiators have ideas about and where they can demonstrate their legal, diplomatic and indeed artisanal skills. The development and construction of bodies through which parties establish the architecture necessary for the implementation of the future treaty is a great subject to work on. Creating the bodies that will make a treaty function brings a distinct element of architectural prowess, as such bodies will underpin a treaty's long-term stability or at least that is anticipated.

Yet, new bodies are not created in a void, as in many cases relevant examples may exist that can be used as a model for the new bodies to be created. Using an existing institution as an example has a number of advantages. It is not only about not reinventing the wheel, but also about being able to rely on the successful practice of other bodies – such as referring to existing rules of procedure when setting out to formulate rules of procedures for the new body. However, this presupposes that relevant examples *are* available, and this has not always been the case for all the organs created under the Law of the Sea Convention.

There are of course examples of courts that could be referred to. These could be the institutions such as the Court of Justice of the European Union (CJEU) or the European Court of Human Rights (ECtHR). These have in a way become courts of second instance, given the role of the chambers in ECtHR, or the General Court within the European Union system. The ECJ has 27 judges (one judge per member State of the European Union) and the General Court has 54 judges (two per member State).[3] The ECtHR has 46 judges which also means one for each member State of the Council of Europe, and works in a chamber system.[4] A system in which every member State has one or two judges implies that the membership of a court grows or declines incrementally with changes in the number of States participating in the organization.

This is different for the International Court of Justice (ICJ), the International Tribunal for the Law of the Sea (ITLOS) and the International Criminal Court

3 For the European Court of Justice, see Art. 19 TEU and Art. 252 TFEU; for the General Court see Art. 254 TFEU and Art. 8 Protocol 3 to the Statute.

4 For the European Court of Human Rights, see Art. 20 ECHR, for the composition of the chambers see Art. 26 ECHR.

(ICC) where elections take place for a limited amount of judges' positions. Article 7(1) UN Charter lists the International Court of Justice as one of the principal organs of the United Nations, a provision directly followed by Article 8 which proclaims that the United Nations shall place no restrictions on the eligibility of men and women to participate in any capacity and under conditions of equality in its principal and subsidiary organs. Chapter XIV of the UN Charter then in Articles 92–96 provides a brief description of the work of the ICJ and the obligations following from its decisions. Further detail is to be found in the ICJ Statute, which determines that the Court shall consist of 15 members, no two of whom may be nationals of the same State. The Statute then describes the election process in Article 4, and the nominations process in Articles 5–7 (in reverse order) before returning to the elections process in Articles 8–12. Article 9 refers to the required qualifications of the candidates for the position of judge, as well as the importance of the representation on the court of the principal legal systems of the world. The ICJ Statute indicates in Articles 25–29 that it may work in chambers.[5]

The ICC has 18 judges as described in Article 36(1) of the Statute of the ICC.[6] This Court tends to work in chambers,[7] which is not surprising as it is a criminal law institution which caters to the characteristics of a penal procedure, including the availability of an appeals procedure.

3 Bodies under the United Nations Convention for the Law of the Sea

The UN Convention on the Law of the Sea has established a number of bodies with specific tasks that contribute to the implementation and application of the law contained in UNCLOS. Not all of them are judicial bodies: there are also expert bodies that either make determinations on the basis of geological and hydrographical information (the Commission on the Limits of the Continental

5 The ICJ Statute itself had not been drafted from scratch but is largely based on the Statute of the Permanent Court of International Justice which (already) had a composition of fifteen members in its Art. 3 in the final version of the Statute of 1936. Art. 3 of the Statute of the PCIJ reads: "The Court shall consist of fifteen members". It has been suggested that the number of 15 judges went back to the International Prize Court of Hague Convention XII of 1907 (Art. 14) which was never established. See Mariano J. Aznar and Felix Boos, "Article 3 ICJ Statute", in Andreas Zimmermann a.o. (eds.) *The Statute of the International Court of Justice: a Commentary* (3rd ed., Oxford UP, 2019), pp. 307–313 at para.1.

6 The International Criminal Court started its work on 1 July 2002 after ratification of the Rome Statute by 60 States, see Art. 126 ICC Statute.

7 Art. 39 ICC Statute.

Shelf, CLCS) or have a role in the preparation of secondary rules with respect to deep seabed mining (the Legal and Technical Commission of the International Seabed Authority, LTC). These bodies will be discussed here in relation to their membership including from the perspective of their role and mandate.

3.1 *The International Tribunal for the Law of the Sea*

Annex VI of the UN Convention on the Law of the Sea contains the Statute of the International Tribunal for the Law of the Sea (ITLOS). Article 2 of the Statute indicates that it has 21 independent members, who shall have the highest reputation for fairness and integrity as well as recognized competence in the field of the law of the sea.[8] There may not be two members with the same nationality, and all regional groups of the UNGA will have at least three members each.[9] The meeting of the States Parties to the Convention (SPLOS) has since determined the distribution of the remaining six seats over the regional groups.[10] The jurisdiction of the Tribunal comprises all disputes and all applications submitted to it in accordance with the Convention, and all matters specifically provided for in other agreements conferring jurisdiction on the Tribunal, including if all parties agree disputes concerning treaties already in force and concerning the subject-matter of the Convention.[11]

Article 287 provides for compulsory dispute settlement with a choice out of four methods for the settlement of disputes: ITLOS, the ICJ, arbitration and special arbitration. An example for the Tribunal already existed in the shape of the International Court of Justice, but this was not followed, as many delegations did not consider the ICJ to be an appropriate comparison at the time. Clearly the intention was that the Tribunal should be different from the Court, it was an example not to be followed. Distinguishing between ICJ and ITLOS had a reason: the ICJ was particularly unpopular with developing States at the time of drafting. The drafters of UNCLOS specifically chose to establish the Tribunal alongside the International Court of Justice, and to refer to arbitration

8 Note that the judges of the Tribunal are called members, except for Art. 26 of the Statute.

9 Art. 3(2) ITLOS Statute.

10 SPLOS/201 of 26 June 2009.

11 Artt. 21 and 22 ITLOS Statute; see for example Art. 30 Agreement for the Implementation of the Provisions of the United Nations Convention on the Law of the Sea of 10 December 1982 relating to the Conservation and Management of Straddling Fish Stocks and Highly Migratory Fish Stocks (UNFSA), or Art. 60 Agreement under the United Nations Convention on the Law of the Sea on the Conservation and Sustainable Use of Marine Biological Diversity in Areas beyond National Jurisdiction (BBNJ Agreement).

and special arbitration, thus creating a multiple-choice system through the so-called Montreux compromise.[12]

During the negotiations of the Convention, initially the composition of the Tribunal had been set at 15 members in the Informal Single Negotiating Text (1975). This was raised to 21 members in the subsequent Revised Single Negotiating Text (1976).[13] The reasons given for this number of judges were related to the need for a speedy dispatch of business, the creation of the Seabed Disputes Chamber and other standing or *ad hoc* chambers, as well as the need to ensure the geographical distribution of the members.[14] Thus the Tribunal is a body with 21 Members, which may be extended with 2 judges *ad hoc*. The Tribunal is relatively large when compared to the ICJ or the ICC: the number of judges may to some extent also have been due to the enthusiasm the drafters had for this new institution. Although ITLOS, like the ICJ, does have the possibility to work in chambers, this possibility is rarely used.[15] To date, four contentious cases have been dealt with by special chambers of the Tribunal, and the Seabed Disputes Chamber has dealt with one Advisory Opinion (Case 17, Responsibilities and Obligations of States sponsoring persons and entities with respect to activities in the Area).[16]

The Tribunal has set rules with respect to the handling of the two types of urgent procedures available: provisional measures[17] and the prompt release of ships on the posting of a reasonable bond.[18] These procedural rules imply

12 About Art. 287 see Center for Oceans Law and Policy, University of Virginia, "Article 287 – Choice of Procedure (V)", in *United Nations Convention on the Law of the Sea Online* (Brill Nijhoff, n.d,), par. 287.1–287.8 at pp. 41–45. For the genesis of the Montreux compromise, see Shabtai Rosenne, "UNCLOS III: The Montreux (Riphagen) compromise", in Adriaan Bos and Hugo Siblesz (eds.) *Realism in Law-Making, Essays on International Law in honour of Willem Riphagen* (Asser Institute, 1986), pp. 169–178.

13 Center for Oceans Law and Policy, *ibidem*, "Annex VI Statute of the International Tribunal for the Law of the Sea(V)", para. A.VI.2 at pp. 341–342.

14 See Patrick H.P. Vrancken, "Annex VI Article 2", in Alexander Proelß (ed.), *UN Convention on the Law of the Sea, A Commentary* (Beck, 2017), para. 2 at p. 2238.

15 The Tribunal has two permanent chambers, the Chamber for Summary Procedure (Art. 15(3) ITLOS St.), and the Seabed Disputes Chamber (Artt. 14 and 35–40 ITLOS St.). The Tribunal may form chambers as it considers necessary for particular disputes (these are chambers constituted by the Tribunal for particular categories of disputes), as well as a Special Chamber dealing with a particular dispute if the parties so request.

16 Not all chamber cases have been litigated until the end, one case was withdrawn as participants found other ways to resolve their differences: *Conservation and Sustainable Exploitation of Swordfish in the South-Eastern Pacific Ocean* (Case 7, *Chile v European Union*).

17 See Art. 290 UNCLOS, and Artt. 89–95 Rules of the Tribunal.

18 See Artt. 73(2), 220(7) and 226(1)(b) UNCLOS, and Artt. 110–114 Rules of the Tribunal.

that such urgent proceedings will generally be dealt with within a month. ITLOS has its own specific procedures such as prompt release or provisional measures pending the constitution of an arbitral tribunal that are not available elsewhere, and there have not been concerns about the speedy dispatch of business. The drafters expected a caseload well beyond what has materialized in the more than 30 years the Tribunal has existed. A total of 32 cases over a period of more than 30 years is not a shocking amount of work.

3.2 *Commission on the Limits of the Continental Shelf*

The contemporary definition of the continental shelf is to be found in Article 76 UNCLOS.[19] The (geological) continental shelf as it existed in customary law and under the 1958 Convention on the Continental Shelf has largely been absorbed in the concept of the Exclusive Economic Zone (EEZ), which according to Article 57 of the Convention has a maximum width of 200 nautical miles (nm). The seabed underneath the EEZ belongs to the coastal State, which may exercise its sovereign rights and jurisdiction over the living and non-living natural resources in this maritime space, as follows from Article 56.

However, if a State would have a (geological) continental shelf going beyond those 200 nm, it ought to submit information about that extended continental shelf to the Commission on the Limits of the Continental Shelf (CLCS). Such a claim beyond 200 nm may not exceed 350 nm from the baselines, nor exceed 100 nm from the 2500 m isobath.[20]

Aside from instructions as to how to delineate the extended continental shelf provided in paragraphs 4–7, Article 76(8) refers to Annex II to the Convention which briefly describes the role of CLCS as "making recommendations to coastal States on matters related to the establishment of the outer limits of their continental shelf".[21] As a body, CLCS plays a crucial role in the delimitation of what are marine spaces under the authority of coastal States, and the Area as managed by the International Seabed Authority (ISA).[22]

19 Annex II to the Final Act of the Third United Nations Conference on the Law of the Sea (entitled "Statement of Understanding concerning a Specific Method to be used in Establishing the Outer Edge of the Continental Margin") provides a specific request from the Conference to CLCS relevant to the establishment of the continental margins in the southern part of the Bay of Bengal. See also Surya P. Subedi, "The role of the Commission on the Limits of the Continental Shelf", in David Joseph Attard a.o. (eds.), *The IMLI Treatise on Global Ocean Governance* vol. I (Oxford UP, 2018), at pp. 99–100.

20 Isobaths are lines on charts indicating the depth of the ocean floor.

21 Art. 3(1)(a) Annex II UNCLOS.

22 Art. 1(1) UNCLOS determines: "Area" means the sea-bed and ocean floor and subsoil thereof, beyond the limits of national jurisdiction.

The details of CLCS are in Annex II to the Convention, indicating that CLCS consists of 21 members who will have expertise in geology, geophysics, or hydrography and serve in their personal capacity. Thus, it is also a body with a permanent number of members. The requirements of technical expertise pertain to the individual members of the Commission which as a body should have an equitable geographic representation. There is however no specific requirement for these members to be independent or impartial: the focus is on specialist expertise. The requirement of the adequate geographical representation within the Commission has received some attention in literature, but mostly the question was raised whether, with the types of expertise explicitly mentioned, it had been a smart idea to omit legal expertise from the Commission.[23]

The size of its membership has rarely been discussed. During the negotiations there had been an initial proposal by Canada (in 1976) to have a CLCS membership of 30, to be elected by the Intergovernmental Oceanographic Commission (IOC) of UNESCO. A later redraft of the provision by the United Kingdom (in 1979) downsized the number to 21 for reasons that are hard to trace, and a connection with the IOC did not materialize.

The workload of CLCS soon became an issue of concern.[24] CLCS has attracted an increasing and not anticipated number of submissions from coastal States, far exceeding the predictions about how many States would have continental shelf beyond 200 nm as existed at the time of the drafting of the Convention. States have an interest in their continental shelves and its minerals (such as oil and gas, or manganese nodules), and the possibility to control and manage these natural resources off their coasts. While in 1978 it had been estimated that 35 coastal States would submit a claim to an extended continental shelf, the Commission has by now received as many as 104 submissions,[25] including several revised submissions. 74 States Parties have made submissions, including some submissions by States made jointly.[26] A total of 40 recommendations

23 Subedi (*supra* note 19), at pp. 99–100. See about the absence of lawyers also Andrew Serdy, "Annex II Article 2", in Proelß (*supra* note 14), para. 4 at p. 2072.

24 James Harrison, "The Law of the Sea Institutions", in Donald R. Rothwell a.o., *Oxford Handbook of the Law of the Sea* (Oxford UP, 2017), pp. 373, 382–385. See also Serdy (*supra* note 23), para. 5 at p. 2068.

25 Gwenaëlle Le Gurun, "Le Rôle des Entités établies par la Convention de Montego Bay", in Mathias Forteau, Jean-Marc Thouvenin (eds.), *Traité de Droit International de la Mer* (Pedone, 2017), pp. 128–133.

26 For a summary of the workload of CLCS, see <https://www.un.org/Depts/los/clcs_new/clcs_workload.html>, last accessed 2 April 2024.

have been issues by CLCS so far.[27] The growing number of submissions is in part due to the economic prospects that a continental shelf may hold, which created a rush of claims being put forward. Also, the development of technology in this field has had an impact on the type and amount of information required for a good submission.

This growth put pressure on the principle of States paying for their candidates who were now required to work more often for the Commission than anticipated, as meeting time necessarily grew to deal with more and increasingly complex submissions.[28] The expenses of Commission members (including travel and hotel costs in New York) are to be paid by the State that has nominated them, which may influence their independence.[29] Steps have been taken to extend meeting time of the Commission including for plenary sessions, and to increase the number of sub-commissions. The Commission itself tried to improve 'turn-around time' of the submissions by working more in sub-commissions,[30] and at one point the CLCS chair suggested that with existing working patterns the Commission would likely be busy until 2035. It has been suggested that a Commission working full time would be necessary, but this debate has so far not had a conclusion. The meeting of States parties to UNCLOS suggested to establish a trust fund for the expenses of CLCS members from developing States. This was established by the Secretary General of the United Nations (SGUN), but does not seem to have made a genuine difference to experts from developing States.[31] Another trust fund was later created by the United Nations General Assembly (UNGA) to support developing States in preparing their submissions to CLCS, including training for such work.[32] Consequently, some developed coastal States can already benefit from their extended continental shelf, whereas developing coastal States are not at that stage yet.[33]

27 See the list at <https://www.un.org/Depts/los/clcs_new/commission_submissions.htm>, last accessed at 2 April 2024.

28 Serdy (*supra* note 23), para. 5 at pp. 2072–2073, refers to the problem of the absent members of the Commission.

29 Art. 2(5) Annex II UNCLOS.

30 Artt. 5 and 6 Annex II UNCLOS.

31 For the long road that this discussion had see <https://www.un.org/depts/los/clcs_new/voluntary_fund_membersCLCS.htm>.

32 Annex II to UNGA Res. 55/7 (27 February 2001, UN doc A/RES/55/7), amended by the Annex to UNGA Res. 58/240 (5 March 2004, UN doc A/RES/58/240); and the annex to UNGA Res. 70/235 (15 March 2016, UN Doc A/RES/70/235).

33 Subedi (*supra* note 19), pp. 97–99.

The idea seems to have been that the Commission was being set up for a limited amount of time, that is until all possible claims with respect to an extended continental shelf would have been submitted and had been dealt with. At such a point in time the work would be done, and the Commission could be abolished.[34] Even if, on the drawing board, there is nothing against the idea of considering claims to an extended continental shelf beyond 200 nm as finite, there are many reasons why the end of the work of the Commission is nowhere near being concluded. Seafloors may naturally change or may be badly charted which makes the submission of a claim difficult. Issues with respect to overlapping claims have arisen, as well as situations that are politically complex, or where non-parties to UNCLOS (who as third States are under no obligation to submit their claims to an extended continental shelf to CLCS) may still become parties at a later point in time and may make a submission to an extended continental shelf.

With the benefit of hindsight, it may be observed that the original idea of 30 CLCS members might have helped prevent the huge backlog the Commission has today. At any rate, CLCS is an example of how a rigid number of members, a restrictive system for the expenses of its members, as well as a miscalculation with respect the amount of work that needed to be carried out, have the unfortunate consequence of creating both an overburdened Commission and huge delay in the necessary work.

3.3 *The Legal and Technical Commission of the International Seabed Authority*

During the drafting of UNCLOS Part XI, various suggestions were made with respect to creating specialized advisory organs that might support the work of the Council of the International Seabed Authority (ISA). Eventually two organs survived and Article 163 sets a number of generic rules for both the Economic Planning Commission (EPC) and the Legal and Technical Commission (LTC).[35]

---

34 There is no provision that explicitly states that the work is finite, or at what point in time CLCS could 'close its shop', but this may be implied in the 10 years' time limit in Art. 4 of Annex II UNCLOS. Le Gurun (*supra* note 25) at p. 127: "Elle n'a pas de vocation à durer. En effet, sa disparition est programmée avec la fin de son mandat qui certes ne se produira pas avant plusieurs décennies".

35 Art. 163(1) also established the Economic Planning Commission, which has since been put on hold as a consequence of the 1994 Agreement on Part XI. Section 1(4) of the Annex to the Agreement reads in the final sentence: "The functions of the Economic Planning Commission shall be performed by the Legal and Technical Commission until such time as the Council decides otherwise or until the approval of the first plan of work for exploitation". At this stage steps are being taken to restart the Economic Planning Commission in

As a consequence of the adoption of the 1994 Agreement,[36] the Economic Planning Commission has not come into being (yet) and it was decided that whatever work remained for the EPC would be taken over by the LTC.[37]

Article 163 is followed by two provisions dealing with the two advisory organs separately. Article 165 provides a list of the tasks of the LTC. The LTC has an important role in – amongst others – reviewing plans of work, assessing environmental implications of activities in the Area and the formulation of rules, regulations and procedures. It reports to and works for the ISA Council, at the very start of the legislative process within the Seabed Authority.

Both Commissions have a membership of 15, which may be increased by the ISA Council "having due regard to economy and efficiency". Article 163 gives a general description for the composition of both commissions, as well as the qualifications required for a role on either commission that need to be "adequate" in the area of competence of their commission. States parties should nominate candidates of the highest competence and integrity with qualifications in the relevant fields for the effective exercise of the functions of the commission. These members will hold office for five years and are re-eligible, there is a need to ensure equitable regional distribution and the representation of special interests, and no State may nominate more than one candidate for a commission. There are no provisions referring to either impartiality or independence of the members of the Commissions, further rules relate to the exercise of their function. Rules of procedure as well as on decision-making are to be established by the International Seabed Authority.[38]

Of significance is paragraph 2 of Article 163, stating that "Each Commission shall be composed of 15 members, elected by the Council from among the candidates nominated by the States Parties. However, if necessary, the Council may decide to increase the size of either Commission *having due regard to economy and efficiency*". This is the only provision in the Convention on membership that contains a certain amount of flexibility with respect to membership numbers. An extension of the Commission is possible having due regard

view of the future presentation of a first plan of work for exploitation (doc. ISBA/27/C/25 of 6 May 2022). Operationalization of deep seabed mining is currently under active consideration, and an interim director of the Enterprise has been appointed within the ISA Secretariat, which may imply the return of the EPC (doc. ISBA/27/C/25 of 6 May 2022).

36 Agreement relating to the Implementation of Part XI of the United Nations Convention on the Law of the Sea of 10 December 1982, 29 July 1994, 1836 UNTS 42 (hereafter: 1994 Agreement).

37 E.J. van Doorn, "Article 163", in Proelß (*supra* note 14), pp. 1160–1174 at p. 1172.

38 Art. 163 (9–11) UNCLOS.

to economy and efficiency on the basis of a decision of the Council.[39] The two criteria seem to imply that only if economy *and* efficiency in the work of the Commission are served, may the Commission be extended. These are cumulative requirements, the text suggests, not alternatives. Whether economy refers to meeting costs (of the LTC) or the economy of deep seabed mining is unclear, as is the notion of efficiency: larger meetings are not necessarily more efficient than smaller meetings.

Ever since the first election of the LTC, its membership has been higher than the 15 members mentioned in Article 163(2), with lip service being paid to the relevance of flexibility.[40] Whether this growth of the membership was the consequence of having due regard for economy and efficiency is not clear, as all 22 candidates were considered elected at the very first election. The quorum or the regular size of the membership do not appear to be a maximum membership limit in reality.[41] Also, it has correctly been observed that Article 163(2) does not provide rules as to a reduction of its membership.[42]

Apart from not following the text of the relevant provision, the growth in membership seems to mostly be a consequence of frequent calls for equitable geographical participation on the Commission. That is a puzzling idea as equitable geographical participation is most of all a relative notion: it is not just a matter of more people but of a balance of people and their expertise, skills and backgrounds, which could be achieved within the given number of 15 members as much as with 41 members. While an equitable geographical balance is an important consideration, it is not directly clear how this would fit with the notions of either economy or efficiency in the LTC as the meaning of both

39 Presumably this Council decision is the decision relating to the election of the members of the Legal and Technical Commission, in which the Council in operational paragraph 1 "Decides on an exceptional and temporary basis, and with due regard to economy and efficiency, to increase the election of the members of the Legal and Technical Commission as provided for in the present decision" (ISA Doc. ISBA/27/C/41 of 29 July 2022).

40 ISA Doc. ISBA/27/C/23 of 22 April 2022 in operational paragraph 4 recalls the following with respect to the first election and Article 163(2): "After failing to reach agreement on the balance of regional representation on the Commission, the Council *took advantage of the flexibility* provided in Article 163, paragraph 2, of the Convention and decided to increase the number of seats on the Commission from 15 to 22" (emphasis added). This is an interesting way of reading Article 163(2) which, by pointing out specific considerations, does clearly *not* provide flexibility in general. The composition of the LTC grew from 15 to 22 in 1996, to 24 in 2001, to 25 in 2006 and 2011, to 30 in 2016 and 41 in 2022 respectively.

41 For the quorum, see LTC Rules of Procedure, ISA doc. ISBA/6/C/9 of 13 July 2000, Rule 28.

42 Van Doorn (*supra* note 37), p. 1172: "The Convention does not provide for any decrease in the size of either Commission although such action might very well improve the economy and efficiency".

notions is not addressed in the various Commentaries or other literature about the institutional structure of the International Seabed Authority.

In reality this growth beyond the agreed number of members is directly and increasingly related to the role the LTC has in the workflow towards the establishment of the section of the Mining Code dealing with the exploitation of polymetallic nodules, and its role in reviewing plans of work and contracts for deep seabed mining. These are important activities as the ISA is on the brink of transitioning to commercial deep seabed mining amidst calls for a 'moratorium' on deep seabed mining. It is a strategically important time for States to have people on the LTC who will be able to steer the content of the work, irrespective of the restrictive membership rules in Articles 163 and 165 UNCLOS.

4 Conclusions

It is intriguing that in all three instances discussed, the drafters did get it wrong with respect to the numbers of members of the various organs discussed above. The membership is either too small to do the work (CLCS) or has grown to be unusually large (LTC). Membership grows informally without reference to the given criteria but mostly as a consequence of a political decision (LTC). It is difficult to trace the exact reasons for the choices that were originally made with respect to the number of members, and if so, what the motives were for such choices. Unlike the case of ITLOS, the numbers do not seem to have had a very thorough underpinning: they just 'seemed like a good idea at the time'.

Sometimes negotiators get the numbers wrong in anticipation of how much (or how little) work will end up with the new body. In part this is related to how predictable the future workload of organs can be. A lot of litigation before the Tribunal was anticipated, which explains its large number of judges. This suggested that much litigation would take place before chambers, which in reality is quite rare. Perhaps the drafters thought there would be a lot of litigation about the new Convention, not only because it was new and contained many new law of the sea concepts, but also because of the way in which the Convention had been negotiated as a series of inter-related concessions that had led to a consensus agreement that should not be disturbed as this would mean putting the final solution in danger. From the perspective of preserving the Convention as a crucial agreement, a solid judicial institution was required. This Pandora's Box argument has been important in setting up a system of compulsory dispute settlement. But it overestimated what the future held: not many cases were brought, in part also because of the distributive system of dispute settlement of Article 287, which implied that cases could go to the ICJ, and in many situations to arbitration as the default mechanism.

With CLCS the opposite happened: the likely number of claims to an extended continental shelf was seriously underestimated. Also, the time, expertise and costs it would take for States to formulate their submissions and prepare the relevant documentation was underestimated, as was the time the Commission itself would be spending on the work. The development of the technology required for analysing the extended continental shelf further complicated matters, both for the States concerned as well as for the Commission. With the increasing workload it became clear that the idea that States' whose candidates had been elected would also pay for their expenses while on Commission duty had been a very bad idea: as the work grew, participation in meetings went down which was something that could not easily be repaired by yet another trust fund. These misconceptions meant that the set-up of the Commission and the burden on the individual CLCS members – who are essentially experts on loan – is very heavy, if not unacceptably heavy.

On the other side of the picture there is the Legal and Technical Committee of the International Seabed Authority. From day one, this body has grown well beyond the membership that had been determined in the Convention. Moving away from 15 members on paper already at the very start to 41 members today is an impressive leap. Although the Convention provides a smallish door towards growth of membership, referring to due regard to economy and efficiency, it is a moot point whether the growth has been necessitated by these two criteria or what the relevance of those criteria is now that the membership of LTC has been elected six times, with a tendency to grow at each new election, in spite of language suggesting that this growth was exceptional and without prejudice to future elections.

Perhaps the drafters did not reflect thoroughly on how many people were needed to do the work or what would be the ideal conditions to do the work, or perhaps these discrepancies are specific to the Law of the Sea Convention. In fact anticipation is not the same as a rational prediction of what the future could bring – whether in litigation, in ocean science or in deep seabed mining. What is anticipated may not become reality.

CHAPTER 25

Falling through the Cracks

Exploring the Role of Law in the Interaction between International Organizations

*René Urueña**

1 Introduction

Interaction among international organizations is the rule rather than the exception in global governance. And yet, it has yet to be prioritized by international institutional law. An early and notable exception was Niels Blokker's 2001 essay, which explored precisely the legal issues surrounding the proliferation of international organizations.[1] The piece tackles the challenges of inter-institutional interaction with characteristic clarity, legal acuity, and a wealth of case studies, and concludes that a kind of "inter-organizational principle of good-neighbourliness" might prove useful in providing a legal basis for orderly interaction. Ultimately, Blokker argues, interaction between international organizations is a legally relevant phenomenon that can be fruitfully addressed with international legal tools that go beyond the mere distribution of competencies among organizations and instead consider the broader institutional landscape in which these institutions operate.

Building on this valuable insight, this chapter explores the different roles that law plays in interorganizational interaction. First, law constitutes international organizations as autonomous actors, serving as a 'background norm' that creates the conditions of possibility for interaction. Second, it assigns competencies and distributes rights and obligations for these organizations to operate – that is, the role of international institutional law that will be more familiar to international lawyers. And third, in a context of inter-institutional interaction, international institutional law could (but often does not) provide criteria for assigning 'normative weight' to the decisions of some organizations over the decisions of others. These different roles occur in a context of organizational decoupling, in which organizational practices deviate from their

* The author is Professor of Law, Universidad de los Andes (Colombia).

1 Niels Blokker, "Proliferation of International Organizations: An Exploratory Introduction", in Niels Blokker and Henry G Schermers (eds.), *Proliferation of International Organizations* (Brill Nijhoff, 2001).

 | DOI:10.1163/9789004699939_027

mandates – not as a matter of non-compliance with the founding document, but rather as a strategy for adapting to external pressures arising from interaction with other international organizations.

To make this argument, the chapter first describes the dynamics of decoupling, while the second section explores the three roles of law in the interaction between international organizations described above. Finally, the final section focuses on the role of organizational practices in this interaction and offers some concluding remarks.

2 Organizational Decoupling and International Institutional Law

The law of international organizations has developed little vocabulary to speak of interaction. While innovative contributions, such as Laurence Boisson de Chazournes's courses at the Hague Academy,[2] have given us an important map of possible interactions and their legal problems, we have little to go on in terms of a distinctive legal theory of such interactions. Part of the challenge is that the law of international organizations derives its normative horizon from a principal/agent model in which the main criterion for deciding the legality of organizational behaviour is the mandate of the member states. In this sense, the 'function' of the organization becomes key, as it defines the horizon of what the organization should do and thus provides the normative underpinning to justify most doctrines of international institutional law.[3]

However, when organizations interact, they are not rational, functionally driven actors. Organizational scholars have observed that external pressures (e.g., regulation or civil society activism) make organizations more responsive to their external environment. However, their internal organizational culture is not as responsive to change. Thus, *decoupling* occurs when organizations adopt policies to conform to external pressures in terms of formally stated goals, but fail to change their behaviour in practice. This means that international organizations are semi-open entities; that is, they are fully structured organizations that are nonetheless sensitive to external pressures.[4]

2 Laurence Boisson de Chazournes, "Les Relations Entre Organisations Régionales et Organisations Universelles", in *The Hague Academy of International Law Collected Courses* vol. 347 (Brill, 2011).

3 On the challenges of functionalism in the law of international organizations, see generally Jan Klabbers, "The EJIL Foreword: The Transformation of International Organizations Law", in *European Journal of International Law* (EJIL) vol. 26 (2015), p. 9.

4 The following discussion on international organizations and decoupling is drawn in part from René Urueña, "Interaction between International Organizations", in Jan Klabbers (ed.), *The Cambridge Companion to International Organizations Law* (Cambridge UP, 2022), p. 222.

Through the idiom of 'decoupling', organizational theory has provided a vocabulary to speak of just such phenomena, at least since the 1960s.[5] Classical organization research took a strict functional view of the formal purposes of an organization, in which formal goals were aligned ('coupled') with their practices. However, critical organizational studies soon began to realize that organizations were open to their environment. And, in that open context, organizational practices were decoupled of formally stated goals – not as a problem of incoherence or lack of compliance with internal regulation, but rather as a way in which the organizations adapted to external pressures, while leaving formal goals unchanged.

While a standard insight of organizational sociology, decoupling has been less studied in international organizations. Notably, both international institutional law and most work in organizational ecology consider each organization as a closed unit, not able to adapt.[6] Only recently have ecological studies started to account for processes of organizational openness and adaptation.[7] Similarly, recent work on the United Nations (UN) Security Council[8] and, particularly, two key studies in the field of international financial institutions

5 The following description of decoupling theory is based on P. Bromley and W. Powell, "From Smoke and Mirrors to Walking the Talk: Decoupling in the Contemporary World", in *Academy of Management Annals* vol. 6 (2012), p. 483.

6 Initially, organizational ecology was mostly concerned with issues of entry, permanence and exit of organizations (that is, their birth, life-length, and death) and understood each of these events as function of their environment, without recognizing any internal process of adaptation on behalf of the organization (see, e.g., M. Hannan and J. Freeman, "The Population Ecology of Public Organizations", in *American Journal of Sociology* vol. 82 (1977). Later work on organizational ecology gave more space for adaptation and learning processes by the organizations. Overall, though, ecological international organizations work seems to be draw more from the first mindset than from the second. Underscoring this blind spot in current International Relations scholarship, see C. Downie, "Competition, Cooperation and Adaptation: The organizational ecology of international organizations in global energy governance", in *Review of International Studies* (2021). On the first phases of organizational ecology as field, see T. Amburgey and H. Rao, "Organizational Ecology: Past, Present, and Future Directions", in *Academy of Management Journal* vol. 39 (1996), p. 1265.

7 Downie, *ibidem*, pp. 7–8. Similarly, underscoring the limits of current organizational ecology approach, Kranke has recently applied an "open system" framework (that is, "a relational understanding of organizations as collective actors that interact with and adapt to their environment") to international organization interaction. M. Kranke, "Pathologies of a Different Kind: Dysfunctional Interactions between International Organizations", in *Global Studies Quarterly* vol. 2 (2022), pp. 1, 2. International organizations law seems not to have taken that step yet. See, for example, H. Gött, "Interactions between International Organizations: Approaching a Neglected Governance Dimension", in *International Organizations Law Review* vol. 17 (2020), p. 75.

8 M. Stephen, "Legitimacy Deficits of International Organizations: Design, Drift, and Decoupling at the UN Security Council", in *Cambridge Review of International Affairs* vol. 31 (2018), p. 96.

provide some evidence that the phenomenon is readily visible in international governance. Reviewing all policy conditionality in loan agreements concluded by the International Monetary Fund (IMF) between 1985 and 2014, Kentikelenis, Stubbs and King found that, despite nominally aiming to allow borrowers more space for the protection of labour and social policies, particularly after the 2008 financial crisis, the organization's programs reincorporated, in practice, many of the mandated reforms that the organization claimed to no longer advocate.[9] On a similar vein, Sarfaty's ethnographic research at the World Bank has shown that, despite formally adopting an indigenous population policy in its organizational culture, the Bank's culture failed to buy into the human rights mindset and, rhetorical flourishes notwithstanding, still sees the protection of human rights as marginal to its mandate.[10]

Decoupling implies that an international organization's function, expressed through a legal mandate, is only partially useful to think of the normative horizon of its actions. Put shortly, decoupling means that organizations often do different things than those defined in their mandate, not as a breach of their institutional law, but as behaviour that is somehow not prohibited by it. This is not to say that international organizations go beyond their mandate to exert their inherent powers, as Seyersted's seminal work would have it.[11] In fact, the opposite process is at play: decoupling means that external pressures, and not inherent powers, bring the organization to go beyond their mandate. Instead of turning their gaze within, to their institutional essence, they have to look out, to what other institutions do, and act accordingly. In that context, international institutional law, with its focus on state delegation, provides a particularly poor map of institutional power, and of the effects of such a power on those governed. Decoupling is thus not a problem, but one of several organizational strategies of adaptation and resilience.

9 A. Kentikelenis, Th. Stubbs and L. King, "IMF Conditionality and Development Policy Space", in *Review of International Political Economy* vol. 23 (2016), p. 543.

10 G. Sarfaty, *Values in Translation: Human Rights and the Culture of the World Bank* (Stanford UP, 2012).

11 See F. Seyersted, *Common Law of International Organizations* (Martinus Nijhoff, 2008), at pp. 65–70, 359–362. See, furthermore, the dissenting opinion of Judge Cançado Trinidade in ICJ, *Certain Activities Carried Out by Nicaragua in the Border Area (Costa Rica v. Nicaragua)*, Joinder of proceedings, Order of 17 April 2013, *ICJ Reports* 2013, p. 166, at pp. 173–174.

3 Three Roles of Law in Inter-institutional Interaction

Decoupling, with its underlying concept of a semi-open organization, is a useful starting point to explore the varying roles of law in international organization interaction. Interaction triggers decoupling: it is because the organization interacts with its external environment that the pressure to decouple appears. This process is deeply intertwined with the law. International organizations are constituted by law, but are more than legal regimes: they are autonomous organizations that govern through law.[12] Law plays, therefore, a key role in structuring and regulating interaction, as international organizations use the law to adapt to the pressure to decouple emerging from interaction. In this section, I map three different roles of law in this context: first, law constitutes international organizations as autonomous actors; second, it assigns competences, and distributes rights and obligations for these organizations to operate; and, third, it could play a crucial role in providing a normative criterion to regulate interaction among organizations.[13]

3.1 *International Institutional Law as Background Norm of Autonomy*

In its first role, international law serves as the background norm for international organization interaction. This is, for lack of a better word, a 'deep' process of organizational constitution. This is obviously true for notions of statehood and state consent, through which international law constitutes the building blocks of the international 'reality' that create international organizations. More directly related to the interaction between international organizations, international law also creates the doctrinal vocabulary that allows the very existence of international organizations to be taken for granted. In this regard, the background idea of autonomy is key. Through the vocabulary of international law, the ontological existence of international organizations becomes possible, as does the idea of international organizations as autonomous actors, and not, say organs of a state, parts of decentralized networks, or private actors.

To be sure, functionalism seems not to work as a theory for this kind of proto-law of international organizations, as there is no specific function being

12 As Besson has rightly put it, international organizations are ruled *and* rule by international law. Samantha Besson, *Reconstruire l'ordre institutionnel international: Leçon inaugurale prononcée le jeudi 3 décembre 2020* (Collège de France, 2021), paras. 30–31.

13 This discussion on the different roles of international law in the interaction between international organizations is drawn from a paper the author presented in the workshop *International Organizations Engaging the World* (Helsinki, 2021).

assigned. Instead, the law of international organizations seems to play here a role more akin to that assigned to property rights by Robert L. Hale. For the realist author, the rules that define the rights of property owners are more than recognition of rights to individual actors, but in fact distribute bargaining power between competing interests, and thus power, in society.[14] Similarly, the notion of autonomy distributes bargaining power between the organization, member states, and other actors: states get a strong bargaining position, as their consent is required to create the organization, but then the idea of autonomy gives the organization an enhanced position, as it is able to increasingly adopt decisions without such consent. Third parties, of course, are given no bargaining power at all.

3.2 *International Institutional Law as Distribution of Powers and Competences*

The second role of law in the interaction between international organizations derives from that legally constituted idea of autonomy, and the distribution of bargaining power it entails. International law creates the 'foreground' institutional law; that is, it provides the vocabulary for states to create particular organizations, and provides the doctrinal tools to define how that particular entity will act in the world – for example, by establishing rules applicable to delegated powers, legal personality, funding, internal structure, and internal decision-making powers, among others. This is, in a way, the more familiar face of international institutional law.

Such a delegation of powers around a particular formal function, though, is only the beginning. As we have seen, international organizations are semi-open entities, that need to adapt to their environment (even if their law fails to recognize such a wider environment). In that process, it is likely that their actual practice is decoupled from the formal goals and powers as established, for example, through its constituent document. This process of decoupling does not register in a narrowly functionalist reading of the organization, but it still takes place, through legal means: organ competences are expanded, implied powers are found, international legal personalities are presumed.[15]

---

14 R. Hale, "Bargaining, Duress, and Economic Liberty", in *Columbia Law Review* vol. 43 (1943), p. 603. This reading of Hale is based on D. Kennedy, "The Stakes of Law, or Hale and Foucault", in *Legal Studies Forum* vol. 15 (1991), pp. 327, 332–334.

15 Alternatively, one could make the opposite argument that this kind of behavior would be, in fact, fully explained from a wider functionalist perspective, as the function in this case would be organizational survival. For that argument, see K. Daugirdas, "Review: Advanced Introduction to the Law of International Organizations, Written by Jan Klabbers", *International Organizations Law Review* vol. 13 (2016), p. 396.

Overall, the organization takes advantage of the flexibilities provided by the open-ended texture of international law to adapt to its environment by shifting the shape of its practices, while keeping its overall formal function untouched. Again, this is not a problem of non-compliance with the internal law of the organization, but rather a process of adaptation that is performed through legal interpretation.

Importantly, interaction among international organizations also occurs in this space. That is, the internal law of the organization is not sheltered from interaction – and thus from the pressure to decouple. Part of the stimuli that enters the semi-open organization is the friction with other international organizations, which is dealt with through law. Explicit delegation of powers is an important starting point: some international organizations have explicit provisions concerning powers to engage in external relations, as in the case of ASEAN, which has explicit treaty-making powers,[16] or the East African Community, which has the explicit power to "foster co-operative arrangements with other regional and international organizations whose activities have a bearing on the objectives of the Community".[17] More often than not, though, the friction generated by interaction with other international organizations needs to be internally managed by recurring to the flexibility offered by the internal law of the organization, for example, by finding the implicit power to engage in external relations, as is the case of the European Union.[18]

3.3 *International Institutional Law as a Theory of Relative Normative Weights*

Finally, international institutional law could provide an overarching legal framework for the interaction among organizations – something akin to Niels Blokker's "inter-organization principle of good neighbourliness", described at the beginning of this chapter. To do so, perhaps a productive staring point is to see that international organizations are not discrete utterances of law, but are instead expressions, and form part, of a changing global "regulatory space",[19] in

16 Article 41(7) of the ASEAN Charter.

17 Article 130(3) of the EAC Treaty.

18 See Panos Koutrakos, *EU International Relations Law* (Hart, 2006), pp. 77–91.

19 Leigh Hancher and Michael Moran, "Organizing Regulatory Space", in Leigh Hancher and Michael Moran (eds.), *Capitalism, culture, and economic regulation* (Clarendon Press, 1989), p. 271. On global governance, see Benedict Kingsbury, Richard B. Stewart and Niko Krisch, "The Emergence of Global Administrative Law," in *Law and Contemporary Problems* vol. 68 (2005), pp. 15–61.

which they interact.[20] In this 'space', international organizations seem to have a 'mass' that exerts a certain pull towards them.[21] This phenomenon has been observed before. Thomas Franck noted a similar 'pull', exerted by international norms in his classic theory of legitimacy.[22] In a similar fashion, each organization draws toward it whatever is around: it exerts a sort of 'gravitational pull' that attracts other institutions. The situation of particular international organizations in the global regulatory space is, therefore, the result of a relative equilibrium of all the 'gravitational pulls', as exerted by each and institutions.

We know, though, that some institutions' 'pull' is greater than others, due to funding, prestige or support by powerful states. Thus, beyond describing which international organization has more 'pull', we need a normative criterion to define which international organization *should* have more 'pull' – that is, a normative theory of relative institutional 'weights' in the global regulatory space. International institutional law could provide such a theory drawing, for example, on Franck's work, for whom the normative pull that characterises legitimacy in the community of states features four indicators: (a) determinacy, meaning the literary (text-based) quality of a rule that "makes its message clear";[23] (b) symbolic validation, that occurs when "a signal is used as cue to elicit compliance with a command";[24] (c) coherence, meaning the attribution whereby "distinctions in the treatment of 'likes' be justifiable in principled terms";[25] and, finally, (d) adherence, referring to the "quality of being validated by an infrastructure of rules about rules".[26]

Or we could consider Kingsbury's attempt to fill a parallel void, by arguing that not all practices of global governance can be interpreted as 'law'. Instead, only those practices that fulfil the requirement of 'publicness' can be considered law, and thus entitled to the benefits of using such language (publicness, for his purpose, is "the claim made for law that it has been wrought by the

20 The following discussion of the global regulatory space is based on Rene Uruena, "Temporariness and Change in Global Governance", in *Netherlands Yearbook of International Law* vol. 45 (2014), pp. 19–40.

21 For a similar argument outside the space metaphor, see B. Simma and D. Pulkowski, "Of Planets and the Universe: Self-Contained regimes in International Law", in EJIL vol. 17 (2006), p. 483.

22 Th. Franck, *The Power of Legitimacy among Nations* (Oxford UP, 1990).

23 *Ibidem*, at p. 52.

24 *Ibidem*, at p. 92.

25 *Ibidem*, at p. 144.

26 *Ibidem*, at p. 184.

whole society, by the public, and the connected claim that law addresses matters of concern to the society as such").[27]

Finally, one last strategy could be along the lines of global constitutionalism; that is, evaluating interaction among institutions and their 'gravitational pull' through the prism of certain core legal standards, just as a national constitution limits the exercise of authority in a domestic setting. Many other options are available – regardless of its actual content, I argue that it is important to think of international institutional law in this latter sense, complementing the other two roles described above.

4 International Institutional Law and Communities of Practice

Thinking in terms of a regulatory space allows us to see that a central challenge for international institutional law is to establish a normative theory of weights, according to which it is possible to establish the relative 'weight' that institutions should have in the global regulatory space. But this is a paradoxical task. It seems impossible to derive a normative theory of weights from a criterion that exists outside the practice of the very institutions that are interacting. This task somehow presupposes a point of view that is external to the interaction, which would allow an external observer to apply a threshold of legality, thus defining what international institutional law is. But, in fact, the opposite is true. The law of international organizations is the result of interaction, thus turning paradoxical its task of creating a legal framework for that very interaction.

Building from the insights of the idiom of decoupling, a possible way out of this contradiction is to focus on the *practice* of the international organizations that interact (and not solely in their expressed functions or mandates) and derive a normative theory of weights from such practice.[28] Indeed, the process of interaction is less chaotic than one may expect. Part of the reason behind this surprising stability in interaction between international organizations is a practical 'common sense', that seems to keep together inter-actual structures of governance. Thus, interaction often forms in practice a sense of identity and appropriateness that guides the actions of staff that goes beyond the institution's mandate, or its stated policies, instead allowing decoupling and giving

27 Benedict Kingsbury, "The Concept of 'Law' in Global Administrative Law", in *EJIL* vol. 20 (2009), p. 31.

28 The following discussion of a community of practice is based in part on Urueña, *supra* note 4.

practical predictability and stability to what could otherwise be constant collision between international organizations.

In that context, it seems fruitful to focus on practical reasoning, and the necessary community that accompanies such reasoning: after all, it seems extremely hard to reason practically if one is completely isolated from others. Such was Brunnée and Toope's key insight, inserting the notion of a community of practice in the creation international legal obligation.[29] From this perspective, the most important role of international organizations is not that of lawmakers, but of nodes of interaction of communities of legal practice. Around them, communities gather to create meaning, which in turn creates international institutional law and, with it, a plausible normative theory of institutional weights. The normative criterion emerges not from the outside, but from within: an acceptable theory of institutional weight in the global regulatory space will result from the acceptance of the relevant community of practice.

Of course, a community of practice does not imply homogeneity. Its members often have different, even conflicting, projects and views. This is crucially important in a theory of weight in international institutional law: a community of practice is not constituted by a single goal, but requires common practices as well as a shared understanding of the social meaning of those practices. Such disagreements, though, do not undermine the claim that a community emerges around institutional interaction. The added value of the community of practice approach is that it underscores the fact that, for all the differences in approach and interpretation, all actors in the community shared a minimal understanding, a mutual agreement, on the kind of practice they are engaging with. As Terry Eagleton put it in his introduction to ideology: "conflict presupposes a degree of mutual agreement: we are not politically conflicting if you hold that patriarchy is an objectionable social system and I hold that it is small town in upper New York state".[30] It is such a basic level of understanding that the community of practice is built upon, which is not in contradiction with heated controversy over which international organization should be given more normative weight by international institutional law.

29 J. Brunnée and S. Toope, *Legitimacy and Legality in International Law: An Interactional Account* (Cambridge UP, 2010).

30 T. Eagleton, *Ideology: An Introduction* (Verso, 2007), p. 13.

5 Conclusion

A top-down approach that would impose an overall rule for interaction between international organizations seems difficult to muster. The iterative interaction between international organizations creates a dynamic that is qualitatively different from that of discrete contact. Such interaction is, in that sense, at the centre of a community of practice which, through iterative interactions, shapes learning and thus the behaviour of international organizations. In that context, international institutional law might want to open its scope and consider the scope of interinstitutional interaction. For that purpose, as this chapter has argued, the crucial step is to consider, on the one hand, the wider global regulatory space and, on the other, the problem of decoupling. Only by navigating the challenges posed by interaction in these two fronts, and by pondering how such dynamics challenges the standard narrative of functionalism, will the law of international organizations provide the required grammar for the construction of unity among institutional diversity through law.[31]

---

31 Henry G. Schermers and Niels Blokker, *International Institutional Law: Unity within Diversity* (6th ed., Brill, 2018).

PART 5

Preserving International Organizations

CHAPTER 26

The European Union as a Democratic International Organization

Laurens-Jan Brinkhorst and Jaap Hoeksma***

1 Introduction

Participants in the ongoing debate about the nature of the EU are well-advised to bear in mind the wisdom of the preamble to the 1992 Treaty on European Union (TEU), stipulating that "this Treaty marks a new stage in the process of European integration …".[1] The implication of this recital is that the identity of the EU is not set in stone and may be subject to change. Indeed, 15 years later, in the Treaty of Lisbon, the dynamic nature of the European Union (EU) was again reflected in the preamble, where the Member States expressed the desire "to complete the process started by the Treaty of Amsterdam and by the Treaty of Nice with a view to enhancing the efficiency and democratic legitimacy of the Union and to improving the coherence of its action".[2] The purpose of this contribution in honour of our learned friend and colleague Niels Blokker is to give an impression of the bearing which the architecture of the 2007 Lisbon Treaty has had, and continues to have, on the debate about the nature and the identity of the EU.

---

* Laurens-Jan Brinkhorst was Director of the Europa Instituut, University of Leiden (1965–1967); professor of European Law, University of Groningen (1967–1973); member of the European Parliament (1994–1999); minister of Agriculture (1999–2002) and of Economic Affairs (2003–2006) of the Netherlands.

** Jaap Hoeksma is Constitutional law philosopher, author, developer of the board game called *Eurocracy*.

1 As formulated in the first recital of the Treaty of Maastricht (*Official Journal* C 191, 29 July 1992). Article A, second sentence, of this treaty adds: "This Treaty marks a new stage in the process of creating an ever closer union among the peoples of Europe, in which decisions are taken as closely as possible to the citizen".

2 Treaty of Lisbon amending the Treaty on European Union and the Treaty establishing the European Community (*Official Journal* C 306, 17 December 2007).

 | DOI:10.1163/9789004699939_028

2 Beyond *Bundesstaat* or *Staaten(ver)bund*?

The omens for the Treaty of Lisbon were not particularly promising. It came to replace the rejected Constitution for Europe and was regarded by federalist politicians at best as a mere surrogate thereof.[3] The confusion which this course of events brought about, can be illustrated by the comments of contemporary politicians and judicial authorities. While the President of the European Commission Barroso described the EU on the basis of the new treaty at a press conference in July 2007 as "a non-imperial empire",[4] the Dutch Council of State suggested that the future direction of the EU had become uncertain because its conceptualisation as a polity of states and citizens had been abandoned.[5] At the time it was also observed that the European Union and its Member States formed a new transnational structure with an own and distinct identity.[6] As the constitutional architecture of the EU had a considerable impact on the organisation of society as well, notably as a result of the recognition of fundamental rights and freedoms, it was concluded by the same observer that Europe had changed beyond recognition. This on-going impact on the construction of the polity and the functioning of its societies continues to inspire the debate about the nature of the European Union. Can the EU still be identified in terms of the traditional template of the modern state system – as either a state or an association of states – or has the drive towards ever closer union propelled the polity beyond the prevailing paradigm?

3 A Persistent Political Problem

Recent developments in the EU have given this debate an unexpected urgency. After the entry into force of the Lisbon Treaty on 1 December 2009, the global trend of democratic backsliding hit the EU too. While the United Kingdom decided, pursuant to its Brexit decision, to resume what it perceived to be its full national sovereignty by voluntarily withdrawing from the Union, other member states developed a different strategy.

In alliance with some like-minded Member States, the Hungarian Prime Minister Orbán set out to reform the EU from within. He propagated the view,

---

3 See, e.g., G. Verhofstadt, *The United States of Europe* (Taurus Publ., 2006).
4 J.M. Barroso, Press Conference, Brussels, 10 July 2007, available at Youtube Euractiv.
5 Raad van State [Council of State], *Kamerstukken II* 2007/08, 31 384 (R 1850, nr. 4, para. 2).
6 L.J. Brinkhorst, *Europese Unie en nationale soevereiniteit* (inaugural lecture Leiden, 2008), available at <https://hdl.handle.net/1887/19623>.

and continues to do so, that the EU must be seen as a traditional association of states, which functions within the boundaries of the Westphalian system of international relations. Orbán – who prefers to describe himself as an "illiberal democrat" – insists that efforts by the institutions of the EU to encourage his government to respect the rule of law and the democratic principles of the Union amount to unwanted interference in the internal affairs of a sovereign state. Although the European Court of Justice has explicitly rejected this approach in its seminal Conditionality judgments of 16 February 2022,[7] the Hungarian PM defies both the Court and the other EU institutions. Most recently, in December 2023, he did so by submitting to the Hungarian Parliament the Defence of Sovereignty Act. The aim of this Act was said to be to protect Hungary against foreign influences and against the "increasing unlawful attacks against the sovereignty of Hungary". An 'Office for the Defence of Sovereignty' was to be established, tasked with investigating activities allegedly carried out in the interest of other States or foreign organisations and which might jeopardise the sovereignty of Hungary; as well as organisations using foreign funding to influence the outcome of elections or the will of voters. In practice this would affect human rights activities by NGOs from other Member States and probably even verdicts of the EU Court of Justice. Still in December 2023, the Hungarian National Assembly adopted the Defence of Sovereignty Law.

This development could not remain unanswered, and indeed in February 2024 the European Commission sent a letter of formal notice to Hungary raising its concerns. Finding that the response provided by Hungary was unsatisfactory, in May 2024, the Commission sent a reasoned opinion reiterating its grievances concerning the violation of fundamental rights enshrined in the EU Charter of Fundamental Rights, the internal market fundamental freedoms, and EU data protection legislation. On 3 October 2024 the European Commission decided to refer the matter to the Court of Justice.[8]

In the past PM Orban had succeeded to reduce the impact of EU decision-making by his use of the veto power on major decisions within the EU. But it has now become clear that even in such a case a very large majority of member States can break a deadlock. After multiple meetings the European Council

7 CJEU, judgments of 16 February 2022, *Hungary v European Parliament and Council of the European Union*, Case C-156/21, ECLI:EU:C:2022:97, and *Poland v European Parliament and Council of the European Union*, Case C-157/21, ECLI:EU:C:2022:98.

8 European Commission, *The Commission decides to refer Hungary to the Court of Justice of the European Union considering its national law on the Defence of Sovereignty to be in breach of EU law* (press release, 3 October 2024), available at <https://ec.europa.eu/commission/presscorner/detail/en/ip_24_4865>.

decided to overrule the Hungarian refusal to continue to finance the Ukraine. Thus, it agreed in its meeting of 1 February 2024 on an additional €50 billion package for the Ukraine within the EU budget.[9] It is a sign of newly found EU leadership to indicate that the use of a veto has its limitations, especially when major decisions are at stake.

What do these developments tell us about the current state of the project of European integration?

4 The Westphalian System of International Relations

The key word of the Westphalian system is sovereignty. The modern state system, which emerged in the aftermath of the Middle Ages, is built on the principle of absolute sovereignty. The notion was championed by the French philosopher Jean Bodin, who identified the diffuse sovereignty of the feudal system of the Middle Ages as one of the main conceptual reasons for the endless bloodshed of the religious wars, which plagued the old continent in the 16th and 17th century. He insisted that the law of the land should be crystal clear and that the sovereign should have absolute power to proclaim and enforce it. The substitution of the principle of absolute sovereignty for the medieval concept of feudal power symbolises the transition from the Middle Ages to the Modern Era. Taking absolute sovereignty as its point of departure, the Westphalian system sanctioned war as the ultimate means of conflict resolution between states.

Contrary to claims about the eternity of this template, it may be observed that the two world wars in the first half of the 20th century have taught the old continent in a hard way that absolute sovereignty leads to absolute destruction.

The overriding motive of the six Western-European countries which founded the European Coal and Steel Community in 1951, was that they wanted to break the vicious circle of war. They agreed to share the exercise of sovereignty in exchange for the guarantee of peace between them. The subsequent seventy years of increased cooperation and integration can be seen in this light as a further deviation from the Westphalian system. The process was implemented by various generations in order to construct the foundations for an ever closer union among the peoples of Europe. This is currently resulting in the EU's departure from the Westphalian system.[10]

9 European Council, *European Council conclusions, 1 February 2024*, available at <https://www.consilium.europa.eu/en/meetings/european-council/2024/02/01/>.

10 Klabbers rightly observes that the distinctive hallmark of the EU does not consist of its regionality (see Jan Klabbers, "Institutional Ambivalence by Design: Soft Organizations

Amidst the vast literature concerning the rise and growth of the European polity, some scholars continue to perceive and discuss the current EU in terms of the Westphalian template, even if – in our opinion – the Union has outgrown this model. This academic mindset may explain why the discussion about the nature of the EU is still conducted in terms of the Westphalian categories of either state or association of states.

Admittedly, the EU at first sight appears to meet a number of the criteria for statehood as laid down in the 1933 Montevideo Convention on the Rights and Duties of States.[11] Let us, by way of experiment, see if this is the case in reality.

5 The Population of the EU

The first question that must be addressed in order to determine if the EU can be regarded as a state, is whether it has a population. The treaties governing the European Union, namely the Treaty on European Union (TEU) and the Treaty on the Functioning of the European Union (TFEU), leave no room for doubt. Article 9 TEU stipulates in clear and unambiguous terms that every national of each Member State shall also be a citizen of the Union. In reaction to the rejection of the 1992 Maastricht Treaty by the Danish electorate, the European Council clarified that

> The provisions of Part Two … relating to citizenship of the Union give nationals of the Member States additional rights and protection as specified in that Part. They do not in any way take the place of national citizenship. The question whether an individual possesses the nationality of a Member State will be settled solely by reference to the national law of the Member State concerned.[12]

---

in International Law", in *Nordic Journal of International Law* vol. 70 (2001), pp. 403–421). This essay argues that, while the EU is indeed a regional organization as membership is confined to the European continent, its distinguishing character is constituted by its system of democratic governance. Hence its qualification as a democratic international organization (DIO).

11 W. van Gerven, *The European Union: a Polity of States and Peoples* (Stanford UP, 2005).

12 European Council, *Declaration of Edinburgh* (12 December 1992), p. 53, available at <https://www.consilium.europa.eu/media/20492/1992_december_-_edinburgh__eng_.pdf>.

In political terms the implication is that the introduction of EU citizenship cannot be regarded as a first step towards the creation of a federal State.[13] Taking this historical background into account, it can be concluded that Article 9 TEU answers the question concerning the EU's population in a most unequivocal manner. As a consequence of this construction, the nationals of a Member State, which volunteers to withdraw from the Union in line with article 50 TEU, lose their status of EU citizens.[14] Another remarkable aspect of EU citizenship is that – in the present stage of its evolution – the citizens do not pay direct taxes for the maintenance of their Union.[15]

6 The Territory of the Union

The territory of the Union is addressed in Article 3 TEU, in which the EU promises to give its citizens "an area of freedom, security and justice without internal frontiers".[16] As the Member States have established the EU with the view to give their – and the Union's – citizens an area of freedom, the territory on which the law of the land is applicable consists of the sum total of the territories of the Member States. While in many cases the border controls at the internal frontiers separating the Member States from each other have been lifted, the Union's external borders are becoming more significant by the day.[17] Although the European Border and Coast Guard Agency was founded in 2004 specifically to protect the EU's external borders, it is not entitled to act of its own accord. Sovereignty in the field of border control remains with the Member States and Frontex' mission is merely to support the Member States and the associated countries in the management of the EU's external borders and the fight against cross-border crime. Although the mandate of Frontex is evolving and its missions are increasingly coming under critique, its very existence corroborates the conclusion that the EU has a territory and that its frontiers are marked in line with international law.

13 J. Fischer, *Vom Staatenverbund zur Föderation* (lecture at the Humboldt-Universität Berlin, 12 May 2000).

14 CJEU, judgment of 15 June 2023, *Shindler a.o. v. Council of the European Union*, Case C-501/21 P, ECLI:EU:C:2023:480.

15 A reversal of the American principle 'no taxation without representation', Boston 1765.

16 K. Lenaerts and P. van Nuffel, *EU Constitutional Law* (Oxford UP, 2021).

17 As exemplified by the Belarussian attempts to 'flood the EU with refugees' against the backdrop of Russia's invasion of Ukraine. See Human Rights Watch, *Violence and Pushbacks at Poland-Belarus Border* (7 June 2022), available at <www.hrw.org/news/2022/06/07/violence-and-pushbacks-poland-belarus-border>.

7 The Will to Be a State

In addition, it may be posited that the EU also meets the extra criterium of having the capacity to conduct relations with other participants in the system of global governance. The EU has a High Representative for Foreign Affairs, its own diplomatic service, the EEAS, and numerous embassies in all parts of the world.[18]

At first glance, then, it would seem that, as the EU has a clearly defined population, well-marked and increasingly defended borders, a transparent structure of governance and the capacity to maintain international relations, it fulfils all criteria for statehood set by the 1933 Montevideo Convention. Another argument in favour of statehood that could be brought forward is that the EU also has its own currency, although at present this is not used in each of its Member States.

Despite these most relevant qualities, however, the European Union has never submitted a request for recognition as a State to the United Nations. The reason for this self-restraint is that the EU lacks the will to be a sovereign State in the sense of the Westphalian system of international relations. The EU has been created with the aim to emulate the Westphalian system by introducing a different concept of sovereignty. So, Westphalian sovereignty is not in the DNA of the EU.[19] Legally speaking, Article 4 TEU instructs the EU to "respect the essential State functions of the Member States, including ensuring their territorial integrity". As if to erase any doubt on the issue, the following sentence underlines that "national security remains the sole responsibility of each Member State".

8 The Concept of Sovereignty

The caution which the EU's executive has applied in this respect, has been validated by the Court of Justice in 2014. In its Opinion on the possible accession of the EU to the European Convention for the Protection of Human Rights and Fundamental Freedoms, the Court stated without any reservation that "the EU

18 The Office of the High Representative for Foreign Affairs was established by virtue of the 1997 Treaty of Amsterdam, while the European External Action Service was launched on 1 January 2011.

19 Cf J. Weiler, "Deciphering the Political and Legal DNA of the European Union", in J. Dixon and P. Eleftheriadis (eds.), *Philosophical Foundations of European Union Law* (Oxford UP, 2012). Weiler argues that "democracy is not in the legal DNA of the EU".

is, under international law, by its very nature precluded from being regarded as a State".[20] While this outcome of the process of European integration, which started in the wake of the Second World War, may come as a surprise to those theorists and politicians who unremittingly propagated that it was destined to lead to the creation of the federal State of Europe, it is the result of the EU's fundamental break with the concept of absolute sovereignty as developed by the Westphalian system of international relations.

In defiance of Bodin's claim that sovereignty must be absolute,[21] the precursors of the EU have developed and practised a concept of relative, tamed or shared sovereignty. That does not imply, as Bodin would have suggested in the aftermath of the Middle Ages, that the EU should have abolished the concept of sovereignty altogether. Instead, the EU exercises sovereignty in a different manner. As their countries had been devastated in the first half of the 20th century by two consecutive World Wars, waged on each other by absolute sovereign states, the peoples of Europe cried out that they wanted 'no more war'. Their call was heeded by politicians of six Western-European states, who agreed to rein in absolute sovereignty for the sake of achieving peace. In hindsight, their pragmatism has been exemplary. They decided to make the renewed outbreak of war between them impossible by transferring the exercise of sovereignty over coal and steel – the raw materials indispensable for the conduct of war – to a higher authority. After having established that their revolutionary method worked and that their states had not lost statehood, they broadened their cooperation to the entire economy and later to their constitutional democracies.

Seventy years onward, the practice of shared exercise of sovereignty continues to underlie the functioning of the European Union, which currently consists of 27 Member States and around 450 million citizens. The principle of their cooperation is enshrined in Article 4 TEU, which plainly states that competences not conferred upon the Union remain with the Member States. In addition, Article 5, para. 1, TEU lays down that the limits of Union competences are governed by the principle of conferral. In consequence, Article 5, para. 2, TEU underlines that the Union shall act only within the limits of the competences conferred upon it by the Member States. However, these articles cannot be perceived by the Member State as a licence to act as they please. By signing the 2007 Lisbon Treaty, they have committed themselves to uphold the values of the EU and to recognise the authority of the Union to defend these values,

20 CJEU, Opinion of the Court of 18 December 2014, *Accession of the EU to the ECHR*, Case C-2/13, ECLI:EU:C:2014:2454.

21 J. Bodin, *Les Six Livres de la République* (Paris, 1576).

even against violations thereof by themselves. Intricate as this construction may be, it demonstrates that the EU functions on the basis of a division of competences laid down in the Treaties. The hallmark of the EU from the viewpoint of international law is that it divides the exercise of sovereignty between the Union and its Member States on the basis of treaties.

9 A Democratic International Organization

In hindsight, the evolution of the EU can be divided into three stages. The initial purpose of the Member States of the European Coal and Steel Community was to prevent the renewed outbreak of war.[22] The subsequent European Communities aimed to create an internal market, while the current European Union has been established with the view to function as a European democracy, that is as an unprecedented democratic Union of democratic States. While the creation of the ECSC implied a revolutionary breakaway from the traditional pattern of international organization, the EU has outgrown the Westphalian system entirely. The implication of the verdicts of the European Court of Justice with respect to the conditionality mechanism is that the Member States have voluntarily accepted the EU as a higher authority with the competence to guarantee the continued respect for the values of the Union by the Member States. In a traditional association of states, such actions would amount to an undue interference in the internal affairs of a sovereign State. So, the EU has ceased to rely upon the Westphalian system as guiding paradigm for its internal functioning.

In the present stage of its evolution to an ever closer union among the peoples of Europe, the hallmark of the EU is that it applies the constitutional principles of human rights, democracy and the rule of law in an international organization. By doing so, the EU supersedes the traditional dichotomy between states and international organizations and establishes itself as an innovative subject of international law. In consequence, it is no longer possible to identify the EU in Westphalian terms as either a state or a union of states.

In turn, this conclusion signifies that the EU has also outgrown the traditional debate between the intergovernmentalists and the federalists about the end goal or *finalité politique* of the Union. Hence, the EU's outdated ideologists should bury the hatchet and concentrate on the improvement of the Union as it is 70 years after the start of the process of European integration. In view

22 P.J.G. Kapteyn and P. VerLoren van Themaat, *Introduction to the Law of the European Communities* (1st edition, Kluwer, 1973).

of the fact that the EU has evolved from a 'Union of democratic States' to a democracy of its own, theorists may find it not too difficult to describe the EU in the present stage of its evolution as 'a democratic Union of democratic States'.[23]

Once the Westphalian spell has been broken, the former antagonists may also agree on the identification of the nature of the European Union from the global perspective. In fact, the well over hundred states participating in the Summits for Democracy, which the Biden administration has been organising with a view to highlight the vitality of the democratic model, have already given the answer by allowing the EU as the only regional organization to participate along all but one of its Member States in their gatherings.[24] They do so precisely because they regard the EU as a democratic regional organization. Other regional organizations like the African Union, the Association of Southeast Asian Nations, Mercosur, the Council of Europe or the Arab League do not have democratic aspirations of their own. So, the EU can be identified from the perspective of international law as a 'Democratic International Organization' (DIO).[25]

In the traditional template, known as the Westphalian system of international relations, the term democratic international organization contains an internal contradiction. According to the Westphalian paradigm, international organizations are *a priori* undemocratic. As the gist of this essay is to posit that the EU has outgrown the Westphalian paradigm, the term democratic international organization symbolises the evolution of the EU to a European democracy. The EU can be described from the internal perspective of the citizens as 'a democratic Union of democratic States', while it may be identified from the UN viewpoint of global governance with a new term as 'a democratic international organization'.

The unexpected benefit of this incremental process is that the EU has established itself indeed as a democratic international organization at the moment of its identification as such. It already has a population, a well-defined territory and a unique structure of governance. Moreover, it has developed its own

23 J. Hoeksma, *The European Union: a democratic Union of democratic States* (Oisterwijk, 2021).

24 See *The Summit for Democracy*, available at <www.state.gov/summit-for-democracy>.

25 J. Hoeksma, *The Democratisation of the European Union* (Eleven Publ., 2023). For the sake of academic comparison it may be recalled that Brendan O'Leary launched the term "confederation with consociational characteristics" for this purpose, while Philippe Schmitter proposes the terms "condominio" and "consortio" for the identification of the EU. See P. Schmitter, *The Europolitan Papers*, available at <https://europeangovernanceandpolitics.eui.eu/the-europolitan-papers/>.

institutions, including a directly elected Parliament, a Court of Justice as well as a Central Bank. Imperfect as it may be, the EU works already as a democratic international organization. Time has come for Europeans to learn to handle their own creation and to provide a correct description of the nature of the EU.

10 Global Perspectives

This concise investigation into the nature of the European Union in the present stage of its evolution also yields a result in the domain of the quest for Eternal Peace, to which Rousseau dedicated his essay in the 18th century. The gist of the present contribution to the study and understanding of the EU is that the original aim to prevent the renewed outbreak of war between former archenemies has succeeded so far because they were able and willing to break with the Westphalian principle of absolute sovereignty.

France and Germany had learnt the hard way that absolute sovereignty leads to absolute destruction. While radical federalists argued in the post-war period that the national states had to be replaced with an overarching federal state in order to attain lasting peace, mature scholars like the Dutch historian Huizinga proposed to rein in absolute sovereignty and to use national states in the construction of a new European order.[26] While their approach fitted in practice well with the neo-functionalist method of Schuman and Monnet, their aim reached further than that of the advocates of intergovernmentalism. The conclusion to be drawn from Huizinga's writings is that, in the final analysis, the attainment of perpetual peace is incompatible with the Westphalian system. Almost a century onward, this conclusion has become more urgent than ever. The threat of nuclear war continues to haunt mankind already since the end of the previous war. Moreover, pandemics recognise no borders and climate change may endanger the entire planet. Problems of this magnitude cannot be tackled globally on the basis of a system which is based on the principle of absolute state sovereignty and which sanctions war as the ultimate means of the solution of conflicts between states.

26 J. Huizinga, *Geschonden Wereld* (Haarlem, 1945).

CHAPTER 27

Unity within Diversity: The Continuing Rise of Consensus

Helena Loutas-Paraskeva and Anmol Gulecha***

1 Introduction

Schermers and Blokker, in their seminal work, explained the decline of majority voting and rise of consensus in decision-making within international organizations after 1945.[1] Today, with the proliferation of regional international organizations consisting of diverse Member States, this study aims to build upon Schermers' and Blokker's work to give examples of two such organizations where consensus continues to remain relevant – the European Union (EU) and the Association of Southeast Asian Nations (ASEAN). We will examine the practice of the Council of the European Union and the European Council on the one hand, and the ASEAN Summit and the ASEAN Coordinating Council on the other.

These two organizations have been selected for comparison in this article precisely because of their differences – in terms of membership, geopolitical interests, and decision-making frameworks. The examination of their decision-making processes against the backdrop of these differences will contribute to an interesting study. Further, some members of ASEAN view the EU as 'the' supranational organization, and have hoped that ASEAN would adopt similar features.[2] Although these ideas were rejected, it appears that the EU still serves as an inspiration for ASEAN. Given this influence between two diverse organizations, a comparison of the two will provide valuable insights in the decision-making process.

* Helena Loutas-Paraskeva is a Legal and Policy Officer at the European Commission and former Managing Editor of *International Organizations Law Review*.

** Anmol Gulecha is a PhD Candidate at Tilburg University Law School and Managing Editor of *International Organizations Law Review*.

1 Henry G. Schermers and Niels M. Blokker, *International Institutional Law* (6th ed., Brill Nijhoff, 2018), p. 574.

2 Tommy Koh and Yeo Lay Hwee, *ASEAN and EU: The untold story* (Ministry of Foreign Affairs, Singapore, 2020), available at <https://www.mfa.gov.sg/Overseas-Mission/Ministry-of-Foreign-Affairs---Permanent-Mission-of-the-Republic-of-Singapore/Recent-Highlights/2020/10/ASEAN-and-EU-The-untold-story>.

 | DOI:10.1163/9789004699939_029

The European Council serves as the highest political entity of the European Union.[3] It is responsible for defining the general political direction and priorities of the EU.[4] It establishes the EU's policy goals in the short and long term.[5] The European Council is made up of the political leaders of each Member State, each having an equal voice.[6] The European Council, however, has no legislative function. It is the Council of the EU, made up of delegates from each EU Member State at ministerial level, that is tasked with negotiating and reaching decisions on specific policy and legislative proposals for the EU, often in co-decision with the European Parliament.[7]

ASEAN is another regional international organization that was established on 8 August 1967 in Bangkok, Thailand, with the signing of the ASEAN Declaration (Bangkok Declaration). On 20 November 2007, the ten member states of ASEAN adopted the ASEAN Charter, which serves as a foundation in achieving the ASEAN Community by providing legal status and an institutional framework for ASEAN. The ASEAN Summit is the highest policy-making organ in ASEAN and it comprises of the Heads of State or Government of ASEAN Member States.[8] The ASEAN Coordinating Council has no policy-making function but is responsible for preparing the ASEAN Summit and coordinating the implementation of agreements and decisions of the ASEAN Summit.[9]

The EU and ASEAN, while both regional international organizations, are different from each other in terms of decision-making procedure. The Council of the European Union (composed of representatives of EU Member States at ministerial level), responsible for adopting EU legislation, officially decides on the basis of a voting system. This differs from the consensus-based decision-making process mandated in the more politically driven European Council (composed of the heads of state or government). Meanwhile, ASEAN has codified consensus-based decision-making. However, when consensus cannot be achieved, the ASEAN Charter empowers the ASEAN Summit to decide how a specific decision can be made.[10] Schermers and Blokker explain that the

3 *How the European Council Works* (2024), available at <https://www.consilium.europa.eu/en/european-council/how-the-european-council-works/>.

4 *Ibidem.*

5 *Ibidem.*

6 *Ibidem.*

7 *The Decision-Making Process in the Council* (2024), available at <https://www.consilium.europa.eu/en/council-eu/decision-making/>.

8 Article 7 of the ASEAN Charter (signed and came in to force in 2008), available at <https://asean.org/book/the-asean-charter-30th-reprint/>.

9 Article 8 of the ASEAN Charter.

10 Article 20 (2) of the ASEAN Charter.

practice of international organizations originally gave rise to consensus-based decision making. This practice was subsequently codified into the founding documents of certain international organizations. This explanation suggests that international organizations naturally tend towards consensus-decision making as a preferred mode of operation.

The evolution of the codified voting system in the Council of the EU into a practice of consensus decision-making, and the codification of consensus decision making in the ASEAN Charter, provides a compelling illustration of the principles discussed by Schermers and Blokker. In this article, we will closely examine both the Council of the EU and ASEAN Summit and the ASEAN Coordinating Council, exploring their origins, the rationale behind their establishment, and the choice between voting and consensus as decision-making mechanisms. Additionally, we will touch upon the diversity among their member states, as well as delve into the intricacies of their decision-making processes.

Beginning with the Council of EU, we will trace the trajectory of its decision-making process. Despite the Council of the EU's initial reliance on voting as mandated by its founding document, member states have gradually gravitated towards consensus-based decision-making in practice. This transition underscores the organic evolution of decision-making norms within the Council of the EU, mirroring the observations made by Schermers and Blokker regarding the emergence of consensus as a prevailing practice despite formal provisions for voting.

Turning our attention to ASEAN and the ASEAN Summit, we encounter a deliberate incorporation of consensus-based decision-making into its Charter. However, the practical application of this principle has posed challenges, as member states often struggle to reach important decisions under this framework. Despite the ASEAN Summit being the final arbiter on matters related to the failure to reach a consensus,[11] member states remain committed to the consensus model. Thus, we observe two distinct trajectories: one where consensus has evolved over time through practice within the Council of the EU, and another where ASEAN, established later, enshrined consensus in its foundational document from the outset and chooses not to break away from the procedure.

Through this comparative analysis, we gain insights into the complexities of decision-making processes within regional international organizations and the dynamics between formal rules and informal practices. The cases of the

11 Daniel Seah, "The ASEAN Charter", in *The International and Comparative Law Quarterly* vol. 58 (2009), p. 197.

Council of the EU and ASEAN serve as valuable studies in understanding how decision-making mechanisms evolve and adapt within diverse institutional contexts.

2 Consensus Decision-Making in European Union: The European Council and the Council of the European Union

2.1 *Decision-Making in the European Council*

The dominant feature of decision-making in the European Council is the requirement of consensus. This is established in Article 15(4) of the Treaty on the European Union, which states that: "Except where the Treaties provide otherwise, decisions of the European Council shall be taken by consensus".

Finding consensus involves often protracted and complex negotiations to find a compromise, and no formal vote takes place. Due to the requirement of consensus, the shadow of a vote cannot be used by the President as leverage to broker an agreement.[12] Member States simply deliberate until a common agreement is reached. The consensus translates into the 'European Council conclusions', a document which specifies the key areas of concern for the EU and the pathway to address these concerns, and sets deadlines for agreement on a particular issue or legislative proposal.[13]

2.2 *Decision-Making in the Council of the European Union*

The Council of the EU plays a key role in EU decision-making and legislating. Negotiations on policy and legislation take place in the Council of the EU, in most cases decided together with the European Parliament through the ordinary legislative procedure.[14] In specific areas, for example in EU Common Foreign Security Policy, the Council takes decisions using special procedures, which do not involve the European Parliament.[15]

Decision-making in the Council requires several stages at different levels. The first stage is carried out by the working parties and committees, which help prepare the work to be approved by the ministers examining legislative

---

12 Steffen Bartsch and Wolfgang Wessels, *The European Council: Tasks and Decision making – A teaching offer* (TRACK – Teaching and Researching the European Council), available at <https://track.uni-koeln.de/sites/jean_monnet/user_upload/TRACK_-_TEDO_Dossie.pdf>.

13 *European Council, Council of the European Union – what is the difference?* (2023), available at <https://www.consilium.europa.eu/en/european-council-and-council-of-the-eu>.

14 *The Decision-Making Process in the Council,* (2024), available at <https://www.consilium.europa.eu/en/council-eu/decision-making/>.

15 *Ibidem.*

proposals in the later stages of the process in Council.[16] The working parties and committees are made up of officials from all member states. During the second stage, the European Commission presents legislative proposals to be examined by the working groups of the Council and, where relevant, the European Parliament.[17] If the legislative proposal is approved at the working party level, it progresses to the Council's Permanent Representatives Committee (COREPER) for approval and further discussion if needed.[18] If COREPER approves the proposal, the proposal will go to the final stage: the Council configuration. There are ten configurations of the Council, for example the General Affairs Council configuration, the Foreign Affairs Council configuration, or the Economic and Financial Affairs Council configuration. The Council operates as a single legal entity, meaning that any of the ten configurations are empowered to adopt a piece of legislation, even if it falls under the remit of another configuration.[19]

The voting system used by the Council to make decisions varies depending on the issue under discussion. The Council votes by simple majority (14 member states voting in favour); qualified majority (55% of member states, representing at least 65% of the EU population, voting in favour); or a unanimous vote (all Member States voting in favour).[20]

Unanimity is required by the Council on several areas considered to be particularly sensitive. These are, for example: common foreign and security policy; citizenship; EU membership; harmonisation of national legislation on indirect taxation; EU finances including the multiannual financial framework; certain provisions in the field of justice and home affairs; and harmonisation of national legislation concerning social security.[21]

2.3 *Qualified Majority Voting in the Council of the EU and the 'Climate of Consensus'*

In cases of qualified majority voting, the Member States nevertheless show a tendency towards taking decisions by consensus. Consensus decision making is defined as the adoption of a collective decision without contesting votes.[22]

16 *Ibidem.*

17 *Ibidem.*

18 *Ibidem.*

19 *Ibidem.*

20 *The Council of the EU – voting system* (2024), available at <https://www.consilium.europa.eu/en/council-eu/>.

21 *Ibidem.*

22 Fiona Hayes-Renshaw a.o., "When and Why the EU Council of Ministers Votes Explicitly", in *Journal of Common Market Studies* vol. 44 (2006) pp. 161–194; Dorothee Heisenberg, "The Institution of 'Consensus' in the European Union: Formal versus informal

From the time when voting results began being made public in 1993 until 2011, on average, approximately 80% of legal acts subject to qualified majority voting were adopted unopposed.[23] Similarly, a study published in 2024 showing the voting records in the Council of the EU from 2009 to 2023 shows consensus is found in 83% of decisions made – decisions which could have been taken by a qualified majority.[24] This trend has been described as a general "climate of consensus" between EU Member States,[25] and shows no signs of slowing. By adopting decisions by consensus even under qualified majority voting procedure, it has been argued that Member States avoid the reputational risk associated with lodging a formal vote, especially when those states perceive that their position will not prevail.[26] A tendency towards decision-making by consensus, even where qualified majority is the formal requirement, could therefore be driven by a desire for Member States to avoid losing face. This idea was encapsulated in 2001 by the Council of the EU Secretariat itself in response to a question from the European Parliament, stating "qualified majority voting can in practice promote the agreement of all the delegations on a text to the extent that delegations who do not agree with it can be inclined to vote in favour of it once they know that they are going to be outvoted".[27] Today, this idea still holds weight.[28] It is possible therefore that it is the requirement of qualified majority voting itself that propagates the apparent 'climate of consensus' amongst Member States.[29] The mere threat of the shadow of a vote compels Member States to find consensus out of fear of 'losing face' as part of the out-voted minority.

---

decision-making in the Council", in *European Journal of Political Research* vol. 44 (2005) pp. 65–90.

23 Stephanie Novak, "Qualified majority voting from the Single European Act to present day: an unexpected permanence", *Notre Europe* (2011), available at <https://institutdelors.eu/wp-content/uploads/2018/01/etud88_en-qualifiedmajority-voting-novak.pdf>.

24 Nicolai von Ondarza and Isabella Stürzer, "The State of Consensus in the EU", in *SWP Comment* 2024/C 16, 19 April 2024, available at <https://www.swp-berlin.org/10.18449/2024C16/>.

25 Stephanie Novak, "Decisions made by consensus in the Council of the European Union are often far more contentious than the voting record would suggest", *LSE Europp blog*, January 8, 2014, available at <https://blogs.lse.ac.uk/europpblog/2014/01/08/decisions-made-by-consensus-in-the-council-of-the-european-union-are-often-far-more-contentious-than-the-voting-record-would-suggest/>.

26 Novak (*supra* note 23).

27 Written question E-3938/00 asked by Christopher Huhne (ELDR) to the Council. Number of qualified majority votes, Official Journal C 364 E of 20/12/2001 p. 0004–0005.

28 Von Ondarza and Stürzer (*supra* note 24).

29 Novak (*supra* note 23).

There are, however, other explanations for the trend towards consensus decision-making in areas of the Council requiring only qualified majority. One suggests that much of the work done towards consensus decision-making does not occur during the confines of the Council meetings, but rather is achieved by Member States forming coalitions among groups of 'like-minded' Member States on a given matter to block certain decisions. The apparent consensus is merely a product of compromise reached between coalitions of Member States in order for a proposal to pass.[30]

The structure of the EU is such that implementation and enforcement of policies adopted by the Council is in the hands of the Member States. It is therefore in the interest of the Council that its decisions have the lowest levels of opposition possible, to encourage strong compliance throughout all Member States. One theory suggests that, in the event of a qualified majority vote being used for a proposal, an out-voted opposing Member State might oppose 'through the backdoor' at the domestic implementation level.[31] This would ultimately undermine the purpose and effectiveness of EU policy adopted by the Council.

3 ASEAN Decision-Making Procedure

The ASEAN Charter diverges from the decision-making approach seen in the Council of the EU by mandating decisions to be made by consultation and consensus.[32] This focus on consensus-driven decision-making has deep roots within ASEAN's history. Scholars suggest that ASEAN member states emerged from former colonies with a strong emphasis on protecting sovereignty, historical rivalries, mutual distrust, and unresolved territorial disputes, many of which continue to affect regional dynamics.[33] To foster unity among these

30 Frank M. Hage, "Coalition Building and Consensus in the Council of the European Union", in *British Journal of Political Science* vol. 43 (2013), pp. 481–504, available at <https://www.cambridge.org/core/journals/british-journal-of-political-science/article/coalition-building-and-consensus-in-the-council-of-the-european-union/3F4AB4FCDDE0299E8E36C6531247F6C4>.

31 Falkner a.o., "Non-Compliance with EU Directives in the Member States: Opposition through the Backdoor?", in *West European Politics* vol. 27 (2004), pp. 452–473.

32 See Article 20 of the ASEAN Charter.

33 Policy Brief, *Reviewing the ASEAN Charter An Opportunity to Reform ASEAN Processes*, available at <https://www.siiaonline.org/wp-content/uploads/2016/10/2014-10-Policy-Brief-Reviewing-the-ASEAN-Charter-An-Opportunity-to-Reform-ASEAN-Processes.pdf>, accessed 6 February 2024.

historically contentious states, the organization's founders embraced an informal working style and emphasised quiet diplomacy, which facilitated consensus-building through regional mechanisms.[34] The informal nature of consultations, combined with the regularity of ASEAN-related meetings at various government levels, has allowed leaders and officials from member states to develop familiarity with each other, thereby fostering trust and facilitating consensus-building processes.[35]

However, when ASEAN cannot reach a decision by consensus, the ASEAN Charter empowers the ASEAN Summit to "decide how a specific decision can be made".[36] This exception suggests that the ASEAN Charter may leave the possibility of forcing a vote open. However, such exceptions should not be overstated, aligning with what Schermers and Blokker referred to as a 'shadow of a vote'. The reason for this is that the ASEAN Charter neither endorses nor prohibits the ASEAN Summit from using voting to break an impasse in decision-making. Furthermore, Seah argues that the ASEAN Summit would unlikely resort to voting to resolve impasses on important matters like foreign policy and security.[37] Furthermore, studies suggest that the ASEAN Summit prefers to maintain consensus-based decision-making.[38] Here, the distinction between ASEAN and the EU becomes more apparent. While the Council of the EU also operates on the basis of consensus, it differs from ASEAN in that it has formal voting or procedural mechanisms to break deadlocks if consensus fails.

Scholars have criticised the informality and consensus-based decision-making approach, known as the 'ASEAN Way',[39] for contributing to shortcomings but also praised it for the successes achieved by ASEAN. Tan Sri Fuzi, the first speaker of the tenth plenary of the 22nd Asia-Pacific Roundtable (APR),[40] conceded that the ASEAN Charter was not perfect. He was aware of various

---

34 Atena S. Feraru, "ASEAN Decision-Making Process: Before and after the ASEAN Charter", in *Asian Development Policy Review* vol. 4 (2016), p. 26.

35 *Ibidem.*

36 See Article 20(2) of the ASEAN Charter.

37 Seah (*supra* note 11).

38 Siti Darwinda Mohamed Pero, "Summitry and Leadership in Regional Organisations: Comparing ASEAN Summit and the European Council Summit", in Siti Darwinda Mohamed Pero (ed.), *Leadership in Regional Community-Building: Comparing ASEAN and the European Union* (Springer, 2019), p. 185.

39 Hiro Katsumata, "Reconstruction of Diplomatic Norms in Southeast Asia: The Case for Strict Adherence to the 'ASEAN Way'", in *Contemporary Southeast Asia* vol. 25 (2003), p. 104.

40 The 22nd APR provided a forum to discuss the ASEAN Charter. At the 10th plenary of the 22nd APR, core intra-Asean views on the Charter and its perceived effectiveness were tabled.

criticisms made, which included that the Charter was not forward-looking enough as it preserved the consensus principle on decision-making.[41] However, Fuzi went on to state that these criticisms were somewhat unfair and lacked understanding of the working of ASEAN and the complexity of the drafting process which involved ten sovereign ASEAN states that came from different backgrounds. Furthermore, scholars have also taken note of the ASEAN Summit's choice to maintain consensus-based decision-making in the face of failure to make a decision.[42]

Expanding on Fuzi's argument, proponents of consensus decision-making assert that it bolsters ASEAN's cohesion and resilience. By striving for consensus, ASEAN members can avoid internal conflicts and maintain unity.[43] Loke contends that despite the time-consuming nature of consensus-building, it serves to safeguard the interests of smaller and less powerful states within ASEAN Summit.[44] Moreover, consensus-building efforts demonstrate ASEAN Summit's solidarity with external observers by seeking common ground on issues and resolving disputes without public blame or damaging the organization's reputation.[45] Additionally, Natoli suggests that consensus and the informal decision-making approach within ASEAN Summit have facilitated cooperation in specialised situations such as disaster management, enabling collaboration that might otherwise be hindered by conflicting sovereignty claims.[46] This underscores why consensus was enshrined in the ASEAN Charter as the organization and its organ's preferred method of operation. It also elucidates why newer members like Laos, Cambodia, Myanmar, and Vietnam

41 Terrence Too, *The ASEAN Charter and the Future of the ASEAN Community* (Institute of Strategic and International Studies, 2008), available at <https://www.jstor.org/stable/resrep13540.8>, accessed 6 February 2024.

42 Pero (*supra* note 38), p. 185. For instance, in the 45th ASEAN Ministerial Meeting (AMM), Phnom Penh, 2012, ASEAN member states failed to issue a joint communiqué regarding the South China sea due to failure of consensus. See also note 49 *infra*.

43 Donald Emmerson, "ASEAN between China and America: Is It Time to Try Horsing the Cow?", in *Trans-Regional and -National Studies of Southeast Asia* vol. 5 (2017), pp. 2–3.

44 Beverley Loke, "The 'ASEAN Way': Towards Regional Order and Security Cooperation?", in *Melbourne Journal of Politics* vol. 30 (2005), pp. 8–38.

45 Amitav Acharya, "Culture, security, multilateralism: The 'ASEAN way' and regional order", in *Contemporary Security Policy* vol. 19 (1998), p. 63.

46 Tommaso Natoli, "Regionalization and Sub-Regionalization of Disaster Management between Sovereignty and Solidarity", in *International Organizations Law Review* vol. 18 (2021), p. 206.

opposed alternatives such as a majority voting system, recognising the value of consensus in preserving ASEAN's unity and effectiveness.[47]

However, the other argument is that ASEAN is vulnerable to non-decision making on contentious issues.[48] For example, ASEAN Summit's failure to project a strong, collective voice against China's aggressive actions in the South China Sea in 2012 came under strong scrutiny,[49] questioning the relevance of ASEAN's consensus based decision-making processes and failure to break the consensus by the ASEAN Summit. Based on such non-decisions, Desker argues that the ASEAN Charter is a weak document because it failed to transform ASEAN into a supranational organization with a majority voting system.[50] As stated by Schermers and Blokker, consensus decision-making is time-consuming and may lead to no decision at all.[51]

Then in a way it could be said that ASEAN Summit's religious adherence to consensus-based decision-making may be ineffective in dealing with urgent or controversial issues concerning national sovereignty or territorial integrity – one recent example is the case of South China Sea.[52] Nevertheless, the ASEAN Summit made a conscious choice to strictly adhere to the Charter's consensus-based decision-making all these years. In light of the codification of the consensus-based decision-making and the ASEAN Summit not exercising powers to break the consensus, the rightful conclusion will be that ASEAN rejects 'majoritarianism'.

47 Expert Roundtable Discussion on the Road to Ratification Implementation of the ASEAN Charter, and Pavin Chachavalpongpun, *The Road to Ratification and Implementation of the ASEAN Charter* (ASEAN Studies Centre, Report no. 3, 2009), p. 58.

48 Shaun Narine and Linda Quayle, "The New ASEAN in Asia Pacific & Beyond", in *Contemporary Southeast Asia* vol. 40 (2018), pp. 527–529.

49 In 2012, the 45th ASEAN Ministerial Meeting in Phnom Penh failed to issue an agreed statement, the first ever such failure since ASEAN was founded in 1967, on the situation in the South China Sea. Shaun Narine, "ASEAN's Half Century: A Political History of the Association of Southeast Asian Nations", in *Contemporary Southeast Asia* vol. 41 (2019), pp. 466–468; Pero (*supra* note 38), p. 185; Nattapat Limsiritong a.o., "The Difficulty of ASEAN Decision Making Mode on South China Sea Dispute: The ASEAN Charter Perspective", in *Asian Political Science Review* vol. 3 (2019), p. 25; Heng Pek Koon, *The 'Asean Way' and Regional Security Cooperation in the South China Sea* (Robert Schuman Centre for Advanced Studies Research Paper No. 2014/121), available at <https://ssrn.com/abstract=2540049 or http://dx.doi.org/10.2139/ssrn.2540049>.

50 Barry Desker, "Is the ASEAN Charter Necessary?", in *RSIS Commentaries* (S. Rajaratnam School of International Studies), July 17, 2008.

51 Schermers and Blokker (*supra* note 1), p. 575.

52 For information on the ASEAN's lack of decision due to consensus based decision-making in the South China Sea, see Pero (*supra* note 38), p. 185; Narine (*supra note* 49); Limsiritong (*supra note* 49); Pek Koon (*supra* note 49).

4 Conclusion

Despite the vast majority of policy areas requiring qualified majority voting in the Council, unopposed decision-making, often with no formal vote at all, prevails as the preferred practice of the Member States when adopting legislative proposals in the Council.[53] Indeed, studies have demonstrated that even in areas requiring qualified majority, voting rarely occurs at all, "except in a few areas where decisions could not be indefinitely delayed or postponed (…) most decisions, even on routine issues, come to be made by letting deliberations and negotiations run until an agreement finally emerged".[54] While several explanations have been put forward to explain this trend, it can be said that fostering a 'climate of consensus' makes for a more harmonious Union. While the decisions ultimately reached using consensus might fall short of the ideal for all Member States, the decisions are palatable to all. Such decisions promote proper implementation at national level, create solutions that work for all Member States, and, perhaps most importantly, foster a spirit of good-will in the decision-making process.

The incorporation of consensus-based decision-making in the ASEAN Charter shares similar underlying motivations with the Council. Just as consensus fosters harmony within the Council, it also promotes unity among ASEAN Summit. Hence, the rationale for both organizations to adopt consensus-based approaches remains analogous. According to Schermers and Blokker, although these organizations' founding documents initially included voting provisions, consensus gradually became the prevailing practice.[55] ASEAN Charter's distinctiveness lies in its formal codification of consensus-based decision-making within Article 21 of the Charter and the choice of the ASEAN Summit to hold on to consensus despite other options, setting it apart from other entities where consensus evolved as a practice over time. Building on Schermers and Blokker's analysis, this paper argues consensus is increasingly being formalised as the preferred method of decision-making between the EU and the ASEAN. Given the trend observed between the EU and ASEAN, future research could explore additional regional organizations to determine whether consensus remains the preferred mode of decision-making

Schermers' and Blokker's research reveals a nuanced evolution of consensus-based decision-making within international organizations. They argue that this approach originated organically from practical experience,

53 Von Ondarza and Stürzer (*supra* note 24).

54 Heisenberg (*supra* note 22), pp. 65–90.

55 Schermers and Blokker (*supra* note 1), p. 575.

gradually formalised into a foundational mechanism. The examination of the decision-making processes in two regional international organizations offers valuable insights. Despite the lack of regional overlap between the two selected organizations – they do not share common membership, address different geopolitical concerns, and have different procedural frameworks – they both adhere to consensus-based decision-making. Whereas the Council of the EU exemplifies a consensus-driven model stemming directly from preferred practice, despite a requirement in many cases of only qualified majority voting, ASEAN's system demonstrates a deliberate codification of consensus-based decision-making. Despite occasional impasses resulting from the consensus requirement, ASEAN Summit remains committed to this method, emphasising its role in preserving unity and cohesion within the organization. Despite their differences, both organizations have chosen, whether through codification or through practice, to follow a consensus approach – truly a finding that supports the phrase 'Unity in Diversity'.

CHAPTER 28

Attaching Member State's Financial Contribution to the Organization to Circumvent the Organization's Immunity from Execution

Let the State Pay?

*Paolo Palchetti**

1 Introduction

Belgian and Italian courts have long been credited with having contributed to the development of the law of sovereign immunity, and in particular to the formation of the rule limiting the scope of state immunity on the basis of the distinction between *acta iure imperii* and *acta iure gestionis*. As observed by the Italian Constitutional Court, in a rather self-congratulatory statement, "it is well known that this limit to the application of the norm of immunity was progressively established mainly thanks to Italian judges and to Belgian judges – the so called 'Italian-Belgian theory'".[1]

The contribution of Belgian and Italian judges has not been confined to the law of state immunity. It has also extended to the rules of immunity of international organizations. In this context, Belgium and Italy have sometimes been presented as countries "with a tradition of judicial activism against international organizations".[2] It is perhaps because of this tradition that the case law of Belgian and Italian courts provides a rich source of inspiration for those who are interested in finding ways for limiting, if not for circumventing, the immunity which is granted to international organizations. Indeed, a number of extremely imaginative strategies have been deployed before the courts of these two countries in order to convince judges of the need to remove the

* The author is Professor of public law, Sorbonne Law School, University Paris 1 Panthéon Sorbonne.

1 Italian Constitutional Court, *Judgment*, Case No. 238/2014, 22 October 2014, para. 3.3, available at <www.cortecostituzionale.it/documenti/download/doc/recent_judgments/S238_2013_en.pdf>.

2 G.L. Burci, "Immunity of Property, Funds, and Assets (Article III Section 4 Specialized Agencies Convention)", in A. Reinisch (ed.), *The Conventions on the Privileges and Immunities of the United Nations and its Specialized Agencies: A Commentary* (Oxford UP, 2016), p. 113.

 | DOI:10.1163/9789004699939_030

barriers which prevent claimants to bring actions against organizations. These imaginative legal strategies have also been employed against the most impenetrable of these legal barriers, namely the immunity from execution.

State immunity from execution has been famously qualified as "the last bastion of State immunity".[3] This is so because "the question of immunity from execution does not arise until after the question of jurisdictional immunity has been decided in the negative and until there is a judgment in favour of the plaintiff".[4] Moreover, as observed by the International Court of Justice, "immunity from enforcement enjoyed by States in regard to their property situated on foreign territory goes further than the jurisdictional immunity enjoyed by those same States before foreign courts"; even when a foreign state could not claim immunity from jurisdiction, "it does not follow *ipso facto* that the State against which judgment has been given can be the subject of measures of constraint on the territory of the forum State".[5]

In the case of international organizations, the bastion of immunity from execution appears even more impenetrable if one considers that some treaties, including the 1946 Convention on the Privileges and Immunities of the United Nations, go so far as to deny international organizations the possibility itself of waiving this immunity.[6]

How can then a claimant, who has been able to obtain a judgment against an international organization, enforce that judgment before a domestic court? Is there any new 'Italian-Belgian theory' on which claimants can rely to satisfy their claims against international organizations? Apparently, an attempt has been made in this direction. In two distinct cases brought before Belgian and Italian courts, claimants sought to convince the judges that, since the organization refused to make voluntary payment in execution of the judgment, they could satisfy their claims by attaching the annual financial contribution owed by the forum state to the organization. So far, this attempt to remove the last bastion of immunity seems to have failed.

---

3 *Yearbook of the International Law Commission* 1991, vol. II (2), p. 56, para. 2.

4 *Ibidem.*

5 ICJ, *Jurisdictional Immunities of the State (Germany v. Italy: Greece intervening)*, [2012] ICJ Reports 146, para. 113.

6 See for instance Art II Section 2 of the 1946 Convention on the Privileges and Immunities of the United Nations ("The United Nations, its property and assets wherever located and by whomsoever held, shall enjoy immunity from every form of legal process except insofar as in any particular case it has expressly waived its immunity. It is, however, understood that no waiver of immunity shall extend to any measure of execution"). On this issue, see A Reinisch, "Immunity of Property, Funds, and Assets (Article II Section 2 General Convention)", in Reinisch (*supra* note 2), p. 97, and Burci (*supra* note 2), at p. 120.

The cases before Belgian tribunals concerned actions brought by International Hotels Worldwide in order to collect a sum of money owed to it by NATO on the basis of a decision rendered by an arbitral tribunal which had received *exequatur* in Belgium. The claimant first attempted to obtain the payment directly from NATO. It then served garnishee orders to a number of commercial contractors and other subjects owing a sum of money to NATO. These orders targeted also Belgium's annual contribution to NATO. Belgium attempted to obtain the annulment of the order by claiming that, under the Ottawa Convention of 20 September 1951, NATO enjoyed immunity. Apparently, in a decision rendered in 2011, the Tribunal of First Instance rejected Belgium's request on the ground that, in the absence of any alternative remedy available to the claimants for obtaining redress from NATO, no immunity could be recognized to NATO.[7] In a separate but related proceedings, the Brussels Court of Appeal upheld the appeal brought by Belgium against the decision recognizing the *exequatur* of the arbitral decision, finding that such decision was contrary to the immunity enjoyed by NATO under the Ottawa Convention.[8] However, on 4 October 2013 the Court of Cassation quashed the decision as it considered that Belgium, not being a party to the proceeding before the arbitral tribunal, did not have the capacity to make an appeal against the decision granting *exequatur*.[9] While the judgment of the Court of Cassation was based on the application of domestic procedural rules, and not on the rule of immunity, its effect was substantially that of precluding Belgium to invoke the immunity of NATO in order to vacate the decision granting *exequatur* to the arbitral award.[10]

The Italian case concerned the execution of a judgment rendered by the Tribunal of Venice in an employment dispute involving the Venice office of

7 On this unreported judgment, see Eric De Brabandere, "Measures of Constraints and the Immunity of International Organizations", in Tom Ruys and Nicolas Angelet (eds.), *The Cambridge Handbook of Immunities and International Law* (Cambridge UP, 2019), p. 343, fn. 107.

8 Court of Appeal (Brussels), *Belgian State v International Hotels Worldwide*, Case No. 2011/AR/558, 26 June 2012, available at <http://www.cahdidatabases.coe.int/Contribution/Details/319>.

9 Court of Cassation, *International Hotels Worldwide v Etat belge et Banca Monte dei Paschi di Siena Belgio*, Case No C.12.0614.F, 4 October 2013, available at <https://www.stradalex.com/fr/sl_src_publ_jur_be/document/cass_F-20131004-2>.

10 As observed by Gerard Cahin, "L'exécution des décisions juridictionnelles internationales rendues à l'encontre des organisations internationales", in *Revue générale de droit international public* vol. 121 (2017), p. 644: "la Cour fonde sa solution sur le fait que la Belgique, n'étant pas partie au procès intenté devant elle contre la société par l'OTAN, ne peut pas invoquer à la place de cette dernière son immunité".

the UNESCO Regional Bureau for Science and Culture in Europe. Here again, the claimant served garnishee order to the Italian Ministry of Foreign Affairs targeting the annual contribution of Italy to UNESCO. Italy brought an action before the Tribunal of Venice for the vacation of this measure. In its order of 8 October 2020, the Tribunal of Venice accepted the Italian Government's request for vacation.[11] Firstly, the Tribunal found that the Ministry of Foreign Affairs had the capacity to request the vacation of the measure since, under the 1947 United Nations Convention on the Privileges and Immunities of Specialized Agencies, to which Italy is a party, and under the 1995 Headquarter Agreement between Italy and UNESCO, Italy was under a duty to ensure UNESCO's immunity from execution. It also observed that Italy, as a member of the organization, had an obligation to provide its financial contribution to UNESCO and that, since in principle UNESCO enjoyed immunity, Italy had no guarantee that it could deduce the sum of money owed by UNESCO to the employer from the total amount owed by Italy to UNESCO. Moving then to assessing whether the rule on immunity from execution was applicable in the case at hand, the Tribunal excluded that UNESCO enjoyed absolute immunity from execution. It considered that the rule of immunity applicable to international organizations only covers properties and assets which are necessary for the organization to perform its functions. Concerning the annual financial contribution owed by member states to the organization, however, the Tribunal found that, unless otherwise provided, there was a presumption that the annual contribution constituted an asset which was used by the organization for the exercise of its specific functions.[12] On the basis of these considerations, the Tribunal concluded by ordering the suspension of the measure of constraint.

Should one conclude that, when it comes to immunity of execution, international organizations remain "the Untouchables"?[13] Perhaps, but there seems to be more than that. As Niels Blokker has warned, "immunity should not leave complainants without a remedy".[14] In this respect, these two cases may also be taken as hinting at a possible alternative remedy.

11 Unpublished order, copy on file with the author.

12 To be more precise, instead of speaking of acts which are necessary for performing the organization's function, the Tribunal referred to acts *iure imperii* ("non è possibile escludere che tutte le somme di cui al capitolo di spesa oggetto di espropriazione siano destinate al compimento di atti iure imperii").

13 Niels Blokker, "International Organizations: The Untouchables?", in *International Organizations Law Review* vol. 10 (2013), pp. 259–275.

14 *Ibidem*, p. 260.

2 Is the Annual Contribution of a Member State Covered by the Organization's Immunity from Execution?

It is not rare in international practice that, in order to satisfy claims against a foreign state, post-judgment measures of constraints are requested against third subjects – in most cases companies – in order to seize sums of money that these subjects owe to the state. In principle, debts owed to the state are to be regarded as property of the state for the purposes of the law of immunity.[15] They are therefore protected against execution if they are not intended to be used for a commercial purpose. The same should apply to sums of money that a third subject owes to a state for the payment of taxes or other social claims. Thus, in cases brought before French courts, the applicant, in order to satisfy its claims against Argentina, sought to attach sums of money that the French companies Air France and Total owed to that state for the payment of overflight charges and other taxes. In a judgment rendered on 28 March 2013, the French Court of Cassation found that the attached assets were covered by immunity, as the action concerned "créances fiscales et sociales de l'Etat argentin, c'est-à-dire [...] des ressources se rattachant nécessairement à l'exercice par cet Etat des prérogatives liées à sa souveraineté".[16] In 2016, France adopted a law expressly providing that "tax and social claims of the state" are to be considered as property of the state which are covered by immunity from execution.[17]

Treaty provisions establishing the immunity from execution of an international organization do not generally provide a precise list of the properties and assets which are covered by immunity. Yet, they frequently use a very broad formulation that allows to include, among the properties and assets covered by immunity, the debts owed to the organization by third subjects. A broad formulation also can be found in the two treaties that were at stake before the Belgian and Italian courts in the two abovementioned cases. Article V of the Ottawa Convention provides that "[t]he Organization, its property and assets, wheresoever located and by whomsoever held, shall enjoy immunity from every form of legal process". Article III Section 4 of the Specialized Agencies Convention refers to "property and assets wherever located and by whomsoever held". The fact that these provisions do not require the organization's

15 See Jean-Marc Thouvenin and Victor Grandaubert, "The Material Scope of State Immunity from Execution", in Ruys and Angelet (*supra* note 7), p. 248.

16 Cour de cassation, Chambre civile, *Société NML Capital c République argentine et Air France*, Case No. 11-13.323, 28 March 2013, available at <https://www.legifrance.gouv.fr/juri/id/JURITEXT000027251612>.

17 LOI n°2016-1691 of 9 December 2016, Art. 59, available at <www.legifrance.gouv.fr/codes/article_lc/LEGIARTI000033563438>.

physical control over the properties and assets allows to consider debts owed to the organization as also covered by immunity.[18]

The Court of Appeal of Brussels and the Tribunal of Venice referred, respectively, to the Ottawa Convention and to the Specialized Agency Convention to justify their conclusion that the measures of restraint requested by the applicant were contrary to the immunity from execution enjoyed by the organization. By so doing, they in fact interpreted the notion of "property and assets" of the organization as including the financial contribution owed to the organization by a member state. This stretches significantly the scope of application of the rule of immunity set forth in the two conventions. One may wonder whether Belgian and Italian courts went too far.

In fact, it is hard to see how an immunity, which is designed to protect properties and assets belonging to, or possessed by, an international organization, could be invoked by a state in order to protect an asset which belongs to it. The fact that a sum of money is used by the state to comply with its international obligation vis-à-vis the organization does not appear to be sufficient for rendering that assets as one belonging to, or possessed by, the organization. In this respect, a member state's international obligation to contribute to the budget of the organization can hardly be assimilated to the debt owed by a company to a state under private law or under tax law. An important difference in this regard concerns the role itself of domestic judges in ensuring compliance with such obligation. It is difficult to imagine that an international organization could address domestic courts in order to enforce its rights to obtain from the member state the annual contribution to its budget. The same should then apply to a private actor who attempts to seize the assets of the state in order to satisfy a claim it has vis-à-vis the organization.

This is not to say that international law has nothing to say when it comes to measures of constraints targeting the state's annual contribution to the organization's budget. Such measures may indeed have the effect of preventing the state from complying with its international obligations. However, the international obligation which may eventually be breached does not appear to be the obligation to accord immunity from execution to the international organization. It is rather the obligation to contribute to the budget of the organization.[19]

18 As observed by Burci (*supra* note 2), p. 107, "the formulation makes it clear that the protection of the property and assets continues even when they are not held physically by the agencies, for example, bank accounts and investments in commercial banks".

19 Indeed, before the Tribunal of Venice the Italian Ministry of Foreign Affairs had also advanced the argument that no measure of constraint could be taken as the sum of money at hand was to be employed to fulfil Italy's obligation to contribute to the budget of UNESCO ("facendo valere la impignorabilità dello stesso [...] in ragione della sussistenza

In other words, Belgian and Italian courts were right in invoking international law in order to justify their refusal to adopt measures of restraints attaching the state's national contribution to the organization. But they should have justified their decision not by relying on the immunity of the organization, which does not benefit the member state, but by referring to the obligation of the state to contribute to the budget of the organization.

3 In Search for Alternative Remedies: Should the State Pay?

Beyond the question of whether a member state's financial contribution is covered by the immunity from execution of the organization, a broader issue may be raised: when a domestic court condemns an international organization to pay pecuniary compensation but the same court subsequently prevents the individual from enforcing the judgment because of the immunity from execution of the organization, would it be a reasonable to expect that the state granting immunity assumes the burden of compensating the individual by paying the sum of money owed by the organization?

To be clear, the point here is not to suggest that the state should deduce from the annual contribution it owes to the organization the sum of money that it is necessary to compensate the individual. Such an action would amount to a breach of the state's obligation to contribute to the budget of the organization. Indeed, it is hard to expect that the organization would consent to such deduction. Moreover, there seems to be no other legal grounds on which such action could be justified. In particular, while the possibility of a member state withholding its financial contribution by way of countermeasure has sometimes been evoked,[20] it is difficult to apply this excuse to the situation at hand. First, this would require demonstrating that, by not compensating the individual, the organization has breached an international obligation. Moreover, if one accepts to follow the indications coming from the Articles on the Responsibility of International Organizations adopted in 2011 by the International Law Commission, the conditions for admitting the possibility of having recourse to countermeasures in the relationship between the

di un vincolo di destinazione al finanziamento obbligatorio delle attività istituzionali dell'UNESCO").

20 See for instance Elisabeth Zoller, "The 'Corporate Will' of the United Nations and the Rights of the Minority", in *American Journal of International Law* vol. 81 (1987), pp. 631–632. For a criticism, see Henry G. Schermers and Niels M. Blokker, *International Institutional Law* (6th ed., Brill, 2018), p. 683.

organization and its member states are so restrictive that in most cases this possibility is substantially ruled out.[21]

In fact, it is difficult to find in international law a possible legal basis for imposing on the state granting immunity the obligation to assume the burden of providing redress to the claimants. When an obligation of this kind has been recognized, it was generally based on the internal law of the state. This probably explains why so far international law scholars do not appear to have paid much attention to this solution. Yet, this alternative form of protection of individual rights has much to be praised. On the one hand, shifting the burden from the individual to the State may be regarded as the price to be paid for limiting access to justice by individuals. On the other, if the state considers that the claim of the individual derives from a breach by the organization of one of its international obligations, it can attempt to obtain redress from the organization through diplomatic protection or any other available means.[22]

Alternative forms of redress of this kind are not infrequent in international practice. Among the most recent examples, one may refer to Law No. 79 adopted by the Italian Parliament on 29 June 2022.[23] This law was adopted in order to put a remedy to the situation created by the 2014 judgment of the Italian Constitutional Court. Following that decision, which established that, in cases of grave breaches of human rights, the individual right to access to justice, set forth in Article 24 of the Italian Constitution, prevailed over the customary international rule granting immunity from jurisdiction, dozens of judgments condemned Germany to pecuniary compensation for the crimes committed against the claimants. In order, essentially, to avoid the risk that measures of restraints be taken against German properties in Italy, in breach of

21 On the conditions for adopting countermeasures in the relations between an organization and its member state, see Art. 52 of the Articles on the Responsibility of International Organizations, *Yearbook of the International Law Commission* 2011, vol. II (2), p. 96. Some authors have criticized these conditions for being excessively restrictive. See Antonios Tzanakopoulos, "L'invocation de la théorie des contre-mesures en tant que justification de la désobéissance au Conseil de sécurité", *Revue belge de droit international* vol. 56 (2013), p. 97; Simone Vezzani, "Countermeasures by Member States Against International Organizations", in Maurizio Ragazzi (ed.), *Responsibility of International Organizations. Essays in Memory of Sir Ian Brownlie* (Martinus Nijhoff, 2013), p. 383.

22 On this option, see Martina Buscemi, *Illeciti delle Nazioni Unite e tutela dell'individuo* (Editoriale scientifica, 2020), pp. 98 ff.

23 See Alessandro Bufalini, "The Italian fund for the victims of the Nazi crimes and the International Court of Justice: Between compliance and dispute settlement", SIDIBlog 2023, available at <http://www.sidiblog.org/2023/05/16/the-italian-fund-for-the-victims-of-nazi-crimes-and-the-international-court-of-justice-between-compliance-and-dispute-settlement/>.

Germany's immunity from execution, Italy accepted to compensate the individuals who had been recognized by Italian courts as being entitled to receive compensation. Law No. 79 of 2022, on the one hand, precludes any proceedings aiming at enforcing against Germany the judgments that condemn that state to compensate Italian victims of Nazi crimes. On the other hand, it established a special fund aimed at granting compensation to individuals who had obtained a judgment against Germany.

As regards the possibility of a member state having to bear subsidiary responsibility in relation to cases brought against international organizations, French judicial practice is of particular interest. In a number of decisions, the French *Conseil d'Etat* recognized that France has to bear responsibility for the damage caused to individuals who had no access to French courts as a consequence of the immunity granted to an international organization. In a judgment rendered in 1976, this principle was affirmed in relation to a case in which an individual was precluded from having access to French courts because of the immunity from jurisdiction recognized to the respondent person under the Headquarter Agreement between France and UNESCO.[24] In a judgment of 2011, the *Conseil d'Etat* found, "sur le fondement de l'égalité des citoyens devant les charges publiques", that France was responsible for the prejudice caused to the applicant as a consequence of the application of the rule on immunity from execution provided by the same treaty.[25] Interestingly, in the latter case the French Government was condemned to pay the same amount of money that the *cour administrative d'appel de Paris* had awarded to the individual. In other words, France took the place of UNESCO in compensating the claimant.

4 Concluding Remarks

Confronted with the question of determining whether the immunity from execution enjoyed by international organizations covers also a member state's financial contribution to the budget of the organization, Belgian and Italian

24 Conseil d'Etat, *Ministre des Affaires étrangères c Dame Burgat et autres*, 29 October 1976, reproduced in *Journal de droit international* vol. 104 (1977), p. 631. On this judgement see August Reinisch, *International Organizations before National Court* (Cambridge UP, 2004), p. 329.

25 Conseil d'État, *Mlle A.C. c Ministre des Affaires étrangères*, 11 February 2011, Judgment No. 325253, available at <www.legifrance.gouv.fr/ceta/id/CETATEXT000023604405>. See Isabelle Pingel, "Les privilèges et immunités de l'organisation internationale", in Evelyne Lagrange and Jean-Marc Sorel (eds.), *Droit des organisations internationales* (LGDJ, 2013), p. 643.

courts appears to have refrained from displaying any form of judicial activism against international organizations. To the contrary, they relied on a solution that stretches considerably the scope of application of the rule of immunity from execution. In fact, this rule was used as a tool for protecting properties and assets of the member state. By refusing to the claimants the possibility of attaching a member state's assets for satisfying claims against the organization, domestic courts refused substantially to lift the veil of the organization and to make the member state responsible for the conduct of the organization. While, given the specific circumstances of these cases, this solution appears a reasonable one, the question remains as to whether, at least in certain cases, it is the state granting immunity to the organization that should bear the burden of providing compensation to the claimants. No doubts, this alternative remedy presents its shortcomings, particularly if one takes into account the interest of taxpayers. But until when "there are no judicial or quasi-judicial remedies in place where they should exist",[26] it is a solution that deserves attention.

26 Niels Blokker, "Jurisdictional Immunities of International Organizations. Origins, Fundamentals and Challenges", in Ruys and Angelet (*supra* note 7), p. 200.

CHAPTER 29

The Privileges and Immunities of International Organizations and Equality

Some Reflections on Their Justifications from an Egalitarian Perspective

*August Reinisch**

1 Introduction

Niels Blokker has greatly contributed to the law of international organizations, both as a practitioner, working in the Dutch ministry of foreign affairs, as well as a professor of international law at the University of Leiden. His initiative to establish a law journal specifically devoted to the law of international organizations, the *International Organizations Law Review* (IOLR) some twenty years ago, his many writings in the field and the devoted updating of the major treatise in this area, *International Institutional Law*, founded by Henry G. Schermers, today already in its sixth edition (and soon in its seventh), bear witness to his outstanding work. It is a particular pleasure to develop a few thoughts on a recurrent theme of international institutional law in honour of Niels Blokker.

That international organizations enjoy privileges and immunities seems fairly commonplace. Most of their constituent instruments make a brief reference to them, often multilateral treaties spell them out in more detail and headquarters agreements equally customize the types and extent of various privileges and immunities to be enjoyed by specific international organizations, their staff as well as delegates.

What is often less clear is the rationale for the enjoyment of privileges and immunities, and even the specific nature of these two concepts. This uncertainty might be even increased as a result of a growing scepticism towards the enjoyment of privileges and immunities in general under a growing push towards egalitarianism. It thus seems interesting to comprehend the notions of privileges and immunities and analyse both their history and current use.

* The author is Professor of international and European law at the University of Vienna and a Member of the International Law Commission as well as of the *Institut de droit international*.
My particular thanks to Fritz Maya Kainz for his excellent research assistance.

 | DOI:10.1163/9789004699939_031

2 Privileges and Immunities

Privileges are often considered to be certain special rights.[1] In the context of international law, a 'privilege' is, however, most often associated with the exemption from the applicability of national law that would otherwise apply. We find this particularly in diplomatic law, providing for envoys of foreign states to be exempted from the duty to pay taxes as well as from some customs regulations of the receiving state.[2] 'Immunity' by contrast does not exempt from the applicability of legal provisions. Rather, it merely exempts from the jurisdiction of courts and administrative bodies to adjudicate and enforce the law.[3]

These concepts of privileges and immunities, developed in the law of diplomatic relations, have also been integrated into international organizations law. Pursuant to the definition of Schermers and Blokker, the term 'privilege' stands for situations in which local legislation is not or is differently applicable, and the expression 'immunity' signifies only an exception from the jurisdiction of courts which implies that "local courts cannot assess the applicability of the law and specific cases".[4] In spite of this clear definition, however, even Schermers and Blokker blur the line to some extent when they do not only assert that "no sharp distinction between privileges and immunities" exists, but introduce their distinction by the statement that the "immunity from tax legislation is usually considered to be the most important privilege".[5] Of course, according to their definition the exemption from tax legislation is a privilege, not an immunity, and referring to an immunity as a privilege more resembles the colloquial idea of any exemption being a special preferential right or treatment.

---

1 See Heinz Mohnhaupt, "Privileges", in Stanley N. Katz (ed.), *The Oxford International Encyclopaedia of Legal History* (Oxford UP, online version 2009) ("Privileges represent an individual norm-type, which – as an individual right, a subjective special right, or a personal prior claim – constitutes the opposite of a general law").

2 See Artt. 34 and 36 Vienna Convention on Diplomatic Relations (adopted 18 April 1961, entered into force 24 April 1964), 500 *UNTS* 95 ("VCDR").

3 See Art. 31 para. 1 VCDR.

4 Henry Schermers and Niels Blokker, *International Institutional Law: Unity Within Diversity* (6th ed., Brill Nijhoff, 2018), p. 268, § 323: "We shall use the word 'privilege' for all cases in which local legislation is not, or is differently, applicable, and the word 'immunity' for the immunity from jurisdiction (unless indicated otherwise). This is the most basic distinction: in the case of immunity from jurisdiction, local legislation is fully applicable and no privileged position is granted. The only consequence of immunity from jurisdiction is that local courts cannot assess the applicability of the law in specific cases" (footnote omitted).

5 *Ibidem*, p. 267, § 323.

3 The Ordinary Meaning of 'Privileges' and 'Immunities'

But what is the colloquial use of privileges and immunities? In regard to the first term, most dictionaries would refer us to "privileges", implying special rights. According to the Oxford Dictionary of English Etymology, the expression 'privilege' is most likely to stem from the combination of the Latin term "*privus*" (separate, distinctive) combined with the plural of *lex* (law, right), "*leges/legum*", meaning a peculiar right, somebody enjoys a privilege if he or she has individual special rights.[6] In classical canonical law or mediaeval law up until modern time, a privilege was usually associated with individuals of a particular social hierarchical rank, enjoying special rights.[7] Such notion is, of course, inherently incompatible with the modern idea that all persons are equal and that any special rights of individuals are unacceptable.

In parallel to the class-based concept of privileges, enjoyed by members of certain social groups like the clergy, aristocracy, military, etc., a functional notion of privilege has evolved in the narrower category of diplomatic exchanges between states. The representatives of foreign states are generally considered to enjoy a limited exemption from the law of the receiving countries (and a rather broad immunity from their courts and administrative bodies).[8] It appears that diplomatic law has thus contributed to the modern understanding of the term 'privilege' as an exemption from the (otherwise applicable) law.

As opposed to the special rights-connotation of a 'privilege', the term 'immunity' focuses on the idea of an exemption. It also derives from Latin; "*immunis*" meaning being exempt from or not subject to ("*in/im*") a public service or obligation ("*munus*").[9]

6 Charles T. Onions (ed.), *The Oxford Dictionary of English Etymology* (1966, reprint 1995), p. 711; see also "privilege", in Angus Stevenson (ed.), *Oxford Dictionary of English* (Oxford UP, online version 2015), at <https://www.oed.com/dictionary/privilege_n>, last accessed 27 February 2024; Gerhard Wesenberg, "Privilegium", in Konrat Ziegler (ed.), *Paulys Realencyclopädie der Classischen Altertumswissenschaft* vol. 45 (1957), pp. 17–29, at p. 17.

7 Alain Boureau, "Privilege in Medieval Societies from the Twelfth to the Fourteenth Centuries, or: How the Exception Proves the Rule", in Peter Linehan a.o. (eds.), *The Medieval World* (2nd ed., Routledge, 2018), pp. 720–733. Note, however, that paradoxically, privileges also led to increased liberties within specific groups which enjoyed them (e.g., cities and monasteries). Moreover, medieval debates about privileges informed in no small part the development of the modern understanding of generally applicable law, "for it was through them that ideas of sovereignty, liberty and equality came to be clarified" (Boureau at p. 722).

8 See above, footnotes 3 and 2.

9 Charles T. Onions (ed.), *The Oxford Dictionary of English Etymology* (1966, reprint 1995), p. 463; see also Konrat Ziegler, "Immunitas", in Ziegler (*supra* note 6), pp. 1134–1136, at p. 1134.

Immunity is generally understood as referring to the exemption from certain obligations, but even more broadly as an inapplicability of the law. Thus, both terms ('privilege' and 'immunity') are very close,[10] and again, it was probably the law of diplomatic relations that clarified the distinguishing traits that we currently associate with 'immunity' in international law. The envoys of foreign states were not only exempt from some parts of the law in the receiving state, more importantly, they were 'immune' in the sense of being exempt from the jurisdiction of the local courts and administrative bodies, so immunity focuses on the exemption from jurisdiction and not from the law.

4 The Privileges and Immunities of International Organizations

International organizations regularly enjoy privileges and immunities. Whether they do so on the basis of customary international law remains contested.[11] However, in most cases, specific treaty provisions provide for the enjoyment of privileges and immunities. Where multilateral or bilateral treaties lay them down specifically, the precise extent of these exemptions from local law and local jurisdiction are also relatively clear.[12] Where constituent instruments only generally refer to "functional" privileges and immunities,[13] it may remain questionable what that exactly implies.

10 See, e.g., "Privilege" in Bryan Garner (ed.), *Black's Law Dictionary* (11th ed., Thomson Reuters 2019): "A special legal right, exemption, or immunity granted to a person or class of persons; an exception to a duty. A privilege grants someone the legal freedom to do or not to do a given act. It immunizes conduct that, under ordinary circumstances, would subject the actor to liability".

11 Michael Wood, "Do International Organizations Enjoy Immunity Under Customary International Law?", *International Organizations Law Review* (IOLR) vol. 10 (2013), pp. 287–318; Schermers and Blokker (*supra* note 4), pp. 1076–1079, § 1610; Edward Chukwuemeke Okeke, *Jurisdictional Immunities of States and International Organizations* (Oxford UP, 2018), pp. 269–272; August Reinisch, "Transnational Judicial Conversations on the Personality, Privileges, and Immunities of International Organizations – An Introduction", in August Reinisch (ed.), *The Privileges and Immunities of International Organizations in Domestic Courts* (Oxford UP, 2013), pp. 1–16, at pp. 6–11.

12 See, e.g., Convention on the Privileges and Immunities of the United Nations (adopted 13 February 1946 in New York, entered into force 17 September 1946), 1 *UNTS* 15 ("General Convention"); Convention on the Privileges and Immunities of the Specialized Agencies (adopted 21 November 1947 in New York, entered into force 2 December 1948) 33 *UNTS* 261. See also August Reinisch (ed.), *The Conventions on the Privileges and Immunities of the United Nations and its Specialized Agencies. A Commentary* (Oxford UP, 2016).

13 See, e.g. Art. 105(1) UN Charter.

The most widely conferred 'privilege' enjoyed by international organizations themselves as well as by their employees is the exemption from direct taxation.[14] In addition, both organizations and their staff are regularly exempt from customs regulations as well as military service requirements.[15] The typical 'immunity' enjoyed by international organizations is a broad, regularly absolute immunity from legal process[16] and in case of their staff members functional immunity.[17]

5 Challenges to the Privileges and Immunities of International Organizations

The underlying rationale for granting privileges and immunities, i.e. to ensure the effective and independent functioning of international organizations, is largely accepted.[18] However, there seem to be increased challenges to the special exceptions from the otherwise applicable law or otherwise applicable jurisdiction of host states. These challenges may derive from a broad egalitarian drive, which even leads some states to become eager to avoid the term 'privilege' in the context of international organizations. An example is national legislation that used to refer to privileges,[19] and now rather cautiously employs more neutral terms such as host state/country legislation.[20]

14 See, e.g. Art. II Section 7(a), Art. V Section 18(b) General Convention.

15 See, e.g. Art. II Section 7(b), Art. V Section 18(g) and (c) General Convention.

16 See, e.g. Art. II Section 2 General Convention.

17 See, e.g. Art. V Section 18(a) General Convention.

18 See Schermers and Blokker (*supra* note 4), at pp. 268–296, § 324 ("[T]he raison d'être of privileges and immunities of international organizations is their functional necessity: their existence is necessary for the independent exercise of its functions by an international organization"); August Reinisch, "Privileges and Immunities", in Jacob Katz Cogan, Ian Hurd and Ian Johnstone (eds.), *The Oxford Handbook of International Organizations* (Oxford UP, 2016), pp. 1048–1068; see also, in the context of privileges and immunities of experts on UN missions pursuant to Section 22 General Convention, ICJ, *Applicability of Article VI, Section 22, of the Convention on the Privileges and Immunities of the United Nations* (Advisory Opinion), [1989] ICJ Reports, p. 177, para. 50 ("[T]he intent of Section 22 is to ensure the independence of such experts in the interests of the Organization by according them the privileges and immunities necessary for the purpose").

19 See, e.g., Bundesgesetz vom 14. Dezember 1977 über die Einräumung von Privilegien und Immunitäten an internationale Organisationen, Federal Gazette No. 677/1977 [Austria, "Federal Law of 14 December 1977 on the Granting of Privileges and Immunities to International Organizations"]; see also Privileges and Immunities Act, Act No: CAP. 179, No. 3 of 1970, last amended by Act No. 23 of 2019 (Kenya) (still in force).

20 Bundesgesetz zur Stärkung Österreichs als internationaler Amtssitz- und Konferenzstandort, Federal Gazette I No. 54/2021 [Austria, "Federal Law to Strengthen Austria as an International Headquarters and Conference Location"]. See also Gesetz über die Vorrechte,

At the same time, questioning immunities stems from an increased awareness of the need for accountability, and even human rights or constitutional law demands, ensuring access to justice, which is likely to lead to an inherent tension with the traditional concept of immunity.

In order to assess to what extent traditional privileges and immunities are justified for international organizations, it is thus necessary to look at their underlying rationale.

6 The Rationale for Privileges and Immunities of International Organizations

The fiscal privileges accorded to international organizations may superficially appear like an expression of inequality in the form of privileging some individuals working for an organization as well as their employer. However, a closer look at the underlying rationale reveals that its justification lies in the generally accepted idea of equal treatment of the member states. Organizations and employees are exempted from taxation because giving taxation rights to individual states where work is performed would imply an indirect financing/subsidisation of the host or seat state of organizations at the expense of all member states.[21] With this rationale it becomes evident that the privilege of

Immunitäten, Befreiungen und Erleichterungen in der Bundesrepublik Deutschland als Gaststaat internationaler Einrichtungen (Gaststaatgesetz) vom 30. November 2019, Federal Gazette I. 1929 [Germany, "Act on Privileges, Immunities, Exemptions and Facilities in the Federal Republic of Germany as a Host State of International Organizations (Host State Act)"]; Bundesgesetz über die von der Schweiz als Gaststaat gewährten Vorrechte, Immunitäten und Erleichterungen sowie finanziellen Beiträge, AS 2007 6637 [Switzerland, "Federal Act on the Privileges, Immunities and Facilities and Financial Contributions Granted by Switzerland as a Host State"]. Note that the latter two do contain the word "Vorrecht" ("privilege") in their long form, but are commonly referred to, including by the German and Swiss Foreign Ministries, by the short form "Gaststaatgesetz" ("Host State Act") (see Federal Foreign Office (Germany), *Deutschland: Attraktiver Standort für Internationale Organisationen*, online at <https://www.auswaertiges-amt.de/de/aussenpolitik/int-organisationen-in-deutschland/2258564>, last accessed 27 February 2024; Federal Department of Foreign Affairs (Switzerland), *Host State Act*, online at <https://www.eda.admin.ch/eda/en/fdfa/foreign-policy/international-law/privileges-and-immunities/host-state-act.html>, last accessed 26 February 2024).

21 See Secretariat of the United Nations, Office of Legal Affairs, "Memorandum to the Chief of the Field Operations Service, Office of General Services" (21 April 1972), in *United Nations Juridical Yearbook 1972*, 190, at 191 (the purpose of tax privileges "is to achieve equality of treatment for all officials independently of nationality and to ensure that funds contributed by all Members to the budget of the Organization are not channelled into the Treasury of a State by levying taxes on staff members' salaries").

tax exemption is not an expression of unequal special rights, but quite to the contrary a necessary tool in order to ensure equal treatment of the member states of an international organization.[22] When recognizing this 'egalitarian' purpose, it seems that such kind of privilege will no longer be too controversial.

The exemption from jurisdiction in the form of immunity, however, has become much more controversial over time. The root of the challenge in the form of calls for accountability may also be conceived as an egalitarian one. The rule of law requires that no one is above the law,[23] everyone is equal before the law and therefore everyone can be sued. This may lead to an inherent tension with any form of immunity excepting some subjects from the jurisdiction of courts. In the field of diplomatic and state immunity, the exemption from the adjudicative power of the courts in a foreign state is mitigated by the fact that diplomats are regularly amenable to suit in their sending states,[24] and that states themselves can regularly be sued not only before their own courts, but also in foreign courts in regard to their non-sovereign activities.[25] The so-called commercial activity exception to immunity – also referred to as an exemption of *iure gestionis* acts – has led to a situation whereby particularly private parties entering into commercial or other private law relationships with foreign states are usually able to sue those states before national courts.[26]

It is worth dwelling on the rationale of state immunity, as well as the evolving exception to state immunity because both are based on equality concerns that may be linked to a general egalitarian consideration. The traditional justification for state immunity is that it is based on sovereign equality requiring states not to sit in judgement over their equals, i.e. other states.[27] To exempt

22 August Reinisch, *International Organizations before National Courts* (Cambridge UP, 2000), p. 241.

23 See Albert V. Dicey, *An Introduction to the Study of the Law of the Constitution* (Pt II, London, 1885), pp. 177–178: "[…] not only that with us no man is above the law, but (what is a different thing) that here every man, whatever be his rank or condition, is subject to the ordinary law of the realm and amenable to the jurisdiction of the ordinary tribunals […]".

24 See Art. 31 para. 4 VCDR; see also ILC, 'Draft Articles on Diplomatic Intercourse and Immunities with commentaries', in *Yearbook of the International Law Commission*, 1958, vol. II, 89, at Art. 31, para 12.

25 See, e.g., Hazel Fox and Philippa Webb, *The Law of State Immunity* (3rd ed., Oxford UP, 2015), pp. 399–416; Xiaodong Yang, *State Immunity in International Law* (Cambridge UP, 2012), pp. 75–131.

26 See, e.g., Art. 10 United Nations Convention on Jurisdictional Immunities of States and Their Property (adopted 2 December 2004 in New York, not yet in force) C.N.141.2005.

27 ICJ, *Jurisdictional Immunities of the State* (Germany v. Italy: Greece intervening) (Judgment), [2012] ICJ Reports, p. 99, para. 57; see also European Court of Human Rights, judgment of 21 November 2001, *Al-Adsani v. United Kingdom* (no. 35763/97), para. 54; Fox

commercial activities may fit into this rationale by arguing that states, when acting like a trader or like a private party, are no longer equal sovereigns. Thus, it may appear acceptable for states to decide over other states which have 'stepped down' on the level of ordinary private citizens by entering into commercial relations and that, in this regard, they should be equally amenable to suit just like any private party would be.[28]

In the case of the jurisdictional immunity of international organizations, the equality paradigm does not appear to work on either level. International organizations are not sovereign and are not equal to states. Thus, the rationale for bestowing them immunity, excepting them from the jurisdiction of state courts, is not based on equality considerations, but rather on the functional necessity of guaranteeing their independence. When it comes to exceptions to jurisdictional immunity, it is obviously tempting for some national courts to apply the restrictive state immunity approach, using some variation of a commercial activity exception to the immunity of international organizations, as courts in Italy[29] and the United States[30] have regularly done. The idea that when international organizations act like private parties they should be subject to the adjudicatory power of national courts, just like their private counterparts, has some intuitive appeal. However, this may still conflict with the underlying rationale to protect their functioning, which often is premised on the performance of activities that might be qualified as commercial. Further, the very express grants of immunity "from every form of legal process" in various treaties[31] seem to exclude such an approach.

Scepticism against according immunity, whether to foreign states or international organizations, has also found support in fundamental/human rights arguments. According to most human rights instruments, individuals enjoy a right of access to justice, among others, in the determination of their (civil) rights and obligations.[32] Such access to justice is often based on more general

---

and Webb, *The Law of State Immunity*, p. 26; Lee M. Caplan, "State Immunity, Human Rights, and Jus Cogens: A Critique of the Normative Hierarchy Theory", in *The American Journal of International Law* vol. 97 (2003), pp. 741–781, at pp. 748–757.

28 See, e.g., Rosanne van Alebeek, *The Immunity of States and Their Officials in International Criminal Law and International Human Rights Law* (Oxford UP, 2008), p. 49.

29 See Riccardo Pavoni, "Italy", in Reinisch (*supra* note 11), pp. 155–171, at pp. 157–162.

30 See Charles H. Brower II, "United States", *ibidem*, pp. 303–327, at pp. 317–23. See also recently the US Supreme Court in *Jam v. International Finance Corporation*, 586 US ##, 139 S. Ct. 759 (2019).

31 See above, text at footnote 16.

32 Art. 10 Universal Declaration of Human Rights, GA Res. 217(III), UN GAOR, 3d Sess., Supp. No. 13, UN Doc. A/810 (1948), 71 ("Everyone is entitled in full equality to a fair and public hearing by an independent and impartial tribunal, in the determination of his rights and

rule of law considerations[33] and overlaps with some customary international law principles concerning the right to a fair trial and the prohibition of a denial of justice.[34]

In the case of state immunity, the development towards a restrictive immunity has, in practice, reduced the problem of an immunity obstacle to access to justice by allowing lawsuits in regard to commercial activities, since such commercial activities often coincide with the determination of civil rights and obligations claimed by individuals.[35] By upholding the absolute immunity of international organizations, however, no corresponding limitation of immunity manages to take care of such fundamental/human rights considerations. It seems, though, that this problem has been recognised on two levels.

---

obligations and of any criminal charge against him"); Art. 14(1) International Covenant on Civil and Political Rights ('ICCPR'), 19 December 1966, 999 *UNTS* 171 (1976) ("All persons are equal before the courts and tribunals. In the determination of any criminal charge against him, or of his rights and obligations in a suit at law, everyone shall be entitled to a fair and public hearing by a competent, independent and impartial tribunal established by law"); Art. 6(1) European Convention on Human Rights, European Convention for the Protection of Human Rights and Fundamental Freedoms, adopted 4 November 1950, entered into force 3 September 1953, 213 *UNTS* 221 ("In the determination of his civil rights and obligations or of any criminal charge against him, everyone is entitled to a fair and public hearing within a reasonable time by an independent and impartial tribunal established by law"); Art. 8(1) American Convention on Human Rights: 'Pact of San José, Costa Rica' (signed 22 November 1969, entered into force 18 July 1978) 1144 *UNTS* 123 ("Every person has the right to a hearing, with due guarantees and within a reasonable time, by a competent, independent, and impartial tribunal, previously established by law, in the substantiation of any accusation of a criminal nature made against him or for the determination of his rights and obligations of a civil, labor, fiscal, or any other nature").

33 United Nations General Assembly, *The Rule of Law at the National and International Levels*, A/RES/69/123, 18 December 2014, para. 14 ("*Recalls* the commitment of the Member States to take all necessary steps to provide fair, transparent, effective, non-discriminatory and accountable services that promote access to justice for all, including legal aid, encourages further dialogue and the sharing of national practices in strengthening the rule of law through access to justice, including with regard to legal aid, where appropriate, in both criminal and civil proceedings, and in this regard stresses the need to intensify the assistance extended to Governments upon their request").

34 Jan Paulsson, *Denial of Justice* (Cambridge UP, 2005), pp. 57–99; Francesco Francioni, "The Rights of Access to Justice under Customary International Law", in Francesco Francioni (ed.), *Access to Justice as a Human Right, Collected Courses of the Academy of European Law* (Oxford UP, 2007); regarding denial of justice in the context of international legal protection of foreigners, see already Charles de Visscher, "Le Déni de Justice en Droit International", in *Collected Courses of the Hague Academy of International Law* vol. 52 (1936), p. 369.

35 Bailey Roe, "Slaying the Leviathan: How Inconsistent Restrictions on State Immunity Undermine the Rule of Law Immunity Undermine the Rule of Law", *American University International Law Review* vol. 36 (2020), pp. 105–132, at pp. 122–125.

On the one hand, human rights bodies and national, often constitutional, courts have developed a jurisprudence pursuant to which access to justice must remain effective even in face of immunities. This implies that exemptions from the jurisdiction of otherwise available national courts are granted only where alternative ways of dispute settlement are available. According to the European Court of Human Rights' judgment in *Waite and Kennedy*,[36] (civil) claims against international organizations involved the right of access to court under Article 6 of the ECHR. And while such right of access to justice might be limited for legitimate purposes, such as protecting the independent functioning of an international organization, this limitation was only legitimate and permissible if it was also proportionate. In the Court's view, the proportionality of the grant of immunity depended upon the availability of "reasonable alternative means".[37] In practice this has led to numerous national courts ascertaining whether alternative forms of dispute settlement are available to private parties when they uphold the immunity of international organizations,[38] though only few courts have taken the step to deny immunity where they consider that no such alternative exists or that it would not be an adequate alternative.[39]

On the other hand, treaty negotiators have already expressly required international organizations for quite some time to provide for alternative means of dispute settlement in regard to contractual disputes as well as other disputes of a private law character. These clauses obligate international organizations to make such forms of dispute settlement available.[40] In other words,

36 European Court of Human Rights, judgments of 18 February 1999, *Waite and Kennedy v Germany* (no. 26083/94) and *Beer and Regan v Germany* (no. 28934/95). The case arose from the fact that German courts granted the European Space Agency jurisdictional immunity from suit by two individuals who claimed to be employees of the organization. The claimants considered that this violated their right of access to court under Article 6 ECHR.

37 *Waite and Kennedy v Germany* (*supra* note 36), para. 68: "[…] a material factor in determining whether granting […] immunity from […] jurisdiction is permissible is whether the applicants had available to them reasonable alternative means to protect effectively their rights under the Convention".

38 See Cedric Ryngaert, "The Immunity of International Organizations Before Domestic Courts: Recent Trends", *IOLR* vol. 7 (2010), p. 121; August Reinisch and Ulf A. Weber, "In the Shadow of Waite and Kennedy. The Jurisdictional Immunity of International Organizations, the Individual's Right of Access to the Courts and Administrative Tribunals as Alternative Means of Dispute Settlement", *IOLR* vol. 1 (2004), p. 59.

39 See, however, *Siedler v Western European Union*, Brussels Labour Court of Appeal (4th chamber), 17 September 2003, *Journal des Tribunaux* 2004, 617, ILDC 53 (BE 2003).

40 See, e.g., Art. VIII Section 29 General Convention: "The United Nations shall make provisions for appropriate modes of settlement of: (a) Disputes arising out of contracts or other disputes of a private law character to which the United Nations is a party".

the accountability gap deriving from according immunity from every form of legal process to international organizations, and the ensuing inequality of private parties, being unable to pursue their rights, because organizations are not amenable to the jurisdiction of the ordinary tribunals, may be closed by the availability of effective alternatives.[41] Devising such mechanisms prevents the unequal outcome of immunity and at the same time permits organizations to function without the interference of national courts in various states where they operate.

7 Conclusion

Where alternative means of dispute settlement are in fact available, individuals are not deprived of means of dispute settlement employed to adjudicate their (civil) rights and obligations vis-à-vis international organizations. It seems to be increasingly recognized that this is the most promising way of keeping and protecting fundamental rights and at the same time safeguarding the independent functioning of international organizations. The latter continue to be usefully protected by their jurisdictional immunity, ensuring that their acts and omissions are not controlled by national courts. Understanding the rationale of other immunities as a safeguard of such independent functioning may also support a more nuanced view of such exemptions. The same is true for the most important privilege enjoyed by international organizations and their staff, their exemption from national taxation. What appears to be the epitome of unequal treatment proves to be a device to achieve equal treatment of its members.

41 See also Niels Blokker and Nico Schrijver, "Afterwords", in *IOLR* vol. 10 (2013), pp. 601–616.

CHAPTER 30

The Personality and Responsibility of International Organizations

Dan Sarooshi[*]

1 Introduction

I am delighted to contribute to this volume in honour of Professor Niels Blokker. Niels has throughout his illustrious career been at the forefront of shaping developments in the law of international organizations, through his teaching at Leiden University, his seminal work with Henry Schermers as well as many other publications, and indeed his work in practice at the Dutch Ministry of Foreign Affairs.

This contribution also focuses on aspects of the law of international organizations. It is an area of public international law that is undergoing profound changes. This has been caused in large part by the increasingly important role that international organizations have played in exercising powers conferred on them by national governments. This phenomenon has led to concerted attempts by States, international courts and tribunals, and domestic courts to seek to ensure accountability for these exercises of power by imposing corresponding limits on international organizations.

This chapter focuses, first, on the development of international law relating to the legal personality of international organizations, using the legal status of the Global Fund to Fight AIDS, Malaria, and Tuberculosis as an example; and then, secondly, turns to discuss the relationship between States and international organizations and the implications of this relationship for the responsibility of States and in some cases the responsibility of international organizations.

* The author is Professor of Public International Law, University of Oxford; King's Counsel & Barrister, Essex Court Chambers, London; and Senior Research Fellow, The Queen's College, Oxford.

 | DOI:10.1163/9789004699939_032

2 The Development of International Law Relating to International Legal Personality: The Curious Case of International Organizations

One of the landmark cases in this area is, of course, the advisory opinion of the International Court of Justice (ICJ) in the *Reparation for Injuries* case.[1] The ICJ clearly established that an international organization can possess international legal personality and pursuant to that personality may well be able to exercise certain powers and have certain capacities on the international plane and indeed the domestic plane.

But the Court was equally clear in saying that this recognition of the international legal personality of the United Nations (UN) is not the same thing as saying that the competences of the Organization are analogous to those of a State: it is States, in the Court's view, that are the omniscient beings on the international legal plane and international organizations by comparison are at best mere mortals. The ICJ stated in its *Reparations* Opinion that

> the [UN] Organization was intended to exercise and enjoy, and is in fact exercising and enjoying, functions and rights which can only be explained on the basis of the possession of a large measure of international personality and the capacity to operate upon an international plane. ... Accordingly, the Court has come to the conclusion that the Organization is an international person. That is not the same thing as saying that it is a State, which it certainly is not, or that its legal personality and rights and duties are the same as those of a State. Still less is it the same thing as saying that it is 'a super-State', whatever that expression may mean. It does not even imply that all its rights and duties must be upon the international plane, any more than all the rights and duties of a State must be upon that plane. What it does mean is that it is a subject of international law and capable of possessing international rights and duties, and that it has capacity to maintain its rights by bringing international claims.[2]

This approach was later confirmed by the ICJ in the *Legality of the Threat or Use of Nuclear Weapons* case, when it stated that international organizations are subjects of international law which do not, unlike States, possess a general competence. Rather, they are governed by the "principle of speciality": i.e.,

1 ICJ, *Reparation for Injuries suffered in the Service of the United Nations*, [1949] ICJ Reports, p. 174.

2 *Ibidem*, p. 179.

they are invested by States with powers, the "limits of which are a function of the common interests whose promotion those States entrust to them".[3]

International organizations have been established in a variety of ways, but what is common in all cases is some form of international agreement or instrument between States governed by international law.[4] The existence of such an international agreement was previously the main criterion employed by the law to distinguish international organizations from non-governmental organizations: this is certainly the approach adopted by the UN,[5] and also the approach taken by the International Law Commission (ILC) in its work on the responsibility of international organizations.[6] International law has, however, developed to be agnostic on the related issue of how an organization can be created. International law recognizes that it is possible for an international organization to be created by evolution over time so long as there is some form of agreement between three or more States establishing the organization.[7]

What is also of interest is that international law does allow an entity to evolve over time into an international organization. The following section provides a case-study which considers the transformation of the Global Fund to Fight AIDS, Malaria, and Tuberculosis (GF) – initially established as a Swiss private law foundation – into something akin to an international organization with international legal personality, possessing powers and functions on both the international and domestic planes.

The GF was established in 2002 in Switzerland, ostensibly as a private Swiss foundation established under Swiss law. It is an international financing

3 ICJ, *Legality of the Threat or Use of Nuclear Weapons case*, [1996] ICJ Reports, p. 66, at para. 24.

4 See, e.g., in the case of the European Union, N.M. Blokker, "The Macro Level: The Structural Impact of General International Law on EU Law: International Legal Personality of the European Communities and the European Union: Inspirations from Public International Law", in *Yearbook of European Law* vol. 35 (2016), pp. 471–483; and in the case of the OSCE, N.M. Blokker and R.A. Wessel, "Revisiting Questions of Organisationhood, Legal Personality and Membership in the OSCE: The Interplay Between Law, Politics and Practice", in M. Steinbrueck Platise, C. Moser and A. Peters (eds.), *The Legal Framework of the OSCE* (Cambridge UP, 2019), pp. 135–164.

5 See also ECOSOC Resolutions 1296 (XLIV), 23 May 1968 and Resolution 1996/31, 25 July 1996.

6 See *Report of the ILC*, 55th Session (2003), UN Doc. A/58/10, p. 38.

7 For example, a decision to establish an organization may be by government representatives assembled in a conference without using a treaty and thus without the formal requirement of subsequent ratification of the treaty by States. This was the way the Asian-African Legal Consultative Committee was originally established and the basis on which it was operated. It is also the way that the Organization of the Petroleum Exporting Countries (OPEC) was created by a resolution adopted by a conference of States in 1960: it was only at the 43rd Session in 2004 that a new and revised Text of Statutes – in effect a constituent instrument – was adopted by States.

institution dedicated to attracting and distributing resources to prevent and treat AIDS, malaria, and tuberculosis and its work is estimated to have saved millions of lives. The GF seeks to work below the formal level of the nation State to promote and fund partnerships between government, civil society, the private sector, and the communities directly affected by the three diseases to reduce the causes and incidences of the diseases.

The GF has 59 States who participate in its work, but it also has a strong civil society component: for example, full members of the GF Board include persons who actually suffer from the three diseases as well as various major donors to the GF such as the Bill & Melinda Gates Foundation. The GF is one of the best-funded international organizations in the world. Between the period 2002 to 2015, 54 donor governments have pledged US$ 28.8 billion and have already paid US$ 24 billion to the GF,[8] quite apart from the very significant contributions made by private foundations such as the Gates Foundation.[9] The GF is continually giving away its money to fund the fight against the three diseases and it has supported more than 1,000 programs in 151 States.

Initially the GF had concluded with the World Health Organization (WHO) an Administrative Services Agreement (ASA) such that GF officials were formally employed by the WHO so that these GF officials enjoyed the privileges and immunities of WHO officials. The GF (despite its formal status as a Swiss private law foundation) and its officials have also been given extensive privileges and immunities within Switzerland pursuant to the Headquarters Agreement between the GF and the Swiss Federal Council dated 13 December 2004.[10] The Headquarters Agreement also states in relation to the GF's legal personality that Switzerland recognizes for the purposes of this Agreement "the international juridical personality and legal capacity in Switzerland" of the GF. Moreover, the GF had also entered into a Trust Fund arrangement with the World Bank with whom it kept its assets in the United States, thereby allowing GF property to enjoy the Bank's immunity from legal process and execution within the United States pursuant to the US International Organizations Immunities Act 1945. Finally, in terms of privileges and immunities, the GF has been granted extensive privileges and immunities within the United States by its designation as an international organization enjoying privileges and immunities.[11]

8 See <http://www.theglobalfund.org/en/donors/public/>.

9 See <http://www.theglobalfund.org/en/donors/private/gatesfoundation/>.

10 The formal title being the Agreement between the Swiss Federal Council and the GF in view of determining the legal status of the GF in Switzerland.

11 Pursuant to s. 288 of the U.S. International Organizations Immunities Act of 1945. This designation was by the U.S. President in an Executive Order dated 13 January 2006.

The GF at a certain point decided that it wanted to terminate the ASA, and did so with effect from January 2009. With the termination of the ASA there was a real need for the GF to enjoy privileges and immunities under international law to ensure that the GF and its officials could continue to do their important work focused on the fight against the three diseases without having to pay significant sums of money – through taxes of various types and forms, including, e.g., taxes on currency transfers – to the various States where it had programs, and also to protect GF staff who may, e.g., have to investigate a country program for fraud or other potentially problematic reasons. As the ICJ held in the *Reparations* case, it is necessary for officials of an international organization to enjoy immunities precisely so that they can exercise their international functions efficiently and independent of States, including their State of nationality.[12]

The GF subsequently engaged with a number of its donor and recipient States and together they drafted a treaty that confers privileges and immunities on the GF.[13] This treaty – the Agreement on Privileges and Immunities of the GF – was adopted by the GF Board in 2010 when it adopted a decision recommending to all GF States, and indeed all States, that they ratify this treaty, and the process of ratification of this treaty is now ongoing.

The rationale here for the conferral by States of such privileges and immunities on the GF, despite its formal status as an international organization being unclear, is that this was possible since the conferral of privileges and immunities on an organization is within the sole gift and discretion of States. The generally accepted privileges and immunities of international organizations operate to exempt an organization from the adjudicative and enforcement jurisdictions of the State[14] – in practice, international organizations and their officials are immune from all forms of legal process within States, they do not have to pay certain taxes, and the police and other arms of the executive branch of government cannot exercise certain of their powers in relation to the international organization or its officials. As such, it is entirely open to States to conclude a treaty that confers privileges and immunities on an entity with an international mandate and objectives, and this is precisely what happened in the case of the GF.

12 *Reparation for Injuries* (*supra* note 1), at p. 183.

13 This author had the privilege of assisting the GF in drafting this treaty.

14 An international organization is still bound by the laws of the States in which it operates: see H.G. Schermers and N.M. Blokker, *International Institutional Law* (6th ed., Brill Nijhoff, 2018), p. 1084.

Indeed there is precedent for a similar – though certainly not identical – approach in the case of the International Committee of the Red Cross (ICRC). The ICRC like the GF is a private association under Swiss Law, and they are both listed by the Swiss Federal Department of Foreign Affairs in its document entitled *International organizations in Switzerland* under the heading "Other [i.e. non-UN System] international organizations in Switzerland".

The ICRC, however, is widely recognized as enjoying privileges and immunities that are comparable to those of the United Nations and other international organizations. These privileges and immunities are largely contained in the Headquarters Agreements and concomitant legislation in the nearly 80 countries in which the ICRC carries out significant operations, but before an international tribunal the ICRC has had to rely on privileges and immunities under customary international law, most notably before a Trial Chamber of the UN International Criminal Tribunal for the former Yugoslavia (ICTY) in the 1999 decision in the *Simić* case.[15]

The ICTY decision concerned the Prosecutor's proposal in the criminal trial of Simic and others to call a former ICRC employee who was willing to give evidence of facts that came to his knowledge by virtue of, and during, the course of his official acts as an ICRC employee. The ICRC opposed this before the ICTY on the basis that the testimony of a former ICRC employee would involve a violation of, *inter alia*, the ICRC's international mandate and its privileges and immunities under customary international law. The ICTY in the *Simic* case held "[i]t is widely acknowledged that the ICRC, an independent humanitarian organization, enjoys a special status in international law, based on the mandate conferred upon it by the international community".[16] An important way in which this mandate is conferred on the ICRC is by the Geneva Conventions, and the ICTY went on to state that

> As is well known, the Geneva Conventions enjoy nearly universal participation as virtually all States are parties to the four Geneva Conventions. … The Trial Chamber is of the view that, by accepting to be bound by the Geneva Conventions, the States party to them have agreed to the special role and mandate of the ICRC.[17]

---

15 ICTY, *Prosecutor v. Simić et al.*, Case No. IT-95-9-PT, 27 July 1999.

16 *Ibidem*, para. 46.

17 In large part on this basis, the ICTY found the ICRC has a right under customary international law to non-disclosure of the information in the knowledge of a former employee before the ICTY, and thus the ICTY decided that the evidence sought to be presented by the Prosecutor should not be given.

While the GF may not be able to claim that it operates on the basis of a mandate conferred upon it by a treaty as such, all this means is that it would not be easy at present for the GF to claim that it enjoys the privileges and immunities of an international organization under customary international law.

But there is nonetheless a strong case to be made that the GF is carrying out a mandated conferred by the international community. In the case of the GF, Section II of the Framework Document of the GF, entitled "Purpose", provides as follows:

> The purpose of the Fund is to attract, manage and disburse additional resources through a new public-private partnership that will make a sustainable and significant contribution to the reduction of infections, illness and death, thereby mitigating the impact caused by HIV/AIDS, tuberculosis and malaria in countries in need, and contributing to poverty reduction as part of the Millennium Development Goals.

It is arguable that in order to achieve these purposes it is necessary for the GF to be able to operate on the international plane with a large degree of independence from its donor and recipient States. Otherwise it would not, e.g., be possible for the GF to ensure that the grants it makes are being used effectively and in a financially accountable way by recipient States to reduce in a "sustainable and significant" way the impact caused by HIV/AIDS, tuberculosis, and malaria. The GF has also concluded a number of agreements with recipient States which imposes obligations on these States in relation to use of GF grants, and this requires the GF to have a position of detachment in order to ensure these States are complying with their obligations.[18] All of this is quite apart from the requirement for the GF to provide functional protection to its officials as explained above.

3 The Relationship between States and International Organizations and the Issue of Responsibility for Unlawful Acts by an International Organization

States confer powers on international organizations to allow them to achieve specified objectives. However when considering issues of responsibility – whether of the organization or State or both – there needs to be consideration

18 Moreover, the GF in its Foundation Board and Secretariat possesses a power of binding decision-making that is independent from that of its participant States.

given to the nature of the *specific relationship* between a State and an international organization since these vary greatly in practice. Indeed the mechanism by which these powers can be conferred by States on an organization also varies – they may be conferred by means of a State's ratification of a constituent treaty which provides for such conferrals[19] or they may be conferred by States on an *ad hoc* basis outside the context of a membership scenario.

A useful way of analysing these relationships is to consider the degree to which a State has given away, or conferred, its powers to an international organization. These conferrals of powers can be considered as being on a spectrum that has at one end a conferral of power which establishes an agency relationship between the State and the international organization and at the other extremity there is a conferral of power which involves the 'transfer' of powers to the international organization. The intermediate category of conferral can usefully be characterized as a 'delegation' by States of powers to an international organization.

There are three characteristics of conferrals that can be used to ascertain the degree to which powers have been given away by a State, and thus within which category a particular conferral of powers can be placed. First is the question of revocability: can a State lawfully revoke its conferral of powers onto an international organization? Second is the degree to which States retain control over the exercise of powers by the international organization. The third is whether an international organization possesses an exclusive right to exercise conferred powers or whether States have retained the right to exercise powers concurrently with the international organization.

In the case of an 'agency relationship',[20] the conferral of powers is revocable on a unilateral basis; States can exert direct control over the international organization's exercise of powers; and States retain the right to exercise powers concurrent with, and independent of, the organization's exercise of powers. In the case of a 'delegation of powers',[21] the conferral of powers is revocable on a unilateral basis; States cannot exert direct control over the international organization's exercise of powers, but States retain the right to exercise powers concurrent with, and independent of, the international organization's exercise

19 ICJ, *Legality of the Threat or Use of Nuclear Weapons*, [1996] ICJ Reports, at p. 79, para. 25.

20 On the existence of such agency relationships, see D. Sarooshi, "Conferrals by States of Powers on international organizations: The Case of Agency", in *British Yearbook of International Law* vol. 74 (2004), pp. 291–332.

21 On such delegations of powers, see D. Sarooshi, *International Organizations and Their Exercise of Sovereign Powers* (Oxford UP, 2005), Chapter 4.

of powers. An example of a delegation of powers is the conferral by States of powers on the United Nations.

Finally, in the case of a 'transfer of powers', the conferral of powers is irrevocable according to law; States cannot exert direct control over the international organization's exercise of powers and nor do States retain the right to exercise powers concurrent with, and independent of, the international organization's exercise of powers, that is, a State has consented to be bound by obligations that flow from the international organization's exercise of conferred powers. It is particularly difficult to measure the precise degree to which States have given away their powers in the case of transfers. It is for this reason that there is a need to distinguish between 'partial transfers' and 'full transfers'. The difference between these two sub-categories depends on the extent to which States can be said to have consented to be bound by obligations that flow from an international organization's exercise of conferred powers.

In the case of 'partial transfers', a State agrees to be bound by obligations that flow from the international organization's exercise of powers on the international plane. An example of a partial transfer is provided by the case of the WTO dispute settlement system where States have consented to be bound on the international plane by decisions of the WTO panels and Appellate Body in a case. In the case of 'full transfers', however, the State has also agreed to give direct effect within its domestic legal order to the obligations that flow from the international organization's exercise of powers such that they can be relied on by persons within the State without the need for separate domestic legislation. The best, and most obvious, instance of a 'full transfer' is the case of the European Union where, for example, Council regulations have direct effect within the legal systems of member States and will, in the view of the European Court of Justice, prevail over all domestic law sources.

These categories are not watertight compartments and especially in the 'delegation' and 'transfer' categories a State's relationship with an international organization may well have elements of both types of conferrals of power. Yet these categories are very useful when considering the differing relationships between States and international organizations and can help clarify a number of the consequences that flow from these relationships, including, for present purposes, issues of responsibility. This chapter will limit itself to a consideration of the issues of responsibility relating to transfers and delegations of power.[22]

22 In the case of agency relationships between States and international organizations, see *ibidem*.

3.1 *Transfers of Powers to International Organizations and the Issue of Responsibility*

The question here is whether States can be held responsible on a primary or secondary basis for an internationally wrongful act (wrongful act) committed by an international organization exercising transferred powers. It is useful to consider this matter in relation to the separate categories of a 'partial' and 'full' transfers of powers since they have differing consequences. We recall from above that a partial transfer of powers is where the decision by an international organization in the exercise of transferred powers imposes an international legal obligation on the State to comply with the decision; while the case of a full transfer is where the international organization's decision has direct effect within the State's internal legal order without the need for domestic legislative enactment.

3.1.1 Partial Transfers of Powers

In case of a 'partial transfer of power' the State is bound on the international plane to comply with decisions of an international organization over which the State has no direct control. But the lack of direct control by a State over a wrongful act committed by an international organization does not exclude all potential bases of responsibility for the State. Control is sufficient but not of course always necessary for establishing attribution for the purposes of State responsibility. There is still arguably a potential basis for attributing the wrongful acts of an international organization to transferring States by application of Article 5 of the ILC's Articles on State Responsibility which provides:

> The conduct of. … [an] entity … not … [a State] organ but which is empowered by the law of that State to exercise elements of the governmental authority shall be considered an act of the State under international law, provided the … entity is acting in that capacity in the particular instance.

In my view, such an "entity" may include an international organization exercising powers of government conferred by a State on that international organization, and it would apply in the case of a full transfer of powers since this transfer of powers will, by its nature, have taken place pursuant to an internal law of the State. But Article 5 is also arguably applicable in the case of a partial transfer of powers where a State will have *agreed under its internal law* to be bound by the organization's exercise of powers on the international plane.

In addition to this potential case of attribution there are arguably three other potential bases for States being held responsible for wrongful acts of an international organization exercising partially transferred powers. Two of these bases flow from the State's *own* acts or omissions.

The first is where a State's implementation within its domestic legal system of a decision by an international organization involves the State committing a wrongful act. In the case of a partial transfers of powers, the organization's decision does not have direct effect within the State's legal system and thus the State may choose not to give domestic legal effect to a decision where it would involve the commission of a wrongful act. If the State were, however, to implement the organization's decision and commit a wrongful act, then it should be held responsible under international law for this act pursuant to Article 1 of the ILC Articles on State Responsibility. And yet this is obviously problematic for the State concerned, since it is being required in such a case to disobey an obligation on the international plane which flows from the organization's exercise of transferred powers. It is for this reason that, when States transfer powers to an international organization, they must try and ensure that the organization's exercise of powers would not lead to the imposition on them of obligations that are inconsistent with a treaty obligation owed to another State that is not a party to the treaty that transfers powers.

In practice, however, it may be very difficult for a State to determine in advance whether the transfer of powers to an international organization may lead to such a conflict of treaty obligations. A possible way to avoid such a conflict is for the negotiating States to decide, where possible, to 'delegate' and not 'transfer' their powers to an organization so that they will not be bound to comply with decisions taken by the organization when exercising conferred powers.

The second case where a State's responsibility can be engaged in relation to the exercise by an organization of partially transferred powers, is where a State aids or assists the organization in the commission of a wrongful act. This responsibility flows from the application, *mutatis mutandis*, of Article 16 of the ILC Articles, which provides that a State is responsible if it "aids or assists" another State to commit a wrongful act if, *inter alia*, it does so with knowledge of the circumstances of the wrongful act. Thus a State may be held responsible for the act of rendering assistance to an international organization in its commission of a wrongful act in the exercise of partially transferred powers. However, in the case of a partial transfer of powers, the primary responsibility of the State would only arise in relation to the actions taken by the State to implement the organization's decision within its domestic legal system.

An important element of the acts of aid or assistance covered by Article 16 is that they are entirely voluntary and, since in the case of partial transfers the

State is bound on the international plane by decisions of the organization, the State can only be held primarily responsible for those voluntary acts of aid or assistance rendered to an organization within its domestic legal system where it is not so bound.

Finally, there is a potential secondary responsibility of States that flows from the commission by an international organization of a wrongful act in the exercise of partially transferred powers. This secondary responsibility is arguably engaged where States actively pursue or support the particular decision in the organization that causes the commission of the wrongful act.

It is even arguable that States should take action within the international organization – e.g., by voting against a decision – to try and ensure that the organization does not commit a wrongful act, and that the failure to do so may engage a secondary responsibility of the State for the organization's act. This rule of secondary responsibility is necessary, arguably, to ensure the systemic integrity of international law. Otherwise it would be a simple matter for States to avoid their obligations under international law by establishing an organization to which they transfer powers and then disclaim all responsibility for the way in which those powers are exercised within the international organization.

3.1.2 Full Transfers of Powers

In the case of a full transfer of powers – such as in relation to the European Union – the decision of the organization binds the State on the international plane but also has direct effect within a State's legal system. In these cases the main basis for the wrongful acts of an organization being attributable to a transferring State is by application of Article 5 of the ILC Articles on State Responsibility. Cases of full transfers are clearly instances where States have conferred on an international organization "the exercise of certain elements of governmental authority" and thus, according to Article 5, "shall be considered an act of the State under international law".

Moreover, the main limitation placed by the Commission's commentary on the scope of application of Article 5 – that it is limited "to entities which are empowered by internal law to exercise governmental authority" – is more than adequately fulfilled in the case of full transfers where decisions of the international organization go further to have a direct effect within the State's legal system. A good example of the potential application of Article 5 is where an international organization exercises transferred powers in such a way that it violates the human rights obligations owed by States. In such cases, a State cannot successfully contend that its hands were tied by the international organization's exercise of transferred powers. The jurisprudence of the European Court of Human Rights is instructive on this point, particularly the decision of the

Court in the *Matthews* case. The Court was concerned, in part, with the question whether the United Kingdom could be held responsible on an individual basis for acting pursuant to Council Decision 76/787 whereby provisions were laid down concerning the election of the members of the European Parliament which in effect excluded those persons who were living in Gibraltar, a dependent territory of the UK, from having the right to participate in the election. This was said to be in violation of the European Convention on Human Rights.

The UK Government contended, *inter alia*, that, while there may be circumstances where a party to the ECHR might infringe its Convention obligations by entering into other treaty obligations that were incompatible with the Convention, they considered that in the present case the position was not the same since "acts adopted by the Community or consequent to its requirements could not be imputed to the member States, together or individually, particularly when those acts concerned elections to a constitutional organ of the Community itself".[23] Moreover, at the hearing the Government suggested – based presumably on Article 8 of the ILC Articles on State Responsibility – that to engage the responsibility of a State under the Convention requires the State to have a power of effective control over the act complained of and that, in the case of the Community provisions relating to the election of the European Parliament, the UK Government had no such control. This argument lacks cogency. In addition to Article 8 there is still in the case of full transfers by State of powers to international organizations the potential basis of attribution provided by Article 5 on State responsibility. The European Court in the *Matthews* case made several pronouncements in support of the application of Article 5 in cases of full transfers (*in casu*, to the EU). The Court found in its judgment that, although the ECHR does not exclude States parties being able to confer powers on international organizations, it does require, however, that if such conferrals take place then Convention rights must continue to be "secured". The Court held that member States' responsibility under the ECHR "continues even after such a transfer".[24]

In the end, however, the European Court of Human Rights did not have to deal directly with the issue of UK responsibility for a Community act since it found that the 1976 Act was not a "'normal' act of the Community, but is a treaty within the Community legal order". Accordingly, the Court based the UK's responsibility on its subsequent acceptance of the Act, being as it was an international instrument "freely entered into by" the UK. In the context of our

23 European Court of Human Rights, judgment of 18 February 1999, *Matthews v the United Kingdom* (no. 24833/94), para. 26.

24 *Ibidem*, para. 32.

discussion above, this represents the commission by the UK of its own wrongful act rather than having an EU wrongful act attributed to the UK.

There is, finally, a potential secondary responsibility of States in the case of full transfers where States have actively pursued or supported within the international organization the decision that mandates the commission of the wrongful act. The considerations relating to this secondary responsibility are the same as those pertaining in the case of a partial transfer of powers already considered earlier.

3.2 *Delegations of Powers to International Organizations and Issues of Responsibility*

In the case where an international organization commits a wrongful act then Article 3 of the ILC Articles on the Responsibility of International Organizations makes clear that this engages the international organization's responsibility. The remaining question is whether such an act can be attributed to a State that has delegated powers to an international organization thus establishing a State's primary responsibility under international law. In the case of agency relationships, the issue of responsibility is clear: effective control (a definitional element of agency) exercised by States over an international organization means that its acts are attributable to States. In cases of delegations, however, such control does not exist and, applying by analogy the ILC's Articles on State Responsibility, there would seem to be no other possible bases for attribution of an international organization's wrongful acts to delegating States. But this only relates to the issue of State responsibility for an international organization's acts. There are three other circumstances where a State should arguably be held responsible in connection with a wrongful act by an international organization that exercises delegated powers. In all three cases the responsibility of the State does not flow from its relationship with the international organization to which it has delegated powers, but from its own acts or omissions.

In the case of delegations a State is not bound by the international organization's exercise of delegated powers. Thus where a State chooses to participate in, or implement domestically, a wrongful act committed by an international organization exercising delegated powers, then the State will be held responsible on a primary basis for its own commission of a wrongful act pursuant to the Commission's Article 1 on State Responsibility. The State cannot seek to escape responsibility for its own acts in such cases by hiding behind the non-binding decision of an international organization in the case of delegations of powers.

The second case where a State's responsibility can be engaged in relation to the exercise by an international organization of delegated powers is where a State aids or assists the international organization in the commission of a wrongful act pursuant to the application, *mutatis mutandis*, of Article 16 on State Responsibility as already explained above in the case of a transfer of powers. However, the argument in relation to Article 16 applies with greater force in the case of delegation of powers, since any aid or assistance given by a State to an international organization in such cases is entirely voluntary and as such a State will very likely be caught by Article 16.

Finally, there is also the arguable secondary responsibility of the State that is engaged where States actively pursue or support within the international organization the decision that causes the commission of the wrongful act.

4 Concluding Remarks

The modern history of international law comprises the history of States. The future history of international law will likely be written to a greater extent by international organizations. International organizations are today increasingly exercising sovereign powers – whether it is the European Union or the United Nations – and the exercise of these powers is effecting important normative and societal changes within States. This area requires a far greater engagement by the legal academy. It will require no less than the development of a truly international public law that regulates the exercise of powers of government on the international plane.

CHAPTER 31

The Great Unknown

General Principles Governing the Law of International Organizations

*Kirsten Schmalenbach**

1 Introduction

In his article entitled *International Organizations and Customary International Law*, Niels Blokker raised one of the key provocative questions on the minds of all those involved in the workings of international organizations: "Is the International Law Commission taking international organizations seriously?"[1] This question is not only valid regarding the *Draft Conclusions on the Identification of Customary International Law* that were adopted by the International Law Commission (ILC) in 2018,[2] but also for the ILC's more recent project on *General Principles of Law*.[3] All three reports on the latter topic, authored by ILC Special Rapporteur Marcelo Vázquez-Bermúdez, as well as the ILC comments attached to its 2023 draft conclusions on general principles of law, give the reader the impression that the Commission does not know what to do with international actors that are not states. In these draft conclusions, the ILC dealt with both general principles of law derived from national legal systems and general principles of international law (draft conclusion 3). Only the former are of interest here. According to the ILC, general principles of law are derived from national legal systems (draft conclusion 4) and must be transposed to the international legal order (draft conclusion 6), the latter of which requires a compatibility test. Transposability due to compatibility implies that the general principle under consideration is recognized as a part of international law by the "community of nations" (draft conclusion 2).

---

* The author is Professor of International and European Law, Paris-Lodron University of Salzburg.

1 Niels Blokker, "International Organizations and Customary International Law – Is the International Law Commission Taking International Organizations Seriously?", in *International Organizations Law Review* (IOLR) vol. 14 (2017), p. 1.

2 ILC, *Draft Conclusion on identification of customary international law*, 25 May 2018, UN Doc A/73/10, at p. 119.

3 ILC, *General principles of law – Text of the draft conclusions provisionally adopted by the Drafting Committee on first reading*, 12 May 2023, UN Doc A/CN.4/L.982.

 | DOI:10.1163/9789004699939_033

Those closely following the ILC's work cannot be surprised by its state-centred approach to international legal sources. However, the concern remains that the Commission deliberately leaves blind spots in areas that may be too controversial. That said, it is worth examining the few passages where the ILC comments on the role that international organizations can play within the context of the general principles of law. To start with, draft conclusion 2 appears to offer more complexity than its seemingly straightforward wording suggests, when it stipulates that "(f)or a general principle of law to exist, it must be recognized by the community of nations". The ILC in its commentary clarifies in the vaguest language possible that the term "community of nations" does not preclude that, in certain circumstances, international organizations may also contribute to the formation of the general principles of law.[4] The three reports of the Special Rapporteur do not help to substantiate this claim, although they do clarify that recognition – explicit or implicit – has to take place on the international plane, not within states' legal systems.[5] However, despite international organizations being well-recognized international actors, the ILC does not support the assumption that they play a decisive role as far as the recognition of general principles of law is concerned. Rather, the Special Rapporteur opined that the practice of international organizations helps to ascertain that certain principles common to various legal systems of the world exist (draft conclusion 4 (a)),[6] thereby reducing the role of international organizations and their international administrative tribunals to sources of legal knowledge.

This contribution argues that there is more to the practice of international organizations than the ILC is prepared to openly admit. In light of the many general principles that shape the legal order of international organizations, especially in their internal employment relations but also beyond, the following contribution explores the idea of general principles governing the internal law of a large number, if not all, international organizations and thereby forming a *corpus iuris communis*. Along the way, several issues which the ILC turns a blind eye to need addressing, starting with the fundamental questions of whether the general principles of internal international organizations law fall within the ambit of Article 38 of the Statute of the International Court of Justice (ICJ) (paragraph 2), how the ILC methodological approach relates to

4 ILC, *Draft Conclusion on general principles of law adopted by the Commission on first reading with commentaries*, UN Doc A/78/10, at p. 14, para. 5.

5 ILC Special Rapporteur Marcelo Vázquez-Bermúdez, *First report on the general principles of law*, para. 174, UN Doc A/CN.4/732, 5 April 2019; *Second report on the general principles of law*, para. 22, UN Doc A/CN.4/741, 9 April 2020.

6 Second Report (*supra* note 5), para. 72.

these general principles of international organizations law (paragraph 3) and, finally, whether there are general principles of law common to all international organizations' legal orders (paragraph 4).

2 General Principles Pursuant to Article 38 ICJ Statute and Beyond

Unsurprisingly, the ILC took Article 38 para. 1 (c) ICJ Statute as the starting point of its work on the general principles of law, considering the provision as an authoritative statement on their legal nature.[7] This inevitably raises the question of whether the general principles forming part of international organizations' internal legal orders fall within the scope of the ILC's work programme on 'general principles of law as a source of international law'.[8] At first glance, the report of the Special Rapporteur appears to provide a negative answer. Administrative tribunals are briefly mentioned in the first report as one of the many international judicial bodies that apply the general principles of law.[9] However, that is as far as it goes. At no point did the ILC consider in more detail the extensive practice of these tribunals in the identification, invocation and application of general principles of law when dealing with international organizations' employment relations.[10] Without speculating on the reasons for this, the ILC's omission did serve to avoid a controversial issue: is the legal order of international organizations, including the general principle of law governing their employment relations, a part of the corpus of public international law? The discussion here is as old as international organizations themselves and despite authoritative voices such as Amerashinghe,[11] Schermers and Blokker[12] having given decisively affirmative answers, their arguments have not persuaded the 'separatists'[13] among international scholars.[14] Whereas the internal law of international organizations clearly derives from the relevant

7 First Report (*supra* note 5), para. 14.
8 Report of the ILC, 69th Session (2017), UN Doc A/72/10 at p. 224, Annex A, para. 4.
9 First report (*supra* note5), para. 138.
10 However, see the extensive footnote 324 on August Reinisch's opinion on the matter, in ILC Special Rapporteur *First report*, p. 55.
11 C.F. Amerasinghe, *The Law of the International Civil Service* vol. I (Clarendon Press, 1994), pp. 22–25.
12 Henry Schermers and Niels Blokker, *International Institutional Law* (6th ed., Brill, 2018), § 1196.
13 Other authors label them as "constitutionalist", cf. Lorence Gasparri, *The Concept of an International Organization in International Law* (Oxford UP, 2021), p. 34.
14 Philippe Cahier, "L'ordre juridique interne des organisations internationales", in: René-Jean Dupuy (ed.) *Manuel sur les organisations internationales* (2nd ed., Brill, 1998), p. 237;

constituent instrument, the international legal nature of which is undisputed, it has some unique characteristics that have been considered indicative of its separate legal character.[15] At least those rules of international organizations that concern their administration and operability are largely inward-looking and statutory and, therefore, share more characteristics with national law than consent-based international law. However, member states consent to an international organization's internal rule-setting powers which are necessary to carry out its functions within the framework of the constituent instrument, as the ICJ stressed in the *Effect of Awards* Advisory Opinion.[16] Ultimately, the legal classification of internal international organizations law depends on which of the two faces of Janus you prefer to look at, the one facing the member states or the other facing the internal administration.

Of course, the legal nature of the general principles of law which are applicable within the legal order of international organizations can be determined independently from the latter's overall legal nature. Just as international treaties are a part of the legal order of international organizations, first and foremost constituent instruments, general principles of law recognized as a part of international law pursuant to Article 38 ICJ Statute can also be part of this order. In this regard, it is worth recalling that the ICJ's advisory jurisdiction puts the Court in the position to apply and, if necessary, review internal international organizations law.[17] Although Article 38 ICJ Statute determines first and foremost the international legal sources relevant in contentious proceedings, the provision is also applicable in advisory proceedings via Article 68 ICJ Statute. Therefore, when the ICJ established in the *Effect of Awards* Advisory Opinion that judgments of the UN Administrative Tribunal are *res judicata*, it applied a "well-established and generally recognized principle of law"[18] within the meaning of Article 38 ICJ Statute. If there were any doubts in this respect, because the ICJ refrained from mentioning Article 38 ICJ Statute, they should have been resolved when, in *Territorial and Maritime Dispute*

Christiane Ahlborn, "The Rules of International Organizations and the Law of International Responsibility", in *IOLR* vol. 8 (2011), pp. 397, 417.

15 Fernando Lusa Bordin, *The Analogy between States and International Organizations* (Cambridge UP, 2018), pp. 52, 54.

16 ICJ, *Effect of awards of compensation made by the UN Administrative Tribunal*, Advisory Opinion, [1954] ICJ Reports, pp. 47, 57.

17 Art. 11 of the Statute of the United Nations Administrative Tribunal, as amended in GA Res. A/RES/957 (X) of 8 November 1955. The jurisdiction was abolished in 1996 by GA Res. A/RES/50/54 of 11 December 1995. The ICJ jurisdiction pursuant to Art. XII of Annex to Statute of Administrative Tribunal of International was removed in 2016.

18 ICJ, *supra* note 16, pp. 47, 53.

(*Nicaragua v. Colombia*), the Court referred to its *Effect-of-Awards* findings on *res judicata*.[19] Fully in line with the ILC draft conclusions, it can be maintained that the *res iudicata* effect of international organizations' tribunal awards is based on a general principle of law common to most if not all national legal systems and recognized by the "community of nations" – including international organizations – as part of international law. However, can the same be said of those general principles of law that the international administrative tribunals have identified as governing the international organizations' employment relations?

3 General Principles within the Internal Law of Individual Organizations

To answer the question raised above, it helps to look at the general principles of law within the international organizations' legal order, especially those identified by administrative tribunals in the context of staff disputes (3.1) and beyond (3.2).

3.1 *Employment Relations*

In the 1930s, the Administrative Tribunal of the League of Nations sought guidance on the general principles of law where League of Nations staff regulations were deemed incomplete.[20] In the almost 100 years since, other administrative tribunals have adopted the same approach and today there is a large body of case law dealing with the general principles of law governing international organizations' employment relations. The range of principles that administrative tribunals have identified is wide: good faith, the concomitant duty of care, non-retroactivity, non-discrimination, proportionality, unjust enrichment, protection of legitimate expectation, acquired rights, right to be heard and foreseeability to name but few. What is of more interest than their number and substance is the methodological approach that administrative tribunals take towards general principles of law. Unsurprisingly, their decisions are not forthcoming with information on which collection of laws they base the

---

19 ICJ, *Territorial and Maritime Dispute (Nicaragua v. Colombia), Application for Permission to Intervene*, Judgment, [2011] ICJ Reports, p. 420, para. 67.

20 [1932] League of Nations Administrative Tribunal Judgment No. 5, p. 5: "the Administrative Tribunal, which must rule in accordance with legal rules, cannot subscribe to this submission which is unsupported by any of the positive provisions of the Staff Regulations or by general principles of law".

identification of these principles. It is not farfetched that, as Amerasinghe suggests, tribunal judges base their view on the domestic law they know best.[21] That said, several general principles governing international organizations' employment relations are based on universal human rights and equally well-recognized principles of procedural law that safeguard the rights of the parties to proceedings. In addition, over time, administrative tribunals have developed a consolidated body of general principles which they refer to as "principles of the law of the international civil service".[22] As the term indicates, this set of principles is tailored to the specifics of international organizations' employment relationships. Legal principles, such as the *Fleming*[23] and *Noblemaire* principles,[24] both of which serve to correlate the employment conditions of international organizations staff with those of the host country, illustrate that some general principles are not drawn from domestic laws but from the functionality requirements of international organizations.[25] For example, in *Reparation for Injuries*, the ICJ offered a strictly functional rationale for the UN's legal right and duty to protect its agents against encroaching states by emphasising that the functional-protection principle safeguards agents' ability to effectively and independently perform their duties for the organization.[26] With reference to the *Reparation for Injuries* Advisory Opinion, the Administrative Tribunal of the International Labour Organization (ILOAT) in the *Jurado* case referred to the ILO's duty to provide functional protection as "a general principle concerning the rights of international civil service".[27]

It is clear from the above that the question of who recognizes the general principles governing international organizations' employment conditions has differentiated answers. Insofar as these principles have their origins in

21 Amerasinghe (*supra* note 111), p. 158.

22 Cf. [1974] ILOAT Judgment 242, paras. 2, 12.

23 According to the *Flemming* principle, general service conditions of employment are based on best prevailing local conditions. The principle was developed by a UN Committee of Experts on Salary in 1949: UNAT Judgment No. 1100 (2003), p. 4.

24 According to the *Noblemaire* principle, salaries of the professional category are determined by reference to those applicable in the civil service of the country with the highest pay levels. The name stems from the Chairman of a Committee of the League of Nations which first formulated the principle in 1921. Back then, the comparator for the League of Nations was the British civil service; for the UN it is the US's national civil service: [1987] ILOAT Judgment 831, 1st consideration.

25 Gerhard Ullrich, *The Law of the International Civil Service* (Duncker & Humblot, 2018), p. 82.

26 ICJ, *Reparation for Injuries Suffered in the Service of the United Nations* (Advisory Opinion), [1947] ICJ Reports, pp. 174, 183.

27 [1964] ILOAT, Judgment No. 70, para. 3.

universally recognized human rights law, the answer is evident: the international community of states. The same can be said of general principles of procedural law identified *in foro domestico*, which are not only applied by administrative tribunals but also by international courts and tribunals that are not concerned with international organizations' staff disputes.[28] These principles embody universal standards and rules of conduct that must always be applied, as the ICSID tribunal noted in *Inceysa Vallisoletana*.[29]

However, the general principles of law which emerged from functional necessities and particularities unique to international organizations create methodological difficulties. These principles either originated from the legal sphere of one major international organization, for example the League of Nations (*Noblemaire*) or UN (*Flemming*), or are derived from the functionality of the international organizations applying them (e.g. principles of independence[30] and functional protection). In other cases, it is unclear whether various administrative tribunals originally used national employment laws to source general principles (e.g. acquired rights of staff). Whatever the specifics, today there are simply 'general principles of international civil service'. What these examples have in common is that a given principle's transposition into an international organization's legal order has little if anything to do with the broader "community of nations", the latter of which, according to the ILC, is at the centre of Article 38 para. 1 (c) of the ICJ Statute. Rather, in the context of staff disputes, it is the respondent international organization which explicitly or implicitly recognizes the principles after the administrative tribunal decides on the suitability of the principle's application within the relevant internal international organization's legal order. This was emphasised by the World Bank Administrative Tribunal (WBAT) in the *de Merode* decision: "Another source of the rights and duties of the staff of the Bank consists of certain general principles of law, the applicability of which has in fact been acknowledged by the Bank in its written and oral pleadings".[31]

3.2 *Contractual and Non-contractual Claims of Third Parties*

The general legal principles governing international organizations' employment conditions are well studied. However, other general principles are equally important to international organizations, even though less obvious. These are

28 Charles T. Kotuby and Luke A. Sobota, *General Principles of Law and International Due Process: Principles and Norms Applicable in Transnational Disputes* (Oxford UP, 2017), p. 35.

29 [2006] ICSID Case No. ARB/03/26, Award, para. 227.

30 [2003] ILOAT No. 2232, para. 6.

31 [1981] WBAT Reports, Decision No. 1, para. 25.

hidden from scrutiny as no administrative tribunal has jurisdiction to identify them, even though they are relevant in disputes between an international organization and a private party over contractual and non-contractual third-party claims (cf. Article VIII Sec 29 of the UN Immunity Convention[32]). Normally, the applicable law that governs the contractual relationship between an international organization and a private party is determined by a choice-of-law clause in the contract. This can refer either to specific national law or to the general principles of international commercial law.[33] The latter belong neither to the body of general international law nor to any international organization's internal legal system but are part of transnational commercial law and thus outside of the scope of this contribution.

Of more interest here are general principles of law applicable to non-contractual relationships between an international organization and third parties. Internal rules of international organizations are often concerned with non-contractual relationships because, understandably, international organizations and their officials can cause harm and/or damage to private parties. With regard to third-party injury suffered in the UN's headquarters, the General Assembly adopted the so-called 'Headquarters Regulation No. 4' in 1986 to limit the UN's financial liability.[34] The UN's practice is now to review such headquarters claims internally to determine whether they fall under the UN's self-insurance plan for general liability risks with respect to acts occurring in the headquarters.[35] In part, the claims settlement practice in UN peacekeeping missions follows the same pattern. General Assembly Resolution 52/247 of 1998 imposed financial and temporal limitations on third-party claims arising from peacekeeping missions.[36] This Resolution provides the legal framework for UN officers charged with internally assessing incoming third-party claims and then negotiating their settlement with individual claimants. Both pieces of General Assembly legislation, the 1986 Headquarters Regulation No. 4 and

32 Convention on the Privileges and Immunities of the United Nations, 13 February 1946, 1 *UNTS* 14.

33 See United Nations General Conditions of Contracts for the Provision of Goods and Services (Rev. 2012), para. 17.2; Michael Joachim Bonell, "The Law governing international commercial contracts and the actual role of the UNIDROIT principles", in *Uniform Law Review* vol. 23 (2018), p. 15.

34 A/RES/41/210 (1986), Limitation of damages in respect of acts occurring within the Headquarters district, 11 December 1986, in: Resolutions and decisions adopted by the General Assembly during its 41st session, 16 September–19 December 1986, p. 210.

35 General Assembly, *Proposed programme budget for 2024*, Part X Section 32, Para. 32.17, UN Doc A/78/6 (Sec.32).

36 GA Res. A/52/247 *Third-party liability: temporal and financial limitations*, UN Doc A/RES/52/247, 17 July 1998.

the 1998 Third-Party Liability Resolution, do not specify all of the relevant substantive rules on the basis of which the UN secretariat evaluates the merits of a third-party claim. What remains unregulated are, for example, the relevant legal concepts of negligence and causality, to name but two. Admittedly, how the UN fills these legal gaps is largely veiled as the UN cloaks its third-party liability practice in secrecy.[37] That said, the Under-Secretary-General for Legal Affairs, Miguel de Serpa Soares, summed up the UN's longstanding (since 1956) claims settlement practice at a 2019 summer course on the responsibility of international organizations by stating: "Traditionally, third-party claims have been dealt with based on general principles of tort law and the amount of compensation paid to third-party claimants was determined by reference to local compensation standards, the prevailing practice in the mission area, as well as the past practice of the Organization".[38] Even though Soares considered the 1998 Third-Party Liability Resolution a game-changer with regard to the applicable law, it stands to reason that the resolution's many lacunae are still filled with a mixture of general principles of tort law, general principles of international human rights and humanitarian law.[39] If this were not the case, there would be serious doubts about the UN following the rule of law in its internal claim settlement procedure, especially since the outcome of these procedures informs the UN's final settlement offer submitted to a private claimant who is inherently pressured to accept it because of the lack of an available judicial review.

All of this begs the question, what exactly are the general principles of tort law and how do they relate to the ILC draft conclusions? Evidently, the general principles of tort law are common to various legal systems of the world (ILC draft conclusion 5), even though undertaking a comparative analysis is probably not the most pressing concern of UN claims officers in the field. As to the recognition of these general principles as a part of international law (ILC draft conclusion 7), the question that needs answering is whether they are of legal relevance for the broader community of nations or whether they

37 Since 2014 the UN Secretariat pursues a strict confidentiality-policy covering all relevant internal UN files from 1945 onwards which deal with non-contractual third-party claims.

38 Miguel de Serpa Soares, "Responsibility of International Organisations", in International and Comparative Research Center (ed.), *Courses of the Summer School on Public International Law* vol. 7 (Moscow, 2022), p. 132.

39 The claim settlement practice of the UN may also have legal relevance ("rule of the organisation" pursuant to Art. 2 (b) draft articles on the responsibility of the organizations"), provided it is established practice. This cannot be determined with certainty due to the UN's policy of non-disclosure.

are tailored to the functional needs of the international organization in question in relation to affected individuals. For example, states which engage in autonomous peace operations often apply their own domestic laws when dealing with third-party claims. An example is the 2020 US Foreign Claims Act, which determines causality based on "general principles of U.S. tort law found in federal case law and standard legal publications".[40] Other states, such as Australia when participating in the US-led UNITAF Mission in Somalia in 1992, applied a combination of local laws (*lex loci delicti commissi*) and international law, especially the law of military occupation.[41] The application of national laws illustrates that from a legal perspective, the proper law governing the relationship between the foreign public actor and the aggrieved individual is first and foremost national law, with international law being used by some actors to incorporate the universally accepted *ordre public*. The same is valid for the UN's non-contractual relationship with aggrieved individuals in mission areas. Therefore, general principles of tort law applied by the UN in its internal claims settlement practice exclusively serve the purpose of supplementing the incomplete 1998 Third-Party Liability Resolution, just like the general principles of law common to EU member states are the source material for the EU's non-contractual liability rules (Article 340 TFEU).[42] Even if the UN legal order is considered a subsystem of international law, it is clear from the above that the general principles of tort law, as internally applied by the UN, are outside the scope of Article 38 para. 1 (c) ICJ Statute, at least if one considers the ILC's understanding of the provision as authoritative. These principles are not recognized by the community of nations but exclusively by the UN to settle third-party claims addressed to it. In the unlikely event that an aggrieved individual succeeds in initiating arbitral proceedings against the UN under the rules of the Permanent Court of Arbitration (PCA), the tribunal will *inter alia* apply "the rules of the organization" to which the transposed general principles of tort law belong (Article 33 of the 1996 Optional Rules for Arbitration between International Organizations and Private Parties).

40 § 842.56 Foreign Claims, 1 July 2020, 10 U.S.C. 2734.

41 Michael J Kelly, *Restoring and Maintaining Order in Complex Peace Operations* (Brill, 1999), pp. 38–39.

42 Art. 340 para. 2 Treaty on the Functioning of the European Union: "In the case of non-contractual liability, the Union shall, in accordance with the general principles common to the laws of the Member States, make good any damage caused by its institutions or by its servants in the performance of their duties". *OJ EU*, 26.10.2012, C326/193.

4 General Principles of Law Common to All International Organizations

Article 33 of the 1996 Optional Rules goes a step further and recognizes another potential source of law when a dispute between an international organization and a private party is submitted to arbitration: "general principles governing the law of international organizations". Even though there is little PCA practice regarding this source of law, the phrase "... governing the law of ..." indicates that these principles, without necessarily taking precedence, have decisive influence on the "rules of the organization" as they are recognized by several international organizations. In addition, it is worth noting that Article 33 mentions this source of law alongside "general international law" as the applicable law. Therefore, it stands to reason that "general principles governing the law of international organisations" cover more than simply "general principles of international law". For example, the ILOAT stated in *V.H. v Interpol*: "the Tribunal recalls that the requirement to pay such interest arises even without such a provision pursuant to the general principles governing the liability of international organisations".[43] In *Da v. Intergovernmental Council of Copper Exporting Countries*, the ILOAT had to decide what was a fair amount of compensation that the organization had to offer in negotiations with staff members even when no staff regulation covers the case: "(The negotiations) also had to abide by the general principles that govern the international civil service, including the respect and consideration due to staff members, as well as such criteria as seniority, record of service and qualifications".[44] The question of whether a body of general principles of law exists which are common to several if not all international organizations is not a new one. The WBAT decision in *de Merode* back in 1981 saw the tribunal contemplate this question, highlighting the differences between individual international organizations with regard to function, membership and institutional structure. It concluded that "the notion of a common law of international organization must be subject to numerous and sometimes significant qualifications", but the fact that these differences exist "does not exclude the possibility that similar conditions may affect the solution of comparable problems".[45] Even though the WBAT refused to decide whether a true *corpus iuris* of international organizations exists, it considered itself "free to take note of solutions worked out in sufficiently

43 [2023] ILOAT, Judgment No. 4671, para. 11.

44 [1987] ILOAT, Judgment No. 873, para. 7.

45 [1981] WBAT Reports, Decision No. 1 para. 28.

comparable conditions by other administrative tribunals, particularly those of the United Nations family."[46] Since the World Bank rules and regulations to be applied by the tribunal (Article II WBAT Statute) can hardly be supplemented by way of 'creative borrowing', the WBAT recognized that, under certain conditions, general principles common to international organizations are a proper source of law in their own right. Indeed, the administrative tribunals' case law on 'general principles of the international civil service' supports this notion.

Even beyond international organizations' employment relations, certain principles have transcended the legal sphere of one organization to other international organizations operating under similar circumstances. By way of example, in its early peacekeeping years, the UN developed and began applying the operational necessity principle to shield the Organization from certain mandate-related third-party tort claims. Unsurprisingly, other international organizations conducting peace operations, such as NATO[47] and the EU,[48] incorporated this principle in their own approach to dealing with non-contractual third-party claims.[49] The operational necessity principles can therefore be regarded as a general principle of law common to international organizations operating on the basis of an operational mandate in a host country. The consequence thereof is that international organizations with no explicit operational-necessity rule remain within the boundaries of the law when applying the principle in their non-contractual relations.

The foregoing considerations are not without bearing on the perception of international organizations and their legal order. If one remains faithful to the language of the ILC in its 2023 draft conclusion, the existence of general principles of law common to international organizations suggests there is a community of international organizations – possibly a subcategory of the community of nations – that creates a *corpus iuris communis* through interrelated recognition of principles in areas where their regulatory topics and interests are comparable.

46 *Ibidem.*

47 Jody M. Prescott, "Operational Claims in Bosnia-Herzegovina and Croatia", *The Army Lawyer* vol. 6 (1998), pp. 1, 7.

48 Kirsten Schmalenbach, "Dispute Settlement (Article VIII Section 29 General Convention)", in A. Reinisch (ed.) *The Convention on the Privileges and Immunities of the United Nations and its Specialized Agencies, A Commentary* (Oxford UP, 2016), para. 79.

49 Art. 15 Draft Model Agreement on the status of the European Union-led forces between the European Union and a Host State, Council of the European Union, Doc 8720/05, 18 May 2005.

5 Conclusion

Niels Blokker, a sympathetic yet critical observer of international organizations, was right to voice doubts as to whether the ILC takes international organizations seriously, as the latter's draft conclusions on general principles of law do not suggest so. That said, the ILC's work provides a useful methodological framework which helps to place general principles governing the law of international organizations into their wider legal context. Many general principles identified by administrative tribunals in connection with international organizations' employment law do not fall within the scope of Article 38 ICJ Statute, at least if one agrees with the ILC's understanding of the provision. However, these tribunals' case law also demonstrates that some general principles are more than just useful supplements to one single international organization's legal order; under certain conditions, they can be applied across international organizations. In this shared legal space, international organizations can be perceived as members of a legal community which are tasked with the recognition of these principles. While the possible implications of this *corpus iuris* are not fully explored here, the purpose of this short contribution was to point out that general principles common to international organizations can supplement fragmentary international organizations law in a manner that is more accessible than elusive international organizations practice and thus contributes to international organizations' wider accountability.

CHAPTER 32

We the Peoples in International Organizations: An Unfinished Agenda

*Nico Schrijver**

1 Introduction

This chapter is meant to serve as a tribute to the lifelong dedication of my *collega proximus* Nicolaas Maximus Blokker to the study and practice of public international law, particularly the law of international institutions. Few people, if any, have gathered such an in-depth knowledge of and insights into international institutional law, the practice of international organizations and the potentials as well as the deficiencies in their functioning.

It could well be argued that so far, the law of international institutions focuses nearly exclusively on the international cooperation between States and their international institutions, although professor Blokker has tirelessly spelled out the independent legal personality of international organizations, their own free will and their established practices.[1] Notwithstanding this, the participation of people is generally rather limited.[2] However, if the international community were to reduce the democratic deficit in global governance and increase confidence in and support for international consultation and decision-making, it would only be logical to enhance the role of people in international organizations. Just like at domestic level, also at an international level uncontrolled powers may lead to a dangerous bureaucracy, technocracy or even autocracy. After all, also international organizations and global governance should serve the people, current as well as future generations.

* The author is Emeritus professor of international law, Leiden University. Co-editor, with Niels Blokker, of *The Security Council and the Use of Force. Theory and Reality – A Need for Change?* (2005), *Immunity of International Organizations* (2015) and *Elected Members of the Security Council. Key Players or Lame Ducks?* (2020).

1 See among many other publications of N.M. Blokker, "International Organizations and their Members", in *International Organizations Law Review* vol. 1 (2004), pp. 139–161, and "Legal Facets of the Practice of International Organizations", in *Recueil des Courses/Collected Courses of the Hague Academy of International Law* vol. 435 (Brill/Nijhoff, 2024), pp. 73–324.

2 See also H.G. Schermers, "We the Peoples of the United Nations", in *Max Planck Yearbook of United Nations Law* vol. 1 (1997), pp. 111–128.

 | DOI:10.1163/9789004699939_034

Confidence in their functioning will be strengthened if international decisions are supported or at least controlled by organs directly representing, if not elected by people to whom the decisions will apply. This requires that people have a voice in global affairs and decision-making.

This chapter first briefly discusses the background and origin of the famous opening words of the UN Charter: "We the Peoples of the United Nations" (section 2). Next, it engages in an examination of the various ways to provide people with a voice in international organizations. Section 3 discusses control by national parliaments with respect to the policies of their respective States in international organizations and the concept of parliamentary diplomacy. Section 4 reviews the existence of parliamentary organs within international organizations. Section 5 pays attention to the role of the Inter-Parliamentary Union, in a way the oldest political international organization founded in 1889. Section 6 takes up the bold proposal for establishing a kind of world parliament, for example by establishing within the United Nations Organization an United Nations Parliamentary Assembly. Section 7 concludes with some thoughts and reflections on the participation of people in international organizations, which so far is an unfinished agenda.

2 *We the Peoples* in the Charter of the United Nations

Initially, it was not envisaged to add a Preamble to the United Nations Charter. Preparatory documents such as the Atlantic Charter (1941) and the Dumbarton Oak Proposals (1944) did not contain any text proposal for this. However, the influential delegate from South Africa and its then prime minister, Field Marshal Jan Smuts, who had attended the Versailles Conference in 1919 establishing the League of Nations, felt that there should be a preamble just like the League of Nations Covenant had one. In his view the Charter should be introduced "[b]y a Preamble setting forth, in language which should appeal to the heart as well as the mind of men, the purposes which the United Nations were setting to achieve for themselves".[3] Smuts submitted a draft for this. At the San Francisco Conference (April–June 1945) it was agreed that the Preamble was meant to set forth the intentions of the participating governments of the peoples. Reportedly, the first seven words of the draft Preamble submitted by Smuts gave rise to considerable debate: "We the Peoples of the United

3 See S.C. Schlesinger, *The Act of Creation. The Founding of the United Nations – A Story of Superpowers, Secret Agents, Wartime Allies and Enemies, and Their Quest for a Peaceful World* (Westview Press, 2004), pp. 236–237.

Nations …".[4] The formulation "We the Peoples" was taken from the preamble of the American Constitution. In the words of an American delegate, they were meant to express the democratic basis of the Organization for peace and human welfare.[5]

The term "peoples" features twelve times in the Charter, mostly in connection with the principle of self-determination or self-government of peoples.[6] In the latter's context the word "peoples" has a national, ethnic connotation. From the legislative history of the Preamble, it follows that "peoples" in the Preamble refers to the populations of the member States of the new world organisation. A Colombian amendment to proclaim that the principles of democracy and co-operation as enshrined in the Atlantic Charter constituted a minimum standard to be respected by every civilised State was rejected by 9 to 17 votes.[7] Furthermore, at the end of the Preamble a clause was inserted providing that "our respective Governments, through representatives assembled in the city of San Francisco … have agreed to the present Charter" which qualifies in part the opening words "We the Peoples of the United Nations determined". The two phrases should be read "in conjunction".[8] While these facts of the legislative history of the Charter may constitute a bar for a too sweeping interpretation of the famous opening words of the UN Charter, in practice these words have often served as a source of inspiration for calls for more democracy and public participation in the United Nations and global governance in general. At the very least, the prominent reference to "We the Peoples" was instrumental in lifting the status of peoples in international law from a mere object of concern to a legal subject with legal personality and some accompanying rights.[9] Furthermore, these words have also provided the United Nations a mandate to promote democratization at the international level. In the words of former UN Secretary-General Boutros Boutros-Ghali, who issued during his term of

4 See R. Wolfrum, "Preamble", in B. Simma a.o. (eds.), *The Charter of the United Nations. A Commentary* vol. 1 (3rd ed., Oxford UP, 2012), pp. 101–106.

5 See United Nations, *Documents of the United Nations Conference on International Organization, San Francisco, 1945* (*UNCIO*) vol. VI (United Nations Information Organizations and Library of Congress, 1945), p. 45. Notably the Dutch delegation opposed this formulation: "In the Netherlands sovereignty was not vested in the people under the Constitution, and the Crown (with authority from above), not the people, concluded treaties". See *UNCIO* VI, p. 366 and p. 371.

6 See Preamble, Artt. 1 (2), 55, 73, 76 and 80 of the UN Charter.

7 On the Colombian proposal, see *UNCIO* vol. VI, p. 373 and p. 528, sub II.

8 *UNCIO vol. VI*, p. 362.

9 Cf J.-P. Cot et A. Pellet (eds.), *La Charte des Nations Unies. Commentaire article par article* (2nd ed., Economica, 1991), pp. 18–20: "… c'est une mutation grande, grâce à la Charte, les peoples cessent d'être les 'grand muets' du droit international" (at p. 20).

office (1992–1996) the tryplitch of *An Agenda for Peace* (1992), *An Agenda for Development* (1994) and *An Agenda for Democratization* (1996):

> The United Nations strengthens the context for support to democratization through information-gathering and awareness-raising and by offering Member States and the wider international community a universally legitimate global forum for dialogue, debate and consensus-building. Through the United Nations, multilateral agreements can be reached – whether embodied in the form of non-binding norms, internationally recognized standards or binding obligations – which help to define a common political and legal framework for action. Indeed, it is to a certain extent through the forum of the United Nations that a consensus on democracy and its practical importance has begun to take shape.[10]

3 Control by National Parliaments Over International Agreements and Organizations

The most conventional way for democratic control over international agreements and international organizations is still that national parliaments exercise control over national governments. Whereas in the past foreign policy was the exclusive domain of the government, in modern times this has changed drastically. In most countries parliamentary control extends to foreign affairs, defence and international co-operation. This includes not only parliamentary debate on current world affairs, but also the legislative process of approving the ratification of or accession to treaties. In most parliamentary systems the rule applies that treaties can only enter into force for the State and the people concerned upon prior approval by the national parliament. It is also increasingly the practice that in an early stage parliaments are being informed of the negotiations on draft international agreements and can have a say in the negotiating position on behalf of its State. Parliaments may issue instructions or directives to their governments during the negotiation process or require at least to be informed on it. When the treaty is in force and there is a treaty organization, parliaments should be able to reach out to the treaty bodies, both the plenary assembly of treaty parties and supervisory bodies, for example human

10 B. Boutros-Ghali, *An Agenda for Democratization* (1996), UN Doc. A/51/176, para. 14. See also the Millennium Report of former Secretary-General Kofi Annan (1997–2006), *We the Peoples: the role of the United Nations in the Twenty-first Century* (2000), UN Doc. A/54/2000.

rights treaty bodies, and to have a voice in these organs when it relates to matters of concern to their State and population.

However, decisions of international organizations do not require ratification at the national level. Notwithstanding this, parliaments have developed various practices for exerting influence by calling governments to account for their positions as regards draft decisions of international organizations. For example, parliaments may issue instructions or directives to their governments before international decisions are adopted in the context of an international organization. Secondly, national delegations to an international organization can include members of parliament in order to improve the understanding of the way in which the international organizations function and to involve them in the work of national delegations to international conferences. This also enables them to meet fellow parliamentarians from other countries. Thirdly, when exercising their national budgetary powers, parliaments may discuss the policies of international organizations and exert some influence on the budget and policies of the international organizations under review. Lastly, it is now a well-established practice in most international organizations to provide national parliamentary commissions with direct access to all relevant information regarding their activities.

These are some of the ways in which national parliaments can be effective in addressing the democratic deficit of international organizations. Parliamentary diplomacy is the common term used to describe this wide range of national and international activities undertaken by members of parliament in order to increase mutual understanding between countries, to improve scrutiny of government, to represent their people better, and to increase the democratic legitimacy of inter-governmental institutions.[11]

The next sections address various ways how this can be done at the international level.

4 International Organizations with Parliamentary Organs

Quite a number of regional and international organizations do have their own parliamentary organs.[12] Obviously, the prime example is the European

11 See Memorandum on Parliamentary Diplomacy of the Senate of the States General of the Netherlands, 16 November 2010, available at <www.eerstekamer.nl>; F.W. Weisglas and G. de Boer, "Parliamentary Diplomacy", in *The Hague Journal of Diplomacy* vol. 2 (2007), pp. 93–99; S. Stravidis and D. Jančić (eds.), *Parliamentary Diplomacy in European and Global Governance* (Brill/Nijhoff, 2017).

12 For a comprehensive overview and analysis, see H.G. Schermers and N.M. Blokker, *International Institutional Law* (6th ed., Brill/Nijhoff, 2018), chapter 5.1, pp. 420–457;

Parliament which from 1979 is directly elected by the peoples of the now 27 member States of the European Union. The European Parliament is the only one which can be viewed as a direct co-legislator with substantial powers (even to dismiss an individual Commissioner or the European Commission) and as the representative of an electorate all endowed with European citizenship, overarching the nationalities of the individual member States.[13] Therefore, there are good reasons to view the European Parliament as a *supra*national parliament rather than as an international parliamentary assembly.[14]

Also, a number of other regional organizations have parliamentary organs, albeit not directly elected but rather as representatives of national parliaments. Their main function is to facilitate parliamentary supervision of intergovernmental decision-making processes. Examples include the Parliamentary Assembly of the Council of Europe (1949) as the frontrunner,[15] the Latin American Parliament (*Parlatino's* founding treaty 1987) charged also with the special task of the defence of democracy, the Pan-African Parliament (from 2004), the Benelux Parliament, the Nordic Council in Scandinavia, and the Assemblies of the Association of Southeast Asian Nations (ASEAN), the Andean Parliament and the Mercosur Parliament in Latin America and the Parliament of the Economic Community of West African States (ECOWAS). Also the North Atlantic Treaty Organization (NATO) and the Organization for Security and Co-operation in Europe (OSCE) each have a Parliamentary Assembly. Likewise the EU-ACP Partnership (an association, not an international organization) for international co-operation between the EU and its 27 member States on the one hand and 79 developing countries in Africa, the Caribbean and the Pacific on the other, has a Joint Parliamentary Assembly.[16]

Obviously, the functions and powers of all these parliamentary assemblies differ and so does their legal and institutional structure and political influence. Few of them are vested with decision-making powers, with the European Parliament as the main exception. Yet, each in their own way seeks to exercise some control over the executive organs, control over the budget and – perhaps most importantly – serve as a platform for public debate and perform advisory

F. Arndt, "Parliamentary Assemblies, International", in R. Wolfrum and A. Peters (eds.), *Max Planck Encyclopedia of Public International Law*, online version, update of 2013, available at <http://opil.ouplaw.com> and <www.mpepil.com>.

13 See Treaty on the Functioning of the European Union, Lisbon, 13 December 2007, *Official Journal European Union*, C115/47, Art. 234 and Part II.

14 See Arndt (*supra* note 12), para. 4.

15 See Art. 22 of the Statute of the Council of Europe, 5 May 1949, CETS No. 1.

16 See the EU-ACP Conventions of Lomé (1975–2000), Cotonou (2000–2022) and São Tomé (2023–), respectively.

functions. Furthermore, the interparliamentary assemblies can also indirectly exercise some influence by providing the national delegates with information, insights and political ideas which they can use in their domestic parliamentary activities. In doing so, the international parliamentary assemblies are to a varying extent all instrumental in contributing to the legitimacy, transparency and accountability of the international organizations through their interparliamentary diplomacy.

5 The Role of the Inter-Parliamentary Union

Founded in 1889, the Inter-Parliamentary Union (IPU) has already a long history. The IPU is an offspring of the politically enlightened period of the late 19th and early 20th century. The main original aim of the founding parliamentarians from France and Great Britain was to promote international arbitration as a method of peaceful settlement of international disputes. On this particular issue the first Hague Peace Conference in 1899 adopted the landmark Convention on the Pacific Settlement of International Disputes, which among other matters established the Permanent Court of Arbitration.[17] This Convention is still valid and a relevant early framework for good offices, inquiry, mediation and arbitration as means of international dispute settlement, "before an appeal to arms" as still was added in 1899.[18] Over time, the promotion of peace has remained the central focus of this interparliamentary organization. Apart from its calls and input for the first and second Hague Peace Conferences (1899 and 1907), the IPU sought after the horrifying Great War (1914–18) to promote the establishment of the League of Nations (1919) and the call for the abandonment of war as an instrument of national policy during the 1920s, ultimately resulting in the adoption of the Briand-Kellogg Pact of 1928.[19]

After WW II, the purposes and principles of the United Nations, now including promoting respect for human rights apart from peace and socio-economic development, have served as the main goals in the work of the IPU.[20] This

17 Convention for the Pacific Settlement of International Disputes, The Hague, 18 October 1907, Chapter II.

18 *Ibidem*, Art. 2.

19 General Treaty for the Renunciation of War as an Instrument of National Policy, Paris, 27 August 1928.

20 See Art. 1 of the IPU Statutes (version of May 2023), providing that the "IPU shall work for peace and co-operation among peoples and for the firm establishment of parliamentary institutions". Available at <www.ipu.org>.

is also reflected in the names of the three main Standing Committees of the IPU: Peace and International Security; Democracy and Human Rights; and Sustainable Development, Finance and Trade. Building up firm parliamentary institutions and strengthening its working methods for purposes of parliamentary control and parliamentary diplomacy is a consistent Leitmotiv in IPU's activities.

IPU has four permanent bodies: (a) the Assembly, which meets twice a year and which is composed of delegations from the participating national parliaments (the corporate members of the IPU) as well as 15 associated international parliamentary assemblies, including the European Parliament, the Parliamentary Assembly of the Council of Europe and the Latin American Parliament; (b) a Governing Council composed of three representatives from each member parliament and serving as the central decision-making organs for internal matters including the election of the IPU President, the adoption of the budget and annual work programme and the establishment of committees; (c) the Executive Committee as the main administrative organ and composed of 15 members elected by the Governing Council, the President of the IPU and the President of the Coordinating Committee of the Meeting of Women Parliamentarians; and (d) the General Secretariat, headed by the Secretary-General. As of September 2024, IPU has 180 member parliaments. A major absentee is the parliament of the United States of America. Having been a founding member since 1889, the latter withdrew in the late 1990s following a controversy on the size of the American financial contribution.[21]

The IPU is *stricto sensu* not an international organization, now that it is a common undertaking by parliamentarians and not based upon a multilateral treaty concluded by States.[22] Nonetheless, IPU is vested with legal personality, established a status agreement with the Swiss Federal Council in 1971 and concluded over time various relationship agreements with the United Nations.[23]

21 In October 1999, the then Secretary of State Madeleine Albright sent an official communication to the IPU announcing the US Congress' withdrawal from the IPU. However, the IPU Executive Committee did not accept this notification since it came from the government, not from the Congress. Consequently, the US Congress remained IPU Member until they accumulated three years of dues and were liable for suspension. Thereupon, US membership was formally suspended by the IPU itself another two years later, in March 2003.

22 Art. 1, para. 1, of the Statutes describes the IPU as "the international organization of the Parliaments of sovereign States".

23 See Art. 1, para. 4, of the Statutes: "The IPU has legal personality and has the authority to enter into international agreements, including cooperation agreements with national

Since 2002, the United Nations General Assembly (UNGA) has granted the IPU permanent observer status with the United Nations.

In 1997, during the politically conducive post-Cold War period, the IPU adopted the Universal Declaration of Democracy, which also pays ample attention to promotion and protection of human rights. Following an initiative by the IPU, the UNGA designated 15 September as the International Day of Democracy in reference to IPU's Universal Declaration on Democracy of 1997.[24] In 2017, the IPU adopted a follow-up resolution entitled "Sharing our Diversity: The 20th anniversary of the Universal Declaration of Democracy". In the Resolution, the IPU Assembly "[r]eaffirms that democracy is a universal value and that democracy does not belong to any country or region, and as a system of government, democracy contributes to the fulfilment of human potential, the eradication of poverty, the development of open and peaceful societies and the improvement of relations among nations" (para. 1). It notes that "peace, security and development are major enablers of democracy" and also recognizes "the importance of democratic principles in international relations and the important role of international and regional organizations in upholding these principles" (preamble). The Resolution reiterates that "building a democratic society requires respect for international law and for the principles of the rule of law, human rights, respect for diversity and the equitable inclusion of all citizens" (para. 14) and urges "respect for democratic principles in inter-State relations as well as in international organizations, and underlines its conviction that principles of democracy must be applied to the international management of issues of common concern to humankind, in particular the human environment" (para. 15).

Felix Arndt rightly notes that on the one hand the IPU represents "a unique form of parliamentary co-operation", but that on the other "a concrete impact of the IPU on the policy-making of international organizations or its Member States appears to be hardly traceable". Rather the relevance of the IPU lies in its "contribution to the promotion of fundamental democratic values and the improvement of working methods of parliamentary institutions".[25]

parliaments and inter-parliamentary organizations, as well as with international inter-governmental and non-governmental organizations".

24 UN Doc. A/RES/62/7, 8 November 2007.

25 See Arndt (*supra* note 12), para. 21. Here Arndt refers to the work by B.M. Habegger, *Parliamentarismus in der internationalen politik: Europarat, OSZE und Interparlamentarische Union* (Nomos, 2005).

6 Strengthening Parliamentary Legitimacy by Establishing a United Nations Parliamentary Assembly

From ancient times proposals have been made for a world parliament, also during the days of the formation of the United Nations in order to give substance to the words "We the Peoples of the United Nations".[26] Under the current constellations one cannot but conclude that a global parliamentary election is an utopia. Somewhat less unrealistic is the idea of an interparliamentary organ composed of representatives of the national parliaments, for example a United Nations Parliamentary Assembly (UNPA) with consultative functions. Here the IPU as the global association of national and regional parliaments could also have an important role. A UN parliamentary network could serve as a major new advisory body consisting of people's representatives to the UN General Assembly. This could be a way of "renewing and strengthening global governance", as Secretary-General Antonio Guterres called for on the occasion of the 75th anniversary of the UN in 2020. An UNPA would directly represent the world's citizens and national parliaments and could serve as a kind of Second Chamber or Citizen Chamber to complement the current intergovernmental UNGA.

It could well be argued that such a UN Parliamentary Assembly could be established without embarking on the cumbersome process of amending the UN Charter[27] and could build on the current relationship agreement between IPU and the UN. Under Article 22 of the UN Charter, the UN General Assembly has the power to create such a new organ.[28] The UNPA could be instrumental in moving the UN General Assembly towards a more vibrant, inclusive and democratic body. Starting as a largely consultative body and being composed of members of national parliaments, the UNPA would have the right of access to all information, the right to discuss all matters relating to the functioning of the UN, scrutinise the budget and the expenditures. Most of all, it would function as a major platform for public debate and discussion of global problems

---

26 See for an insightful and inspiring plea for this J. Leinen and A. Bummel, *World Parliament. Governance and Democracy in the 21st Century* (2nd ed., Democracy Without Borders, 2024).

27 See Art. 108 of the UN Charter.

28 Art. 22 of the UN Charter reads: "The General Assembly may establish such subsidiary bodies as it deems necessary for the performance of its functions". A large number of UN organs have been established under this provision, among them the International Law Commission (1947), the United Nations Conference on Trade and Development (1964), the United Nations Development Programme (1966) and the Human Rights Council (2006).

and make proposals on how to solve these. It would also enable its members to engage in parliamentary diplomacy at the world stage.

To exert maximum parliamentary influence, it is certainly better to be within and part of the UN than remaining outside its institutional structure. Initially, the IPU could serve as the *de facto* Secretariat of the UNPA. The UNPA could establish committees, just as IPU has these, e.g., on Peace, on Human Rights and on Sustainable Development and Finance. Hence, UNPA would function as an independent watchdog of the UN system and as a democratic reflection of world public opinion, rendering advice to the United Nations and making full use of IPU's advisory and organisational services, including through its offices in Geneva, New York and Vienna.

7 Final Reflections

The impressive proliferation of international organizations in response to the transnational and global nature of many policy issues have frequently led to calls for democratic legitimacy of international organizations, transparency and accountability. Schermers and Blokker have enumerated and analysed a host of measures to respond to such calls within the existing framework of international institutional law. A somewhat underexposed topic in the literature is how parliamentary participation on behalf of "We the Peoples of the United Nations" could be instrumental in reducing these legitimacy, democracy and accountability gaps.[29]

This chapter concluded, firstly, that there is still a wide variety of opportunities for national parliaments as the prime representative of *demos* to contribute to and exercise control on global governance, through access to information and participation in consultations and decision-making, and engaging in parliamentary diplomacy at the international level. Secondly and in a similar vein, international parliamentary assemblies also serve as important pillars of democratization at the international level, albeit mostly in the context of regional and interregional organizations and with a varying extent of formal decision-making and control powers. Currently, the IPU serves as the global parliament of nearly all national parliaments and associated regional parliamentary assemblies. However, it hardly has any supervisory and control powers, let alone a legislative role. The IPU functions at best as a soft power for the promotion of fundamental democratic values and the promotion of

29 Cf. M. Krajewski, "International Organizations or Institutions, Democratic Legitimacy", in Wolfrum and Peters (*supra* note 12), online version, update of 2019.

the strengthening of effective parliamentary working methods. Thirdly, at the global level more efforts could be made with new forms of parliamentary participation, next to increased recognition of the important role of civil society organisations and increased level of transparency and accountability. Somewhat thriftly, "We, the Heads of State and Government, representing the peoples of the world", resolve in their *Pact for the Future* (2024):

> We will strengthen our partnerships to deliver on existing commitments and address new and emerging challenges … [and] decide to: […]
>
> (d) Deepen United Nations engagement with national parliaments in United Nations intergovernmental bodies and processes, in accordance with national legislation, including through building on the efforts of the United Nations and the Inter-Parliamentary Union to engage parliamentarians to maintain support for the implementation of relevant United Nations agreements and resolutions.[30]

In response to the frequent calls for more legitimacy, democracy and accountability in global governance, this chapter draws inspiration from the Preamble of the nearly eighty years old Charter of the United Nations and offers some proposals for some meaningful first steps to embark on the undoubtedly long journey to strengthen the "*We the Peoples*" dimension in international organizations.

30 *Pact for the Future*, para. 1 and Action 55, para. 83, sub b, *UN Doc.* A/RES/79/1, 22 September 2024.

PART 6

Some Concluding Reflections on the Discipline of International Institutional Law

CHAPTER 33

International Institutional Lawyers as Masters of Modern Philosophy

*Jean d'Aspremont**

1 Introduction

International institutional lawyers often downplay their philosophical moves.[1] Such modesty is surely instrumental in the field being often demoted as poorly theorized.[2] This small contribution, whose aim is to pay tribute to the *oeuvre* of Niels Blokker and the latter's foundational contribution to the discipline,[3] seeks to challenge such disciplinary self-representation and shed light on the key philosophical moves embraced by most of those who engage with the law of international organizations. This essay particularly argues that two very common moves of modern philosophy are pervasive in international legal thought and practice related to international organizations, namely dualism and dialectics. It shows that, notwithstanding their modest self-representations, international institutional lawyers are masters of dualism and of dialectics.

---

* The author is Professor of International Law, Sciences Po Law School and University of Manchester.

1 For instance, Niels Blokker describes his magnum opus as "practice-inspired and practice-oriented", claiming later that "the whims of practice do not always follow the templates of theory". He also argues that his book follows "a rather modest approach" which he sees as being "bottom up". See Henry G. Schermers and Niels M. Blokker, *International Institutional Law* (6th rev. ed., Brill, 2018), at pp. xxviii, 5, and 15.

2 On that very common claim, see Schermers and Blokker (*supra* note 1), p. 10; Jan Klabbers and Guy Fiti Sinclair, "On Theorizing International Organizations Law: Editors' Introduction", in *European Journal of International Law* (*EJIL*) vol. 31 (2020), p. 489; Jan Klabbers, "The EJIL Foreword: The Transformation of International Organizations Law", in *EJIL* vol. 26 (2015), p. 9; Jan Klabbers, "Reflections on Role Responsibility: The Responsibility of International Organizations for Failing to Act", in *EJIL* vol. 28 (2017), p. 1133; Laurence Boisson de Chazournes a.o., "Foreword", in *International Organizations Law Review* (*IOLR*) vol. 6 (2009), p. 316; José E. Alvarez, *International Organizations as Law-makers* (Oxford UP, 2005), p. xii; Nigel D. White, *The Law of International Organizations* (2nd ed., Manchester UP, 2006), pp. 14–23.

3 No other book is more constitutive of the field of international institutional law that the world famous *International Institutional Law* (*supra* note 1). On the constitution of international institutional law as a field, see H.G. Schermers, *The Birth and Development of International Institutional Law*, *IOLR* vol. 1 (2004), pp. 5–8.

 | DOI:10.1163/9789004699939_035

This contribution starts by sketching out these two common patterns of thought theorized and systematized by modern philosophy, namely dualism and dialectics (section 2). It then illustrates the extent to which these two moves are everywhere in international legal thought and practice related to international organizations (sections 3 and 4). It ends with a few concluding remarks on the distinction between theory and practice around which international institutional lawyers commonly describe the field as well as their own work (section 5).

2 Two Salient Modes of Thinking of Modern Philosophy: Dualism and Dialectics

Postulating binaries and articulating one's claims in dualist terms is a common pattern of thought of modern philosophy.[4] Dualism of thought is usually traced back to Descartes, who allegedly put forward the first articulated form of dualism in a modern sense.[5] Indeed, Descartes is remembered for his distinction between the undoubted, central, and knowing self (i.e. the absolute subject) and the world-in-itself external to the self but knowable by it (the object).[6] Yet, Cartesian dualism is only one of the many variants of dualism of thought. Kant, for his part, rejecting the possibility of an absolute knowing by the self of the world-in-itself but still acknowledging the possibility of a world-in-itself, put forward a type of dualism less dogmatic and more transcendental, which turns the attention to the relation between the world-in-itself

4 On the idea that dualism is an important part of the modern mind, see Bruno Latour, *Nous n'avons jamais été modernes. Essai d'anthropologie symétrique* (La Découverte, 1997) p. 24; see also Henri Bergson, *La pensée et le mouvant* (Flammarion, 2014), p. 228.

5 It is interesting to note that, in pre-modern times, dualism of thought, and especially the understanding of Christ as having two distinct natures, while supported by Nestorianist school, came to be severely repressed by the Catholic Church after the Council of Chalcedon (451 AC) in favour of a monophysitist approach to the nature of Christ, whereby the latter would have only one inseparable nature, partly divine, partly human. For some remarks, see Roland Minnerath, *Histoires des Conciles* (Presses Universitaires de France, 1996) pp. 17–23. See also the remarks of Régis Debray, *Vie et mort de l'image* (Gallimard, 1992), pp. 99–141.

6 This is not to say that dualism of thought is unknown from pre-modern thought. Previously, the distinction between the body and the spirit brought about an important mode of dualistic thinking. See Jacques Le Goff, "L'homme médiéval", in Jacques Le Goff (ed.), *L'Homme médiéval* (Seuil, 1989), p. 15.

and its representation.[7] Since Kant, dualism, especially in the form of modes of thinking articulated around identity and differences,[8] has continued to thrive. For instance, structuralism,[9] in the 20th century, came to reaffirm dualism, possibly constituting dualist of thought at its best. It can be said that, in the West, the history of modern thinking until today can primarily be read as a history of dualist thinking.

It is well known that Hegel challenged the dualist modes of thinking of both Descartes and Kant by seeking to show that dualism is bound to be caught in idealism.[10] In doing so, Hegel, re-appropriating a notion invented by Greek philosophy,[11] introduced a new form of non-contradictory dualism: dialectics.[12] Indeed, for Hegel, the thing and the thought are caught in a dialectical relation: the thing cannot be thought without the thought of the thing whilst the thought cannot be a thought of the thing without the thing. From a Hegelian perspective, dialectics is a mode of thinking that overcomes contradictions[13] by creating unity through the contradiction itself.[14] After Hegel, dialectics continued to inform modern philosophy, for instance through Marxism which elevated dialectics into a method properly so-called.[15] Dialectics even became of

7 Quentin Meillassoux has claimed that Descartes's dualism is a type of dogmatic dualism, whereas Kant's dualism constitutes a form of transcendental dualism. See Quentin Meillassoux, *Après la Finitude. Essai sur la nécessité de la contingence* (Seuil, 2006), pp. 13–49.

8 On the idea that modernity generalised modes of thinking articulated around identity and differences, see Timothy Mitchell, *Questions of Modernity* (University of Minnesota Press, 2000), p. 17; Michel de Certeau, *L'écriture de l'histoire* (Gallimard, 1975), p. 59; Michel Foucault, *Les mots et les choses* (Gallimard, 1966), p. 68.

9 On the dualism of structuralism, see Jacques Derrida, *L'écriture et la différence* (Seuil, 1967), p. 426. See also the remarks of Jonathan Culler, *Structuralist Poetics. Structuralism, Linguistics, and the Study of Literature* (Routledge, 2002), pp. 5–6.

10 For Hegel, only the idea provides the self with access to the thing-in-itself, idealism simultaneously enabling the possibility of absolute knowledge. For an impressive and yet accessible interpretation of Hegel, see Jean Hyppolite, *Logique et existence* (Presses universitaires de France, 1952).

11 In Greek philosophy, dialectics was a shorthand for dialogue and was opposed to the rhetorical techniques of the sophists.

12 On the idea that dialectics is necessarily grounded in dualism, see Latour (*supra* note 4), p. 77.

13 Michel Foucault, *Dits et écrits, II* (Gallimard, 2001), at p. 50.

14 Louis Althusser, *Être Marxiste en Philosophie* (Presses Universitaires de France, 2015), at p. 82.

15 On the dualism of Marxism, see Peter Singer, *Marx, A Very Short Introduction* (Oxford UP, 2000), pp. 27–30. See also the remarks of Régis Debray, *Le Scribe* (Editions Grasset

mode of theorizing sciences.[16] In the 20th century, Adorno sought to repudiate Hegelian identity dialectics through his notion of negative dialectics, understood as a form of thinking of non-identity.[17] Although rejected in critical theory precisely because it irons out and obfuscates conflicts,[18] dialectics has remained a very central mode of thinking of modern philosophy, and more generally, of Western thought as a whole. It constitutes, together with dualism, one of the two main modes of thinking of modern philosophy.

3 A Mastery of Dualism

Although too modest to acknowledge their philosophical moves, international institutional lawyers have proved very gifted at wielding the two abovementioned patterns of thought so central in modern philosophy. This is certainly the case of dualism which is a mode of thinking that is omnipresent in international legal thought and practice related to international organizations.[19] Dualism particularly manifests itself, in international institutional law, as the constant and systematic postulation of a contradiction or tension.[20] Indeed, findings of contradictions and tensions always presuppose the postulation of a

---

et Fasquelle, 1980), pp. 161–70; Cornelius Castoriadis, *L'Imaginaire comme tel* (Hermann Editeurs, 2007), p. 38.

16 Gaston Bachelard, *Le nouvel esprit scientifique* (PUF, 1934): "la pensée scientifique est dialectique", at p. 18.

17 T. Adorno, *Negative Dialectics* (Continuum, 1981), at p. 5; T.W. Adorno, Lectures on Negatic Dialectics. Fragments of a lecture course 1965/1966 (edited by Rolf Tiedmann and Translated by Rodney Livingstone) (Polity Press, 2008), at pp. 6–7. On this aspect of Adorno's works, see the remarks of Ross Wilson, *Theodor Adorno* (Routledge, 2007), pp. 59–65.

18 See the rejection of dialectics by Michel Foucault, *Naissance de la biopolitique. Cours au Collège de France (1978–1979)* (Gallimard Seuil, 2004), at p. 44; Foucault (*supra* note 13), p. 471; see also Gilles Deleuze, *Différence et Répétition* (PUF, 1968), at p. 339.

19 For a very thorough examination of the manifestations of dualism in relation to the law of international organizations, see Anne Vianin, *Le dualisme et le concept d'organisation internationale en droit* (Université Laval, 2023).

20 Viljam Engström, "Powers of Organizations and the Many Faces of Autonomy", in Richard Collins and Nigel D. White (eds.), *International Organizations and the Idea of Autonomy: Institutional Independence in the International Legal Order* (Routledge, Abingdon 2011), p. 224; Catherine Brölmann, *The Institutional Veil in Public International Law: International Organisations and the Law of Treaties* (Hart, 2007), p. 30. For a more dated recognition of that tension, see Michel Virally, "La notion de fonction dans la théorie de l'organisation internationales", in *Mélanges offerts à Charles Rousseau: La Communauté internationale* (Pedone, 1974), p. 277. See also Arnold D. McNair, "Functions and Differing Legal Character of Treaties", in *British Yearbook of International Law* vol. 11 (1930), pp. 110, 112; and Manuel

binary relation between two distinct elements, which is the hallmark of dualist thinking. Niels Blokker, to whom these lines are dedicated, is certainly among those that have studied the contradictions and tensions in the law of international organizations, and thus the dualist modes of thinking that they presuppose, in the most extensive and systematic way.[21]

Among the many contradictions and tensions that are the object of such systematic scholarly discussions and which are the expression of dualist thinking, a few can be mentioned here: those pertaining to States being members of a collective entity while simultaneously being autonomous entities,[22] those pertaining to the diverging capacities in which States act in their relation with an organization of which they are a member,[23] those between the internal role and the external role of member States,[24] those related to international organizations' need for independence to carry out their mission while remaining dependent on member States,[25] those between the openness of international organizations and their transparency,[26] those related to the different facets of the autonomy of international organizations,[27] those between functionalism and constitutionalism (the former being then construed as freedom and the latter as control),[28] those between contractual and constitutional elements

---

Rama-Montaldo, "International Legal Personality and Implied Powers of International Organizations", in *British Yearbook of International Law* vol. 44 (1970), p. 111.

21 See generally the remarks of Niels Blokker, "International Organizations and Their Members. 'International Organizations Belong to All Members and to None' – Variations on a Theme", in *IOLR* vol. 1 (2004), p. 139. See also Jan Klabbers, *An Introduction to International Institutional Law* (2nd ed., Cambridge UP, 2009), esp. pp. 1–6; Jan Klabbers, "Two Contending Approaches to the Law of International Organizations", in Jan Klabbers and Asa Wallendahl (eds.), *Research Handbook on International Organizations Law: Between Functionalism and Constitutionalism* (Edward Elgar, 2010); and Jan Klabbers, "Two Concepts of International Organization", in *IOLR* vol 2 (2005), p. 277.

22 Blokker (*supra* note 21), p. 139; Schermers and Blokker (*supra* note 1), p. 2. See also Lorenzo Gasbarri, *The Concept of an International Organization in International Law* (Oxford UP, 2021).

23 Blokker (*supra* note 21), p. 139; Collins and White (*supra* note 20).

24 Schermers and Blokker (*supra* note 1), para. 66; Blokker (*supra* note 21), p. 139.

25 Niels Blokker, "Comparing Apples and Oranges? Reinventing the Wheel? Schermers' Book and Challenges for the Future of International Institutional Law", in *IOLR* vol. 5 (2008), pp. 197, 210.

26 Brölmann (*supra* note 20), p. 32.

27 See Jean d'Aspremont, "The Multifaceted Concept of the Autonomy of International Organizations and International Legal Discourse", in Collins and White (*supra* note 20).

28 Klabbers, "Two Contending Approaches" (*supra* note 21), pp. 3–30; see also Klabbers, "Two Concepts" (*supra* note 21), p. 277. For an attempt to explain how this tension works in practice, see Andrew Guzman, "International Organizations and the Frankenstein

of international organizations,[29] those between the doctrine of functionalism and the idea of international organizations pursuing the common good and universal peace,[30] those pertaining to international organizations being forces for good while being a product of sovereign States,[31] those between international organizations' rules and practices falling in the realm of international institutional law and international organizations' simultaneous subjection to public international law, those related to the ways in which the rules of international organizations are construed,[32] those related to the ambiguous nature of the constituent instrument of organizations,[33] those between

Problem", in *EJIL* vol. 24 (2013), pp. 999, 1013. For a previous use of the Frankenstein analogy, see generally Alvarez (*supra* note 2).

29 I have examined this type of dualist thinking elsewhere. See Jean d'Aspremont, "The Law of International Organizations and the Art of Reconciliation: From Dichotomies to Dialectics", in *IOLR* vol. 11 (2014), pp. 428–453.

30 Jan Klabbers, "Schermers' Dilemma", in *EJIL* vol. 31 (2020), pp. 565, 575. For a history of the consolidation of the concept of functionalism, see Jan Klabbers, "The Emergence of Functionalism in International Institutional Law: Colonial Inspirations", in *EJIL* vol. 25 (2014), p. 645; Klabbers, "The EJIL Foreword" (*supra* note 2) pp. 9, 15–22; see also Jan Klabbers, "Beyond Functionalism. International Organizations Law in Context", in Jan Klabbers (ed.), *Cambridge Companion to International Organizations Law* (Cambridge UP, 2022), pp. 8–17.

31 Klabbers, "Schermers' Dilemma" (*supra* note 30), pp. 565, 582.

32 Christiane Ahlborn, "The Rules of International Organizations and the Law of International Responsibility", in *IOLR* vol. 8 (2011), p. 397; Gasbarri (*supra* note 22), p. 14; Lorenzo Gasbarri, "The Dual Legality of the Rules of International Organizations", in *IOLR* vol. 14 (2017), p. 87; Klabbers, "Two Concepts" (*supra* note 21), pp. 277, 278. For an older study of this debate, see Riccardo Monaco, "Le caractère constitutionnel des actes institutifs d'organisations internationals", in *Mélanges offerts à Charles Rousseau* (Pedone, 1994); see also the three-tiered construction of Seyersted, according to which all international organisations possess their own internal law governing the relations between their the organs, officials and member States in their capacity as members; they are subject to international law in their relations with States and other international organizations; and they also enter into relations of a private nature with both public and private entities (Finn Seyersted, *Common Law of International Organizations* (Martinus Nijhoff, 2008), esp. pp. 21–24). See also Schermers and Blokker (*supra* note 1), paras 1142–1144, according to whom the separation between the organization's internal law and general international law has never been settled.

33 Gasbarri, "The Dual Legality" (*supra* note 32), pp. 87, 103; Ahlborn (*supra* note 32), p. 397; McNair (*supra* note 20), pp. 110, 112. On this debate, see also Brölmann (*supra* note 20), p. 144; Collins and White (*supra* note 20), p. 14; or Anne Peters, "L'acte constitutif de l'organisation internationale", in Evelyne Lagrange and Jean-Marc Sorel (eds.), *Droit des organisations internationales* (LGDJ, 2013), esp. p. 206. For an earlier study on the dual nature of the constitutive instruments of international unions, see Andrea Rapisardi-Mirabelli, "Théorie Générale des Unions Internationales", in *Collected Courses of the Hague Academy of International Law* vol. 7 (1925), p. 348.

considerations of flexibility and considerations of stability,[34] those between the idea of functionality and the idea of centralisation,[35] etc. All those commonly studied contradictions and tensions are grounded in a deeply dualist type of thinking. The dualist modes of thinking about international organizations sometimes materializes in the common claims that the constitutive instruments,[36] the rules,[37] or the legal orders[38] of international organizations are hybrid. Hybridity, although it allows international institutional lawyers to temper tensions and contradictions, always starts by the postulation of two distinct elements which relate to one another in a binary manner, thereby always being accompanied by dualist thinking.

The account provided in the previous paragraph, albeit necessarily cursory, should suffice to show that dualist patterns of thought are prominent modes of engagement with international organizations in international institutional law. Dualism, and thus the postulation of two distinct elements that are in a binary relation with one another, are actually everywhere in international legal thought and practice pertaining to international organizations. This is why it is possible to claim that international institutional lawyers are truly great masters of dualism, thereby continuing the distinguished dualist thinking that was made so central in modern philosophy.

4 A Mastery of Dialectics

International institutional lawyers have not only been great masters of dualist constructions. They have also shown that they have a great command of

34 Klabbers, *Introduction* (*supra* note 21), p. 230.

35 Brölmann (*supra* note 20), p. 30. For Brölmann, functionality corresponds to the sovereignty of States whilst centralisation reflects the independence of the organization.

36 Peters (*supra* note 33), pp. 206–207.

37 Ahlborn (*supra* note 32); Mathias Forteau, "Organisations Internationales et Sources du Droit", in Lagrange and Sorel (*supra* note 33), esp. pp. 281–285; Brölmann (*supra* note 20), p. 144.

38 In this respect, an interesting shift is to be observed in the terminology of the European Court of Justice which, in its much celebrated 1963 decision in the case *Van Gend en Loos*, claimed that the European legal order was "a new legal order of international law" (Case 26-62, [1963] ECR 1). It later dropped the reference to "international law" (see, in particular, *Parti écologiste 'Les Verts'* v. *European Parliament*, Case 294/83, [1986] ECR 1339). See also the remarks of Jean Allain, "The European Court of Justice as an International Court", in *Nordic Journal of International Law* vol. 68 (1999), p. 255; and see also Jean d'Aspremont and Frédéric Dopagne, "Two Constitutionalisms in Europe: Pursuing an Articulation between the European and the International Legal Orders", in *Zeitschrift für Ausländisches Öffentliches Recht und Völkerrecht* vol. 68 (2008), p. 939.

dialectics. What is more, their use of dialectics has been very Hegelian in that they have resorted to it for the sake of unifying and reconciling otherwise distinct objects and concepts. For instance, such Hegelian approach to dialectics is very conspicuous in international institutional lawyers' very common use of the notion of *dédoublement fonctionnel* (role-splitting).[39] In the context of the law of international organizations, the resort to this notion of *dédoublement fonctionnel* is commonly meant to overcome the antinomies at work in the nature and functioning of international organizations by contending the existence of a permanent role-shifting by states and international organizations, for the concept of *dédoublement fonctionnel* allows actors to act in several capacities. As a result, tensions and contradictions can always be bypassed by shifting to the capacity that has the greatest explanatory and justificatory force. As it is employed in the law of international organizations, the idea of *dédoublement fonctionnel* thus brings about a dialectical image of the law of international organizations, whereby capacities never need to be fixed and are left oscillating between opposite poles. Of course, in doing so, international institutional lawyers have taken some liberty with the idea of *dédoublement fonctionnel* as it was first conceived by Georges Scelle. Indeed, it is well known that *dédoublement fonctionnel* as it was originally envisaged by Scelle was the very means by which the objective law (*droit objectif*) was to be translated into positive law (*droit positif*).[40] For Scelle, such a *dédoublement fonctionnel* was an expression of solidarity between the components of an overarching and all-embracing order (and of the political project associated with it).[41] It is far from certain the role-splitting function that is nowadays ascribed to the notion of *dédoublement fonctionnel* in the law of international organizations corresponds to the monist understanding (and the political project) that informed Scelle's original notion. But that does not matter. What is interesting to note is that Scelle's *dédoublement fonctionnel* was probably not as dialectical as this notion is nowadays construed in the law of international organizations and that international institutional lawyers appropriated the concept to make it a

39 See Schermers and Blokker (*supra* note 1), para. 200, p. 1160; para. 919, p. 632; para. 1886, p. 1261. See also N. Blokker, "Organizations and their members", in *IOLR* vol. 1 (2004), pp. 139–161; Brölmann (*supra* note 20), p. 32.

40 See G. Scelle, *Précis, du droit du gens*, vol. I (Dalloz 1932), at p. 298.

41 H. Thierry writes: "The law-making function, which in the international legal system is accomplished by means of a 'dédoublement fonctionnel', does not imply the settlement of conflicting or discordant interests in the international community, but is the expression of solidarity requirements within the international society". See H. Thierry, "The European Tradition of International Law: Georges Scelle", in *EJIL* vol. 1 (1990), p. 193, at pp. 199–200.

full dialectical device to play down some of the fundamental tensions of the law of international organizations.

Other dialectical devices have been constructed and tested in international institutional law and must be mentioned here. The most refined of them is probably the concept of "institutional veil" that has famously been proposed by Catherine Brölmann.[42] According to this idea, international organizations are neither open nor closed but transparent.[43] They constitute "open structures that are vehicles for states and, at the same time, closed structures that are independent legal actors".[44] It ensues, according to this construction, that there exists a dynamic relation between the entity and member states, whereby member states continue to shine through the institutional veil of the organizations,[45] such veil being occasionally pierced to reveal the states behind it.[46]

Another illustration of the resort by international institutional lawyers to dialectics is found in discussions about the relation between the legal order of international organizations and the international legal order as a whole. Often the legal order of the international organizations is said to be an autonomous sub-legal order which nonetheless remains permeable to international law and its rules, especially those deemed of a peremptory character.[47] In that sense, the sub-legal order of the organization is said to be oscillating between some autonomy necessary for the realisation of the political project of the organization and some limited overture to the most important rules of the international legal order. Such a dialectical position came to be defended, for instance, by a majority of international institutional lawyers on the occasion of the notorious controversy surrounding the review by European courts of

42 See generally Brölmann (*supra* note 20), p. 32.

43 Brölmann (*supra* note 20), p. 32. Transparency is meant to be "an endemic condition of intergovernmental organisations in general international law, partly due to the other two features counteracting: it indicates that organisations are neither entirely closed-off to international law in the way of states, nor entirely open, as instances of non-institutionalized inter-state cooperation would be" (p. 11). This transparency is also multi-layered (p. 33).

44 *Ibidem*, p. 1.

45 C. Brölmann, "A Flat Earth? International Organizations in the System of International Law", *Nordic Journal of International Law* vol. 70 (2009), p. 320.

46 In doing so, Brölmann (*supra* note 20, p. 30) seeks to nuance P. Weil's emphasis on the nudity of States behind the immaterial veil of organisations. See P. Weil, "Le droit international en quête de son identité: cours général de droit international public", in *Recueil des Cours*, vol. 237 (1992), at p. 104.

47 Brölmann (*supra* note 20), p. 60. See also P. Klein & P. Sands, *Bowett's Law of International Institutions* (Sweet & Maxwell, 2009), p. 16.

the legality of sanctions taken against *Kadi* as a result of the Security Council's anti-terrorist measures.[48]

The resort to dialectics is similarly witnessed in the findings made by international institutional lawyers of an oscillation between two theorizations of international organizations,[49] in their claims about the oscillations between the law of treaty and the law of the organization concerned,[50] in their recognition of a mutual and ontological need between international organizations and their member States,[51] in their stories about the interactions between law and politics in international institutional law,[52] etc. Even the doctrine of functionalism has been approached in a dialectical way, one that allows to make the world of international organizations commensurable and unitary.[53]

The dialectical constructions mentioned in this section are only a few of the many that permeate international institutional law. The present observations, although not exhaustive, should however provide enough support to the argument made here that international institutional lawyers have also shown a great mastery of dialectical modes of thinking inherited from modern philosophy.

5 Concluding Remarks

This short essay has tried to demonstrate that international institutional lawyers masterfully wield dualism and dialectics as they were introduced by modern philosophy. It must be acknowledged that international institutional lawyers are not alone in embracing dualist and dialectical modes of thinking. In fact, these modes of thinking pervade international legal thought and practice as a whole.[54] Yet, international institutional lawyers, as is illustrated by

48 On this question, see the special issue of *IOLR* vol. 5, issue 2 (2008). For a different non-dialectical position, see J. d'Aspremont & F. Dopagne, "Kadi: The ECJ's Reminder of the Elementary Divide between Legal Orders", in *IOLR* vol. 5 (2008), pp. 371–379. See also d'Aspremont & Dopagne (*supra* note 38).

49 Brölmann (*supra* note 20), p. 5.

50 Catherine Brölmann a.o., "Exiting International Organizations", in *IOLR* vol. 15 (2018), pp. 243, 251.

51 Blokker (*supra* note 21), p. 139; Ige F. Dekker and Ramses A. Wessel, "Identities of States in International Organizations", in *IOLR* vol. 12 (2015), p. 293.

52 Simon Chesterman a.o., *Law and Practice of the United Nations. Documents and Commentary* (2nd ed., Oxford UP, 2016), p. xxxi.

53 See d'Aspremont (*supra* note 29), pp. 428, 445–448.

54 On the idea that critical legal scholarship has relied on a certain type of dualism, be it the concreteness and the normativity, the centre and the periphery, the form and the

the *oeuvre* of Niels Blokker and has been discussed in this chapter, have surely been among the deftest of all international lawyers in their use of dualism and dialectics, even pushing such use to an extent witnessed nowhere elsewhere in international legal thought and practice.

There are at least two implications from the claim developed in the previous paragraphs. First, if international institutional lawyers are deft users of some of the central modes of thinking of modern philosophy, the common narrative according to which international institutional law is poorly theorized and practice-oriented should be discontinued once and for all. The field is awash with theory, some of which is directly inherited from modern philosophy. Second, and maybe more fundamentally, the aptitude of international institutional lawyers to constantly mobilize and deploy patterns of thoughts developed in modern philosophy reminds us that the traditional distinction between theory and practice should similarly be abandoned. As is illustrated by the law of international organizations, there is no practice that is out there and not the product of abstract categories, if only that of the language. Likewise, thinking and arguing about the law of international organizations is a type of professional practice, if only that of an inscription.[55] If, as this essay has shown, international institutional lawyers are able to skillfully mobilize and deploy modes of thinking inherited from modern philosophy, there is no reason why they could not appreciate the inanity of the distinction between theory and practice and revamp the way they describe their work and their field.

---

content, the male and the female, the universal and the particular, etc, see e.g. Rose Parfitt, *The Process of International Legal Reproduction. Inequality, Historiography, Resistance* (Cambridge UP, 2019), p. 21; Ntina Tzouvala, *Capitalism as Civilisation. A History of International Law* (Cambridge UP, 2020), pp. 38–40. See also the remarks of Akbar Rasulov, who argues that Martti Koskenniemi's engagement with structuralism in *From Apology to Utopia* is much more on the side of traditional French(-speaking) structuralism and that it is more a structuralism *à la* Saussure. See Akbar Rasulov, "From Apology to Utopia and the Inner Life of International Law", in *Leiden Journal of International Law* vol. 29 (2016), p. 641.

55 In the same vein, see Louis Althusser, *Initiation à la Philosophie pour les Non-Philosophes* (Presses Universitaires de France, 2014), at pp. 112–113 and 137. See also Gaston Bachelard, *Le nouvel esprit scientifique* (PUF, 1934), pp. 9–10.

CHAPTER 34

Reading International Organizations

Between Legal Construction and Social Existence

*Catherine Brölmann**

1 Introduction

This contribution in honour of Niels Blokker considers the identity of international organizations as international 'actors' over the past century. This dynamic approach seems fitting, as Niels Blokker's wide-ranging work on international organizations frequently involves development over time, as well as movement between contrasting concepts ('unity' and 'diversity'). The chapter proposes an alternative account of the history of international organizations as legal actors, tracing in broad strokes their transformation from a 'legal construction' to a creature with 'social existence', somewhat in the way of states. The identity of international organizations logically is in a mutually constitutive relation with international organizations law.

On other occasions the particular (legal) persona of international organizations has been examined, for example by their dual appearance (as a platform for states on the one hand and as an independent actor on the other), or by the nature of their institutional sphere or 'order'. These are key elements in understanding the socialization of international organizations in international legal life. Yet, their existence in the social world is a distinctive aspect in the contemporary imaginary of international organizations, which deserves separate mention.

A few initial remarks are warranted. To be sure, this is an account about how international organizations as legal actors have been perceived, or in other words: how they have appeared in the eyes of other participants in international life and law. It is not about what international organizations *are*. Secondly, the notion of 'legal construction' in this case does not point to a theoretical approach. Rather, it refers to the view of international organizations as legal fabrications – literally put together by building blocks of law. Of course, international organizations, similar to all (arrangements of) law, are 'socially

* The author is Professor of Public International Law, University of Amsterdam.

 | DOI:10.1163/9789004699939_036

constructed' – but that is not the point this chapter seeks to make. Finally, 'social existence' refers to a presence in the social (as opposed to legal) reality or 'real world' – regardless of whether we think of that world as a shared imaginary, as an individual experience, or as an objective, material space.

The following sections address international organizations as legal constructions (section 2); international organizations with a social existence (section 3); followed by concluding observations (section 4).

2 International Organizations as Legal Constructions

In the mid-nineteenth century, an international organization would be taken as the pure equivalent of a legal arrangement between states. Otto von Gierke thus held administrative unions to be "merely contractual relationships".[1] The view of 'international organs' as treaty *regimes*, to some extent detached from the original treaty instrument, soon gained ground. Continental legal scholarship was actively engaged in shaping the necessary doctrinal context, for instance with the iconic concept of the *Gemeinwillen*,[2] distinct from the sum of 'wills' of states parties. Doctrinal examinations remained inconclusive, possibly facilitated by the fact that organizations in the nineteenth and early twentieth century were relatively self-contained in their field of operation, with little need for prominent 'external relations' (other than from the perspective of states' coexisting treaty obligations). In the early days, an important focus was on the collaboration between member states within the organization's framework, in turn conceptualized as a regime created by the constituent treaty.[3] While the identity of organizations thus had become akin to a treaty regime, it is doubtful whether at the time this engendered an *institutional* dimension – even in the case of some arrangements, such as the 19th century River Commissions, with an exceptional degree of independence vis-à-vis the member states.

In the interwar period came unprecedented impact of the League of Nations due to the universality of its membership combined with the generality of its

1 Otto von Gierke, *Community in Historical Perspective* (Cambridge UP, 2002), edited by A. Black and translated by M. Fischer, which includes much of *Das Deutsche Genossenschaftsrecht* (1868); reference in David Bederman, "The Souls of International Organizations: Legal Personality and the Lighthouse at Cape Spartel", in *Virginia JIL* vol. 36 (1996), pp. 275–377, at pp. 354–356.

2 Famously introduced by Heinrich Triepel (see *Völkerrecht und Landesrecht*, 1899) – the basis for the binding force of the *Gemeinwillen*, Triepel himself admitted, had to be found in an extra-legal context.

3 See on pre-war doctrine Bederman (*supra* note 1), at pp. 344–347.

purposes.[4] Several authors classified the League as a 'confederation' on the basis of an accepted definition,[5] with the advantage of safeguarding the territorial (sovereignty) element. Oppenheim in one of his last writings offered what was taken as a far-reaching view: the League was "[neither] a super-state, nor a confederation of States, nor an Alliance", but an entity *sui generis*.[6] Oppenheim thus rejected standard classifications – and in fact received criticism for "the surrender of his *sui generis*"[7] – but he also avoided analytical and doctrinal categories such as 'international organization' and 'legal personality'.

The *denouement* came soon after the establishment of the United Nations (UN), with the 1949 *Reparation* Opinion. The International Court of Justice (ICJ) – mindful of the political economy of international relations in the post-war international order – squarely affirmed the independence of the UN, couched in terms of (even 'objective') international legal personality.[8] The well-known reference to the 'super-state'[9] underscores how this was precarious at a time when the prevailing discourse on organizations was *contractual*, with its emphasis on state sovereignty, voluntarist underpinnings, and the law of treaties as primary legal toolbox.

A significant and generally unobserved aspect of the *Reparation* Opinion is that on this occasion the Court brought in an *institutional* discourse regarding international organizations. Now the perspective shifted to organizations as self-standing institutional orders. One key subject of study would be international organizations' independence – vis-à-vis the member states in terms of 'autonomy' (also referred to as 'a will of its own'),[10] and vis-à-vis participants in general international law in terms of 'legal personality'. Another question was

4 Background on the League, e.g., in Inis Claude, *Swords into Ploughshares: The Problems and Progress of International Organization* (1971), at p. 43 ff.

5 Georg Jellinek, *Allgemeine Staatslehre* (1890), chapter XXI: "[A confederation is a] permanent union of independent states, based on agreement, and having for its object the protection of the territory (…)".

6 Lassa Oppenheim, "Le caractère essentiel de la société des nations", in *Revue Générale de droit International Public* vol. 26 (1919), pp. 234–244.

7 Percy Corbett, "What is the League of Nations?", in *British Yearbook of International Law* vol. 5 (1924), pp. 119–148, at p. 119.

8 See Catherine Brölmann, *The Institutional Veil in Public International Law* (Hart, 2007), pp. 65–96.

9 "[…] the Organization is an international person. That is not the same thing as saying that it is a State […] Still less it is the same as saying that it is a 'super-State' whatever that expression may mean", in [1949] ICJ Reports, at p. 179 – echoing concerns voiced at the San Francisco conference (*UNCIO* vol. 12, p. 703, at p. 710) also in relation to the League.

10 Henry Schermers & Niels Blokker, *International Institutional Law* (6th rev. ed., Brill, 2018), paras. 44 and 44A.

the basis of organizations' legal personality and capacity. For some time that debate would be dominated by the 'will theory',[11] which situated the basis for international legal personality in the agreement ('will') between the founding states. This made sense in light of the original contractual image of organizations, even if it was problematic given that legal personality in any legal system is by definition granted by that system and never by aspiring legal participants themselves. It is not surprising that in recent decades, as organizations have assumed an identity of creatures with an objective existence in 'social reality' (see below), legal doctrine has come to emphasize the 'objective theory'.[12] In that view international law attributes 'legal personality' on the basis of objective features, in a way somewhat similar to the 'Montevideo criteria' for states. The constitutive treaty, on the other hand, would express the 'will' of founding states to create an entity with the particular features of an international organization. A case in point is that organizations with a self-proclaimed *lack* of personality have seemed to incur legal personality even against their will (or that of the founders) if they objectively meet the criteria of an 'organization', as borne out by the recent history of the EU and the OSCE.[13]

The contractual discourse and the institutional discourse on organizations existed alongside each other, and were each bolstered further with the notion of *objectiveness*. The category of treaties creating objective regimes (articulated as such around the 1960s),[14] then was often taken to include also non-territorial arrangements, notably organizations' constitutive treaties.[15] The 'objective legal personality' attributed by the ICJ to the United Nations (and essentially to all international organizations in its wake) on the other hand would be frequently likened and conceptually linked to the 'objective effect' of a treaty.[16]

Yet, it is clear that from the UN era organizations were increasingly read as *institutional* structures. As mentioned, this came with an interest in the operation of organizations as legal organisms, certain institutional or even 'constitutional' mechanisms, autonomous development and *Kompetenz*

11 *Ibidem*, paras. 1562–1568.

12 See Jan Klabbers, *An introduction to International Organizations Law* (Cambridge UP, 2022), pp. 43–51.

13 See Niels Blokker and Ramses Wessel, "Revisiting Questions of Organisationhood, Legal Personality and Membership in the OSCE: The Interplay Between Law, Politics and Practice", in Mateja Steinbrück Platise et al. (eds.), *The Legal Framework of the OSCE* (Cambridge UP 2019), pp. 135–64.

14 Carlos Fernández de Casadevante Romani, "Objective Regimes", in *Max Planck Encyclopedia for Public International Law* (2010).

15 See Paul Reuter, *Introduction to the Law of Treaties* (Geneva, 2nd ed., 1995), at pp. 124–125.

16 *Ibidem*, at p. 121.

Kompetenz – while the treaty at the origin of the organization faded into the background. That lens has been the starting point for the impressive work of scholars such as, among others, Jenks, Virally, Schermers, and Blokker. The body of institutional rules had been first developed by practitioners in the newly established organizations.[17] As a disciplinary field, somewhat later, 'international institutional law' fittingly started out with a focus on the systematization and stocktaking of institutional rules, and a comparative methodology.

International law and doctrine, by mouth of the ICJ, had formalised the apparent agency of international organizations through the attribution of 'international legal personality'. However, as argued elsewhere, this amounted to a 'thin' version,[18] with organizations accepted as legal persons but not quite as '*personnes morales*'.[19] For example, organizations seemed incapable of the 'states of mind' or 'psychological states' ascribed to recognized participants in any legal order, such as *assent, acquiescence, intention, opinion, aim,* and *good* or *bad faith*. In contrast, international law since at least two centuries seems to be at ease with this when it comes to states – even if these are composite, non-natural legal persons in their own right.[20]

So, notwithstanding their status as legal participant, organizations retained a mechanical and partly transparent legal image. This is borne out by the 1986 *Vienna Convention on the Law of Treaties* and its long and winding legislative history.[21] International organizations of course could engage in treaty-making by producing an agreed symbol for legal 'will', as with an 'expression of consent to be bound by a treaty'. But, as one of many examples, up until the last version of the draft Articles in order to establish fraud by an organization in the conclusion of a treaty, one would have to resort to the internal institutional order of the organization – in other words: to the member states – while no such engagement with a state's domestic order was prescribed.[22] Echoes of this

17 Jan Klabbers, "Theorizing International Organizations", in Anne Orford, Florian Hoffmann and Martin Clark (eds.), *The Oxford Handbook of the Theory of International Law* (Oxford UP, 2016), pp. 618–634.

18 Brölmann (*supra* note 8), pp. 245–247.

19 On 'moral personality' in the civil law tradition see, e.g., Frederic W. Maitland, "Moral Personality and Legal Personality", in *Journal of Comparative Legislation and International Law* vol. 6 (1905), p. 192.

20 See Catherine Brölmann, "Capturing the Juridical Will of International Organisations", in Sufyan Droubi and Jean d'Aspremont (eds.), *International Organizations and Non-State Actors in the Formation of Customary International Law* (Manchester UP, 2019).

21 1986 Vienna Convention on the Law of Treaties between States and International Organizations or between International Organizations (UN Doc. A/CONF.129/15); the argument is elaborated in detail in Brölmann (*supra* note 8).

22 Cf. *Yearbook ILC* 1982 Vol. II (Part Two) at p. 5, para. 2 (re Draft Art. 48 (2)).

cautious perspective on organizations are found in the 2018 ILC *Conclusions on the identification of customary international law*, as was pointed out by, *inter alia*, Niels Blokker.[23]

As organizations' interaction with non-member states and other actors and stakeholders intensified, it made sense that the existing rules of general international law were assessed on their applicability to organizations. Thus the body of law and the disciplinary field of 'international institutional law' expanded and came to encompass rules of general international law, classic examples being the law of privileges and immunities,[24] the law of treaties,[25] and later the law of international responsibility.[26] It brought further changes to the style and the epistemological underpinnings of the disciplinary field, which increasingly was named 'the law of international organizations' or 'international organizations law'[27] – as confirmed by the title of the first dedicated journal in the field, the *International Organizations Law Review*, founded in 2004 by Niels Blokker and Ramses Wessel.

The changed legal image of international organizations – from treaty regime to institutional structure – and doctrine's acceptance of organizations as independent legal persons in international law, however, had not fundamentally changed the identity of the international organization, viz. of a *legal* construction made of law and through law.

3 The Social Existence of International Organizations

But change was in the air. With some simplification it can be argued that in the course of the 1990s organizations transformed further, from legal constructions into creatures with a degree of social existence. In the same way as today we generally feel that states "are not metaphysical entities but political

23 Niels Blokker, "International Organizations and Customary International Law: Is the International Law Commission Taking International Organizations Seriously?", in *International Organizations Law Review* (*IOLR*) vol. 14 (2017), p. 1.

24 1946 Convention on the Privileges and Immunities of the United Nations, 1 *UNTS* 15; and development of doctrine through judicial decisions up until this day.

25 1986 Vienna Convention on the Law of Treaties between States and International Organizations or between International Organizations, UN Doc. A/CONF.129/15.

26 UN Doc. A/66/10, 9 December 2011.

27 See, e.g., the changed title in editions of Jan Klabbers' textbook (Cambridge UP): *An introduction to International Institutional Law* (2002 and 2012) and *An introduction to International Organizations Law* (2015 and 2022).

communities"[28] in the real world, organizations seem to have assumed an objective presence in 'social reality'.

For one, the entrenched mechanistic view of international organizations had increasingly become untenable, as its negative effects persisted and its positive ambitions were not met. As for the latter, the 'thin' legal image had once been tied to organizations' 'neutrality' and their ability of "pooling sovereign interests or as neutral appliers of the real interests of all states".[29] Similarly, it had supported the trope of organizations as 'technical' and 'a-political'.[30] But the optimism about 'institutionalisation' of international law in the 1970s and 1980s – and in the early 1990s, linked to the vision of a new world made up of liberal-democratic states – would fade rapidly in the 2000s.[31] It gave way to disenchantment and a sobering of expectations, triggered for example by information about misconduct of United Nations military missions[32] and self-enrichment of United Nations staff members.[33] Already there were long-time misgivings about the manifestation of international organizations as a Western-hegemonic project,[34] and criticism for instance on the idea of distributing power and authority[35] along functional lines, with ensuing single issue agendas in international affairs.

Meanwhile the negative associations of the mechanical, 'thin' legal image of organizations – the abovementioned legal incongruencies, and detrimental

---

28 Gleider Hernàndez, *International Law* (2nd ed., Oxford UP, 2022), p. 22.

29 José Alvarez, "International Organizations: Then and Now", in *The American Journal of International Law* vol. 100 (2006), pp. 324, 342.

30 See also Catherine Brölmann, "Regional Organizations in International Law: Exploring the Function-Territory Divide", in *IOLR* vol. 21 (2024), pp. 132–145, referring to Anne Peters and Simone Peter, "International Organizations: Between Technocracy and Democracy", in Bardo Fassbender and Anne Peters (eds.), *The Oxford Handbook of the History of International Law* (Oxford UP, 2014).

31 One of the first papers (written just before '9/11') to note and articulate this trend is Jan Klabbers, "The Changing Image of International Organizations", in Jean Marc Coicaud and Veijo Heiskanen (eds.), *The Legitimacy of International Organizations* (Tokyo, UN University, 2001).

32 Catherine Lutz a.o., "Conduct and Discipline in UN Peacekeeping Operations: Culture, Political Economy and Gender", in *Watson Institute for International Studies Research Paper* (2009), available at <http://dx.doi.org/10.2139/ssrn.2323758>.

33 Susan A Notar, "The Oil-for-Food Program and the Need for Oversight Entities to Monitor UN Sanctions Regimes", in *Proceedings of the Annual Meeting of the American Society of International* Law vol. 101 (2007), p. 163.

34 Bhupinder Chimni, "International Institutions Today: An Imperial Global State in the Making", in *European Journal of International Law* (*EJIL*) vol. 15 (2004), pp. 1, 23–24.

35 Günther Teubner, "Globale Zivilverfassungen: Alternativen zur staatszentrierten Verfassungstheorie", in *Zeitschrift für ausländisches öffentliches Recht und Völkerrecht* vol. 63 (2003), p. 1.

effects to the legal protection of other actors – had also become more prominent. As international organizations increasingly gained an existence in the 'real world', questions came to be less about institutional and formal-juridical issues, or the role of member states as *Herren der Verträge*, and more about legitimacy and ethics. A sign of this in positive law and doctrine is that the notorious gap in individual legal protection vis-à-vis international organizations – created by a concurrence of attribution of conduct on the one hand and immunity on the other, or attribution of conduct on the one hand and a (lack of) *locus standi* on the other – was considered ever more problematic.

The manifestation of organizations in the social world is exemplified by the activities of the UN (Secretariat) rolling out its agenda of the 'international rule of law' on member states through a consistent discursive practice, and struggling to subject also itself to it.[36] Another example from the 1990s are the episodes of the UN engaging in high politics operations that entered into the domestic order of states, under the flag of 'transitional justice'.

A key sign of the organization's social presence in contemporary international organizations *law* is that the longtime idea of impossibility of an international organization's 'wrongdoing' ("[i]s it really conceivable that … organisations may … employ the threat or use of force …?"[37] and "it must not be forgotten that, by their very nature, international organizations normally behave in such a manner as not to commit internationally wrongful acts"[38]) was abandoned – witness the adoption of the 2011 ILC *Articles on the Responsibility of International Organizations*.[39]

International organizations and international organizations law are mutually constitutive. It is thus likely that the new manifestation of international organizations, with '*personalité morale*' and a presence in the social world, strengthened the call for accountability of international organizations, while conversely, the call for accountability helped to forge the new identity of international organizations. Either way, it led to an innovative project on non-legal

36 *The rule of law and transitional justice in conflict and post-conflict societies*, Report of the Secretary-General to the Security Council (UN Doc. S/2004/616 (2004)); also the call upon the UN ("The duty of non-recognition specified above also applies to international organizations") by the ICJ in the 2024 Opinion on the *Legal Consequences Arising From The Policies and Practices of Israel in the Occupied Palestinian Territory, Including East Jerusalem* (para. 280) can serve as an example.

37 *Yearbook ILC* 1982 Vol. II (Part Two), p. 55, para. 2.

38 Statement by the ILC in relation to an early version of the Draft Articles on State Responsibility – *Yearbook ILC* 1975 Vol II, p. 87, para. 3 (emphasis added); both the article and the commentary were adopted in an unaltered version in 1996.

39 UN General Assembly resolution 66/100 of 9 December 2011.

accountability processes of international organizations (with the involvement of Niels Blokker as ILA member)[40] as well as to the development of a formal legal responsibility mechanism by the ILC. More generally, space opened for concerns about the compatibility of international organizations' actions with human rights,[41] and for questions such as whether organizations could be bound by rules of international law which they – i.e., independently – did not create.[42] The cutting face between the old identity of the organization as an unanimated, mechanical legal actor and its new identity as an actor with a social existence and a capacity for 'legal will' somewhat in the way of a state, could give rise to 'dilemmas', as for professor Schermers in the 1970s when organizations were found to breach human rights.[43]

As for international organizations *law*, the aforementioned inclusion of general rules into the body of international organizations law was followed, especially since the 2000s, by a 'constitutional turn' looking to the incorporation of substantive norms, notably 'fundamental values' linked to human rights or theories of justice. It is perhaps not a coincidence that at this time it also became increasingly clear that 'functionalism' – once the prime candidate for a theoretical underpinning of international organizations law – was not equipped, as Jan Klabbers himself has pointed out,[44] to explain all the ups and downs of organizations. It makes sense that precisely the manifestation of organizations as creatures with a 'real world' presence would bring to light the limitations of an explanatory model focused on 'internal' interaction between the institution and the member states, or: between the sum and the parts. Recent years have seen further endeavours at theorizing international organizations law.[45] Theoretical scholarship reflecting on international organizations has also come to the fore, building on earlier rapprochements between

40 ILA Committee on *Accountability of International Organisations* (final report of 2002 at the 70th conference in New Delhi).

41 Cf. Jan Wouters a.o. (eds.), *Accountability for Human Rights Violations by International Organisations* (Intersentia, 2010), at p. 2: "How could one imagine international organisations violating human rights?".

42 An early study to raise this question, in the context of human rights, is Rick Lawson, *Het EVRM en de Europese Gemeenschappen – Bouwstenen voor een aansprakelijkheidsregime voor het optreden van internationale organisaties* (Kluwer, 1999); see also Kristina Daugirdas, "How and Why International Law Binds International Organizations", in *Harvard International Law Journal* vol. 57 (2016), p. 325.

43 Jan Klabbers, "Schermers' Dilemma", in *EJIL* vol. 31 (2020), p. 565.

44 Jan Klabbers, "The EJIL Foreword: The Transformation of International Organizations Law", in *EJIL* vol. 26 (2015), p. 9.

45 Jan Klabbers and Guy Fiti Sinclair, "On Theorizing International Organizations Law: Editors' Introduction", in *EJIL* vol. 31 (2020), p. 489; also Klabbers (*supra* note 17).

international law and different brands of international relations scholarship;[46] sharp analyses by TWAIL;[47] and more generally critical scholarship on international organizations (law). One example is enlightening work on international organizations through a post-colonial lens, setting out how 'international organizations law' followed quite late after the actual creation of organizations, with as a prime incentive its promise for both colonizer and decolonized states.[48] The dimension of organizations as an actual entity in social reality, and perhaps an actual space, was highlighted by the role of 'caretaker' brought up in a recent take on organizations from a phenomenological perspective.[49]

4 Conclusion

This account proposes that the identity of international organizations has transformed from a legal construction – appearing as an (objective) treaty regime, and then predominantly as an institutional structure – to a creature with a social existence. That transformation can be plausibly connected to the scope and meaning of international organizations *law*.

Admittedly, this is presented as a linear 'development' and in some ways a 'coming of age' story. That could seem to point to an ideal type legal actor – the state – as if that were the highest possible attainment in international law. Obviously, this is not the proposition. "The progress narrative that characterized the turn to international organizations"[50] in fact revolved around offsetting the disadvantages of states. What it could point to, is that participants in the legal world at some point will also cross over to the social world, with in turn a response from the applicable legal frameworks. The question is where it ends. Will we see a *Badinter Committee* for the acceptance or recognition of new international organizations (including 'authoritarian organizations')?[51]

---

46 Apt observations, e.g., in Jan Klabbers, "Review of Jens Steffek, International Organization as Technocratic Utopia (Oxford 2021)", in *EJIL* vol. 33 (2022), p. 720.

47 Chimni (*supra* note 34), p. 1.

48 Guy Fiti Sinclair, "Towards a Postcolonial Genealogy of International Organizations Law", in *Leiden Journal of International Law* vol. 31 (2018), p. 841: "(…) pictures a world of nation-states in opposition to the hegemonic territorialism of colonialism".

49 See the work of Jean d'Aspremont, e.g., "The Love for International Organizations", in *IOLR* vol. 20 (2023), pp. 111–159, at pp. 118–121.

50 Alvarez (*supra* note 29), pp. 324, 346.

51 Christina Cottiero and Stephan Haggard, "Stabilizing Authoritarian Rule: The Role of International Organizations", in *International Studies Quarterly* vol. 67 (2023).

What is certain is that the handbook by Schermers and Blokker would not hesitate to include an accurate description and categorisation of such a new phenomenon.[52] In conclusion it is worth mentioning that the brief account of international organizations (law) proposed here underscores the enduring value of that formidable reference work – which never changed its name. It operates from "the general consensus that despite their legal differences (which are associated, in turn, with different objectives and powers), organizations confront similar problems and are governed by common rules or principles".[53] The organization of the subject matter – a systematic treatment of institutional facets (by resorting to both specific institutional rules and general international law), with final chapters on "Legal Status" and "External Relations" – suggest an approach to the global order through the lens of international organizations as the centre of the universe, somewhat in the way of *äusseres Staatsrecht*. And that is helpful for many of the questions regarding organizations that are a topic of conversation today – as these must always rely on a foundation of knowledge on the setup of international organizations as legal actors, even if organizations have meanwhile also gained an existence in the social world.

---

52 Schermers & Blokker (*supra* note 10).

53 Kelly Vinopal, "Review of H. Schermers and N. Blokker, *International Institutional Law*, Sixth Rev. Ed.", in *The American Journal of International Law* vol. 99 (2005), p. 311.

CHAPTER 35

Law and Lawyering in International Organizations

*Edward Chukwuemeke Okeke**

1 Introduction

International organizations matter! They matter because they have become the fulcrum of international cooperation among States. International organizations have competences across a wide spectrum of human activities and interests. They do not only impact their member States but also the daily lives of individuals. They have, therefore, become indispensable in the international legal order. The United Nations and its specialized agencies were founded on the idea of an international legal order where nations agree to work together in their collective interest through international organizations. In other words, the multilateral system is a rules-based system built on international cooperation. Because of the place of international organizations in the international legal order and their presence in present-day international life, it is important to understand the role of law in them. It is equally important to understand the role of lawyers in international organizations – who are the custodians of the law of international organizations in the sense it is their responsibility to interpret the law and provide legal advice to various organs within the institution. "While the formal role of lawyers in international organizations may be limited, they have tremendous influence in developing both international institutional law and in developing their organization".[1]

A century ago, a good many legal scholars did not know what to make of the legal status of international organizations. They were considered an enigmatic oddity, especially amongst lawyers who were steeped in the understanding of international law as the law of nations. It took the *Reparations Case* to resolve the issue of the international personality of the United Nations and other such international organizations.[2] Previously, States alone were thought to be the only subjects of international law. The consequence of the international

* The author is the Lead Counsel, Global Knowledge and Research, World Bank.

1 Jan Klabbers, *An Introduction to International Organizations Law* (Cambridge UP, 2015), p. 256.

2 ICJ, *Reparation for Injuries Suffered in the Service of the United Nations* (Advisory Opinion), [1949] ICJ Reports, p. 174.

 | DOI:10.1163/9789004699939_037

personality of international organizations is that they are subjects of international law, with some rights and responsibilities on the international plane. For example, as subjects of international law, international organizations can enter into treaties with States or other international organizations. Even though States are still the primary and principal subjects of international law, and are central to the international system, international organizations have become major actors in their own right. With the recognition of international organizations as subjects of international law, the field of international law has expanded from the *law of nations* to include the *law of international organizations*. This recognition also cemented the law of international organizations as a field within international law. As the law of international organizations has taken hold so also has the role of lawyers in them. However, more needs to be known about law and lawyering in international organizations.

Over a century ago when the League of Nations was established and even a quarter of a century later when the United Nations was created, there was a dearth of scholarship on the law of international organizations. Thanks to the scholarship of international law scholars like Niels Blokker, amongst others, such is no longer the case.[3] I first met Professor Blokker during the conference on *Immunity of International Organizations: Functional Necessity or Out of Date*, which he had organized in June 2013 at Leiden University, and subsequently met him during a seminar organized by August Reinisch at the University of Vienna in connection with a book project in which we were all contributors.[4] I, however, knew of Professor Blokker before these meetings through his writings and had benefitted from his scholarship in my research, practice and writings. In fact, his *magnum opus*, *International Institutional Law*, has served me as a vade mecum throughout my career as a lawyer in international organizations.[5] Professor Blokker is the model of the international law scholar

3 C. Wilfred Jenks, a legal scholar and practitioner, was a pioneer in this area and his scholarly writings were pivotal to the emergence and development of the discipline. Among his works is "The Legal Personality of International Organizations", in *British Yearbook of International Law* vol. 22 (1945), p. 267. Other early writings on the subject are D.W. Bowett, *The Law of International Institutions* (Stevens & Sons, 1963), and Henry G. Schermers, *International Institutional Law* (Sijthoff, 1972).

4 The 2013 conference at Leiden University gave birth to Niels Blokker and Nico Schrijver (eds.), *Immunity of international organizations* (Brill Nijhoff, 2015) while the conference at the University of Vienna resulted in August Reinisch (ed.), *The Conventions on the Privileges and Immunities of the United Nations and its Specialized Agencies: A Commentary* (Oxford UP, 2016).

5 *International Institutional Law* was first published in 1972 by Henry G. Schermers and has been co-authored with Niels M. Blokker since the fourth edition, which was published in 2003. The Sixth Revised Edition was published in 2018.

who has left an indelible impact on the law of international organizations. As an academic, he has contributed to the development and understanding of the law of international organizations through his scholarly writings. The functions, structure and competences of international organizations are the province of the law of international organizations. In sum, the law of international organizations is the body of laws dealing with all aspects of their creation, existence and dissolution, including their relations with other international persons, i.e., member States, non-member States and international organizations. This contribution to the *liber amicorum* in honour of this legal luminary discusses the role of law and lawyers in international organizations.

2 Origin, Nature and Purposes of International Organizations

1815 was a critical year in the development of international organizations. 1815 marked the end of the years of war between Britain and France, when the Duke of Wellington defeated Napoleon Bonaparte at the Battle of Waterloo, ending the Napoleonic Wars. 1815 ushered the Concert of Europe which lasted till the outbreak of the First World War in 1914. The Concert of Europe was the system of international cooperation between governments in the form of either diplomatic conferences or administrative bodies. It started with the Congress of Vienna as the first such diplomatic conference and the Commission for the Navigation of the Rhine as the first permanent administrative body set up by governments. During the Concert of Europe, the International Telegraphic Union (ITU) was established in 1865, followed by the Universal Postal Union (UPU) in 1874.

The First World War ended with the Treaty of Versailles which gave birth to the modern or contemporary international organizations, with the establishment in 1920 of both the League of Nations for cooperation between governments in the political arena, and the International Labour Organization (ILO) for the international improvement and maintenance of labour standards and conditions. The League of Nations was the forerunner of the United Nations which was created in 1945. The ILO, on the other hand, with the promise of the usefulness of international organizations dealing with specialized areas of concerns, was the impetus for the concept of specialized agencies which became an integral part of the United Nations system as provided for in Articles 57 to 59 of the Charter of the United Nations.

Articles 2 of the Draft Articles on the Responsibility of International Organizations defines international organization to mean "an organization established by a treaty or other instrument governed by international law and possessing its own international legal personality. International organizations may include as members, in addition to States, other entities".[6] Article 2(1)(i) of the Vienna Convention on the Law of Treaties defines an international organization to mean an "intergovernmental organization".[7] The nature of international organizations is that they are typically created by States under a treaty as a constituent instrument, also known as Charter, Constitution, or Articles of Agreement, etc. International organizations are diverse in their composition, functions, and membership but share some basic characteristics. Most have only States as members while some have other international organizations or other non-State actors as members.[8] The common thread is that there must be States in their membership. As a result of this characteristic, international organizations are also known as intergovernmental organizations, which exclude international non-governmental organizations, such as the International Federation of the Red Cross and Red Crescent Societies. Thus, the definitional delimitation of international organizations is usually with how they are created and by whom: they are created by States under international law in the form of a treaty and governed by international law as its subject.[9]

An international organization has its own international personality which is separate from that of its members.[10] It is rare to find an explicit provision on the international personality of international organizations in constituent instruments.[11] The legal or juridical personality of international organizations

6 International Law Commission, "Draft Articles on the Responsibility of International Organizations", in *Yearbook of the International Law Commission* 2011 vol. II (2), UN Doc A/66/10.

7 Vienna Convention on the Law of Treaties (done at Vienna on 23 May 1969 and entered into force on 27 January 1980), 1155 *UNTS* 331.

8 See Article 4 of the Statute of the World Tourism Organization, which is an international organization that has non-State actors in its membership. Its membership includes 137 countries as Full Members, six Associate Members, and 500 Affiliate members representing the private sector, educational institutions, tourism associations, and local tourism authorities. The Universal Postal Union and the International Telecommunication Union both have non-State actors as members. The Joint Vienna Institute is an international organization that was created by six international organizations and Austria.

9 The Organization for Security and Cooperation in Europe (OSCE) is an odd exception to the rule in that it was created without a treaty. The Helsinki Final Act signed by 35 nations on 1 August 1975 concluded the Conference on Security and Cooperation in Europe held in Helsinki, Finland.

10 See Edward Chukwuemeke Okeke, *Jurisdictional Immunities of States and International Organizations* (Oxford UP, 2018), pp. 243–264, for a discussion of the legal status of international organizations.

11 There is no explicit provision on international personality in the Charter of the United Nations and the constituent instruments of its specialized agencies. A rare example of an

in their member States, on the other hand, are usually provided for in their constituent instruments.[12] The standard provision is that the organization shall have the capacity in the territories of its member States to contract; acquire and dispose of immovable and movable property; and institute legal proceedings. The legal personality in national or municipal law includes the capacity to perform other legal acts necessary to fulfil the functions of the international organization in the State.

The raison d'être of international organizations is that States opt for international cooperation through the creation of international organizations to achieve their common objectives. Even though some of these objectives could be accomplished by States acting unilaterally, most require multilateral cooperation. Multilateralism through international organizations tends to give legitimacy to actions that could be taken by any State individually. At the same time, an international organization is not an alter ego of any particular member State even though that member State may have undue or immense influence within the organization. International cooperation is born, oftentimes, not out of altruism but out of strategic national interest. There is no gainsaying that the strategic national interest of the United States informed its championing the creation of the United Nations and the Bretton Woods institutions. In this regard, the United States Treasury Secretary, Henry Morgenthau, in his closing address at the Bretton Woods Conference stated: "We have come to recognize that the wisest and most effective way to protect our national interest is through international cooperation – that is to say, through united efforts for the attainment of common goals".[13]

International organizations have become indispensable in international life as they are involved in virtually every field of human endeavour. Take for instance, the work of the International Civil Aviation Organization (ICAO) in helping 193 countries to cooperate and share their skies to their mutual benefit, and in developing policies and standards for aviation safety. Another

---

explicit provision on international personality is Article 50 of the Articles of Agreement of the African Development Bank which provides: "To enable it to fulfil its purpose and the functions with which it is entrusted, the Bank shall possess full international personality. To those ends, it may enter into agreements with members, non-member States and other international organizations".

12 See, e.g., Article 104, UN Charter; Article VII, Section 2, Articles of Agreement of the World Bank.

13 Address by Henry Morgenthau at the Closing Plenary Session, 22 July 1944, 1944, United Nations Monetary and Financial Conference, Bretton Woods, New Hampshire, July 1 to July 22, Final Act and Related Documents. Available at <https://fraser.stlouisfed.org/files/docs/historical/eccles/036_17_0004.pdf>.

example is the World Health Organization which connects countries, partners and people to promote health and keep the world safe. The International Maritime Organization (IMO) has the responsibility for the safety and security of shipping and the prevention of marine and atmospheric pollution by ships. International organizations pursue global public interest and produce global public goods which no State alone could furnish. The solution to global problems like climate change, humanitarian and economic crises, especially in countries affected by fragility, conflict and violence (FCV), require robust multilateral systems and strong international cooperation. The ideals for which international organizations were created have not spared them the criticism that they lack accountability for wrongful acts and must therefore be constrained or controlled. In addition, one can always question whether international organizations, like the United Nations and its specialized agencies, have lived up to the ideals for which they were created.

The activities of international organizations are informed by the purposes for which they were created under their constituent instruments. Even though international organizations are recognized to have implied powers, it would be *ultra vires* for them to act outside of their mandates. The competence of international organizations is limited under the principle of attributed powers, which the International Court of Justice (ICJ) articulated as follows: "International organizations are governed by the 'principle of speciality', that is to say, they are invested by the States which create them with powers, the limits of which are a function of the common interests whose promotion those States entrust to them".[14] To carry out their functions under their mandates, international organizations are imbued with certain privileges and immunities by their member States. This has given rise to controversy about how to hold international organization accountable, considering that their jurisdictional immunity may result in denial of access to justice.[15]

14 ICJ, *Legality of the Use by a State of Nuclear Weapons in Armed Conflict (Request for an Advisory Opinion by the World Health Organization)*, [1996] ICJ Reports, p. 66, para. 25 (rejecting the request by WHO for an advisory opinion on the legality of nuclear weapons on the grounds that the request was outside the scope of its mandate).

15 See Edward Chukwuemeke Okeke, "The Tension between the Jurisdictional Immunity of International Organizations and the Right of Access to Court", in Peter Quayle (ed.), *The Role of International Administrative Law at International Organizations* (Brill Nijhoff, 2021), pp. 25–53.

3 Role of Law in International Organizations

Law is vital to the life of international organizations. To carry out their functions, international organizations may enter into relationships with (a) member States, (b) staff, (c) non-member States, (d) other international organizations, (e) non-state private entities, and (f) other third parties. These relationships variously implicate the role of law in international organizations. International organizations are created by international law and operate under it. Because international organizations are created by interstate action, their dealings with States are unquestionably governed by international law.

However, international law is not the only law that applies to or governs the activities of international organizations. In addition, there is a *corpus* of law that regulates the institutional framework and structure of international organizations. This is variously known as the Law of International Organizations or International Organizations Law or International Institutional Law. In their *magnum opus, International Institutional Law*, Henry G. Schermers & Niels M. Blokker state that the "institutional law of international organizations comprises those rules of law which govern their legal status, structure and functioning".[16] Thus, the law of international organizations refers to the norms, principles and processes of the international organizations which are contained in their constituent instruments, including the applicable norms and principles of international law.

The application of the institutional law of international organizations is both international and internal in nature. Internationally, it applies in the relations of the international organizations with other international persons. Internally, it applies to the relations between persons and organs within the organization, as well as between States as members of the organization. The constituent instrument is part of the institutional law of an international organization, and as a treaty, it is international law that applies to the relations between the member States as parties to a treaty, and between the member States and the organizations as international persons. In addition, the constituent instrument may contain rules that govern the internal functioning of the organization. Other than treaties, the law of international organizations includes bylaws of plenary organs, regulations, rules, institutional policies and procedures. In sum, the law of the organization relates to those rules that are applicable to its functions, powers and duties.

16 Schermers & Blokker, *supra* note 5, p. 4, § 7.

4 Role of Lawyers in International Organizations

As important as the role of lawyers in international organizations is, it must be noted that most positions in international organizations are for carrying out the functions and activities of the organizations under their respective mandates and missions. Together, all these positions, including lawyers, are key to the functioning of international organizations. The roles and responsibilities of lawyers differ across international organizations but there are essential features and common characteristics.[17] Lawyering in international organizations entails the typical role of lawyers, such as interpreting legal instruments, drafting and negotiating agreements and other legal instruments, issuing legal opinions, litigation and dispute resolution, etc. Some lawyers advise on international law, international administrative law, employment law, and institutional law. The primary role of lawyers in international organizations is to provide legal advice or opinion on an array of issues. They also provide legal advice to the constituent organs of the organization on the legal aspects of the organization's activities and operations. Some act as in-house counsel with various and varied tasks. In some international organizations, lawyers provide legal services and advice in the area of law-making and standard-setting that fall within their mandates. For some legal services, lawyers may seek the opinion of outside counsel or retain outside counsel to represent the international organization, such as in litigation or arbitration.

Lawyers in international organizations are, first and foremost, international civil servants and, as such, they owe an exclusive duty of loyalty to their respective organizations, and the member States of the organization are required to respect the international character of that duty.[18] As staff of the organization, they are subject to the overall authority of the executive head of the organization, i.e., the Secretary-General, Director-General or President of the organization. Legal practitioners in international organizations exercise their functions in a legal office or department under the leadership of a general counsel, legal counsel or legal adviser as the role is variously known.[19] Typically, in the United Nations system, the legal adviser heads the legal office and reports directly to the executive head of the organization. To ensure that the legal adviser and the

---

17 For an extensive discussion of the role of legal advisers and functioning of lawyers in various international organizations, see Jan Wouters (ed.), *Legal Advisers in International Organizations* (Edward Elgar, 2023).

18 See, e.g., Article 101 of the United Nations Charter, and Article v, Section 5(c) of the Articles of Agreement of the World Bank.

19 Some international organizations may employ lawyers in other areas outside of the legal office but the focus of this article is with those lawyers that serve as legal advisers and their staff.

lawyers working in the legal office provide independent legal advice directly to its clients within the organization, the legal office is usually a separate and independent office. According to the Interoffice Memorandum on Certain Aspects Regarding the Legal Adviser/Legal Office:

> It should also be clearly understood that the role of the legal service in any organization is to independently assist the secretariat and its divisions, branches and sections in the day-to-day administration of their mandates and programmes through the provision of legal services. In accordance with its terms of reference, the role of any legal service is advisory. It does not administer.[20]

The clients or recipients of the legal services from the legal office are varied as the legal functions in a particular organization. At the World Bank, for example, among the responsibilities of the general counsel is the management of the legal office, preparation of draft resolutions for the Board of Governors and Board of Executive Directors, provision of advice to the President, Management, Offices and Departments of the Bank on legal and policy matters; and defending or overseeing the defence of the Bank in litigation and other dispute resolution mechanisms. In the performance of these responsibilities, the general counsel is assisted by a team of lawyers in the Legal Vice Presidency Unit.[21] As noted by a former General Counsel of the International Monetary Fund, "one of the General Counsel's most important duties is to empower each of the lawyers around him/her to exercise greater responsibility in carrying out the mission of the Legal Department. The Fund's General Counsel is only as effective as the team he/she leads".[22] There may be units, offices or departments within international organizations that employ lawyers but those lawyers do not perform the legal function under the auspices of the legal office or provide legal services to the organization per se.[23]

---

20 Independence and reporting of the Legal Advisor of an agency of the United Nations system—Structure and role of the Legal Office—Specialized agencies v. subsidiary organs of the United Nations. *United Nations Juridical Yearbook* 2003, p. 564, para. 9.

21 See Ibrahim F.I. Shihata, "The Role of the World Bank's General Counsel", in *Collection of Essays by Legal Advisers of States, Legal Advisers of International Organizations and Practitioners in the Field of International Law* (United Nations, 1999).

22 Sean Hagan, "The Role of Law – and Lawyer – in the International Monetary Fund", in Asif H. Qureshi & Xuan Gao (eds.), *International Economic Organizations and Law: The Perspective and Role of the Legal Counsel* (Kluwer, 2012), p. 45.

23 The focus of this essay is more on what lawyers in the legal office of international organizations generally do as their functions under the mandate of the office.

To effectively perform the role of lawyers in international organizations calls for a certain skillset. Lawyers should be politically savvy, but not political, as international organizations are increasingly becoming political – even those whose mandate eschews politics. In the life and activities of international organizations, some political issues are couched as legal issues and presented to the legal adviser for advice. Lawyers and legal advisers in international organizations are supposed to be independent in the discharge of their duties. Since they are independent, their legal advice to various organs or clients within the organization should be consistent. In providing legal advice, an effective lawyer tries to find solutions that are both practical and defensible on legal grounds. It is not enough that the legal advice be sound and correct, it must be able to enable the clients carry out their respective mandates. In short, lawyers in international organizations are pre-eminently problem-solvers and, as such, need to be innovative and proactive. They should be able to apply their legal acumen and expertise to complex or novel issues, and develop sound, innovative and creative solutions to enable the organization to successfully respond to the evolving needs, while protecting it from legal and reputational risks in a demanding global environment.

Lawyering in international organizations calls for collaboration and coordination, both within the legal office of a particular organization and those of other international organization, with colleagues whose experience and expertise are varied. An effective legal adviser is principled but at the same time works for compromise or consensus to defuse conflict where possible. Lawyers are called upon to advise on the legality or lawfulness of some decisions and policies based on applicable legal instruments. For this task, they have to interpret these instruments and advise on the correct application of rules and policies. Lawyers, even though they are not policymakers per se, sometimes help policymakers such as management and organs think through the potential ramifications of a proposed policy decision or course of action. An astute lawyer must be able to distinguish between legal and policy advice, and to discern where the exclusive responsibility lies with respect to each category of advice. For advice on legal issues, the buck stops with the legal adviser.

Considering that lawyers in international organizations are international civil servants and do not practice in national jurisdictions but in the international sphere, it would not be an aggrandizement to characterize them as international lawyers. Some of these lawyers have distinguished themselves as international law scholars.[24] Others have gone on to serve as judges in

24 Oscar Schacter of the United Nations, Joseph Gold of the International Monetary Fund, Aron Broches and Ibrahim Shihata of the World Bank are some examples.

the ICJ.[25] Lawyers in international organizations play a role in international intercourse and discourse. These lawyers are no longer invisible because they have left their footprints all over the landscape of international law.[26] This does not mean that all lawyers that perform legal functions in international organizations are international lawyers in the traditional sense or even have knowledge of or expertise in public international law.

5 Conclusion

International organizations have developed to become major actors in international affairs. Accompanying this development is their proliferation to the point that they now far outnumber States. They are the major fora for international cooperation. They are created by international law and have also become part of the lawmaking apparatus of the international community. They are no longer the curiosities that they were over a century ago when they were coming into existence. Much more is known about them now because of the writings of some international law scholars and practitioners. The law of international organizations has become a discipline and a major field of study in universities around the world.

More is also known about the role of lawyers in international organizations. These lawyers have become a veritable and visible college of international lawyers with networks for knowledge-sharing and collaboration. For example, the legal advisers of the United Nations System have a forum where they try to meet annually and discuss issues of common interest. The general counsels of the international financial institutions (IFIs) and multilateral development banks (MDBs) have a similar forum. There are other network of lawyers in international organizations that serve as communities of practice, such as the Association of Lawyers in Intergovernmental Finance and Development Organization (ALIFDO) and the Forum on Institutional Law in International Organizations (FILIO). The role and responsibilities of lawyers in international organizations are evolving to meet the ever-changing needs and missions of the organizations. These are interesting times for law and lawyers in international organizations.

---

25 Carl-August Fleischhauer, former UN Legal Counsel, and Abdulqawi Yusuf, former UNESCO Legal Adviser.

26 Cf. Oscar Schachter, "The Invisible College of International Lawyers", in *Northwestern University Law Review* vol. 72 (1977), p. 217. Schachter wrote about the "invisible college of international lawyers" which he described as a "professional community, though dispersed throughout the world and engaged in diverse occupations, dedicated to a common intellectual enterprise".

Index

accountability 13–14, 22, 239, 245, 248, 282–293
accountability, for atrocities 74, 78, 81–86
acquiescence 151
advisory proceedings 339–352
Agenda for Democratization (1996) 454
aggression 11–18
animal health 132–138, 158, 163–173
animal welfare 158–175
Articles on the Responsibility of International Organizations (ARIO) 24, 28*n*21, 408–409, 436, 483, 489, 490*n*6
  See also International Law Commission (ILC)
Assembly of States Parties (ASP), to the Rome Statute of the ICC 266, 270, 278–280
Association of Southeast Asian Nations (ASEAN) 390–401
autonomy, of international organizations 370–371

Budgets of international organizations 165, 251–264, 283, 382, 407–410

Chagos Archipelago 149, 223–231, 340–352
China, actions in the South China Sea 398*nn*42–43, 399
climate change 119–131, 311, 322
  and trade policy 325, 327, 332
  United Nations Framework on Convention on Climate Change (UNFCCC) 171, 332
climate crisis, and industrial meat production 168, 175
climate security 119, 123–130
Collective security 41, 67, 88, 209
Common Foreign and Security Policy (CFSP) 207–221
Commission of Small Island States on Climate Change and International Law (COSIS) 150*n*29, 153, 154
Commission on the Limits of the Continental Shelf (CLCS) 146–149, 178–181, 358
comparative research 390–401
compensation mechanism 13–22
competence, to conclude treaties 139–142
complementarity 265–280
composition, of bodies of international organizations 353–357, 362, 363*n*40
Concert of Europe 489
consensus 332–338, 390–401
Council of Europe 13–21, 202, 217, 284–287, 305, 354, 388, 456
  Enlarged Partial Agreement (EPA) 17
Court of Justice of the European Union (CJEU) 207–221
  application of international law 299
  relations with other European courts 297
COVID-19 108–111, 116–118, 324–338
COVID-19, and WIPO 322

decision – making, in international organizations 390–401
decoupling 366–371, 374, 376
delegation, of powers 41
delegations of powers, to international organizations 430*n*21, 436
dialectics, in modern philosophy 465–475
dialogue, between courts 309
dualism, in modern philosophy 465–474

EFTA Court, relations with other European courts 298–309
enforcement actions 56
environment 107–110, 119–131
  See also UNEP
erga omnes obligations 235, 240, 243
European Convention on Human Rights (ECHR)
  EU accession to 208, 217
European Court of Human Rights
  Al-Adsani v. United Kingdom (Judgment, 2001) 418
  application of EU law 297–299, 301, 306
  Beer and Regan v Germany (Judgment, 1999) 421*n*36

European Court of Human Rights (*cont.*)
Bosphorus v. Ireland (judgment, 2005) 305–309
Dhabi v. Italy (judgment, 2014) 306*n*34
Matthews v. UK (Judgment, 1999) 435
relations with other European courts 297
Waite and Kennedy v. Germany (judgment, 1999) 204*n*38, 421
European Union (EU)
accession to ECHR 208, 217
decision-making 392–400
sanctions 208–220
Exclusive Economic Zone (EEZ) 358
Extraordinary Chambers in the Courts of Cambodia (ECCC) 250, 255*n*24

Food and Agriculture Organization (FAO) 133, 134, 139, 171*n*81
food security 330–332
fragmentation 142
functional privileges and immunities 415
functionalism 58, 61, 367–376

Gaza 234–248
general principles, governing the law of international organizations 438–450
Global Fund to Fight AIDS, Malaria, and Tuberculosis (GF) 423–425

Hammarskjöld, Dag 58–72, 152

immunity, of international organizations 402, 404*n*7, 419–421, 427
implementation, of judicial decisions 222–231, 237, 240–241
implied powers 149–151
impunity 74–75, 86–87
independence, of international criminal tribunals 249–264, 266*n*3
independence, of international courts and tribunals 282, 285–291, 293
indigenous peoples, and intellectual property 311, 320, 321
'INJUGOVIN' 176–177, 181, 183, 190, 282–293
intellectual property (IP) 310–323
interaction, between international organizations 366–375
inter-organizational collaboration 132
Inter-Parliamentary Union (IPU) 452, 457–462
International Committee of the Red Cross (ICRC) 428
International Court of Justice (ICJ)
advisory proceedings, in general 339–352
Allegations of Genocide under the Convention on the Prevention and Punishment of the Crime of Genocide (Ukraine v. Russian Federation) (Order of 16 March 2022) 223*n*4, 236*n*23
Alleged Breaches of Certain International Obligations in respect of the Occupied Palestinian Territory (Nicaragua v Germany) (Provisional Measures: Order of 30 April 2024) 238*n*31
Applicability of Article VI, Section 22, of the Convention on the Privileges and Immunities of the United Nations (Advisory Opinion, 1989) 416*n*18
Application of the Convention on the Prevention and Punishment of the Crime of Genocide in the Gaza Strip (South Africa. v. Israel) (Order of 24 May 2024) 223*n*4, 236–239
Arbitral Award made by the King of Spain (Honduras v. Nicaragua) (Judgment, 1960) 200–201
Certain Expenses of the United Nations (Advisory Opinion, 1962) 57*n*1
Difference Relating to Immunity from Legal Process of a Special Rapporteur of the Commission on Human Rights (Advisory Opinion, 1999) 151*n*36
Effects of Awards of Compensation Made by the United Nations Administrative Tribunal (Advisory Opinion, 1954) 345, 346*n*32, 441*n*16
Jurisdictional Immunities of the State (Germany v. Italy: Greece intervening) (Judgment, 2012) 403*n*5, 418*n*27
Legal Consequences arising from the Policies and Practices of Israel in the Occupied Palestinian Territory (Advisory Opinion, 2024) 339, 345*n*27

International Court of Justice (ICJ) (*cont.*)
- *Legal Consequences Arising from the Policies and Practices of Israel in the Occupied Palestinian Territory, Including East Jerusalem* (Advisory Opinion, 2024) 223*n*3, 227, 234, 235*n*13
- *Legal Consequences for States of the Continued Presence of South Africa in Namibia* (Advisory Opinion, 1971) 77*n*81
- *Legal Consequences for States of the Continued Presence of South Africa in Namibia (South West Africa) notwithstanding Security Council Resolution 276 (1970)* (Advisory Opinion, 1971) 223*n*3, 227
- *Legal Consequences of the Construction of a Wall* (Advisory Opinion, 2004) 75*n*7
- *Legal Consequences of the Construction of a Wall in the Occupied Palestinian Territory* (Advisory Opinion, 2004) 223*n*3, 227, 234*n*6
- *Legal Consequences of the Separation of the Chagos Archipelago from Mauritius in 1965* (Advisory Opinion, 2019) 223*n*3, 340*n*8
- *Legality of the Use by a State of Nuclear Weapons in Armed Conflict* (Advisory Opinion, 1996) 30, 33, 340*n*8, 346, 492*n*14
- *North Sea Continental Shelf Cases* (Judgment, 1969) 38
- *Obligations of States in respect of Climate Change* (request for advisory opinion, pending) 339
- *Military and Paramilitary Activities in and Against Nicaragua (Nicaragua v. U.S.)* (Judgment, 1986) 77*n*20, 223*n*4
- *Pulp Mills on the River Uruguay* (Argentina v. Uruguay) (Judgment, 2010) 197*n*11
- *Reparation for Injuries Suffered in the Service of the United Nations* (Advisory Opinion, 1947) 424*n*1, 443*n*26
- *Reparation for Injuries Suffered in the Service of the United Nations* (Advisory Opinion, 1949) 487*n*2
- *Right to Strike under ILO Convention No. 87* (request for advisory opinion, pending) 342
- Statute, Article 38 439–441, 444, 447, 450
- Statute, Article 66(2) 340, 341, 342
- *Territorial and Maritime Dispute (Nicaragua v. Colombia), Application for Permission to Intervene* (Judgment, 2011) 441, 442*n*19

International Criminal Court (ICC)
- arrest warrants against Prime Minister and Defence Minister of Israel 246
- *Prosecutor v. Tadić* (Decision on the Defence Motion for Interlocutory Appeal on Jurisdiction, 1995) 268
- *Prosecutor v. Simone Gbagbo* (Judgment, 2014) 272
- *Prosecutor v. Saif Al – Islam Gaddafi* (Judgment, 2013) 272*n*34, 273*n*37
- *Prosecutor v. Alfred Yekatom and Patrice – Edouard Ngaïssona* (2020) 273*n*38
- Statute, Article 17 271, 277–279
- Statute, Article 18 272, 273*n*40, 279
- Statute, Article 19 272–273
- Statute, Article 54 279
- Statute, Article 93 (10) 279

international criminal tribunals 86, 249–253, 258, 263

International Criminal Tribunal for the Former Yugoslavia (ICTY) 249, 428
- *Prosecutor v. Simić et al.* (Judgment, 1999) 428n15

International Criminal Tribunal for Rwanda (ICTR) 250–263

international dispute settlement 194

International, Impartial and Independent Mechanism for Syria (IIIM – Syria) 84

International Law Commission (ILC)
- Articles on the Responsibility of International Organizations (ARIO, 2011) 24, 28*n*21, 408, 409*n*21, 436, 483, 489, 490*n*6
- Articles on the Responsibility of International Organizations (ARIO, 2011), Article 52 408, 409*n*21
- Draft Articles on Diplomatic Intercourse and Immunities (1959) 418

International Law Commission (ILC) (*cont.*)
  Draft Conclusions on the Identification of Customary International Law (2018) 438
  Draft Conclusions on Subsequent Agreements and Subsequent Practice in General Principles of Law 438–450
  Relation to the Interpretation of Treaties (2018) 77*n*18
  Study Group on Fragmentation of International Law (2006) 30
  The Settlement of International Disputes to which International Organizations are Parties (2016) 204*n*42
International Seabed Authority 145–155
International Tribunal for the Law of the Sea (ITLOS) 177–190, 225, 284*n*14, 339, 353–357
  advisory proceedings 339–352
  Delimitation of the maritime boundary in the Bay of Bengal (Bangladesh/Myanmar) (Judgment, 2012) 147*n*11
  Delimitation of the Maritime Boundary in the Indian Ocean (Mauritius/Maldives), (Judgment, 2023) 148–149
  Dispute Concerning Delimitation of the Maritime Boundary Between Mauritius and Maldives in the Indian Ocean (Mauritius v. Maldives) (Judgment, 2021) 225*n*8
  Request for an Advisory Opinion submitted by the Sub – Regional Fisheries Commission (Advisory Opinion, 2015) 150*n*27, 341
  Request for an Advisory Opinion submitted by the Commission of Small Island States on Climate Change and International Law (Advisory Opinion, 2024) 150–154, 341
  Rules of the Tribunal, Article 133 341
  Rules of the Tribunal, Article 138 150, 341
International Union for the Conservation of Nature (IUCN) 342, 348*n*43
Israel 232–248
ITLOS. *See* International Tribunal for the Law of the Sea

judicial governance 282–293
judicial protection 217–218

lawyers, role in international organizations 487–497
League of Nations, Administrative Tribunal 441–445
Legal and Technical Commission of the International Seabed Authority (LTC) 356, 361–365
legal personality, of international organizations 154, 423–426, 478–479, 490, 491
lex generalis 25, 28, 29
lex specialis 23–40, 112
liability, of international organizations 23–40
local communities, and intellectual property 311, 320, 321

masters of the treaty, States Parties as 190
MH17 86

NGOs, participation of advisory proceedings before the ICJ or ITLOS 340–343
North Atlantic Treaty Organisation (NATO) 88–100

One Health 109–110, 132–143, 166–174
Opération des Nations Unies au Congo (ONUC) 57–72
Orchestration, governance by 160
organizational ecology 368
organizational theory 368

Palestine 232–248
pandemic 103, 105, 108–118
Pandemic Influenza Preparedness (PIP) Framework 114
parliamentary diplomacy 452, 455, 458, 461
parliaments, and international organizations 452–458
peace and security 120–131
peacekeeping 57–73
peacekeeping operations 23–40, 41–56
philosophy, and international law 465–475
privileges, of international organizations 412–422, 426–429

Quadripartite (of WOAH, WHO, FAO and UNEP) 157–175
Qualified Majority Voting 394–401

regime complexity 103–118, 159*n*9, 160*n*15
responsibility, of international organizations 423–436
Rinderpest 134–137, 143
rule of law 287, 290–293
Russia
  aggression against Ukraine 12
  expulsion from Council of Europe 16
  EU, sanctions against 209, 211
  position of NATO vis-à-vis 92, 97
Register of Damage Caused by the Aggression of the Russian Federation Against Ukraine 11–22

Schachter, Oscar 58–72
small and medium – sized enterprises (SMEs) 311, 321, 327
Special Court for Sierra Leone (SCSL) 250–264, 284*n*10
Special Tribunal for Lebanon (STL) 249–263
SPLOS (Meeting of States Parties to the 1982 United Nations Convention on the Law of the Sea) 177–190, 356
State immunity 402–403
status of forces agreement (SOFA) 24–40
Statute, of the ICJ. *See* International Court of Justice (ICJ) 340, 341, 343, 348
strategic litigation 232–247
subsequent agreement, between the parties regarding the interpretation of the treaty 181
supply chains 327, 328, 329
sustainable development 119–131, 317–323
Sustainable Development Goals (SDGs) 317–323

theorizing international organizations law 484
third-party claims, against international organizations 445–449
transfers of powers, to international organizations 432–434
TRIPS. *See* WTO
Trump, Donald 90, 97–100

UN Charter
  Article 12 77
  Article 33 193, 199
  Article 42 42
  Article 43 42
  Article 51 43, 44
  Article 53 42–47
  Article 54 43, 51
  Article 94(2) 201–202
  Article 104 491*n*12
  Preamble 452–453, 459, 462
UN Convention on Biological Diversity (CBD, 1992) 113–118
  Nagoya Protocol (2010) 113–117
UN Liability Rules 23–40
UN Security Council 12, 41–56, 57–69, 74–87, 90, 119–131, 199–201, 216, 228, 250–264
UNAIDS (Joint United Nations Programme on HIV/AIDS) 104, 106
Ukraine
  invasion of 2022 11–22, 90, 94, 208–209
  Russian aggression against 12, 22, 82
United National Environmental Program (UNEP) 110, 139, 157–174
United Nations Convention on the Law of the Sea (UNCLOS) 144–155, 176–190, 353, 362
  Article 319 177–190
  Meeting of States Parties. *See* SPLOS
United Nations Emergency Force (UNEF) 57–71
United Nations General Assembly 459–460
  and the law of the sea 184, 187–189
  ensuring accountability, for atrocities 74
  Resolution ES–11/5 12*n*4, 14–20
  Resolution 37/66 (1982) 188
  Resolution 52/247 (1998) 23, 25, 26, 27, 28, 33, 34, 35, 36, 37, 445
  Resolution 69/123, The Rule of Law at the National and International Levels (2014) 420
  Resolution 76/262 80
United Nations Secretary-General 177–190
  Uniting for Peace (Resolution 377 A, 1950) 74–75, 79–80
United Nations Parliamentary Assembly (UNPA), proposals for 452, 460–461

United Nations Stabilisation Mission in Haiti (MINUSTAH) 35–37
United Nations Security Council
  authorisation of military action 50
  setting up international criminal tribunals 249–263
  veto 80
United Nations Sustainable Development Goals. *See* SDGS
United States, and NATO 88–90

Venezuela, sanctions against 211
Vienna Convention on the Law of Treaties
  Article 2(1)(i) 490
  Article 31 279

Women, and IP 311, 317–320
World Bank Administrative Tribunal (WBAT) 444, 448–449
World Health Organization (WHO) 104, 133, 134, 139, 159, 160*n*14
World Intellectual Property Organization (WIPO) 310–323, 326
World Organization for Animal Health (WOAH) 109–110, 132–134, 158
World Trade Organization (WTO)
  Administrative Services Agreement (ASA) with GF 426
  Agreement on Trade – Related Aspects of Intellectual Property Rights (TRIPS) 106
  new roles and responsibilities 338
  response to the COVID–19 crisis 324, 328

Youth, and IP 311, 319, 320

Printed in the United States
by Baker & Taylor Publisher Services